Get the eBooks FREE!

(PDF, ePub, and Kindle all included)

We believe that once you buy a book from us, you should be able to read it in any format we have available. To get electronic versions of this book at no additional cost to you, purchase and then register this book at the Manning website following the instructions inside this insert.

That's it!

Thanks from Manning!

tion

on't use Post-

Wood, NIWA

Asoft Pty Ltd.

k pulls it off!
rin Solutions

er.
ction District

WeoGeo.com

development.
stem (EFFIS)

the Aha!
its kind.
Software Ltd.

nologies, Inc.

PostGIS in Action

SECOND EDITION

REGINA O. OBE
LEO S. HSU

MANNING
SHELTER ISLAND

For online information and ordering of this and other Manning books, please visit www.manning.com. The publisher offers discounts on this book when ordered in quantity. For more information, please contact

Special Sales Department
Manning Publications Co.
20 Baldwin Road
PO Box 761
Shelter Island, NY 11964
Email: orders@manning.com

♾ Recognizing the importance of preserving what has been written, it is Manning's policy to have the books we publish printed on acid-free paper, and we exert our best efforts to that end. Recognizing also our responsibility to conserve the resources of our planet, Manning books are printed on paper that is at least 15 percent recycled and processed without the use of elemental chlorine.

Manning Publications Co.
20 Baldwin Road
PO Box 761
Shelter Island, NY 11964

Development editor: Jeff Bleiel
Technical development editor: Deepak Vohra
Copyeditors: Benjamin Berg, Andy Carroll
Proofreader: Katie Tennant
Technical proofreader: David Pombal
Typesetter: Dottie Marsico
Cover designer: Marija Tudor

ISBN 9781617291395
Printed in the United States of America
1 2 3 4 5 6 7 8 9 10 – EBM – 20 19 18 17 16 15

To Dr. Ernest Olagbade Obe (1935–2012),
professor, chief, daddy

brief contents

contents

foreword

As children, we were probably all told at one time or another that "we are what we eat," as a reminder that our diet is integral to our health and quality of life. In the modern world, with location-aware smartphones in our pockets, GPS units in our vehicles, and the internet addresses of our computers geocoded, it has also become true that "who we are is where we are"—every individual is now a mobile sensor, generating a ceaseless flow of location-encoded data as they move about the planet.

To manage and tame that flow of data, and the parallel flow of data opened up by economical satellite imaging and crowdsourced mapping, we need a tool equal to the task—a tool that can persistently store the data, efficiently access it, and powerfully analyze it. We need a spatial database, like PostGIS.

Prior to the advent of spatial databases, computer analysis of location and mapping data was done with geographic information systems (GIS) running on desktop workstations. When it was first released in 2001, the project name was just a simple play on words—naturally, a spatial extension of the *PostgreSQL* database would be named *PostGIS.*

But the name has come to have further significance as the project has matured. Each year, new functions have been added for data analysis, and each year users have pressed those functions further and further, doing the kinds of work that in earlier years would have required a specialized GIS workstation. PostGIS is actually creating a world that is post-GIS—we don't need GIS software to do GIS work anymore. A spatial database suffices.

In March of 2002, not even one year after the first release of PostGIS, I asked on the user mailing list for examples of how people were using PostGIS. In her first post to the list, Regina Obe answered this way:

> We use it here [city of Boston] for proximity analysis. Part of our department is in charge of distributing foreclosed property to developers, etc., to build houses, businesses, etc. We use PostGIS to list properties by proximity ... so that if a developer wants to develop on a piece of land that is, say, X in size, they will be able to get a better sense of whether it can be done.

Even at that early date in the project, Regina Obe was already testing the capabilities of PostGIS and creating clever analyses.

Since the first edition of *PostGIS in Action* in 2011, PostGIS has itself remained very much in action, adding new features for raster analysis, 3D, and more. And the world has kept on moving, too.

Only a decade ago, when PostGIS was brand new, the idea that almost every person would have a GPS unit (a phone) in their pocket was pretty crazy, and now it's commonplace. The features of PostGIS for managing location are now being used widely by developers who only a few years ago had never heard of spatial data.

Within the next few years, satellite and aerial imagery will move into the mass market, as drone systems and new low-cost satellite systems become affordable. The raster-management capabilities of PostGIS are now there for the next generation of developers to work with.

Enjoy this book and enjoy the insights it provides in putting location data to work. Regina and Leo have distilled a huge body of information into a concise guide that is truly one of a kind.

PAUL RAMSEY
CHAIR, POSTGIS PROJECT STEERING COMMITTEE

preface

PostGIS (pronounced *post-jis*) is a spatial database extender for the PostgreSQL open source relational database management system. It's the most powerful open source spatial database engine. It adds to PostgreSQL several spatial data types and over 300 functions for working with these spatial types. It does for PostgreSQL what Oracle Spatial and Oracle Locator do for Oracle, what IBM DB2 Spatial Extender and IBM Informix Spatial DataBlade do for DB2 and Informix, and what the geometry and geography types packaged in Microsoft SQL Server 2008+ do for SQL Server. PostGIS supports many of the OGC/ISO SQL/MM–compliant spatial functions you'll find in these other OGC-compliant databases, as well as numerous additional ones that are unique to PostGIS.

Readers coming from other ANSI/ISO–compliant spatial databases, or other relational databases such as those we've mentioned, will feel right at home with PostgreSQL and PostGIS. PostgreSQL is the most ANSI/ISO SQL–compliant database management system around. In a similar vein, PostGIS supports many of the industry-standard OGC/ISO SQL/MM spatial database functions, types, and operations.

The main raison d'être of this book is to provide a companion volume to the official PostGIS documentation—to serve as a guidebook for navigating through the hundreds of functions offered by PostGIS. We wanted to create a book that would catalog many of the common spatial problems we've come across and various strategies for solving them with PostGIS.

Above and beyond our primary mission, we hope to lay the foundation for thinking spatially. We hope that you'll be able to adapt our numerous examples and recipes to your own field of endeavor, and perhaps even spawn creative scions of your own.

acknowledgments

We thank each other for making this book possible. If only one of us was writing this book, it would have been either a random stream of consciousness or an obsessively organized masterpiece that would never have been finished in our lifetime.

We thank our technical reviewer, David Pombal, who went above and beyond the call of duty in reviewing all chapters of our book, testing the code, and providing invaluable constructive criticism. We'd also like to thank Paul Ramsey for contributing the foreword, and our illustrators, Gary Battiston and Alejandro Gomez.

We thank everyone at Manning Publications. In particular, we acknowledge publisher Marjan Bace; review editor Aleksandar Dragosavljevic for organizing reviewer feedback; our development editor, Jeff Bleiel, who endured many revisions of our chapters; and our production team of Benjamin Berg, Andy Carroll, Katie Tennant, Dottie Marsico, Janet Vail, Mary Piergies, and others for keeping us focused during the production process.

Our exposure to PostGIS would not be possible without the City of Boston Department of Neighborhood Development (DND), particularly the MIS and Policy Development and Research divisions where Regina was first exposed to GIS and PostGIS. A special thanks to fellow members of the PostGIS development team and Steering Committee: Bborie Park, Paul Ramsey, Sandro Santilli, Nicklas Avén, Olivier Courtin, Mateusz Loskot, Pierre Racine, Jorge Arévalo, and others; each ensures that every new release of PostGIS has great features and that bug reports get immediate attention. We also thank the PostGIS community of newsgroup subscribers who answer questions as best and as quickly as they can, PostGIS bloggers, and package maintainers; each in their own way gives newcomers to PostGIS a warm and fuzzy feeling.

Finally, we thank our Early Access readers and the reviewers who flagged errors and ambiguities in our text and code before publication, in particular, Alban Thomas, Alfredo Alessandrini, Amit Kulkarni, Andrew Parker, Bborie Park, Charlie Gaines, Federico Ferreri, Guy Ndjeng, Jiří Fejfar, Jonathan DeCarlo, Kulwadee Somboonviwat, Marcus Brown, Matthew Kenny, Nicklas Aven, Paolo Corti, Phillip Warner, Sarah Goodwin, Sergio Arbeo, Stephen Mather, Steven Parr, and Tarin Gamberini.

about this book

This second edition is updated for and focused on the PostGIS 2.0 and 2.1 series and PostgreSQL 9.1–9.3 with highlights of PostgreSQL 9.4 and the upcoming PostGIS 2.2. This book isn't a substitute for either the official PostGIS or PostgreSQL documentation. The official PostGIS documentation does a good job of introducing you to the myriad of functions available in PostGIS and provides examples on how to use each. But it won't tell you how to combine all these functions into a recipe to solve your problems. That's the purpose of our book. Although it doesn't cover all the functions available in PostGIS, this book does cover the more commonly used and interesting ones and gives you the skills you need to combine them to solve classic and more esoteric but interesting problems in spatial analysis and modeling.

Although you can use this book as a reference source, we recommend that you also visit the official PostGIS site at http://postgis.net.

This book focuses on two- and three-dimensional non-curved Cartesian vector geometries, two-dimensional geodetic vector geometries, raster data, and network topologies.

Although the main purpose of this book is the use of PostGIS, we'd fall short of our mission if we neglected to provide some perspective on the landscape it lives in. PostGIS is not an island and rarely works alone. To complete the cycle, we also include the following:

- An extensive appendix that covers PostgreSQL in great detail from setup, to backup, to security management. The appendix also covers the fundamentals of SQL and creating functions and other objects with it.

- Several chapters dedicated to the use of PostGIS in web mapping, viewing using desktop tools, PostgreSQL PL languages commonly used with PostGIS, and extra open source add-ons such as the PostGIS-packaged TIGER geocoder and separately packaged pgRouting.

This book in no way attempts to provide a rigorous treatment of the math underlying the PostGIS libraries. We rely on intuitive understanding for concepts such as points, lines, and polygons. In the same vein, we're not able to delve into database theory. If we predict that a particular index should be more effective than another, we're making educated guesses from experience, not from having mastered relational algebra and dissecting a few computer chips along the way.

Who should read this book?

This book provides an introduction to PostGIS, and it assumes a basic comfort level with programming and working with data. The types of people we've found are most attracted to PostGIS and are best suited for reading this book are listed here.

GIS PRACTITIONERS AND PROGRAMMERS

You know everything about data, geoids, and projections. You know where to find sources of data. You can create stunning applications with ArcGIS, MapInfo, Google Earth, OpenLayers, Adobe Flex, Silverlight, or other Ajax-enabled toolkits. You're adept at generating data sources in Esri shapefiles, using MapInfo, and creating cartographic masterpieces. You may even be able to add and extract data from a spatially enabled database, but when asked questions about the data, you're stuck. Being able to draw all the Walmarts in the United States on a map is one thing, but being able to answer the question, "How many Walmarts are east of the Mississippi?" without counting individual pushpins is a whole different ball game. Sure, you may have used desktop tools and written procedural code to answer these questions, but we hope to show you a much faster way.

So what does a spatially enabled database offer that you don't already have at your fingertips?

- It provides the ability to easily intermingle spatial data with other corporate data, such as financial information, observational data, and marketing information. Yes, you can do these with Esri shapefiles, KML files, and other GIS file formats, but that requires an extra step and limits your options for joining with other relevant data. A database such as PostgreSQL has features such as a query planner that improves the speed of your joins and many commonly used statistical functions to make fairly complex questions and summary stats relatively fast to run and quick to write.
- When collecting user data, whether that user is drawing a geometry on the screen and inputting related information or clicking a point on the map, there's so much infrastructure built around databases that the task is much easier if you're using one. Take, for example, rolling your own web application in

.NET, PHP, Perl, Python, Java, or some other language. Each already has a driver for PostgreSQL to make inserting and querying data easy. Add to that mix the text-to-geometry functions, geometry-to-SVG, -KML, and -GeoJSON functions, and other processing functions that PostGIS provides, along with the geometry generation and manipulation functions that platforms like OpenLayers, MapServer, and GeoServer have, and you have a myriad of options to choose from.

- A relational database provides administrative support to easily control who has access to what, whether that be a text attribute or a geometry.
- PostgreSQL offers triggers that can allow the generation of other things like related geometries in other tables when certain database events happen.
- PostgreSQL has a multi-version concurrency control (MVCC) transactional core to ensure that when 100 users are reading or updating your data at the same time, your system doesn't come screeching to a halt.
- PostgreSQL provides the ability to write custom functions in the database that can be called from disparate applications. PostgreSQL offers several choices of languages to choose from when writing stored functions.
- If you're married to your preferred GIS desktop tools, don't worry. Choosing a spatial DBMS such as PostGIS doesn't mean you need to abandon your tools of choice. Manifold, Cadcorp, MapInfo 10+, AutoCAD, Esri ArcGIS, ArcMap, Server tools, and various commonly used desktop tools have built-in support for PostGIS. Safe FME, an extract-transform-load (ETL) favorite of GIS professionals, has supported PostGIS for a long time.

DB PRACTITIONERS

At some point in your database career, someone might have asked you a spatially oriented question about the data. Without a spatially enabled database, you're forced to limit your thinking in terms of coordinates, location names, or other geographical attributes that can be reduced to numbers and letters. This works fine for point data, but you're at a complete loss once areas and regions come into play. You may be able to find all the people named *Smith* within a county, but if we were to ask you to find all the Smiths living within 10 miles of the county, you'd be stuck.

We want readers coming from a standard relational database background to realize that data is more than just numbers, dates, and characters, and that amazing feats of SQL can be accomplished against non-textual data. Sure, you might have stored images, documents, and other oddities in your relational database, but we doubt you were able to do much in the way of writing SQL joins against these fields.

SCIENTISTS, RESEARCHERS, EDUCATORS, AND ENGINEERS

A lot of highly skilled scientists, researchers, educators, and engineers use spatial analysis tools to analyze their collected data, model their inventions, or train students. Although we don't consider ourselves the same as them, we admire these people the most because they create knowledge and improve our lives in fundamental ways. They may know a lot about mathematics, biology, chemistry, geology, physics, engineering, and so forth, but they aren't trained in database management, relational database use, or GIS. If you're one of these people, we hope to provide just enough of a framework to get you up to speed without too much fuss.

What does PostgreSQL/PostGIS hold for you?

- It gives you the ability to integrate with statistical packages such as R, and you can even write database procedural functions in PL/R that leverage the power of R.
- PostgreSQL also supports PL/Python, which allows you to leverage the growing Python libraries for scientific research right in the database, where it can work even closer with the data than in a plain Python environment.
- While many think of PostGIS as a tool for geographic information systems, and that's implied by the name, we see it as a tool for spatial analysis. The distinction is that whereas geography focuses on the earth and the reference systems that bind the earth, spatial analysis focuses on space and the use of space. That space and coordinate reference system may be specific to an anthill, or to a map of a nuclear plant whose location is yet to be defined, or it may be used as a visualization tool to model the inherently non-visual, such as in process modeling. Although you may think of your particular area of interest as not being touched by spatial analysis, we challenge you to dig deeper.
- A database is a natural repository for large quantities of data and has a lot of built-in statistical/rollup functions and constructs for producing useful reports and analyses. If you're dealing with data of a spatial nature or using space as a visualization tool, PostGIS provides more functions to extend that analysis.
- Much of the data needed for scientific research can be easily collected by machines (GPS, alarm systems, remote sensing devices) and directly piped to the database via automated feeds or standard import formats. In fact, collection tools such as smartphones and unmanned aircraft are becoming cheaper each day and more accessible to the general population, and the hardware to store the data is also getting cheaper.
- Portions of data are easily distributed. A relational database is ideal for creating what we call "data dispensers" or "datamarts," which allow other researchers to easily grab just the subset of data they need for their research or to provide data for easy download by the public.

These profiles are the basic groups of spatial database users, but they're not the only ones. If you've ever looked at the world and thought "Wouldn't it be great if I could correlate crime statistics with the locations where we've planted trees?" or "Where's the best place and time to plant our crops given the elevation model and temperature fluctuations of an area?" then PostGIS might be the easiest and most cost-effective tool for you.

Roadmap

This book is divided into three major parts and has several supporting appendixes.

PART 1: LEARNING POSTGIS

Part 1 covers the fundamental concepts of spatial relational databases and PostGIS/PostgreSQL in particular. The goal of this part is to introduce you to industry-standard GIS database concepts and practices. By the end of this part, you should have a solid foundation in the various geometry, geography, raster, and topology types, and what problems each strives to solve. You should have a basic understanding of spatial reference systems and database storage options. Most important, you'll have the ability to load, query, and view spatial data in a PostGIS-enabled PostgreSQL database.

PART 2: PUTTING POSTGIS TO WORK

This part focuses on using PostGIS to solve real-world spatial problems and on optimizing for speed. You'll learn how to do a variety of things:

- How to do proximity analysis using both geometry and geography
- How to use different kinds of vector operations to optimize your data
- How to perform seamless raster processing using raster and vector data
- How to create new vector data using raster processing, map algebra, histograms, and other raster statistics functions to compute statistics about an area of interest
- How to create big rasters from smaller rasters using raster aggregate functions
- How to use the packaged PostGIS TIGER geocoder for address normalization, geocoding, and reverse geocoding
- How to use topology to ensure consistency of editing
- How to simplify a whole network of geometries and still maintain connectedness in your simplified dataset

PART 3: USING POSTGIS WITH OTHER TOOLS

Part 3 encompasses the tools most commonly used with PostGIS for building applications. We'll cover pgRouting, a tool you can use with PostGIS directly in the database for creating network routing applications. In addition, we'll cover PostgreSQL stored procedure languages: PL/Python, PL/R, and PL/V8 (a.k.a. PL/JavaScript). Finally, we'll end with a brief study of PostGIS in web applications. We'll cover the various mapping servers used with PostGIS as well as mapping JavaScript APIs: OpenLayers and Leaflet.

APPENDIXES

There are four appendixes.

Appendix A provides additional resources for getting help on PostGIS and the ancillary tools discussed in the book.

Appendix B shows how to get up and running with PostgreSQL and PostGIS.

Appendix C is an SQL primer that explains the concepts of `JOIN`, `UNION`, `INTERSECT`, and `EXCEPT`. It discusses the fundamentals of rolling up data with aggregate functions and aggregate constructs, as well as the more advanced topic of using window functions and frames.

Appendix D covers features of PostgreSQL that are rarely found in other databases.

Code and other conventions

The following typographical conventions are used throughout the book:

- Courier typeface is used in all code listings.
- Courier typeface is used within the text for certain code words.
- Sidebars and notes are used to highlight key points or introduce new terminology.
- Code annotations are used in place of inline comments in the code. These highlight important concepts or areas of the code. Some annotations appear with numbered bullets like this, ❶, that are referenced later in the text.

Code downloads

The examples and data for all chapters of this book can be downloaded via http://www.postgis.us/chapters_edition_2. On the book site you'll also find descriptions of each chapter with related links for each chapter. Each chapter page has a link where you can download the full data and code for that chapter.

The code can also be downloaded from the publisher's website at http://www.manning.com/PostGISinActionSecondEdition. Two free sample chapters are also available for download from this site.

Author Online

The purchase of *PostGIS In Action, Second Edition* includes free access to a private forum run by Manning Publications where you can make comments about the book, ask technical questions, and receive help from the authors and other users. You can access and subscribe to the forum at http://www.manning.com/PostGISinActionSecondEdition. This page provides information on how to get on the forum once you're registered, what kind of help is available, and the rules of conduct in the forum.

Manning's commitment to our readers is to provide a venue where a meaningful dialogue among individual readers and between readers and authors can take place. It's not a commitment to any specific amount of participation on the part of the authors, whose contribution to the book's forum remains voluntary (and unpaid). We suggest you try asking the authors some challenging questions, lest their interest stray!

The Author Online forum and the archives of previous discussions will be accessible from the publisher's website as long as the book is in print. Lastly, there will be additions to the content added to the author's online website for the book, located at www.postgis.us.

You may also visit the authors at the PostgreSQL and Open Source GIS companion sites: www.postgresonline.com and www.bostongis.com.

About the title

By combining introductions, overviews, and how-to examples, the *In Action* books are designed to help learning and remembering. According to research in cognitive science, the things people remember are things they discover during self-motivated exploration.

Although no one at Manning is a cognitive scientist, we are convinced that for learning to become permanent it must pass through stages of exploration, play, and, interestingly, retelling of what's being learned. People understand and remember new things, which is to say they master them, only after actively exploring them. Humans learn *in action.* An essential part of an *In Action* book is that it's example driven. It encourages the reader to try things out, to play with new code, and to explore new ideas.

There's another, more mundane, reason for the title of this book: Our readers are busy. They use books to do a job or solve a problem. They need books that allow them to jump in and jump out easily and learn just what they want just when they want it. They need books that aid them in action. The books in this series are designed for such readers.

About the cover illustration

The figure on the cover of *PostGIS in Action, Second Edition* is captioned "A woman from Ubli, Croatia." The illustration is taken from a reproduction of an album of Croatian traditional costumes from the mid-nineteenth century by Nikola Arsenovic, published by the Ethnographic Museum in Split, Croatia, in 2003. The illustrations were obtained from a helpful librarian at the Ethnographic Museum in Split, itself situated in the Roman core of the medieval center of the town: the ruins of Emperor Diocletian's retirement palace from around AD 304. The book includes finely colored illustrations of figures from different regions of Croatia, accompanied by descriptions of the costumes and of everyday life.

Ubli is the main ferry port on the island of Lastovo, located in an archipelago of islets in the Adriatic Sea off the coast of Croatia. The main characteristic of an Ubli woman's costume is the rich and colorful embroidery. Over a white linen dress that is trimmed with red bands, women typically wear a long blue vest decorated with red woolen roses as well as an embroidered apron. Colorful woolen socks and a little red hat decorated on the edges complete the costume. Live flowers are often added to the back of the hat.

Dress codes and lifestyles have changed over the last 200 years, and the diversity by region, so rich at the time, has faded away. It is now hard to tell apart the inhabitants of different continents, let alone of different hamlets or towns separated by only a few miles. Perhaps we have traded cultural diversity for a more varied personal life—certainly for a more varied and fast-paced technological life.

Manning celebrates the inventiveness and initiative of the computer business with book covers based on the rich diversity of regional life of two centuries ago, brought back to life by illustrations from old books and collections like this one.

Part 1

Introduction to PostGIS

Welcome to *PostGIS in Action, Second Edition.* PostGIS is a spatial database extender for the PostgreSQL database management system. This book will teach you the fundamentals of spatial databases in general, key concepts in geographic information systems (GIS), and more specifically how to configure, load, and query a PostGIS-enabled database. You'll learn how to perform actions with single lines of SQL code that you thought were possible only with a desktop GIS system. By using spatial SQL, much of the heavy lifting that would require many manual steps in desktop GIS tools can be scripted and automated.

This book is divided into three sections and four appendixes. Part 1 covers the fundamentals of spatial databases, GIS, and working with spatial data. Although part 1 is focused on PostGIS, many of the concepts you'll learn in part 1 are equally applicable to other spatial relational databases.

Chapter 1 covers the fundamentals of spatial databases and what you can do with a spatially enabled database that you can't do with a standard relational database. It also introduces features that are fairly unique to PostGIS. It concludes with a fast-paced example of loading fast-food restaurant longitude/latitude data and converting it to geometric points, loading road data from Esri shapefiles, and doing spatial summaries by joining these two sets of data.

Chapter 2 covers all the spatial types that PostGIS has to offer. You'll learn how to create these using various functions and learn about concepts unique to each spatial type.

Chapter 3 is an introduction to spatial reference systems, and we'll explain the concepts behind them, why they're important for working with geometry, raster, and topology, and how to work with them.

Chapter 4 covers how to load spatial data into PostGIS using packaged tools as well as additional third-party open source tools. You'll learn how to load geometry and geography data using the shp2pgsql command-line tool packaged with all PostGIS distributions, as well as the shp2pgsql-gui GUI loader/exporter that's packaged with some desktop distributions of PostGIS. You'll also learn how to load raster data using the PostGIS-packaged raster2pgsql command-line tool and how to import and export both raster and vector data of various formats using the GDAL/OGR suite. You'll also learn how to load OpenStreetMap data using the commonly available osm2pgsql command-line tool.

Chapter 5 covers some of the more common, open source, desktop tools for viewing and querying PostGIS data.

Chapter 6 starts getting into the simpler core functions that are used with geometry and geography functions. These all take single geometry or geography objects and morph them or take text representations of them and convert them to PostGIS spatial objects.

Chapter 7 is an introduction to raster functions. It covers some functions for creating rasters, interrogating rasters, and setting pixel values.

Chapter 8 covers geocoding with the packaged PostGIS TIGER geocoder. You'll learn how to load U.S. Census TIGER data using functions packaged with the TIGER geocoder. Once the data is loaded, you'll learn how to use the packaged functions to normalize, geocode, and reverse geocode data.

Chapter 9 concludes this first part by introducing you to spatial relationships. Spatial relationships are most important when working with sets of data. In later sections of the book, we'll use these concepts to do things like spatial joins.

1 What is a spatial database?

This chapter covers

- Spatial databases in problem solving
- Spatial data types
- Modeling with spatial in mind
- Why you might use PostGIS/PostgreSQL for a spatial database
- Loading and querying spatial data

Most folks experience their first spatially enabled application when they see pushpins tacked onto points of interest on an interactive map. This provides a glimpse into the vast and varied field of geographic information systems (GIS).

We'll begin this chapter with a pushpin model. As we demonstrate its limited usefulness, we'll introduce the need for a spatial database—not just any database, but PostGIS. PostGIS is a spatial database extender for the PostgreSQL database management system. We'll provide a brief introduction to the entire PostGIS suite and whet your appetite with an example that goes far beyond what you can accomplish with pushpins. The data and code used in this chapter can be found at http://www.postgis.us/chapter_01_edition_2.

1.1 Thinking spatially

Popular mapping sites such as OpenStreetMap, Google Maps, Bing Maps, MapQuest, and Yahoo have empowered people in many walks of life to answer the question "Where is something?" by displaying teardrop shapes on a gorgeously detailed, interactive map. No longer are we restricted to textual descriptions of "where," like "Turn right at the supermarket and it'll be the third house on the right with a mangy dog out front." Nor are we faced with the frustrating problem of not being able to figure out our current location on a paper map.

Going beyond getting directions, organizations large and small have discovered that mapping can be a great resource for analyzing patterns in data. By plotting the addresses of pizza lovers, a national pizza chain can assess where to locate the next grand opening. Political organizations planning grassroots campaigns can easily see on a map where the undecided or unregistered voters are located and target their route walks accordingly. Even though the pushpin model offers unprecedented geographical insight, the reasoning that germinates from it is entirely on visual.

In the pizza example, the chain might be able to see the concentration of pizza lovers in a city by means of adding pushpins. But what if they need to differentiate pizza lovers by income level? If the chain has a gourmet offering, it would be a good idea to locate new restaurants in the midst of mid- to high-income pizza lovers. The pizza chain planners could use pushpins of different colors on an interactive map to indicate various income tiers, but the heuristic visual reasoning will now be much more complicated, as shown in figure 1.1. Not only do the planners need to look at the concentration of pushpins, they must also keep the varying colors or icons of the pins in mind. Add another variable to the map, like households with lactose-intolerant adults, and the problem overwhelms our feeble minds. Spatial databases come to the rescue. A *spatial database* has column data types specifically designed to store objects in space—these data types can be added to database tables. The information stored is usually geographic in nature, such as a point location or the boundary of a lake. The spatial database also provides special functions and indexes for querying and manipulating that data, which can be called from a query language such as Structured Query Language (SQL). A spatial database is often used as just a storage container for spatial data, but it can do much more than that. Although a spatial database need not be relational in nature, most are.

A spatial database gives you a storage tool, an analysis tool, and an organizing tool all in one. Presenting data visually isn't a spatial database's only goal. The pizza shop planners can store an infinite number of attributes of the pizza-loving household, including income level, number of children in the household, pizza-ordering history, and even religious preferences and cultural upbringing (as they relate to topping choices on a pizza). More important, the analysis need not be limited to the number of variables that can be juggled in the brain. The planners can make very specific requests, like "Give me a list of neighborhoods ranked by the number of high-income pizza lovers who have more than two children." Furthermore, they can easily

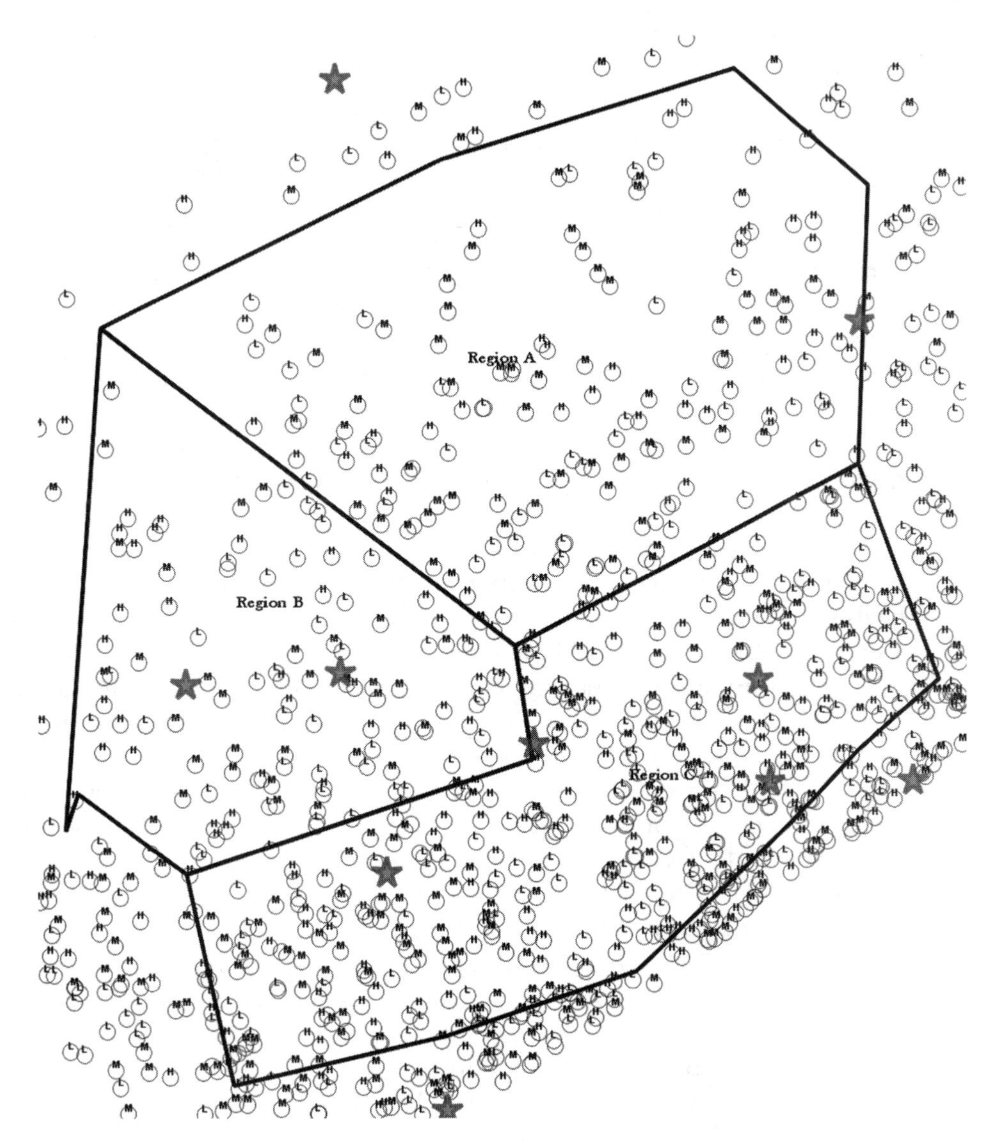

Figure 1.1 Pushpin madness!

incorporate additional data from varied sources, such as the location and rating of existing pizzerias from restaurant review sites or the health-consciousness level of various neighborhoods as identified by the local health commission. Their questions of the database could be as complicated as "Show me the region with the highest number of households where the average closest distance to any pizza parlor with a star-ranking below 5 is greater than 16 kilometers (10 miles). Oh, and toss out the health-conscious neighborhoods."

Table 1.1 shows what the results of such a spatial query might look like.

Table 1.1 Results of a spatial query

Region	Households	Restaurants	Distance
Region A	194	1	17.1 km

Suppose you aren't a mapping user, but are more of a data user. You work with data day in and day out, never needing to plot anything on a map. You're familiar with questions like, "Give me all the employees who live in Chicago," or "Count up the number of customers in each postal code." Suppose you have the latitude and longitude of all the employees' addresses; you could ask questions like "Give me the average distance that each employee must travel to work." This is the extent of the kind of spatial queries that you can formulate with conventional databases, where data types consist mainly of text, numbers, and dates.

Suppose the question posed is "Give me the number of houses within two miles of the coastline requiring evacuation in the event of a hurricane" or "How many households would be affected by the noise of a newly proposed runway?" Without spatial support, these questions would require you to collect or derive additional values for each data point. For the coastline question, you'd need to determine the distance from the beach, house by house. This could involve algorithms to find the shortest distance to fixed intervals along the coastline or require a series of SQL queries to order all the houses by proximity to the beach and then make a cut. With spatial support, all you need to do is reformulate the question slightly as "Find all houses within a two-mile radius of the coastline." A spatially enabled database can intrinsically work with data types like coastlines (modeled as linestrings), buffer zones (modeled as polygons), and beach houses (modeled as points).

As with most things in life worth pursuing, nothing comes without some effort. You'll need to climb a gentle learning curve to tap into the power of spatial analysis. The good news is that unlike other good things in life, the database that we'll introduce you to is completely free—moneywise.

If you're able to figure out how to get data into your Google map, you'll have no problem taking the next step. If you can write queries in non-spatially enabled databases, we'll open your eyes and mind to something beyond the mundane world of numbers, dates, and strings. Let's get started.

1.2 Introducing PostGIS

PostGIS is a free and open source library that spatially enables the free and open source PostgreSQL object-relational database management system (ORDBMS). We want you to choose PostgreSQL as your relational database and PostGIS as your spatial database extender for PostgreSQL.

1.2.1 Why PostGIS

PostGIS started as a project of Refractions Research and has since been adopted and improved on by government, public organizations, and private companies.

The power of PostGIS is enhanced by other supporting projects:

- *Proj4*—Provides projection support
- *Geometry Engine Open Source (GEOS)*—Advanced geometry-processing support
- *Geospatial Data Abstraction Library (GDAL)*—Provides many advanced raster-processing features
- *Computational Geometry Algorithms Library (CGAL/SFCGAL)*—Enables advanced 3D analysis

Most of these projects, including PostGIS, now fall under the umbrella of the Open Source Geospatial Foundation (OSGeo). The foundation of PostGIS is the PostgreSQL ORDBMS, which provides transactional support, gist index support for spatial objects, and a query planner out of the box. It's a great testament to the power and flexibility of PostgreSQL that Refractions chose to build on top of PostgreSQL rather than on any other open source database.

STANDARDS CONFORMANCE

PostGIS and PostgreSQL conform to industry standards more closely than most products. PostgreSQL supports many of the newer ANSI SQL features. PostGIS supports Open Geospatial Consortium (OGC) standards and the new SQL Multimedia Spec (SQL/MM) spatial standard. This means that you aren't simply learning how to use a set of products; you're garnering knowledge about industry standards that will help you understand other commercial and open source geospatial databases and mapping tools.

What are OGC, OSGeo, ANSI SQL, and SQL/MM?

OGC stands for *Open Geospatial Consortium*, and it's the body that exists to standardize how geographic and spatial data is accessed and distributed. Towards that goal, they have numerous specifications that govern accessing geospatial data from web services, geospatial data delivery formats, and querying of geospatial data.

OSGeo stands for *Open Source Geospatial Foundation*, and it's the body whose initiative is to fund, support, and market open source tools and free data for GIS. There's some overlap between the OSGeo and OGC. Both strive to make GIS data and tools available to everyone, which means they're both concerned about open standards.

You'll also often hear the term *American National Standards Institute (ANSI)* or *International Organization of Standardization (ISO) SQL*. The ANSI/ISO SQL standards define general guidelines that SQL implementations should follow. These guidelines are often year-dated like ANSI SQL 92 and ANSI SQL:2011 and they build upon prior-year

> ***(continued)***
> specs. You'll find that many relational databases support most of the ANSI SQL 92 spec but not as much of the later specs. PostgreSQL supports many of the newer guidelines, some of which we'll cover in appendix C. The ANSI/ISO SQL Multimedia spec (SQL/MM) is a specification that, among other things, defines standard functions for spatial data used in SQL.
>
> As spatial became *not so special* and almost an expected part of high-end relational databases, much of what OGC governed fell under the ANSI/ISO SQL–making body. As a result, you'll often see the newer SQL/MM specs referring to spatial types with an ST_ prefix, like `ST_Geometry` and `ST_Polygon`, instead of the unadorned `Geometry` and `Polygon` from the older OGC/SFSQL (Spatial Features for SQL) specs.

If your data and your APIs implement standards supported by many kinds of software—Cadcorp, Safe FME, AutoCAD, Manifold, MapInfo, Esri ArcGIS, ogr2ogr/GDAL, OpenJUMP, QGIS, deegree, MapGuide, UMN MapServer, GeoServer, or even standard programming tools like PHP, Python, Perl, ASP.NET, SQL, or new emerging tools—then everyone can use the tools that they feel most comfortable with, or that fit their work processes, or that they can afford, and share information with one another. OSGeo tries to ensure that regardless of how small your pocketbook is, you can still afford to view and analyze GIS data. OGC and ANSI/ISO SQL try to enforce standards across all products so that regardless of how expensive your GIS platform is, you can still make your hard work available to everyone. This is especially important for government agencies whose salaries and tools are paid for with tax dollars; for students who have a lot of will, the intelligence to learn, and advanced technology but have small pockets; and even for smaller vendors who have a compelling offering for specific kinds of users but who are often snubbed by larger vendors because they can't support (or lack access to) the private API standards of the big-name vendors.

PostGIS is supported by a vast number of GIS proprietary desktop and server tools. You can find a listing of some of these in appendix A, section A.3. PostGIS is also the preferred spatial relational database of most open source geospatial desktop and web-mapping server tools. We'll cover some of the more common ones in chapters 5 and 17.

PostGIS is powerful

PostGIS provides many spatial operators, spatial functions, spatial data types, and spatial indexing enhancements to PostgreSQL. If you add to the mix the complementary features that PostgreSQL and other related projects provide, then you have a jam-packed powerhouse at your disposal that's well suited for sophisticated GIS analysis and is a valuable tool for learning GIS.

You'll be hard pressed to find the following features in other spatial databases:

- Functions to work with GeoJSON and Keyhole Markup Language (KML), allowing web applications to talk directly to PostGIS without the need for additional serializing schemes or translations
- Comprehensive geometry-processing functions that go far beyond basic geometric operations, including functions for fixing invalid geometries and for simplifying and deconstructing geometries
- Built-in 3D and topology support
- Over 150 seamless operations for working with vectors and rasters in tandem, as well as for converting between the two families

GeoJSON and KML data formats

Geographic JavaScript Object Notation (GeoJSON; http://geojson.org) and Keyhole Markup Language (KML; http://en.wikipedia.org/wiki/Keyhole_Markup_Language) are two of the most popular vector formats used by web-mapping applications:

- GeoJSON is an extension of JSON that's used for representing JavaScript objects. It adds to the JSON standard support for geographic objects.
- KML is an XML format developed by Keyhole (which was purchased by Google), first used in Google's mapping products and later supported by various mapping APIs.

These are only two of the many formats that PostGIS can output.

BUILT ON TOP OF POSTGRESQL

The major reason PostGIS was built on the PostgreSQL platform was the ease of extensibility PostgreSQL provided for building new types and operators and for controlling the index operators. PostgreSQL was designed to be extensible from the ground up.

PostgreSQL has a regal lineage that dates back almost to the dawn of relational databases. It's a cousin of the Sybase and Microsoft SQL Server databases, because the people who started Sybase came from UC Berkeley and worked on the Ingres or PostgreSQL projects with Michael Stonebraker. Michael Stonebraker is considered by many to be the father of Ingres and PostgreSQL and to be one of the founding fathers of object-relational database management systems. The source code of Sybase SQL Server was later licensed to Microsoft to produce Microsoft SQL Server.

PostgreSQL's claim to fame is that it's the most advanced open source database in existence. It has the speed and functionality to compete with the popular commercial enterprise offerings, and it's used to power databases terabytes in size. As time has moved on, new usability features have been added, making it not only the most advanced, but perhaps the most flexible relational database out there. For more details about the features of PostgreSQL and the key enhancements in newer versions that are lacking in most other databases (including expensive proprietary ones), please refer to appendix B.

PostgreSQL is becoming a one-size-fits-all database that doesn't sacrifice the needs and wants of any database users. Most OS distributions carry a fairly new version that provides a quick and painless install process. Since the last edition of this book, cloud offerings have come on board that provide PostgreSQL with PostGIS out of the box. Some popular cloud versions of PostgreSQL that PostGIS users enjoy are CartoDB, Heroku PostgreSQL, and Amazon RDS for PostgreSQL.

FREE—AS IN MONEY

The starting package of Esri's ArcGIS for Server is well over $10,000 and gets higher as you add more cores. Licenses for SQL Server start at $5,000 and can easily cost you $20,000 for a modest server. The commercial version of Oracle's Spatial starts at $20,000 per core and doesn't even include the cost of the Enterprise license.

Oracle Standard ships with Oracle Locator, but this elementary tool lacks most of the medium and advanced functionality that PostGIS offers. The comparable Oracle Spatial requires the purchase of Oracle Enterprise.

PostGIS is free. 'Nuff said.

FREE—AS IN FREEDOM

PostGIS and PostgreSQL are open source. PostGIS is under a GPL v2 license; PostgreSQL is under a BSD-style license, which means you can both see and modify the source code. If you find a feature missing, you can contribute a patch or pay a developer to add the feature. Adding features to PostGIS and PostgreSQL generally costs much less than the licensing costs for proprietary counterparts. If you discover a bug in PostGIS, you can fix it instead of just reporting it. You have more freedom to control your destiny with PostGIS and PostgreSQL than you do with comparable proprietary offerings. You can install them on as many servers as you want, and you aren't limited by artificial restrictions on how many cores you can use.

The openness of PostGIS has spawned an explosion of user-contributed add-ons and community-funded features. These are the most notables ones to date: raster support, geodetic support, topology support, improved 3D support, faster spatial indexes, and Topologically Integrated Geographic Encoding and Referencing (TIGER) geocoder enhancements.

The release cycles for PostGIS and PostgreSQL are radically shorter than those of commercial offerings. With contributions from users, PostgreSQL evolves at a rate of one minor version per year and one micro version per two months, with bugs getting immediate attention. You don't have to wait years in anticipation of features promised in subsequent releases. If you choose to live on the bleeding edge, you can even download a new build every other week.

1.2.2 Alternatives to PostGIS

Admittedly, PostGIS isn't the only spatial database in use today. Early entrants were dominated by proprietary offerings, and PostGIS broke this mold. Successors to PostGIS are gravitating towards installations with lightweight footprints for use on mobile devices. We're also beginning to see rudimentary spatial features in NoSQL databases like MongoDB, CouchDB, and Solr.

Oracle Spatial

Oracle was the one that started it all. In Oracle 7, joint development efforts with Canadian scientists gave birth to SDO (Spatial Data Option). In later releases, Oracle redubbed this lovechild *Oracle Spatial*.

Oracle Spatial isn't available with lower-priced editions of Oracle. Only when you fork out the money for Oracle Enterprise Edition will you have the luxury of being able to buy the Oracle Spatial option.

Standard Oracle installations do come with something called *Oracle Locator*, which offers the basic geometry types, proximity functions, and some spatial aggregates, but it lacks processing features like union aggregation functions and intersection functions.

Microsoft SQL Server

Microsoft introduced spatial support in their SQL Server 2008 offering with its built-in Geometry and Geodetic Geography types and companion spatial functions. To Microsoft's credit, you'll get the same feature set with their express, standard, enterprise, and data center offerings. You may just be limited regarding database size, how many processors you can use, and what query plan features you're allowed.

Microsoft's spatial feature, except their curved and geodetic support, pales in comparison to PostGIS. Admittedly, Microsoft SQL Server 2012 has probably got the best curve and geodetic support of any database—it's the only one to support curved geometries in geodetic space. But don't expect to find numerous output/input functions, such as input/output for KML and JSON, or raster support, or the numerous processing functions that PostGIS has.

SpatiaLite

Our favorite kid on the block is SpatiaLite, which is an add-on to the open source SQLite portable database. SpatiaLite is especially interesting because it can be used as a low-end companion to PostGIS and other high-end, spatially enabled databases. It can run on an Android smartphone, and it can be used to create master/slave applications to provide basic lightweight spatial support for portable devices.

SpatiaLite also has a companion, RasterLite, that's mostly focused on raster data storage and display, and so makes a great companion to the raster analysis that's present in PostGIS. SpatiaLite and RasterLite also use many of the core libraries that PostGIS uses: GEOS, PROJ, and GDAL. This makes it an even more fitting companion to PostGIS, because many of the conventions are the same and much of the ecosystem around PostGIS also supports or is starting to support SpatiaLite/RasterLite.

What SpatiaLite lacks is a strong enterprise database behind it that allows for writing advanced functions and spatial aggregate functions. That's why some spatial queries possible in PostGIS are harder to write or are not even possible in SpatiaLite.

SpatiaLite/SQLite stores data as a single file that's easily transportable. This makes it less threatening to deploy for users new to databases or GIS, and easier to deploy as a lightweight offline database companion to a server-side database like PostGIS/PostgreSQL.

MySQL

MySQL has had elementary spatial support since version 4, but as a database MySQL is handicapped by its lack of a powerful SQL engine. Its primary audience is still developers who are looking for a database that will *store* something, rather than *do* something. Earlier MySQL spatial support made a fatal mistake of not providing indexing capabilities except on MyISAM tables—spatial queries rely heavily on indexing for speedy performance. In version 5.6, MySQL extended geometric operations to work beyond bounding boxes and also allowed spatial indexes on its InnoDB storage engine.

Oracle MySQL and other MySQL forks like MariaDB have made strides in the 5.6 variants by improving the performance of subqueries, but the query planner and SQL feature set in the MySQL family is still a kid when compared to the likes of PostgreSQL, SQL Server, and Oracle, so MySQL is not suitable for doing anything as complex as most spatial analysis.

ArcGIS by Esri

We must give a nod to Esri, which has long packaged its spatial database engine (SDE) with its ArcGIS for Server product. The SDE engine is integrated into the ArcGIS line of products and is often used to spatially enable or augment legacy or weak database products, such as Microsoft SQL Server 2005 and Oracle Locator.

Older versions of ArcGIS desktop required going through an SDE middle tier to get at the native offerings of your spatial database. Newer versions, starting around ArcGIS 10.0, allow for direct read-only access to PostGIS and other databases. By sidestepping the middleware, you're free to use any version of PostGIS with ArcGIS desktop. Although their proprietary model doesn't sit well with us, we must give them credit—a lot of credit, in fact—for being one of the first major companies to introduce GIS analysis to commercial and government organizations. They paved the way, but still stand in the way, for the rise of free and open source GIS.

1.2.3 Installing PostGIS

We encourage you to install the latest version of PostgreSQL and PostGIS—PostgreSQL 9.4 and PostGIS 2.1 at the time of writing. The introduction of the extension model in PostgreSQL 9.1 greatly simplified the installation of add-ons (such as PostGIS) to two steps. First, you locate and install the binaries for your particular OS into your PostgreSQL directories. Second, you individually enable the extensions for each database as needed. For instance, if you have ten databases on your server, but only two require PostGIS, you'd only enable PostGIS for the two.

> **PostGIS must be enabled in each database**
>
> One characteristic of PostgreSQL that confuses many people coming from other database systems is that custom extensions like PostGIS, `hstore`, PL/JavaScript, and PL/Python must be enabled in each database they will be used in. This isn't the case for built-in types like Full-Text, XML, PostgreSQL 9.2+ JSON, and so on, which are always present.

Many of the popular Linux/Unix distributions include PostGIS 2.1 in their repository. Use `yum` or `apt-get` to install the binaries. For Mac users, there are a couple of popular distributions, all itemized on http://postgis.net/install. For Windows, we recommend using the EnterpriseDB StackBuilder. Please refer to appendix A for more details on where to obtain binaries for your OS.

Once you've successfully installed the binaries, you can create a database with a command such as this:

```
CREATE DATABASE postgis_in_action;
```

You next enable PostGIS in your database by connecting to the database and running the single-line SQL command in the following listing. Enabling the extension rarely fails, but you may encounter dependency errors, especially if you have earlier versions of PostGIS floating around.

Listing 1.1 Enabling PostGIS in a database

```
CREATE EXTENSION postgis;
```

Two popular tools come packaged with PostgreSQL: *psql* and *pgAdmin*. You use these tools to create databases, users, and compose queries.

Psql is strictly a command-line tool. If you don't have a GUI, psql is your only option.

If you have the luxury of a graphical interface, we encourage you to use the more newbie-friendly pgAdmin. PgAdmin can be installed separately from PostgreSQL. You can find source code as well as precompiled binaries at the pgAdmin site, http://www.pgadmin.org.

To enable extensions in pgAdmin, use the extension install section pictured in figure 1.2.

If postgis isn't listed, you can install it by right-clicking the Extensions branch, choosing New Extension, and picking postgis from the menu. You should see postgis listed in the Add Extension menu if you installed the binaries and don't have it already installed in your selected database.

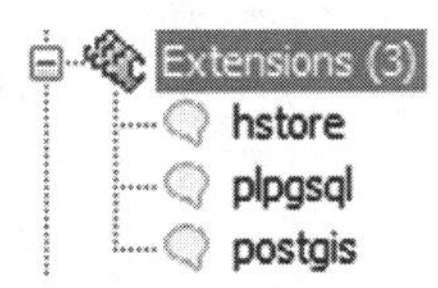

Figure 1.2 Database with postgis extension installed

VERIFYING VERSIONS OF POSTGIS AND POSTGRESQL

After a PostGIS install, do a quick verification of the version to make sure the installation succeeded. Execute the following query:

```
SELECT postgis_full_version();
```

If all is well, you should see the version of PostGIS, as well as the versions of the supporting GEOS, GDAL, PROJ, LIBXML, and LIBJSON libraries, as shown here:

```
POSTGIS="2.1.2 r12389"
GEOS="3.4.2-CAPI-1.8.2 r3924"
PROJ="Rel. 4.8.0, 6 March 2012"
GDAL="GDAL 1.10.0, released 2013/04/24"
LIBXML="2.7.8" LIBJSON="UNKNOWN" RASTER
```

Installing visualization tools

Unlike conventional character-based databases, spatial databases must be experienced visually. When you view a bitmap file, you'd much rather see the rendered bitmap than the bits themselves. Similarly, you'd much rather see your spatial objects rendered rather than their textual representations.

Many visualization tools are available for free download, with OpenJump and QGIS being two of the more popular ones. We encourage you to install multiple viewing tools for comparison. Chapter 5 offers a quick comparison and installation guide to get you started with these tools.

1.3 Spatial data types

There are four key spatial types offered by PostGIS: geometry, geography, raster, and topology. PostGIS has always supported the *geometry* type from its inception. It introduced support for *geography* in PostGIS 1.5. PostGIS 2.0 raised the bar more by incorporating *raster* and *network topology* support. Although PostGIS 2.1 introduces many more functions, perhaps the most important feature it provides is faster speed, particularly for *raster* and *geography* operations:

- *Geometry*—The planar type. This was the very first model and it's still the most popular type that PostGIS supports. It's the foundation of the other types. It uses the Cartesian math you learned about in high school geometry.
- *Geography*—The spheroidal geodetic type. Lines and polygons are drawn on the earth's curved surface, so they're curved rather than straight lines.
- *Raster*—The multiband cell type. Rasters model space as a grid of rectangular cells, each containing a numeric array of values.
- *Topology*—The relational model type. Topology models the world as a network of connected nodes, edges, and faces. Objects are composed of these and may share these with other objects. There are really two related concepts in topology—the *network*, which defines what elements each thing is composed of, and *routing*. PostGIS 2+ packages the *network topology* model, which is often just referred to as *topology*. Network topology ensures that when you change the edge of an object, other objects sharing that edge will change accordingly. *Routing* is commonly used with PostGIS via a long-supported add-on called *pgRouting*. Routing not only cares about connectedness, but also how costly that connectedness is. PgRouting is mostly used for building trip navigation applications (taking into account the cost of tolls or delays due to construction), but it can be used for any application where costs along a path are important. We'll cover pgRouting in later chapters of this book.

These four types can coexist in the same database and even as separate columns in the same table. For example, you can have a geometry that defines the boundaries of a plant, and you can have a raster that defines the concentration of toxic waste along each part of the boundary.

1.3.1 Geometry type

In two dimensions, you can represent all geographical entities with three building blocks: points, linestrings, and polygons (see figure 1.3). For example, an interstate highway crossing the salt flats of Utah clearly jumps out as linestrings cutting through a polygon. A desolate gas station located somewhere along the interstate can be a point.

But you need not limit yourself to the macro dimensions of road atlases. Look around your home. Use rectangular polygons to represent rooms. The wiring and the piping running behind the walls would be linestrings. You can use either a point or a polygon to stand in for the dog house, depending on its size. Just by abstracting the landscape to 2D points, linestrings, and polygons, you have enough to model everything that could crop up on a map or a blueprint.

Don't be overly concerned with the rigorous definition of the geometries. Questions such as how many angles will fit into a point, and what is the width of a linestring are best left for mathematicians and philosophers. To us, points, linestrings, and polygons are simplified models of reality. As such, they'll never perfectly mimic the real thing. Also, don't worry if you feel that we're leaving out other geometries. Two good examples are beltways around a metropolis and hippodromes. The former could be well represented by circles; the latter by ellipses. You'll do fine by approximating them using linestrings with many segments, and polygons with many edges.

The geometry type treats the world as a flat Cartesian grid. The mathematics behind the model requires nothing more than the analytic geometry you learned in high school. The geometry model is intuitively appealing and computationally speedy, but it suffers from one major shortcoming—the flat earth.

1.3.2 Geography type

The curvature of the earth comes into play when you're modeling anything that extends beyond the visual horizon. Although geometry works for architectural floor plans, city blocks, and runway diagrams, it comes up short when you model shipping lanes, airways, or continents, or whenever you consider two locations that are far apart. You can still perform distance computations without abandoning the Cartesian

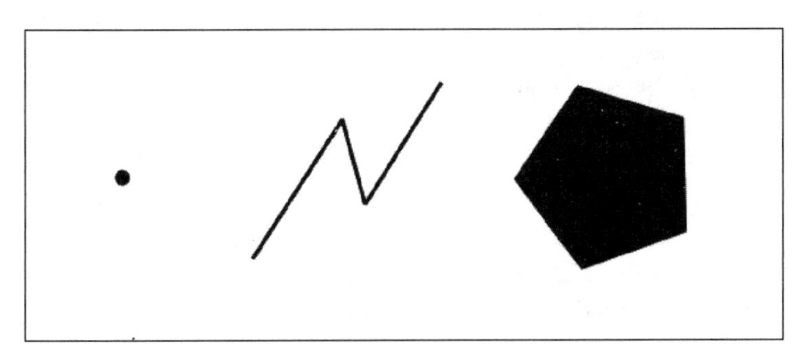

Figure 1.3 Basic geometries: a point, a linestring, and a polygon

underpinnings by sprinkling a few sines and cosines into your formulas, but the minute you need to compute areas, the math becomes intractable.

A better solution is to use a new family of data types based on geodetic coordinates—geography. This new family shields the PostGIS user from the complexity of the math. As a trade-off, geography offers fewer functions, and it trails geometry in speed. You'll find the same point, linestring, and polygon data types in geography; just keep in mind that the linestrings and polygons conform to the curves of the earth.

Are geometry and geography standard or not?

The geometry type is a long-accepted OGC SQL/MM type that you'll find in other relational databases. Geography, on the other hand, isn't a standard type and is only found in PostGIS and SQL Server.

The PostGIS geography type is loosely patterned after the SQL Server 2008+ geography type. For general use cases, you can think of the SQL Server geography type and PostGIS geography type as the same kind of animal.

1.3.3 Raster type

Geometry and geography are vector-based data types. Loosely speaking, anything you can sketch with an ultra-fine pen without running short on ink lends itself to vector representation. Vectors are well suited to modeling designed or constructed features, but suppose you snap a colored photo of the coral-rich Tasmania sea. With its motley colors and fractal patterns, you're going to have a hard time constructing lines and polygons out of the photo. Your best hope is to quantize the photo into microscopic rectangles and assign a color value to each. *Raster data* is exactly this—a mosaic of pixels.

Perhaps the best example of a raster is the television you stare at every day, for hours on end. A TV screen is nothing more than a giant raster with some 2 million pixels. Each pixel stores three different color values: the intensity of red, green, and blue (hence the term RGB). In raster-speak, each color is called a *band.* The scale of each pixel's edges corresponds to the underlying spatial reference system—if you're measuring in meters, the pixel represents one square meter of area.

If you're buying a TV set, the physical number of pixels will matter greatly to you: the larger the number of pixels, the bigger the viewing area and the more money it'll cost you. For GIS purposes, the pixel has no physical meaning. It's nothing more than a bundle of data. Terms like pixel length or size don't apply. Each pixel *represents* a certain unit of area in reality, nothing more.

Raster data almost always originates from instrumental data collection and often serves as the raw material for generating vector data. As such, you'll encounter plenty more sources of raster data than vector data. PostGIS will let you overlay vector data atop raster data and vice versa. The satellite view of Google maps is a perfect example of such an overlay. You see roads superimposed on top of the satellite imagery.

Rasters appear in the following applications:

- Land coverage or land use.
- Temperature and elevation variations. This is a single-band raster where each square holds a measured temperature or elevation value.
- Color aerial and satellite photos. These have four bands—one for each of the colors of the RGBA color space.

1.3.4 Topology type

When you gaze down at the terrain from your private jet, what you witness is not distinct geometries on a barren terrestrial plane, but an interwoven network of points, linestrings, and polygons. A cornfield abuts a wheat field, abuts a pasture, abuts a large expanse of prairie. Roads, rivers, fences, or other artificial boundaries divide them all. The surface of the earth (at least the parts that host humanity) resembles a completed jigsaw puzzle. Topology models take on this jigsaw perspective of the world. Topology recognizes the inherent interconnection of geographic features and exploits it to help you better manage data.

Consider a historical example where you want to model the United States and Mexico as two large polygons. Prior to the Gadsden Purchase, the northern boundary of Mexico extended well into present day Arizona and parts of New Mexico. For 33 cents per acre, the U.S. "purchased" 30 million acres from Mexico. The U.S. polygon grew as the Mexico polygon shrank. If you were using the geometry family to model the two polygons, you'd have to perform two operations to get your record-keeping straight: enlarge the U.S. and shrink Mexico. Using the topology model, you only need to perform one operation—either the enlargement or the shrinkage—because topology tracks the fact that the U.S. abuts Mexico. If the U.S. grows on its southern border, Mexico must shrink on its northern border. One operation implies the other.

Topology isn't concerned with the exact shape and location of geographic features, but with how they're connected to each other.

Topology is useful in the following applications:

- Parcel (land lot) data, where you want to ensure that the change of one parcel boundary adjusts all other parcels that share that boundary change as well.
- Road management, water boundaries, and jurisdiction divisions. U.S. Census MAF/Topologically Integrated Geographic Encoding and Referencing system (TIGER) data is a perfect example (http://www.census.gov/geo/www/tiger/).
- Architecture.

1.4 Hello real world

In this section, we'll walk you through a full example from start to finish. Unfortunately, PostGIS is not a programming language where a few lines of code will print a Hello World message on your screen. Instead, to provide you with a true taste of PostGIS, we'll guide you through the following steps:

- Digesting a problem and formulating a solution
- Modeling
- Gathering and loading data
- Writing a query
- Viewing the result

If you're completely new to PostGIS, just perform the tasks we ask of you for now. You won't understand most of what you're typing, but you'll have the rest of this book for that. Right now, we want to give you an overview of the steps involved in writing a spatial query.

Before going further, you'll need to have a working copy of PostGIS 2.0 or higher and PostgreSQL 9.0 or higher (preferably 9.1+ to take advantage of the new, simpler extension installation feature), as well as ancillary tools such as pgAdmin III to compose and execute your queries. Information about acquiring and installing these can be found in appendix B. As always, if you're starting from scratch, we recommend that you install the latest versions.

1.4.1 Digesting the problem

Here's the scenario you're faced with: you need to find the number of fast-food restaurants within one mile of a highway. As for why someone might want to do this, any of the following reasons could apply:

- A fast-food chain is trying to locate a new store where supply falls short.
- A highway commissioner wants to satisfy the needs of motorists, who will be paying tolls.
- A health-conscious parent is trying to cut down the availability of fast food in the neighborhood.
- Hungry travelers are looking for their next meal.

First, you need to realize that you're not going to be able to answer this question quickly or accurately with your usual arsenal of Google Maps, MapQuest, or even the latest paper map you picked up from the auto association. Learning PostGIS may not be any quicker, but you'll have at your disposal the tools and skills to solve any and all problems of this kind in the future. Replace the highway with a lake, and you can determine how many homes surrounding the lake can be considered waterfront property. On a geodetic scale, replace the highway with the continent of Australia, and you can determine the number of islands within territorial waters. From there, you can even go on to a planetary scale and ask how many moons are within 10 million kilometers at perigee.

Once you have an initial understanding of the problem, we recommend that you immediately perform a feasibility study, even if it's just in your mind. You don't want to devote time to a solution if the problem itself is impossible to solve, lacking specificity, or, worse, you have no available data source.

Before going further, you need the postgis_in_action database you set up in section 1.2.3.

1.4.2 Modeling

You need to translate the real world to a model that is composed of database objects. For this example, you'll represent the highway as a geometric linestring and the locations of fast-food restaurants as points. You'll then create two tables: highways and restaurants.

Using schemas

First, you need to create a schema to hold your data for this chapter. A schema is a container you'll find in most high-end databases. It logically segments objects (tables, views, functions, and so on) for easier management.

```
CREATE SCHEMA ch01;
```

In PostgreSQL it's very easy to back up selected schemas and also to set up permissions based on schemas. You could, for example, have a big schema of fairly static data that you exclude from your daily backups, and also divide schemas along user groups so that you can allow each group to manage their own schema set of data. The postgis_in_action database schemas are chapter-themed so that it's easy to download just the set of data you need for a specific chapter. Refer to appendix D for more details about schemas and security management.

Restaurants table

Next, you need to create a lookup table to map franchise codes to meaningful names. You can then add all the franchises you'll be dealing with.

Listing 1.2 Create franchise lookup table

```
CREATE TABLE ch01.lu_franchises (
    id char(3) PRIMARY KEY,                    <-- Create table
    franchise varchar(30)
);

INSERT INTO ch01.lu_franchises(id, franchise)      <-- Populate table
VALUES
  ('BKG', 'Burger King'), ('CJR', 'Carl''s Jr'),
  ('HDE', 'Hardee'), ('INO', 'In-N-Out'),
  ('JIB', 'Jack in the Box'), ('KFC', 'Kentucky Fried Chicken'),
  ('MCD', 'McDonald'), ('PZH', 'Pizza Hut'),
  ('TCB', 'Taco Bell'), ('WDY', 'Wendy's');
```

Finally, you need to create a table to hold the data you'll be loading.

Listing 1.3 Create restaurants table

```
CREATE TABLE ch01.restaurants (
    id serial PRIMARY KEY,              <-- 1 Create dummy primary key
    franchise char(3) NOT NULL,
    geom geometry(point,2163)           <-- 2 Create spatial geometry column
);
```

The restaurant data has no primary key, and nothing in the data file lends itself to a good natural primary key, so you create a dummy one ❶. For your later analysis, you'll need to uniquely identify restaurants so that you don't double-count them. Also, certain mapping servers and viewers, such as MapServer and QGIS, balk at tables without integer primary keys or unique indexes, so you need to create an autonumber primary key on the restaurants table.

Next, you use a point geometry column to store your restaurant locations ❷. The second argument to the geometry function indicates the spatial reference ID (SRID) that you've selected for the restaurant data. The SRID denotes the coordinate range and how the spherical space is projected on a flat surface. We'll get into more detail about spatial reference systems in chapter 3. If you're coming from a GIS background, you'll know that you must have common projections before you can compare two data sets. This example uses EPSG:2163, which is an equal-area projection covering the continental United States.

Next, you need to place a spatial index on your geometry column:

```
CREATE INDEX idx_code_restaurants_geom ON ch01.restaurants USING gist(geom);
```

As part of the definition of an index in PostgreSQL, you must specify the type of index as we did in the preceding `CREATE INDEX`. PostGIS spatial indexes are of the gist index type.

Although it's not necessary for this particular data set, because it won't be updated, you'll create a foreign key relationship between the franchise column in the restaurants table and the lookup table. This helps prevent people from mistyping franchises in the restaurants table. Adding `CASCADE UPDATE DELETE` rules when you add foreign key relationships will allow you to change the franchise ID for your franchises if you want, and have those changes update the restaurants table automatically. By restricting deletes, you prevent inadvertent removal of franchises with extant records in the restaurants table. (One added benefit of foreign keys is that relational designers, such as those you'll find in OpenOffice Base and other ERD tools, will automatically draw lines between the two tables to visually alert you to the relationship.)

```
ALTER TABLE ch01.restaurants
ADD CONSTRAINT fk_restaurants_lu_franchises    FOREIGN KEY (franchise)
REFERENCES ch01.lu_franchises (id) ON UPDATE CASCADE ON DELETE RESTRICT;
```

You can then create an index to make the join between the two tables more efficient:

```
CREATE INDEX fki_restaurants_franchises ON ch01.restaurants (franchise);
```

HIGHWAYS TABLE

Next you need to create a highways table to contain the road segments that are highways.

Listing 1.4 Create highways table

```
CREATE TABLE ch01.highways (          <-- Create highways table
  gid integer NOT NULL,
```

```
  feature character varying(80),
  name character varying(120),
  state character varying(2),
  geom geometry(multilinestring,2163),        <-- Multilinestring equal area
  CONSTRAINT pk_highways PRIMARY KEY (gid)
);

CREATE INDEX idx_highways ON ch01.highways USING gist(geom);   <-- Add spatial index
```

In this case, you're creating the spatial index before loading the data, but for large tables that are loaded only once, it's more efficient to create the indexes after you have loaded the data.

1.4.3 Loading data

To give this example some real-world flavor, we'll scope out real data sources.

In this chapter, you first created the data tables and are now chasing after data to populate them. Ideally, these are the steps you'd want to take. In reality, though, you'll sometimes find yourself subservient to the available data and begrudgingly have to alter your ideal table structure to fit what's available.

But don't surrender to the availability of real data too easily. You can often create SQL scripts that will translate the less-than-perfect data from your source into your perfected data structure. Always give primacy to your model. A well-thought-out model can often ride out the vagaries of a data source. We'll follow this mantra as we continue.

IMPORTING A CSV FILE

Fastfoodmaps.com graciously provided us with a comma-delimited file of all fast-food restaurants circa 2005. To import a CSV file, you need to create a table beforehand. After quickly studying the CSV file, you can create a staging table:

```
CREATE TABLE ch01.restaurants_staging (
  franchise text,
  lat double precision,
  lon double precision
);
```

Use the psql `\copy` command to import the CSV file into your staging table:

```
copy ch01.restaurants_staging
 FROM '/data/restaurants.csv' DELIMITER as ',';
```

Your purpose here is to get the CSV data into a table so you can scrutinize it more carefully and write any additional queries to sanitize the data before you insert it into the production table. In this case, the data passes the quality check, so you can proceed with the insert:

```
INSERT INTO ch01.restaurants (franchise, geom)
SELECT
    franchise,
    ST_Transform(ST_SetSRID(ST_Point(lon,lat),4326),2163) As geom
FROM ch01.restaurants_staging;
```

In this example, we use SRID 4326 (which corresponds to WGS 84 lon/lat), but then transform all the data to our desired planar projection for faster analysis.

> **Spatial reference IDs (SRID) and spatial reference systems (SRS)**
> You'll often find number identifiers such as `4326` and `2163` in PostGIS and other spatial database code. These refer to records in the spatial_ref_sys table, where srid is the column that uniquely identifies the record. The ID 4326 is the most popular and refers to an SRS that often goes by the name WGS 84 lon/lat. We'll go into spatial reference systems in more detail in chapter 3.

IMPORTING FROM AN ESRI SHAPEFILE

You'll find Esri shapefiles to be a common storage format for spatial data, mostly due to Esri's early preponderance in GIS. To load data from shapefiles into a PostGIS database, use the shp2pgsql command-line utility that comes with all PostGIS installations. If you're on Windows or Linux/Unix with a graphical desktop, you can also use the GUI version of the utility, dubbed shp2pgsql-gui. Both shp2pgsql and shp2pgsql-gui can load DBF files in addition to the Esri shapefile format.

We'll use shp2pgsql-gui to demonstrate loading the road network data we downloaded from the National Atlas website and packaged with this chapter's download. Using pgAdmin III, you can first highlight the database and then fire up shp2pgsql-gui using the plug-in menu or button. See figure 1.4.

> **What if the shp2pgsql-gui plug-in doesn't show in plug-ins?**
> There are generally two reasons why the PostGIS Shapefile and Dbf-Loader option doesn't show in your pgAdmin plug-ins menu. The first is that your distribution doesn't install this GUI. The second is that the .ini file that pgAdmin is looking for isn't in the right place. Refer to the "Configured shp2pgsql-gui in pgAdmin III" page (www.postgresonline.com/journal/archives/180-shp2pgsql-gui.html) for troubleshooting help.

You can use the Add File button to add one or more shapefiles, and each file appears in the Import List. Each shapefile will load into its own table. Clicking in any cell in the file list allows you to change the preset value.

You know your projection to be NAD 83 lon/lat, so you indicate this by changing the SRID to 4269, but be careful here! You're simply telling the importer what the SRID is for the data coming in. You're not transforming it! In this example, we also changed the name of the imported table to highways_staging. Click the Import button once you're ready.

Once the import finishes, you should see the new highways_staging table in your database. You may have to refresh the browse tree in pgAdmin. Both shp2pgsql-gui and its command-line sibling automatically add a column named geom during the

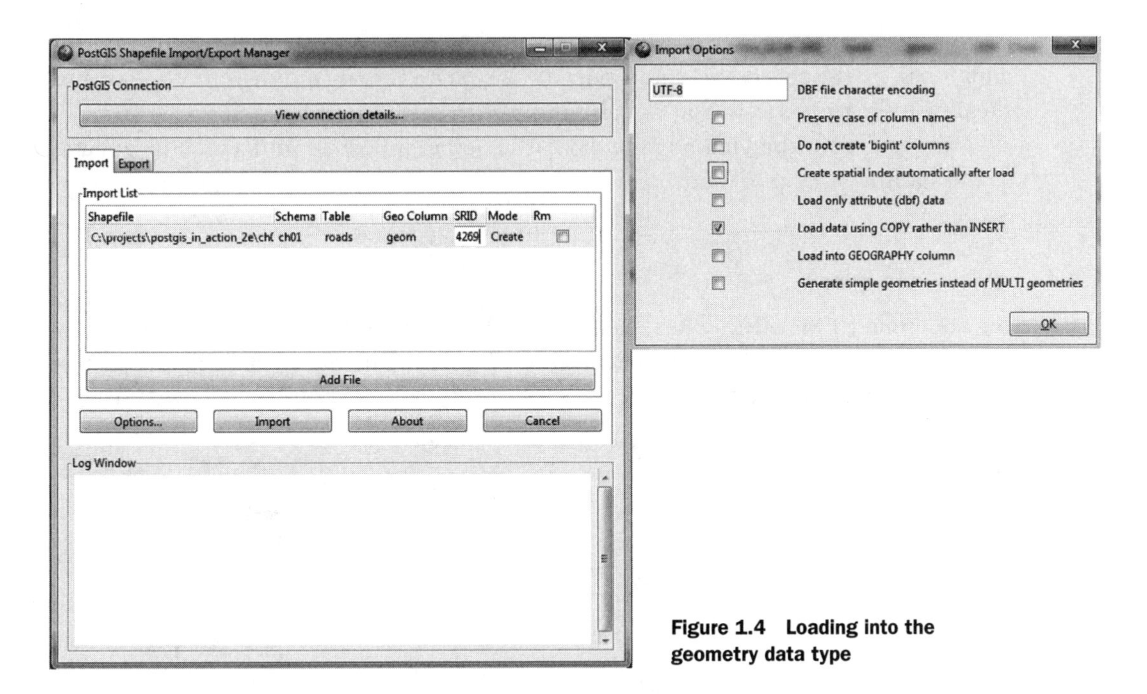

Figure 1.4 Loading into the geometry data type

import and set its data type by reading information contained in the shapefile. If you're unfamiliar with the raw data, this is the time to study it. Perform general sanity checks, such as checking the total record count, inspecting columns that came in without data, and so on.

After you're satisfied that the importer did its job without dropping any information, you can write an insert query to move the data from your staging table to the production table. In the query, you want to transform the SRID from 4269 to 2163 and only select columns that you defined in your production table. You can also filter the data to only the needed rows. The highway data has approximately 47,000 rows and includes every major and state highway in the U.S., and you're only going to be looking at major highways, so you can add a filter that will bring the row count down to about 14,000.

Listing 1.5 Populating the highways table

```
INSERT INTO ch01.highways (gid, feature, name, state, geom)
SELECT gid, feature, name, state, ST_Transform(geom, 2163)
FROM ch01.highways_staging
WHERE feature LIKE 'Principal Highway%';
```

If you'd rather use the command-line shp2pgsql tool, open up the psql console and type in the following command:

```
shp2pgsql -s 4269:2163 -g geom
➥ -I /data/roadtrl020.shp ch01.highways_staging
➥| psql -h localhost -U postgres -p 5432 -d postgis_in_action
```

As you might have noticed, the command line lets you transform the SRID with an additional `-s` switch, so you could skip the `ST_Transform` step in your code or use the data more or less as is. You can also index with the `-I` switch.

After you've finished loading the data, it's good to follow up with a vacuum analyze so the statistics are up to date:

```
vacuum analyze ch01.highways;
```

1.4.4 Writing the query

It's now time to write the query. Remember the question we set out to answer: *How many fast-food restaurants are within one mile of a highway?* The query that will answer this question is shown in the following listing.

Listing 1.6 Restaurants within one mile of a highway

```
SELECT f.franchise, COUNT(DISTINCT r.id) As total        ❶ Remove duplicates
FROM
    ch01.restaurants As r INNER JOIN
    ch01.lu_franchises As f ON r.franchise = f.id INNER JOIN
    ch01.highways As h ON ST_DWithin(r.geom,h.geom,1609)        ❷ Spatial join
GROUP BY f.franchise
ORDER BY total DESC;
```

The crux of this example is where you join the restaurants table with the highways table using the `ST_DWithin` function ❷. This commonly used function accepts two geometries and returns true if the minimum distance between the two geometries is within the specified distance. In this case, you pass in a point for the restaurant, a multilinestring for the highway, and 1609 meters as the distance. All restaurant-highway pairs matching the join condition will filter through.

The join condition does allow for duplicate restaurants. For example, a McDonalds located at the intersection of two major highways would show up twice. To only count each restaurant once, you use the `COUNT(DISTINCT)` construct ❶.

The rest of the code is elementary SQL. If you're a little rusty on SQL, please see appendix C for a refresher. As fair warning, the SQL we use in this book will get harder.

Finally, here's the fruit of your labor.

```
     franchise_name      | total
-------------------------+------
 McDonald's              | 5343
 Burger King             | 3049
 Pizza Hut               | 2920
 Wendy's                 | 2446
 Taco Bell               | 2428
 Kentucky Fried Chicken  | 2371
:
```

1.4.5 Viewing spatial data with OpenJump

What's more gratifying than to see your query output displayed on a map? You don't want to display some 20,000 dots on a map of the U.S.—you can find that on each chain's restaurant locator. Instead, you're going to draw a buffer zone around highway segments and see how many dots fall within them.

For this you'll use the `ST_Buffer` function. This function will take any geometry and radially expand it by a specified number of units. The post-expansion polygonal geometry is called a *buffer zone* or *corridor*.

> **INSTALLING OPENJUMP** If you haven't installed OpenJump, do so now before continuing. Chapter 5 discusses the installation and use of OpenJump, among other tools.

For this example, we'll locate Hardee's restaurants within a 20-mile buffer of U.S. Route 1 in the state of Maryland. Here's the query to get the count:

```
SELECT COUNT(DISTINCT r.id) As total
FROM ch01.restaurants As r INNER JOIN ch01.highways As h
ON ST_DWithin(r.geom, h.geom, 1609*20)
WHERE r.franchise = 'HDE' AND h.name  = 'US Route 1' AND h.state = 'MD';
```

Let's see where the three Hardee's are located. Fire up OpenJump and connect to your PostgreSQL database. You can first draw U.S. Route 1 using the following query:

```
SELECT gid, name, geom
FROM ch01.highways
WHERE name = 'US Route 1' AND state = 'MD';
```

Next, overlay the 20-mile corridor:

```
SELECT ST_Union(ST_Buffer(geom, 1609*20))
FROM ch01.highways
WHERE name = 'US Route 1' AND state = 'MD';
```

Finally, position the Hardee's in the buffer zone routes.

```
SELECT r.geom
FROM ch01.restaurants r
WHERE EXISTS (
    SELECT gid
    FROM ch01.highways
    WHERE
        ST_DWithin(r.geom, geom, 1609*20) AND
        name = 'US Route 1' AND
        state = 'MD' AND
        r.franchise = 'HDE'
);
```

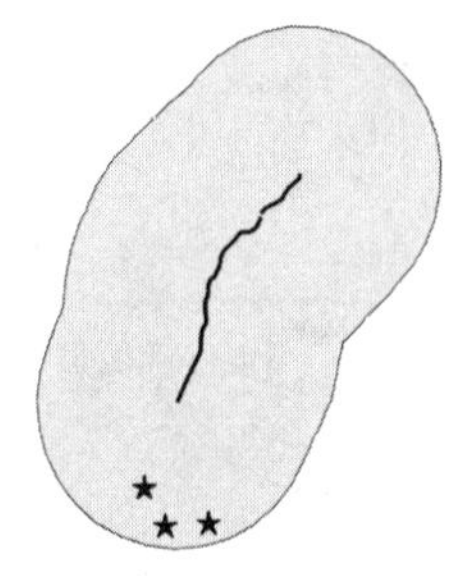

Figure 1.5 U.S. Route 1 in Maryland, with three Hardee's restaurants in the 20-mile buffer, and the 20-mile buffer around the route

The results are shown in figure 1.5.

Play around with this example. Use your home state and your favorite restaurant chain to see how far you have to go to grab your next nutritious meal.

1.5 Summary

In this chapter, we've given you a small taste of how a spatially enabled database can fit in with a relational database system. We sowed the idea of how you can model real-world objects in space with spatial constructs.

We championed PostgreSQL and its spatial companion PostGIS. We demonstrated how PostgreSQL and PostGIS can be used together to analyze spatial patterns in data. We hope we've convinced you that the PostgreSQL/PostGIS combination is one of the best choices (if not *the* best) for spatial analysis.

Some of the SQL examples we demonstrated were at an intermediate level. If you're new to SQL or spatial databases, these examples may have seemed daunting. In the chapters that follow, we'll explain the functions we used here and the SQL constructs in greater detail. For now, we hope that you focused on the general steps we followed and the strategies that we chose.

Although spatial modeling is an integral part of any spatial analysis, there's no right or wrong answer in modeling. Modeling is inherently a balance between simplicity and adequacy. You want to make your model as simple as possible so you can focus on the problem you're trying to solve, but you must retain enough complexity to simulate the world you're trying to model. Therein lies the challenge.

Before we can continue our journey, we must first analyze the different spatial types that PostGIS offers and show you how to create these and when it's appropriate to do so. We'll explore the geometry, geography, and raster types in greater detail in the next chapter and revisit topology in chapter 13.

2 Spatial data types

This chapter covers

- Geometry, geography, and raster spatial types and subtypes
- Geometry and geography type modifiers
- Spatial catalog tables
- How to create spatial columns and populate them

In the first chapter, we teased you with the potential that you can unlock with PostGIS. This chapter will start to show you how, by delving deeper into the core spatial data types bundled with PostGIS. We'll discuss each spatial type in detail. Once you've completed this chapter, you'll know how to create table columns of these various types and how to populate them with spatial data.

Do keep in the back of your mind that PostgreSQL has its own built-in geometric types. These are `point`, `polygon`, `lseg`, `box`, `circle`, and `path`. PostgreSQL geometry types are incompatible with the PostGIS geometry type and have little or no third-party visualization support. These geometry types have existed since the dawn of PostgreSQL and don't follow the SQL/MM standards, nor do they support spatial coordinate systems. Using them as mathematical tools is fine, but stay away from them for GIS use or if you need visualization support.

If you're in too deep, PostGIS 2.1 introduced functions and casts to convert the PostgreSQL types to PostGIS `geometry`. For example, this line converts a PostgreSQL `polygon` to an equivalent PostGIS `geometry`:

```
SELECT polygon('((10,20),(30,40),(35,40),(10,20))')::geometry;
```

> **LAYERS** Geometry, geography, and raster columns in a spatial table are often referred to as *layers* or *feature classes* when displayed in mapping applications.

Before you begin, you'll need to create a schema to house the data for this chapter:

```
CREATE SCHEMA ch02;
```

The data and code used in this chapter can be found at http://www.postgis.us/chapter_02_edition_2.

2.1 Type modifiers

Before we get into data types, we must explain type modifiers (a.k.a. typmods). You use type modifiers all the time in PostgreSQL, perhaps not knowing what they're called. When you declare a column as `varchar(8)`, the number `8` is a type modifier. In this particular case, it's the character length type modifier for the `varchar` data type. When you write `numeric(8,2)`, you're declaring the data type to be `numeric`, the length (precision) type modifier to be `8`, and the scale type modifier to be `2`.

You specify type modifiers when you declare the data type of a column. Alternatively, you can use check constraints to achieve the same effect as type modifiers. For example, you can declare a column as `varchar` and then add a check constraint that limits the length to be `8`. Loosely speaking, only constraints involving attributes that are often used are promoted to be type modifiers. In the `varchar` example, the length check qualified as a type modifier, but a lesser attribute, such as the number of vowels in the `varchar`, would not.

2.1.1 Subtype type modifiers

The `geometry` and `geography` data types have hierarchical structures. You can declare a column to be a `geometry` or `geography` type, but you can and should be more specific where possible and use subtypes. Subtypes are not data types, but for `geography` and `geometry` are type modifiers. Some examples of geometry subtypes are `POINTZ`, `POINT`, `LINESTRING`, `LINESTRINGM`, `POLYGON`, `POLYGONZ`, `POLYHERALSURFACE`, `POLYHEDRALSURFACEZ`, `TIN`, and `TINZ`. A typical type declaration in PostGIS is `geometry(POINT,4326)`, where `geometry` is the data type, `POINT` is the subtype type modifier, and `4326` is the SRID type modifier. To make the subtype stand out from other type modifiers, we'll capitalize subtypes in the code listings and in the narrative, where needed for clarification. PostgreSQL ignores casing in types and type modifiers, so you don't need to follow our convention.

In the early years of PostGIS, type modifiers for non-built-in types didn't exist. Because PostGIS-packaged data types are custom types (not packaged with PostgreSQL), you had to first create your table excluding the geometry column, and then use the `AddGeometryColumn` function to add the geometry column and apply SRID and subtype check constraints to the column in order to ensure that it only contained a particular subtype of a particular spatial reference system. You can still use this function, but the behavior has changed. In PostGIS 2.0+, the `AddGeometryColumn` function will by default create the column using the new type-modifier approach instead of the old check-constraint approach. In PostGIS 2.0 and later, you should make use of the subtype type modifier in the type declaration itself, as in `geometry (POINT)`, so that you can create the table in a single step. To draw a parallel example with other PostgreSQL data types, the constraint approach would be akin to declaring a column as `varchar` and then adding a check constraint that limits the length to be `8` instead of declaring the column as `varchar(8)` to begin with.

Only the `geometry` and `geography` data types support type modifiers. The PostGIS `raster` data type doesn't, nor does the `topogeometry` data type you'll learn about in later chapters.

> **TYPMOD** We use the term *typmod* both as an abbreviation for *type modifier* and also to refer to the practice of adding type modifiers in parentheses during column creation.

2.1.2 Spatial reference identifier

One attribute that all data types have is a spatial reference identifier (SRID). We'll cover SRIDs and spatial reference systems in chapter 3. For now, it's enough to know that if two different spatial objects have the same SRID, then you can determine spatial relationships between them, like how far are they from each other or whether one is contained in another. If they are different but known types, you can transform one to match the other. You can even determine spatial relationships between two spatial objects that have different data types, but have the same SRID. To overlay a geometry atop a raster and have everything line up perfectly, you just need to make sure they both share the same SRID.

In order to use a particular SRID, it must be present in the spatial_ref_sys table. You can leave the SRID as unknown—since PostGIS 2.0, an unknown SRID takes on the value of `0`. An unknown SRID means that the geometry in question doesn't take on geographical meaning, but that it still resides in Cartesian space. Suppose you're trying to map out your living room on a blueprint—the SRID is unimportant, but the geometry is still useful for modeling.

2.2 Geometry

At the dawn of PostGIS, `geometry` was the only data type available. The `geometry` data type was so named because its basis is analytical geometry (Cartesian geometry). All `geometry` subtypes assume a Cartesian coordinate system: parallel lines never meet, the Pythagorean theorem applies, the distances between coordinates are uniform throughout, and so on.

Often, you'll find people using latitude and longitude to specify a point geometry, but don't let this mislead you into thinking that they've abandoned the Cartesian plane. The use of lon/lat coordinates in geometry means that the area under consideration is small enough that you can treat degrees of longitude and latitude as uniform, and that the curvature of the earth doesn't come into play. When dealing with distances on a global scale, however, the `geometry` data type is grossly inadequate. For these, you should use the `geography` data type.

2.2.1 Points

Subtypes of points differentiate themselves by the dimension of the Cartesian space they occupy. Here's a complete listing of `POINT` subtype modifiers for `geometry` and `geography`:

- `POINT`—A point in 2D space specified by its X and Y coordinates
- `POINTZ`—A point in 3D space specified by its X, Y, and Z coordinates
- `POINTM`—A point in 2D space with a measured value specified by its spatial X and Y coordinates plus an M value
- `POINTZM`—A point in 3D space with a measured value specified by its X, Y, and Z coordinates plus an M value

The code in the following listing creates a table with one column for each of the points subtypes and appends one record.

Listing 2.1 Points

```
CREATE TABLE ch02.my_points (
    id serial PRIMARY KEY,
    p geometry(POINT),
    pz geometry(POINTZ),
    pm geometry(POINTM),
    pzm geometry(POINTZM),
    p_srid geometry(POINT,4269)
);
INSERT INTO ch02.my_points (p, pz, pm, pzm, p_srid)
VALUES (
    ST_GeomFromText('POINT(1 -1)'),
    ST_GeomFromText('POINT Z(1 -1 1)'),
    ST_GeomFromText('POINT M(1 -1 1)'),
    ST_GeomFromText('POINT ZM(1 -1 1 1)'),
    ST_GeomFromText('POINT(1 -1)',4269)
) ;
```

In the preceding listing, you don't specify the SRID of any point except for the last one. The unknown SRIDs will take on the value of `0`, whereas the last column has an SRID of 4269. This common SRID is the North America 1983 lon/lat (NAD 83).

POINTZ versus POINT Z

In the `ST_GeomFromText` function in listing 2.1, you use the SQL/MM format `ST_GeomFromText('POINT Z(1 -1 1)')`. PostGIS will also allow the representation of `ST_GeomFromText('POINTZ(1 -1 1)')` or even `ST_GeomFromText('POINT(1 -1 1)')`. For cross-compatibility with other spatial relational databases, you should stick with the more conventional form of `ST_GeomFromText('POINT Z(1 -1 1)')`, which includes the space. The same goes for `POINT ZM`, `LINESTRING ZM`, and so on. But when defining columns, these subtypes must not have spaces, though the casing is not important. For instance, `geometry(PointZM)` is equivalent to `geometry(POINTZM)`, but `geometry(POINT ZM)` won't work.

2.2.2 Linestrings

Connected straight lines between two or more distinct points form *linestrings*. Individual lines between points are called *segments*. Segments aren't data types or subtypes in PostGIS, but it is possible for a linestring to have just one segment.

Although a linestring is defined using a finite set of points, in reality it's composed of an infinite number of points, and each line segment defines a straight line. This distinction becomes clear when you need to determine something like the closest point on a linestring to a polygon or other geometric form. The closest point rarely coincides with any point used to define the linestring.

Like points, linestrings have four dimensional variants:

- `LINESTRING`—A linestring in 2D specified by two or more distinct `POINT`s
- `LINESTRINGZ`—A linestring in 3D space specified by two or more distinct `POINTZ`s
- `LINESTRINGM`—A linestring in 2D space with measure values specified by two or more distinct `POINTM`s
- `LINESTRINGZM`—A linestring in 3D space with measure values specified by two or more distinct `POINTZM`s

The following listing adds some 2D linestrings.

Listing 2.2 Add linestrings

```
CREATE TABLE ch02.my_linestrings (                    <-❶ Create table
    id serial PRIMARY KEY,
    name varchar(20),
    my_linestrings geometry(LINESTRING)
);

INSERT INTO ch02.my_linestrings (name, my_linestrings)
VALUES
    ('Open', ST_GeomFromText('LINESTRING(0 0, 1 1, 1 -1)')),           <-❷ Insert open linestring
    ('Closed', ST_GeomFromText('LINESTRING(0 0, 1 1, 1 -1, 0 0)'));    <-❸ Insert closed linestring
```

In this listing, you create a new table to hold 2D linestrings of an unknown spatial reference system ❶. The first INSERT statement adds a linestring starting at the origin, going to (1,1) and terminating at (1,-1) ❷. This is an example of an open linestring. The second INSERT statement adds a closed linestring ❸.

Figure 2.1 illustrates the linestrings created in listing 2.2.

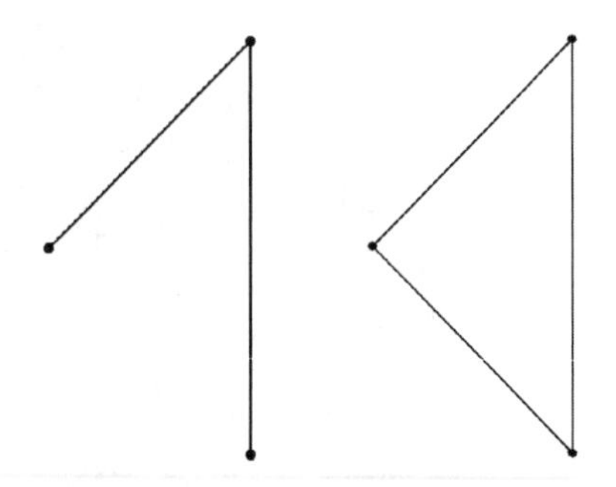

Figure 2.1 Open and closed linestrings created using the code in listing 2.2. The points that make up the lines are shown as well.

In listing 2.2 we introduced the concept of open and closed linestrings. In open linestrings, the starting and ending points aren't the same, whereas they are the same in closed linestrings. In modeling real-world geographic features, open linestrings predominate over closed linestrings. Rivers, trails, fault lines, and roads rarely start where they end. However, as you'll soon see, closed linestrings play an indispensable part in constructing polygons.

The concept of simple and non-simple geometries also comes into play when describing linestrings. A simple linestring can't have self-intersections (can't cross itself) except at the start and end points—all points in the linestring are unique. A linestring that crosses itself isn't simple.

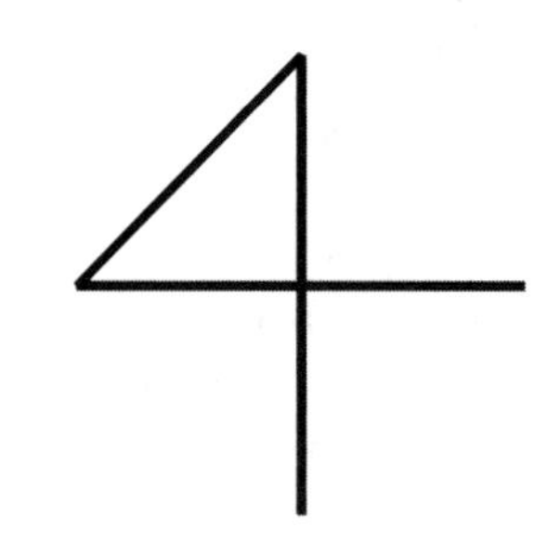

Figure 2.2 A non-simple linestring

PostGIS provides a function, ST_IsSimple, that tests to see if a geometry is simple. The following query will return false:

```
SELECT ST_IsSimple(ST_GeomFromText('LINESTRING(2 0,0 0,1 1,1 -1)'));
```

Figure 2.2 displays the non-simple linestring.

2.2.3 Polygons

Closed linestrings are the building blocks of polygons. Let's start by creating a triangle. Any closed linestring with three distinct, non-collinear points will build a triangle. By definition, a polygon contains all the enclosed area, and its boundary is the linestring that forms it. All points enclosed by the linestring and the points on the linestring itself form the polygon. The closed linestring outlining the boundary of the polygon is called the *ring* of the polygon when used in this context; more specifically, it's the *exterior ring*.

Listing 2.3 demonstrates forming a solid polygon whose exterior matches the closed linestring defined in listing 2.2.

Listing 2.3 Triangular polygon with no holes

```
ALTER TABLE ch02.my_geometries ADD COLUMN my_polygons geometry(POLYGON);
INSERT INTO ch02.my_geometries (name, my_polygons)
VALUES (
    'Triangle',
    ST_GeomFromText('POLYGON((0 0, 1 1, 1 -1, 0 0))')
);
```

Figure 2.3 illustrates the solid triangular polygon formed with listing 2.3.

Figure 2.3 Triangular polygon

A single ring surrounds most polygons used in geographical modeling, but polygons can have multiple rings, carving out holes. To be precise, a polygon must have exactly one exterior ring and can have one or more inner rings. Each interior ring creates a hole in the overall polygon. You can see such a hole generated in listing 2.4 and shown in figure 2.4. This is why you need the seemingly redundant set of parentheses in the text representations of polygons. The well-known text representation (WKT) of a polygon is a set of closed linestrings. The first one designates the exterior ring, and all subsequent ones designate inner rings. Always include the extra set of parentheses in the WKT, even if your polygon has just a single ring. Some tools may tolerate single-ringed polygons with only one pair of parentheses, but not PostGIS.

Figure 2.4 Polygon with interior rings (holes)

Listing 2.4 Polygon with two holes

```
INSERT INTO ch02.my_geometries (name,my_polygons)
VALUES (
    'Square 2 holes',
    ST_GeomFromText('POLYGON(
        (-0.25 -1.25,-0.25 1.25,2.5 1.25,2.5 -1.25,-0.25 -1.25),
        (2.25 0,1.25 1,1.25 -1,2.25 0),(1 -1,1 1,0 0,1 -1))'
    )
);
```

In the real world, multi-ringed polygons play an important part in excluding bodies of water within geographical boundaries. For example, if you were planning a surface transit system in the greater Seattle area, you could start by outlining a big polygon bounded by Interstate 5 on the west and Interstate 405 on the east, as shown in figure 2.5. You could then start to pin down starting and terminal points of popular bus lines and let the computer choose the shortest path within the polygon. Soon enough, you'd realize that most of those popular routes are over water, Lake Washington to be specific. To have the computer pick routes correctly, your polygon of greater Seattle would need an inner ring outlining the shape of Lake Washington. This way, if you were to run a query asking for the shortest path between two points on the polygon and completely within the polygon, you wouldn't end up with buses driving into the water.

> **MULTIPOLOYGONS** This simple model overlooks the existence of Mercer Island in Lake Washington, which would make this a collection-type geometry called a *multipolygon*. We'll cover multipolygons in the next section.

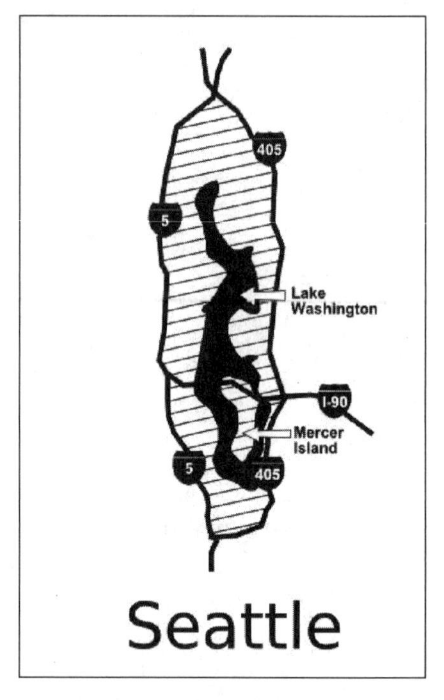

Figure 2.5 The Seattle area modeled as a polygon with two rings (Lake Washington fills up the hole.)

With polygons, you have the concept of *validity*. The rings of a valid polygon may only intersect at distinct points—rings can't overlap each other, and two rings can't share a common boundary. A polygon whose inner rings partly lie outside its exterior ring is also invalid.

Figure 2.6 shows an example of a single polygon with self-intersections. Visually, you can't discern that it's an invalid geometry because such a visual can also be created with two valid polygons or with one valid multipolygon that happens to be touching at a point. We'll cover multipolygons in the next section.

Not every invalid polygon lends itself to a pictorial representation. Degenerate polygons, such as polygons that don't have enough points and polygons with non-closed rings, are difficult to illustrate. Fortunately these polygons are difficult to generate in PostGIS and don't serve any purpose in real-world modeling.

Figure 2.6 A self-intersecting polygon with a text representation of `POLYGON((2 0,0 0,1 1,1 -1, 2 0))')`. This is an invalid polygon, but just by looking it's impossible to see that it's not one valid multipolygon or two valid polygons.

2.2.4 Collection geometries

To demonstrate the concept of collection geometries, try mentally picturing the 50 states of the United States as polygons. Interior rings allow you to handle states with large bodies of water within their boundaries, such as Utah (the Great Salt Lake), Florida (Lake Okeechobee), and Minnesota with its 10,000-plus lakes. There's at least one state that you'll have trouble handling: Hawaii. Hawaii has at least five big pieces.

You could conceivably model Hawaii as five separate polygons, but this would complicate your storage. For example, if you wanted to create a table of states, you'd expect to have 50 rows. Breaking states into different polygons would call for storing a state using a state-polygon table, where each state could have up to hundreds of geometries depending on how fractured the state is. You'd lose the simplicity associated with one geometry per state.

To overcome this problem, PostGIS and the OGC standard offer geometry collections as data types in their own right. A collection of geometries groups separate geometries that logically belong together. With the use of collections, each of the 50 states becomes a collection of polygons—a multipolygon.

U.S. states as multipolygons

To give you a taste of real-world GIS, consider the state polygon data set you can download from the U.S. Census Bureau's TIGER (Topologically Integrated Geographic Encoding and Referencing) data set: ftp://ftp2.census.gov/geo/tiger/TIGER2014/STATE/. In this data set, only the following states are modeled as multipolygons: Alaska, California, Hawaii, Florida, Kentucky, New York, and Rhode Island.

In reality, more states are really multipolygons based on geography alone. Almost all states border large bodies of water and have detached islands. Because the census data is more concerned with people living in the states than their physical outlines, it uses the political boundaries for its table of states. State political boundaries extend to adjacent bodies of water and stretch for a few miles into oceans. These more encompassing boundaries eliminate most states as multipolygons.

In PostGIS and other spatial databases, each of the single geometry subtypes we've just covered has a collection counterpart: multipoints, multilinestrings, and multipolygons. In addition, PostGIS has a data type called `geometrycollection`. This data type can contain any kind of geometry as long as all geometries in the set have the same spatial reference system and the same coordinate dimensions.

MULTIPOINTS

We'll start with multipoints, which are nothing more than collections of points. Figure 2.7 shows an example of a multipoint.

Let's look at the WKT syntax for multipoints. If you have only X and Y coordinates for a multipoint, each comma-delimited value would have two coordinates. The following example is pictured in figure 2.7:

```
MULTIPOINT(-1 1, 0 0, 2 3)
```

For a 3DM multipoint, having X, Y, Z, M, you'd have four coordinates:

```
MULTIPOINT ZM(-1 1 3 4, 0 0 1 2, 2 3 1 2)
```

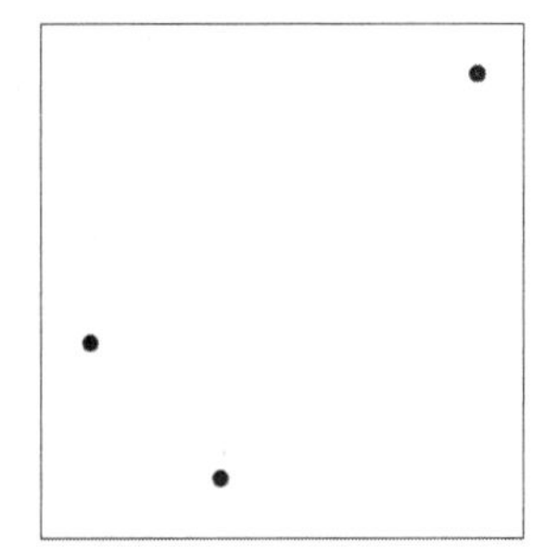

Figure 2.7 A single multipoint geometry (not three distinct points!)

For a regular 3D multipoint composed of X, Y, Z, you'd have the following:

```
MULTIPOINT Z(-1 1 3, 0 0 1, 2 3 1)
```

For a multipoint where each point is composed of X, Y, M, you must use `MULTIPOINTM` to distinguish it from an X, Y, Z multipoint:

```
MULTIPOINT M(-1 1 4, 0 0 2, 2 3 2)
```

> **3D COORDINATE DIMENSIONS** When we use the term *3D*, we're almost always referring to coordinate dimensions, not geometry dimensions. PostGIS doesn't have any 3D geometries. At best, it has 2D geometries living in 3D or 4D coordinate dimensions. In other words, PostGIS has no solids.

An alternate and acceptable WKT representation for multipoints uses parentheses to separate each point as follows: `MULTIPOINT ((-1 1), (0 0), (2 3))`. PostGIS will accept this format as well as `MULTIPOINT (-1 1, 0 0, 2 3)` but will output the non-parenthetical version with the `ST_AsText` and `ST_AsEWKT` functions.

PostGIS 2.0 changed the way it handles higher dimensional input so that it's now more in line with other spatial relational databases, but it differs from how PostGIS 1.5 handles these inputs and expresses these outputs. As such, if you're working with data above 2D, you may experience some backward compatibility issues in working with older and newer PostGIS versions.

MULTILINESTRINGS

It will be no surprise that a multilinestring is a collection of linestrings. Be mindful of the extra sets of parentheses in the WKT representation of a multilinestring that surround each individual linestring in the set. The following examples of multilinestrings are shown in figure 2.8:

```
MULTILINESTRING((0 0,0 1,1 1), (-1 1,-1 -1))
MULTILINESTRING ZM ((0 0 1 1,0 1 1 2,1 1 1 3), (-1 1 1 1,-1 -1 1 2))
MULTILINESTRING M((0 0 1,0 1 2,1 1 3), (-1 1 1,-1 -1 2))
```

Note that because the M coordinate can't be visually displayed, the `MULTILINESTRING` and `MULTILINESTRING M` code examples have the same visual representation.

Before moving on to multipolygons, let's return to the concept of simplicity. In section 2.2.2 we tested a linestring for simplicity. Simplicity is relevant for all linestring type geometries. Multilinestrings are considered *simple* if all constituent linestrings are simple and the collective set of linestrings doesn't intersect each other at any point except boundary points. For example, if you create a multilinestring with two intersecting simple linestrings, the resultant multilinestring isn't simple.

Figure 2.8 Multilinestrings

MULTIPOLYGONS

The WKT of multipolygons has even more parentheses than its singular counterpart. Because you use parentheses to represent each ring of a polygon, you'll need another set of outer parentheses to represent multipolygons. With multipolygons, we highly recommend that you follow the PostGIS conventions and not omit any inner parentheses for single-ringed polygons.

Following are some examples of multipolygons, the first of which is shown in figure 2.9:

Figure 2.9 `MULTIPOLYGON(((2.25 0,1.25 1,1.25 -1,2.25 0)),((1 -1,1 1,0 0,1 -1)))`

```
MULTIPOLYGON(
    ((2.25 0,1.25 1,1.25 -1,2.25 0)),
    ((1 -1,1 1,0 0,1 -1))
)

MULTIPOLYGON Z(
    ((2.25 0 1,1.25 1 1,1.25 -1 1,2.25 0 1)),
    ((1 -1 2,1 1 2,0 0 2,1 -1 2))
)

MULTIPOLYGON ZM(
    ((2.25 0 1 1,1.25 1 1 2,1.25 -1 1 1,2.25 0 1 1)),
    ((1 -1 2 1,1 1 2 2,0 0 2 3,1 -1 1 4))
)

MULTIPOLYGON M(
    ((2.25 0 1,1.25 1 2,1.25 -1 1,2.25 0 1)),
    ((1 -1 1,1 1 2,0 0 3,1 -1 4))
)
```

Recall from our discussion of single polygons that a polygon is considered valid if its rings don't intersect or they intersect only at distinct points. For a multipolygon to qualify as valid, it must pass two tests:

- Each constituent polygon must be valid in its own right.
- Constituent polygons can't overlap. Once you lay down a polygon, subsequent polygons can't be laid on top.

GEOMETRYCOLLECTION

The `geometrycollection` is a PostGIS `geometry` subtype that can contain heterogeneous geometries. Unlike multi-geometries, where the constituent geometries must be of the same subtype, `geometrycollection` can include points, linestrings, polygons, and their collection counterparts. It can even contain other geometrycollections. In short, you can stuff every `geometry` subtype known to PostGIS into a `geometrycollection`.

The following listing presents the WKT for geometrycollections, but instead of building the geometries using `ST_GeomFromText` and the WKT representation, we'll build them by collecting simpler geometries using the `ST_Collect` function.

Listing 2.5 Forming geometrycollections by collecting constituent geometries

```
SELECT ST_AsText(ST_Collect(g))
FROM (
    SELECT ST_GeomFromText('MULTIPOINT(-1 1, 0 0, 2 3)') As g
    UNION ALL
```

```
    SELECT ST_GeomFromText(
        'MULTILINESTRING((0 0, 0 1, 1 1), (-1 1, -1 -1))'
    ) As g
    UNION ALL
    SELECT ST_GeomFromText(
        'POLYGON(
            (-0.25 -1.25, -0.25 1.25, 2.5 1.25, 2.5 -1.25, -0.25 -1.25),
            (2.25 0, 1.25 1, 1.25 -1, 2.25 0),
            (1 -1, 1 1, 0 0, 1 -1)
        )'
    ) As g
) x;
```

The output of listing 2.5 is as follows:

```
GEOMETRYCOLLECTION(
    MULTIPOINT(-1 1, 0 0, 2 3),
    MULTILINESTRING((0 0, 0 1, 1 1), (-1 1, -1 -1)),
    POLYGON(
        (-0.25 -1.25, -0.25 1.25, 2.5 1.25, 2.5 -1.25, -0.25 -1.25),
        (2.25 0,1.25 1,1.25 -1,2.25 0),
        (1 -1, 1 1, 0 0, 1 -1)
    )
)
```

The visual representation of the `geometrycollection` is shown in figure 2.10.

In real-world applications, you should rarely define a data column as `geometrycollection`. Although having a collection is perfectly reasonable for storage purposes, using it within a function rarely makes any sense. For example, you can ask what the area of a multipolygon is, but you can't ask for the area of a geometrycollection that has linestrings and points in addition to polygons. Geometrycollections almost always originate as the result of queries rather than as predefined geometries. You should be prepared to work with them, but avoid using them in your table design.

Finally, a geometrycollection is considered valid if all the geometries in the collection are valid. It's invalid if any of the geometries in the collection are invalid.

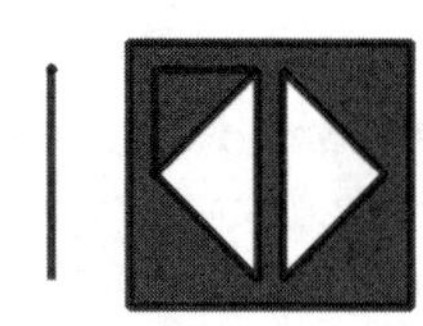

Figure 2.10 Geometrycollection formed from listing 2.5

2.2.5 The M coordinate

The M coordinate is an additional coordinate added for the convenience of recording measured values taken at various points along spatial coordinates. The benefit of using M to store additional information becomes clear as soon as you move beyond points. Suppose that you have a linestring made up of many points, each with its own measure. Without the M coordinate, you'd always need an additional table to store the measurement data.

The M coordinate need not have any spatial interpretation and is therefore impervious to the reference system of the other spatial X, Y, Z coordinates. It can be negative or positive, and its units have no relationship to the units of the other spatial coordinates. The M coordinates of a geometry are unchanged when you transform a geometry to another spatial reference system. All functions of PostGIS that work with M treat the coordinate as linear, allowing you to interpolate along the M dimension.

The M coordinate is a full-fledged coordinate, and as such we offer the following recommendations:

- Support for M is limited, so don't use it unless you absolutely need to.
- Don't use M for sparsely populated data. Once you introduce the M dimension, all your geometries must live in this space. If most of your data points don't have an M value, you'll have to resort to some convention to tag the missing data. A coordinate can't have null values.
- You should be consistent in your use of the M value. For instance, if you're using M to measure temperature or ocean depth, keep the units consistent.
- Try to use M for linear measures, as opposed to logarithmic ones, even though you're free to populate the coordinate with any numeric value. All PostGIS functions that take M coordinates into consideration assume that the M dimension is linear like its spatial counterparts. For instance, if you take a pH measure for a linestring with points spaced far apart, and you try to estimate the pH at the midpoint, PostGIS only has linear interpolation functions, which will be woefully inadequate for your logarithmic measurements. In this case, you're better off storing the pH as an additional attribute of each point or writing your own functions to do the correct interpolation.
- Once you introduce M, avoid using interrogative functions and applying spatial concepts. For instance, you probably can't trust the answer if you ask if a `LINESTRINGM` is closed or open. Did the function consider the M coordinate? If so, what is closure for an M coordinate? Spare yourself the headache; don't ask and PostGIS won't tell.

The M coordinate can also exist in a geometrycollection. Listing 2.6 is a `GEOMETRYCOLLECTIONM` example similar to listing 2.5 but with an M component.

Listing 2.6 Forming GEOMETRYCOLLECTIONMs from constituent geometries

```
SELECT ST_AsText(ST_Collect(g))
FROM (
    SELECT ST_GeomFromEWKT('MULTIPOINTM(-1 1 4, 0 0 2, 2 3 2)') As g
    UNION ALL
    SELECT ST_GeomFromEWKT(
        'MULTILINESTRINGM((0 0 1, 0 1 2, 1 1 3), (-1 1 1,-1 -1 2))'
    ) As g
    UNION ALL
    SELECT ST_GeomFromEWKT(
        'POLYGONM(
```

```
                (-0.25 -1.25 1, -0.25 1.25 2, 2.5 1.25 3,
            ➥ 2.5 -1.25 1, -0.25 -1.25 1),
                (2.25 0 2, 1.25 1 1, 1.25 -1 1, 2.25 0 2),
                (1 -1 2,1 1 2,0 0 2,1 -1 2)
            )'
    ) As g
) x;
```

The output of listing 2.6 is as follows:

```
GEOMETRYCOLLECTION M (
    MULTIPOINT M (-1 1 4, 0 0 2, 2 3 2),
    MULTILINESTRING M ((0 0 1, 0 1 2, 1 1 3), (-1 1 1, -1 -1 2)),
    POLYGON M (
        (-0.25 -1.25 1, -0.25 1.25 2, 2.5 1.25 3, 2.5 -1.25 1, -0.25 -1.25 1),
        (2.25 0 2, 1.25 1 1, 1.25 -1 1, 2.25 0 2),
        (1 -1 2, 1 1 2, 0 0 2,1 -1 2)
    )
 )
```

PostGIS does offer PolygonMs, PolyhedralZMs, TINZMs, and so on, but we have yet to see any real-world need for these more abstruse dimensional types.

2.2.6 The Z coordinate

First, to clear up any misconceptions, just because a geometry has a Z coordinate doesn't make it a volumetric geometry. A polygon in three-coordinate dimensional space is still a planar 2D geometry. It has an area but no volume. The story will get a little more interesting when we get to polyhedral surfaces in the next section.

PostGIS 2.0 introduced new relationship and measurement functions prefixed with `ST_3D`, specifically designed to work with subtypes in X, Y, Z coordinate space. Common ones are `ST_3DIntersects`, `ST_3DDistance`, `ST_3DDWithin` for 3D radius searches, `ST_3DMaxDistance`, and `ST_3DClosestPoint`. PostGIS 2.0 also introduced the *n*D spatial index, which considers the Z coordinate. The default spatial index ignores the Z coordinate.

PostGIS 2.1 introduced additional 3D functions based on the SFCGAL library, which is a 3D enhancement built atop the Computational Geometry Algorithms Library (CGAL); the *SF* stands for *spatial features.* SFCGAL adds functions such as `ST_3DIntersection` and `ST_3DArea`. It also brings its own implementation of some existing `ST_3D` functions such as `ST_3DIntersects`. For more details about the PostGIS SFCGAL, visit www.sfcgal.org.

In order to take advantage of these additional 3D functions and 3D enhanced functions, you need to compile PostGIS 2.1 with SFCGAL support or find a distribution of PostGIS already compiled with it. If you happen to be on Ubuntu, Oslandia may have something ready for you (http://www.oslandia.com/full-spatial-database-power-in-2-lines-en.html).

Regardless of how you get a SFCGAL-fortified version of PostGIS 2.1, be sure to run the sfcgal.sql SQL script, generally located in the PostgreSQL contrib folder after installing PostGIS in your database. This script will add the additional functions to your database provided via the SFCGAL library.

In PostGIS 2.2, SFCGAL will be packaged as an extension named postgis_sfcgal. This means that in PostGIS 2.2, you can install SFCGAL support using the standard `CREATE EXTENSION postgis_sfcgal;` command instead of running the sfcgal.sql script required in PostGIS 2.1.

Experimental Windows builds of PostGIS 2.2 with SFCGAL support
If you're a Windows user and can't wait, or you wish to help us test SFCGAL, you can download experimental Windows binaries from here: http://postgis.net/windows_downloads.

Some functions provided by SFCGAL, such as `ST_Intersects` and `ST_3DIntersects`, are named the same as the ones packaged with PostGIS but behave differently or support more geometry types than those packaged with the postgis extension. By default, the PostGIS ones are used. If you instead want the SFCGAL ones to be used where they have the same names, then you'll want to set `postgis.backend=sfcgal`. This is covered in more detail in the PostGIS manual.

To fully appreciate geometries in 3D space, you'll need rendering software. The PostGIS `ST_AsX3D` function will output geometry in X3D XML format, which you can view with various X3D viewers. The JavaScript x3dom.js library (http://www.x3dom.org) has logic for rendering X3D in HTML5-compatible browsers. We've created a PostGIS X3D web viewer for PHP and ASP.NET built on the x3dom.js library to demonstrate the process. You can download the code for that at https://github.com/robe2/postgis_x3d_viewer. We used our minimalist X3D viewer to render the images of polyhedral surfaces and TINs you'll see in this chapter. Oslandia (http://www.oslandia.com), the company spearheading the SFCGAL work, is working on an enhancement to the popular QGIS package to allow viewing of all geometries in 3D space regardless of complexity.

Prior to PostGIS 2.0, support for the Z coordinate was sketchy. PostGIS relied on a library called *GEOS*, which is not well known for 3D support. When using PostGIS functions against your 3D geometry, the functions won't error out if they can't handle the Z coordinate; they'll either pretend the Z isn't there or do some interpolation to give you some semblance of processing the Z dimension. For example, when you use `ST_Intersection` and `ST_Union` with geometries having Z coordinates, both functions will handle the X and the Y perfectly but only approximate the Z coordinate. This may be acceptable when you don't need precision, such as when mapping a mountainous hiking trail. But the outcome could be deadly if you used it to program a flight GPS to navigate around mountainous terrain. The PostGIS reference guide will tell you how each function behaves when the Z coordinate is present. If you're doing serious modeling in 3D, consult the manual to make sure Z behaves within your specifications.

There's no support for `ST_Transform` for geometries with a Z coordinate. You can still use it, but it'll leave the Z coordinate alone. This should be fine, because reprojections rarely affect Z anyway. Mount Everest stays the same height regardless of how you draw your map.

2.2.7 Polyhedral surfaces and TINs

Float a bunch of polygons in three-coordinate space and glue them together at their edges, and you'll form a patchwork referred to as a *polyhedral surface.* Although polygons make up both multipolygons and polyhedral surfaces, there is one fundamental difference: polygons in multipolygons can't share edges; polygons in a polyhedral surface almost always do. There are two other notable restrictions in the construction of polyhedral surfaces: polygons can't overlap, and each edge can be mated with at most one other edge.

> **POLYHEDRAL SURFACE DEFINITION** You can read the more rigorous definition of polyhedral surfaces in the OGC and SQL/MM specifications at http://www.opengeospatial.org/standards/sfa.

Some real-world examples of polyhedral surfaces that come to mind are geodetic domes, a jigsaw puzzle that you pieced together but later spilled drinks on so now it's warped, a honeycomb, the surface of the space shuttle with its mosaic of heat-deflecting tiles, or the checkered flag at a car race as it furls in the wind.

Polyhedral surfaces allow you to create closed surfaces in three coordinate dimensions. The simplest example is the triangular pyramid formed by four equilateral triangular polygons. PostGIS is still vacillating on whether such a geometry should be treated as a solid, with a geometry dimension of three, or as a surface, with a geometry dimension of two. A solid would mean that all points inside the surface would count as part of the geometry, and the intersection of two solids could generate another solid. Solid or planar? At this point, PostGIS doesn't provide a definitive answer. Some functions, such as `ST_Dimension`, will return `3` for closed polyhedral surfaces. But if you apply the native `ST_3DIntersects` built into PostGIS for two closed polyhedral surfaces, the result just considers the surface. However, if you have the SFCGAL engine enabled, `ST_3DIntersects` and the SFCGAL `ST_3DIntersection` treat them as solids if created via SFCGAL functions. Perhaps more troubling is that you currently have no means of indicating whether a closed polyhedral surface should be treated as a solid or not. This may change in the future.

TINs stands for *triangular irregular networks.* They're a subset of polyhedral surfaces where all the constituent polygons must be triangles. TINs are widely used to describe terrain surfaces. Recall from basic geometry (or common sense) the minimum number of points needed to form an area? Three—a triangle. The mathematical underpinning of TINs is based on triangulating key peak and valley point locations of a surface to form non-overlapping connected area pockets. The most common form of triangulation used in GIS is Delaunay triangulation (explained on Wikipedia: http://en.wikipedia.org/wiki/Delaunay_triangulation).

PostGIS 2.1 specifically added a powerful `ST_DelaunayTriangles` function to convert a "well-behaved" polygon collection into a TIN. But one shortcoming of `ST_DelaunayTriangles` is that it can't convert polyhedral surfaces to TINs. For that conversion, you need to use `ST_Tesselate`, which is packaged with SFCGAL and will convert polygon collections as well.

PostGIS 2.0 added many new functions specifically for use with polyhedral surfaces and TINS; go to http://postgis.net/docs/PostGIS_Special_Functions_Index.html #PostGIS_TypeFunctionMatrix to find the full list. Many existing functions, such as `ST_Dump` and `ST_DumpPoints`, were augmented to accept these two subtypes as well. Because most polyhedral surfaces and TINs specimens live in 3D space, they face the same limitations and vagaries of PostGIS's current handling of the Z coordinate, if not more. If you're planning on doing serious work with these two subtypes and can't wait until PostGIS 2.2, we recommend that you go ahead and install a version of PostGIS 2.1 compiled with SFCGAL now rather than later.

GENERATING POLYHEDRAL SURFACES

The next listing demonstrates two ways of generating a three-faced polyhedral surface.

Listing 2.7 Three-faced polyhedral surface

```
SELECT ST_GeomFromText(
    'POLYHEDRALSURFACE Z (
        ((12 0 10, 8 8 10, 8 10 20, 12 2 20, 12 0 10)),
        ((8 8 10, 0 12 10, 0 14 20, 8 10 20, 8 8 10)),
        ((0 12 10, -8 8 10, -8 10 20, 0 14 20, 0 12 10))
    )'
);

SELECT ST_Extrude(ST_GeomFromText(
    'LINESTRING(12 0 10, 8 8 10, 0 12 10,-8 8 10)'),
    0, 2, 10
);
```

Both examples in listing 2.7 generate the same polyhedral surface. The second example uses the SFCGAL `ST_Extrude` function, whereas the first uses the WKT representation of the resulting geometry when extruding the linestring. A rendering of listing 2.7 is shown in figure 2.11. If you were to extrude a polygon, you'd end up with a closed polyhedral surface (a volume).

Figure 2.11 A three-faced polyhedral surface generated from the code in listing 2.7

Note that like the `MULTIPOLYGON`, the `POLYHEDRALSURFACE` has double-braced rings with coordinates of each `POLYGON Z` that makes up the element.

GENERATING TINs

A TIN is a collection subtype formed from a geometry subtype called `TRIANGLE`. You'll rarely see the `TRIANGLE` subtype in use, especially not in its column data type form of `geometry(TRIANGLE)`. But you may come across it if you use the `ST_Dump` function to dump out all the triangles in a TIN.

In the next example, we'll demonstrate a four-triangled TIN and we'll color-code each triangle so it's clear where the delineations are. Many rendering packages won't delineate the triangles by design, so that the result ends up looking like a regular polyhedral surface.

Listing 2.8 TIN made up of four `TRIANGLE`s

```
SELECT ST_GeomFromText(
    'TIN Z (
        ((12 2 20, 8 8 10, 8 10 20, 12 2 20)),
        ((12 2 20, 12 0 10, 8 8 10, 12 2 20)),
        ((8 10 20, 0 12 10, 0 14 20, 8 10 20)),
        ((8 10 20, 8 8 10, 0 12 10, 8 10 20))
    )'
);
```

The visual output of listing 2.8 is shown in figure 2.12.

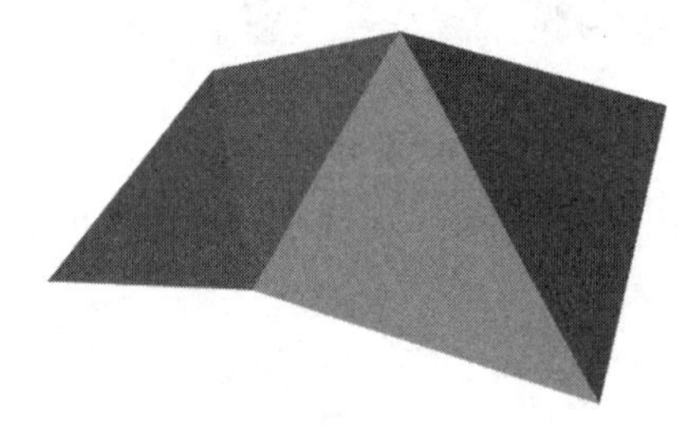

Figure 2.12 Four-faced polyhedral surface generated from the code in listing 2.8

2.2.8 *Curved geometries*

Curved geometries came into existence with the OGC SQL/MM Part 3 specs, and PostGIS 2.0 has almost complete support for what's defined in the specs, but tools for rendering PostGIS curved geometries still lag behind and are somewhat spotty on what they support.

Curved geometries aren't as mature as other geometries and aren't widely used. Natural terrestrial features rarely manifest themselves as curved geometries. Architectural structures and artificial boundaries do have curves, but linestrings will adequately serve as approximations for many modeling cases. Aeronautical charts are full of curves because the sweep of radar is circular. Dams, dikes, breakwaters, stadiums, hippodromes, coliseums, Greek and Shakespearean theaters, and crop circles (both those made by humans and aliens) are other curved structures that come to mind. Some highway segments come close to being curves, but linestrings are often more appropriate for modeling them when processing speed is more important than accuracy. Because of the lack of support, consider the following points before you decide to go down the path of using curved geometries:

- Few third-party tools, either open source or commercial, currently support curved geometries.
- The advanced spatial library called GEOS that PostGIS uses for much of its functionality, such as performing intersections, containment checks, and other spatial relation checks, doesn't support curved geometries. As a workaround, you can convert curved geometries to linestrings and regular polygons using the `ST_CurveToLine` function and then convert back with `ST_LineToCurve`. The downside of this method is the loss of speed and the inaccuracies introduced when interpolating arcs using linestrings.
- Many native PostGIS functions don't support curved geometries. You can find a full list of functions that do support curved geometries in the PostGIS reference manual. Again, for cases where you need to use functions that don't support curved geometries, you can apply the `ST_CurveToLine` and then apply the `ST_LineToCurve` function to convert back if needed.
- PostGIS hasn't supported curved geometries for as long as the other geometries, so you're more likely to run into bugs when working with them. More recent releases of PostGIS have cleaned up many of the bugs and have expanded the number of functions that support curved geometries.

Given all the drawbacks of curved geometries, you might be wondering why you'd ever want to use them. Here are a few reasons:

- You can represent a truly curved geometry with less data. A perfect circle is defined by a centroid and a radius. A perfect circle described using linestrings would require an infinite number of points.
- More tools are planning to add support for curved geometries. Safe FME and uDig are two tools we know of that already support PostGIS curved geometries.
- Even if you don't ultimately store your data as curved geometry types, it's often easier to use such types as intermediaries. For example, if you have a closed linestring that comes close to a circle, you can create a curved geometry and then convert it to a linestring using `ST_CurveToLine`, rather than typing out all the points to form the linestring.
- PostGIS 2.1 has more robust support for curves than prior versions.

Let's now take a closer look at the wide variety of curved geometries. For simplicity, you can think of curved geometries in PostGIS as geometries with arcs. To build an arc, you must have exactly three distinct points. The first and last points denote the starting and ending points of the arc. The point in the middle is called the control point because this point controls the degree of curvature of the arc.

CIRCULARSTRINGS

A series of one or more arcs where the endpoint of one is the starting point of another makes up a geometry called a *circularstring*. Figure 2.13 illustrates a five-point circularstring.

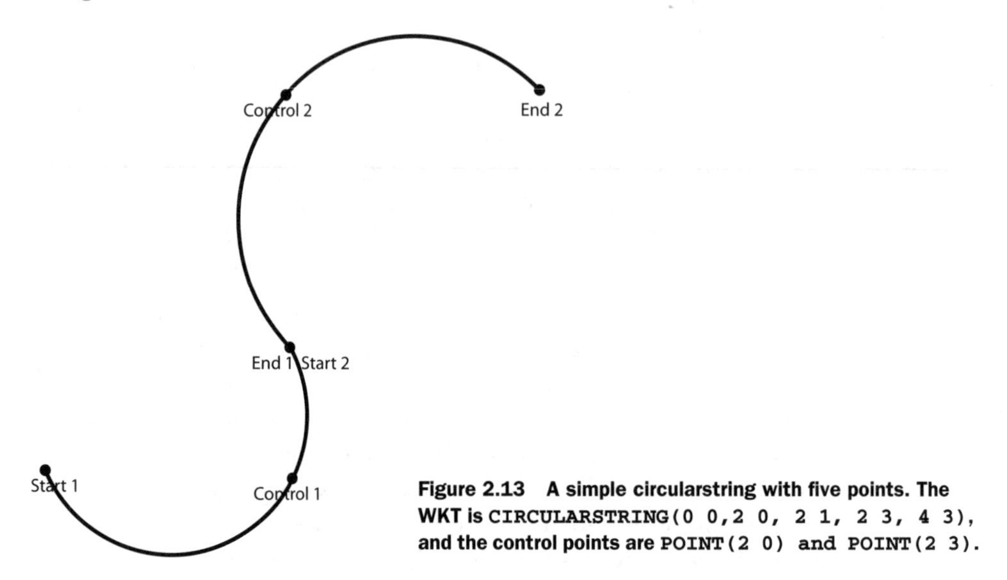

Figure 2.13 A simple circularstring with five points. The WKT is `CIRCULARSTRING(0 0,2 0, 2 1, 2 3, 4 3)`, and the control points are `POINT(2 0)` and `POINT(2 3)`.

The circularstring is the simplest of all curved geometries and contains only arcs. The following listing contains more examples of circularstrings and how you'd register them in the database.

Listing 2.9 Building circularstrings

```
ALTER TABLE ch02.my_geometries
ADD COLUMN my_circular_strings geometry(CIRCULARSTRING);

INSERT INTO ch02.my_geometries(name, my_circular_strings)
VALUES
    ('Circle',
    ST_GeomFromText('CIRCULARSTRING(0 0, 2 0, 2 2, 0 2, 0 0)')),
    ('Half circle',
    ST_GeomFromText('CIRCULARSTRING(2.5 2.5, 4.5 2.5, 4.5 4.5)')),
    ('Several arcs',
    ST_GeomFromText('CIRCULARSTRING(5 5, 6 6, 4 8, 7 9, 9.5 9.5,
➥  11 12, 12 12)'));
```

The output of listing 2.9 is shown in figure 2.14.

As you can see from these examples, a circularstring must have an odd number of points. If you were to number them starting with one, all odd-numbered points would be starting or ending points and all even-numbered points would be control points.

You'll discover that not all rendering tools can handle curved geometries. When faced with this situation, don't ditch the tool. Use the `ST_CurveToLine` function to fit a linestring atop your curve.

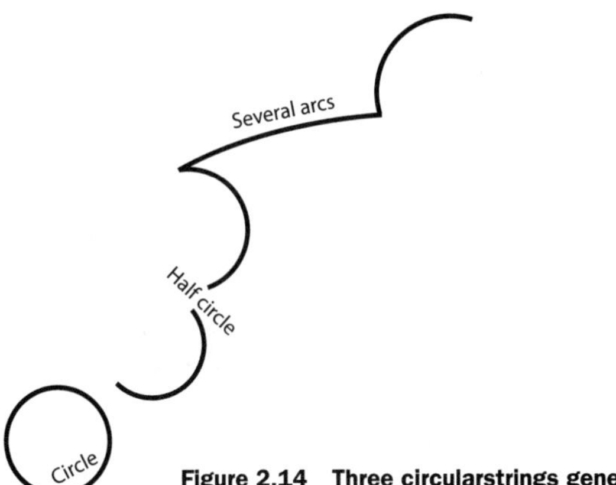

Figure 2.14 Three circularstrings generated from the code in listing 2.9

COMPOUNDCURVES

Circularstrings and linestrings in series make up a collection geometry subtype called COMPOUNDCURVEs. A polygon constructed using a compoundcurve is called a CURVEPOLYGON.

A closed compoundcurve is a geometry composed of both circularstring and regular linestring segments, where the last point in the prior segment is the first point of the next segment. A square with rounded corners is a nice representation of a closed compoundcurve (with four circular strings and four straight linestrings).

Following is an example of a compoundcurve composed of an arc sandwiched between two linestrings. The output is shown in figure 2.15.

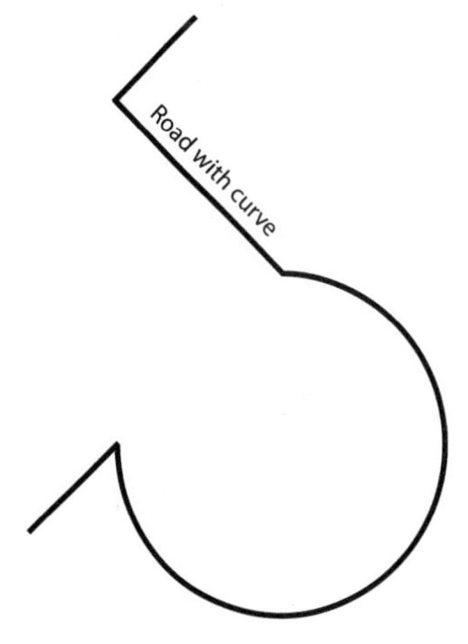

Figure 2.15 A compoundcurve generated from listing 2.10

Listing 2.10 Creating a compoundcurve

```
ALTER TABLE ch02.my_geometries
ADD COLUMN my_compound_curves geometry(COMPOUNDCURVE);
INSERT INTO ch02.my_geometries (name, my_compound_curves)
VALUES (
    'Road with curve',
    ST_GeomFromText(
        'COMPOUNDCURVE(
            (2 2, 2.5 2.5),
            CIRCULARSTRING(2.5 2.5, 4.5 2.5, 3.5 3.5),
            (3.5 3.5, 2.5 4.5, 3 5)
        )'
    )
);
```

As you can see in the WKT in listing 2.10, the circularstring portion of the curve is identified as such, and the rest of the components are linestrings. You might be tempted to make everything clearer by adding the word LINESTRING, but refrain from doing so because you'll get an error.

CURVEPOLYGONS

A curvepolygon is a polygon that has exterior or inner rings of circularstrings. Listing 2.11 and figure 2.16 show some examples of curvepolygons.

Listing 2.11 Creating curvepolygons

```
ALTER TABLE ch02.my_geometries
ADD COLUMN my_curve_polygons geometry(CURVEPOLYGON);

INSERT INTO ch02.my_geometries (name, my_curve_polygons)
VALUES
    ('Solid circle',
    ST_GeomFromText('CURVEPOLYGON(
        CIRCULARSTRING(0 0, 2 0, 2 2, 0 2, 0 0)
    )')),
    ('Circles with triangle hole',
    ST_GeomFromText('CURVEPOLYGON(
        CIRCULARSTRING(2.5 2.5, 4.5 2.5, 4.5 3.5, 2.5 4.5, 2.5 2.5),
        (3.5 3.5, 3.25 2.25, 4.25 3.25, 3.5 3.5)
    )')),
    ('Triangle with arcish hole',
    ST_GeomFromText('CURVEPOLYGON(
        (-0.5 7, -1 5, 3.5 5.25, -0.5 7),
        CIRCULARSTRING(0.25 5.5, -0.25 6.5, -0.5 5.75, 0 5.75, 0.25 5.5)
    )'));
```

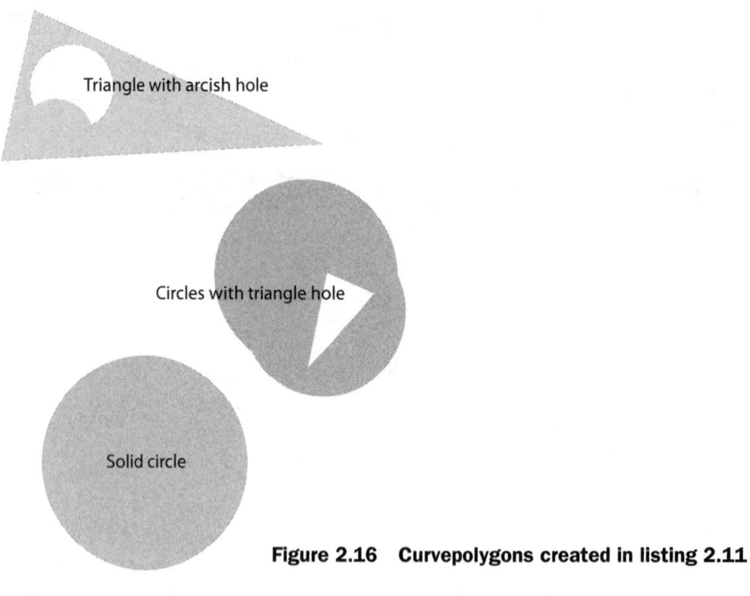

Figure 2.16 Curvepolygons created in listing 2.11

2.2.9 Spatial catalog for geometry

PostGIS comes packaged with a read-only view named *geometry_columns* that lists all geometry columns within the database.

Prior to version PostGIS 2.0, geometry_columns didn't read from the PostgreSQL systems catalog and was a table—not a view—that you could update and mess up. This meant that you needed to maintain meticulous bookkeeping to make sure that your geometry_columns table accurately reflected the structure of the PostGIS data type columns in your data tables. For instance, if you manually added a linestring column to a table with SRID 4326, you had the additional responsibility of recording all the information about this column in the geometry_columns meta-table. PostGIS does offer a set of management functions that will take care of both steps for you, but the need to use supplemental functions to add columns, instead of using SQL, created some annoyance, and the greatest worry was that the geometry_columns table could easily get out of sync with the actual data structure.

Thankfully, in version 2.0, geometry_columns is now under the hood, and you no longer have to be cognizant of its existence and fret over your data definitions getting out of sync. You're still welcome to access the information in it, but because it now reads from the PostgreSQL system catalog, it's strictly a read-only view.

PostGIS will automatically register views that contain columns of the geometry data type. You can retrieve this registration information from the geometry_columns view just as you do with tables. To ensure registration with all the relevant metadata, such as subtype, dimension, and SRID, you may need to take the extra step of casting the geometry column in your view definition. For example, if you create a view as follows,

```
CREATE VIEW my_view AS
 SELECT ST_Transform(geom,4326) geom FROM some_table;
```

PostGIS is not smart enough to infer the SRID from your view definition nor to know that `ST_Transform` will always result in same geometry type as the input. It'll lazily record the column as just geometry without additional info. This is especially likely to happen if you use check constraints to restrict the subtype or if you use any PostGIS function to morph the geometry, such as `ST_Transform` or `ST_Centroid`, in your view definition. If any of these apply to your view, you should create your view with an extra cast, like this:

```
CREATE VIEW my_view AS
 SELECT ST_Transform(geom,2163)::geometry(POINT,2163) geom
 FROM some_table;
```

The structure of the geometry_columns view is shown in table 2.1.

The last two rows merit more discussion: coord_dimension and SRID.

Table 2.1 The structure of the geometry_columns view

Column	Description
f_table_catalog	Name of the database (catalog in computer-science parlance)
f_table_schema	Name of the schema
f_table_name	Name of the table
f_geometry_column	Name of the column holding the geometry
type	Subtype of the geometry column. If this isn't specified or is specified with `geometry(GEOMETRY)`, then it will just show `GEOMETRY`.
coord_dimensions	Coordinate dimensions
SRID	Spatial reference identifier

COORD_DIMENSION

Coord_dimension is the coordinate dimension of the geometry column; permissible values are 2, 3, and 4. Yes, PostGIS supports up to four dimensions: X, Y, Z, M. Don't forget M.

In spatial speak, there are two kinds of dimensions: the coordinate dimension and the geometry dimension:

- The *coordinate dimension* defines the number of linearly independent axes in your space. Mathematically speaking, the coordinate dimension is the number of vectors forming the basis. For example, geometries that occupy X, Y, Z or X, Y, M have a coordinate dimension of 3. Those that have X, Y, Z, M have a coordinate dimension of 4.
- The *geometry dimension* describes the size and shape of a geometry. A flat polygon is a two-dimensional geometry because you can speak in terms of length and width. A linestring is a one-dimensional geometry because only the length is a relevant measure. A point, by definition, has zero dimensions.

Most people expect you to know which kind of dimension, coordinate or geometry, is being referred to from the context alone, but this becomes confusing when you use both simultaneously. For example, a cobra emerging out of a snake charmer's basket is a one-dimensional geometry (the serpentine linestring has a geometry dimension of one) living in three-dimensional space (the wicker basket has three coordinate dimensions). A cobra slithering around your checkered kitchen floor is a one-dimensional geometry linestring in a two-dimensional coordinate space (your kitchen floor). PostGIS 2.0 introduced polyhedral surfaces and triangulated irregular network (TIN) geometries. Think of the former as a flying carpet and the latter as the shell of Spaceship Earth (the famous dome at Epcot). Points and linestrings always have zero and one geometry dimensions, respectively, but be careful when people start talking about polygons in 3D or 4D space. Polygons are still two-dimensional. One rule that you can always count on is this: a geometry dimension can never exceed the coordinate dimension that it's living in.

SRID

SRID stands for *spatial reference identifier* and it's an integer that relates back to the primary key of the spatial_ref_sys table. PostGIS uses this table to catalog all the spatial reference systems available to the database. The spatial_ref_sys table contains the name of the SRS, the parameters needed to reproject from one SRID to another, and the organization that gave rise to the particular SRID. Even though the spatial_ref_sys table has close to 4,000 entries, you'll encounter plenty of instances where you have to add SRIDs not already in the table. You can also be adventurous and define your own custom SRS and add it to the spatial_ref_sys table in any PostGIS database.

Be aware of a similar term in GIS lingo called *SRS ID* (spatial reference system identifier). This identifier adds the authority that created the SRID. For example, the common WGS 84 lon/lat has an SRID of 4326 but an SRS ID of EPSG:4326, where EPSG stands for European Petroleum Survey Group (www.epsg.org). Most of the SRIDs in PostGIS came from EPSG, so the SRID used in the table is by PostGIS convention the same as the EPSG identifier. Keep in mind that the SRID column in spatial_ref_sys is just a user-input (or in this case PostGIS-distributed) primary key in the spatial_ref_sys table. This isn't the case with all spatial databases, so from database vendor to database vendor you can't guarantee that SRID 4326 corresponds to the global SRS EPSG:4326.

Prior to PostGIS 2.0, a value of `-1` represented the unknown or unspecified SRID. Since PostGIS 2.0, the default value is `0` to conform to the SQL/MM standard. Should you use the unknown SRID? The answer is no if you're working with geographic data. If you know the SRS of your data, and presumably you should if you have real geographic data, then you should explicitly specify it. If you're using PostGIS for non-geographical purposes, such as modeling a localized architecture plan or demonstrating analytic geometry principles, it's perfectly fine to keep your spatial reference as unknown. For most functions that require an SRID, you can leave out the SRID and it'll default to the unknown value. The `ST_Transform` function is an obvious exception.

Finally, keep in mind that switching SRIDs doesn't alter the fact that the coordinate system underlying the geometry data type is always Cartesian.

2.2.10 Managing geometry columns

A big pre-PostGIS 2.0 headache when adding new columns was the need to manage your geometry columns. For instance, if you manually added a geometry column with an `ALTER TABLE` statement, you had the additional task of adding check constraints to restrict the column to a particular subtype and SRID and of recording this information in geometry_columns. PostGIS 2.0 introduced the type-modifier syntax that allows you to add new columns using the SQL data definition language (DDL) and not have to worry about adding constraints for subtype and SRID. PostGIS will now also automatically list the column in geometry_columns for you.

To ease all the additional management tasks in the pre-2.0 days, PostGIS made available a few helper functions. These are AddGeometryColumns, DropGeometryColumn, UpdateGeometrySRID, and DropGeometryTable. They're still around for backward compatibility, but we strongly discourage you from using them. In fact, should you run into them, replace them with equivalent DDLs. Let's look at two DDL examples that you'll probably come across often.

CHANGING THE SRID OF AN EXISTING GEOMETRY COLUMN

Should you stamp the wrong SRID on your geometry column, you'll want to change it to the right SRID. Use the ALTER TABLE syntax as follows:

```
ALTER TABLE us_states
ALTER COLUMN geom TYPE geometry(MULTIPOLYGON,4326)
USING ST_SetSRID(geom,4326);
```

CONVERTING A GEOMETRY COLUMN TO A GEOGRAPHY COLUMN

This example will convert a geometry column called way in osm_roads from its current spatial reference geometry to geography by first transforming and then casting to geography:

```
ALTER TABLE osm_roads
ALTER COLUMN way TYPE geography(MULTIPOLYGON,4326)
USING ST_Transform(way,4326)::geography;
```

THE POPULATE_GEOMETRY_COLUMNS FUNCTION

Although most alterations are easier to do with SQL, we find that the old Populate_Geometry_Columns management function is still handy at times. This powerful function will scan all unregistered geometry columns in your database or in a table that you specify. If the column is a generic geometry column or has an unknown SRID, it will examine the data to try to pinpoint the subtype and SRID. If it can identify a uniform subtype, it will add the subtype to your column definition using typmod syntax or check constraints. Similarly, if it can determine the SRID, it will add the SRID to your column definition using typmod syntax or check constraints. Populate_Geometry_Columns will obviously be unable to arrive at a subtype and SRID for columns with no data or for tables with mixed subtypes.

2.3 Geography

PostGIS hit the scene with only the geometry data type. As devotees grew in number, a common need arose to perform calculations taking the spherical nature of Mother Earth into consideration. Remember that the geometry data type is based on a Cartesian grid? As people began to plot cities using geometry points and calculating distances where the curvature of the earth came into play, they had to constantly resort to the rather hairy formula for finding distances on a sphere. Soon all this became a nuisance, and PostGIS introduced a new data type—geography.

2.3.1 Differences between geography and geometry

Unlike its geometry forebears, geography starts by assuming that all your data is based on a geodetic coordinate system, specifically the WGS 84 lon/lat SRID of 4326. No exceptions. This greatly simplified matters for people using PostGIS on a global scale because lon/lat is a coordinate system familiar to everyone.

Prior to PostGIS 2.1, geography only supported SRID 4326. In PostGIS 2.1, geography changed to support any lon/lat-based spatial reference system. 4326 is still the default, and if no SRID is specified, then 4326 is assumed.

Because the geography data type is specialized for geodetic applications, you're going to find yourself missing support for all but the basic subtypes of points, linestrings, and polygons. Furthermore, don't expect much support for anything above 2D space. PostGIS has yet to enter the space age.

Because the structure of the geography data subtypes mimic those of geometry, everything you already know about geometry applies to geography with no changes except for swapping out the term *geometry* for *geography* in both data type and function names. For example, ST_GeomFromText becomes ST_GeogFromText. Let's look at a few examples.

Listing 2.12 Using the geography data type

```
CREATE TABLE ch02.my_geogs (
    id serial PRIMARY KEY,
    name varchar(20),
    my_point geography(POINT)
);
INSERT INTO my_geogs (name, my_point)
VALUES
    ('Home',ST_GeogFromText('POINT(0 0)')),
    ('Pizza 1',ST_GeogFromText('POINT(1 1)')),
    ('Pizza 2',ST_GeogFromText('POINT(1 -1)'));
```

The difference between the two becomes apparent when you ask the question "How far is my house from each pizza restaurant?" as shown in the following listing.

Listing 2.13 How far am I from pizza (spheroid distance)

```
SELECT
    h.name As house, p.name As pizza,
    ST_Distance(h.my_point, p.my_point) As dist
FROM
    (SELECT name, my_point FROM ch02.my_geogs WHERE name = 'Home') As h
    CROSS JOIN
    (SELECT name, my_point FROM ch02.my_geogs WHERE name LIKE 'Pizza%') As p;
```

For listing 2.13, the distance is 156899.568... meters for both pizza parlors. Points in geography correspond to longitude and latitude, and distances are always computed in meters. This example puts your home on the Republic of Null Island (http://www.nullisland.com), and the pizza stores are on islands to the northeast and the southeast. If you performed the same distance computation using geometry, you'd end up with 1.414... (the square root of 2)—a straightforward Pythagorean calculation. At the equator, one degree is approximately 110.944 meters, so the previous geometry answers tell you that you're about 156,874 meters from pizza.

Here's another example to drive home the difference:

```
SELECT ST_Distance(ST_Point(0,180)::geography, ST_Point(0,-180)::geography)
```

```
SELECT ST_Distance(ST_Point(0,180)::geometry, ST_Point(0,-180)::geometry)
```

Geography is smart enough to know that you're measuring the distance between the same point on the globe and returns a result of 0. Geometry continues to assume that you're on a flat earth and returns 360 "degree" units, close to 40,000 kilometers!

2.3.2 Spatial catalogs for geography

The geography_columns view is very similar to the geometry_columns view, except it lists columns in your database that are of type `geography`. You'll find this view in PostGIS 1.5 and above. Most of the columns in geography_columns are the same as those in geometry_columns except for one. In the geography_columns view, f_geometry_column is replaced with f_geography_column.

2.4 Raster

Rasters are all around us. You're probably staring at one now. Rasters organize information using pixels; pixels, sometimes called *cells*, form the basis of rasters. Unlike when you're shopping for a color TV, the actual shape and size of the pixels don't matter for database applications. Each pixel is really a space holder for data, nothing more.

Pixels are organized in rows and columns to form tiles. To make life easier, all tiles should be rectangular. When we speak of the size of a raster tile, we're referring to the number of horizontal pixels and vertical pixels. For example, your 1080-px HDTV can be said to have 1920 columns and 1080 rows of pixels, a 1920×1080 raster tile, giving you a total count of 2.1 megapixels. Remember that pixels are positional designations, not data. The actual data elements rest in *bands* (sometimes known as *channels* or *dimensions*). On your RGB TV raster, you can have three bands of data—one for each of the primary colors. PostGIS rasters can have as many as 255 bands in PostGIS 2.0, and even more in later versions.

Let's consider an example of raster modeling. Many city districts are laid out in grids: midtown Manhattan, the Chicago Loop, and the French Quarter of New Orleans, just to name a few. You can model each city block as a pixel, and you can then add bands to store data about each block. You could have a band that records the height of the tallest building in the block, another band to record the number of inhabitants, another to record the average property value, and another to record the number of pizzerias in the block. Rasters are more than pretty JPEGs and LCD displays—they're a powerful way to organize data.

GIS makes frequent use of georeferenced rasters. Pixels in a georeferenced raster correspond to actual geographical locations, and the physical size of the pixels takes on a real unit of measure. You can even assign an SRID to a georeferenced raster. For example, when flattened out, the globe can be modeled as a raster with 360 vertical columns and 180 horizontal rows for a total of 64,800 pixels. Each pixel is one degree high and one degree wide. This example has conveniently created a raster data structure that has geographic meaning. Remember that for data modeling, the actual shape and size of the pixels don't matter. The physical size of the globe raster goes from tiny triangles near the poles to big squares at the equators.

2.4.1 Properties of rasters

Rasters have more common properties than other data types, and more than PostgreSQL allows to be stored as type modifiers, so you should use check constraints whenever possible to enforce property values.

PostGIS raster data is stored in a table with a column of type `raster`. Data is usually evenly tiled so that one row holds the same rectangular size of pixels as other rows. We recommend that you keep each row between 50 and 500 pixels for both width and height. You'll experience faster processing if you break large rasters into tiles for storage in multiple rows rather than keeping them in a single row.

The raster2pgsql loader packaged with PostGIS is capable of taking larger rasters and chunking them into smaller tiles for database storage. We'll talk more about selecting suitable tile sizes in later chapters.

RASTER WIDTH AND HEIGHT

Each raster tile (a row in the `raster` column) has a width and height that's measured in pixels.

BANDS

Each raster can have multiple bands, but you must have at least one. PostGIS 2.0 allows up to 255 bands, but PostGIS 2.1 and above allow more.

BAND PIXEL TYPES

Rasters can only store numeric values in their pixels. The number of bands determines the number of values that each pixel can store. For example, a 100-band raster can store 100 values in each pixel; an RGB raster can store 3.

Pixel types describe the type of numbers that a given band in a pixel can accommodate. There are several possible choices:

- 1-bit Boolean, abbreviated as 1BB
- Unsigned integer of 2, 8, 16, or 32 bits, abbreviated as 2BUI, 8BUI, 16BUI, 32BUI
- Signed integers of 8, 16, or 32 bits, abbreviated as 8BSI, 16BSI, 32BSI
- Two float types of 32 bits and 64 bits, abbreviated as 32BF and 64BF

The most common pixel type by far is 8BUI. Each band has a single pixel type defined for all pixels. You can't vary the pixel type except across bands. Use the `ST_BandPixelType` function to obtain the pixel type of a specific band. We'll cover its use in chapter 7.

RASTERS AND SRIDS

Georeferenced rasters have spatial coordinates defined within a spatial reference system and therefore have an SRID to denote the SRS. Transformation functions are available to convert rasters from one SRS to another.

PIXEL WIDTH AND HEIGHT

For georeferenced rasters, pixels do have heights and widths that reflect units of measure. For example, if you're using a raster to represent downtown Manhattan's grid of streets and avenues, the width of your cell would be 274 meters and the height would be 80 meters (the typical area of a city block).

Two functions are useful for reading off a pixel's width and height: `ST_PixelWidth` and `ST_PixelHeight`.

PIXEL SCALE

In order to reference a particular pixel on a raster, you must have some pixel-numbering convention relative to spatial coordinates. This convention is generally positive in the X direction and negative in the Y direction of coordinate space, though it need not be. A raster's pixel cell numbering always starts at the top-left corner of the tile rectangle, whereas when we talk about coordinate space we generally start numbering from the bottom-left corner. A negative Y pixel scale means increasing pixel row cell numbers correspond to decreasing Y spatial coordinates, and a positive X pixel scale means increasing column cell numbers correspond to increasing X coordinates.

If you assign a unit grid to your rasters, you can speak in terms of scale for georeferenced rasters. For the Manhattan raster example, the width of each pixel represents 274 meters, so it would be said to have an X scale of 1:274. Similarly, the Y scale is 1:80. You often encounter scales on a printed map. If you use a unit grid of 1 mm to map Manhattan, then each block would occupy 274 by 80 mm on paper, and the map could be said to have a 1:1000 scale.

SKEW X AND Y

The skew values are generally `0`. Most rasters are aligned with the spatial reference coordinate axis, but on occasion they may be rotated, and the skew angle would define the rotation from the geocoordinate axis.

2.4.2 Creating rasters

People generally use a loader such as raster2pgsql to import or register external rasters in the database. We'll demonstrate this technique in chapter 4. For now, we want to show you how to create raster data from scratch and how to insert the data using SQL. Remember that you can't add type modifiers during column creation for rasters, so the common practice is to first get data into a raster table and then apply constraints using the `AddRasterConstraints` function.

The `AddRasterConstraints` function has some intelligence built into it. You don't need to specify the particular constraint you're adding. The function will scan the data and try to apply as many check constraints as possible, namely SRID, width, height of each tile, alignment, bands, and so on, but it will skip over any constraints where the data is already in violation. It can also take additional arguments specifying the constraint types to enforce, if you only want certain constraints enforced.

In the next listing you'll generate a raster table consisting of tiles that cover the world. To do so, you'll project the earth out in a simple way: one degree of longitude and one degree of latitude corresponds to one pixel. Each raster tile will be 90 pixels wide and 45 pixels high. There will be one band to hold temperature readings in each pixel.

Listing 2.14 Creating a raster table of the world

```
CREATE TABLE ch02.my_rasters (
    rid SERIAL PRIMARY KEY,
    name varchar(150),
    rast raster
);

INSERT INTO ch02.my_rasters (name, rast)
SELECT
    'quad ' || x::text || ' ' || y::text,
    ST_AddBand(                                    <-- 1 Add temperature band
        ST_MakeEmptyRaster(
            90, 45,
            (x-2) * 90,
            (2-y) * 45,                            2 Add 90×45 pixel raster rows, WGS 84 lon/lat
            1, -1, 0, 0,
            4326
        ),
        '16BUI'::text,
        0
    )
FROM generate_series(0,3) As x CROSS JOIN generate_series(0,3) As y;
```

In listing 2.14, you first create a table to hold your raster tiles. You then add 16 raster tiles (rows) to the table ❷. Each tile is 90 pixels wide by 45 pixels high. Given that you're using WGS 84 lon/lat, each pixel represents 1 square degree. Then, as part of the creation process, you add a single band to hold temperature fluctuations around the world and initialize the temperature to 0 ❶. For this example, the temperature is recorded in Kelvin; just like when you're using the M coordinate, you should consistently use a given band to store the same type of measurement using the same unit of measurement.

ADDING BANDS

You might later decide to add more bands to your rasters, and you can do so with an update statement. Generally, though, it's best to add all the bands when you create the raster.

The next example creates an 8BUI band to store some measure of vegetation, with 0 being bad and 255 being really good:

```
UPDATE ch02.my_rasters SET rast = ST_AddBand(rast, '8BUI'::text,0);
```

APPLYING CONSTRAINTS

Once you're done adding bands, you'll want to add constraints to get the raster table column to register properly in the raster_columns view:

```
SELECT AddRasterConstraints('ch02', 'my_rasters'::name, 'rast'::name);
```

2.4.3 Spatial catalog for rasters

The raster_columns view is a catalog of all the columns in your database that are of type `raster`.

When you create a table with a `raster` column data type or import rasters with the raster2pgsql utility, you'll see entries in the raster_columns view. As you add additional constraints using the `AddRasterConstraints` function, this view will show the relevant constraint information. This manual registration is identical to how PostGIS recorded `geometry` column data types prior to version 2.0, but unlike the old model, PostGIS can infer the information from the constraints rather than requiring manual registration in a table.

You can query raster_columns much like any other table or view with a query like this:

```
SELECT
    r_table_name As tname,r_raster_column As cname,
    srid,
    scale_x As sx, scale_y As sy,
    blocksize_x As bx, blocksize_y As by,
    same_alignment As sa,
    num_bands As nb,
    pixel_types As ptypes
FROM raster_columns
WHERE r_table_schema = 'ch02';
```

This is the output of the preceding query:

```
   tname   | cname | srid | sx | sy | bx | by | sa | nb |     ptypes
-----------+-------+------+----+----+----+----+----+----+------------
 my_rast..| rast  | 4326 |  1 | -1 | 90 | 45 | t  |  2 | {16BUI,8BUI}
```

The raster2pgsql raster loader is capable of creating overview tables. These are tables that have the same data as the main table, but at lower resolutions. They're particularly useful for running fast calculations for showing raster data zoomed out on a map. We'll cover overview tables in more detail when we discuss loading raster data. For now, just keep in mind that the raster_overviews view lists these tables, their resolutions, and their parent tables. The raster_columns view lists columns from the overview tables. At times, you may need to join raster_columns with raster_overviews to obtain all the columnar details you need.

2.5 Summary

In this chapter, we took a closer look at the major data types packaged in the PostGIS extension: `geometry`, `geography`, and `raster`. We showed you how to create these types from scratch, and you should be able to discern which family works best for the modeling task at hand, at least in cut-and-dried cases. You should also know the basic properties for each type and subtype, and in which meta-tables or catalog views to look for information on existing data.

In chapter 3, we'll explore spatial reference systems before returning to our core coverage of PostGIS.

3 Spatial reference system considerations

This chapter covers

- Characteristics of spatial reference systems
- How to determine and select spatial reference systems

Up to this point we've been working mostly with fictitious data. Using sample data to learn the basics of PostGIS is an excellent beginning. You're immediately rewarded with results without facing the distractions and the obstacles of real-world data. From this chapter forward, though, we're not going to shield you anymore.

We'll start this chapter by discussing different types of spatial reference systems. We'll then follow up with sections on selecting suitable SRSs for storage and on determining the spatial reference of source data.

The art and science of modeling our bulbous earth and getting a 2D representation on paper have been around since antiquity. *Geodetics* is the science of measuring and modeling the earth, and *cartography* is the science of representing the earth on flat maps. The intricacies of these two venerated sciences are far beyond the scope of this book, but together with a lot of math, they produce something that's of utmost importance to GIS: spatial reference systems (SRSs).

In this chapter, we're not going to take the easy way out by accepting spatial reference systems without understanding them. We'll also avoid the path of arcane mathematics necessary to study the science in all its glory. We'll take a middle road so that you can at least have more than a one-sentence explanation of SRSs when your kids finally get around to asking you about them. Our journey into the real world begins.

3.1 Spatial reference systems: what are they?

The topic of spatial reference systems is one of the more abstruse in GIS. This is mainly due to the loose way in which people use the term *spatial reference system* and secondly due to its unglamorous nature compared to other areas of GIS. If GIS is Disneyland, think of SRSs as the bookkeeping necessary to keep the Disneyland operation afloat.

Take any two paper maps having one point in common, and overlay one atop the other using the common point as a reference. Both maps represent the whole or a part of the earth, but unless you're extremely lucky, the two maps have no relation to each other. Travel five centimeters right on one map and you can end up on another street. Five centimeters on the other map could put you on another continent. Your two maps don't overlay well because they don't have the same spatial reference system.

The main reason for the GIS data consumer to become acquainted with SRSs is to bring in data from disparate sources that use different SRSs and be able to overlay one atop another. Many standards exist to make this task easy without you having to delve into the nuances of SRSs. The most common one is the European Petroleum Survey Group (EPSG) numbering system. Take any two sources of data with the same EPSG number, and they'll overlay perfectly. But EPSG is a fairly recent SRS numbering system. If you uncover data from a few decades ago, you won't find an EPSG number. You'll have no choice but to delve into the constituent pieces that form an SRS: ellipsoid, datum, and projection. So what is a spatial reference system?

3.1.1 Geoids

From outer space, our good earth appears spherical, often described as a blue marble. To anyone living on its surface, though, nothing could be further from the truth. The slick glossy surface seen from outer space actually comprises mountain ranges, deep canyons, and ocean trenches. The surface of the earth with all its nooks and crannies resembles a slightly charred English muffin much more than a lustrous marble. Even the idea of the earth being spherical isn't accurate, because the equator bulges out, making a trip around the equator about 42.72 km longer than a trip on one of the meridians.

In light of the fact that we have a deeply pitted and somewhat squashed orange under our feet, what should we do? With our new GPS toys we could conceivably represent every square meter on earth as a satellite map, assigning it a spherical 3D coordinate, and be done with it. This is the approach taken by many digital elevation models. Though this brute force computation method could certainly become the standard one day, we still need a simpler and more computationally cost-effective model for most use cases.

A *model*, by definition, is a simplified representation of reality. All models are inherently flawed in some way or other, but in exchange for their shortcomings, they provide us with a more cost-effective way of doing things. A key factor in selecting a model is finding one that balances cost of computation (in speed and complexity) with observed failure. Some models may fail in ways you don't care about because you'll never exercise their points of failure. Until the time when we can afford to carry around portable holograms of the earth, we need several cheap models.

A starting point for any 3D model is choosing the definition of the surface of the earth. Do you use the mean sea level? An average of the peaks and valleys? Quite a few options are available, but they all suffer from a common problem; you can't really go out and set up a standard of measurement that's applicable around the entire world. Take the notion of sea level, for instance. Someone in Cardiff, Wales, can say that her house is 50 meters above the sea during low tide and use this as a reference against her neighbor's house. Suppose a fellow in Pago Pago has a small house and measures his house also to be 50 meters above sea level. What can we say about the elevation of the two houses relative to each other? Not much. Sea level varies from place to place relative to the center of the earth. And even the notion of *center of the earth* is ambiguous.

Along comes Gauss, who, with the help of a crude pendulum, determined in the early nineteenth century that the surface of the earth can be defined using gravitational measurements. Though he lacked a digital gravity meter, he envisioned the idea of going around the surface of the globe with such a device, like a simple pendulum, and measuring out a surface where gravity was constant—an equipotential surface. This is the basic idea of what we call *the geoid*. We take gravity readings at various sea levels to come up with a consensus and then use this constant gravitational force to map out an equigravitational surface around the globe. Many consider the geoid to be the true figure of the earth.

Surprisingly, the geoid is far from spherical; see figure 3.1. You must not forget that the core of the earth isn't homogenous. Mass is distributed unevenly, giving rise to bulges and craters that rival those found on the lunar surface. The advent of the geoid didn't simplify matters. On the contrary, it created even more headaches. The true surface of the earth is now even less marble-like, and even a slightly squashed orange is no longer a faithful representation.

Figure 3.1 The geoid representing the earth seen from different angles

Although the geoid is rarely talked about in GIS, it's the foundation of both planar and geodetic models. In the next section, we'll discuss the more commonly used ellipsoids, which are simplifications of the geoid and are generally good enough for most geographic modeling needs.

3.1.2 Ellipsoids

As early as ancient Greek times, ellipsoids have been used to model the earth. An ellipsoid is merely a 3D ellipse.

> **Ellipsoids**
> An ellipsoid is composed of three radii: *a* and *b* are equatorial radii (along the X and Y axes), and c is the polar radius (along the Z axis). In geodesy, only two axes are considered: semi-major and semi-minor. Spheroids are a subclass of ellipsoids where $a = b$. A spheroid where $c > a$ is called an *oblate spheroid*. If $a = b = c$, you have a perfect sphere.

By varying the equatorial and polar radii on the ellipsoid, you can model the equatorial bulge. At some point in the history of cartography, it was postulated that one ellipsoid could be used all around the world as a reference ellipsoid. Everyone could locate each other by finding their placement on the reference ellipsoid.

The discovery of the geoid shattered the idea of using a single ellipsoid. One look at the geoid will show why. The geoid paints a picture where the curvature varies from place to place. An ellipsoid that fits the curvature for one spot may be awfully inaccurate for another; see figure 3.2. Instead of one ellipsoid to rule us all, people on different continents wanted their own ellipsoids to better reflect the regional curvature of the earth. This gave rise to the multitude of ellipsoids we have today.

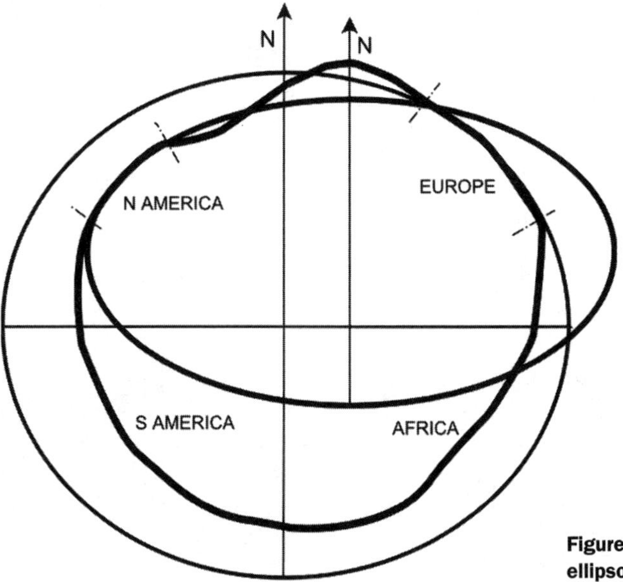

Figure 3.2 The geoid and the ellipsoid seen together

This was all well and good when we didn't have much communication with people far away from us. This use of different systems became more of an issue over time because scientists and governments needed to collaborate and because of the rise of oil surveying and aviation. Fortunately, today the world is settling on the World Geodetic System (WGS 84) and Geodetic Reference System (GRS 80) ellipsoids, with WGS 84 becoming the standard of choice. WGS 84 is what all GPS systems are based on.

NOTE The 80 and 84 in GRS 80 and WGS 84 stand for 1980 and 1984, when the standards came out, and the ellipsoids are very similar.

To call WGS 84 simply an ellipsoid isn't quite accurate. The WGS 84 GPS systems we use have a geoid component as well. The present WGS 84 system uses the 1996 Earth Gravitational Model (EGM96) geoid and is the ellipsoid that best fits the geoid model for the selected survey points in the set.

Many ellipsoids have been used over the years, and some continue to be used because of their better fit for a particular region. All historical data is still referenced against other ellipsoids. Table 3.1 lists some common ellipsoids and their ellipsoidal parameters.

Table 3.1 Common ellipsoids

Ellipsoid	Equatorial radius (m)	Polar radius (m)	Inverse flattening	Where used
Clarke 1866	6,378,206.4	6,356,583.8	294.9786982	North America
NAD 27	6,378,206.4	6,356,583.8	294.978698208	North America
Australian 1966	6,378,160	6,356,774.719	298.25	Australia
GRS 80	6,378,137	6,356,752.3141	298.257222101	North America
WGS 84	6,378,137	6,356,752.3142	298.257223563	GPS (World)
IERS 1989	6,378,136	6,356,751.302	298.257	Time (World)

One common old ellipsoid is Clarke 1866, and it's so close to the NAD 27 ellipsoid that they're synonymous for most purposes.

In the next section we'll discuss the concept of datums and how they fit into the overall picture of the spatial reference system.

Lon/lat, but which ellipsoid?

Even though old data points are measured in longitude and latitude, they aren't the same longitude and latitude we use today, and they also use different grounding points. They're shifted. This is why it's important to not just call things lon/lat. You can have NAD 27 lon/lat, NAD 80 lon/lat, and WGS 84 lon/lat, and each will be subtly different.

As a rule, when people nowadays refer to lon/lat, they mean WGS 84 datum and WGS 84 ellipsoid in lon/lat units. NAD 27 is the most different because it was created a long time ago. (Note that *datum* is the shift of a spheroid, as explained in the next section.)

3.1.3 Datum

The ellipsoid only models the overall shape of the earth. After picking out an ellipsoid, you need to anchor it to use it for real-world navigation. Every ellipsoid that's not a perfect sphere has two poles. This is where the axis arrives at the surface. These ellipsoid poles must be tagged permanently to actual points on earth. This is where the datum comes into play. Even if two reference systems use the same ellipsoid, they could still have different anchors, or datum, on earth.

The simplest example of a datum is to look at the tilt between the geographic pole and the magnetic pole. In both models, the earth has the same spherical shape, but one is anchored at the North Pole, and the other is somewhere near northern Canada.

To anchor an ellipsoid to a point on earth, you need two types of datum: a horizontal datum to specify where on the plane of the earth to pin down the ellipsoid and a vertical datum to specify the height. For example, the North American Datum of 1927 (NAD 27) is anchored at Meades Ranch in Kansas because it's close to the geographical centroid of the United States. NAD 27 is both a horizontal and a vertical datum.

Here are some commonly used datums:

- NAD 83 (North American Datum 1983, which is often accompanied by the GRS 80 ellipsoid)
- NAD 27 (North American Datum 1927, which is generally accompanied by the Clarke 1866/NAD 27 ellipsoid)
- European Datum 1950
- Australian Geodetic System 1984

3.1.4 Coordinate reference system

Many people confuse coordinate reference systems with spatial reference systems. A coordinate reference system is only one necessary ingredient that goes into the making of an SRS and isn't the SRS itself. To identify a point on your reference ellipsoid, you need a coordinate system.

The most popular coordinate reference system for use on a reference ellipsoid is the geographical coordinate system (also known as *geodetic coordinate system* or simply as *lon/lat*). You're already intimately familiar with this coordinate system. You find the two poles on an ellipsoid and draw longitude (meridian) lines from pole to pole. You then find the equator of your ellipsoid and start drawing latitude lines.

Keep in mind that even though you may only have seen geographical coordinate systems used on a globe, the concept applies to any reference ellipsoid. For that matter, it applies to anything resembling an ellipsoid. For instance, a watermelon has nice longitudinal bands on its surface.

3.1.5 Spatial reference system essentials

Let's summarize what we've discussed thus far about spatial reference systems:

- You start by modeling the earth using some variant of a reference ellipsoid, which should be the ellipsoid that deviates least from the geoid for the regions on earth you care about.
- You use a datum to pin the ellipsoid to an actual place on earth, and you assign a coordinate reference system to the ellipsoid so you can identify every point on the surface. For example, the zero milestone in Washington, D.C., is W -77.03655 and N 38.8951 (in spatial, x: -77.03655, y: 38.8951) on a WGS 84 ellipsoid using the WGS 84 datum; on the NAD 27 datum and Clarke 1866 ellipsoid, this would be W -77.03685, N 38.8950.

We can quit at this point, because we have all the elements necessary to tag every spot on earth. We can even develop transformation algorithms to convert coordinates based on one ellipsoid to another. Many sources of geographic data do stop at this point and don't go on to the next step of projecting the data onto a flat surface. We term this data *unprojected data*. All data served up in the form of latitude and longitude is unprojected.

You can do quite a bit with unprojected data. By using the great circle distance formula, you can get distances between any two points. You can also use it to navigate to and from any points on earth.

3.1.6 Projections

The concept of *projection* generally refers to taking an ellipsoidal earth and squashing it onto a flat surface. Projection has distortion built in. Because geodetic and 3D globes are ellipsoidal, they by definition don't refer to a flat surface. So why do we have 2D projections of our ellipsoid or geoid? The obvious reason is eminently practical: you can't carry a huge globe everywhere you go. Less obvious but more relevant is the mathematical and visual simplicity that comes with planar (Euclidean) geometry.

As we've repeated many times, PostGIS works for the most part on a Cartesian plane, and most of the powerful functions assume a Cartesian model. Your brain and the quite different brain of PostGIS can perform area and distance calculations quickly on a Cartesian plane. On a plane, the area of a square is its side squared. Distance is calculated simply by applying the Pythagorean theorem. A planar model fits nicely on a piece of paper. In contrast, calculating the area of a square directly on the surface of an ellipsoid is quite a challenge, not the least aspect of which is deciding what constitutes a square on an ellipsoid in the first place.

How exactly you squash an ellipsoidal earth on a flat surface depends on what you're trying to optimize for. There are several classes of Cartesian coordinate systems,

PostGIS 1.5 supports geodetic data, and PostGIS 2.1 improves support

PostGIS 1.5 introduced support for geodetic data using the new `geography` data type, which is similar in concept to SQL Server 2008 geography types. There are many fewer functions for `geography` than there are for the `geometry` type.

In PostGIS 2.1, various enhancements were made to improve speed, yielding in many cases 10-fold or higher speed increases in proximity checks compared to PostGIS 1.5 geography support. PostGIS 2.1 also introduced new geography-aware functions, such as `ST_Segmentize`.

which we call kinds of projections, that are named for how they flatten the earth. Each class tries to optimize for a set of features. Each specific instance of a coordinate system is bounded by a particular region on earth and uses a particular unit (usually meters or feet) for units of Cartesian space.

In creating a projection, you try to balance four conflicting features. The importance you place on each will dictate your choice of coordinate system and eventually the spatial reference system:

- Measurement
- Shape—how accurately does it represent angles?
- Direction—is north really north?
- Range of area supported

The general tradeoff is that if you want to span a large area, you have to either give up measurement accuracy or deal with the pain of maintaining multiple SRSs and some mechanism to shift among them. The larger your area, the less accurate and potentially unusable your measurements will be. If you try to optimize for shape and to cover a large range, your measurements may be off, perhaps way off.

There are a few flavors of projections you can use to optimize for different things:

- *Cylindrical projections*—Imagine a piece of paper rolled around the globe, imprinting the globe on its surface. Then you unroll it to make it flat. The most common of these is the Mercator projection, which has the bottom of the rolled cylinder parallel to the equator. This results in great distortion at the polar regions, with measurement accuracy better the closer you are to the equator, because there the approximation of flat is most accurate.
- *Conic projections*—These are sort of like cylindrical projections, except you wrap a cone around the globe, take the imprint of the globe on the cone, and then roll it out.
- *Azimuthal projections*—You project a spherical surface onto a plane tangential to the spheroid.

Within these three kinds of projections, you must also consider the orientation of the paper you roll around the globe. These are the possibilities:

- *Oblique*—Neither parallel nor perpendicular to the equator; some other angle
- *Equatorial*—Perpendicular to the plane of the equator
- *Transverse*—Parallel along the equator

Combinations of these categories form the main classes of planar coordinate systems:

- *Lambert Azimuthal Equal Area (LAEA)*—These are reasonably good for measurement and can cover some large areas, but are not great for shape. The one we like most when dealing with United States data and when we're concerned with somewhat decent measurement is U.S. National Atlas (EPSG:2163). This is a meter-based spatial reference system. LAEAs are generally not good at maintaining direction or angle.
- *Lambert Conformal Conic (LCC)*—These preserve shape more than they preserve area and are generally good for measurement for the regions they serve. They distort poles. The projection commonly uses two lines of latitude for its bounds of a portion of a cone. The closer the two lines of latitude, the better the measurement accuracy. LCCs are best used for middle latitudes with east-west orientation. They are often used for aeronautical charts, U.S. State Plane coordinate systems, and national and regional mapping.
- *Universal Trans Mercator (UTM)*—These are generally good for maintaining measurement and shape and direction, but they only span six-degree longitudinal strips. If you need to cover the whole globe and you use one of these, you'll have to maintain about 60 SRS IDs. You can't use them for the polar regions.
- *Mercator*—These are good for maintaining shape and direction and spanning the globe, but they're not good for measurement, and they make the regions near the poles look huge. The measurements you get from them are nothing less than cartoonish, depending on where you are. The most common Mercator projections in use are variants of World Mercator (SRID 3395) or Spherical Mercator (a.k.a. Google Mercator (SRID 900913)), which is now an EPSG standard with EPSG:3857 (but for a time was EPSG:3785). This last one is fairly new, so you may not find it in your spatial_ref_sys table if your PostGIS version is older. Mercator systems are common favorites for web map display because you only have to maintain one SRID, and they look good to most people.
- *National grid systems*—These are generally a variant of UTM or LAEA but are used to define a restricted region, such as a country. As mentioned, U.S. National Atlas (SRID 2163, U.S. National Atlas Equal Area) is common for the United States. These are generally decent for measurement (but not super-accurate; they don't always maintain good shape), but cover a fair amount of area, which is in many cases the national area you care about.
- *State plane*—These are U.S. spatial reference systems. They're usually designed for a specific state, and most are derived from UTM. Generally there are two for a state—one measured in meters and one measured in feet—although some larger states have four or more. Optimal for measurement, these are commonly

used by state and city land surveyors but, as we said, they can deal with only a single state.

- *Geodetic*—PostGIS can store WGS 84 lon/lat (4326) as a `geometry` data type, but more often than not you'll want to transform it to another SRS or store it in the `geography` data type so it's usable. You can sometimes get away with using it as a `geometry` data type for small distances along the same longitude and when two things intersect, but keep in mind that when you use it, PostGIS is really projecting it. It squashes it on a flat surface, treating longitude as X and latitude as Y, so even though it looks unprojected, in reality it's projected and in a mostly unusable way. The colloquial name for this kind of projection is *plate carrée.*

Given all these different options for SRSs, determining which one your source data is in and choosing one for storage is often a tricky undertaking. In the next section, we'll show you how to select a spatial reference system as well as some simple exercises for determining which SRS your source data is in.

3.2 Selecting a spatial reference system for storing data

One of the most common questions people ask is what spatial reference system is appropriate for their data. The answer is, "It depends."

Table 3.2 lists the most commonly used SRSs and their PostGIS/EPSG SRIDs. PostGIS SRIDs follow the EPSG numberings, so you can assume for sake of argument that they're the same. This isn't necessarily true for other spatial databases, so keep in mind that a spatial reference system can have several different IDs. Although EPSG is the most common authority on SRSs, it isn't the only one. Many people, for example, load up their tables with Esri definitions, which are sometimes identical to EPSG definitions, but under SRID codes that are more ArcGIS-friendly.

Table 3.2 Common spatial reference systems and their fitness for particular purposes

EPSG/PostGIS SRID	Colloquial name	Range	Measurement	Shape
4326	WGS 84 lon/lat	Excellent	Bad	Bad
3785/900913 (old number)	Spherical Mercator	Good	Bad	Good
900913 (deprecated)	Google Mercator	Good	Bad	Good
32601-32760	UTM WGS 84 zones	Medium	Good	Good
2163	U.S. National Atlas EA	Good	Medium	Medium
State planes	U.S. state planes	Medium	Good	Good

RANGE, MEASUREMENT, AND SHAPE In table 3.2 the range, measurement, and shape values are relative. For range, *excellent* means it covers the globe, *good* means it covers a largish country like the U.S., and *medium* covers several degrees or a large state. For measurement, *good* means the measurements for the area served are usually within a meter for length, area, and distance calculations; *medium* means the measurements are accurate within meters, but distances can be as much as 10 meters off if two things are far from each other; and *bad* means the measurements don't have useful units, or they exaggerate areas as you get closer to the poles. Shape refers to how distorted shapes are and how well angles are preserved.

If you deal with mostly regional data, such as for a country or state, then it's generally best to stick with one of the national grid or state planes systems. You'll get fairly good measurement accuracy, and it will also look good on a map.

NOTE Cartesian coordinate systems that are measure-preserving only support a limited region, so if you use the `geometry` type, you may have to use several spatial reference systems if you need to span large areas and maintain measurement accuracy.

3.2.1 Pros and cons of using EPSG:4326

The most common SRS people use is WGS 84 lon/lat (EPSG:4326). It's used by many people who don't know anything about SRSs, but knowledgeable people use this system for a couple of main reasons:

- It covers the whole globe and is the most common SRS for sharing data. For example, all GPS data is stored in this SRS. If you need to cover the world, dish out data to lots of people, and deal with lots of GPS data, this isn't a bad choice.
- Most commercial mapping toolkit APIs accept data to be mapped only in WGS 84 lon/lat (although they use some variant of Mercator for display). `ST_Transform` also introduces some rounding errors as you retransform data, so it's best to transform only once from the source format. `ST_Transform` is a fairly cheap process, so it's okay to run it for each geometry if you keep functional indexes on the transformations of the form `CREATE INDEX idx_geomt ON sometable USING gist(ST_Transform(geom,some_srid)` and then use `ST_DWithin(a.geom, ST_Transform(sometable.geom,some_srid), some_distance)` for distance checking. Now when `ST_DWithin` is used with the transformed geometry, the function spatial index will kick in to help.

There are also reasons not to use EPSG:4326:

- It's bad for measurement. If measurement is something you do often, and especially if you're concerned about small regions such as a country or state, you'll spend a lot of time transforming back and forth if you use EPSG:4326. There are hacks for avoiding this with point data using a combination of `ST_Distance_Spheroid`, `ST_Distance_Sphere`, and `ST_DWithin`, and in PostGIS 1.5+ you can just use the `geography` data type instead (in exchange for many fewer functions).
- Things like intersects, intersections, and unions generally work fine for small geometries but fall apart for large geometries; for example, continents or long fault lines.

- It's bad for shape and it doesn't look good on a map. It's squashed because you're showing longitude and latitude, which are meant to be measured around an ellipsoid, and you're showing them on planar axes (X and Y).

3.2.2 Geography data type for EPSG:4326

If you'll be storing your data in a WGS 84 spatial reference system and are using PostGIS 1.5 or above, you should consider using the new `geography` data type that was introduced in PostGIS 1.5. The key benefit it provides over the `geometry` EPSG:4326 data type is that it's ideal for measurement because it's not projected, and measurements are always in meters. The pros are as follows:

- It will more or less work out of the box for you.
- Distance and area measurements are as good as or better than UTM, so if your data covers the globe and you just need distance, area, and length measurements, this is probably the best option.
- Most web-mapping layers, such as Google, Virtual Earth (Bing), and the like, expect data to be fed to them in WGS 84 coordinates, so `geography` will work fine out of the box.

If `geography` is great, why should you use `geometry` instead?

- Processing functions for `geography` are limited. As of PostGIS 1.5, you can do an `ST_Intersection` and an `ST_Buffer`. But these are just wrappers around the `geometry` implementations that perform a transformation to a suitable planar projection behind the scenes, so it's not too hard to roll your own functions.
- Although you can piggyback on the `geometry` processing functions by casting and transforming to `geometry` and casting back, the `ST_Transform` operation isn't a lossless operation. `ST_Transform` introduces some floating-point errors that can quickly accumulate if you do a fair amount of geometry processing.
- If you're dealing with regional data, WGS 84 is generally not quite as accurate for measurements as regional SRSs.
- If you're building your own mapping app, you'll still need to learn how to transform your data to other SRSs if you want them to look good on a map. Although the transformation process is fairly cheap, it can quickly become taxing with the more data you pull, the more users hitting your database, or the greater number of points you have in a geometry.
- Not as many tools support `geography`. In theory, though, any tool that just uses the `ST_AsBinary` and other output functions of PostGIS geometries will work fine with `geography` without any change.

3.2.3 Mapping just for presentation

Although the basic Mercator projections are horrible for measurement calculations, especially far from the equator, they're a favorite for web mappers because they look good on a map. The advantage of Google Mercator, for example, is that the whole globe is covered with just one spatial reference system.

So if your primary concern is looking good on a map and overlaying Google Maps with something like OpenLayers, Leaflet, or some other JavaScript API, Mercator isn't a bad option for native data storage. If you're concerned with distances and areas, your choice depends on the accuracy you need.

Table 3.3 (generated from code in chapter 10) lists the distances between city pairs measured using various SRSs: WGS 84 sphere (sp), WGS 84 spheroid (spwgs84), and Web Mercator (wm). The WGS 84 spheroid or sphere calculations are generally what most applications use for doing long-distance measurement. The sphere is a little less accurate because it treats the earth as a sphere rather than the more accurate ellipsoid model. The WGS 84 spheroid is as accurate as you can get for long-distance measurement. As you can see, the Web Mercator distance precision is very different from the WGS 84 spheroid, and therefore much worse for measurement, and it gets worse the farther away two cities are from each other or for regions farther from the equator. The computed distance between Beijing and Philadelphia, for example, is really poor with Mercator. The sphere calculations are pretty good for long-range/short-range rule-of-thumb calculations.

Table 3.3 Results of distance calculations in kilometers

city1	city2	sp	spwgs84	wm
Beijing	Jerusalem	7119	7135	9104
Beijing	Melbourne	9128	9095	9938
Beijing	Philadelphia	11060	11085	21330
Beijing	Sao Paulo	17600	17601	19656
Beijing	Shanghai	1066	1065	1315
Cairo	Jerusalem	423	424	494
Cairo	Melbourne	13977	13973	15024
Cairo	Philadelphia	9154	9173	11928
Cairo	Sao Paulo	10224	10216	10667
Cairo	Shanghai	8351	8367	10045
Rio de Janeiro	Jerusalem	10323	10315	10808
Rio de Janeiro	Melbourne	13221	13240	21078
Rio de Janeiro	Philadelphia	7706	7680	8250
Rio de Janeiro	Sao Paulo	338	338	368
Rio de Janeiro	Shanghai	18249	18256	19399
Sydney	Jerusalem	14114	14111	15040

Table 3.3 Results of distance calculations in kilometers *(continued)*

city1	city2	sp	spwgs84	wm
Sydney	Melbourne	694	694	858
Sydney	Philadelphia	15895	15895	26702
Sydney	Sao Paulo	13357	13377	22041
Sydney	Shanghai	7878	7849	8354

Table 3.3 covers distance, but what about the areas of geometries? How bad is the story there? Again, this depends on where you are on the globe, but in general the situation is bad. Table 3.4 shows the areas of 10-meter buffers around the globe. The table shows the area of the buffers in the UTM (utm), geography (geog), and web Mercator (wm) spatial reference systems. The two columns at the right show the differences between UTM and the other two buffer sizes. The buffer is created by picking a specific point and drawing a circle polygon around it with a 10-meter radius centered at the point, generated from code in chapter 8.

Table 3.4 Ten-meter buffer areas in different regions of the world

City	utm	geog	wm	diff_utm_geog	diff_utm_wm
Honolulu	312	312	362	0.13	49.48
San Francisco	312	312	500	0.22	188.03
Boston	312	312	572	0.02	260.22
Paris	312	312	722	0.24	409.54
Oslo	312	312	1240	0.18	927.74
Saint Petersburg	312	312	1241	0.09	929.03
Helsinki	312	312	1260	0.15	947.76
Bergen	312	312	1272	0.11	959.40
Arkhangelsk	312	312	1681	0.20	1368.54
Murmansk	312	312	2412	0.25	2100.22

Why is a PostGIS 10-meter buffer of a point 312 and not 314 sq m?

If you do the calculation, a perfect 10-meter buffer will give you an area of 10*10*pi(), which is around 314 square meters. The default buffer in PostGIS is a 32-sided polygon (eight points approximate a quarter segment of a circle). You can make this more accurate by using the overloaded version of the `ST_Buffer` function that allows you to pass in the number of points used to approximate a quarter segment.

3.2.4 Covering the globe when distance is a concern

If you're in the unfortunate predicament of needing to cover the whole globe with good measurement and shape accuracy, then a single spatial reference system isn't likely to cut it. A common favorite for measurement accuracy that also preserves shape is the UTM family of SRSs. The UTM family has coordinates in meters so it's easy to use for measurement. There are about 60 UTM SRIDs in the spatial_ref_sys table covering the globe that are based on the WGS 84 ellipsoid. Each UTM SRS covers six-degree longitudinal strips. There are also a series of UTMs for the NAD 83 ellipsoid, but the WGS 84 series is more common.

You'll need to figure out the WGS 84 UTM SRID for your particular data set, and there's a function for that in the PostGIS wiki at http://trac.osgeo.org/postgis. The following listing shows a slight variant of that function that takes any geometry and returns the WGS 84 UTM SRID of the centroid of that geometry.

Listing 3.1 Determining the WGS 84 UTM SRID of a geometry

```
CREATE OR REPLACE FUNCTION upgis_utmzone_wgs84(geometry)
    RETURNS integer AS
    $$
    DECLARE
        geomgeog geometry;
        zone int;
        pref int;
    BEGIN
    geomgeog:=ST_Transform(ST_Centroid($1),4326);          ❶ Convert to a lon/lat point

    IF (y(geomgeog))>0 THEN
         pref:=32600;
     ELSE                                                   ❷ Determine UTM start
         pref:=32700;                                         and number of zones
     END IF;                                                  to add to get SRID
     zone:=floor((ST_X(geomgeog)+180)/6)+1;

    RETURN zone+pref;
    END;
    $$ LANGUAGE 'plpgsql' immutable;
```

You convert your geometry to a point ❶ and then transform it to WGS 84 lon/lat. This function assumes the SRIDs are named the same as the EPSG for UTMs, which is the case with the default spatial_ref_sys that comes packaged with PostGIS. For example, the SRID of WGS 84 UTM Zone 1N is 32601, and the corresponding EPSG code is `EPSG:32601`.

You determine whether latitude is positive or negative ❷. UTM EPSG numbers start with 32600 and increment every six degrees. Negative latitude, or 0, starts at 32700. The final SRID will be between these numbers.

If you need to maintain multiple SRIDs, you have three approaches:

- Store one SRID (usually 4326) and transform on the fly as needed.

- Maintain one SRID for each region and possibly partition your data by region using table inheritance.
- Maintain multiple geometries—one field for each you commonly use.

There are many philosophies about the correct way to go, and none is right or wrong. For our cases, we've found that keeping one SRID (usually 4326) and transforming as needed works best, provided we maintain functional indexes on transforms used for distance calculations. We also like using views as an abstraction layer, where the view contains the calculated transform.

PostgreSQL supports not only functional indexes but also partial ones. A partial index allows you to index only part of your data. In general, you should only apply an `ST_Transform` function for the region defined for a given UTM; otherwise you'll run into coordinate bounds issues. It's also generally best to partition your data using table inheritance, and use different transform indexes for each table.

The next listing is an example of a functional `ST_Transform` index and of a possible view you might create to take advantage of it.

Listing 3.2 Using functional indexes

```
CREATE INDEX feature_data_the_geom_utm
     ON feature_data
     USING gist
     (st_transform(the_geom, 32611));

CREATE VIEW vwfeature_data AS
     SELECT gid, f_name, the_geom,
         ST_Transform(the_geom,32611) As the_geom_utm
     FROM feature_data;
```

In this view, you're transforming your native data to SRID 32611, which is one of the UTM SRIDs for a region of California in the United States.

Functional indexes on ST_Transform

Putting functional indexes on `ST_Transform` is something we do when building a view on our data with the transformed version of the data. It's a gray zone, in the sense that we're exploiting a small violation by treating `ST_Transform` as an immutable function, when technically it isn't.

In PostGIS, `ST_Transform` is marked as immutable mostly for performance reasons, which means when you calculate it for a given geometry, it can be assumed to never change. PostgreSQL kindly believes PostGIS and often caches the answer to `ST_Transform` and allows `ST_Transform` to be used in functional indexes as well. Only functions marked as immutable can be used in functional indexes, and in theory a function that relies on a table (except possibly for a static system table in pg_catalog) is at best considered stable (meaning it won't change within a query given the same inputs). In actuality, it's a bit of a lie that `ST_Transform` is immutable because it relies on entries in the spatial_ref_sys table. If you change the entry for

(continued)
your transform in the table, you'll need to re-index your data; otherwise it will be wrong (this would also be the case if you kept a second transformed geometry column). We tend to think a bit liberally and consider the spatial_ref_sys table to be immutable in practice because existing entries in the table rarely change. You might add entries to the table, but it's rare that you'd change the definitions of entries distributed with PostGIS or that you'd update an entry after you add it, so the immutability argument is valid.

The other issue with functional indexes is they're dropped when you restore your data, unless you set the `search_path` of the `ST_Transform` function to include the schema that the spatial_ref_sys table resides in (supported only in PostgreSQL 8.3 and above). Read our diatribe on this topic for more details:

http://www.postgresonline.com/journal/index.php?/archives/121-Restore-of-functional-indexes-gotcha.html.

So why do we use functional indexes on `ST_Transform` even though it's a bit of a no-no? The alternative is to keep a geometry field for your alternative spatial references. This is annoying for two reasons:

- You have to ensure the second geometry field is updated when your main geometry field is, which means putting in a trigger. Someone may get confused and update the secondary geometry field instead of the primary geometry field.
- If you have big geometries, having a second big geometry in your table slows down updates considerably, because PostgreSQL creates a copy of the original record during update and marks the original as deleted. It probably slows down selects too, because you have a fatter row to contend with.

Using `ST_Transform` on the fly is cheap, but doing an index search on this calculated call isn't possible without a gist index on this transformed data.

Often you'll have to load spatial data that you didn't create into your database. Before you worry about what spatial reference system you should use to transform your source data for storage, you first have to figure out what SRS your source data is in. If you guess wrong about that, all your spatial transformations will be wrong. In the next section, we'll look at how you can determine the SRS of your source data.

3.3 Determining the spatial reference system of source data

In this section, we'll go through some exercises that will help you determine the spatial reference system of source data. This will prepare you for the next chapter, where we'll finally start loading real data.

Determining the SRS of your source data is sometimes a fairly easy task and sometimes not. Sometimes a site will tell you the EPSG code for its data, and your work is done. Often, it will give you a text representation of the SRS either in WKT SRS notation or some sort of free text. In these cases you'll need to match up the description with a record in the spatial_ref_sys table.

With newer Esri shapefiles, there is often a file with a .prj extension giving the SRS information in WKT SRS notation. This file is often used by third-party tools to derive the projection in cases where different layers need to be transformed to the same SRS to be overlaid on a map. In the following exercises, we'll present some SRS text descriptions and demonstrate how you can match these to an SRID in the spatial_ref_sys table. In some cases, your task may be difficult, especially if the record you're looking for doesn't exist and you need to add it. We'll go over that too.

More shockingly, some data comes with no SRS or (even worse) the wrong information. The easiest way to determine if you have the wrong information is to overlay a map where you suspect this to be the case on top of a layer for the same region with a known SRS and reproject to the suspected projection. Common errors include using NAD 27 data in a NAD 83 spatial reference system. In cases like this, you'll see a shift when you overlay the two because the same degree is not in the same spot between NAD 27 and NAD 83 spatial reference systems. If things are way off, one of your layers won't even show when you transform it to the same SRS as your known layer. This is the cause for a well-known beginner's FAQ: "Why don't I see anything?"

3.3.1 Guessing at a spatial reference system

Let's go over some simple but common exercises for determining the SRS of source data. In these examples, we'll pick out key elements in spatial reference system text representations.

Exercise 1: The U.S. states data

We downloaded a states data file that includes a states020.txt file, which gives spatial reference information as well as lots of details about how the data set was made and its licensing.

The spatial reference information at the bottom of the file reads as follows:

```
Spatial_Reference_Information:
    Horizontal_Coordinate_System_Definition:
    Geographic:
    Latitude_Resolution: 0.000278
    Longitude_Resolution: 0.000278
    Geographic_Coordinate_Units: Decimal degrees
    Geodetic_Model:
    Horizontal_Datum_Name: North American Datum of 1983
    Ellipsoid_Name: GRS1980
    Semi-major_Axis: 6378137
    Denominator_of_Flattening_Ratio: 298.257222
```

This is an important piece of information. It tells us that the data is in decimal degrees and that it uses ellipsoid GRS1980 and the North American Datum of 1983. These are the three ingredients you need to know about every data source you have:

- Unit: degrees
- Ellipsoid: GRS 80
- Datum: NAD 83

If you're dealing with projected data (non-degree data), there are some other fuzzy pieces you'll need to know. One is the projection, and each type of projection has additional parameters you'll want to look for. These are the common projections you'll find in spatial reference system text files:

- Degree (`longlat`)
- Lambert Azimuthal Equal Area (`laea`)
- Universal Trans Mercator (`utm`)
- Trans Mercator (`tmerc`)
- Lambert Conformal Conic (`lcc`)
- Stereographic (`stere`)

The short corresponding lowercase acronym is how you'll see these referred to in the `spatial_ref_sys.proj4text` field. For example, you'll see a proj4text entry start with `proj=utm` to denote a Universal Trans Mercator projection.

Once you've figured out these pieces, the next thing to do is match your source to an SRS defined in the spatial_ref_sys table and then record the SRID number for it. Sometimes the record you're seeking isn't in the table and you'll need to add it, or there may be multiple matches. Living without an SRID is only an option if you know that your data is planar, you know the units, and you know that all the data you'll be getting is from the same source and was made using the same SRS. In this case, you're using the unknown SRID, which is `-1` in pre-PostGIS 2.0 and `0` in the OGC standard and PostGIS 2+ series.

Two fields of information in the spatial_ref_sys table can help you guess at the projection. For the previous data, you can do a simple `SELECT` query to determine the SRID and use the PostgreSQL `ILIKE` predicate to do a case-insensitive search:

```
SELECT srid, srtext,proj4text
FROM spatial_ref_sys
WHERE srtext ILIKE '%nad83%' AND
 srtext ILIKE '%grs%80%' AND proj4text ILIKE '%longlat%';
```

The `SELECT` query will return five records (SRIDs: 4140, 4152, 4269, 4617, 4759) that all have the same `proj4text`. Although the `srtext` is useful for matching up textual representations with SRSs in the table, PostGIS only uses `proj4text`. Any records that have the same `proj4text` are equivalent, so it doesn't matter which one of the set you use as long as you consistently use the same one for the same projected data.

> **PROJ4TEXT DIFFERENCES IN POSTGIS 1.5 AND POSTGIS 2.0/2.1** The way the `proj4text` value is presented is different in PostGIS 1.5 than it is in PostGIS 2.0/2.1. The details behind the coding logic of this change are beyond the scope of this book, but you can find more information on the PROJ.4 site (http://trac.osgeo.org/proj/wiki/GenParms#towgs84-DatumtransformationtoWGS84).

EXERCISE 2: SAN FRANCISCO DATA (READING FROM .PRJ FILES)

For this second exercise, we grabbed a zip file of San Francisco data that included a .prj file. The .prj contents look like this:

```
PROJCS["NAD_1983_StatePlane_California_III_FIPS_0403_Feet",
    GEOGCS["GCS_North_American_1983",
    DATUM["D_North_American_1983",
      SPHEROID["GRS_1980",6378137.0,298.257222101]],
       PRIMEM["Greenwich",0.0],
    UNIT["Degree",0.0174532925199433]],
    PROJECTION["Lambert_Conformal_Conic"],
     PARAMETER["False_Easting",6561666.666666666],
    PARAMETER["False_Northing",1640416.666666667],
    PARAMETER["Central_Meridian",-120.5],
    PARAMETER["Standard_Parallel_1",37.06666666666667],
    PARAMETER["Standard_Parallel_2",38.43333333333333],
    PARAMETER["Latitude_Of_Origin",36.5],
    UNIT["Foot_US",0.3048006096012192]]
```

You can surmise from this that the units are feet, it uses the NAD 83 datum, and the projection is some California state plane. Now you can guess by doing a query:

```
SELECT srid, srtext,proj4text
    FROM spatial_ref_sys
    WHERE srtext ILIKE '%california%' AND srtext ILIKE '%nad83%'
        AND proj4text ILIKE '%ft%';
```

This query yields several records. When you look at the `srtext` fields, each has something of the form NAD83/California zone 1 (ftUS), where the number ranges from 1 to 6. You may recall that III (which shows up in the .prj file) is the Roman numeral for 3. So the answer must be SRID 2227, 2872, or 3494, each of which has an `srtext` field with all those elements. SRID 2227 seems closest in the `srtext` representation to what's in the file and is shown next. Keep in mind that all three SRIDs returned have essentially the same `proj4text` definition and so are equivalent.

```
"PROJCS["NAD83 / California zone 3 (ftUS)",
    GEOGCS["NAD83",DATUM["North_American_Datum_1983",
    SPHEROID["GRS 1980",6378137,298.257222101,AUTHORITY["EPSG","7019"]],
    AUTHORITY["EPSG","6269"]],
    PRIMEM["Greenwich",0,AUTHORITY["EPSG","8901"]],
    UNIT["degree",0.01745329251994328,AUTHORITY["EPSG","9122"]],
    AUTHORITY["EPSG","4269"]],
    UNIT["US survey foot",0.3048006096012192,AUTHORITY["EPSG","9003"]],
    PROJECTION["Lambert_Conformal_Conic_2SP"],
    PARAMETER["standard_parallel_1",38.43333333333333],
    PARAMETER["standard_parallel_2",37.06666666666667],
    PARAMETER["latitude_of_origin",36.5],
    PARAMETER["central_meridian",120.5],
    PARAMETER["false_easting",6561666.667],
    PARAMETER["false_northing",1640416.667],
    AUTHORITY["EPSG","2227"],
    AXIS["X",EAST],AXIS["Y",NORTH]]"
```

Now that you have some idea of how to match a spatial reference system to one in your table, what can you do if you guess wrong?

EXERCISE 3: IF YOU GUESS WRONG

Let's imagine you guessed the wrong SRID, and you've already loaded in all your data. What do you do now?

There are two ways to solve this problem. First, you can use the longstanding maintenance function in PostGIS called `UpdateGeometrySRID`, which will correct the mistake:

```
SELECT UpdateGeometrySRID('ch03', 'bayarea_bridges', 'geom', 2227);
```

The newer way from PostGIS 2.0+ on is to use a typmod conversion:

```
ALTER TABLE ch03.bayarea_bridges
 ALTER COLUMN geom TYPE geometry(LINESTRING,2227)
  USING ST_SetSRID(geom,2227);
```

If we brought our San Francisco data in as unknown with a 0 SRID or the wrong SRID, this would become quite apparent if we tried to transform our data. We'd get errors such as `NaN` when doing distance checks on the transformed data, or a transform error when doing the transformation.

In the next section we'll talk a bit about what to do when you've concluded that your spatial_ref_sys table doesn't have the spatial reference you're looking for.

3.3.2 When the spatial reference system is missing from spatial_ref_sys table

Sometimes you may come up short, and no record in the SRS matches what you're looking at. The best place to go at that point is the Spatial Reference site (http://spatialreference.org). This site contains thousands of user-contributed SRSs in addition to the standard ones. Best of all, if the record you're looking for can't be found, and you happen to have a .prj file, you can submit the contents of that (via the Upload Your Own link), and the site will magically determine the `INSERT` statement you need to use to insert the new item into your spatial_ref_sys table.

> **Spatialreference.org uses the auth_srid field instead of the SRID**
>
> The Spatial Reference site by default assigns an SRID starting with 9 to indicate that it was grabbed from the spatialreference.org site. For the sake of consistency, we replace this SRID with what's listed in the `auth_srid` field. By following this convention, you won't accidentally insert a record into spatial_ref_sys that's already in the table.

Although it's possible to create your own custom spatial reference system to suit your specific needs, this topic is beyond the scope of this book. PostGIS uses the PROJ.4 library to underpin its projection support. If you're interested in how to do this, appendix A has links to articles on SRSs and PROJ.4 syntax that may be of use.

3.4 Summary

In this chapter, we explained the details of spatial reference systems. We hope that you now understand their importance, as well as the general rules of thumb for selecting one and determining which one your source data is using.

In chapter 4 we'll continue our journey into the real world by loading real geographic data. We'll also cover some of the more popular free and open source tools, both packaged and not packaged with PostGIS, that are useful for importing and exporting data.

4 Working with real data

This chapter covers

- PostGIS backup and restore utilities
- Utilities for downloading and uncompressing files
- Importing and exporting Esri shapefile data
- Importing and exporting vectors using ogr2ogr
- Importing OpenStreetMap data
- Importing and exporting raster data
- PostGIS raster output functions

In this chapter, we'll look at how you can load real-world data into PostGIS and export it. We'll point you to specific data sources for the examples in this chapter, but if you're interested in other sources, see the list in appendix A. Note that appendix A is not a comprehensive list, so we encourage you to explore on your own and report back on any discoveries at our Manning author forum: www.manning.com/obe2.

NOTE Geographic data that covers large areas on our spheroidal earth needs a little special care. You'll need to understand, at least on a rudimentary level, ellipsoids, datums, and projections in order to understand the pros and cons of each spatial reference system and determine which ones are suitable for your use cases. We hope the fundamentals we provided in the previous chapter are sufficient to get you started working with real data.

Before we get started, we recommend you create a separate schema to house the raw data you import. We generally name this schema *staging*, but you're free to call it whatever you like. We recommend that you group your database assets into schemas instead of stuffing everything into the default *public* schema, which gets unwieldy after it grows to about 30 tables. We find the use of staging schemas especially important. During imports, you may have to cleanse the data and create intermediate tables, and you should shield these from the production tables by segregating them into their own schema. Furthermore, you should set permissions on this schema to keep out general users.

The data and code used in this chapter can be found at www.postgis.us/chapter_04_edition_2.

4.1 General utilities

In this section we'll cover general non-PostGIS utilities that you can use to load PostGIS data. These include the packaged PostgreSQL command-line tools as well as tools for downloading and extracting files.

4.1.1 PostgreSQL built-in tools

PostgreSQL has some command-line tools that are useful for getting data into and out of PostgreSQL.

PSQL

Psql is a standard PostgreSQL command-line tool. If you're working in a non-GUI environment, you should already be intimately familiar with it.

Psql has both interactive and non-interactive modes:

- *Interactive mode*—Psql executes commands as you type them after a `psql` prompt. You can use the `\copy` command to load comma- and tab-delimited data, as you saw in chapter 1. The copy command copies to and from the *client* machine—this is the machine from which `psql` was launched and need not necessarily be the PostgreSQL server.
- *Non-interactive mode*—You prepare script files and feed them to `psql` for execution. This mode allows you to load data in batches.

The PostGIS `shp2pgsql` tool, which we'll cover shortly, relies on `psql` to silently process the SQL it generates.

When you invoke `psql`, you can add switches to indicate host name (`--host` or `-h`), user (`--user` or `-u`), and database (`--database` or `-d`). If you're authenticating via trust, peer, or ident, these settings will be sufficient. Authentication requiring a password is the trickiest because you can't specify a password. Psql will prompt or read the password from the pgpass.conf file (or ~/.pgpass), should you have one defined in your home directory. Psql will also honor passwords set using environment variables.

If you intend to use psql as your main workhorse, you ought to set the following variables so you can call psql without always having to string along a chain of switches:

- PGPORT—The port that the PostgreSQL service is running on
- PGHOST—The IP address or host name of the PostgreSQL server
- PGUSER—The PostgreSQL role to connect as
- PGPASSWORD—The password for the role
- PGDATABASE—The database to connect to

For a full list of PostgreSQL environment variables, refer to the PostgreSQL documentation at www.postgresql.org/docs/current/static/libpq-envars.html.

PGADMIN III

PgAdmin III is a graphical interface tool packaged with PostgreSQL, and it's also available as a separate install via the www.pgadmin.org site. It can run only on machines with a graphical interface, such as OS X, Windows, Linux/BSD, Unix with Gnome, or KDE. It has functionality similar to psql, but it doesn't support a client-side `\copy` command—you can only use the SQL `COPY` command. Via the pgAdmin interface, you can launch a psql session, and it will automatically fill in the credentials of the database you're connected to.

PG_DUMP AND PG_RESTORE

If you want to distribute large amounts of data, or you just need to do simple backups and restores to other databases, then pg_dump and pg_restore are the tools you'll want to use. Pg_dump backs up data, even that of a spatial nature, and it can run in a compressed format to save space. You can then use pg_restore to restore these tables, functions, and the like to another PostgreSQL database.

If you want to use the postgis_restore.pl script packaged with PostGIS, you'll want to back up your data in the pg_dump custom compressed format (using the `-Fc` switch of `pg_dump`). Postgis_restore.pl only supports the custom format and not the plain-text backup format because behind the scenes it utilizes the `pg_dump` PostgreSQL restore utility that restores custom format backups. The other nice thing about the custom compressed format is that you can restore tables in parallel (using the `-j` switch of `pg_restore`), which can result in speeds as high as eight times faster than loading serially.

We have various PostgreSQL cheat sheets for psql, pg_dump, pg_dumpall, and pg _restore on our Postgres OnLine Journal site: www.postgresonline.com/specials.php.

4.1.2 Downloading files

Wget is a command-line tool for grabbing files from the internet, and it generally comes prepackaged with Linux and Unix systems. It can also be downloaded for free for Windows at http://gnuwin32.sourceforge.net/packages/wget.htm. Get the binaries and the dependencies, and extract them to the same folder.

If you're on Windows or any OS with a GUI, you can also download files using your browser, but you may still find Wget handy for automating the download of many files.

The following listing demonstrates some handy command-line switches for Wget. These apply to both Unix/Linux and Windows.

Listing 4.1 Using Wget to download a batch of files

```
cd /gisdata
wget http://www2.census.gov/geo/tiger/TIGER2012/ROADS/*_72*    ❶
➥--no-parent --relative
➥--recursive --level=2 --accept=zip --mirror    ❷
```

❶ Download just Puerto Rico—FIPS 72

❷ Mirror folder structure; recurse only two folders down; download just zip

Listing 4.1 will download all the Puerto Rico roads zip files into the gisdata folder. The FIPS code for Puerto Rico is 72, and TIGER 2012 data is prefixed with the year and the FIPS ❶, so this command will grab all files that have a segment in the name beginning with 72.

Wget maintains the folder structure of the FTP/HTTP site with the mirror option ❷, so the folder structure created on your disk will be www2.census.gov/geo/tiger/TIGER2012/ROADS. The other nice thing about the mirror option is that it won't redownload a file if you already have it. This is great if you lose your internet connection—you can just pick up where you left off.

If you just need to pull down a single file, use the following Wget syntax:

```
wget http://www2.census.gov/geo/tiger/TIGER2012/ZCTA5
➥/tl_2012_us_zcta510.zip
```

This will put the file in your current directory. It won't create subfolders like the previous mirror example.

If the site exposes a directory listing of files, you can also use a wildcard such as `*zcta510.*` to pull down multiple files with the same command.

4.1.3 Extracting files

Most files you'll download will be compressed in tar.bz, tar.gz, or zip format. Most Unix-like systems have command-line tools to extract these files. Here's an outline of the basics.

Linux/Unix uncompress examples

Unzip a single zip file:

```
unzip somefile.zip
```

Unzip all zip files in folders, recurse down, and put them in the same folder:

```
for z in */*.zip; do unzip -o $z; done
```

Unzip a single .tar gzipped file and extract its contents (two equivalent commands):

```
tar xvfz somefile.tar.gz
gzip -d -c somefile.tar.gz | tar xvf
```

For Windows users, we recommend the 7-Zip extraction/compression tool. 7-Zip is free for both personal and commercial use, and it can extract all the aforementioned formats plus more. For simple zip files, you can also use the built-in uncompress in Windows. We've found 7-Zip to be better than the built-in Windows tool because it can handle compressing and extracting files over 4 GB and gives you many more compression options, such as password protection and level of compression. You can download 7-Zip from www.7-zip.org, and after you install it, you can right-click a file in Windows Explorer and choose to extract it with 7-Zip.

Although most people think of 7-Zip as a nice GUI tool for extracting various compression formats, it also has a handy command-line interface (the 7z.exe file) that's useful for automating zip and unzip processes. To make this portable, you can copy the 7z.exe and 7z.dll files to a USB flash drive or folder and use them from anywhere without doing an install. Followoing are some simple tips for using the 7-Zip command-line interface.

Example uses of the 7-Zip command-line interface

Extract a single file (tar.gz) in the same directory. The first example creates the .tar file and the second extracts the .tar:

```
7z e statesp020.tar.gz
7z x statesp020.tar -o"C:\gisdata\states"
```

Extract all zip files in the current folder to a new folder called extracteddata using a flat folder structure:

```
7z e C:\gisdata\*.zip -oC:\gisdata\extracteddata
```

Extract all zip files in the current folder to a new folder called extracteddata, and keep the same folder structure as in the archive:

```
7z x *.zip -y -oC:\gisdata\extracteddata
```

Extract all zip files in the current folder to a new folder called extracteddata, and recursively search for .zip files:

```
for /r %%z in (*.zip ) do 7z e %%z  -oC:\gisdata\extracteddata
```

4.2 Importing and exporting shapefiles

PostGIS comes packaged with a pair of command-line tools, shp2pgsql and pgsql2shp, that import and export Esri shapefiles, respectively. A GUI version of both exists: shp2pgsql-gui. Despite its name, the GUI does a fine job of both exporting and importing.

What is an Esri shapefile? Esri produces some of the most widely used commercial GIS software, and Esri's preponderance during the early days of GIS desktop systems allowed it to popularize its proprietary file format—Esri shapefiles. Shapefiles continue to be the most widely used format for transporting GIS data.

The term *shapefile* refers to an entire entourage of files. The main file containing the geographical data ends in a .shp extension. The contained files include a mandatory dBase file (.dbf), which contains the non-GIS portion of the data; a projection file (.prj), which describes the projection of the main shapefile; and one or more index files (.shx).

4.2.1 Importing with shp2pgsql

If you launch shp2pgsql from the command line without any arguments, the help will come up with a plethora of switches. The most important ones are as follows:

- `-s`—Specifies the spatial reference system (SRS) of the source data; you should always include this switch. Even if a projection is present, PostGIS still can't make an accurate determination of the SRID. Since PostGIS 2.0, you can also indicate the SRID of the destination, effectively letting you perform a transformation during the load. The format of the switch is `-s` *`srid_from:srid_to`*. For example, `-s 26986:4326` means that the source data is in Massachusetts State Plane Meters but should be reprojected to WGS 84 lon/lat during the load.
- `-W`—Specifies the encoding of the source dBase file. Since PostGIS 2.0, shp2pgsql will assume an encoding of UTF-8 if you omit this switch. Regardless of the encoding of the source, shp2pgsql will always convert the data to UTF-8. Should shp2pgsql find characters outside of those expected, it will write a line to the console for each encounter, but you'll probably miss these messages as they fly by and unknowingly end up with incomplete data. If the encoding of your destination database is set to UTF-8, you should encounter no problems while inserting the data from shp2pgsql. If your database encoding is less encompassing than UTF-8, and if PostgreSQL encounters a character unrecognized by your database, you may get an error message.
- `-I`—Creates a spatial index on the geometry column after loading. You may wish to hold off adding indexes to a table until you're done with loading, because indexes retard insertions. This switch is useful if you aren't going to append data to this table in the future.
- `-g`—Sets the name of the geometry or geography column in the table created by shp2pgsql. The default is *geom* for geometry and *geog* for geography.
- `-G`—Loads to the `geography` type instead of the `geometry` type; the default is the `geometry` type. Shp2pgsql will only honor this switch if your data is in WGS 84 lon/lat (SRID 4326). You can, however, transform during the load to WGS 84 with the `-s` switch, as in `-G -s 26986:4326`.

Additional switches let you take advantage of other useful shp2pgsql features, such as naming an SQL file for processing later, converting column names to PostgreSQL standards, and loading just the non-geographical data from the dBase file.

Since PostGIS 2.2, you can also specify a mapping file with `-m`; this allows you to specify a file that contains name mappings between the dBase file and the PostgreSQL table column names. Any names that match the dBase in the file will be renamed, and others will retain their original name.

Let's go through a step-by-step example of loading data with shp2pgsql. For this exercise, we'll load U.S. state boundaries from United States Census. You can find the data file here: ftp://ftp2.census.gov/geo/tiger/TIGER2012/STATE/tl_2012_us_state.zip.

First, download and extract the file using your tool of choice. You should end up with three files: tl_2012_us_state.shp, tl_2012_us_state.dbf, and tl_2012_us_state.shx.

Next, figure out the spatial reference system. For this dataset, we know the SRS to be NAD 83 lon/lat, which has an EPSG code and PostGIS SRID number of 4269. In chapter 3 we showed you how to arrive at this SRID.

Finally, open up a console and execute shp2pgsql using this command:

```
shp2pgsql -s 4269 -g geom_4269 -I -W "latin1"
➥"tl_2012_states" staging.tl_2012_states |
➥psql -h localhost -p 5432 -d postgis_in_action -U postgres
```

The tl_2012_states can include an extension of .shp or .dbf or no extension. Generally, if you just have dBase data, with no accompanying shapefile, then you specify it with the .dbf extension.

Shp2pgsql outputs SQL, and the preceding command immediately executes the SQL by piping it to `psql`. Loading the data should take just a few seconds. After it's done, you should see a new table in your staging schema with one geometry column named *geom_4269*. Shp2pgsql also loads the textual information, creating additional columns to match the original dBase file.

If you don't want the data loaded immediately but only want to store the SQL file for future loading, execute the following command instead:

```
shp2pgsql -s 4269 -g geom_4269 -I -W "latin1"
➥"tl_2012_states" staging.tl_2012_states > tl_2012_states.sql
```

The SQL output is then dumped to a .sql file named tl_2012_states.sql . You can edit this file, fixing any misbehaving data points. If the file is so large that it can't fit into memory for loading, you can break it apart so you can load the pieces piecemeal. When you're ready to perform the loading, run the `psql` command.

If you don't specify a user with the `-u` option, then the user defaults to what psql defaults to, which is usually the logged-in OS user name:

```
psql -h localhost -p 5432 -d postgis_in_action -f tl_2012_states.sql
```

Shp2pgsql can provide much of the importing functionality you'll need, but you might rather work with a GUI interface. In that case, you can use shp2pgsql-gui. The main difference between the two is that shp2pgsql is a command-line tool just for importing data, whereas shp2pgsql-gui provides a graphical interface for both importing and exporting.

4.2.2 Importing and exporting with shp2pgsql-gui

Shp2pgsql-gui is the graphical wizard counterpart of shp2pgsql. It isn't available in all PostGIS installs, because not all PostgreSQL installations run on machines with GUIs.

For Windows, shp2pgsql-gui is part of the StackBuilder installer as well as the OpenGeo installer. You also have the option to install it as a pgAdmin III plug-in by adding a .ini file to the plugins.d folder of your pgAdmin install. For detailed installation instructions, read our article, "PgAdmin III plug-in registration: PostGIS shapefile and DBF loader," at http://bit.ly/Sjzhyu.

> **StackBuilder and OpenGeo suite**
>
> PostgreSQL StackBuilder is distributed as part of EnterpriseDb desktop installations and is used to get and upgrade PostgreSQL extensions and utilities. The EnterpriseDb installer is the most widely used tool for installing PostgreSQL/PostGIS on Windows.
>
> The OpenGeo suite is a whole stack of open source GIS tools, packaged by Boundless. The package includes PostgreSQL and PostGIS. The OpenGeo offering also has shp2pgsql-gui for all the OSs it supports (OS X, Windows, and Linux).

Shp2pgsql-gui is user-friendly and obviates the need to memorize and look up command-line syntax and switches. The version packaged with PostGIS 2.0 allows you to load more than one shapefile at the same time. The main deficiencies of shp2pgsql-gui are that you can't create an SQL file to save for later and it's generally slower than shp2pgsql for loading large files. Shp2pgsql-gui takes you straight from Esri shapefiles to PostGIS tables.

We're not going to show you how to use shp2pgsql-gui because the GUI is intuitive enough. Figure 4.1 shows what shp2pgsql-gui looks like after you've specified an import path by browsing to the states table using the browser icon and filled in the relevant information.

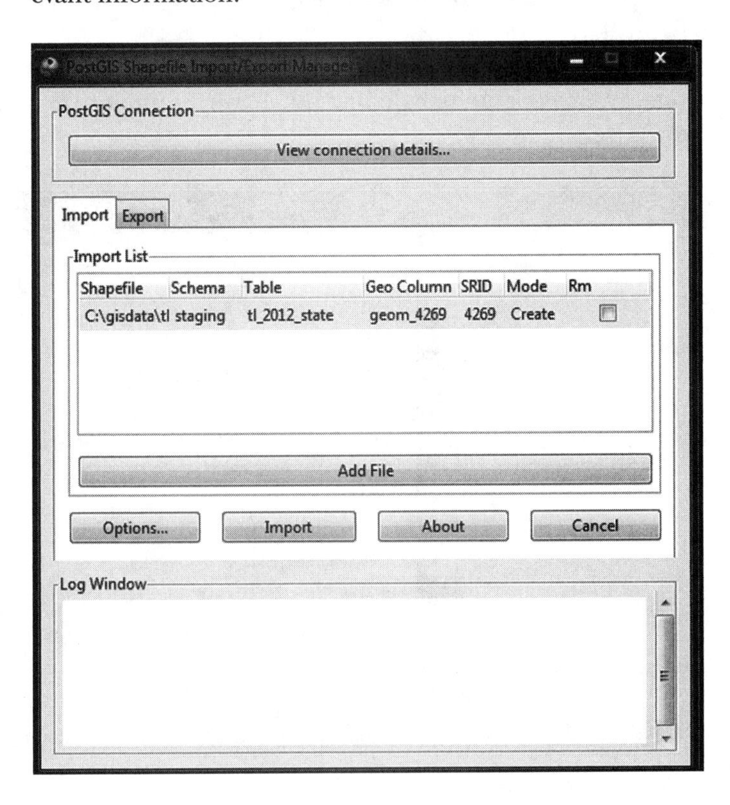

Figure 4.1 Using shp2pgsql-gui

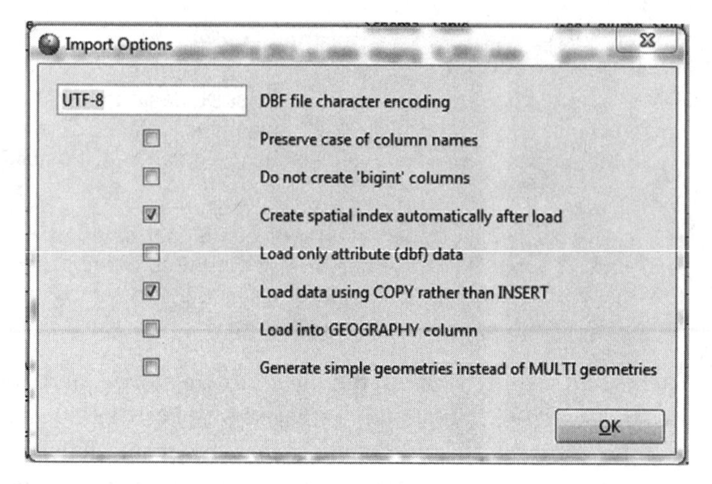

Figure 4.2 The shp2pgsql-gui Import Options dialog box showing the advanced options

Next, you need to click Options to verify the other settings (see figure 4.2).

The shp2pgsql-gui name became somewhat misleading as of version 2.0, because you can now also use it to export data. To export, switch to the Export tab, click the Add Tables, and select all the tables you'd like to export. Yes, you can export many tables at once (see figure 4.3).

Once you've picked your tables, they'll appear on the Export tab. For tables with more than one geometry or geography column, you have the option to stipulate which column to export (see figure 4.4).

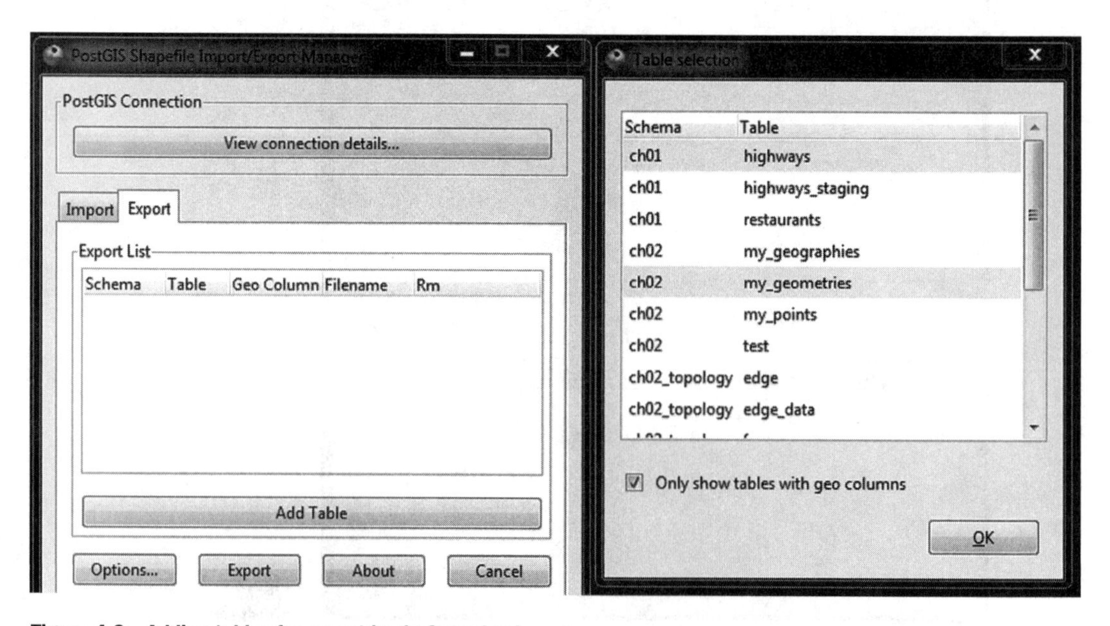

Figure 4.3 Adding tables for export in shp2pgsql-gui

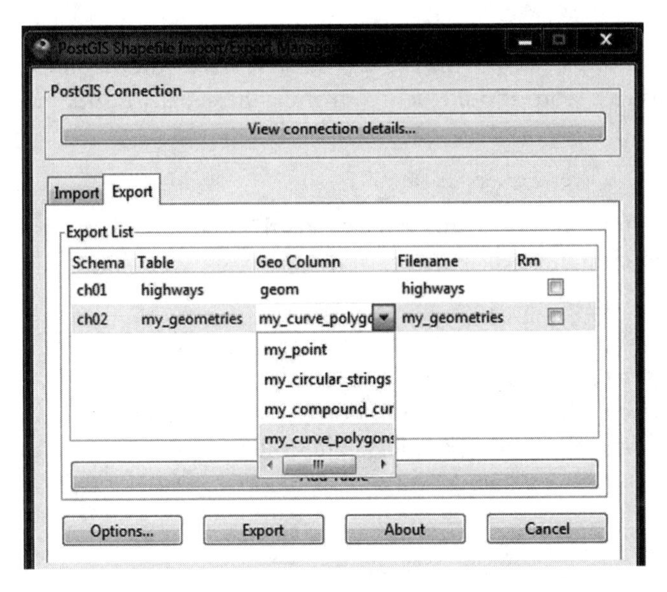

Figure 4.4 Selecting a column for export in shp2pgsql-gui

Finally, click Export, and a browse window will pop up asking you where to save the exported files.

4.2.3 *Exporting with pgsql2shp*

You can use pgsql2shp to export PostgreSQL tables, views, and queries to Esri shapefiles. Remember that a shapefile isn't a single file but a container for a number of files. In most cases, pgsql2shp outputs .dbf, .shp, .shx, and .prj files. It will omit the projection file (.prj) if it can't determine the SRID of the geometry or geography column. If you export a table without a geometry or geography column, pgsql2shp will create a dBase file (.dbf) and nothing else. This means you can use pgsql2shp as a dBase export utility for PostgreSQL. You can find a cheat sheet for getting up to speed with pgsql2shp on our BostonGIS site: www.bostongis.com/pgsql2shp_shp2pgsql_quickguide_20.bqg.

You'll find pgsql2shp in the bin folder of your PostgreSQL install. As with many commands, you can launch it without any arguments to see the help. There are two caveats to keep in mind:

- Column names longer than ten characters will be truncated. If this creates duplicate column names, pgsql2shp will add a sequence number. In PostGIS 2.0 and later, you can define a mapping file to exercise more control over column names.
- Esri shapefiles can't handle textual columns with more than 255 characters and will silently include only the first 255 characters of your data field.

Let's look at two examples of pgsql2shp: one where it's used to export a table, and another that exports an ad hoc query.

USING PGSQL2SHP TO EXPORT A TABLE

This example exports a table called zips in the ca schema of the database named gisdb. Once it's finished, you should see four new files: cazips.shp, cazips.dbf, cazips.shx, and cazips.prj.

```
pgsql2shp -f /gisdata/cazips gisdb ca.zips
```

The next example accomplishes the thing same as the first, but it includes switches to indicate hostname and credentials.

```
pgsql2shp -f /gisdata/cazips -h localhost -u pguser
➥-P somepassword -p 5432 gisdb ca.zips
```

USING PGSQL2SHP TO EXPORT AN AD HOC QUERY

Although exporting whole tables is a common need, for large tables you may want to export only a portion of a table using a query. The following query outputs filtered rows:

```
pgsql2shp -f boszips -h localhost -u postgres gisdb

➥"SELECT * FROM ma.zips WHERE city = 'Boston'"
```

The next query reprojects the data and outputs it in the popular WGS 84 lon/lat spatial reference system:

```
pgsql2shp -f boszips -h localhost -u postgres gisdb
➥"SELECT zip5, ST_Transform(the_geom, 4326) As the_geom
➥FROM ma.zips WHERE city = 'Boston'"
```

4.3 Importing and exporting vector data with ogr2ogr

Ogr2ogr is a command-line tool that is part of the GDAL suite. You can use it to import an ever-growing list of spatial and non-spatial formats into PostgreSQL/PostGIS. You can see the complete list at www.gdal.org/ogr/ogr_formats.html. Shp2pgsql does a great job of importing Esri shapefiles, but if your data is in some other format, you'll need ogr2ogr.

Ogr2ogr is available for Linux/Unix, Windows, and OS X. You can download the appropriate version here: http://trac.osgeo.org/gdal/wiki/DownloadingGdalBinaries. This download includes other useful utilities, collectively known as the *GDAL toolkit*. Keep in mind that you can always compile your own version should you not find a ready-made version for your OS.

Ogr2ogr is a rich tool, especially given its small size. We'd have to devote a whole book to it to do it justice, but this section will cover the most common use cases you're likely to encounter. For other use cases, check out the examples on our websites:

- Examples of non-spatial data loading are included in our article, "GDAL ogr2ogr for data loading," at www.postgresonline.com/journal/index.php?/archives/31-GDAL-ogr2ogr-for-Data-Loading.html.
- Additional information about spatial data loading and installation for Windows is available on the Boston GIS site: www.bostongis.com/PrinterFriendly.aspx?content_name=ogr_cheatsheet.

4.3.1 Environment variables

Unlike shp2pgsql, ogr2ogr ignores encoding. If you feed it LATIN-1, it'll try to insert LATIN-1 into PostgreSQL. To ensure that PostgreSQL will perform any conversion necessary, you need to set the client encoding environment variable to the encoding of the incoming data.

The client encoding is the encoding that PostgreSQL honors for each connection session. This is different from database encoding, which varies by database and is set when you first create the database. If PostgreSQL sees a difference between the client encoding and the database encoding, it will automatically convert for you both ways, but you must tell PostgreSQL what the client encoding is. It can't look at the incoming data and make a guess, and it certainly can't read your mind as to how you want to encode the data coming back to you.

The name of the environment variable is `PGCLIENTENCODING`. To set it, use `export` in Linux/Unix/OS X:

```
export PGCLIENTENCODING=latin1
```

Use `set` in Windows:

```
set PGCLIENTENCODING=latin1
```

Another environment variable worth setting is `PG_USE_COPY`. This should be set to `YES` if you want to use the PostgreSQL copy command for inserting data into PostgreSQL. The copy command is much faster than SQL inserts. Newer ogr2ogr versions (GDAL 2.0 and above) automatically use copy, but older versions may need this variable.

4.3.2 Ogrinfo

Ogrinfo is a tool that analyzes the data source and extracts what metadata it can, such as spatial reference system, bounding box, layers (for multilayer formats), and attributes.

What ogrinfo displays varies widely depending on the format of the data source. For GPX, ogrinfo provides little more than the field names and geometry type, but for Esri personal geodatabase, it'll output so much detail that you'll probably need to curtail the output with additional switches. We suggest that you always run a quick ogrinfo prior to every import, especially for large files. You don't want to expend the effort importing a large file only to find that a field you really need is not part of your import file.

To get more information on ogrinfo and see the variety of switches available for it, visit www.gdal.org/ogrinfo.html.

4.3.3 Importing with ogr2ogr

Ogr2ogr can be used to import numerous kinds of vector data formats. In this section, we'll cover the more common vector formats people need to load.

OGR2OGR IMPORT SWITCHES

Ogr2ogr lets you add a `-lco` switch to control various aspects of the tables that it creates during import. These are some common options:

- `GEOM_TYPE`—Options are geometry, BYTEA, or OID to force the type of geometry used for a table. In general, there's no need to set this.
- `GEOMETRY_NAME`—Sets the name of the geometry column in new tables. If omitted, the default is wkb_geometry.
- `LAUNDER`—Set this to `YES`, the default, to force new fields created on this layer to have their field names "laundered" into a form more compatible with PostgreSQL. This converts fields to lowercase and translates special characters that are not suitable as PostgreSQL identifiers.
- `PRECISISON`—Set this to `YES`, the default, and ogr2ogr will choose numeric data types over floats and integers, and char over varchar.

To specify more than one option, repeat the `-lco` switch.

Another often-used switch is `-nln`. This allows you to name the table that ogr2ogr creates.

You can find the full details of the ogr2ogr switches here: http://gdal.org/ogr/drv_pg.html. When you read OGR documentation, keep in mind that *layers* in GIS translates to *tables* in the database world.

LOADING GPS EXCHANGE FILES (GPX)

GPX files are the standard transport format for GPS-generated data. GPX textual data is in XML, so you can take advantage of all the XML functionality built into PostgreSQL. GPX data is also always in the WGS 84 lon/lat spatial reference system, which has a PostGIS SRID/EPSG number of 4326. Ogr2ogr is smart enough to know this, so it puts in the correct SRID for you. For more details about command-line switches specific to the OGR GPX driver, visit www.gdal.org/ogr/drv_gpx.html.

OpenStreetMap is full of user-contributed GPX files uploaded by users worldwide. You can find these at www.openstreetmap.org/traces. We randomly selected one from Australia titled "A bike trip around Narangba" by going to www.openstreetmap.org/traces/tag/australia and downloading the file www.openstreetmap.org/user/Ash%20Kyd/traces/468761.

You can find out more about the data you're about to load by using ogrinfo.

Listing 4.2 Displaying info about GPX file using ogrinfo

```
ogrinfo 468761.gpx                    <-- Command

INFO: Open of '468761.gpx' using driver 'GPX' successful.     <-- Output
1: waypoints (Point)
2: routes (Line String)
3: tracks (Multi Line String)
4: route_points (Point)
5: track_points (Point)
```

Next, you can load this up into a staging schema with the simple ogr2ogr command shown in the next listing.

Listing 4.3 Loading data from GPX into a single table

```
ogr2ogr -f "PostgreSQL"
➥PG:"host=localhost user=postgres port=5432
➥dbname=postgis_in_action password=mypassword"
➥468761.gpx -overwrite -lco GEOMETRY_NAME=geom
➥-nln "staging.aus_biketrip_narangba"
```

This code loads the track_points layer into a single new table called aus_biketrip_narangba in a schema called staging.

The following command loads all the layers, creating new tables for each layer. It skips naming the layers so ogr2ogr will import them all, but it does specify the schema to create all the tables.

```
ogr2ogr -f "PostgreSQL" PG:"host=localhost user=postgres
➥port=5432 dbname=postgis_in_action password=>mypassword"
➥468761.gpx -overwrite -lco GEOMETRY_NAME=geom -lco SCHEMA=staging
```

LOADING AN ESRI PERSONAL GEODATABASE

The Esri personal geodatabase format is nothing more than a Microsoft Access database with geometries stored in BLOB (OLE object) fields along with some metadata tables. The personal geodatabase is convenient in that you can hold a number of tables in a single file, but its size is limited to 4 GB. It's reaching obsolescence and is slowly being replaced by Esri's personal file database (GDB) format, which can handle larger file sizes, although fewer tools can yet read the format.

Ogr2ogr supports reading Esri personal geodatabase files. Versions of ogr2ogr packaged with GDAL 1.8+ also have rudimentary support for reading the new GDB format. Note that the GDB support requires compiling with the Esri FileGDB SDK, so many GDAL packages don't include it.

For the next example, we'll download a personal geodatabase of global political boundaries from www.gadm.org. You can download either the whole world or go country by country. Whichever you choose, make sure to choose the Personal Geodatabase format for this exercise. Once it's extracted, you'll get an MDB file. If you have Access, you can open this file and look around.

The file you pulled down should have only one table, so only one geographic layer. To learn more about your data, you can use ogrinfo, as shown in listing 4.4. If this is a large database, ogrinfo will take a bit of time to churn through it. Note that the following command uses the `-so` switch to let ogrinfo know that you only need summary data.

Listing 4.4 Use ogrinfo to list fields for a personal geodatabase layer

```
ogrinfo gadm_v1.mdb -so -geom=YES gadm1
```

This is the output we got when we ran the preceding command:

```
INFO: Open of 'gadm_v1.mdb' using driver 'PGeo' successful.

Layer name: gadm1
Geometry: Unknown (any)
```

```
Feature Count: 167176
Extent: (-180.000015, -90.000000) - (179.999999
Layer SRS WKT:
GEOGCS["GCS_WGS_1984",
    DATUM["WGS_1984",
        SPHEROID["WGS_84",6378137.0,298.2572235
    PRIMEM["Greenwich",0.0],
    UNIT["Degree",0.0174532925199433]]
FID Column = OBJECTID
Geometry Column = Shape
OBJECTID: Integer (10.0)
UID: Integer (10.0)
ID_0: Integer (10.0)
ISO: String (3.0)
NAME_0: String (75.0)
ID_1: Integer (10.0)
NAME_1: String (75.0)
VARNAME_1: String (150.0)
NL_NAME_1: String (50.0)
HASC_1: String (15.0)
:
ID_5: Integer (10.0)
NAME_5: String (75.0)
TYPE_5: String (25.0)
ENGTYPE_5: String (25.0)
Shape_Length: Real (0.0)
Shape_Area: Real (0.0)
```

The output lists the names of the fields, their sizes, and also the spatial reference system of the data—WGS 84 lon/lat, with the familiar SRID 4326. It also indicates that the geometry is mixed, not all of a single subtype.

You can take this data, filter down to just the USA portion of it, and bring it into your database, transformed to U.S. National Atlas Equal Area:

```
ogr2ogr -f "PostgreSQL"
➥PG:"host=localhost user=postgres port=5432
➥dbname=postgis_in_action password=mypassword" gadm_v0dot9.mdb
➥-lco GEOMETRY_NAME=the_geom
➥-where "ISO='USA'"
➥-t_srs "EPSG:2163"
➥-nln "us.admin_boundaries" gadm1
```

In this example, you select U.S. boundaries with the `ISO='USA'where` clause; you transform from the original SRID of the data (4326) to the SRID of 2163. If you look in the PostGIS spatial_ref_sys table, you'll note that 2163 corresponds to U.S. National Atlas. You load the data into a new table called admin_boundaries that resides in the us schema. In this particular case, ogr2ogr has enough information to guess at the source SRS, so it doesn't need to be provided. To tell ogr2ogr what the source SRID is, you can use the `-s_srs` switch.

If you tried to load the full data set, you might have run into errors because of the multitude of languages that might be in a file containing global data. To accommodate this, you'd need to set the client encoding of the data to LATIN1. Unfortunately, you can't set the client encoding with a switch in ogr2ogr, so you'd have to resort to setting environment variables.

LOADING A MAPINFO TAB FILE

Another popular format is the MapInfo TAB file format. MapInfo files encode the spatial reference information, obviating the need for a separate projection file. Field names can be upper, lower, or mixed case without any character size limitations. Because people use MapInfo files for mapping, they are usually chock full of cartographic formatting instructions that ogr2ogr conveniently ignores.

The next example uses a file from Statistics Canada, which you can download from www12.statcan.gc.ca/census-recensement/2011/geo/bound-limit/files-fichiers /gecu000e11m_e.zip. Go to the Population Ecumene Census Division Cartographic Boundary File and choose MapInfo TAB format. The zip file you download will include several TAB files.

The following listing shows how you can load the entire folder in one swoop, which is a handy feature of ogr2ogr, especially if you have hundreds of files.

Listing 4.5 Loading MapInfo files

```
ogr2ogr -f "PostgreSQL" PG:"host=localhost user=postgres port=5432
➥dbname=postgis_in_action password=mypassword" "/gisdata/canada"
➥-lco GEOMETRY_NAME=geom -lco SCHEMA=canada
➥-a_srs "EPSG:4269"
```

Folder of input files

Name of geometry column in new table, and schema that will house new table

SRS of the source

In listing 4.5, you tell ogr2ogr which folder to look in for the files; it will pull all the files it recognizes and create separate tables named after the fields. You also explicitly specify the source spatial reference system. If you hadn't specified the SRS for this particular file, ogr2ogr would have created an arbitrary SRID and added this to the spatial_ref_sys table with the correct projection. This is highly undesirable, and we have yet to figure out why it can't discern the correct SRID, even though it has no problem getting the projection information.

Now that you've learned how to import data with ogr2ogr, you'll probably want to know how to export data as well. In the next section, we'll cover exporting PostGIS data into various spatial vector formats with ogr2ogr.

4.3.4 Exporting with ogr2ogr

Ogr2ogr allows you to output tables, views, and queries. With ogr2ogr you can export multiple tables at once.

OGR2OGR EXPORT SWITCHES

The most important switches for outputting data with ogr2ogr are the following:

- `-select`—Specifies the fields you want to output. There's no need to include the geometry or geography field here.
- `-where`—Sets the filter condition. The syntax is the same as a SQL `where` clause.

- `-sql`—Use this if you want to output a more complex query than what `-select` and `-where` offer. The output column data types may not reflect the data types of your query columns.
- `-t_srs`—Specifies the SRID that you want ogr2ogr to output to. Ogr2ogr will ignore this if it can't figure out the SRID of the source, or if the source SRID is not in the list of projections included with your particular installation of ogr2ogr.
- `-s_srs`—Specifies the SRID of the data you're exporting. You can usually get away with leaving this out because ogr2ogr does a good job of determining the SRID.
- `-dsco overwrite=YES`—Instructs ogr2ogr to delete the old files first, should they exist. It's useful if you have a nightly scheduled dump where you're constantly overwriting the same files.

Now that you know the fundamental switches used when exporting data from PostgreSQL with ogr2ogr, we'll demonstrate exporting PostgreSQL data to popular geospatial file formats.

EXPORT TO KML USING OGR2OGR

Listing 4.6 demonstrates how you can output a table, a query, and multiple tables to Keyhole Markup Language (KML). KML data is always in WGS 84 lon/lat (EPSG 4326). If your data is in a known projection, then ogr2ogr will transform it to 4326 without you having to specify either the source or the output SRID. If you want finer control, PostGIS offers a `ST_AsKML` function that you can use in lieu of ogr2ogr. (To learn more about the KML driver used by ogr2ogr, follow this link: http://gdal.org/ogr/drv_kml.html.)

Listing 4.6 Export PostGIS table and query to KML

```
ogr2ogr -f "KML" /gisdata/us_adminbd.kml                    # Simple export whole table to KML
➥PG:"host=localhost user=postgres port=5432 dbname=postgis_in_action
➥password=mypassword" us.admin_boundaries -dsco NameField=name_2

ogr2ogr -f "KML"                                             # Export subset of records based on filter to KML
➥/gisdata/biketrip.kml PG:"host=localhost user=postgres port=5432
➥dbname=postgis_in_action password=mypassword" -dsco NameField=time
➥-select "SELECT track_seg_point_id, ele, time"
➥-where "time BETWEEN '2009-07-18 04:33-04' AND '2009-07-18 04:34-04'"
➥staging.aus_biketrip_narangba

ogr2ogr -f "KML"                                             # Export multiple tables to a single KML file
➥/gisdata/biketrail.kml PG:"host=localhost user=postgres port=5432
➥dbname=postgis_in_action password=mypassword" -dsco NameField=time
➥staging.track_points staging.tracks
```

These examples always include a `NameField` argument. This tells ogr2ogr which field to use as the KML title.

When exporting multiple tables, ogr2ogr places them all into the same KML file. Take a look at the KML generated by the preceding multi-table export in Google Earth, and you'll see two layers in the biketrail.kml file: one for track_point and one for tracks.

EXPORT TO MAPINFO TAB FILE FORMAT USING OGR2OGR

The next example outputs to MapInfo TAB format. Unlike KML, which is always in WGS 84 lon/lat (EPSG 4326), MapInfo data can be in any spatial reference system. In many cases, the SRS of the data in PostGIS is not the one you want to use for output.

In the first example in the following listing, you use the `-f_srs` switch to transform the SRID.

Listing 4.7 Export PostGIS tables and queries to MapInfo TAB format

```
ogr2ogr -f "MapInfo file"
➥/gisdata/us_boundaries.tab
➥PG:"host=localhost user=postgres
➥port=5432 dbname=postgis_in_action password=mypassword"
➥-t_srs "EPSG:4326" us.admin_boundaries

ogr2ogr -f "MapInfo file"
➥/gisdata/biketrip.tab
➥PG:"host=localhost user=postgres port=5432
➥dbname=postgis_in_action password=mypassword"
➥-select "SELECT track_seg_point_id, ele, time"
➥-where "time BETWEEN '2009-07-18 04:33-04' AND '2009-07-18 04:34-04'"
➥staging.aus_biketrip_narangba

ogr2ogr -f "MapInfo file"
➥/gisdata/tab_files
➥PG:"host=localhost user=postgres port=5432
➥dbname=postgis_in_action password=mypassword"
➥staging.track_points staging.tracks
```

❶ Export PostGIS data to EPSG 4326 projected MapInfo file

❷ Export PostGIS (no transformation, native projections), but subset of data

❸ Export multiple PostGIS tables to same MapInfo file

In the first example, you transform the data from a National Atlas projection (which is the stored form in the PostGIS table) to WGS 84 lon/lat ❶. In the second example, you keep the data in the native PostGIS form (National Atlas projection), but only output a subset of the data using a `-where` switch ❷.

In the third example, you export two tables ❸. Ogr2ogr creates a set of four files (.tab, .map, .dat, .id) for each table. It also creates a containing folder called tab_files. If the containing folder already exists, you must include the `-dsco overwrite=YES` switch, or ogr2ogr will fail.

4.4 Importing OpenStreetMap data with osm2pgsql

OpenStreetMap (OSM) is an exciting project that makes spatial data available free of charge via mapping web services, similar to Google Maps and MS Virtual Earth. You can then import this data into PostGIS. Having the data in your own PostGIS database is useful for advanced querying, managing your own services, or building your own custom tiles. OSM data is exported in either XML format, which usually ends with a .osm or .osm.bz extension, or in a compressed file format with a .pbf extension.

Most of the data provided through OSM is licensed under the Open Database License or Creative Commons Attribution-ShareAlike 2.0. This means that it can be used for both commercial and non-commercial ventures. In section 4.4.1 we'll discuss how you can carve out specific areas of OpenStreetMap data and download them in OSM XML format and then import the resulting file into your PostGIS-enabled database.

You can import OSM data into PostGIS using the osm2pgsql tool, and newer versions of ogr2ogr also have support for loading OSM data. Imposm is another free, open source, command-line tool that people commonly use for importing OSM data, and it's younger than osm2pgsql. Many claim Imposm is more robust for handling large OSM dumps, but both projects are constantly being updated, so that claim may no longer be valid.

The main downside of Imposm is that it only runs on Linux and OS X, and not on Windows, whereas osm2pgsql has support for all the platforms PostGIS runs on. Imposm also currently doesn't support OSM differential loads, so it's not a good solution if you have a large OSM data set and want to perform differential updates as things get updated on OSM. One key benefit of Imposm is that it supports custom database schemas, so you can better control the table structures of your data as part of the load process.

You can find out more about Imposm at http://imposm.org. Visit www.openstreetmap.org/export to download both utilities.

Now that we've covered the common free options available for loading data, let's test these tools.

4.4.1 Getting OSM data

You can choose to download and load the whole OSM database, which is about 16 GB in size, or you can download extracts of key areas such as those available at http://download.geofabrik.de/ or http://metro.teczno.com.

To export a section from the OSM world map, follow these steps:

1. Go to www.openstreetmap.org/export and type in the lon/lat block you want, or draw a box on the map.
2. Select a region encompassing the Arc de Triomphe (or wherever section you prefer).
3. By selecting a region, the BBOX filters should be filled in. For example, if you picked the Arc de Triomphe area, the min longitude/latitude and max longitude/latitude will be filled in the bounding box coordinates. Something like `2.28568,48.87957,2.30371,48.8676` will appear in the coordinate text boxes.
4. Select OpenStreetMap XML Data as the export format. We called ours arctriump.osm.

You can also use one of the REST APIs provided by OpenStreetMap to achieve the same results. The following listing demonstrates carving out a similar section using a `wget` call. Note that the `bbox` argument corresponds to the minimum longitude/latitude and maximum longitude/latitude of the area you're interested in.

Listing 4.8 Download a bounding box area covering the Arc de Triomphe

```
wget --progress=dot:mega -O "arc.osm"
➥"http://www.overpass-api.de/api/xapi?*
➥[bbox=2.29,48.87,2.30,48.88][@meta]"
```

Listing 4.8 should be run as a single line.

A wizard for using the REST XAPI services for OpenStreetMap can be found at http://harrywood.co.uk/maps/uixapi/xapi.html. Not only does the XAPI service allow you to carve out specific areas of OSM data, but you can also carve out selected elements like hospitals or roads.

Once you have an OSM-formatted file, you can load it using osm2pgsql.

4.4.2 Loading OSM-formatted data with osm2pgsql

Osm2pgsql has numerous options we won't explore, such as on-the-fly projection using the `-E` switch, importing as lon/lat with the `-ll` switch, and so forth. You can get a listing of all the options by calling `osm2pgsql -h`. Osm2pgsql and psql behave more or less the same on all the platforms the utility is compiled for. (Note that psql is located in the bin folder of your PostgreSQL install.)

If you want to use the key/value store feature of PostgreSQL and be able to import the OSM key tags into this structure, you'll need to install hstore located in the contrib folder. For PostgreSQL 9.1+, you can install this in your database with the following SQL command: `CREATE EXTENSION hstore;`.

> **USING OSM2PGSQL ON WINDOWS** If you're using Windows, the best binary to use is the Cygwin one from http://wiki.openstreetmap.org/wiki/Osm2pgsql#Binary. Just extract the zip file into a folder and it should work. At the time of this writing, the Cygwin version seemed most up to date and bug-free.

Now you're ready to load your OSM-formatted data into PostgreSQL with the following statement.

Listing 4.9 Load OSM XML file with osm2pgsql

```
osm2pgsql -d postgis_in_action          <-- 1 Specify database name
➥-H localhost                          <-- 2 Specify database server host
➥-U postgres                           <-- 3 Specify user name
➥-P 5432                               <-- 4 Set PostgreSQL port
➥-S                                    <-- 5 Specify style file
➥default.style --hstore                <-- 6 Create hstore columns
➥arc.osm
```

The commands for database name ❶, database server host ❷, user name ❸, and PostgreSQL port ❹ are pretty much the same as for psql, with two exceptions: for the port (which is only really needed if installing in a PostgreSQL database that's not on the standard port), the switch is an uppercase `P` instead of lowercase `p`; and for the host, the switch is an uppercase `H` instead of lowercase `h`.

The `-S` switch denotes the style file to use ❺. The style file defines how to treat each feature in the OSM file, such as what fields should be created and what goes into or is excluded from tags. If you're missing a style file, you can download one from GitHub (https://github.com/openstreetmap/osm2pgsql/blob/master/default.style) and put it in the same folder as osm2pgsql or specify the full path to the style file.

You denote `--hstore` so that the load creates an hstore column in each of the tables ❻. The name of the hstore column is `tags`. In newer versions of osm2pgsql, `--hstore` will only add to tags values that are not already represented in table columns. If you want all tags, even if they're represented in table columns, use `--hstore-all` instead. Newer versions of osm2pgsql also support the `--hstore-add-index` switch, which will automatically create the gist index on the hstore column for you during load.

> **OLDER OSM2PGSQL COMMAND LINES** If you're running an older osm2pgsql command line that predated the PostGIS 2.0 release, and you have PostGIS 2.0+, you'll need to install some legacy scripts: legacy_minimal.sql and legacy_gist.sql. These are packaged with PostGIS 2.0.2 and above and are located in the share/contrib/postgis-2.* folder of your PostgreSQL installation.

Once you've run this command, you should see a bunch of tables created in the public schema that start with planet_osm.

READING HSTORE TAGS

If you used the `--hstore` flag as shown in listing 4.9, each table should have a column called tags that uses the PostgreSQL key/value `hstore` storage type. Tags can be different for each object, but if you request a tag that doesn't exist, it will return NULL. This is often referred to as a schemaless design. Most of the key OSM tags are already included as database columns in the OSM PostgreSQL output, but querying tags is useful to get at the more obscure ones that may be particularly useful to you.

To demonstrate querying, suppose you wanted to pull out all the cycleways from the lines table and to also have a pipe-delimited list of the other keys each has. You could write a query such as the following:

```
SELECT name, array_to_string(akeys(tags), '|') As keys
  ,tags -> 'cycleway' As cycleway
FROM planet_osm_line
WHERE tags ? 'cycleway' ;
```

The `hstore` data type can use a gist index for added performance, similar to what you'd create against PostGIS geometry, geography, and raster columns. In the preceding example, `tags ? 'cycleway'` means "return only records that contain a tag with the name *cycleway*." It will use a gist index if there is one on the hstore tags column.

If you wanted to pull out each tag as a separate row, which is more suitable for storing tags in other relational databases, you could write a query like the following one, which would create a new table called osm_key_values consisting of a row with three columns: osm_id, key, and value. You'd get a record for each key/value pair, so if you had 10 entries in each tags column, you'd get 10 rows for each row.

```
SELECT osm_id, (foo.e).key, (foo.e).value
INTO osm_key_values
FROM
 (SELECT osm_id, each(tags) As e
  FROM planet_osm_line ) As foo ;
```

As you've seen, there are numerous open source tools freely available for getting vector data into and out of your PostgreSQL/PostGIS database. Many of these tools grew up alongside PostGIS, so the free PostGIS import tools are often more tested and functional than those you'll find for other spatial databases. You can similarly import and export PostGIS raster data, as you'll see in the next section.

4.5 Importing and exporting raster data

GDAL is a suite of utilities for working with raster data. It can be used for importing, exporting to different raster types, transforming raster data from one spatial reference system to another, and converting raster data to a vector form. Although GDAL can export to numerous other raster types and can read PostGIS rasters, it can't be used to import raster data to a PostGIS database. PostGIS provides a utility for importing raster data—*raster2pgsql*.

The command-line GDAL packaged tools commonly used when working with PostGIS rasters are as follows:

- Gdalinfo is used to inspect a raster. This works for both PostGIS and non-PostGIS rasters.
- Gdal_translate is used to export data out of PostGIS into other formats.
- Gdalwarp is used to transform spatial references. It can also export to other formats.

The main difference between gdal_translate and gdalwarp is that gdal_translate works for both spatially referenced and non-spatial rasters alike. Gdal_translate never transforms from one spatial reference to another, whereas that's the main purpose of gdalwarp. You can use gdal_translate to manipulate your selfies!

4.5.1 Using gdalinfo to inspect rasters

When you lay your hands on some raster data, it's worth taking a closer look before you go through the trouble of importing it. Gdalinfo provides detailed information about specific raster sources.

Depending on your installation, gdalinfo will only be able to inspect certain raster formats. To see which, use the `--formats` switch as follows:

```
gdalinfo --formats
```

Besides providing information about the raster, gdalinfo gives you information that will help you troubleshoot when an import goes awry. To get basic information about a raster before you load it, run gdalinfo as shown in the following listing. (This example uses the data file from http://dds.cr.usgs.gov/srtm/version2_1/SRTM3/Eurasia/N48E086 .hgt.zip.)

Listing 4.10 Using gdalinfo on a PostGIS raster table

```
gdalinfo N48E086.hgt
```

The output of listing 4.10 is shown in the next listing.

Listing 4.11 Output of gdalinfo

```
Driver: SRTMHGT/SRTMHGT File Format
 Files: N48E086.hgt
Size is 1201, 1201
Coordinate System is:
GEOGCS["WGS 84",
    DATUM["WGS_1984",
        SPHEROID["WGS 84",6378137,298.257223563,
            AUTHORITY["EPSG","7030"]],
        TOWGS84[0,0,0,0,0,0,0],
        AUTHORITY["EPSG","6326"]],
    PRIMEM["Greenwich",0,
        AUTHORITY["EPSG","8901"]],
    UNIT["degree",0.0174532925199433,
        AUTHORITY["EPSG","9108"]],
    AUTHORITY["EPSG","4326"]]
Origin = (85.999583333333334,49.000416666666666)
Pixel Size = (0.000833333333333,-0.000833333333333)
Metadata:
  AREA_OR_POINT=Point
Corner Coordinates:
Upper Left  (  85.9995833,  49.0004167) ( 85d59'58.50"E, 49d 0' 1.50"N)
Lower Left  (  85.9995833,  47.9995833) ( 85d59'58.50"E, 47d59'58.50"N)
Upper Right (  87.0004167,  49.0004167) ( 87d 0' 1.50"E, 49d 0' 1.50"N)
Lower Right (  87.0004167,  47.9995833) ( 87d 0' 1.50"E, 47d59'58.50"N)
Center      (  86.5000000,  48.5000000) ( 86d30' 0.00"E, 48d30' 0.00"N)
Band 1 Block=1201x1 Type=Int16, ColorInterp=Undefined
  NoData Value=-32768
  Unit Type: m
```

The output will always contain size, bands and type of each band, and corner coordinates of the raster. The corner coordinates correspond to geospatial coordinates, in this case degrees. If a raster isn't georeferenced, these coordinates will range from 0 to the maximum number of columns/rows of the raster. Only with georeferenced rasters will you see a section denoting the coordinate system.

4.5.2 *Importing raster data with raster2pgsql*

Raster-enabled PostGIS distributions come packaged with a command-line tool called *raster2pgsql*, which can usually be found in the bin folder of your PostgreSQL install. This tool is built using GDAL, so it's capable of loading most raster formats supported by your particular version of GDAL. Using wildcard switches, it can load an entire folder of files into a single PostGIS table. You can also use it to break up large raster files into smaller chunks and store each chunk as a separate table row suitable for magnified analysis. It can also create overviews of tables, which are useful for mapping and showing rasters at low zoom levels.

RASTER2PGSQL COMMAND-LINE SWITCHES

To see the available command-line switches, type `raster2pgsql` on the command line by itself. The most frequently used switches are listed here:

- `-s SRID`—Specifies the SRID of the source raster. Raster2pgsql will check the metadata of the incoming raster to determine an appropriate SRID if one is not specified. If it can't discern the SRID, the raster will be imported with an SRID of 0.
- `-t tile size`—Sets the size of the tiles. This divides the raster into tiles (*chunking* in raster lingo), to be inserted one per table row. You express the tile size as width-by-height in pixels. In PostGIS 2.1, you can set the tile size to be auto, and raster2pgsql will compute the appropriate tile size, which is usually between 32 and 100 pixels and as close to evenly dividing the original dimension as possible. Raster2pgsql will never constitute a raster row from more than one original file, so regardless of tiling, the number of rows created during import will always be the same as or more than the number of files.
- `-R`—Registers the raster as an out-of-db (filesystem) raster.
- `-F`—Adds a column with the filename of the raster. The default column name is *filename*. This is especially useful if you're tiling the files during import. Keeping the original filename allows you to easily reconstitute the original file should that ever become necessary.
- `-n column name`—Specifies the name of the filename column. Implies `-F`. This is new in PostGIS 2.1.
- `-l overview factor`—Creates overview tables of the raster. If you have more than one factor, separate them with commas. The overview table name follows the pattern *o_overview_factor_table name* (for example, `o_2_srtm`). The overview is always stored in the database, unaffected by the `-R` switch. The overview factor must be an integer value greater than 0.
- `-I`—Creates a gist spatial index on the raster column. The PostgreSQL `ANALYZE` command will automatically be issued for the created index to update column statistics information.

- `-C`—Sets the standard set of constraints on the raster column after loading. Some constraints may fail if one or more rasters violate the constraint.
- `-e`—Executes each statement individually and doesn't use a transaction.
- `-G`—Prints the supported GDAL raster formats.

The next four switches take a table name as an argument and are mutually exclusive:

- `-d table name`—Drops the table, then re-creates it and populates it with current raster data.
- `-a table name`—Appends the raster into an existing table denoted by *table name*.
- `-c table name`—Creates a new table and populates it. This is the default if you don't specify any options.
- `-p table name`—Creates the table and does nothing else (prepare mode).

Raster2pgsql can't perform transformations and therefore doesn't have a switch where you can specify the destination SRID. Your imported raster will always use the SRID of the source.

RASTER2PGSQL SUPPORTED FORMATS

The raster2pgsql tool has a `-G` switch that lists all the raster formats it supports, as shown in the next listing.

Listing 4.12 Raster2pgsq list of supported formats

```
raster2pgsql -G                  <-- Command

Supported GDAL raster formats:          <-- Output
  Virtual Raster
  GeoTIFF
  National Imagery Transmission Format
  :
  Erdas Imagine Images (.img)
  :
  Arc/Info Binary Grid
  Arc/Info ASCII Grid
  GRASS ASCII Grid
  SDTS Raster
  DTED Elevation Raster
  Portable Network Graphics
  JPEG JFIF
  :
  Graphics Interchange Format (.gif)
  :
  SRTMHGT File Format
  :
  GRIdded Binary (.grb)
  :
  R Object Data Store
  :
  ASCII Gridded XYZ
  :
```

As you can see, you can import many different formats with raster2pgsql. You get even more formats if you compile with additional extensions or if you keep up to date and use the latest version of GDAL.

LOADING A SINGLE FILE WITH RASTER2PGSQL

Let's use raster2pgsql to load some elevation data from http://dds.cr.usgs.gov/srtm/version2_1/SRTM3/Eurasia/N48E086.hgt.zip. You'll extract the zip file to a folder and load the file in as a single record. (We'll demonstrate how you can load entire folders, chunked for easier analysis, in the next section.)

```
raster2pgsql -s 4326 -C N48E086.hgt staging.n48e086
➥| psql -h localhost -U postgres -p 5432 -d postgis_in_action
```

This example loads the single file into a table called staging.n48e086. The `-C` switch tells raster2pgsql to add all necessary constraints, thereby ensuring that the properties of the raster are correctly registered in the raster_columns view. You can specify the SRID of the raster files using the `-s` switch.

LOADING MULTIPLE FILES AND TILING IN SHELL SCRIPT

In this example, we'll load multiple elevation files in one step. This time the data comes from http://dds.cr.usgs.gov/srtm/version2_1/SRTM3/Eurasia/. Download and extract the data using your choice of utility, and then place the files into a folder called usgs_srtm (to match the name used in the following code). Next, create a plain-text script file by copying the following listing.

Listing 4.13 Loading multiple rasters

```
export PGPORT=5432                               ❶ Set environment variables
export PGHOST=localhost
export PGUSER=postgres
export PGPASSWORD=mypassword
export PGDATABASE=postgis_in_action
raster2pgsql -s 4326 -C -F -t 100x100            ❷ Execute raster2pgsql with switches
➥usgs_srtm/*.hgt                                ❸ Pull many files
➥staging.usgs_srtm                              ❹ Load to table
➥| psql                                         ❺ Pipe to psql
```

Listing 4.13 is an example of a raster load shell script. First you set the environment variables that psql will read ❶; this allows you to call psql without any arguments ❺. If you're on Windows, replace the word `export` with `set`. Raster2pgsql will then try to pick a tile size from 32 to 100 so that your file size is close to being evenly divisible by your tile size ❷. You can specify a wildcard to load multiple files in a table ❸. Then you denote the table to be created and loaded ❹. You can include the schema name in the table name if you don't want it loaded in your default schema. Then you send the script generated by raster2pgsql to psql for execution ❺. You can also save the script as a file.

After loading the table, it's a good idea to check the raster_columns view to verify that all constraints were added properly.

4.5.3 Gdal_translate and gdalwarp

Gdal_translate and gdalwarp are command-line tools packaged with GDAL to export rasters to another format. Gdal_translate has the ability to change the resolution of the output and can export both georeferenced and non-georeferenced rasters, but it can't transform spatial reference systems. For this, you'll need gdalwarp.

When you work through the following examples and create output files, it's a really good idea to look at what you export to make sure that the elephant image is still an elephant and the Arc de Triomphe is not sitting in Atlantis, and so on. Viewers built using GDAL, such as the popular QGIS and MapServer, are guaranteed to render every format that gdal_translate exports. See chapter 5 for information about installing one of the GDAL-based viewers.

We'll now look at various uses of gdal_translate.

USING GDAL_TRANSLATE TO SHRINK OR ENLARGE RASTERS

Let's start by shrinking a raster to 10% of its original size and outputting it as a GeoTIFF file:

```
gdal_translate -of GTiff -outsize 10% 10%
➥"PG:host=localhost port=5432 dbname='postgis_in_action'
➥user='postgres' password='xyz'
➥schema=staging table=usgs_srtm mode=2" elev_small.tif
```

In this example, you set `mode` to 2. Since GDAL 1.8, you need to add this `mode` setting when you export a raster spanning multiple rows in a table to a file format that supports only a single raster.

Also take note of the output size percentages: the first is the width, and the second is the height.

USING GDAL_TRANSLATE TO EXPORT A SINGLE BAND

Let's now export only the first band of a multiband raster to a JPEG file:

```
gdal_translate -of JPEG
➥"PG:host=localhost port=5432 dbname='postgis_in_action'
➥user='postgres' password='xyz' schema='staging'
➥table='pele_chunked' column='rast' mode=2" -b 1 pele_grey.png
```

For simplicity, let's assume your picture is RGB, with red, green, and blue bands. This example exports the first band only, giving you a monochromatic elephant. It also specifies the raster column to export. If your table has more than one raster column, you must indicate the one to export, or gdal_translate will pick one arbitrarily.

USING GDAL_TRANSLATE WITH A WHERE CLAUSE

Gdal_translate accepts an SQL-like `where` clause that allows you to filter the rows you wish to export. In this example, you only export rows 1–200 of Kauai:

```
gdal_translate -of GTiff
➥"PG:host='localhost' port='5432' dbname='postgis_in_action'
➥user='postgres' password='whatever' schema='staging'
➥table='usgs_srtm'
➥where='rid BETWEEN 1 and 200' mode=2" subset.tif
```

USING GDAL_TRANSLATE TO EXPORT A REGION

Nothing stops you from building fancy `where` clauses that take advantage of PostGIS functions. In this example, you only output that portion of the raster containing the bounded region centered on the Arc de Triomphe:

```
gdal_translate -of GTiff
➥PG:"host='localhost' port='5432'
➥dbname='postgis_in_action' user='postgres'
➥password='whatever' schema='staging' table='usgs_srtm'
➥where=
➥    'ST_Intersects(
➥        rast,
➥        ST_MakeEnvelope(2.28568,48.8676,2.30371,48.87957,4326)
➥    )'
➥mode=2" arctriomphe.tif
```

This `where` clause gives you a glimpse of how raster and geometry data types can freely interact in the PostGIS world.

USING GDAL_TRANSLATE TO RECONSTITUTE AN IMPORTED FILE

If you imported your rasters with the `-F` option, the name of the original file should be in the database. By filtering for the filename, you can rebuild the original file, even if you tiled it across many rows:

```
gdal_translate -of USGSDEM
➥"PG:host=localhost port=5432 dbname='postgis_in_action'
➥user='postgres' password='whatever' schema=staging table=usgs_srtm
➥mode=2 where='filename=\'N48E086.hgt\' '" N48E086.dem
```

USING GDALWARP TO TRANSFORM SPATIAL REFERENCES

The one deficiency of gdal_translate is that it can't handle spatial reference transformations as part of the export. You need to use gdalwarp to get that feature.

Let's export a subset of data from the PostGIS database and transform it in one command. For this particular example, you need at least GDAL 1.8 compiled with PostGIS raster support. GDAL 1.9 or higher is an even better choice.

Gdalwarp has two switches that distinguish it from gdal_translate:

- `-s_srs`—This switch specifies the spatial reference system of the source raster. Even though gdalwarp can determine the SRS without your help, lend it a hand. It'll reward you with greater speed.
- `-t_srs`—This switch is absolutely required and states the SRS of the output.

These two switches will accept both proj4 and EPSG codes, but to use EPSG, the `GDAL_DATA` path environment variable must be set and must point to an EPSG file that translates EPSG codes to proj4. So even though the EPSG code is infinitely easier to type out than the monstrous proj4 string, you have to do some prep work.

This next example transforms data in the PostgreSQL staging.usdem table that is in EPSG 4326 (WGS 84 lon/lat) and that intersects the geometry envelope in the `where` clause to EPSG 2163 (U.S. National Atlas). If you had multiple raster columns in your database tables, you'd also need to denote the raster column name with `column_name='rast'`.

```
gdalwarp -s_srs "EPSG:4326" -t_srs "EPSG:2163"
➥PG:"host='localhost' port='5432' dbname='postgis_in_action'
➥user='postgres' password='whatever'
➥schema='staging' table='usdem'
➥where='ST_Intersects(
➥  rast,
➥  ST_MakeEnvelope(-115.60, 32.54, -112.96, 26.03, 4326)
➥ )'
➥mode='2'"
➥usdem_sub.tif
```

4.5.4 Using PostgreSQL functions to output raster data

Since PostGIS 2.0, there are a number of output functions for raster data. `ST_AsGDALRaster` is an all-purpose function that outputs to all formats supported by GDAL.

To get a listing of supported formats for your particular GDAL version, execute this query:

```
SELECT short_name, long_name
FROM ST_GdalDrivers()
ORDER BY short_name;
```

> **GDAL formats disabled by default in PostGIS versions 2.1.3+, 2.0.6+, and future releases**
>
> Because of security concerns with some formats that can access network resources, GDAL formats are disabled by default. To enable them, you need to set environment variables `POSTGIS_GDAL_ENABLED_DRIVERS` and `POSTGIS_ENABLE_OUTDB_RASTERS`. Please refer to the PostGIS security releases page (http://postgis.net/2014/05/19/postgis-2.0.6_and_2.1.3) and the PostGIS manuals (http://postgis.net/documentation) for details.
>
> In PostGIS 2.2, in lieu of using OS environment variables, PostgreSQL global unified variables (GUCs) can be set in postgresql.conf, or at the database level for a specific database. PostgreSQL 9.4 allows you to set GUCs using the new `ALTER SYSTEM` command, so editing postgresql.conf is not necessary.

Simpler functions to use if you just want to output in the common PNG, JPEG, or TIFF formats are the `ST_AsPNG`, `ST_AsJPEG`, and `ST_AsTiff` functions, which take fewer arguments because they have many of the common defaults set. In addition, the

ST_AsRaster function allows you to convert any 2D (non-curved) geometry into a PostGIS raster format that can then be converted to any of the GDAL-supported formats, thus allowing you to render your geometries in many raster formats as well.

For example, the following SQL statement will output an image of the planet_osm_roads table containing a geometry data type column (loaded with osm2pgsql in listing 4.9) as a PNG file with maximum dimensions of 400 × 400 pixels.

Listing 4.14 Output OSM roads as a single PNG raster

```
SELECT ST_AsPNG(                          <-- 1 Raster to PNG function
    ST_AsRaster(                          <-- 2 Geometry to raster function
        ST_Union(way),                    <-- 3 Union roads
        400,400,                          <-- 4 Specify 400 × 400 pixels
        ARRAY['8BUI','8BUI','8BUI'],      <-- 5 Specify three bands
        ARRAY[200,0,0],                   <-- 6 Set color to RGB array (very red)
        ARRAY[0,0,0]                      <-- 7 Set no data value to (0,0,0)
    )
)
FROM planet_osm_roads;
```

In listing 4.14 you first take all the roads in planet_osm_roads and spatially union them into a collection of multilinestrings ❸. Then you rasterize that geometry ❷ into a 400 × 400 pixel ❹ raster composed of three 8BUI bands ❺ and set the band value of the multilinestrings to a reddish color during output ❻. You then initialize non-geometry pixels to 0,0,0 ❼ and finally convert the PostGIS raster to a PNG raster ❶.

The output of listing 4.14 is the bytes that make up the PNG image as a PostgreSQL bytea (byte array) data type. You can then use a standard query connection like JDBC, PHP pgsql, ODBC, ADO.NET, or Python psychopg to retrieve the image for rendering in a web application. We have a demonstration of rendering for web applications at www.bostongis.com/blog/index.php?/archives/175-Minimalist-Web-based-PHP-PostGIS-2.0-Spatial-GeometryRaster-Viewer.html.

OpenOffice can also read images stored in a field. With it you can easily incorporate your image in spreadsheets and presentations. We demonstrate the use of OpenOffice and LibreOffice at www.postgresonline.com/journal/archives/244-Raster-LibreOffice-Base-Reports.html.

4.6 Summary

In this chapter, we demonstrated the use of various tools for importing and exporting vector and raster data:

- Shp2pgsql
- Shp2pgsql-gui

- Pgsql2shp for Esri shapefiles
- Ogr2ogr for other vector files
- Osm2pgsql for OpenStreetMap
- Raster2pgsql for importing rasters
- Gdal_translate and gdalwarp for exporting raster data

We advised you to take advantage of useful GDAL tools such as ogrinfo and gdalinfo to inspect the data prior to importing. The examples in this chapter should provide you with enough of a starting point that you can now load and export your own data under most circumstances. If you run into difficulties, each of the tools has switches that you can use to customize the import and export.

Our last bit of advice is this: look at what you've imported and exported with a visualization tool. Just because your routine ran successfully doesn't mean you ended up with what you want. What you thought was Portland, OR, could actually be Portland, ME. Too many times we've seen people go on to subsequent steps assuming the data to be flawless, only to find their later efforts wasted due to bad data sets. Be extra careful when using data from quasi-authoritative sources. For instance, just because you found a source for downloading the borders of all continents doesn't mean it wasn't drawn by some toddler for a kindergarten thesis (and posted online by an overly proud mommy or daddy). Worse yet, the continents could be from 300 million years ago—Pangaea.

Unfortunately, no import or export utility can guard against human error. Save yourself some time and embarrassment down the road. Make it a habit to check your data the minute you import or export.

Now that you know how to load data into your PostGIS spatial database, we'll next look at how you can view this data using popular open source, desktop, spatial-viewing tools.

Using PostGIS on the desktop

5

This chapter covers

- OpenJUMP
- QGIS
- uDig
- gvSIG

In this chapter, we'll cover some popular open source GIS desktop viewing tools often paired with PostGIS. You'll find that each has its own strengths and weaknesses and caters to a certain niche of users or tasks.

We'll start off by providing a brief at-a-glance summary of these tools, liberally ladling out our personal opinions. We hope that once you've read this chapter, you'll have a better understanding of which tools are best for what you're doing and for your particular style of working. We'll focus mostly on the use of these tools to view and query data, but we'll also highlight the features each offers for building custom desktop applications, and the availability of plug-ins and scripting to extend built-in features.

5.1 Desktop viewing tools at a glance

We'll start with a quick summary of the various tools' features. After reading this section, you may be able to rule out some of the tools altogether for your purposes, and you can skip the sections that pertain to them. If you've already invested in one of the tools, we recommend that you go through this section to at least see what you might have missed. New features are being added to these tools more quickly than any book can keep up with. If you've dismissed a tool due to the lack of some critical feature a year ago, you may find it now incorporated.

Table 5.1 provides a quick overview of the four tools that we'll cover in this chapter.

Table 5.1 Summary of tools based on architecture, language, OS, and setup

Feature	OpenJUMP [a]	QGIS	uDig	gvSIG
Current version	1.7.1	2.4.0	1.4.0	2.1
JVM	1.5+	N/A	1.5+/JAI	1.5+/JAI[b]
Plug-in	JARs/Jython/beans	Python/Qt	Eclipse	JARs
Scripting	Jython/BeanShell	Python	No	Jython[c]
Download size	30–50 MB	150–200 MB	150–200 MB	270 MB
Extract and go	Yes	No	Yes	No
Ease of use[d]	Moderate	Easy	Moderate	Difficult
Mobile version[e]	No	Yes	No	Yes

a. The JUMP unified mapping platform is the platform for OpenJUMP, but some other applications use it as a framework, including the namesake desktop application JUMP.
b. Java Advanced Imaging (JAI) is an API created by Sun (now Oracle).
c. Jython is the Java framework that allows you to run Python code in a JVM.
d. Indicates how easy the tool is to get up and running after performing basic configurations.
e. Indicates whether the tool has, or claims to have, a mobile companion version.

5.1.1 Capsule reviews

We've used all four tools in various capacities and have solicited input from other users. In this section, we offer our opinion of each. This is subjective, so YMMV.

OpenJUMP

This is our favorite tool because it's lightweight and lets us write spatial SQL and immediately view the visual results. OpenJUMP also has nice features for fixing and analyzing geometries and has tools to fix up faulty shapefiles. It's probably best suited for people who aren't afraid of querying directly against the database and who appreciate tidy workspaces. For Java and Python/Jython programmers, OpenJUMP automates common tasks.

On the downside, we wish that OpenJUMP would provide support for the PostGIS raster type. OpenJUMP native code plug-ins such as the ECW/JPEG 2000 drivers require running 32-bit JVM, which could hinder Mac users, because many versions of 64-bit OS X have 32-bit mode disabled.

QGIS

New GIS users tend to gravitate towards QGIS for its user-friendly interface, GPS and raster support, Python scriptability, and overall polish. GIS crowd sourcers, Python programmers, and GRASS users also tend to choose QGIS. Its speed and spatial SQL capabilities are fairly decent, and it's the only one of these tools, besides OpenJUMP, with support for SpatiaLite. It's also the only one of the tools we're discussing that has native support for PostGIS topology via additional plug-ins. QGIS supports SQL Server spatial types present in SQL Server 2008 and above. This ability to connect to disparate database products appeals to Windows folks needing to use both PostGIS and SQL Server, like we do.

QGIS provides a user-friendly query interface. If you're strictly an SQL writer, you might find its lack of full SQL support disappointing, but an extension called DB Manager is a one-click install away. QGIS has a huge developer base and following, so new features arrive at a lightning pace, and bugs are quickly worked out.

QGIS is the only tool in this list not built atop Java. It uses the C++ Qt framework (http://qt-project.org), and the newest versions have both 32-bit and 64-bit support. As a bonus, QGIS sports a mapping server that allows you to partially reuse a QGIS desktop workspace as a mapping service. The latest news from QGIS is that a port for Android is in the developmental phase. You can test this out at http://hub.qgis.org/projects/android-qgis.

uDig

uDig distinguishes itself by providing a rich suite of tools for working with OGC web services as well as advanced cartographic features. It caters to an Eclipse Java audience with heavy emphasis on cartography niceties that churns out sweet eye candy. Eclipse programmers might find it to be just what they're looking for.

uDig has both 32-bit and 64-bit JVM support. New in the 1.4 version is support for GeoScript (http://geoscript.org/), which allows for scripting in JavaScript, Python, Scala, and Groovy.

uDig is also EPL/BSD licensed, making it more inviting for companies that want to distribute it as part of their own product. The other desktop products (gvSIG, OpenJump, and QGIS) are all GPL, limiting their use in certain for-profit ventures.

gvSIG

gvSIG has basic support for various databases, OGC services, and non-OGC Esri products. It's also extensible via Java.

As far as PostGIS goes, we found gvSIG to be somewhat clunky. Although it claims to support PostGIS rasters natively, we had a good bit of trouble getting it to work with our PostGIS raster data and eventually gave up. Hopefully the gvSIG team will resolve the PostGIS raster issues prior to the 2.1 release.

If you've invested in Esri and are looking for something to tap into your legacy Esri stack, gvSIG may be your best choice. As a bonus, gvSIG has a mobile edition.

5.1.2 Spatial database support

All four of the desktop tools we're discussing support PostGIS without additional plug-ins. In this section, we'll catalog various features we find important when using the tools to connect to spatial data stores. We reviewed each tool against the following list of features:

- *Support for other databases (SpatiaLite, SQL Server 2008/2012, MySQL, DB2, Oracle)*—Can the tool render geometries stored in these other databases?
- *Multiple geometry columns*—Can the tool handle PostGIS tables with more than one geometry or geography column? Does it randomly pick one or fail?
- *Geography*—Does it support the PostGIS `geography` data type?
- *Save PostGIS*—Can the tool save tables to PostGIS? For instance, if you opened a shapefile, would you be able to save it to PostGIS?
- *Edit PostGIS*—Can the tool load in PostGIS data and permit editing using drawing tools and form fields?
- *Heterogeneous column*—Is the tool capable of rendering a table with a geometry column storing multiple subtypes?
- *SQL queries*—Are you able to compose PostGIS queries in SQL and see their output visually?
- *Integer unique key required*—Does the tool expect an integer to uniquely identify the rows?

In table 5.2, if we marked a tool as supporting a particular feature, we might not have tested it ourselves but instead culled the information from a quick read of the documentation or by exploring the menu options. If we marked a *Yes* entry with an asterisk, the tool claims to support the feature via additional extensions. If we marked a *No* entry with an asterisk, the tool has workarounds to adequately emulate the feature.

Table 5.2 Spatial database support

Feature	OpenJUMP	QGIS	uDig	gvSIG
SpatiaLite	Yes*	Yes	No	No
Oracle Spatial	Yes*	Yes*	Yes	Yes*
SQL Server 2008/2012	No	Yes	Yes	No*
DB2	No	No	Yes	No
ArcSDE	Yes*	No	Yes	Yes
MySQL	Yes*	Yes	Yes	Yes
Multiple geometry columns	Yes	Yes	No	Yes

Table 5.2 Spatial database support *(continued)*

Feature	OpenJUMP	QGIS	uDig	gvSIG
PostGIS geography	No*	Yes*	No	No
PostGIS raster	No*	Yes*	No	Yes*
Read PostGIS	Yes	Yes	Yes	Yes
Save PostGIS	Yes*	Yes*	No	Yes
Edit PostGIS	Yes	Yes	Yes	Yes
Curve support	No	No	No	No
3D geometry	No	Yes*	No	Yes*
Heterogeneous column	Yes	Yes	No*	No
SQL queries	Yes	Yes*	No	No
Integer unique key required	No	Yes	No	No
Views	Yes	Yes*	Yes	Yes*

5.1.3 Format support

Table 5.3 identifies the various vector, raster, and web service formats supported by each tool. This list isn't comprehensive but tries to cover the more common formats that people expect in a desktop tool. A *Yes* entry means the tool supports the format either as an import, export, edit, or all of these. A *Yes** entry means it supports the format via an additional extension not installed by default.

Table 5.3 Vector file data formats

Format	OpenJUMP	QGIS	uDig	gvSIG
Esri shapefile	Yes	Yes	Yes	Yes
SpatiaLite	Yes*	Yes	No	No
Esri Personal Geodatabase (MDB)	No	Yes	No	No
GPX	Yes	Yes	Yes*	No
GML	Yes	Yes	Yes	Yes
KML	Yes*	Yes	Yes	Yes
WKT	Yes	No	No	No
DXF	Yes	Yes	No	Yes
DWG	No	No	No	Yes
MIF/MID	Yes	Yes	No	No

Table 5.3 Vector file data formats *(continued)*

Format	OpenJUMP	QGIS	uDig	gvSIG
TAB	No*	Yes	No	No
Excel	Yes	Yes	No	No
CSV	Yes	Yes	No	No
SVG	Yes	No	No	No

Here are a few notes about some of the formats:

- *TAB*—This is the default MapInfo format.
- *MIF/MID*—These are MapInfo interchange formats that MapInfo can export to and maintain most of the functionality of the default TAB format.
- *SpatiaLite*—This is the spatial database extender for SQLite. It builds on GEOS and PROJ and extends SQLite similar to the way PostGIS builds on GEOS and PROJ and extends PostgreSQL. Think of SpatiaLite as a lightweight single-file PostGIS.
- *Esri Personal GeoDatabase*—This is the old geodatabase format from Esri, which is an extension of the MS Access database format. This is not to be confused with Esri's newer Personal File format.
- *Esri Personal File*—This relatively new storage format has only recently garnered support via the OGR/GDAL library. To our knowledge, only QGIS (if compiled with OGR/GDAL 1.10+) and the commercial tools Esri ArcGIS and Safe FME support this newer file-storage format.

Table 5.4 lists the various raster formats supported by these tools. We didn't investigate their editing and exporting capabilities, so a *Yes* here means that it can render or export the format. A *Yes** means it can render or export that format with an extra downloadable plug-in.

Table 5.4 Raster file data formats

Format	OpenJUMP	QGIS	uDig	gvSIG
JPG	Yes	Yes	Yes	Yes
TIFF	Yes	Yes	Yes	Yes
ECW	Yes*	Yes	Yes*	No
PNG	Yes	Yes	No	Yes
MrSID	Yes*	Yes	No	No

5.1.4 Web services supported

Table 5.5 lists the common OGC web services and the support each tool has for them. We didn't test any of these, so this is based purely on literature or menu items. *Yes* means built-in support, and *Yes** means the support requires an additional downloadable plug-in.

Table 5.5 Web services support

Format	OpenJUMP	QGIS	uDig	gvSIG
WMS	Yes*	Yes	Yes	Yes
WFS	Yes*	Yes	Yes	Yes
WFS-T	Yes*	No	Yes	No
WPS	Yes*	No	Yes	No
WCS	No	No	No	Yes

Following is a brief description of what these different web services are designed for:

- *WMS (Web Mapping Service)*—This is the oldest and most common of these services. It allows you to make requests for image data based on layer names and bounding regions using the `GetMap` method. It also has a simple `GetFeatureInfo` call that can retrieve already-formatted text information.
- *WFS (Web Feature Service)*—This web service generally returns vector-formatted data based on a web query. The standard format is Geography Markup Language (GML). There are also WFS service providers that return other formats, such as KML and GeoJSON.
- *WFS-T (Web Feature Service Transactional)*—This is an extension of the standard WFS protocol that allows for editing geometries across the web via vector formats such as GML or WKT.
- *WPS (Web Processing Service)*—This is the OGC GIS web service protocol for exposing generic work processes. Key parts are `DescribeProcess`, `GetCapabilities`, and `Execute` (`Execute` takes a named process with arguments and executes it).
- *WCS (Web Coverage Service)*—This is the OGC GIS web service protocol for raster coverage and the like.

Now that you have a basic sense of the possibilities of each program, we'll take them for a test drive. Note that in each of these tools, you can get the full extent of a layer (a geometry column in PostGIS terminology) by right-clicking the layer and choosing Zoom To Layer. This is pretty consistent across them all.

5.2 OpenJUMP workbench

OpenJUMP is a Java-based, cross-platform, open source GIS analysis and query tool. It's rich in functions for statistical analysis and geometry processing. It works well with Esri shapefiles, PostGIS data stores, and numerous other data formats. We've found it to be an excellent option for composing ad hoc spatial queries and viewing the rendered results immediately. Its cartography offering is adequate, but nothing to write home about. OpenJUMP is speedy when it comes to editing geometries, but it lags somewhat when it comes to cartography tasks such as printing.

Under the hood, OpenJUMP is powered by the Java Topology Suite (JTS) engine. JTS is the Javanese parent of the Geometry Engine Open Source (GEOS) library, the very library that serves as the foundation of PostGIS. Because JTS leads GEOS in the timing of new releases, you'll find that many new features will appear in OpenJUMP before they become available in PostGIS.

In the sections that follow, we'll continue to expound on the prowess of OpenJUMP, go through setup procedures, detail useful plug-ins, and demonstrate some sample uses.

5.2.1 OpenJUMP feature summary

OpenJUMP is our tool of choice for rendering PostGIS geometries. In fact, we used OpenJUMP to generate most of the geometry figures you see in this book. It has a small download size, provided you have Java Virtual Machine (JVM) already running. Its analytical tools for processing geometries are easy to use, letting you speed through tasks such as performing unions, fixing faulty geometries, and getting stats. For Python aficionados, OpenJUMP sports a Jython scripting and plug-in framework.

We absolutely love OpenJUMP's ad hoc query tool. We can write any SQL query and see our geometry output without fuss. Other tools only allow you to pick tables for display with some filtering capability, which means you have to compose your SQL in PostgreSQL, save the output to a table or the SQL to a view, and then return to the tool to poll the table or view. This back-and-forth really slows us down when we're writing many exploratory queries at once to better understand the data.

INSTALLING OPENJUMP

Installing OpenJUMP is a cinch: extract the zip file and launch the executable. OpenJUMP doesn't package its own JVM like uDig and gvSIG do, so the download is small, but you must have a JVM ready.

You can get a copy of OpenJUMP at the website: www.OpenJUMP.org/.

EASE OF USE

We ranked OpenJUMP behind QGIS in terms of ease of use. Although OpenJUMP has facilities to create new tables, we found it to be a bit quirky. You can't transform between SRIDs without additional plug-ins.

Perhaps the biggest disappointment is that our beloved ad hoc query tool can't handle `geography`, `raster`, or `topology` data types. As a workaround, you can first cast to geometry (PostGIS allows direct casting from geography and topology to geometry), but not being able to display rasters is a big drawback. For output in rasters, we turn to QGIS.

PLUG-INS

OpenJUMP supports plug-ins, extensions, and registries:

- A *plug-in* is a Java archive file (JAR) that you drop in the lib or lib/ext directory of your OpenJUMP install. The plug-ins could be additional database drivers, geometry functions, and so on.
- An *extension* manages a set of plug-ins to accomplish a particular workflow, and it manages the installation and configuration of plug-ins. Extensions come as JAR files or Python or BeanShell scripts. You would also place these in the lib/ext directory.
- A *registry* is nothing more than a dictionary of what's available in an extension.

SCRIPTING

In addition to adding new JARs, you can enhance OpenJUMP using BeanShell and Jython scripting. Place your own scripts and Python classes in either the BeanTools or Jython subdirectory under the lib/ext directory in the OpenJUMP install.

FORMAT SUPPORT

To load a supported vector file, right-click on the workspace and select the Load Dataset option or use the File > Open menu option. To load a raster file, use the File > Open File menu option. To load a spatial database layer, use the Load Data Store or Ad Hoc Query tools.

OpenJUMP can open the following vector formats: GML, JML, Esri shapefile, WKT, and PostGIS. You can save your work to the following vector formats: Scalable Vector Graphics (SVG), Esri shapefile, and GML. You can save to the following raster formats: GIF, TIFF, JPG, and PNG.

With additional plug-ins, you'll find support for MrSID, MIF, ArcSDE, Oracle, GPX, and Excel. Be sure to visit http://sourceforge.net/apps/mediawiki/jump-pilot/index.php?title=Plugins_for_OpenJUMP for all the latest and greatest OpenJUMP plug-ins.

5.2.2 PostGIS support

OpenJUMP has good support for PostGIS. It has two key features:

- *Heterogeneous column*—OpenJUMP is capable of rendering a heterogeneous column of geometries in Add Data Store mode as well as Ad Hoc Query mode, and treats it like a single layer.
- *SQL queries*—OpenJUMP, via its Layer > Run Datastore Query menu option, allows you to type in freehand SQL statements and view them. The only restriction is that the ad hoc query must have at least one geometry column. If more than one geometry column is output, then the first geometry column is rendered.

5.2.3 Register data source

OpenJUMP maintains a list of data sources you can connect to, but you must register these prior to using them. You register a data source by using the OpenJUMP Connection Manager.

Drivers used by data sources

Behind the scenes, OpenJUMP uses JDBC drivers to connect to databases. The latest version of OpenJUMP installs with PostgreSQL 9.3 JDBC drivers. If you live on the bleeding edge and want the 9.4 drivers, swap out the packaged drivers using these simple steps:

- Download the latest PostgreSQL JDBC3 driver from http://jdbc.postgresql.org/download.html.
- Copy the PostgreSQL JDBC driver into your OpenJUMP lib directory and delete the version that's there. The driver filename usually begins with the word *postgresql*.

There are several ways to get to the Connection Manager. Here's one:

1. Select Layer > Run Data Store Query from the menu.
2. Click the database icon next to the connection drop-down list (see figure 5.1) to open the Connection Manager (figure 5.2) and click Add.

Figure 5.1 OpenJUMP drop-down list for database connections

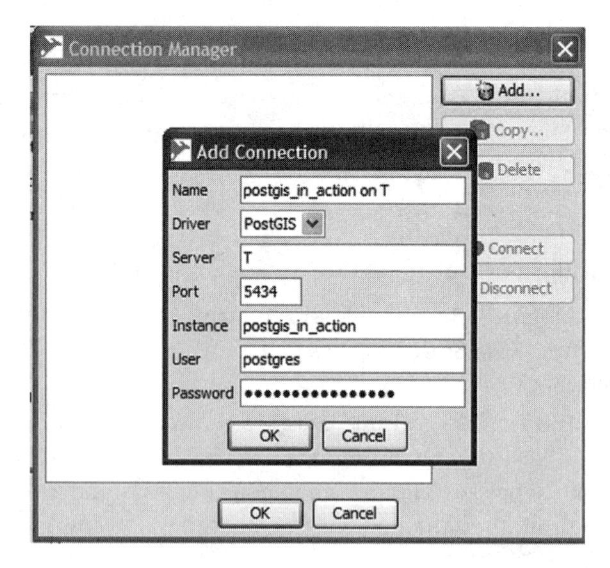

Figure 5.2 Adding a new PostGIS database connection

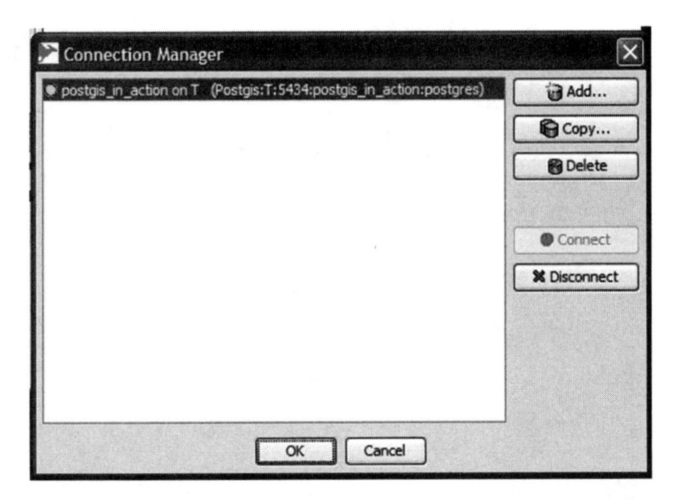

Figure 5.3 OpenJUMP Connection Manager with a new connection

Enter the name you want for the connection, the database name (in the Instance field), and all other relevant information. Then click OK.

Once you've successfully added the connection, you should see it in your Connection Manager list with a green dot at the left (see figure 5.3). Should you end up with a red dot, delete the connection and try again.

One annoyance with OpenJump is that you can't edit connections. You can, however, copy an existing connection, which gives you a screen to edit the values, and you can then save that edited connection under a new name.

5.2.4 Rendering PostGIS geometries

The Add DataStore Layer dialog box is the quickest way to render data that's stored in an existing geometry column. To get to this dialog box, right-click Working and choose Open > Data Store Layer (see figure 5.4).

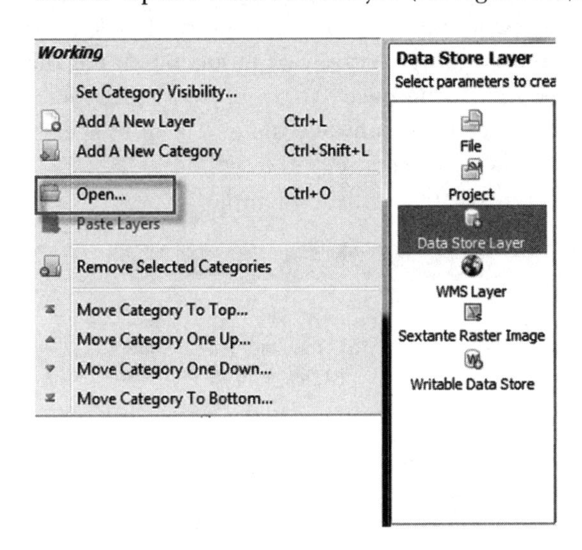

Figure 5.4 Adding a PostGIS table in OpenJUMP

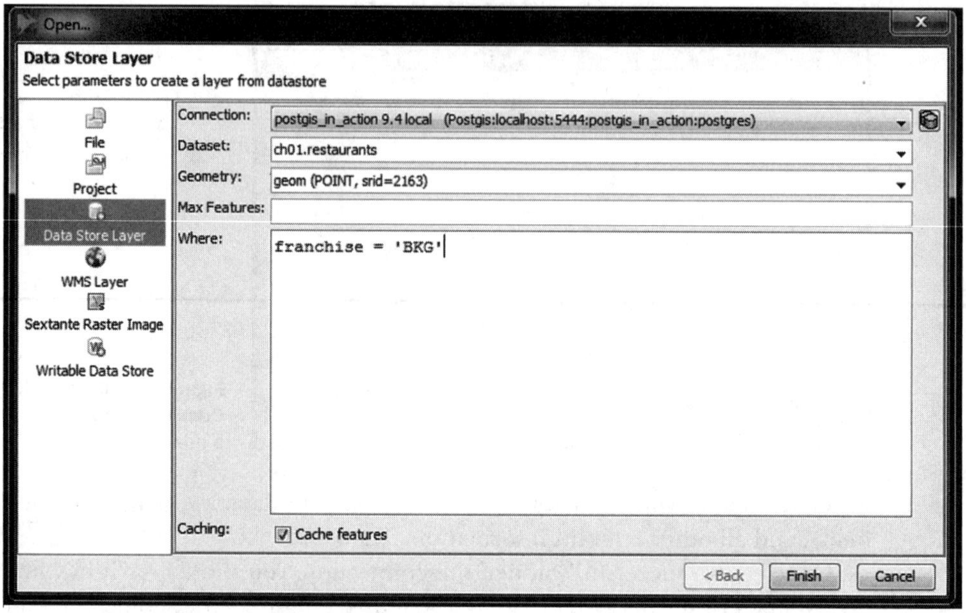

Figure 5.5 Datastore layer setup in OpenJUMP

Select a connection, and then a table and the geometry column you want to display. You can filter the data with an optional WHERE clause (see figure 5.5). Then click OK.

If nothing appears on the main display window after you click OK, select the layer, right-click, and choose Zoom to Layer. OpenJUMP is finicky in that it considers the extent (the area that fully contains all the data) to always be the extent of all records in the table, even when a WHERE clause has shrunk the extent.

To display the result of an ad hoc query, select File > (SQL) Run Data Source Query from the menu. This will present a window where you can copy in a full SQL statement.

If you want to display a query that has geography or topogeometry as the spatial type, you'll need to cast to `geometry` using `geog::geometry or topo::geometry` as part of your SQL statement. You're free to use any SQL statement or to access custom objects you've created in the database you're connected to.

The following listing demonstrates with an artistic example.

Listing 5.1 Abstract SQL art

```
SELECT art.n, art.geom
FROM (
    SELECT
        n,
        ST_Translate(
            ST_Buffer(
                ST_MakeLine(pt), mod(n,6) + 2,
```

ST_Translate moves buffered line randomly up and down

ST_Makeline creates line from random set of points

```
                'endcap=' || endcaps[mod(n,3) + 1] || ' join=' ||
                joins[mod(n,array_upper(joins,1)) + 1] ||
                ' quad_segs=' || n
            ),
        n*10,n*random()*pi()
    ) As geom
FROM (
    SELECT ceiling(random()*100)::integer As n,
        ARRAY['square', 'round', 'flat'] As endcaps,
        ARRAY['round','mitre','bevel'] As joins,
        ST_Point(x*random(),y*random()) As pt
    FROM generate_series(1,200, 7) As x
        CROSS JOIN generate_series(1,500,20) As y
) As foo
GROUP BY foo.n, foo.endcaps, foo.joins
HAVING count(foo.n) > 10) As art;
```

ST_Buffer converts linestring to polygon

The result of the query changes each time you run it.

To apply styles in OpenJUMP, right-click a layer and choose Change Styles > Enable Color Theming. Figure 5.6 shows the output of one run of the query after applying styles.

Figure 5.6 SQL art after applying custom styles

5.2.5 *Exporting data*

OpenJUMP comes with basic import and export capabilities to save files in Esri, GML, WKT, raster, and SVG formats. By installing additional plug-ins, you can export to AutoCAD DXF and print to PDF. Visit http://sourceforge.net/projects/jump-pilot/files for the plug-ins. To export a layer, right-click the layer and choose Save Dataset As. To save the current view to PNG or JPG, select File > Save View As Raster from the menu.

In this section, we've given you a taste of what OpenJUMP offers. We encourage you to explore the plug-ins available for it. You'll find plug-ins that enable WFS, ArcSDE, JGrass, printing, and exporting to many formats. OpenJUMP also has a Jython scripting environment that allows you to write custom plug-ins in Python. We encourage you to explore all these features. In the next section, we'll take a look at QGIS.

5.3 QGIS

QGIS, formerly Quantum GIS, is a free and open source desktop GIS viewing, editing, and analysis tool. Its polished and intuitive interface makes it well suited for GIS novices. QGIS also has a devoted Python and GRASS following. Unlike the other tools we're reviewing, it's not based on Java. Instead, it's built on the Qt framework, a C/C++ cross-platform windowing framework.

What makes QGIS stand out from the pack is its high level of integration with GRASS, its extensive support for rasters, its integration with the OGR/GDAL suite, and its native Python scripting framework. Finally, perhaps the most appealing aspect of QGIS is the user-friendly interface. With the other tools, we often have to second-guess the UI; with QGIS, everything is nicely organized and we find ourselves not having to question whether we're missing a key feature simply because we're unfamiliar with its navigation.

We ranked QGIS as Easy in ease of use because of its tight integration with data tables. With the QGIS interface, you can add tables, edit rows, and filter rows. We particularly like the feature where you can highlight a data row and QGIS will automatically zoom to the corresponding area of the viewing window. One slight annoyance is QGIS's insistence on having a unique key from the table that's an integer, with no characters.

Because QGIS is so intuitively organized, you probably shouldn't need to peruse the 300-plus-page manual, but if you do, you'll find that it comes in many languages and is quite helpful.

5.3.1 Installing QGIS

Installing QGIS is straightforward. QGIS sometimes prompts for a reboot after install, but because QGIS doesn't rely on Java, you avoid the nuisance of installing and updating the Java runtime. You can download QGIS from this link: www.qgis.org/en/download/current-software.html. Both 32-bit and 64-bit flavors are available for most operating systems.

QGIS is part of the OSGeo4W suite, so you can choose instead to install OSGeo4W, which will give you QGIS along with a bevy of GIS-related tools. You can find OSGeo4W here: http://trac.osgeo.org/osgeo4w.

5.3.2 Using QGIS with PostGIS

QGIS matured alongside PostGIS, so QGIS's spatial database support for PostGIS has been time-tested more than any of the other spatial databases it supports. The PostGIS `geometry` type support in QGIS is stronger than its support for other PostGIS spatial types. QGIS has always been first to jump on board to support new PostGIS spatial features, and as such its PostGIS raster and topology support is stronger than you'll find in most other desktop products.

Although the QGIS menu options suggest it now supports the PostGIS `geography` data type, we were disappointed when our geography layer didn't load. On scrutinizing the logs, we found that the query call to PostGIS that was generated is invalid when using the PostGIS Add Layer menu option, but if you use the Add Vector Layer menu option, geographies display flawlessly.

Two plug-ins are available to enable QGIS to work with PostGIS topogeometries: *DB Manager TopoViewer* and *PostGIS Topology Editor*, though the latter is still in the experimental stage. PostGIS raster viewing is available via the *DB Manager* plug-in. For pgRouting, look for the *pgRouting Layer* plug-in. You can install most extensions with a single-click from the extensions menu option. Popular extensions like DB Manager may already be installed during setup.

Adding a PostGIS connection

Adding a PostGIS geometry connection in QGIS is easy. There are two common ways of doing it. Start by going to the Layer menu highlighted in figure 5.7 and select Add Layer > Add PostGIS Layer > New. Alternatively you can create a connection from the Browser pane by right-clicking on PostGIS and choosing the New Connection option, also highlighted in figure 5.7.

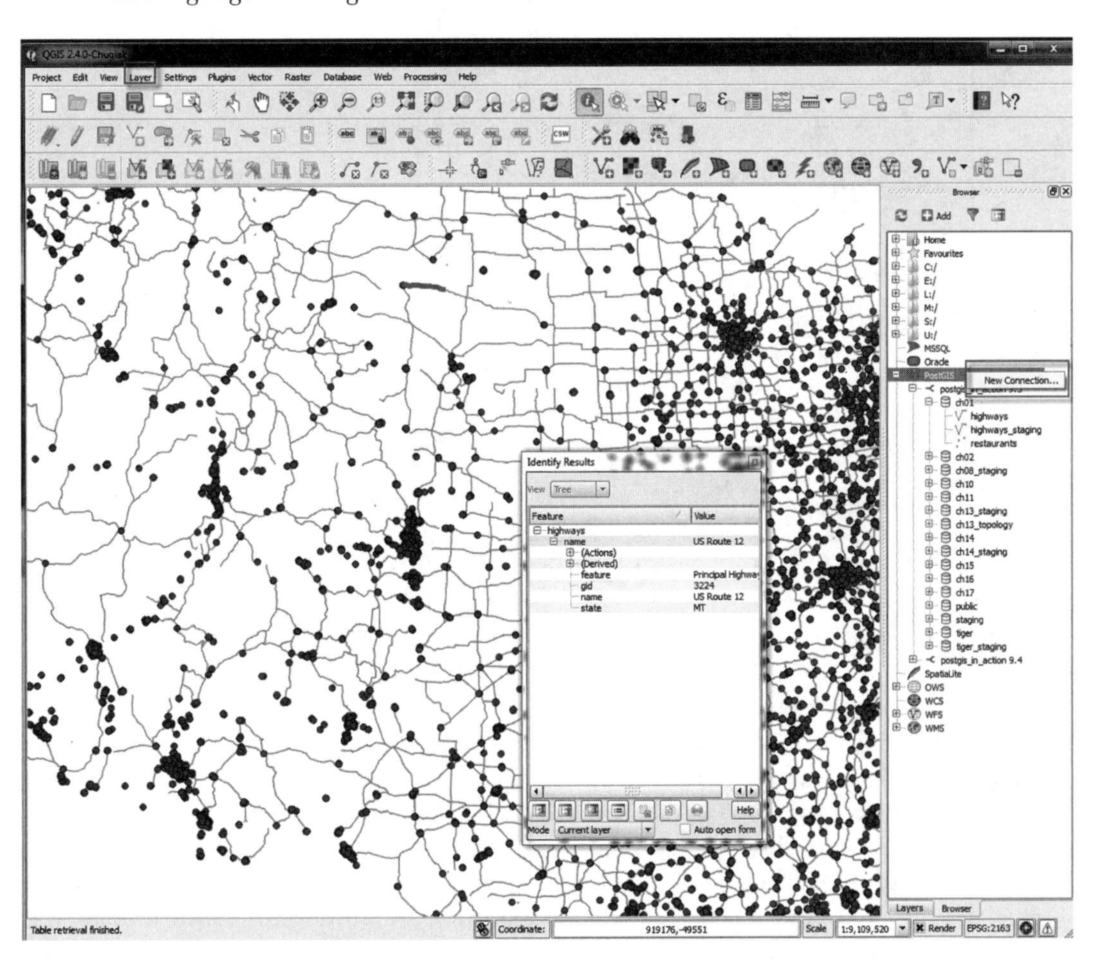

Figure 5.7 Adding a geometry vector layer and PostGIS connection in QGIS

Figure 5.8 shows the QGIS PostGIS connection dialog box you get after clicking New in the Layer menu or New Connection from the Browser pane. You'll get better load speeds for large tables if you check the Use Estimated Table Metadata check box. The drawback is that if your table stats are out of date, you may end up with weird results, like the QGIS viewport not fully containing the extent of your data. The other drawback is that the metadata may be incomplete. For example, if you have a mixed geometry type column that contains both points and linestrings, it may arbitrarily assume the table consists of all one or the other.

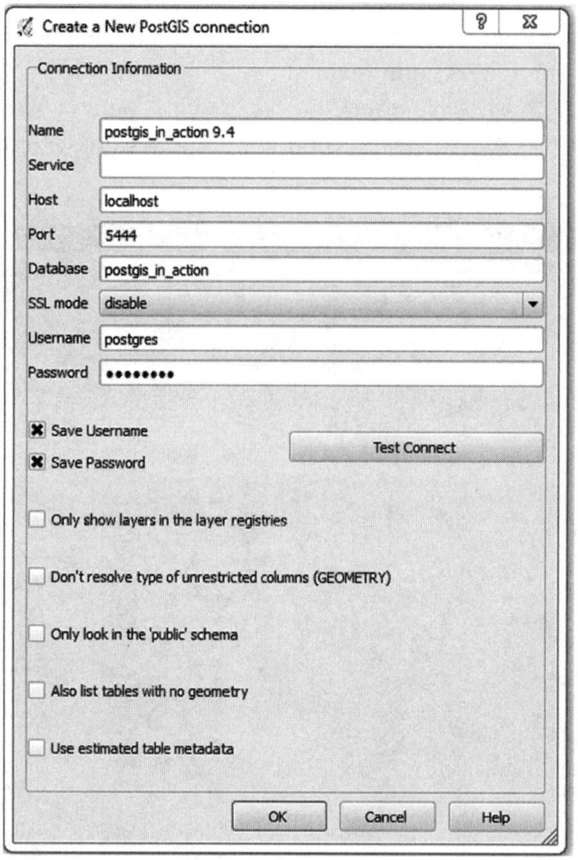

Figure 5.8 Adding a PostGIS connection in QGIS

VIEWING AND FILTERING POSTGIS DATA

When using the Layer > Add PostGIS Layer menu option, you get the QGIS dialog box for adding new tables. This dialog box displays each geometry column with a stylized icon. If a geometry field has more than one kind of geometry, QGIS lists each type as a separate layer, as shown in figure 5.9.

Once you pick a column, you can use a query builder to apply a filter to control the rows retrieved by clicking Set Filter (shown in figure 5.9), which displays the screen shown in figure 5.10. After you're done setting the filter for a column, click OK. This will bring you back to the screen shown in figure 5.9.

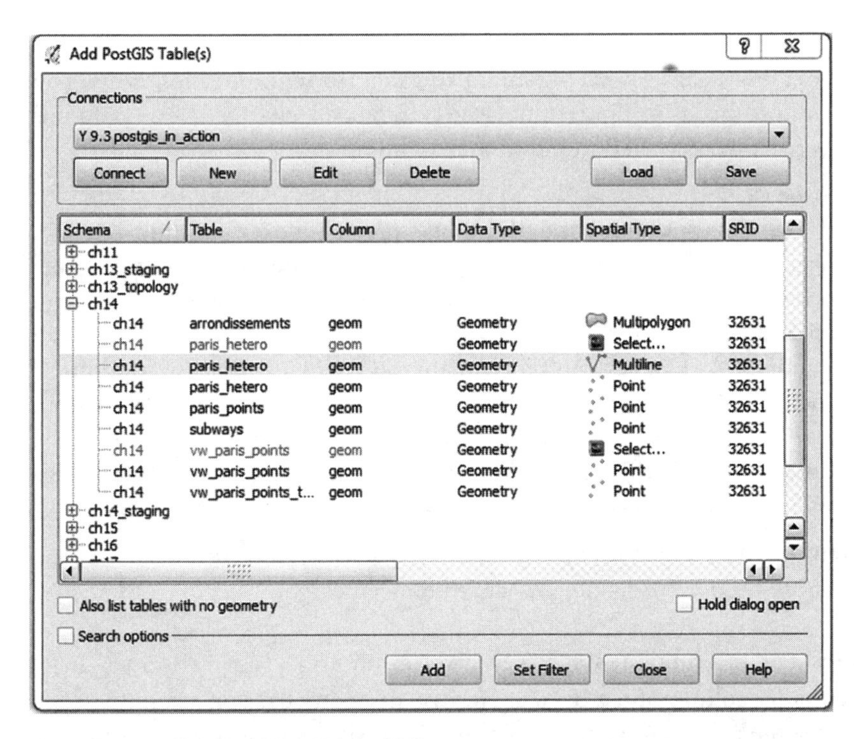

Figure 5.9 Adding PostGIS tables in QGIS

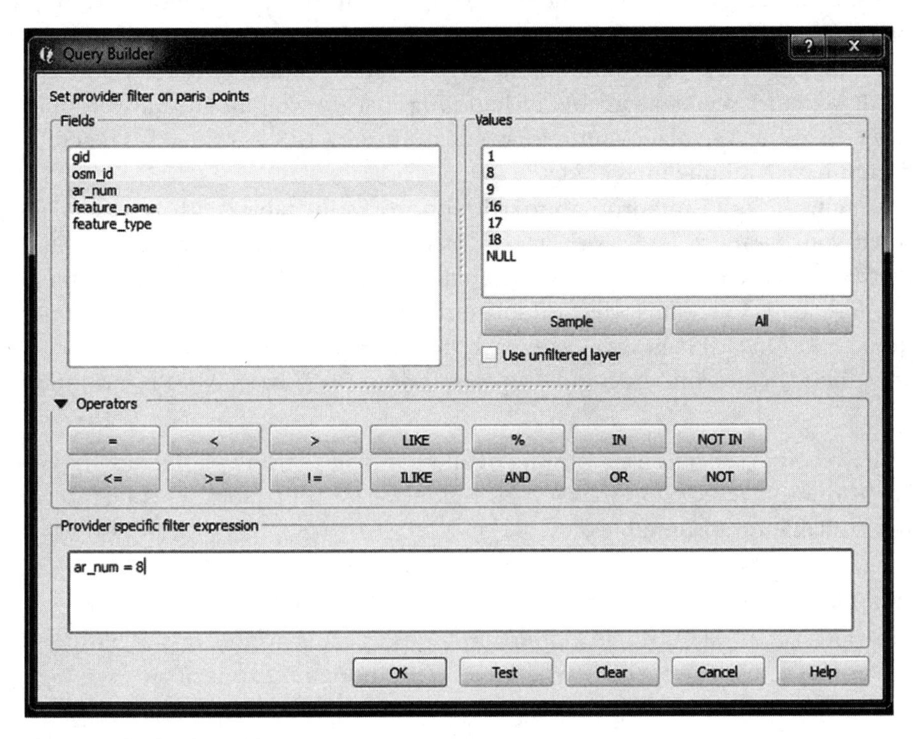

Figure 5.10 Setting a filter

You can click Set Filter again for each column you want to set a filter for. When you click the Add button shown in figure 5.9, QGIS adds all selected geometry columns with their respective filters applied to the viewport.

USING THE DB MANAGER

More-advanced PostGIS users may find the QGIS query building limiting. Luckily, QGIS's DB Manager plug-in lets you write ad hoc queries. In newer versions of QGIS, DB Manager appears to be installed by default, but if you don't see it in your install, go to the Plugins > Manage And Install Plugins menu option to install it. Once it's in place, you can launch DB Manager from the Database > DB Manager menu option.

You can launch DB Manager's SQL window by selecting Database > SQL Window in the main DB Manager window. Figure 5.11 shows the DB Manager window with the SQL window popped open. In this window you can write any query for QGIS to render as long as you abide by some rules:

- Make sure you have one and only one geometry column in your output.
- If you want to render `geography` or `raster` data types, you have to cast to `geometry`.
- You must include a unique integer key in your output.
- Your geometry column must be a single type of geometry. For example, a column with some rows that have points and others with polygons won't work.

If you'd like to see an entire table rendered, you can skip the SQL window and drag and drop tables with a geometry column directly from the DB Manager to the main QGIS map window. But if the column is heterogeneous, containing more than one subtype, DB Manager seems incapable of handling it. We recommend that you only add tables with a single spatial column to avoid confusing QGIS or yourself. The table you add must have a unique integer key.

Surprisingly, the drag-and-drop approach also works for tables with a raster column, but if your raster is large, we suggest that you have accompanying overview tables—QGIS is smart enough to take advantage of them and speed up loading. Another approach is to create a view to isolate the area of interest. All in all, we find that raster support in QGIS improves with each successive release.

Besides the SQL and the drag-and-drop rendering, DB Manager has a few more talents:

- It allows you to see a tree-view listing of all your tables with the ability to browse the attribute data and preview a map rendering of your table. This feature is also available for raster tables.
- It has a PostGIS topology viewer accessible from the DB Manager's Schema > TopoViewer menu option.
- You can use DB Manager to import and export data in and out of PostGIS. Access this via the Table menu option, or the import and export icon.

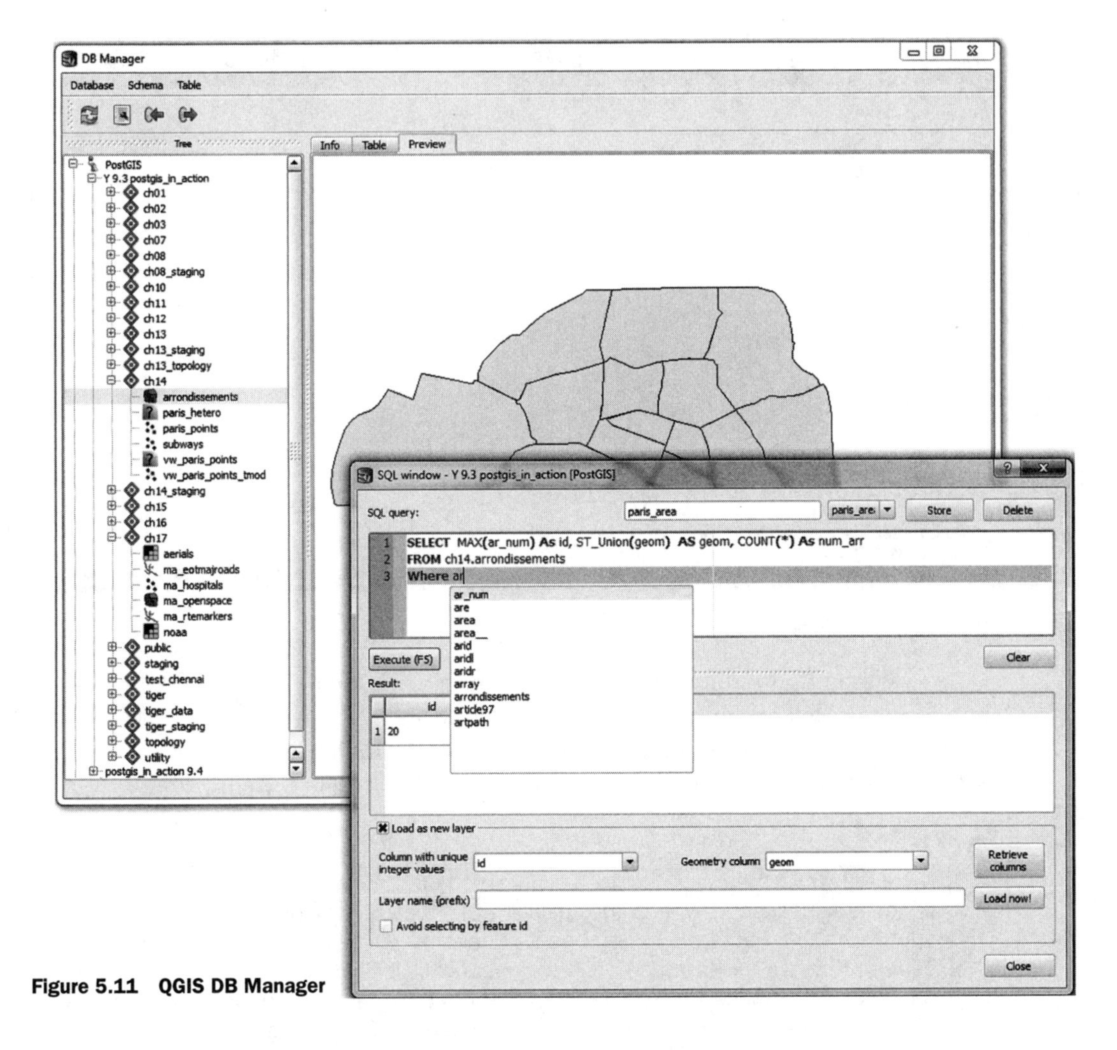

Figure 5.11 QGIS DB Manager

- You can perform database administration tasks like deleting tables, creating new schemas, and so on.
- The SQL window has syntax coloring and type-ahead where table names will drop down for you to pick.
- It has a versioning feature that will add triggers to tables you specify for tracking changes.

5.3.3 *Importing and exporting layers*

QGIS can import files in an incredible number of formats, and the list is ever-growing.

To import a vector file, choose Layer > Add Vector Layer > File Or Directory; you'll be amazed at the number of file types available, as shown in figure 5.12.

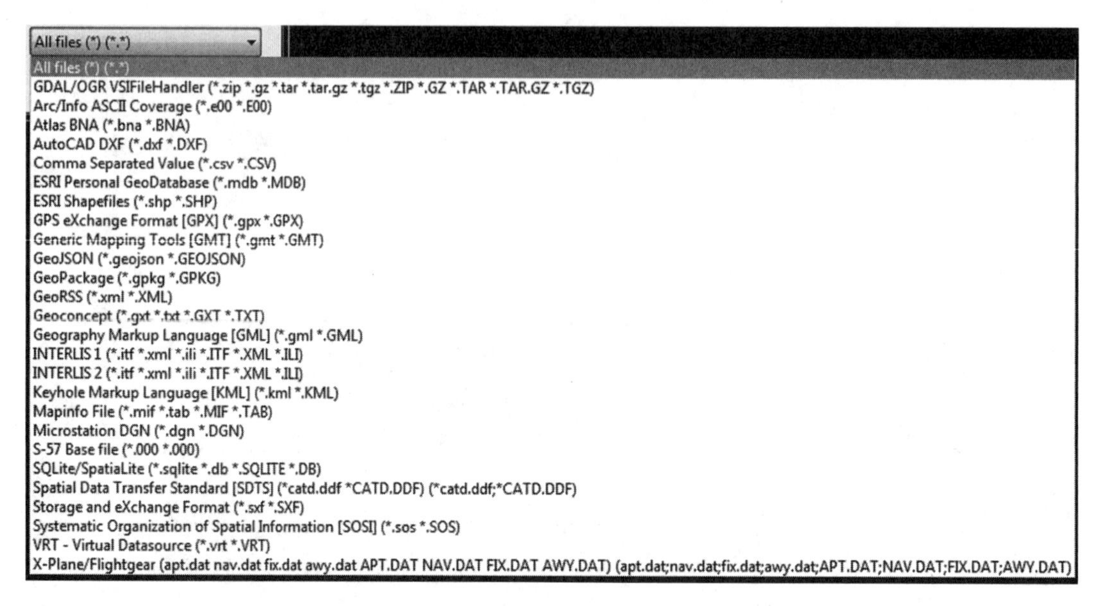

Figure 5.12 QGIS vector file sampling

QGIS can also import a number of raster formats; we last counted 15. Installing additional plug-ins will encompass even more raster formats.

Exporting layers to other file formats is just as easy. Right-click on a layer and select Save Vector Layer As. You'll have a choice of over 10 different formats.

> **QGIS SPIT**
>
> QGIS comes packaged with a tool called SPIT that allows you to batch-load Esri shapefiles into a PostgreSQL database, bypassing rendering. One crippling annoyance with this tool is its automatic conversion of all field names to uppercase. In PostgreSQL, uppercase field names must be double-quoted in queries, and that's a lot of extra typing of quotes. If you're going to use SPIT, we suggest that you create a function to convert everything back to lowercase after import.

In this section, we only touched the surface of all that QGIS has to offer. We encourage you to visit the QGIS website or peruse the well-prepared user manual to learn more. Also keep in mind the growing number of plug-ins, especially for working with PostGIS rasters, PostGIS topology, and PostGIS 3D data types.

Finally, the new QGIS Server can convert your workspace to a web service. Find out more here: http://hub.qgis.org/projects/quantum-gis/wiki/QGIS_Server_Tutorial.

In the next section, we'll cover uDig, another popular GIS desktop tool.

5.4 uDig

User-friendly Desktop Internet GIS, more commonly known as uDig, shines in cartography with unrivaled tools for editing and fixing geometries. It connects with most spatial databases, both open source and commercial, without needing additional plug-ins. Although uDig does have minimal query capabilities, it's clearly geared toward outputting eye-catching presentations and being able to do it quickly.

uDig is built atop of Eclipse, a cross-platform Java framework. Because of this, uDig is extensible and easy to hack if you're a Java programmer. In fact, you can build a complete GIS desktop suite starting with uDig. One living example is JGrass, an interface to GRASS built using the uDig framework. You can tour other projects based on uDig here: http://udig.refractions.net/gallery/. uDig also supports WFS-T, so you can push edits out to any WFS-T–compliant service, such as GeoServer.

uDig stands out from the other desktop tools discussed in this chapter because it's licensed under EPL/BSD rather than GPL. EPL/BSD is much friendlier for those who want to integrate uDig into their proprietary applications.

Installing uDig is easy. The download is a hefty 200 MB, but that includes the JRE. It also has self-extract installed for both 32-bit and 64-bit Windows. uDig installation has certainly improved from earlier versions we faintly remember having struggled with many years ago. You can download a version for your OS from http://udig.refractions.net.

With the default install, uDig only supports exporting to Esri shapefile, KML, PDF, and image formats. To export, right-click a layer and choose Export.

5.4.1 Using uDig with PostGIS

uDig evolved alongside PostGIS, and as such its support for PostGIS is probably stronger and better tested than for any other spatial databases. It started life as a project of Refractions Research, the company that brought us PostGIS.

Loading a PostGIS geometry layer in uDig is easy, and this is a big improvement over prior releases. As always, data paints with amazing speed. If a table has multiple geometry columns, uDig lists them as separate layers, but it didn't display the geometry column we chose. It seemed to display the first geometry column of a table.

uDig can't handle heterogeneous geometry columns. It allowed us to pick a column with mixed subtypes, but it was never able to display it.

Although uDig allows you to write queries, uDig doesn't understand SQL. Instead, you have to resort to a more obscure web query standard called Common Query Language (CQL).

CQL As of version 1.2, CQL renamed itself Contextual Query Language. You can learn more about CQL on Wikipedia at http://en.wikipedia.org/wiki/Contextual_Query_Language.

5.4.2 Connecting to PostGIS

uDig has the easiest interface for connecting to PostGIS. Choose Layer > Add from the menu, and PostGIS appears as a data source (shown at the left in figure 5.13).

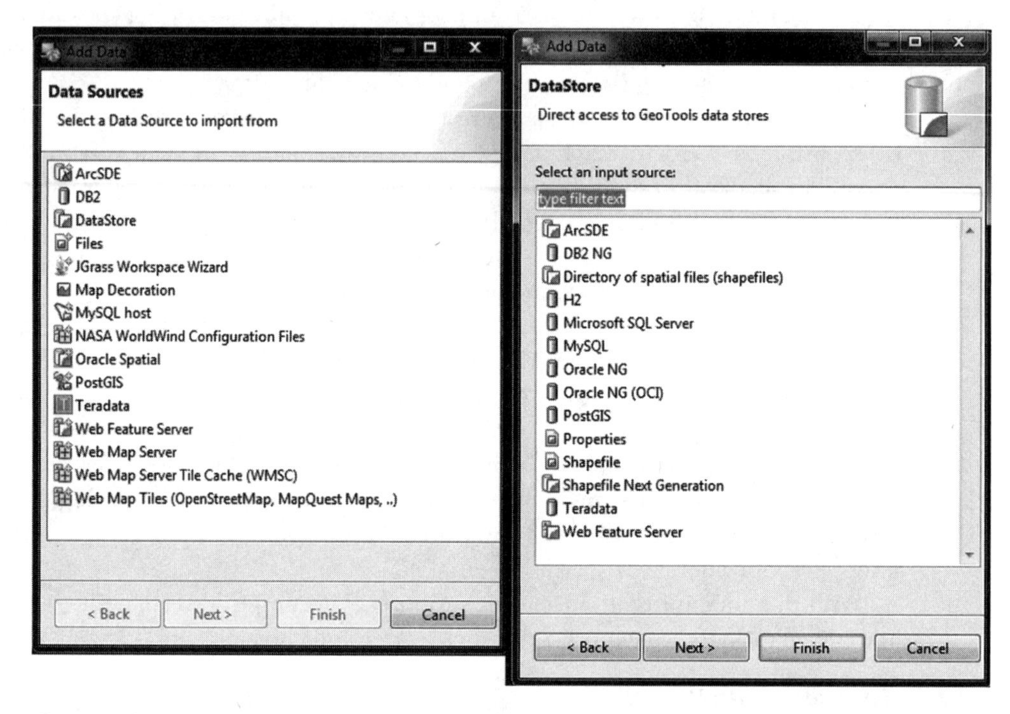

Figure 5.13 Adding database connections in uDig

You can alternatively use the GeoTools built into uDig to connect. Instead of choosing PostGIS, click on DataStore. Another window will pop up listing data stores supported by GeoTools (shown at the right in figure 5.13).

5.4.3 Viewing and filtering PostGIS data

You can filter data using CQL or by using a rudimentary query builder. We found both approaches to be cumbersome, to say nothing of having to contend with CQL. One design flaw we see in uDig is that it first pulls all the data before letting you apply a filter, so if you need only one row in a million, you face an unnecessary wait. The only positive aspect of the preloading is that you'll see the full extent of your data, and uDIG will then highlight the filtered area, as shown in figure 5.14.

CQL does follow SQL conventions, but it offers only a subset of what you can do in SQL. To use CQL, do the following:

1. Add your PostGIS layer.
2. Right-click the layer, and zoom to the layer.
3. Choose the Table tab. Select CQL from the drop-down list, and type in your CQL statement.

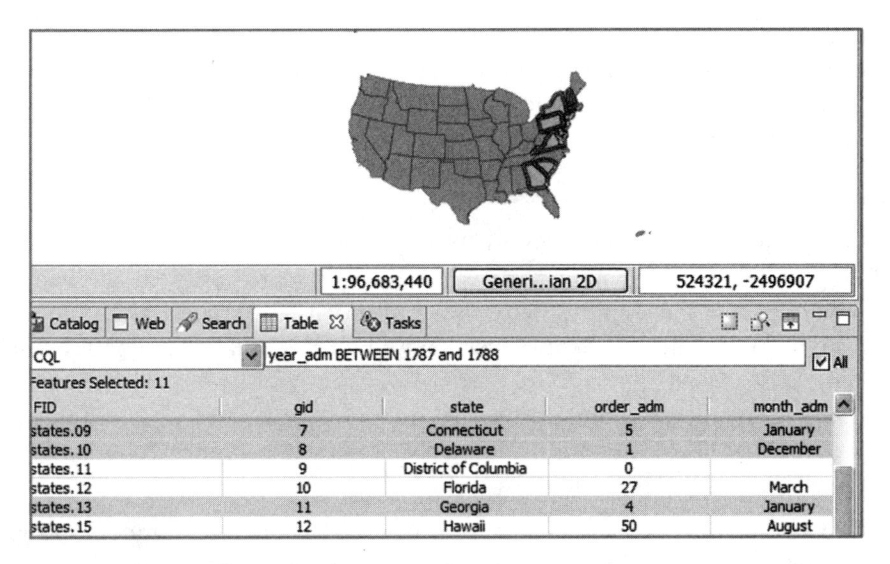

Figure 5.14 Using CQL for filtering data in uDig

From the table tab, you can directly edit textual fields. From the map view (visible in figure 5.14) you can edit geometry fields.

We can't say we're impressed with uDig's support for PostGIS functionality, but uDig does live up to its claim of being a professional cartography tool. uDig has more support for web mapping services than other tools we tested. Finally, its liberal licensing model makes it enticing for developing commercial products.

5.5 gvSIG

gvSIG is an open source desktop GIS tool largely funded by the government of Spain to replace ArcGIS desktop. As a result, you may find that much of the layout, workflow, and idioms in ArcGIS carried over to gvSIG. gvSIG got its start later than the other tools, so gvSIG developers took advantage of the advances in desktop hardware to make gvSIG outperform the rest of the pack.

gvSIG also offers a mobile version geared toward surveyors in the field. We didn't test this version, but we assume it would be similar to ArcGIS ArcPad.

gvSIG is built on top of Java and uses the JAI framework for advanced imaging. It doesn't use Eclipse but has its own Eclipse-like framework, should you wish to extend the base functionality. Like other tools, gvSIG is both a desktop tool and an extensible mapping platform that will let you code your own extensions in Java. All extensions reside in the bin/gvSIG/extensions directory. Each extension gets its own subdirectory and consists of a single JAR file, various language configuration files, and an XML configuration file. In addition to supporting extensions via Java programming, you can also script in Jython.

The process of installing gvSIG is much improved from prior versions. It's still a hefty download, weighing in at around 260 MB with a JVM, but the installation finishes in under ten minutes. One downside is that it runs in a 32-bit JVM, so it won't take full advantage of a 64-bit OS. If you're running on Linux 64-bit or Mac OS X without a 32-bit JVM, you may encounter some issues: http://blog.gvsig.org/2014/03/25/running-gvsig-in-hardwares-with-linux-64-bits/.

5.5.1 Using gvSIG with PostGIS

Figuring out how to connect to PostGIS and render a table was not all that intuitive. After exploring all the menu options, we finally had to resort to the manual and study it for some ten minutes before we succeeded. Fortunately, the PDF manual is thorough, and besides the Spanish version we found translations to both English and Italian.

gvSIG is organized around documents. To add PostGIS data, you must first create a view document. Once you've established a view document, you're free to add as many layers as you like. Follow these steps:

1. Create a new view document from the Project Manager window and give it a name (we used *PostGIS Test* for this example), as shown in figure 5.15.

Figure 5.15 Project manager window in gvSIG

2 Click Open and select View > Add Layer. Switch to the GeoDB tab and click Connect to create a new PostGIS connection, as shown in figure 5.16.

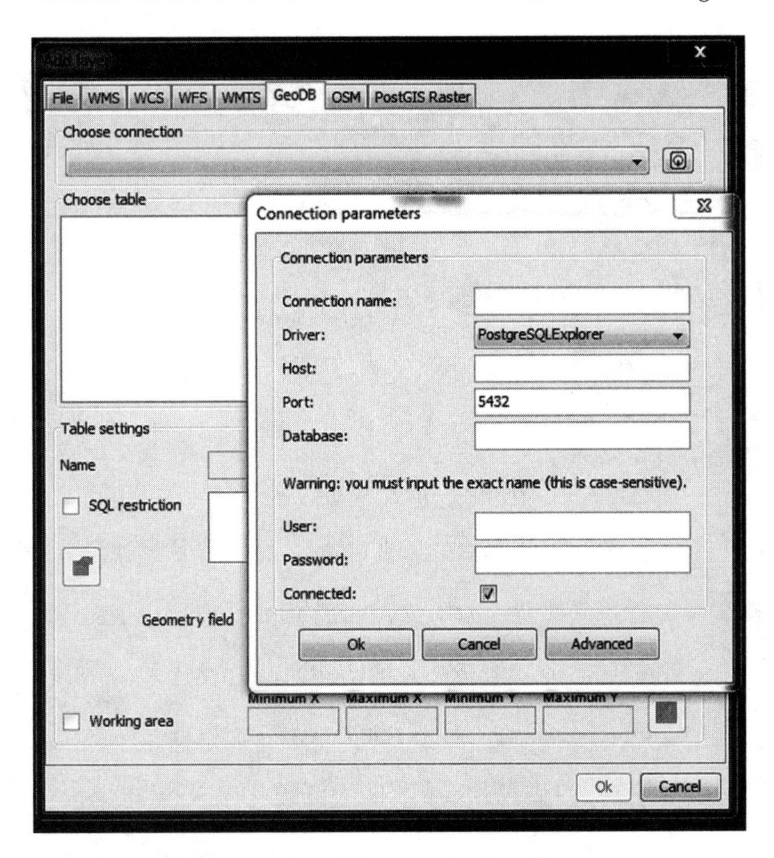

Figure 5.16 Adding a new PostGIS connection in gvSIG

3 Fill in all the connection information and click OK. Then select the connection and the tables you want to add, and fill in the parameters for each, as shown in figure 5.17.

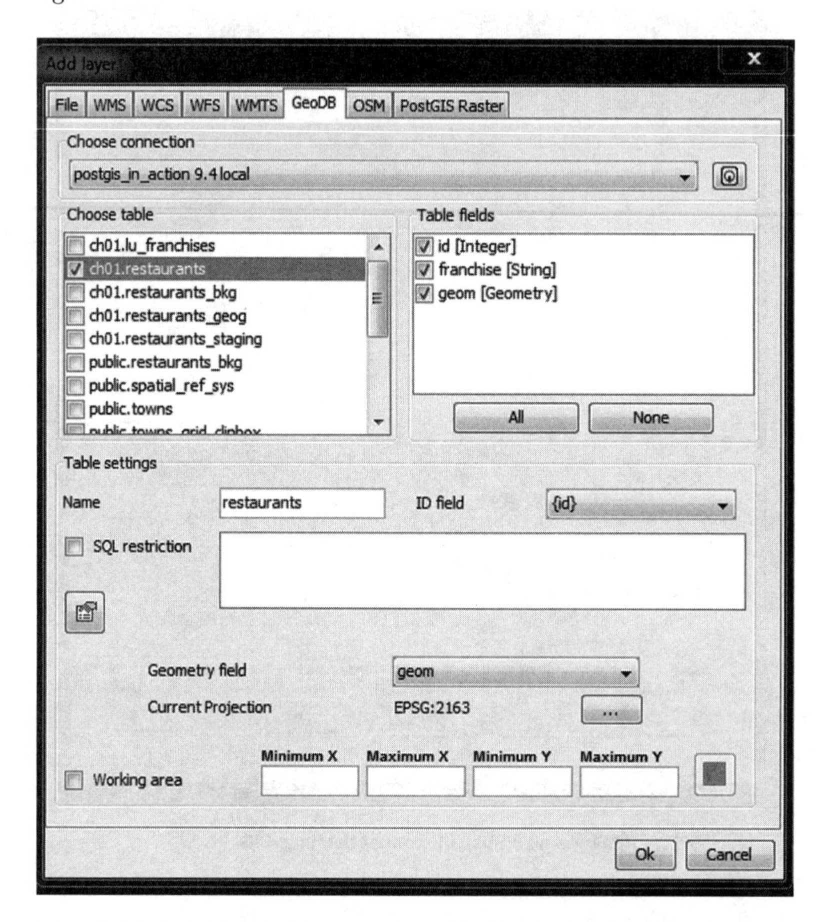

Figure 5.17 Selecting PostGIS layers in gvSIGSelecting PostGIS layers in gvSIG

You can filter rows by typing in a SQL `WHERE` clause, but that's the extent of the SQL at your disposal.

gvSIG can handle heterogeneous geometry columns, but not geography columns. The Add Layers dialog box listed rasters as an option, but it failed to detect all the raster columns in our PostGIS 2.1 database. Of the rasters it found, gvSIG was able to retrieve table stats for them. Sadly, we were unable to view any of the raster columns. Our suspicion is that gvSIG has yet to retool for PostGIS 2.1.

5.5.2 Exporting data

Exporting data to other formats is straightforward in gvSIG. Follow these steps:

1. Select the layer.
2. Select the Layer > Export To menu option.
3. Choose the format to export to, as shown in figure 5.18.

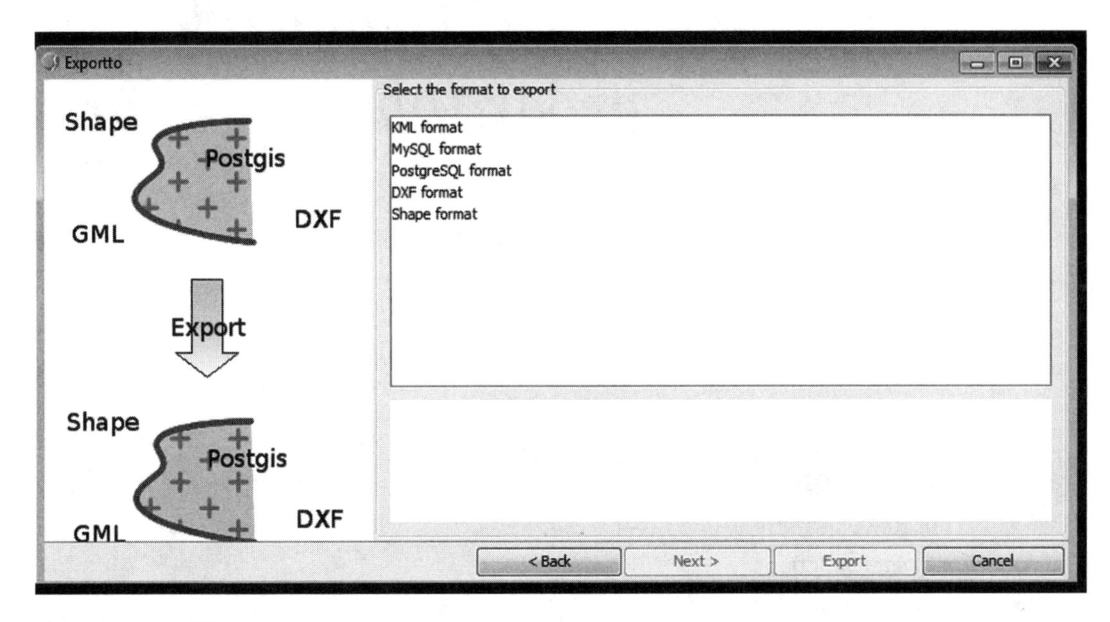

Figure 5.18 gvSIG export options

5.6 Summary

In this chapter, we covered four free, open source desktop tools that can be used to view and edit PostGIS data: OpenJUMP, QGIS, uDIG, and gvSIG. All four have varying levels of support for PostGIS. We hope that you were able to get a sense of what's offered by each of these tools and the target audience of each. Keep in mind that one single tool probably won't serve all your needs.

The pace at which these tools are developed is much faster than the pace of our writing. New features and bug fixes will inevitably invalidate some of our findings over time. We encourage you to bookmark the main site for each tool to keep up with the latest details. And don't forget the manuals—they all have excellent documentation.

In chapters that follow, we'll be using PostGIS for processing and analyzing data. The tools we discussed in this chapter will be tremendously helpful in visualizing that data. In the next chapter, we'll take a look at geometry and geography functions.

6 Geometry and geography functions

This chapter covers

- Output functions
- Constructor functions
- Accessor and setter functions
- Measurement functions
- Composition and decomposition functions
- Simplification functions

In previous chapters, we've discussed PostGIS spatial types—how to create them, and how to add them to your database. In this chapter, we'll introduce the core set of functions that work with spatial types. This chapter concentrates on functions that work with single geometries and geographies.

PostGIS offers lots of functions and operators, and in this chapter we've grouped them by intent of use. This is by no means a rigorous classification, nor one that will neatly sort each function into a unique group without ambiguity, but grouping functions by the type of tasks you're trying to accomplish is the handiest approach, in our experience. We'll refer to geometries and geographies as *spatial objects* when discussing both. This is the classification scheme we'll use:

- *Output functions*—These functions output spatial object representations in various standard formats (WKT, WKB, GML, SVG, KML, GeoJSON).
- *Constructor functions*—These functions create PostGIS spatial objects from a well-known format, such as a well-known text (WKT) format, a well-known binary (WKB) format, or Geography JavaScript Object Notation (GeoJSON).
- *Accessor and setter functions*—These functions work against a single spatial object and return or set attributes of the object.
- *Measurement functions*—These functions return scalar measurements of a spatial object.
- *Decomposition functions*—These functions extract other spatial objects from an input spatial object.
- *Composition functions*—These functions stitch, splice, or group together spatial objects.
- *Simplification functions*—Sometimes you don't need the full resolution of a spatial object. These functions, in the case of geometry and geography, return simplified representations by removing points or linestrings or by rounding the coordinates. The resultant spatial objects still have the basic look and feel of the originals but contain fewer points or elements of lower precision.

In this chapter, we'll introduce a dozen or so commonly used functions. You can find an exhaustive listing of all functions and their usage in the official PostGIS manuals at http://postgis.net/documentation.

6.1 Output functions

We'll start by looking at the various functions PostGIS provides for outputting geometries and geographies in standard formats. These functions allow PostGIS to be used with tools not designed specifically for PostGIS. Output functions return spatial objects in another industry-standard format, allowing third-party rendering tools with no knowledge of PostGIS to be used as display tools for PostGIS.

In this section, we'll summarize the output formats available, give some general usage scenarios, and discuss the PostGIS functions that output them. We'll cover some of the more popular output formats, but you should check the official PostGIS site for the ever-growing list. To learn more about the various output formats themselves, be sure to visit their own sites. We won't go into detail about the various formats.

Finally, we advise that you use good judgment when it comes to determining whether the output format makes sense for your particular geometry types. For example, if you have only known a particular function to support 2D with SRID 4326, make sure your geometries are all 2D with SRID 4326 prior to using the export function, instead of trying your luck. This will save you from having to remember how each function handles exceptions, and it will help make sure your code still works if the default handling of the output functions changes, as sometimes happens with new versions of PostGIS.

Most of the functions we'll describe support both geometry and geography as long as you have PostGIS 2.0 or higher.

6.1.1 Well-known binary (WKB) and well-known text (WKT)

Well-known text and well-known binary are the most common OGC text and binary formats for spatial objects. In fact, many spatial databases, PostGIS included, store their geometry data in a format based on the WKB standard. We've already used the WKT format quite extensively in the book to show the output of queries, because it provides a clear text representation of the underlying geometry.

Two functions that output geometries in WKT format are `ST_AsText` and `ST_AsEWKT`. Recall from earlier discussions that the `ST_AsEWKT` function is a PostGIS-specific extension loosely based on the SQL/MM and OGC SFSQL WKT standards, but it isn't considered OGC-compliant. The OGC-compliant function is `ST_AsText`, but this function won't output the SRID. In PostGIS versions prior to 2.0, it didn't output the M or Z coordinates either. Textual representations will always lack the precision of binary representations and will preserve only about 15 significant digits.

Two functions that output geometries in WKB format are `ST_AsBinary` and `ST_AsEWKB`. `ST_AsBinary` is the OGC- and SQL/MM-compliant version, whereas `ST_AsEWKB` is a PostGIS-specific version that includes the SRID.

6.1.2 Keyhole Markup Language (KML)

Keyhole Markup Language is an XML-based format created by Keyhole, Inc., to render geospatial data in its applications. KML gained enormous popularity after Google acquired Keyhole and integrated KML into Google Maps and Google Earth. OGC accepted KML as a standard transport format in its own right.

The PostGIS geometry and geography function for exporting to KML is called `ST_AsKML`. The default output is KML version 2 with 15-digit precision. `ST_AsKML` isn't one function, but several with the same name that take different arguments. Other variants of the function allow you to change the target KML version and level of precision.

The spatial reference system (SRS) for KML is always WGS 84 lon/lat (SRID 4326). As long as your geometry is in a known SRID (present in the spatial_ref_sys table), `ST_AsKML` will automatically convert it to SRID 4326 for you.

`ST_AsKML` supports both 2D and 3D basic geometries but will throw an error when exporting curved geometries, geometry collections, polyhedral surfaces, or TINs (triangular irregular networks). Also keep in mind that although `ST_AsKML` will accept geometries containing an M coordinate, it won't output the M coordinate.

6.1.3 Geography Markup Language (GML)

Geography Markup Language is an XML-based format and an OGC-defined transport format for both geometry and geography types. It's commonly used in Web Feature Service (WFS) to output the columns of a query. It's also a building block of the budding CityGML standard (http://en.wikipedia.org/wiki/CityGML), used for modeling cityscapes including buildings and bridges.

The PostGIS function for exporting to GML is `ST_AsGML` and it's supported for both `geometry` and `geography` spatial types. There are many variants of `ST_AsGML`, giving you control over GML version and precision. Supported GML versions are 2.1.2 (pass in 2 for version number) and 3.1.1 (pass in 3 for version number). If no version parameter is passed in, GML version 2.1.2 is assumed. Two additional parameters control the number of significant digits and whether to use short CRS (Coordinate Reference Systems).

`ST_AsGML` supports 2D and 3D for both geometries and geometry collections. If a geometry has an M coordinate, the M is dropped. Passing in curved geometries will throw an error in PostGIS versions 1.4 and above and return NULL in older versions. `ST_AsGML` version 3 does support the advanced 3D geometries of TIN and `PolyhedralSurface`. The version 2 variant only supports basic 3D geometries like 3D linestrings, points, and polygons.

6.1.4 Geometry JavaScript Object Notation (GeoJSON)

Geometry JavaScript Object Notation is a format based on JavaScript Object Notation (JSON). GeoJSON is geared toward consumption by Ajax-oriented applications such as OpenLayers and Leaflet because its output notation is in JavaScript format. JSON is the standard object representation in JavaScript data structures, and GeoJSON extends JSON by adding specifications for storing geographic objects. You can read more about GeoJSON here: http://geojson.org/geojson-spec.html.

The PostGIS function for exporting `geography` and `geometry` data types to GeoJSON is `ST_AsGeoJSON` (first introduced in PostGIS 1.3.5). There are six variants of this function as of PostGIS 2. The arguments are similar to those for `ST_AsGML` with overloads for different targeted versions, numbers of decimal places, short or long CRS, an encoded flag denoting whether to include the bounding box, and various other options. `ST_AsGeoJSON` supports 2D, basic 3D, and geometry collections. It will drop the M coordinate and throw an error for TINs, polyhedral surfaces, and curved geometries.

Although the `ST_AsGeoJSON` function in PostGIS only handles the spatial component, the JSON functions introduced in PostgreSQL 9.2 and enhanced in PostgreSQL 9.3 and 9.4 make it relatively easy to create a fully formed GeoJSON object replete with attributes from a row or set of data rows. We cover this in our blog entry, "Creating GeoJSON Feature Collections with JSON and PostGIS Functions," at www.postgresonline.com/journal/archives/267-GeoJSON-Features.html.

6.1.5 Scalable Vector Graphics (SVG)

The Scalable Vector Graphics (SVG) format has been around for a while and is popular among high-end rendering tools as well as drawing tools such as Inkscape. Toolkits such as ImageMagick can easily convert SVG to many other image formats. Most web browsers support SVG, either natively or via an installable plug-in.

The PostGIS function for exporting to SVG is ST_AsSVG. This function outputs only 2D geometries without SRIDs or Z or M coordinates, and it doesn't output curved geometries. Three variants of the function allow you to specify whether the output points are relative to an origin or to the coordinate system and indicate the level of precision desired.

6.1.6 Extensible 3D Graphics (X3D)

Extensible 3D Graphics (X3D: http://en.wikipedia.org/wiki/X3D) is an ISO XML format for defining objects in 3D space. It was born out of the older Virtual Reality Modeling Language (VRML). PostGIS 3D objects such as TINs and polyhedral surfaces translate to IndexedTriangleSet and IndexedFaceSet elements, respectively, in X3D.

Rendering support for X3D is still a bit spotty, and the standard is being incrementally updated with new features. Efforts are in the works to integrate the HTML5 canvas 3D API with X3D. You can get the latest news at the X3D wiki's "X3D and HTML5" page: www.web3d.org/x3d/wiki/index.php/X3D_and_HTML5.

The most popular JavaScript library for X3D is X3DOM (www.x3dom.org/), which is an MIT-licensed open source library for rendering X3D in browsers (including smartphone web browsers) without any plug-ins. We've demonstrated its use in our ASP.NET/PHP postgis_x3d_viewer (https://github.com/robe2/postgis_x3d_viewer) and NodeJS-based node_postgis_express (https://github.com/robe2/node_postgis_express) PostGIS query viewers.

The ST_AsX3D function was introduced in PostGIS 2.0 and only supports geometries, not geographies—it's primarily focused on 3D geometries. It's the only format function, aside from ST_AsGML, that supports TIN and polyhedral surface geometries.

6.1.7 Examples of output functions

Let's now look at an example that brings all the aforementioned output functions together. Listing 6.1 uses the functions to output a 3D linestring in SRID 4326 to a precision of five significant digits. The linestring originates in northern France and terminates in southern England at an altitude of 1 unit (generally assumed to be meters).

Listing 6.1 Outputting geometry in various standard formats

```
SELECT
    ST_AsGML(geom,5) as GML,
    ST_AsKML(geom,5) As KML,
    ST_AsGeoJSON(geom,5) As GeoJSON,
    ST_AsSVG(geom,0,5) As SVG_Absolute,
    ST_AsSVG(geom,1,5) As SVG_Relative,
    ST_AsX3D(geom,6) As X3D
FROM
    (SELECT
        ST_GeomFromText('LINESTRING(2 48 1,0 51 1)',4326) As geom
    ) X;
```

The results of listing 6.1 are shown in table 6.1.

Table 6.1 Results of listing 6.1

Format	Output
GML	<gml:LineString srsName="EPSG:4326"><gml:coordinates>2,48,1 0,51,1</gml:coordinates></gml:LineString>
KML	<LineString><coordinates>2,48,1 0,51,1</coordinates> </LineString>
GeoJSON	{"type":"LineString","coordinates":[[2,48,1],[0,51,1]]}
SVG_Absolute	M 2 -48 L 0 -51
SVG_Relative	M 2 -48 l -2 -3
X3D	<LineSet vertexCount='2'><Coordinate point='2 48 1 0 51 1' /> </LineSet>

All of the types presented in listing 6.1 output the Z coordinate except for the SVG formats, which are strictly 2D.

6.1.8 Geohash

Geohash is a lossy geocoding system for longitudes and latitudes. It's meant more as a tool for the easy exchange of coordinates or as a poor man's indexing strategy than for visual presentation. Geohash is a darling of lightweight spatial apps that don't need precise proximity checks. You'll find many such apps in the NoSQL camp. You can explore more at http://en.wikipedia.org/wiki/Geohash.

PostGIS outputs to Geohash using `ST_GeoHash`. `ST_GeoHash` always outputs WGS 84 lon/lat coordinates, and your data must have a known SRID so that `ST_GeoHash` can automatically transform it for you during output. `ST_GeoHash` supports curved geometries but not M or Z coordinates.

Keep in mind that Geohash is most accurate for points. If you output anything other than points, `ST_GeoHash` will output a hash corresponding to the bounding box of the geometry. The larger the bounding box, the shorter the hash will be. In fact, for some large areas, Geohash will just give up and output nothing. The following listing demonstrates this behavior as you take a point and expand it to ever-larger circles.

Listing 6.2 Computing Geohash of a buffer as radius is expanded from 0.02 meters

```
SELECT i As rad_meters, ST_GeoHash(geog::geometry) as ghash
FROM (
    SELECT i, ST_Buffer(ST_GeogFromText('POINT(2 48)'), i) As geog
    FROM unnest(ARRAY[0.02,1,1000,10000,50000,150000]) AS i
) As X;
```

The output of listing 6.2 is shown in the following listing.

Listing 6.3 Output of Geohash buffer expansion

```
rad_meters | ghash
-----------+-----------
      0.02 | u093jd0k72
         1 | u093jd0k
      1000 | u093j
     10000 | u09
     50000 | u0
    150000 |
```

The reason why the hash decreases in size as your box gets larger is that Geohash is designed as a simple strategy for filtering geometries by bounding box that can be employed even by databases that only support indexes on text. In the preceding example, to find anything within a 1000 × 1000 meter box, you'd look for all geometries that have a hash that starts with `u093j`. In this way you can create a simple mapping application that filters by the hashed box to grab lots of things in the window.

Before we move on to the next section, you need to keep in mind that the output functions we covered here export only geometry and geography components. Many formats carry non-spatial data. For example, KML and JSON data formats often include data such as name, date, and category within JSONed and KMLed data. In chapter 17 we'll demonstrate how you can export attendant data with scripting tools.

PostGIS not only has functions for outputting data in standard formats—it also has functions to do the reverse, constructing geometries and geographies from various representational formats. In the next section, we'll cover these constructor functions.

6.2 Constructor functions

As the name implies, constructor functions create new spatial objects. There are two common ways to create new spatial objects:

- Build them from scratch using raw data in various formats.
- Utilize existing spatial objects and decompose, splice, slice, dice, or morph them to form new ones.

In this section, we'll start with the first approach. We'll go through the list of common representations and the functions used to transform them into bona fide PostGIS geometries and geographies. We'll then cover functions that create new geometries and geographies from existing ones.

6.2.1 Creating geometries from text and binary formats

In this section, we'll look at functions that return geometries when you feed them various text or binary representations. They're especially useful for quickly viewing geometries in various desktop tools. In tools that accept only geometries, and not their textual representations, the use of these functions is necessary.

ST_GEOMFROMTEXT

Well-known text (WKT) representations are a common way to express geometries, and the ST_GeomFromText function builds geometries from WKT. Prior to PostGIS 2.0, this function only accepted 2D geometries; since version 2.0 it accepts geometries of all dimensions. ST_GeomFromText is an SQL/MM function that can be found in other SQL/MM-compliant spatial database products.

The following listing demonstrates its use.

Listing 6.4 Using ST_GeomFromText

```
SELECT * INTO unconstrained_geoms
FROM (
    VALUES
        (ST_GeomFromText('POINT(-100 28 1)',4326)),
        (ST_GeomFromText('LINESTRING(-80 28 1,-90 29 1)',4326)),
        (ST_GeomFromText('POLYGONZ((10 28 1,9 29 1,7 30 1,10 28 1))')),
        (ST_GeomFromText(
            'POLYHEDRALSURFACE(
                ((0 0 0,0 0 1,0 1 1,0 1 0,0 0 0)),
                ((0 0 0,0 1 0,1 1 0,1 0 0,0 0 0)),
                ((0 0 0,1 0 0,1 0 1,0 0 1,0 0 0)),
                ((1 1 0,1 1 1,1 0 1,1 0 0,1 1 0)),
                ((0 1 0,0 1 1,1 1 1,1 1 0,0 1 0)),
                ((0 0 1,1 0 1,1 1 1,0 1 1,0 0 1))
            )'
        ))
) As z(geom);
```

Listing 6.4 creates a table called unconstrained_geoms with a generic geometric column that has no meaningful constraints. Generally, this isn't a good idea because you can easily run into data integrity issues.

The next listing demonstrates how you can specify the SRID as a second argument in the ST_GeomFromText function.

Listing 6.5 Using ST_GeomFromText with an SRID argument

```
SELECT geom::geometry(LineString,4326) INTO constrained_geoms
FROM (
    VALUES
        (ST_GeomFromText('LINESTRING(-80 28, -90 29)', 4326)),
        (ST_GeomFromText('LINESTRING(10 28, 9 29, 7 30)', 4326 ))
) As x(geom);
```

In listing 6.5 you only add linestrings, and all items have an SRID of 4326. Also, you explicitly cast the output: geom::geometry(LineString,4326). This forces the created table to be geometry type- and SRID-constrained. If you left out the cast step, the resulting table geometry column would still be unconstrained.

If you forget to cast to a constrained type and specify the SRID when you do a bulk insert, you can always fix the issue by altering the table as follows:

```
ALTER TABLE constrained_geoms
ALTER COLUMN geom TYPE geometry(LineString,4326);
```

If you only want to constrain the spatial reference system for future inserts, and not the geometry type, you can do this:

```
ALTER TABLE constrained_geoms
ALTER COLUMN geom TYPE geometry(Geometry,4326);
```

ST_GEOMFROMWKB AND ST_GEOMFROMEWKB

On many occasions, you'll find yourself needing to import data from a client application where geometries are already stored in binary representations. This is where the functions `ST_GeomFromWKB` and `ST_GeomFromEWKB` come into play. `ST_GeomFromWKB` is an SQL/MM-defined function, and `ST_GeomFromEWKB` is a PostGIS extension offering SRID encoding.

These two functions accept byte arrays instead of text strings, and PostGIS geometry types derive from byte arrays. In this sense, using byte arrays as input or output formats results in no loss of data.

Any textual representation will only carry about 15 significant digits. Thus, the following operation would result in a loss for geometries having many significant digits:

```
SELECT ST_GeomFromText(ST_AsText(geom));
```

In contrast, the following operation results in no loss:

```
SELECT ST_WKBFromText(ST_AsWKB(geom));
```

The following example uses `ST_GeomFromWKB`:

```
SELECT ST_GeomFromWKB(
    E'\\001\\001\\000\\000\\000\\321\\256B\\312O
    \\304Q\\300\\347\\030\\220\\275\\336%E@',
    4326
);
```

The WKB representation uses a backslash as an internal separator. Because the backslash is a token in SQL, you must escape it with yet another backslash.

To avoid the nuisance of the extra slash, you can set the PostgreSQL variable `standard_conforming_strings` to on (the default setting for PostgreSQL 9.0 and higher) as follows:

```
SET standard_conforming_strings = on;
SELECT ST_GeomFromWKB(
    '\001\001\000\000\000\321\256B\312O\304Q\300\347\030\220\275\336%E@'
);
```

A similar PostgreSQL variable, `bytea_output`, controls the format of the output. The default is generally hex, as you'll see by running the following:

```
SET bytea_output = hex;
SELECT ST_AsBinary(
    ST_GeomFromWKB(
        E'\\001\\001\\000\\000\\000\\321\\256B\\
```

```
        312O\\304Q\\300\\347\\030\\220\\275\\336%E@',
        4326
    )
);
```

The output looks like this:

```
\x0101000000d1ae42ca4fc451c0e71890bdde254540
```

Another option for `bytea_output` is `escape`, which will render the output with single slashes, as in the following:

```
\001\001\000\000\000\321\256B\312O\304Q\300\347\030\220\275\336%E@
```

Canonical representation

If you peek at the data stored in a geometry column, you'll see something that looks like a long string of alphanumeric characters. This is the hexadecimal representation of the Enhanced Well-Known Binary (EWKB) notation, which is what you'd get by using the `ST_AsEWKB` function. You can cast it to a geometry without using any functions and not lose anything:

```
SELECT '0101000020E61000008048BF7D1D20...'::geometry;
```

To conform with OGC-MM, PostGIS offers other functions such as `ST_PointFromText`, `ST_LineFromText`, `ST_PolyFromText`, `ST_GeometryFromText`, and other plain text or binary input functions that require specific geometry subtypes. Our advice, as far as using PostGIS is concerned, is to stay away from them and stick with `ST_GeomFromText` and `ST_GeomFromWKB`. Functions such as `ST_PointFromText` are wrappers for `ST_GeomFromText` and `ST_GeomFromWKB` and perform an additional check to make sure you're feeding in the correct subtype (returning NULL if not), adding additional overhead for the check and also potentially resulting in data loss if you're not aware of this side effect. In the course of setting up your tables, you should have already added the necessary subtype constraints. If you want to filter out rows that don't fit your type constraints and prevent pollution of your table with NULLs, you should filter using the `ST_GeometryType` or `GeometryType` functions.

ST_GeomFromGML, ST_GeomFromGeoJSON, and ST_GeomFromKML

In addition to WKT and WKB functions, PostGIS also offers input functions for various other web mapping formats:

- *Geography Markup Language (GML)*—`ST_GeomFromGML`
- *GeoJSON*—`ST_GeomFromGeoJSON`
- *Keyhole Markup Format (KML)*—`ST_GeomFromKML`

KML is the format used by Google Maps and Google Earth. It differs from other formats in that the spatial reference system is always assumed to be WGS 84 lon/lat (SRID 4326). As such, the `ST_GeomFromKML` function will always output a geometry that's in SRID 4326. You'll need to use `ST_Transform` to convert to another SRID.

6.2.2 Creating geographies from text and binary formats

The geography type has functions, similar to the geometry type, for converting from various formats to geography: ST_GeogFromText, ST_GeogFromWKB, ST_GeogFromKML, ST_GeogFromGML, and ST_GeogFromGeoJSON.

These functions have some notable limitations compared to their geometry siblings:

- They don't support types such as TINs, polyhedral surfaces, or curved geometries because geography itself does not support these.
- Unless you specify otherwise, these functions will always assume the input format to be in SRID 4326.

6.2.3 Using text or binary representations as function arguments

You'll encounter instances where someone might take a text or binary representation of a geometry or geography and use it as a parameter to a function. Although this is convenient, you should avoid doing so. The following example demonstrates what can go wrong:

```
SELECT ST_Perimeter('POLYGON((
    145.007 13.581,144.765 13.21,
    144.602 13.2,144.589 13.494,
    144.845 13.705,145.007 13.581
))');
```

The preceding example throws an "ST_Perimeter(unknown) is not unique" error. PostGIS has no idea what type the WKT representation should be because the ST_Perimeter function exists for both geometry and geography types in PostGIS 2.1+.

You can sometimes get away with text/binary representation input and allowing PostgreSQL to autocast it to the right spatial data type when the function you use has no overloading. For example, the following will work in PostGIS 2.1:

```
SELECT (ST_Centroid('LINESTRING(1 2,3 4)'));
```

But just because something works doesn't mean it's a good idea. The preceding example will break as soon as PostGIS overloads the ST_Centroid function to accept geographies. We recommend that you always use a constructor function, as in the next example:

```
SELECT ST_Centroid(ST_GeomFromText('LINESTRING(1 2,3 4)'));
```

Or you can explicitly cast your textual or binary representation to a type:

```
SELECT ST_Centroid('LINESTRING(1 2, 3 4)'::geometry);
```

Geometry and geography objects have various properties that you can read or set to change the object that can be accessed using accessor and setter functions. In the next section, we'll cover some of the more common accessor and setter functions.

6.3 Accessor and setter functions

If you're experienced with any object-oriented (OO) language, accessor and setter functions will come as nothing new. The terms come from OO programming and refer to any function that accesses or sets the intrinsic properties of an object.

Because quite a large number of functions fall under this classification, we'll use the terms *accessor* and *setter* only for functions that return or set textual values or scalars. For example, if you have a square polygon, only functions that return or set the type, the SRID, and dimensions will be considered *accessors* and *setters*. Functions that return the centroid (a point), the diagonal (a linestring), or the boundary (a linestring collection) we'll call *decomposition* functions and save for discussion in a later section. We also don't consider measurement functions, such as those for computing length, area, and perimeter, to be accessors.

It's important to know a few defining characteristics of spatial objects when you're using spatial accessor functions:

- The *spatial reference identifier (SRID)* defines the projection, ellipsoid or spheroid, and the datum of the coordinates of a geometry or geography.
- The *subtype* is the finer categorization of `geometry` and `geography` types, such as points, linestrings, polygons, multipolygons, multicurves, and so on.
- The *coordinate dimension* is the dimension of the vector space in which your geometry lives. In PostGIS, this can be 2, 3, or 4.
- The *geometric dimension* is the minimal dimension of the vector space necessary to fully contain the geometry. (There are many more rigorous definitions, but we'll stick with something intuitive.) In PostGIS, geometry dimensions can be 0 (points), 1 (linestrings), or 2 (polygons).

In this section, we'll go into detail about these intrinsic properties of geometries and the various functions you can use to retrieve and set them.

6.3.1 Spatial reference identifiers

In PostGIS, the `ST_SRID` function retrieves the SRID of geometries. This function isn't necessary for geographies because the SRID is always 4326. You'll find this OGC SQL/MM standard function in most spatial databases.

The companion setter function is `ST_SetSRID`, which is also an SQL/MM standard. Again, `ST_SetSRID` doesn't exist for geography. This setter function will replace the spatial reference metadata embedded within a geometry. Remember that all geometries must have an SRID, even if it's the unknown SRID (`0` for PostGIS 2 or higher and `-1` for prior versions).

Let's take a look at the uses of this accessor and setter.

Listing 6.6 Example uses of ST_SRID and ST_SetSRID

```
SELECT ST_SRID(ST_GeomFromText('POLYGON((1 1,2 2,2 0,1 1))',4326));   -- Simple use of ST_SRID

SELECT ST_SRID(geom) As srid, COUNT(*) As number_of_geoms   -- Counts number of distinct SRIDs
FROM sometable
GROUP BY ST_SRID(geom);

SELECT
    ST_SRID(geom) As srid,
    ST_SRID(ST_SetSRID(geom,4326)) as srid_new   -- Uses ST_SetSRID to change the SRID
FROM (
    VALUES
        (ST_GeomFromText('POLYGON((70 20,71 21,71 19,70 20))',4269)),
        (ST_Point(1,2))
) As X (geom);
```

If you set up your production tables properly, your geometries should contain only SRIDs found in the spatial_ref_sys table. Although nothing in the OGC specification requires SRIDs to have real-world significance, PostGIS prepopulates the spatial_ref_sys table with only EPSG-approved SRIDs.

You're free to invent your own SRIDs and add them to the table. Esri product users often add spatial reference systems defined by Esri to ease the sharing of data between PostGIS and Esri products.

6.3.2 Transforming geometry to different spatial references

The `ST_Transform` function converts all the points of a given geometry to coordinates in a different spatial reference system. A common application of this function is to take a geometry in longitude and latitude and transform it to a planar SRS so that you can take meaningful measurements.

The following example converts a road somewhere in New York state expressed in WGS 84 lon/lat to WGS 84 UTM Zone 18N meters:

```
SELECT ST_AsEWKT(
    ST_Transform('SRID=4326;LINESTRING(-73 41,-72 42)'::geometry,32618)
 );
```

The output of this code snippet is as follows:

```
SRID=32618;
LINESTRING(
    668207.88519421 4540683.52927698,
    748464.920715711 4654130.89132385
)
```

Now that you've transformed from longitude and latitude to planar coordinates, you can obtain the length with a simple application of the Pythagorean theorem.

People often confuse `ST_SetSRID` with `ST_Transform`. Just remember that `ST_SetSRID` doesn't change the coordinates of a geometry; it only sets an attribute called SRID—there's nothing in PostGIS that says the true SRID of the geometry must match its manifested SRID.

ST_SetSRID comes in useful when you realize that you made a mistake during data import. For example, if you import your geometries as WGS 84 lon/lat (SRID 4326), and you later realize they were defined using NAD 27 lon/lat coordinates (SRID 4267), ST_SetSRID will quickly correct the mistake.

6.3.3 Using transformation with the geography type

The geography type doesn't have ST_Transform, ST_SetSRID, or ST_SRID functions because it always uses WGS 84 lon/lat, at least for now. Nevertheless, the ST_Transform function is crucial when working with the geography type. At times you may need to take advantage of geometry functions that aren't available for geography. The use of geometry functions for geography shouldn't pose a problem as long as you're working with a small area and don't need pinpoint accuracy.

The following listing shows how you can cast to geometry to find the closest point on a line to a geometry and then cast back to geography.

Listing 6.7 Finding the closest point on geographies

```
SELECT
    ST_Transform(
        ST_ClosestPoint(
            ST_Transform(geog::geometry,32618),
            ST_Transform(
                'SRID=4326;LINESTRING(-73 41,-72 42)'::geometry,32618
            )
        ),
        4326
    )::geography;
```

Listing 6.7 operates on a table of geographies, ones in or close to New York State. For each, it finds the closest point on the geography to a specific road. It does so by first casting the geography to a geometry and then transforming to a New York state plane (SRID 32618). The ST_ClosestPoint function only accepts geometries. Like other functions we'll discuss that take two or more geometries, all input geometries must have the same SRID. Once you have the answer in planar coordinates, you transform back to 4326 because only geometries in 4326 can be cast to geography.

A number of geography functions, such as ST_Buffer, piggyback on geometry via a transformation under the hood. These functions are denoted with a *(T)* in the PostGIS manual. You should be cautious when using these functions, especially for large areas where the curvature of the earth becomes a concern and in regions of longitude and latitude singularities, such as the poles.

6.3.4 Geometry type functions

In most situations, you're keenly aware of the geometry types you're working with, but when importing data containing heterogeneous geometry columns, you may not be.

PostGIS offers two functions to help you identify geometry types: GeometryType and ST_GeometryType. We've mentioned that functions in PostGIS without the ST prefix are deprecated functions, but in the case of GeometryType versus ST_GeometryType, not only are they different from each other, but both are very much in use.

The GeometryType function is the older of the two. It's part of the OGC simple features for SQL. It returns the geometry types that you're familiar with in all uppercase. Its younger counterpart, ST_GeometryType, is part of the OpenGIS SQL/MM standard. It outputs the familiar geometry names but prepends *ST_* to comply with the MM geometry class-hierarchy naming standards. The following listing demonstrates the differences between the two.

Listing 6.8 Differences between ST_GeometryType and GeometryType

```
SELECT ST_GeometryType(geom) As new_name, GeometryType(geom) As old_name
FROM (VALUES
    (ST_GeomFromText('POLYGON((0 0,1 1,0 1,0 0))')),
    (ST_Point(1,2)),
    (ST_MakeLine(ST_Point(1,2), ST_Point(1,2))),
    (ST_Collect(ST_Point(1,2), ST_Buffer(ST_Point(1,2),3))),
    (ST_LineToCurve(ST_Buffer(ST_Point(1,2),3))),
    (ST_LineToCurve(ST_Boundary(ST_Buffer(ST_Point(1,2),3)))),
    (ST_Multi(ST_LineToCurve(ST_Boundary(ST_Buffer(ST_Point(1,2),3)))))
) As x(geom);
```

Table 6.2 shows the results of listing 6.8.

Table 6.2 Using ST_GeometryType and GeometryType

new_name	old_name
ST_Polygon	POLYGON
ST_Point	POINT
ST_LineString	LINESTRING
ST_Geometry	GEOMETRYCOLLECTION
ST_CurvePolygon	CURVEPOLYGON
ST_CircularString	CIRCULARSTRING
ST_MultiCurve	MULTICURVE

Determining the geometry type is particularly useful when various functions have to be applied to a heterogeneous geometry column. Remember that some functions accept only certain geometry types or may behave differently for different geometry types. For example, asking for the area of a line is pointless, as is asking for the length of a polygon.

Using an SQL CASE statement is a compact way to selectively apply functions against a heterogeneous geometry column. Here's an example:

```
SELECT
    CASE
        WHEN GeometryType(geom) = 'POLYGON' THEN ST_Area(geom)
        WHEN GeometryType(geom) = 'LINESTRING' THEN ST_Length(geom)
        ELSE NULL
    END As measure
FROM sometable;
```

6.3.5 Geometry and coordinate dimensions

Two kinds of dimensions are relevant when talking about geometries:

- *Coordinate dimension*—The dimension of the space that the geometry lives in
- *Geometry dimension*—The smallest dimensional space that will fully contain the geometry

The coordinate dimension is always greater than or equal to the geometry dimension.

PostGIS provides the `ST_CoordDim` and `ST_Dimension` functions to return the coordinate and geometry dimensions respectively. In the next listing, these two functions are applied to the mixed bag of 3D geometries created in listing 6.4.

Listing 6.9 Coordinate and geometry dimensions

```
SELECT
    ST_GeometryType(geom) As type,
    ST_Dimension(geom) As gdim,
    ST_CoordDim(geom) as cdim
FROM unconstrained_geoms;
```

Table 6.3 shows the output of listing 6.9.

Table 6.3 Differences between geometry dimension and coordinate dimension

type	gdim	cdim
ST_Point	0	3
ST_LineString	1	3
ST_Polygon	2	3
ST_PolyhedralSurface	3	3

In table 6.3, all geometries have a coordinate dimension (cdim) of 3 because all have X, Y, Z components for coordinates. Only the polyhedral surface also has a geometric dimension (gdim) of 3 because it's the only true 3D type.

6.3.6 Retrieving coordinates

`ST_X`, `ST_Y`, and `ST_Z` are functions that you can use to return the underlying coordinates of point geometries. Although geography points don't have this function, you can access this function by casting your `geography` point to `geometry`. These functions are generally combined with `ST_Centroid` to get the X and Y coordinates of a centroid for non-point geometries.

`ST_Xmin`, `ST_Xmax`, `ST_Ymin`, `ST_Ymax`, `ST_Zmin`, and `ST_Zmax` are functions meant to take bounding boxes as input, but feel free to use these functions against geometries too, because PostGIS autocasts a geometry to its bounding box when needed. These functions are used to return the minimum or maximum coordinates of each geometry. They're rarely used alone but are generally combined with each other to obtain approximate widths and heights for mapping the extent of geometries. We'll demonstrate their use when we talk about translation.

6.3.7 Checking geometry validity

We introduced the concept of validity in chapter 2. As you'll recall, pathological geometries such as polygons with self-intersections and polygons with holes outside the exterior ring are invalid. Generally speaking, the higher the geometry dimension of a geometry, the more prone it is to invalidity. Unfortunately, functions for checking validity only work for geometries, not geographies.

The `ST_IsValid` function tests for validity, and `ST_IsValidReason` provides a brief description as to why a geometry isn't valid. `ST_IsValidReason` will offer up a description only for the first offense encountered, so if your geometry is invalid for multiple reasons, you'll see only the first reason. If a geometry is valid, it will return the string "Valid Geometry."

`ST_IsValidDetail` is a new function available since PostGIS 2.0. This function returns a set of `valid_detail` objects, each containing a reason and location for a particular violation, allowing you to review all the violations, not just the first. Also introduced in version 2.0 is the `ST_MakeValid` function, which will try to fix the invalid geometry for you. Both of these functions require PostGIS compiled with GEOS 3.3.0 or above.

All validity-checking functions only check X and Y, not Z. They will automatically reject polyhedral surfaces and TINs.

We remind you again that it's important to make sure your geometries are valid. Don't even try to work with geometries unless they're valid. Many of the GEOS-based functions in PostGIS will behave unpredictably upon encountering invalid geometries.

6.3.8 Number of points that defines a geometry

The `ST_NPoints` function returns the number of points defining a geometry. It won't work for geography, but you can cast your `geography` to `geometry` and then use the function without any loss of information. `ST_NPoints` is a PostGIS creation; you may not find it in other OGC-compliant spatial databases.

Many people make the mistake of using the function `ST_NumPoints` instead of `ST_NPoints`. `ST_NumPoints` only works when applied to linestrings, as dictated by the OGC specification.

You may be wondering why there are two functions when one completely performs the duties of another. This has to do with the fact that most spatial databases, PostGIS included, offer functions that adhere strictly to the OGC specification. After meeting the OGC specifications to the letter, spatial databases continue on to extend OGC functions where they find deficiencies.

In versions prior to PostGIS 2.0, when used with multilinestrings, `ST_NumPoints` exhibited the undocumented behavior of only using the first linestring. To avoid this problem, PostGIS 2.0 and higher removed support for multilinestrings altogether. If you pass in a multilinestring or a collection containing a multilinestring, `ST_NumPoints` will return NULL, to better conform to OGC requirements. Other functions with similar behavior changes are `ST_StartPoint` and `ST_EndPoint`. Our advice is to avoid using all three functions with multilinestrings, even if the multilinestring is made up of only a single linestring.

The following listing demonstrates the difference in results between `ST_NPoints` and `ST_NumPoints`.

Listing 6.10 Example of using `ST_NPoints` and `ST_NumPoints`

```
SELECT
    type,
    ST_NPoints(geom) As npoints,
    ST_NumPoints(geom) As numpoints
FROM (VALUES
    ('LinestringM',
        ST_GeomFromEWKT('LINESTRINGM(1 2 3,3 4 5,5 8 7,6 10 11)')
    ),
    ('Circularstring',
        ST_GeomFromText('CIRCULARSTRING(2.5 2.5,4.5 2.5,4.5 4.5)')
    ),
    ('Polygon (Triangle)',
        ST_GeomFromText('POLYGON((0 1,1 -1,-1 -1,0 1))')
    ),
    ('Multilinestring',
        ST_GeomFromText('MULTILINESTRING((1 2,3 4,5 6),(10 20,30 40))')
    ),
    ('Collection',
        ST_Collect(
            ST_GeomFromText('POLYGON((0 1,1 -1,-1 -1,0 1))'),
            ST_Point(1,3)
        )
    )
) As x(type, geom);
```

Table 6.4 shows the output of listing 6.10.

Table 6.4 Difference between `ST_NumPoints` and `ST_NPoints` in PostGIS 2.1.3

type	npoints	numpoints
LinestringM	4	4
Circularstring	3	3

Table 6.4 Difference between `ST_NumPoints` and `ST_NPoints` in PostGIS 2.1.3 *(continued)*

type	npoints	numpoints
Polygon (Triangle)	4	NULL
Multilinestring	5	NULL
Collection	5	NULL

Table 6.4 demonstrates that `ST_NPoints` works for all geometry subtypes, whereas `ST_NumPoints` works only for linestrings and circularstrings. For multilinestrings, `ST_NumPoints` will return NULL for version 2 or higher, but in prior versions would count the vertices in the first linestring only.

6.4 Measurement functions

Before taking any measurements in GIS, you must concern yourself with the scale of what you're measuring. This goes back to the fact that we live on a spheroid called Earth and that you're measuring something on its surface. When your measurements cover a small area where the curvature of the earth doesn't come into play, it's perfectly fine to assume a planar model that treats the earth as essentially flat.

What distances should be considered *small* depends on the accuracy of the measure you're trying to achieve. We've found that planar measurements are often people's first choice, even across very long measures. People prefer the simplicity and intuitiveness that comes with planar measurements even at the expense of accuracy. Planar measurements are generally in units of meters or feet, and planar models are better supported by GIS tools and are faster to process.

Once measures start to cross continents and oceans, as is the case with areas and perimeters of entire continents or long air travel routes, planar measures deteriorate rapidly. You'll have to use geodetic measurements in these cases, where you must consider the spherical nature of the earth. A geodetic measurement models the world as a sphere or spheroid. Coordinates are expressed using degrees or radians. The classic SRID 4326 (WGS 84 lon/lat) is the most common geodetic spatial reference system in use today.

In this section, we'll cover both kinds of measurements, but we'll only focus on internal measurements like length, perimeter, and area. We'll leave measurements between objects, such as distance measures, as a topic for chapter 10. PostGIS does have dedicated functions that work only on spheroids and can be used with the geometry type. These are used when your application requires you to keep your data in the geometry type, but once in a while you need to measure using a geodetic model.

One last point to keep in mind: Measurement functions are always used as getters. Setting the measurement of a geometry doesn't make sense. To change a measurement, you must change the geometry itself.

6.4.1 Geometry planar measurements

All the planar measurement functions we're about to discuss are in the same units as the spatial reference system that's defined for the geometry. For example, if your spatial reference system is in feet, then the lengths and the areas are in feet and square feet. Common measurement functions are `ST_Length`, `ST_3DLength`, `ST_Area`, `ST_Perimeter`, and `ST_3DPerimeter`. If your spatial reference system is in degrees of longitude and latitude (spherical coordinates), then your units of measure will be in degrees after PostGIS naively maps longitude to X coordinate values and latitude to Y coordinate values. This may only be acceptable for small areas far from the poles, where the longitude and latitude grid still has some semblance of being uniform squares.

Prior to PostGIS 2.0, most of the measurement functions accepted only 2D geometries, with the exception of `ST_Length3D`. Since PostGIS 2.0, you can pass in 3D geometries, but be warned: only the 2D projection of the geometry will be measured. To get true 3D measures, use one of the newer functions: `ST_3DClosestPoint`, `ST_3DDistance`, `ST_3DIntersects`, `ST_3DMaxDistance`, or `ST_3DPerimeter`. `ST_Length3D` was renamed to `ST_3DLength` to better conform to SQL/MM standards. These newer 3D functions support points, polygons, linestrings, and their multi- counterparts. They also work with polyhedral surfaces, but not TINs.

The following example demonstrates the 2D and 3D lengths of a 3D linestring:

```
SELECT ST_Length(geom) As length_2d, ST_3DLength(geom) As length_3d
FROM (
    VALUES
        (ST_GeomFromText('LINESTRING(1 2 3,4 5 6)')),
        (ST_GeomFromText('LINESTRING(1 2,4 5)')))
As x(geom);
```

As you can see in table 6.5, the lengths returned by `ST_Length` and `ST_Length3D` are the same for a linestring in 2D coordinate space and different for the linestring in 3D coordinate space.

Table 6.5 Comparing 2D and 3D lengths

length_2D	length_3D
4.24264068711928	5.19615242270663
4.24264068711928	4.24264068711928

The two other common measurement functions for area and perimeter are fairly intuitive. Obviously, you should use them only with valid polygons and multipolygons. For multi-ringed polygons, `ST_Perimeter` calculates the length of all the rings. You should also keep in mind that both `ST_Area` and `ST_Perimeter` only consider the X and Y coordinates; to consider Z as well, you should use the companion `ST_3DArea` and `ST_3DPerimeter` functions.

6.4.2 Geodetic measurements

All the measurements we've discussed thus far apply to geometries in Cartesian coordinate systems. Because the earth isn't flat, a more appropriate coordinate system to use when looking at large swaths of the planet is a spherical coordinate system. *Geodetic* is a fancier-sounding term for *spherical* as it relates to the earth.

Spherical coordinates literally throw a curve into our commonsense grasp of lengths, areas, and perimeters. Take the simple question of what the length is of the shortest line that connects Houston and Mumbai. The only straight line would pass through the center of the earth. Along the surface of the earth, an infinite number of curved lines connect the two cities. Even if you should always take the shortest curve, there's no guarantee that it will be unique. Try drawing the shortest line between the two geographic poles. You'll end up with not one but infinitely many.

PostGIS created the `geography` type to deal with coordinates in degrees of longitude and latitude, specifically WGS 84 lon/lat (SRID 4326). You should consider using `geography` when your data covers an area wide enough for the curvature of the earth to come into play. But even if you choose not to use the `geography` type, you can still take advantage of spheroidal computations by using the spherical family of functions in `geometry`. These functions piggyback on `geography` geodetic functions, saving you the trouble of converting back and forth.

Let's look at three examples of length measurements between Houston and Mumbai:

```
SELECT ST_Length(
    ST_GeomFromText('LINESTRING(-95.40 29.77,72.82 19.07)')
);
```

This first measure yields an answer of 168.56, and the units would be degrees. Even if you were to convert the degrees to kilometers, assuming that each degree is about 111 km, your answer would still be disastrously wrong, given that at Houston, one degree of longitude is already down to 96 km.

Next, we'll use geography, whose units are always in meters and all distances compute against a spheroid:

```
SELECT ST_Length(
    ST_GeogFromText('LINESTRING(-95.40 29.77,72.82 19.07)')
);
```

The answer in this case is 14,456 km or just shy of 9,000 miles. This is the correct distance between the two cities, also known as the great circle distance. You can arrive at this distance using a spheroid calculation in `geometry`:

```
SELECT ST_Length_Spheroid(
    ST_GeomFromText('LINESTRING(-95.40 29.77,72.82 19.07)'),
    'SPHEROID["GRS_1980",6378137,298.257222101]'
);
```

Again, the answer is 14,456 km, the same as for `geography`. Notice that in this spheroid example, you need to specify the spheroid that you'd like to use. GRS 80 and WGS 84 are virtually identical. But because you're able to dictate the spheroid, you can also use geometry spheroid measures to calculate distances on Mars, the moon, or even Pluto.

When choosing between the `geometry` and `geography` types for data storage, you should consider what you'll be using the data for. If all you do are simple measurements and relationship checks on your data, and your data covers a fairly large area, then you'll likely be better off storing your data using the `geography` type.

Although the `geography` data type can cover the globe, the `geometry` type is far from obsolete. The `geometry` type has a much richer set of functions than `geography`, relationship checks are much faster, and it currently has wider support across desktop and web mapping tools. If you need support for only a limited area, such as a state, a town, or a small country, then you're better off with the `geometry` type. If you do a lot of geometric processing, such as unioning geometries, simplifying, performing line interpolations, and the like, `geometry` will provide that out of the box, whereas `geography` has to be cast to `geometry`, transformed, processed, and cast back to `geography`.

We've now completed our basic study of scalar properties, and we'll move on to the more exciting topic of properties that are themselves spatial objects. First on our journey are decomposition functions, which are functions that explode a spatial object into subelements or return a caricature of a spatial object.

6.5 Decomposition functions

You'll often find yourself needing to extract parts of an existing geometry. You may need to find the closed linestring that encloses a polygon or the multipoint that constitutes a linestring, or to expand a multipolygon into individual polygons. We call functions that extract and return one or more geometries *decomposition* functions. In this section, we'll demonstrate some of the more common PostGIS decomposition functions.

6.5.1 Bounding box of geometries

Boxes are the unsung heroes of geometries. Though rarely useful for modeling terrestrial features, they play an important role in spatial queries. Often, when comparing the relative spatial relationships of two or more geometries, the question can be sufficiently answered much more quickly by comparing the bounding boxes of the geometries. By encasing disparate and complicated geometries in bounding boxes, you only need to work with rectangles and can ignore the details of the geometries within. Borrowing from an engineering concept, bounding boxes are the black boxes of spatial analysis.

By definition, the bounding box of a 2D geometry is a `box2D` object, and it's the smallest axis-aligned, two-dimensional box that fully encloses the geometry. PostGIS also has another kind of box called `box3D`, which is less commonly used but is useful for doing filters with 3D objects and is internally used by 3D indexes introduced in PostGIS 2. The box3D is also axis-aligned.

All geometries have boxes, even points. Boxes aren't geometries, but you can cast boxes into geometries. Naturally, casting a 2D box to geometry will yield a rectangular polygon, but you have to watch out for degenerate cases such as points, vertical lines, horizontal lines, or multipoints along a horizontal or vertical. The syntax and text representation for a 2D box is BOX(p1,p2) where p1 and p2 are points of any two opposite vertices.

box2D and box3D are axis-aligned

box2D and box3D are never rotated, meaning that the edges of the boxes are parallel to the coordinate axes. A true minimum bounding box, in contrast, may not necessarily be axis-aligned.

PostGIS doesn't yet have the facilities to compute a true minimum bounding box for a geometry. In the meantime, you can consider the convex hull and the minimum bounding circle as proxies for a minimum bounding box. Use the ST_ConvexHull and ST_MinimumBoundingCircle functions to get at them.

Although geographies can be thought of as having bounding boxes, these are only internal constructs used by PostGIS for spatial relationship queries and have no physical manifestation.

The following listing demonstrates how to compute box2D and box3D for various geometries.

Listing 6.11 box2D and box3D of various geometries

```
SELECT name, Box2D(geom) As box2d, Box3D(geom) As box3d
FROM (VALUES
    ('2D Line',
        ST_GeomFromText(
            'LINESTRING(121.63 25.03,3.03 6.58,-71.06 42.36)',4326
        )
    ),
    ('3D Line', ST_GeomFromText('LINESTRING(1 2 3,3 4 1000.34567)')),
    ('Vert 2D Line', ST_GeomFromText('LINESTRING(1 2,1 4)')),
    ('Point', ST_GeomFromText('POINT(1 2)')),
    ('Polygon', ST_GeomFromText('POLYGON((1 2,3 4,5 6,1 2))')),
    ('Cube',
        ST_GeomFromText(
            'POLYHEDRALSURFACE(
                ((0 0 0,0 0 1,0 1 1,0 1 0,0 0 0)),
                ((0 0 0,0 1 0,1 1 0,1 0 0,0 0 0)),
                ((0 0 0,1 0 0,1 0 1,0 0 1,0 0 0)),
                ((1 1 0,1 1 1,1 0 1,1 0 0,1 1 0)),
                ((0 1 0,0 1 1,1 1 1,1 1 0,0 1 0)),
                ((0 0 1,1 0 1,1 1 1,0 1 1,0 0 1))
            )'
```

```
        )
    )
)
AS x(name,geom);
```

The following listing displays the output of 6.11.

Listing 6.12 Textual representation of box2d and box3d of geometries

```
name          | box2d                | box3d
--------------+----------------------+------------------------------
2D line       | BOX(-71.06 6.58,...) | BOX3D(-71.06 ..,121.63 42.36 0)
3D line       | BOX(1 2,3 4)         | BOX3D(1 2 3,3 4 1000.34567)
Vert 2D line  | BOX(1 2,1 4)         | BOX3D(1 2 0,1 4 0)
Point         | BOX(1 2,1 2)         | BOX3D(1 2 0,1 2 0)
Polygon       | BOX(1 2,5 6)         | BOX3D(1 2 0,5 6 0)
Cube          | BOX(0 0,1 1)         | BOX3D(0 0 0,1 1 1)
```

6.5.2 Boundaries and converting polygons to linestrings

ST_Boundary works with all geometries, but not geographies, and it returns the geometry that determines the separation between the points in the geometry and the rest of the coordinate space. This particular way of defining boundaries will make matters easy when we discuss interactions between two geometries in chapter 9. Also note that the boundary of a geometry is at least one dimension lower than that of the geometry itself.

One common use of ST_Boundary is to break apart polygons and multipolygons into their constituent rings. ST_Boundary ignores M and Z coordinates and currently doesn't work with geometry collections or curved geometries.

The next listing shows some examples of ST_Boundary in action.

Listing 6.13 Examples of ST_Boundary

```
SELECT object_name,ST_AsText(ST_Boundary(geom)) As WKT
FROM (VALUES
    ('Simple linestring',
        ST_GeomFromText('LINESTRING(-14 21,0 0,35 26)')
    ),
    ('Non-simple linestring',
        ST_GeomFromText('LINESTRING(2 0,0 0,1 1,1 -1)')
    ),
    ('Closed linestring',
        ST_GeomFromText('
            LINESTRING(
                52 218,139 82,262 207,245 261,207 267,153 207,
                125 235,90 270,55 244,51 219,52 218)'
        )
    ),
    ('Polygon',
        ST_GeomFromText('
            POLYGON((
                52 218,139 82,262 207,245 261,207 267,153 207,
```

```
                125 235,90 270,55 244,51 219,52 218))'
            )
        ),
        ('Polygon with holes',
            ST_GeomFromText('
                POLYGON(
                    (-0.25 -1.25,-0.25 1.25,2.5 1.25,2.5 -1.25,-0.25 -1.25),
                    (2.25 0,1.25 1,1.25 -1,2.25 0),
                    (1 -1,1 1,0 0,1 -1))'
            )
        )
)
AS x(object_name,geom);
```

Table 6.6 shows the output of listing 6.13 with the object names and WKT representations.

Table 6.6 Output of ST_Boundary

object_name	wkt
Simple linestring	MULTIPOINT(-14 21,35 26)
Non-simple linestring	MULTIPOINT(2 0,1 -1)
Closed linestring	MULTIPOINT EMPTY
Polygon	LINESTRING(52 218,139 82,262 207,245 261,207 267,153 207,125 235,90 270,55 244,51 219,52 218)
Polygon with holes	MULTILINESTRING((-0.25 -1.25,-0.25 1.25,2.5 1.25,2.5 -1.2 5,-0.25 -1.25),(2.25 0,1.25 1,1.25 -1,2.25 0),(1-1,1 1,0 0,1 -1))

The visual representation of some geometries in listing 6.13 is shown in figure 6.1. We left out the representations of the non-simple linestring and the closed linestring, which is an empty geometry and has no representation.

Figure 6.1 Simple linestring, polygon, and polygon with holes overlaid with their boundaries from ST_Boundary

Looking at the query and its output, you can surmise the following behavior of ST_Boundary:

- An open linestring, either simple or non-simple, will return a multipoint made up of exactly two points, one for each of the endpoints.
- A closed linestring has no boundary points.
- A polygon without holes will return a linestring of the exterior ring.

- A polygon with holes will return a multilinestring made up of closed linestrings for each of its rings. The first element of the multilinestring will always be the exterior ring.
- A multipolygon will always return a multilinestring.

A more specialized cousin of `ST_Boundary` is `ST_ExteriorRing`. This function accepts only polygons and returns the exterior ring. If you're trying to find the outer boundary of a polygon, `ST_ExteriorRing` will perform faster than `ST_Boundary`, but as its name suggests, it won't return the inner rings. You can use `ST_InteriorRingN` to grab individual interior rings or `ST_DumpRings` to get both the exterior ring and all interior rings.

6.5.3 Centroid and point on surface

We've all seen maps where small geometries are reduced to a single point to declutter the visual representation. Most maps use a star to indicate capital cities rather than the city boundaries. Should you zoom in enough on any online map, such as to the street level, you may find a labeled dot where you expect to see a huge polygon. Try this on a top-secret military installation. If you zoom in enough, you won't see any of the details you expect but just a dot telling you that it's a place the government doesn't want you to ever visit.

In PostGIS, `ST_Centroid` and, to a lesser extent, `ST_PointOnSurface` are often used to act as point markers for polygons. These functions only work as advertised for 2D geometries. Although you can use them for 3D polygons, they will ignore the Z and M coordinates. You should think of the centroid of a geometry as the center of gravity, as if every point in the geometry had equal mass. The only caveat is that the centroid may not lie within the geometry itself (think of donuts or bagels). The `ST_Centroid` function doesn't work for curved geometries.

`ST_Centroid` sometimes produces undesirable visual results when the point isn't on the geometry itself. Take the island nation of FSM (Federated States of Micronesia); its `ST_Centroid` is most likely somewhere in the Pacific Ocean. If you provide a mapping service, you probably don't want people sailing to FSM and failing to end up on dry land. For this situation `ST_PointOnSurface` comes to the rescue. It always returns an arbitrary point on the boundary geometry. `ST_PointOnSurface` works for all 2D geometries except curves. For points, linestrings, multipoints, and multilinestrings, it considers the M and Z coordinates and returns a point that's usually one used to define the geometry. For polygons, it cuts out the M and Z coordinates.

The following listing compares the output of `ST_Centroid` with that of `ST_PointOnSurface` for various geometries.

Listing 6.14 Centroid and point on surface of various geometries

```
SELECT
    name,
    ST_AsEWKT(ST_Centroid(geom)) As centroid,
    ST_AsEWKT(ST_PointOnSurface(geom)) As point_on_surface
```

```
FROM (VALUES
    ('Multipoint',ST_GeomFromText('MULTIPOINT(-1 1,0 0,2 3)')),
    ('Multipoint 3D',ST_GeomFromText('MULTIPOINT(-1 1 1,0 0 2,2 3 1)')),
    ('Multilinestring',
        ST_GeomFromText('MULTILINESTRING((0 0,0 1,1 1),(-1 1,-1 -1))')
    ),
    ('Polygon',ST_GeomFromEWKT('
        POLYGON(
            (-0.25 -1.25,-0.25 1.25,2.5 1.25,2.5 -1.25,-0.25 -1.25),
            (2.25 0,1.25 1,1.25 -1,2.25 0),
            (1 -1,1 1,0 0,1 -1)
        )')
    )
)
As x(name,geom);
```

The code in listing 6.14 outputs both the centroid and the point on the surface of various geometries. Although the centroid may not always be part of the geometry, the point on the surface is. Figure 6.2 uses the code in listing 6.14 to show the centroid overlaid with the original geometry.

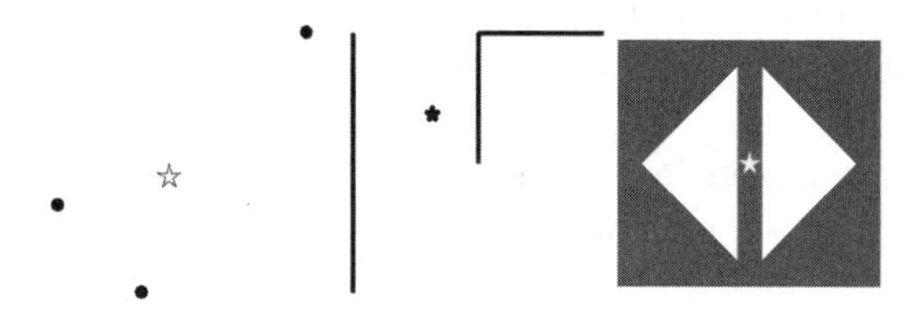

Figure 6.2 Simple linestring, polygon, and polygon with holes overlaid with their centroids from the `ST_Centroid` code.

As demonstrated in the figure, the centroid may not be part of the geometry. In our example, the centroids of the multipoint and multilinestring are outside.

6.5.4 *Returning points defining a geometry*

A convenient little function that works only with linestrings and circularstrings is `ST_PointN`. It returns the *n*th point on the linestring, with indexing starting at 1. Here's a quick example that returns `POINT(3 4)`:

```
SELECT ST_AsText(
    ST_PointN(ST_GeomFromText('LINESTRING(1 2,3 4,5 8)'),2)
);
```

If you wanted to extract all or a good number of the points of a geometry, regardless of what geometry it is, you'd use `ST_DumpPoints`. `ST_DumpPoints` returns a set of `geometry_dump` objects. `geometry_dump` has two components: a one-dimensional path array and a `geometry`. In the case of `ST_DumpPoints`, the `geometry` is always a point, and the path array lists the sequence in which the points were dumped.

`ST_DumpPoints` is particularly useful for deconstructing a geometry and passing it to a tool such as R, which can't work directly with PostGIS types. It's also useful for breaking up large geometries into smaller pieces, such as breaking a long linestring into smaller segments.

ST_DUMPPOINTS IS ENHANCED IN POSTGIS 2.1 In PostGIS 2.1, the `ST_DumpPoints` function was changed to be a pure C function under the hood. This change significantly improved the speed for large geometries with linestrings.

6.5.5 Decomposing multi-geometries and geometry collections

Both `ST_GeometryN` and `ST_Dump` are useful for exploding multi-geometries and collection geometries into their component geometries, but they don't always return the same answers. `ST_Dump` recursively dumps all contained geometries, whereas `ST_GeometryN` drills down only a single level. `ST_Dump`, like its `ST_DumpPoints` sibling, returns a set of `geometry_dump` objects. The `geometry` returned will always be a singleton geometry, never a multi-geometry.

The following listing demonstrates `ST_Dump`.

Listing 6.15 `ST_Dump` in action

```
WITH foo(gid,geom) As (                          ◁ ❶ Common table expression (CTE)
     VALUES (
        1,
        ST_GeomFromText('
            POLYHEDRALSURFACE(
                ((0 0 0,0 0 1,0 1 1,0 1 0,0 0 0)),
                ((0 0 0,0 1 0,1 1 0,1 0 0,0 0 0)),
                ((0 0 0,1 0 0,1 0 1,0 0 1,0 0 0)),
                ((1 1 0,1 1 1,1 0 1,1 0 0,1 1 0)),
                ((0 1 0,0 1 1,1 1 1,1 1 0,0 1 0)),
                ((0 0 1,1 0 1,1 1 1,0 1 1,0 0 1))
            )'
        )
    ),
        (
        2,
        ST_GeomFromText('
            GEOMETRYCOLLECTION(
                MULTIPOLYGON(
                    ((2.25 0,1.25 1,1.25 -1,2.25 0)),
                    ((1 -1,1 1,0 0,1 -1))
                ),
                MULTIPOINT(1 2,3 4),
                LINESTRING(5 6,7 8),
                MULTICURVE(CIRCULARSTRING(1 2,0 4,2 8),(1 2,5 6)))'))
 )

SELECT
    gid,
    (gdump).path As pos,                         ❷ Output path and geometry elements
    ST_AsText((gdump).geom) As exploded_geometry ◁

FROM (SELECT gid, ST_Dump(geom) As gdump FROM foo) As foofoo;   ◁ ❸ Expand using ST_Dump
 ---
```

In listing 6.15, you use a common table expression (CTE) named *foo* to create a set of geometries ❶. (Refer to appendix C to learn more about CTEs.) You then convert each geometry to a set of `geometry_dump` objects ❸ and then break out the path and geometry properties of each dump object as separate columns ❷ to get an idea of what a `geometry_dump` object looks like. The output of this query is shown next.

Listing 6.16 `ST_Dump` output

```
gid | pos    | exploded_geometry
----+--------+----------------------------------------
  1 | {1}    | POLYGON((0 0 0,0 0 1,0 1 1,0 1 0,0 0 0))
  1 | {2}    | POLYGON((0 0 0,0 1 0,1 1 0,1 0 0,0 0 0))
  1 | {3}    | POLYGON((0 0 0,1 0 0,1 0 1,0 0 1,0 0 0))
  1 | {4}    | POLYGON((1 1 0,1 1 1,1 0 1,1 0 0,1 1 0))
  1 | {5}    | POLYGON((0 1 0,0 1 1,1 1 1,1 1 0,0 1 0))
  1 | {6}    | POLYGON((0 0 1,1 0 1,1 1 1,0 1 1,0 0 1))
  2 | {1,1}  | POLYGON((2.25 0,1.25 1,1.25 -1,2.25 0))
  2 | {1,2}  | POLYGON((1 -1,1 1,0 0,1 -1))
  2 | {2,1}  | POINT(1 2)
  2 | {2,2}  | POINT(3 4)
  2 | {3}    | LINESTRING(5 6,7 8)
  2 | {4,1}  | CIRCULARSTRING(1 2,0 4,2 8)
  2 | {4,2}  | LINESTRING(1 2,5 6)
-
```

Note that the pos column in the output is an *n*-dimensional integer array that denotes the position of the subgeometry within the collection. For single-level geometries like the polyhedral surface, the integer array is one-dimensional and contains the index position within the parent. For nested collections, such as a mixed collection of geometries, the first element is the outermost geometry, and each subsequent integer is the index position in inner geometries.

`ST_GeometryN` extracts the *n*th geometry from a multi-geometry or collection geometry. It returns the single extracted geometry, doesn't recurse, and therefore doesn't report depth. Use `ST_GeometryN` when you have just one geometry to extract. If you find yourself needing to repeatedly call `ST_GeometryN` to explode all constituent geometries, switch to `ST_Dump`; otherwise you'll suffer severe performance penalties. `ST_GeometryN` is often used in conjunction with the PostgreSQL `generate_series` function, which provides an iteration index.

Now that we've looked at functions that allow you to decompose a geometry, let's take a look at composition functions that allow you to combine multiple geometries together to form bigger geometries.

6.6 Composition functions

We've already covered creating geometries from non-geometry data, either text or binary. In this section, we'll show you how to put together geometries from other geometries.

6.6.1 Making points

Points are the most elementary geometries. Two functions let you create points from raw coordinates: ST_Point and ST_MakePoint. Coordinates aren't geometries, but we feel they're more related to geometries than text representations, so we classify ST_Point and ST_MakePoint as composition functions.

ST_Point works only for 2D coordinates and can be found in other database products. ST_MakePoint and a variant, ST_MakePointM, can accept 2DM, 3D, and 4D coordinates in addition to 2D, but these two functions are PostGIS-specific. The syntax is the same for all three—just a single argument of coordinates separated by commas. Because these functions don't take an SRID as an argument, you need to combine them with ST_SetSRID to include an SRID.

You may ask yourself what these additional point-making functions offer beyond ST_GeomFromText. To put it concisely: speed and precision. Creating a handful of or even a few hundred points doesn't take much time, but loading files with millions of points with many significant digits (a common task when working with data collected via instrumentation) is a different matter, and you'll certainly come to prefer ST_Point or ST_MakePoint over ST_GeomFromText in that context.

To illustrate these functions, listing 6.17 simulates reading data points from tracking devices attached to gray whales as they make their annual migration from Baja California to the Bering Sea. Depending on the interval of reads and the number of whales tracked, the number of data points coming into the database could be quite overwhelming, making speed an important consideration for importing.

Listing 6.17 Point constructor functions: where is my whale?

```
SELECT whale, ST_AsEWKT(spot) As spot
FROM (VALUES
    ('Mr. Whale', ST_SetSRID(ST_Point(-100.499, 28.7015), 4326)),
    ('Mr. Whale with M as time',
        ST_SetSRID(ST_MakePointM(-100.499,28.7015,5), 4326)
    ),                                                    <-- 1 Whale with time
    ('Mr. Whale with Z as depth',
        ST_SetSRID(ST_MakePoint(-100.499,28.7015,0.5), 4326)
    ),                                                    <-- 2 Whale with depth
    ('Mr. Whale with M and Z',
        ST_SetSRID(ST_MakePoint(-100.499,28.7015,0.5,5), 4326)
    )                                                     <-- 3 Whale with time and depth
) As x(whale, spot);
```

Listing 6.17 demonstrates various overloads to the ST_Point and ST_MakePoint functions. In the first case, you use an extra M unit to store time as a serial ❶. For example, if you take readings every 5 hours, then M=1 would mean this reading was taken 5 hours from the start time, M=2 means 10 hours, and so on. If you're keeping data as individual points, this isn't terribly useful, but if you later decide to stitch them together into a LINESTRINGM, the time slots could be encoded in the line. You may also be interested in knowing how far Mr. Whale dove before coming to the surface for air, so the second variant uses the Z coordinate to store the depth ❷. SRID 4326 is unprojected data, and ST_Transform currently returns the Z coordinate unchanged. The third case includes both Z and M ❸. M is an additional measurement that you're free to use any way you like. In this example, it's used to store time.

The output of listing 6.17 follows.

```
whale                        | spot
-----------------------------+--------------------------------------
Mr. Whale                    | SRID=4326;POINT(-100.499 28.7015)
Mr. Whale with M as time     | SRID=4326;POINTM(-100.499 28.7015 5)
Mr. Whale with Z as depth    | SRID=4326;POINT(-100.499 28.7015 0.5)
Mr. Whale with M and Z       | SRID=4326;POINT(-100.499 28.7015 0.5 5)
-
```

6.6.2 Making polygons

ST_MakeEnvelope, ST_MakePolygon, ST_BuildArea, and ST_Polygonize all build polygons. In addition, the ST_Buffer function, which we demonstrated in chapter 1, is capable of making polygons from linestrings and points. These functions are only supported for geometry.

ST_MAKEENVELOPE

Boxes play an important role in mapping in that they're often used to query for geometries that fit into the viewing area of a map. A common function drafted for this purpose is the ST_MakeEnvelope function, which takes four or five arguments. The first four are the xmin, ymin, xmax, and ymax of the box. The final argument is optional and indicates the SRID of the geometry. If unused, ST_MakeEnvelope assumes the unknown SRID of 0.

ST_MAKEPOLYGON

ST_MakePolygon builds a polygon from a closed linestring representing the exterior ring. Optionally, it can accept as a second argument an array of closed linestrings for interior rings. ST_MakePolygon doesn't validate the input linestrings in any way. This means that if you aren't careful, and you pass in open linestrings or linestrings that can't form polygons, you could end up with an error or a fairly goofy polygon, such as polygons with holes outside the exterior ring or interior rings not completely contained by the exterior ring.

The complete absence of validation does provide an advantage in speed. ST_MakePolygon runs much more quickly than other functions for creating polygons, and it's the only one that won't ignore Z and M coordinates. ST_MakePolygon accepts only closed linestrings as input—no multilinestrings and no collections of linestrings.

ST_BUILDAREA

You can think of `ST_BuildArea` as the neater roommate of `ST_MakePolygon`. Unlike its more reckless counterpart, you can toss it wherever you like and it will organize what you've offered into valid polygons.

`ST_BuildArea` will accept linestrings, multilinestrings, polygons, multipolygons, and geometrycollections. You don't have to worry about the order or the validity of the geometries that you feed into `ST_BuildArea`. It will check the validity of each input geometry, determine which geometries should be interior rings and which one should be the exterior ring, and finally reshuffle them to output polygons or multipolygons. `ST_BuildArea` won't work with arrays, but this shortcoming is mitigated by the fact that it will accept multilinestrings and geometrycollection geometries. If you intend to feed the function an assortment of linestrings and polygons, perform an `ST_Collect` first to gather all the loose pieces into a single geometry.

All this neatness comes at a price: you sacrifice performance and you can't use it to build 3DM polygons. If you've already sanitized your input geometries using another procedure, and speed is of utmost importance, use `ST_MakePolygon`. If your input geometry came from suspect sources and you just want to see what area comes out, the sanitizing feature of `ST_BuildArea` will be worth the wait.

ST_POLYGONIZE

`ST_Polygonize` comes in two forms: an aggregate function and a function that takes an array of linestring geometries. As a database aggregate, its use makes sense only against an existing table with geometry columns. This function takes rows of linestrings and returns a geometry collection consisting of the possible polygons you can form from such linestrings. The array input form of `ST_Polygonize` takes an array of linestrings and returns a geometrycollection of polygons. It's often used when trying to form polygons from a potpourri of open and closed linestrings, which are then passed to `ST_Dump` to dump out the individual polygons as separate rows.

6.6.3 *Promoting single geometries to multi-geometries*

The `ST_Multi` function is used often in PostGIS, mostly to promote points, linestrings, and polygons to their multi counterparts, even if they have only a single geometry. If a geometry is already of a multi variety, it remains unchanged.

The main use case of `ST_Multi` is to ensure that all geometries in a table column are of the same geometry type for consistency. For instance, suppose you obtained polygons for all nations. The Kingdom of Lesotho could come in as a single polygon because it's a tiny, landlocked enclave, whereas Indonesia will come in as a multipolygon with anywhere from 17,508 to 18,306 islands and atolls. To keep your column consistent, you'd promote Lesotho to be a multipolygon.

6.7 Simplification functions

In this section, we'll cover the three functions ST_SnapToGrid, ST_Simplify, and ST_SimplifyPreserveTopology. These functions behave quite differently from one another, but they all try to achieve the same goal: reducing the bytes necessary to describe a geometry.

Simplification functions become important when passing geometries across the internet. Despite recent advances, bandwidth is still a precious commodity, especially with wearable wireless devices. With a tiny, black-and-white, 200 × 300 resolution screen on a GPS watch, transmitting geometries with thousands of vertices or coordinates with a monstrous number of significant digits is certainly overkill.

6.7.1 Grid snapping and coordinate rounding

ST_SnapToGrid reduces the weight of a geometry by rounding the coordinates. If, after rounding, two or more adjacent coordinates become indistinguishable, it will automatically keep only one of them, thus reducing the number of vertices.

There are four variants of this function. The most common one takes one argument for tolerance and rounds the X and Y coordinates while leaving Z and M intact (ST_SnapToGrid doesn't remove Z and M coordinates). Other variants can round all four coordinates or allow you to specify tolerance. For example, a tolerance of 50 means that only coordinates within 50 units of each other can be rounded to the same value.

One common use of ST_SnapToGrid is to trim those extra floating-point decimals introduced by ST_Transform. Those extra digits can degrade performance and are generally a nuisance if the precision isn't needed. Another use of ST_SnapToGrid is to group distinct nearby points into a single representational point. For example, if you obtained point data for every school in the country, but you care only about the location of school districts, then clustering schools down to points would be the way to go.

As with most simplifying operations, you should exercise restraint. Too-ambitious rounding can inadvertently turn a valid polygon into an invalid one or, worse yet, into a single point.

6.7.2 Simplification

ST_Simplify and ST_SimplifyPreserveTopology both reduce the weight of a geometry by reducing the number of vertices of the geometry, using some variant of the Douglas-Peucker algorithm. The ST_SimplifyPreserveTopology function is newer than ST_Simplify and has safeguards against oversimplification, which means it's generally preferred over the older version even though it's a bit slower.

Both ST_Simplify and ST_SimplifyPreserveTopology take a second argument, which we'll term *tolerance*. This can be roughly treated as the unit of length between the vertices at which you'd want to collapse the vertices into one. For example, if you set the argument to 100, the two functions will try to collapse any vertices spaced up to 100 units apart. As you increase the tolerance, you'll experience more simplification.

Putting it another way, the more tolerant you are of losing vertices, the more simplification you can achieve.

These two simplifying functions, unlike ST_SnapToGrid, don't preserve M and Z coordinates and will remove them if present. They also work only for linestrings, multilinestrings, polygons, multipolygons, and geometry collections containing these geometries. For multipoints, they return the same input geometry without any simplification. The reason for this is that ST_Simplify and ST_SimplifyPreserveTopology require edges (lines between vertices) to achieve simplification. Multipoints don't have edges.

Don't use the ST_Simplify function with data in longitude and latitude; ST_Simplify and ST_SimplifyPreserveTopology assume planar coordinates. Should you use these functions with, say, SRID 4326, the resultant geometry can range from slightly askew to completely goofy. First transform to a preferably measure-preserving spatial reference system, then apply ST_Simplify, and then transform back to your lon/lat SRID.

The next listing compares the two functions.

Listing 6.18 Comparing ST_Simplify and ST_SimplifyPreserveTopology

```
SELECT
    pow(2,n) as tolerance,
    ST_AsText(ST_Simplify(geom, pow(2,n))) As simp1,
    ST_AsText(ST_SimplifyPreserveTopology(geom, pow(2,n))) As simp2
FROM
    (SELECT ST_GeomFromText(
        'POLYGON(
            (10 0,20 0,30 10,30 20,20 30,10 30,0 20,0 10,10 0)
        )') As geom) As x
    CROSS JOIN
    generate_series(2,4) As n;
```

You can see the results of listing 6.18 in table 6.7.

Table 6.7 ST_Simplify versus ST_SimplifyPreserveTopology

Tolerance	ST_Simplify	ST_SimplifyPreserveTopology
4	POLYGON((10 0,20 0,30 10,30 20,20 30,10 30,0 20,0 10,10 0))	POLYGON((10 0,20 0,30 10,30 20,20 30,10 30,0 20,0 10,10 0))
8	POLYGON((10 0,30 10,20 30,0 20,10 0))	POLYGON((10 0,30 10,20 30,0 20,10 0))
16	POLYGON((10 0,20 30,10 0))	POLYGON((10 0,30 10,20 30,0 20,10 0))

Notice that once you reach a tolerance of 16 with `ST_Simplify`, the geometry reduces to a triangle. In PostGIS 1.5, it would completely vanish. `ST_Simplify-PreserveTopology` reduces the eight-sided polygon to a four-sided polygon and stops there, regardless of the tolerance.

ST_Simplify behavior changes in PostGIS 2.0 and 2.1 from PostGIS 1.5 behavior

The behavior of `ST_Simplify` has undergone changes with each version of PostGIS. In PostGIS 1.5, it was possible for `ST_Simplify` to reduce to NULL, but in versions 2.0.0 and 2.0.1 the behavior changed to never simplify past its current subtype. For example, oversimplifying a polygon would not result in a point. This had the undesirable side effect of making the function simplification-shy, and polygons weren't quite as simple as they could be, so in version 2.0.2 `ST_Simplify` reverted back to the version 1.5 behavior.

6.8 Summary

In this chapter, we started covering the most commonly used functions in PostGIS. So far we've concentrated on functions with a single geometry or geography as an argument.

We developed a loose classification scheme to organize the myriad of unary functions in PostGIS. We started with output functions and then moved to constructors, getters and setters, and measurement functions, followed by decomposition and composition functions. We ended the chapter with simplification functions.

These popular functions constitute a small subset of all the unary functions available in PostGIS. We didn't cover all the functions PostGIS has to offer, even within this narrowed taxonomy. We highly recommend you peruse the official PostGIS documentation to see the full list of functions available (http://postgis.net/documentation). You may find the number of functions overwhelming at first, but on closer examination you'll find that many functions are closely related and fit nicely into our taxonomy. We also advise you to refer to the documentation before using any of the functions we described, to make sure you discern the nuances between overloads, take notice of exceptional cases, and keep up to date with changes in behavior as PostGIS evolves.

In the next chapter, we'll continue our study with raster functions, covering unary functions that work with rasters and grouping them in a similar way where applicable. One geometry output function we neglected to mention in this chapter is `ST_AsRaster`, which takes a 2D geometry (non-curved) and outputs to raster format. We'll cover this function and many more raster-centric functions in the next chapter.

7 Raster functions

This chapter covers

- Constructor functions
- Output functions
- Raster band and pixel accessors and setters
- Georeferencing functions
- Reclassing functions
- Polygonizing functions

The `raster` type is different in makeup from the `geometry` type covered in chapter 6. Geometries model an object as a set of linear equations, whereas rasters model an object as a tapestry of cells. In PostGIS, you'll find the two types working together, leveraging each other's strengths. For example, you can output a geometry in a raster file format such as PNG. You can also clip raster images with vector boundaries. We'll touch on raster processing in this chapter, but we'll leave the more thorough treatment for chapter 12, where we'll demonstrate advanced raster-processing functions, such as raster aggregate functions, map algebra functions, and set-returning functions.

The PostGIS `raster` type only supports pixels, which are 2D cells on an X-Y grid. It can't yet support voxels, which are pixels with more than two dimensions, but you can compensate by storing higher dimensional data as a band or using multiple rasters with the same coverage area. For example, if you have a raster with elevations and measurements, you can add two more bands: one to hold the Z value, and one to hold the M value.

As always, for the full breadth of raster functions, refer to the official documentation, "PostGIS raster functions reference": http://postgis.net/docs/RT_reference.html.

Let's start with raster constructor functions so that you can create rasters for the examples in this chapter.

7.1 Raster terminology

Before we begin, let's define some raster terminology:

- *Georeferencing*—A georeferenced raster means the pixels are pinned to a geographic reference system, defined in the spatial_ref_sys table. You generally note the spatial reference system by the SRID in the spatial_ref_sys table. Only if you specify the SRID can you transform to other SRSs. The term *georeference* is a bit of a misnomer, in that the SRID doesn't have to be earth-based but could very well be for another planet or an artificial coordinate system such as for building a floor plan, or for a virtual gaming world. Each pixel represents *x* units of the reference system (the pixel width) and *y* units of the reference system (pixel height). Conversely, a non-georeferenced raster means that the pixels have no correlation to any other coordinate system. The most common examples of non-georeferenced rasters are family pictures you snap with your camera. In contrast, if you boarded a high-altitude spy plane intending to snap pictures of enemy targets, you'd be negligent if you didn't include georeferencing.
- *Out-of-database or out-of-db*—You're free to store rasters as files outside of the database. If you choose out-of-database storage, PostGIS records a pointer to the file in the database, and you can then reference the out-of-db raster as if it were any other in-db raster. PostGIS will handle all the behind-the-scenes reading and conversion from the file—PostGIS never modifies out-of-db rasters, treating them as read-only. Out-of-db storage makes sense when you have massive amounts of reference data that must be accessible to other programs. When you're using out-of-db rasters, ensure that the Postgres service account can access the path and that it has read rights to the files. Should some aspect of the out-of-db raster change, such as paths, dimensions, georeferences, number of bands, or band types, you'll need to re-register the out-of-db data.
- *Raster tile*—A raster tile is a raster like any other raster. The main reason we differentiate a raster tile from a raster is to denote that the raster tile was created by chopping a bigger raster into a set of smaller rasters that can be reconstituted together via various raster operations. The main reasons people tile rasters is for speed and manageability.

- *Coverage*—Coverage is only relevant for georeferenced data, and it represents a non-overlapping expanse of space where each *n*th band represents the same reading in each raster tile of a raster column. In the context of a PostGIS raster, the coverage is often stored as a table of rasters where each raster in a particular table column represents a tile of space. When taken as a whole, all the rasters in the table column form a contiguous geographic space. In addition, each tile has the same number of bands, with each *n*th band storing the same kind of information. For example, you could define a grid covering Europe, chopped into tiles with each tile being stored as a raster that has two bands: one representing temperature and another elevation. When considered together, the set of rasters forms one huge raster covering Europe, without any tiles overlapping.
- *Same alignment*—Two rasters have the same alignment if they have the same skew, pixel scale ratio (the size one pixel represents in spatial coordinates), and the rasters' upper-left spatial coordinates are set such that the pixels of both can be put on the same grid. If the two rasters are georeferenced, they must also share the same spatial reference system. Many operations, such as unioning, require rasters to have the same alignment. If you're creating coverage tables, the tiles constituting the coverage must all be of the same alignment. If you're defining a coverage table for rasters, all the tiles must similarly have the same alignment.
- *Map algebra*—Map algebra is a fancy term for mathematical operations on a set of pixels over one or more bands. In PostGIS 2.0, map algebra was limited to one or two bands. PostGIS 2.1 overcame this limitation, and you can use map algebra against as many bands as you wish, but the result of any `ST_MapAlgebra` operation is a single-band raster. Map algebra can use all the PostgreSQL mathematical operations. In addition, PostGIS lets you define your own map algebra functions using any procedural language (PL) supported by PostgreSQL. Map algebra forms the foundation of many functions in PostGIS rasters such as `ST_Union`, `ST_Slope`, and `ST_HillShade`.
- *Neighborhood*—In the context of map algebra, a neighborhood is a contiguous, rectangular grid of pixels centered around a particular pixel. The neighborhood extends both *n* pixels to the right and left and *m* pixels up and down from the central pixel. The neighborhood therefore contains $(2n + 1) \times (2m + 1)$ pixels (note that the width and length will always be odd numbers). In PostGIS 2.1, there are several functions overloaded with the same `ST_MapAlgebra` name. From an API standpoint, because they all have the same name, they can be treated as a single function with many optional arguments. The neighborhood is an optional argument that is either `0` (the default if not specified, meaning the map algebra operation works on a single cell) or *n* pixels left/right, and *m* pixels up/down from the center pixel.
- *Reclass*—Reclassing is an operation that changes the range value of a raster. For example, you can reclassify all positive pixel values to be `+1` and all negative

values to be -1. If your pixel values represented sea-level elevations, instead of storing the actual heights, your raster would now take on the meaning of a location either above water or underwater. Reclassing is often used to remove noise introduced by instrumentation, to simplify a raster, or to convert a raster's floating values into integer values. Although it's similar to map algebra and can even be considered a subset of map algebra, reclassing often performs much more quickly than map algebra—in many cases, orders of magnitude faster.

PostGIS 2.1: more raster, faster raster, more vector raster action

Many improvements to raster functionality happened in the PostGIS 2.1 series. A lot of functions implemented in the PostgreSQL PL/pgSQL language in PostGIS 2.0 were rewritten in native C, providing orders of magnitude of speed improvements. In addition, new functions such as `ST_Tile` and `ST_Resize` were introduced. Support for out-of-database rasters, as well as non-georeferenced rasters, was made more robust and expanded. Map algebra involving *n* bands (instead of just 2 bands) was introduced. `ST_Union` became multiband-aware and was made orders of magnitude faster, significantly simplifying the syntax for unioning multiband rasters and stitching chunked images back together. In addition, a lot of the underlying map algebra was reworked to be more efficient.

Some examples in this chapter will showcase the new features in PostGIS 2.1, so if you want to take full advantage of this chapter, use PostGIS 2.1+. Be warned that some syntax has been deprecated between versions 2.0 and 2.1, so although the 2.0 syntax will usually work in version 2.1, it's best to use the newer syntax if you're running version 2.1 and don't need to support 2.0.

7.2 Raster constructors

There are several ways of creating PostGIS rasters:

- Convert PostGIS geometries to rasters with `ST_AsRaster`.
- Load rasters with the raster2pgsql loader. If you want to maintain the rasters outside of your database, you can use the `-R` switch of the loader to register them instead of importing them into the database.
- Create rasters from scratch using `ST_MakeEmptyRaster` and `ST_AddBand`, and then set pixel values using various other raster functions.
- Build rasters from existing rasters using processing functions such as unioning, tiling, map algebra, reclassifying, resizing, reprojecting, resampling, and so forth.
- Use the new PostGIS 2.1 function called `ST_FromGDALRaster`, which allows you to convert rasters in various formats to PostGIS rasters. All you need to have is the binary BLOB (byte array) of the input raster. This function is especially handy if you need to keep raster data in its source form, but you occasionally want to leverage the PostGIS raster functions.

POSTGIS 2.0.6+ AND 2.1.3+ SECURITY CHANGES AFFECT GDAL INPUT AND OUTPUT FUNCTIONS AND OUT-OF-DB RASTERS From PostGIS 2.0.6 and 2.1.3 on, all GDAL drivers are disabled by default, as is support for out-of-db rasters. Refer to the article "Security releases 2.0.6 and 2.1.3" on the PostGIS website (http://postgis.net/2014/05/19/postgis-2.0.6_and_2.1.3) for details on how to reenable selected drivers and out-of-db support. This default means your `ST_AsPNG` and other GDAL-based input/output functions may not work, and `ST_GDALDrivers`, which we'll discuss in this chapter, will list no drivers if you haven't enabled any.

In this section, we'll demonstrate some of these approaches for creating rasters.

For the purposes of this section, we'll create a table called *bag_o_rasters* to house the rasters we create:

```
CREATE SCHEMA ch07;
CREATE TABLE ch07.bag_o_rasters(
    rid serial primary key, rast_name text, rast raster
);
```

Keep in mind that creating a table of rasters with no constraints is useful for demonstrations, or as a transit table before pushing to other tables, or if you want to use PostGIS to manage your photo gallery. For GIS work, you'll almost always want to have georeferenced rasters with well-defined tiles, bands, SRIDs, and other constraints on the table to ensure that each raster row is a tile of a contiguous coverage.

7.2.1 Converting geometries to rasters with ST_AsRaster

You can convert rasters from geometries using the `ST_AsRaster` function. This is useful if you need to do any of the following:

- Output a geometry to an image format for viewing
- Overlay a geometry on a raster to highlight specific areas or to incorporate boundaries, roads, or points of interest
- Store numerical statistics about a region that you can then query with the raster analytic family of functions

In this section, we'll demonstrate the use of `ST_AsRaster` and how to use various optional arguments. Although `ST_AsRaster` can be used by itself, you'll often want to use it in conjunction with other raster functions, such as `ST_Union`, `ST_MapAlgebra`, and `ST_SetValues`.

Unfortunately, `ST_AsRaster` doesn't support curved or 3D geometries.

CREATE SINGLE-BAND RASTERS FROM GEOMETRY

Listing 7.1 creates two single-band rasters from one geometry. Because you don't specify a band type or band value, `ST_AsRaster` creates bands with the `8BUI` band type, which is the default when a band type is not specified (band types were discussed in chapter 2). A pixel value of `1` represents the geometry and a pixel value of `0` represents empty space.

Listing 7.1 Disproportional and proportional fixed-width rasters

```
INSERT INTO ch07.bag_o_rasters(rast_name, rast)
WITH a1 AS (
    SELECT ST_Buffer(
        ST_GeomFromText(
            'LINESTRING(
                448252 5414206,448289 5414317,448293 5414330,
                448324 5414417,448351 5414495
            )',
            32631),
        10
    ) As geom
)                                                    -- ① Road in Paris

SELECT 'disprop road', ST_AsRaster(geom,50,500) FROM a1    -- ② 50 × 500 pixel disproportional raster
UNION ALL
SELECT
    'proport fixed w road',
    ST_AsRaster(geom,200,(
        (ST_YMax(geom) - ST_YMin(geom)) *  200 /
        (ST_XMax(geom) - ST_XMin(geom))
    )::integer
FROM a1;                                             -- ③ Proportional raster
```

In listing 7.1 a CTE ❶ defines a road in Paris with a UTM SRID (32631), which means that each unit represents a meter. From the Paris road geometry ❷ a raster of 50 × 500 pixels is created. Because the ratio of the road is not 50/500, the raster is disproportional. The `UNION ALL` ❸ creates another raster with the same proportionality as the Paris road geometry, but with a fixed width of 200 pixels by using the Paris geometry bounding box width and height for the ratio factor to compute the pixel height.

The rasters generated by the code in listing 7.1 are shown in figure 7.1, which shows the Paris road drawn by squashing it in a fixed 50 × 500 box. Because the road's dimensional proportions are not 50 × 500, the first image doesn't correctly reflect the slant of the road. In the second image, the width is fixed at 200 pixels, and the height is computed based on the geometric dimensions. As a result, the image at right correctly displays the slanting of the road and the relative road thickness.

Figure 7.1 `ST_AsRaster`: the left line is fixed 50 × 500 and the second is proportional to the road but 200 px wide.

ALIGN ST_ASRASTER

If you plan to union many geometries together into a single raster or to overlay geometries on an existing raster, then you'll want to make sure that your geometries and rasters are in alignment. Perfect alignment requires all geometries and rasters to share the same SRID.

You can think of the reference raster (your canvas raster) as the grid the geometry lives on. If the coordinate region covered by the reference raster doesn't cover your geometry, then part of the geometry will be cut off. If the reference raster covers more area than your geometry, then the resulting geometry raster will be a subset of the reference. You can build that reference raster from scratch using ST_MakeEmptyRaster or use an existing raster.

Listing 7.2 is similar to listing 7.1, but instead of allowing the geometry to occupy the 50 × 500 area, this listing positions it relative to an existing grid, and the final raster will be a subset of that grid.

Listing 7.2 Geometry positioned by coordinates

```
WITH
    r AS
        (SELECT
            ST_MakeEmptyRaster(
                500,500,445000,5415000,2,-2,0,0,32631
            ) As rast
        ),
    g AS
        (SELECT ST_Buffer(
            ST_GeomFromText(
                'LINESTRING(
                    448252 5414206,448289 5414317,448293 5414330,
                    448324 5414417,448351 5414495)',
                32631),
            10) As geom
        )
INSERT INTO ch07.bag_o_rasters(rast_name, rast)
SELECT 'canvas aligned road', ST_AsRaster(geom,rast,'8BUI'::text)
 FROM r CROSS JOIN g;
```

❶ Create 500 × 500 reference raster starting at 445000, 5415000

❷ Road in Paris

❸ 8BUI raster of geometry aligned with reference

Listing 7.2 uses a CTE to define a reference raster that's 500 × 500 pixels with a spatial reference system of 32631, where each pixel represents 2 meters width/height ❶. Next, a CTE called g is created that holds a road in Paris as a geometry ❷. The final step ❸ creates a raster from the geometry road that's aligned with the reference raster. The resulting raster that's inserted into bag_o_rasters will have dimensions 60 pixels wide by 155 pixels high and be labeled *canvas aligned road*.

7.2.2 Loading rasters with raster2pgsql

You can use raster2pgsql to create a raster table and populate it with a set of related raster files. If your raster encompasses a great many pixels, raster2pgsql will create tiles for you with one tile occupying one row.

We covered loading rasters in chapter 4, so we'll only show one example here. We'll load the elephant called *Reo* into the bag_o_rasters table using a command-line command. We're going to keep Reo as an out-of-db elephant.

The following example dispenses with all the niceties of constraint and index switches you'd normally add because you're adding to an existing table that's a mixed bag of rasters. The -a switch indicates that you're loading into an existing table, so a new one won't be created.

```
raster2pgsql -e -R -a C:/pics/adbadge_tall.png ch07.bag_o_rasters
 | psql -U postgres -d postgis_in_action -h localhost -p 5432
```

After this command runs, there should be one unnamed raster in the table corresponding to the elephant image you just loaded. You can then fill in the `rast_name` field with `Reo` for the raster that has no name using this command:

```
UPDATE ch07.bag_o_rasters SET rast_name = 'Reo'
WHERE rast_name IS NULL;
```

7.2.3 Constructing rasters from scratch: ST_MakeEmptyRaster and ST_AddBand

In the followoing listing, you create an empty raster using `ST_MakeEmptyRaster`, add a single `8BUI` band to the raster using `ST_AddBand`, and set all the pixel values to `255` by passing `255` in as a default value for new pixels.

Listing 7.3 Building a raster from scratch

```
INSERT INTO ch07.bag_o_rasters(rast_name, rast)
SELECT
    'Raster 1 band scratch',
    ST_AddBand(                                    <-- Add band
        ST_MakeEmptyRaster(                        <-- Create empty raster
            500,500,445000,5415000,2,-2,0,0,32631
        ),
        '8BUI'::text,255,0                         <-- Initialize new 8BUI band with a value of 255
    ) As rast;
```

All the pixels in listing 7.3 have the same value. It's not all that interesting. We'll liven it up in our next example.

7.2.4 Setting pixels: ST_SetValue and ST_SetValues

Rasters store numeric values in their bands, and PostGIS has two functions for updating a raster band's pixel values with numeric values: `ST_SetValues` and `ST_SetValue`. Yes, one is singular, one is plural.

`ST_SetValue` came first, introduced with rasters in PostGIS 2.0. To use it to set the value of a pixel, indicate the column and row of the pixel (or a geometry) and the new value, as shown in the next listing. The order of the input parameters is as follows: raster, band number, column number, row number, new value.

Listing 7.4 ST_SetValue by column and row position

```
UPDATE ch07.bag_o_rasters AS b
SET rast = ST_SetValue(rast,1,10,20,146)
WHERE b.rast_name = 'Raster 1 band scratch';
```

ST_SetValues came about in PostGIS 2.1, and it allows you to set all the pixel values that intersect with a set of geomvals. A geomval is a composite PostgreSQL data type consisting of a geometry and a floating point value.

> **ST_SetValues and ST_SetValue in PostGIS 2.1**
>
> If burning values into rasters is something you need to do often, we suggest using PostGIS 2.1 or above. In addition to the ST_SetValues function introduced in version 2.1, the ST_SetValue function was augmented to accept more than just points. If you have to use PostGIS 2.0, and you want to burn a geometry image, your best bet is to build a geometry, align it with your raster, and use ST_MapAlgebraExpr to set the values.

PostGIS rasters are capable of generating heat and bubble maps, which show metrics like population, temperature, and vegetation using different colors (where, for example, color becomes redder as temperature increases) or bubble sizes (where the size of the bubble increases by the metric). In order to accomplish this task, you'll want to burn various geometries with a specific pixel value on an existing raster.

Listing 7.5 creates a copy of the previous Raster 1 band scratch and then uses ST_SetValues to burn a set of bubbles into this new raster. ST_SetValues is particularly useful for creating thematic maps where you need to burn in a particular geographic region with a particular value.

Listing 7.5 ST_SetValues: building a heatmap

```
WITH heatmap As (                    <-- 1 CTE heatmap

    SELECT array_agg(                <-- 2 Aggregate geomvals

        (ST_Buffer(
            ST_Translate(
                ST_SetSRID(
                    ST_Point(445500,5414500), 32631
                ),
                -500 + i * 150,
                -200 + 160 * i
            ),
            i * 50),
            50 + i * 15.0
        )::geomval
    ) As gvals
    FROM generate_series(-3,4) As i
)
```

```
INSERT INTO ch07.bag_o_rasters(rast_name, rast)
SELECT
    'Raster 1 band heatmap',
    ST_SetValues(rast,1, heatmap.gvals) As rast          <-3 Burn in gvals
FROM ch07.bag_o_rasters As b CROSS JOIN heatmap
WHERE b.rast_name = 'Raster 1 band scratch';
```

In listing 7.5 you create a CTE called `heatmap` ❶ composed of a single value called `gvals`, which is an array of geomvals accumulated with the PostgreSQL array aggregator function `array_agg` ❷. You buffer and translate the geometries to create ever larger circles, and then burn the array of geomvals onto band 1 of the raster ❸. In order for this operation to be successful, you need to make sure your geometries have the same spatial reference as the reference raster.

Figure 7.2 shows the raster image generated from listing 7.5. As shown in this figure, the different bubbles vary in shades of gray. Both the size of the bubble and the shading intensity depend on the value of `i`. The top bubble is cut off because its area exceeded the borders of the canvas. This grayscaled raster can be colorized using the `ST_ColorMap` function, which converts the single-band raster to one with RGB bands. We demonstrate the use of `ST_ColorMap` in our article, "Using ST_ColorMap for Thematic Maps," on the BostonGIS blog (http://www.bostongis.com/blog/index.php?/archives/222-Using-ST_ColorMap-for-Thematic-Maps.html).

Figure 7.2 `ST_SetValues`: **a heatmap**

7.2.5 Creating rasters from other rasters

PostGIS provides many functions for creating rasters from other rasters. Two commonly used functions are `ST_Band` and `ST_Clip`.

ST_CLIP: CROPPING RASTERS

The `ST_Clip` function allows you to cut out a portion of a raster using a geometry as your cutter. Imagine petits-fours here. The function can take a band number or array of band numbers as arguments. If you omit a band specification, the geometry will clip all bands. Remember, the geometry cutter you use must have the same SRID as the raster.

The following listing creates a single-band Reo using `ST_Clip`.

Listing 7.6 Using `ST_Clip`

```
INSERT INTO ch07.bag_o_rasters(rast_name, rast)
SELECT
    'Reo 1 band crop',
    ST_Clip(
        rast,
        1,
```

```
        ST_Buffer(ST_Centroid(rast::geometry), 75),
        255
    )
FROM ch07.bag_o_rasters
WHERE rast_name = 'Reo';
```

The code in listing 7.6 selects the first band and clips it with a 75 radius circle centered on the middle of the image (a piece of Reo's earlobe, as shown in figure 7.3). The last argument of 255 is an optional no-data value argument—if the clipped region contains pixels without any values, `ST_Clip` fills the clipped raster with the no-data value.

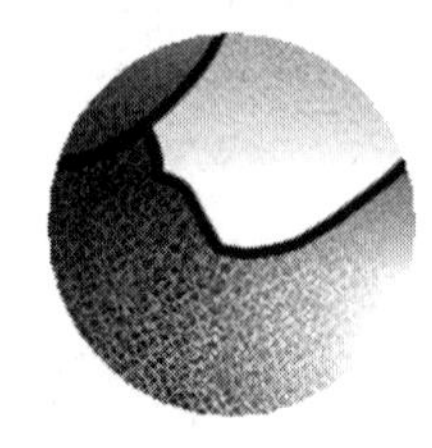

Figure 7.3 Reo's ear

`ST_Clip` has many optional arguments. One worth mentioning is `crop`, which defaults to `true`. With the default setting, the extent of the new raster is the extent of the intersection of the raster and the clipping geometry. If you pass in `false`, the dimensions of the new raster will be the same as those of the original.

Always keep `ST_Clip` in the back of your mind if you're given a giant raster with tens of thousands of pixels and you only need an isolated area. Your life will be easier if you crop out the region of interest into a new raster before starting your scrutiny.

ST_BAND: SELECTING SPECIFIC BANDS

The `ST_Band` function allows you to select one or more bands of a raster to form a new raster with the same dimensions, coordinates, SRID, and pixel values. The number of bands in the new raster will be equal to the number of bands you selected. You can also use this function to reorder bands, and you'll find it used in conjunction with `ST_AddBand` to combine single-band rasters into multiband rasters.

The first argument is always the raster, and the second is either an integer to indicate the band number or an array of integers to indicate more than one band or to indicate a shuffled order. The following example creates a new raster by shuffling the bands of the original Reo:

```
INSERT INTO ch07.bag_o_rasters (rast_name,rast)
SELECT 'Reo band shuffle', ST_Band(rast,ARRAY[3,1,2])
FROM ch07.bag_o_rasters
WHERE rast_name = 'Reo';
```

Reo takes on a purplish hue in the output, which is shown in figure 7.4.

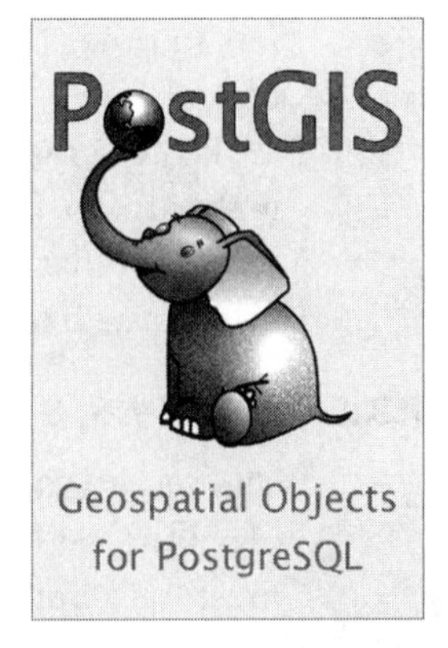

Figure 7.4 Reo shuffled

`ST_Band` doesn't pay attention to whether the raster is in-db or out-of-db. You shouldn't have to worry unless you're going to be saving the output of the `ST_Band` back to the database. If you also use `ST_AddBand`, your source raster can be both in-db and out-of-db. This is perfectly fine.

Creating and manipulating rasters means little if you have no way to share them with the rest of the world. In the next section, we'll show you some raster output functions.

7.2.6 Converting other raster formats with ST_FromGDALRaster

The PostGIS `raster` type is a format specific to PostGIS. When you use raster2pgsql to load rasters and opt for in-db storage, the loader converts the foreign raster format into the PostGIS raster format. But sometimes you already have `bytea` data (byte arrays) in your database that store the bytes of the original image, and you want to manipulate these right in the database, such as to resize them. In order to use the PostGIS raster functions, you'll need to convert these rasters into the PostGIS raster format.

`ST_FromGDALRaster` converts another raster type, such as PNG or JPEG images, to the PostGIS raster format. It's also smart enough to figure out what raster format you're starting with.

Suppose you had a table of pictures of various formats like bitmap (BMP), PNG, and JPEG, which stored the `bytea` (binary BLOB) of each picture. Your table structure would look something like this:

```
CREATE TABLE ch07.pics(pic_name varchar(255), pic bytea);
```

If you wanted to convert them to PostGIS raster format, so you could keep them with the rest of your growing bag of rasters, you'd run a query such as this:

```
INSERT INTO ch07.bag_o_rasters(pic_name, rast)
SELECT pic_name, ST_FromGDALRaster(pic) As rast
FROM pics;
```

This would convert all your pictures (as long as they're in a format supported by your PostGIS GDAL driver) to PostGIS `raster` format and insert them into the bag_o_rasters table. If you wanted to keep your images in a more common format, such as PNG or JPEG, then you'd convert back using one of the PostGIS raster companion output functions (`ST_AsGDALRaster`, `ST_AsPNG`, or `ST_AsJPEG`), which we'll cover in the next section.

7.3 Raster output functions

For distribution and interoperability, you'll want to be able to convert the PostGIS rasters to other raster formats. PostGIS offers several output functions to accomplish this conversion.

PostGIS raster output functions return byte arrays (`bytea`), which are the bytes that make up an image. Many rendering applications easily consume byte arrays. You'll even find that popular report writers, such as OpenOffice Base and Pentaho, can read byte arrays from a database.

7.3.1 ST_AsPNG, ST_AsJPEG, and ST_AsTiff

The `ST_AsPNG`, `ST_AsJPEG`, and `ST_AsTiff` functions output PostGIS rasters to the popular PNG, JPEG, and TIFF graphics formats. In order to use these functions, the raster must have binary unsigned integer (BUI) values as pixels. You may have to perform a reclass or colormap if your raster contains values outside of BUI. Rasters with three or four bands tend to output without problems, but you're not precluded from outputting rasters with fewer bands. To output more than four bands, you'll need to apply some sort of raster operation that will extract at most four bands from your existing raster.

> **Ad hoc raster querying**
> We used `ST_AsPNG` and `ST_AsJPEG` to generate the figures for this chapter. Using these functions, we've also built a simple ad hoc PHP/ASP.NET web application with JQuery and HTML for the front-end interface. You are welcome to download this tool for ASP.NET or PHP from the book's website at http://www.postgis.us/page_web_tools and customize it to suit your needs.

`ST_AsPNG`, `ST_AsJPEG`, and `ST_AsTiff` take optional arguments, such as compression and which band numbers to output, but the only required argument is the raster itself. To output the heatmap generated in figure 7.2, you'd run this query:

```
SELECT ST_AsPNG(rast) As png
FROM ch07.bag_o_rasters
WHERE rast_name = 'Raster 1 band heatmap';
```

7.3.2 Output using ST_AsGDALRaster

In addition to the aforementioned PNG, JPEG, and TIFF formats, PostGIS allows you to output rasters to any formats supported by your GDAL library. Keep in mind that GDAL supports many formats, and that PostGIS is usually only compiled with a subset of the formats possible. You can use `ST_GDALDrivers` to determine your output options and `ST_AsGDALRaster` to output in one of those formats.

USING ST_GDALDRIVERS TO LIST RASTER TYPES AVAILABLE FOR OUTPUT

If the version of GDAL installed with PostGIS didn't compile with any additional libraries, you should still have over 20 formats available. To see a listing, use the `ST_GDALDrivers` function as follows.

Listing 7.7 Listing raster formats available for output

```
SELECT short_name, long_name
FROM ST_GDALDrivers()
ORDER BY short_name;
```

The output of listing 7.7 is shown next. Your output may vary depending on the drivers your GDAL library is compiled with and also the drivers you decide to allow.

```
short_name       | long_name
-----------------+------------------------------------
AAIGrid          | Arc/Info ASCII Grid
DTED             | DTED Elevation Raster
EHdr             | ESRI .hdr Labelled
FIT              | FIT Image
GIF              | Graphics Interchange Format (.gif)
GSAG             | Golden Software ASCII Grid (.grd)
```

```
GSBG              | Golden Software Binary Grid (.grd)
GTiff             | GeoTIFF
:
PNG               | Portable Network Graphics
R                 | R Object Data Store
:
USGSDEM           | USGS Optional ASCII DEM (and CDED)
:
(25 rows)
```

This list of output formats is a subset of what you'd get with `raster2pgsql -G`, which outputs the list of readable formats using raster2pgsql. GDAL can read more formats than it can output to.

If you find your list is much smaller than what we've listed, this may be because GDAL drivers are disabled by default in PostGIS 2.0.6 and 2.1.3 on, as we noted earlier in the chapter. See the sidebar "PostGIS 2.0.6+ and 2.1.3+ security chanages affect GDAL input and output functions and out-of-DB rasters" in section 7.2 for the details.

You may need to meet additional requirements in order to export. `ST_GDALDrivers` outputs a third column, `create_options`, that we didn't list in the previous output. This is an XML column detailing information that must be or can be included with your output to a certain format. The raw XML isn't all that easy to digest, but PostgreSQL has functions that will expand the tags to make the column easier to read. We demonstrate in listing 7.8 how to use the PostgreSQL built-in `xpath` function to extract subelements of an XML field and the PostgreSQL `unnest` function to expand an array of XML elements into separate rows. This is applied to the USGS Digital Elevation Model (USGSDEM) `create_options` raster format.

Listing 7.8 Export options for USGSDEM

```
SELECT
    (xpath('@name', g.opt))[1]::text As oname,
    (xpath('@type', g.opt))[1]::text As otype,
    (xpath('@description', g.opt))[1]::varchar(30) As descrip
FROM (
    SELECT
        unnest(
            xpath('/CreationOptionList/Option',create_options::xml)
        ) As opt
    FROM ST_GDALDrivers()
    WHERE short_name = 'USGSDEM'
) As g;
```

Listing 7.8 truncates the description column to 30 characters with `::varchar(30)` so that it can be easily displayed on the page. The output follows.

```
     oname      |    otype      |          descrip
----------------+---------------+-------------------------------
 PRODUCT        | string-select | Specific Product Type
 TOPLEFT        | string        | Top left product corner (ie. 1
 RESAMPLE       | string-select | Resampling kernel to use if re
```

```
TEMPLATE          | string         | File to default metadata from.
DEMLevelCode      | int            | DEM Level (1, 2 or 3 if set)
DataSpecVersion   | int            | Data and Specification version
PRODUCER          | string         | Producer Agency (up to 60 char
OriginCode        | string         | Origin code (up to 4 character
ProcessCode       | string         | Processing Code (8=ANUDEM, 9=F
ZRESOLUTION       | float          | Scaling factor for elevation v
NTS               | string         | NTS Mapsheet name, used to der
INTERNALNAME      | string         | Dataset name written into file
```

USING ST_ASGDALRASTER TO EXPORT RASTERS

Once you've decided on an output format and met its requirements, use `ST_AsGDALRaster` to perform the output, as demonstrated in the following listing.

Listing 7.9 Raster output as USGSDEM

```
SELECT
    ST_AsGDALRaster(ST_Band(rast,1),
    ARRAY[
        'PRODUCER=' || quote_literal('postgis_in_action'),
        'INTERNALNAME=' || quote_literal(rast_name)
    ]) As dem
FROM ch07.bag_o_rasters
WHERE rast_name='Raster 1 band heatmap';
```

`ST_AsGDALRaster` takes three arguments: the band to output, the output raster format, and an array of optional or required information that GDAL needs to perform the output.

7.3.3 Using psql to export rasters

In all the output discussion thus far, we've only shown you functions. Usually, you have client applications or database connectors that will call these functions and perform the rendering or save the output to a file, as we demonstrate in a couple of ad hoc web-based query tools:

- *Postgis_webviewer (PHP and ASP.NET)*—https://github.com/robe2/postgis_webviewer
- *Pode_postgis_express (NodeJS)*—https://github.com/robe2/node_postgis_express

These tools both output PostGIS-generated images when passed a spatial query from the web browser.

But what if you want to export to a raster file without using another application? PostgreSQL doesn't interact with the OS filesystem, but psql does. You can use one of the output functions to create a binary BLOB, store this BLOB temporarily in the large objects systems table, and then use psql to export the BLOB to a file.

The following listing demonstrates how you can output the query from listing 7.9 to a file.

Listing 7.10 Exporting a raster as a DEM file using psql

```
SELECT oid, lowrite(lo_open(oid, 131072), img) As num_bytes
FROM (
    VALUES (
        lo_create(0),                         <-- Create large object
         (SELECT
            ST_AsGDALRaster(ST_Band(rast,1),
            'USGSDEM',
            ARRAY[
                'PRODUCER=' || quote_literal('postgis_in_action'),
                'INTERNALNAME=' || quote_literal(rast_name)]
            ) As dem
        FROM ch07.bag_o_rasters
        WHERE rast_name = 'Raster 1 band heatmap')   <-- Wrap raster
    )                                                     query output
) As v(oid,img);
                                                   Use oid returned
lo_export 9585208 'C:/temp/heatmap.dem'      <--  by previous query

                                            Delete large object
SELECT lo_unlink(9585208);            <--   after export
```

Run listing 7.10 in a psql client while connected to your database. PostgreSQL lets you include a query as an input to a function as long as a single value is returned (a scalar query)—you must surround the scalar query in parentheses. Psql creates a USGSDEM-formatted file on your local computer. To view the USGSDEM file, fire up QGIS and choose Layer > Add Raster Layer from the menu.

You'll find additional documentation for using psql as well as information on interfacing with various programming languages, such as PL/Python, PHP, Java, and .NET, in the PostGIS documentation, "Outputting Rasters with PSQL," at http://postgis.net/docs/using_raster_dataman.html#RasterOutput_PSQL.

Even though raster output functions only accept rasters as input, you don't need to have rasters to take advantage of them. All you need is an expression that resolves to a PostGIS raster. For example, if you created geometries that you would like to output to JPEG, use `ST_AsRaster` to convert the geometry to a raster, and then use the `ST_AsJPEG` function. There's no need to create `raster` type columns.

7.4 Raster accessors and setters

Rasters have many intrinsic attributes, such as width, height, scale, skew, and SRID, which you can read using raster accessor functions. You'll often constrain these attributes using table constraints, and the table constraints are built using the raster accessor functions. For example, if you're using a table to store high-resolution pictures tiled to rasters of 100 × 100 per row, you'd add check constraints to the table specifying that the width and height must be 100 and use the `ST_Width` and `ST_Height` raster functions to get the values of these attributes for each raster.

7.4.1 Basic raster metadata properties

The bag_o_rasters table defies constraints for the most part because it's a hodgepodge of unrelated rasters. But you can still retrieve attributes by calling the relevant raster accessor functions. We'll first cover accessor functions that return measurement and positional properties.

RASTER ACCESSOR FUNCTIONS: ST_WIDTH, ST_HEIGHT, ST_PIXELWIDTH, AND ST_PIXELHEIGHT

The following listing shows some raster metadata and band metadata functions.

Listing 7.11 Accessing raster properties

```
SELECT
    rid As r, rast_name,
    ST_Width(rast) As w,
    ST_Height(rast) As h,
    round(ST_PixelWidth(rast)::numeric,4) AS pw,
    round(ST_PixelHeight(rast)::numeric,4) As ph,
    ST_SRID(rast) AS srid,
    ST_BandPixelType(rast,1) AS bt
FROM ch07.bag_o_rasters;
```

Here's the output of listing 7.11:

```
r |        rast_name         |  w  |  h  |   pw    |   ph    | srid  |  bt
--+--------------------------+-----+-----+---------+---------+-------+-----
1 | disprop road             |  50 | 500 | 2.3791 | 0.6179 | 32631 | 8BUI
2 | proport fixed w road     | 200 | 519 | 0.5948 | 0.5953 | 32631 | 8BUI
3 | Reo                      | 600 | 878 | 1.0000 | 1.0000 |     0 | 8BUI
4 | canvas aligned road      |  60 | 155 | 2.0000 | 2.0000 | 32631 | 8BUI
5 | Raster 1 band scratch    | 500 | 500 | 2.0000 | 2.0000 | 32631 | 8BUI
6 | Raster 1 band heatmap    | 500 | 500 | 2.0000 | 2.0000 | 32631 | 8BUI
7 | Reo  1 band crop         | 150 | 150 | 1.0000 | 1.0000 |     0 | 8BUI
8 | Reo band shuffle         | 600 | 878 | 1.0000 | 1.0000 |     0 | 8BUI
```

The query in listing 7.11 outputs the width, height, pixel width, pixel height, SRID, and band type of the first band for each raster in the bag_o_rasters table.

ST_METADATA AND ST_BANDMETADATA

If you'd like to retrieve multiple properties all at once, make a call to the `ST_MetaData` or `ST_BandMetaData` function. These two functions spit out all the properties as a composite object. The `ST_MetaData` function outputs properties of the raster such as the width and height, whereas `ST_BandMetaData` outputs properties for a raster band such as the band pixel type and `nodata` value.

The following listing demonstrates the use of these functions.

Listing 7.12 Using `ST_MetaData` and `ST_BandMetaData`

```
SELECT rid As r, (rm).upperleftx As ux, (rm).numbands As nb, (rbm).*
FROM (
    SELECT
        rid,
```

```
        ST_MetaData(rast) As rm,
        ST_BandMetaData(rast,1) As rbm
FROM ch07.bag_o_rasters) As r;
```

The output of listing 7.12 follows.

```
 r|        ux      | nb | pixeltype  |nodatavalue|isoutdb|      path
--+---------------+----+-----------+-----------+-------+-------------
1 | 448242.02..  |  1 | 8BUI       |          0| f     |
2 | 448242.02..  |  1 | 8BUI       |          0| f     |
3 |             0 |  4 | 8BUI       |           | t     | ..ge_tall.png
4 |        448242 |  1 | 8BUI       |          0| f     |
5 |        445000 |  1 | 8BUI       |          0| f     |
6 |        445000 |  1 | 8BUI       |          0| f     |
7 |           225 |  1 | 8BUI       |        255| f     |
8 |             0 |  3 | 8BUI       |           | t     | ..ge_tall.png
```

In listing 7.12 you output only select properties returned by the `ST_MetaData` function, and all properties of the first band of each raster are returned by `ST_BandMetaData`.

7.4.2 Pixel statistics

In addition to supplying functions for obtaining metadata at the raster and band levels, PostGIS provides several functions for getting stats about the composition of the pixels and pixel values within a band. These functions return descriptive statistics that can aid you in making decisions about how to crop or reclass rasters. The functions in this category are `ST_Count`, `ST_Histogram`, `ST_Quantile`, `ST_SummaryStats`, and `ST_ValueCount`. By default, all these functions will ignore pixel values with no data.

In this section, we'll demonstrate the use of `ST_Histogram` and `ST_SummaryStats`. The other functions work in the same way as these two but return a table with different columns. Examples of these functions are in the PostGIS Manual, "Raster band statistics and analytics," at http://postgis.net/docs/RT_reference.html#RasterBand_Stats.

ST_HISTOGRAM

`ST_Histogram` provides summary statistics across the pixel values in a given band. You can ask the function to partition the values into buckets by specifying the number of total buckets or by providing the percentage of pixels you'd like to consider for each bucket. Keep in mind that the location of the pixels doesn't factor into the histogram, only its value.

In listing 7.13 you ask ST_Histogram to partition the pixel data into six buckets. The second argument is the band number. Although it's not demonstrated in this example, you can vary the size of the buckets by passing in a numeric array.

Listing 7.13 `ST_Histogram` band 2 into six buckets

```
SELECT (stats).*
FROM (
    SELECT ST_Histogram(rast,2,6) As stats
    FROM ch07.bag_o_rasters
    WHERE rast_name = 'Reo'
) As foo;
```

The output of listing 7.13 follows.

```
       min          |        max         | count  |       percent
--------------------+-------------------+--------+--------------------
                 29 | 66.6666666666667  |   9433 | 0.0179062262718299
   66.6666666666667 | 104.333333333333  |  10126 | 0.0192217160212604
   104.333333333333 |               142 |  15964 | 0.0303037205770691
                142 | 179.666666666667  |  43079 | 0.0817748671222475
   179.666666666667 | 217.333333333333  |  19205 |  0.036455960516325
   217.333333333333 |               255 | 428993 |  0.814337509491268
(6 rows)
```

Listing 7.13 returned a histogram for band 2 of the Reo raster broken into six buckets. As a result, the preceding output returns six rows corresponding to each bucket of a specific band in a raster, and each row gives the min, max, count of pixels that have values in this range, and percent count for that bucket with respect to the count of all pixels in that band.

ST_SUMMARYSTATS

ST_SummaryStats provides summary statistics for a single band or for the entire raster. In the following code, you ask for summary statistics from the second band. If you omit the band number, ST_SummaryStats will cover only pixel values in the first band.

```
SELECT (stats).*
FROM (
    SELECT ST_SummaryStats(rast,2) As stats
    FROM ch07.bag_o_rasters
    WHERE rast_name = 'Reo'
) As foo;
```

The summary statistics follow.

```
count  |    sum    |       mean        |      stddev       | min | max
-------+-----------+-------------------+-------------------+-----+----
526800 | 119211159 | 226.293012528474  | 43.0372444228884  |  29 | 255
```

Summary statistics do just what it sounds like—they summarize. But at a certain point, you may need to drill down to the pixel level. PostGIS has several accessors for pixels. Some will pinpoint specific pixels, and some will consider a particular region sectioned off using a geometry. We'll look at these next.

7.4.3 Pixel value accessors

There are several functions that return pixel values. Some of the more popular ones are ST_Value, ST_DumpValues, and ST_DumpAsPolygons.

ST_VALUE

ST_Value returns a single pixel value at a geometric point or raster row/column location. It's often used with elevation data to return the elevation at a particular location of interest.

ST_DumpValues

ST_DumpValues, new in PostGIS 2.1, returns a band as a 2D array, where the location in the array corresponds to the raster column/row and the values are the pixel values. The function can also handle multiple bands by returning a set of composites, where each record consists of the band number and the 2D array of pixel values. Some computational environments, such as R, work best with arrays.

ST_DumpAsPolygons

The functions that return geometry pixel-value combos use a special type called a geomval. You saw this type in use in listing 7.5 where you created an array of geomvals that was used to set pixels in a raster.

The ST_DumpAsPolygons function takes as input a raster and outputs a set of geomvals. The geom part of each geomval is a polygon geometry formed when you union all the pixels of a given pixel value. ST_DumpAsPolygons is often used to render a raster in GIS software that can only handle geometry data, such as OpenJUMP. The corresponding value field of the geomval is then used for coloring the polygon.

Listing 7.14 dumps the raster created in listing 7.5 as a set of geomvals and also the accompanying area of the corresponding polygons.

Listing 7.14 ST_DumpAsPolygons applied to heatmap raster

```
WITH X AS (
    SELECT ST_DumpAsPolygons(rast) As gv
    FROM ch07.bag_o_rasters
    WHERE rast_name = 'Raster 1 band heatmap'
)
SELECT
    ST_AsText((gv).geom)::varchar(30) AS wkt,
    ST_Area((gv).geom) As area,
    (gv).val
FROM Z;
```

The textual output of listing 7.14 follows.

```
             wkt               |  area  | val
-------------------------------+--------+-----
 POLYGON((445018 5414962,445018 |      4 | 146
 POLYGON((445410 5415000,445410 |  85992 | 110
 POLYGON((445400 5414922,445400 |  46208 |  95
 POLYGON((445290 5414720,445290 |  28884 |  80
 POLYGON((445140 5414510,445140 |   7840 |  65
 POLYGON((445000 5415000,445000 | 831072 | 255
```

Note how most of the dump consists of a large area with a value of 255, corresponding to the large white space of the raster.

We'll demonstrate another function that returns a geomval set, ST_Intersection, in chapter 12. ST_Intersection works much like ST_DumpAsPolygons except that it first filters the raster by a geometry before dumping the results. ST_Intersection, unlike ST_DumpAsPolygons, can return any kind of geometry for the geom portion of the geomvals.

In this section, you learned how to access the properties of a raster. In the next section, you'll learn how to set raster properties directly or change them indirectly via raster-processing functions.

7.4.4 Band metadata setters

You can set raster bands with a value that indicates they have no data value. We'll look at two related functions in this section: ST_SetBandNoDataValue and ST_SetBandIsNoData.

ST_SetBandNoDataValue

For a given band, ST_SetBandNoDataValue sets the value that represents no data. Remember that all pixels in a raster must have a non-NULL value, so you need to specify a non-NULL value to represent "no data." If you want to remove the ability to specify a no-data value, set the no-data value to NULL. This means that no value can be the no-data value, and your raster will never have a no-data value. Again, the no-data value is not NULL—all pixels must have a numeric value.

In the following example, you set the pixel value of 255 to represent no data. This means that for most operations, the 255 values will be ignored.

```
UPDATE ch07.bag_o_rasters
SET rast = ST_SetBandNoDataValue(rast,1,255)
WHERE rast_name = 'Raster 1 band heatmap';
```

This function is often used in conjunction with ST_Reclass when you need to map more than one value as no data.

ST_SetBandIsNoData

ST_SetBandIsNoData stamps the entire band as containing no useful data. You may find this function useful when working with raster coverages. Suppose that you imported a single-band raster of elevation on a Pacific atoll, which you tiled into 100 rows (100 rasters in their own right). Some 50 rows are ocean and have no analytical interest, but much third-party software expects your coverage to be rectangular. No tiles can be missing. To prevent PostGIS from considering the oceanic tiles when using processing functions, set their band to no data.

A similar situation is when you import a multi-band raster but have no need for the data in some of the bands. You can set entire bands to no data.

Another situation where this function is useful is when you're creating a template raster to accept data. The template may not have all bands populated at once. For example, if you have a ten-year study of the height of glaciers, you may start with one raster for each glacier you're tracking, and prepopulate them with ten bands of no-data value. As your decade-long measurement progresses, you can still write queries that encompass the entire ten bands, but PostGIS will automatically gloss over the bands with no data.

7.5 Georeferencing functions

You can't change all the properties of a raster once it's created. For example, you can reset the upper-left coordinate of a raster, or which pixel value of a band should be considered as representing no data, but you can't outright change the width and height of a raster.

In the following sections, we'll cover some of the properties that you can update using setters. Then we'll look at processing functions that drill down to the pixel level, allowing you to make more fundamental changes to rasters, such as raster width and height.

7.5.1 Metadata setters

Raster data has an origin that starts at the upper left, so pixels have positive X and negative Y values. Spatial coordinates, on the other hand, usually have an origin starting at the lower left, making for both positive X and Y values.

> **World file**
>
> A *world file* is a metadata sister file that lists the six numbers necessary to locate a rotated (or unrotated) raster in its reference system: four numbers for the size and shape of the pixels and two numbers to specify the upper-left corner of the raster.
>
> For some kinds of raster formats, this metadata is embedded directly in the file rather than as a separate text file. If no information is provided, raster2pgsql guesses at the X and Y pixel scale sizes and direction.

In this section, we'll explore the georeferencing functions used to set the orientation and sizing of the pixels relative to spatial coordinates. You'll find a complete listing of these functions in the "Raster Editors" section of the PostGIS official reference manual (http://postgis.net/docs/RT_reference.html#Raster_Editors).

ST_SetGeoReference

`ST_SetGeoReference` sets the basic six georeferencing numbers in one statement. This includes scale X, skew Y, skew X, scale Y, and upper-left corner X and Y coordinates, in that order. For example, `ST_SetGeoReference(rast, '10 0 0 -10 446139 2440440')` would set the `rast` PostGIS raster object to have 1 pixel width represent 10 spatial units, 1 pixel height represent –10 spatial units, and no skew, and it would set the upper-left corner to be X `446139` and Y `2440440`. If your spatial units are meters, then 1 pixel would be 10 meters wide.

ST_SetSRID

`ST_SetSRID` sets the spatial coordinate system that the raster uses. The upper-left corner coordinates and pixel sizes should be expressed in coordinates and units of this system.

This function is used either when you don't set the SRID during loading, or you discover the SRIDs of the rasters are mislabeled. Don't confuse this with `ST_Transform`, which also changes the SRID but reprojects all the pixels from one known SRS to another known SRS. `ST_SetSRID` does not reproject!

ST_SETUPPERLEFT

`ST_SetUpperLeft` sets the X and Y coordinates of the upper-left corner of the raster to coordinates in the SRID.

ST_SETSCALE

`ST_SetScale` sets the pixel width and height in units of the coordinate reference system. It specifies the number of units of spatial coordinate width and height that is represented by each pixel. There are two versions of this function. One takes separate X and Y values to set the ratios differently, and one takes a single XY value to set the ratios the same.

This function just changes the metadata and doesn't actually make changes to the pixels. A related function, `ST_Rescale`, is the processing function that algorithmically changes the underlying pixels of a raster from one known scale ratio to another.

ST_SETSKEW

`ST_SetSkew` sets the georeference X and Y skew (the rotation parameter). If only one coordinate is passed in, the X and Y skew will both take on the same value. The skew of `0` generally works fine for most rasters, but you may need to change this if your raster coordinate axis deviates from your spatial reference coordinate axes. Needing to account for magnetic deviation comes to mind.

This function just changes the metadata and doesn't touch the pixels. A related function, `ST_ReSkew`, is a processing function that algorithmically changes the underlying pixels of a raster from one known skew ratio to another.

GEOREFERENCING EXAMPLE

The next example demonstrates georeferencing a non-georeferenced raster by setting upper-left, upper-right, skew, scale, and SRID values in a single statement:

```
UPDATE ch07.bag_o_rasters
SET rast = ST_SetSRID(
    ST_SetGeoReference(rast, '1 0 0 -1 445139 5415000'),32631
)
WHERE rast_name = 'Reo 1 band crop';
-
```

> **DO NOT GEOREFERENCE OUT-OF-DB RASTERS** Although the system will let you, do not attempt to set georeferencing properties of out-of-db rasters aside from the SRID.

7.5.2 Processing functions

Sometimes, changing only the metadata of a raster is insufficient, and the underlying pixels must be visited. We'll describe the most common of these functions in this section.

All these functions employ a resampling algorithm that dictates how pixels will be transformed to arrive at the new georeferenced state. The default algorithm used by all of these functions is called *nearest neighbor* (NN). NN is fast, but it often leads to less-faithful transformations compared to other algorithms such as bilinear, cubic, cubic spline, or Lanczos. The resampling algorithm is passed in as an optional argument in each of the functions. For example, `ST_Transform(rast, 4326, 'Cubic')` would change the algorithm to be `Cubic`.

ST_TRANSFORM

`ST_Transform` changes the spatial coordinate system by projecting all the pixels from one known spatial reference system to another. It does for `raster` exactly what the geometry `ST_Transform` sibling does for `geometry`.

ST_RESCALE

`ST_Rescale` is the companion of `ST_SetScale`. It changes the pixel size of a raster, but does so by visiting every pixel and either reducing or increasing the number of pixels. As a result, this function affects both pixel scale as well as the raster width and height (the number of pixels per column and number of pixels per row). This function will only work with rasters that have a known SRID.

ST_RESAMPLE

`ST_Resample` is similar to `ST_Rescale`, but instead of giving it a target pixel size, you supply the overall target raster width and height. Versions prior to PostGIS 2.1 only work with rasters with a known SRID.

ST_RESIZE

`ST_Resize` is a new function in PostGIS 2.1 that allows you to set the width and height to a fixed number or a percentage of the original. It doesn't need a raster with a known SRID. Similar to the `ST_Rescale` function, it changes not only the width and height but also the pixel scaling to ensure that the new raster occupies the same geometric space as the old raster.

RASTER-PROCESSING EXAMPLE

Listing 7.15 demonstrates all the aforementioned functions.

Listing 7.15 Effects of various georeference-processing operations

```
WITH
    r As (
    SELECT rast
    FROM ch07.bag_o_rasters
    WHERE rast_name = 'canvas aligned road'
),
    r2 AS (
    SELECT 'orig' As op, ST_MetaData(rast) As rm FROM r
    UNION ALL
    SELECT 'resamp' AS op,
        ST_MetaData(ST_Resample(rast,300,300)) As rm FROM r
```

❶ Resample to 300 × 300 pixels

```
    UNION ALL
    SELECT 'tform' AS op,
            ST_MetaData(ST_Transform(rast,4326)) As rm FROM r        ❷ Transform to lon/lat

    UNION ALL
    SELECT 'resize' AS op,
            ST_MetaData(ST_Resize(rast,0.5,0.5)) As rm FROM r        ❸ Resize to 50%

    UNION ALL
    SELECT 'rescale' AS op,
            ST_MetaData(ST_Rescale(rast,0.5,-0.5)) As rm FROM r
                                      Rescale to 0.5 and –0.5 meters per pixel ❹
)
SELECT
    op,
    (rm).srid,
    (rm).width::text || 'x' || (rm).height::Text as wh,
    (rm).scalex::numeric(7,5)::text || ',' ||
    (rm).scaley::numeric(7,5)::text as sxy,
    (rm).upperleftx::numeric(11,2)::text || ',' ||
    (rm).upperlefty::numeric(12,2)::text As uplxy
FROM r2;
```

The output of listing 7.15 follows.

```
   op     | srid  |   wh    |        sxy        |         uplxy
----------+-------+---------+-------------------+---------------------
 orig     | 32631 | 60x155  | 2.00000,-2.00000  | 448242.00,5414506.00
 resamp   | 32631 | 300x300 | 0.40000,-1.03333  | 448242.00,5414506.00
 tform    |  4326 | 86x143  | 0.00002,-0.00002  | 2.29,48.88
 resize   | 32631 | 30x78   | 4.00000,-3.97436  | 448242.00,5414506.00
 rescale  | 32631 | 240x620 | 0.50000,-0.50000  | 448242.00,5414506.00
```

In listing 7.15 you pass the raster you created in listing 7.2 through various processing functions.

First, you resample, forcing the raster width and height to be 300 × 300 ❶. To compensate, pixel scaling goes from 2 meters to 0.40000 meters in the X direction, and 2 meters to –1.03333 meters in the Y direction.

Then you transform the raster to lon/lat projection, which causes the upper-left corner to show longitude and latitude ❷. The scaling and the width and height change as well.

Then you resize to 50% of the original for both width and height ❸. Because scaling doesn't change, each pixel takes up twice the coordinate space, approximately 4 meters instead of the original 2.

Finally, you rescale the raster so that each pixel represents 0.5 meters by –0.5 meters of coordinate space ❹. Because each pixel now represents less space, the overall dimensions of the raster enlarge four times in both X and Y directions to compensate.

7.6 Reclassing functions

ST_Reclass and its more general cousin, ST_MapAlgebra, are powerful functions that work at the pixel level. You can use these functions for the following purposes:

- Change band type by mapping a band of floating-point numbers to integer values, or vice versa.
- Identify and classify pixel values as having no data.
- Remap numerically close pixel values or neighboring pixels to a single value for easier vectorization. For example, you may want all pixel values from 0–10 to be treated as 0 and all values from 50–60 to be treated as 1. To smooth out spotty areas where values change because of instrumentation noise, you may want all pixels to take on the value of the average of all neighboring pixels.
- Interlace your raster by reducing the number of overall pixels.

Although the ST_Reclass functionality is a subset of what you can do using ST_MapAlgebra, the ST_Reclass syntax is generally easier syntax-wise and faster than map algebra functions.

In the following listing, you use the histogram statistics from section 7.1.1 to isolate the boundary of Reo. The result is shown in figure 7.5.

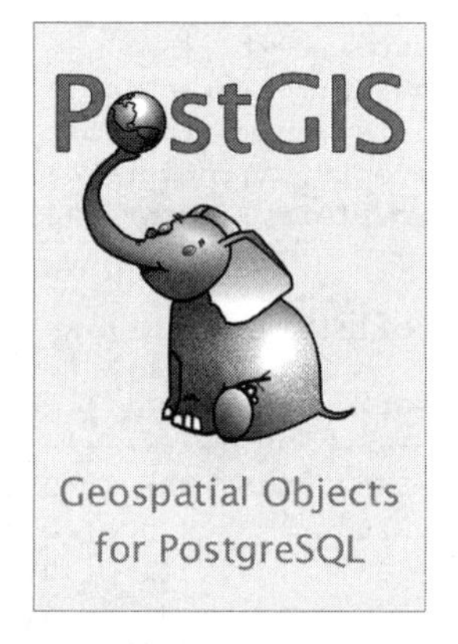

Figure 7.5 ST_Reclass: band 2 before and after reclassification

Listing 7.16 Creating single-band raster from reclassified second band

```
INSERT INTO ch07.bag_o_rasters(rast_name, rast)
SELECT
    'Reo 1 banded band 2 reclass',
    ST_Reclass(
        ST_Band(rast,2),                              <- Form new raster with just the second band
        1,                                            <- Reclass band 1 of new raster
        '[0-66]:0,(66-255]:255'::text , '8BUI'::text, <- Values > 66 and <= 255 are set to 255 and others are set to 0
        255                                           <- Define 255 as no data
)
FROM ch07.bag_o_rasters
WHERE rast_name = 'Reo';
```

ST_Reclass will always return the full raster with the specified bands reclassified. You may want to use ST_Band to limit the input raster, as in the preceding example, if you don't want the full raster back.

We'll leave the thorough treatment of ST_MapAlgebra for chapter 12.

7.7 Polygonizing functions

Polygonizing is the conversion of rasters to polygons. The simplest polygonizing functions take an entire raster, a band, or a set of bands as input and then return a single polygon.

In this section, we'll go over the functions that take a raster or a raster and raster band(s) as input and return a single geometry. In chapter 12 we'll explore more-advanced polygonizing functions that will return multiple polygons or geomvals.

7.7.1 ST_ConvexHull

`ST_ConvexHull` returns the convex hull of a raster, including pixels with no data. `ST_ConvexHull` is fast—only `ST_Envelope` is faster. PostGIS internally uses this function to cast from `raster` to `geometry` and to build spatial indexes.

`ST_ConvexHull` observes the skew of the raster. For non-skewed rasters, the hull will always be a rectangle. For skewed rasters, the hull will be a parallelogram.

7.7.2 ST_Envelope

`ST_Envelope` is similar to `ST_ConvexHull` but always returns the minimum bounding rectangle, and therefore is slightly faster. If your raster has a skew, `ST_Envelope` returns the rectangle that bounds the parallelogram.

7.7.3 ST_Polygon

`ST_Polygon` creates a polygon or multipolygon by unioning all the geometric representations of pixels. In PostGIS 2.1, the function was rewritten completely in C, providing a notable speed improvement. Additional validation was also added to ensure that it always returns a valid multipolygon.

`ST_Polygon`, when used in conjunction with `ST_Reclass`, is indispensable for image recognition. Consider the following scenario: A volcano erupts in Iceland, sending a plume of ash into the stratosphere. A satellite produces a raster image of the dust against the backdrop of the earth below. With this raster, you first use reclassing to pick out the ash-colored pixels, setting all others to no data. You then use `ST_Polygon` to cast the smoke plume to a polygon. Then you can intersect the polygon with the linestrings of the North Atlantic Tracks (http://en.wikipedia.org/wiki/North_Atlantic_Tracks) to figure out which airline routes will be affected. To be more precise, you can use multiple satellites to create multiband rasters—one band for each 5,000 feet. You can pass specific bands or entire rasters to `ST_Polygon`.

7.7.4 ST_MinConvexHull

`ST_MinConvexHull` is a new function in PostGIS 2.1 that returns the same answer as `ST_ConvexHull` but removes `nodata` pixels from the edge inward. `nodata` pixels completely surrounded by data pixels have no chance of being excluded.

You'll find this function useful for removing pesky padding added to rasters to make them fill a given pixel width or height requirement. Think of old Polaroid photos with their uneven white frame that served no purpose.

If you don't yet have PostGIS 2.1, you can achieve the same effect, though much more slowly, by the chain `ST_Envelope(ST_Polygon)`.

The following listing shows the difference between `ST_ConvexHull` and `ST_MinConvexHull`.

Listing 7.17 Comparing `ST_ConvexHull` and `ST_MinConvexHull`

```
SELECT
    rast_name::varchar(10),
    ST_AsText(ST_ConvexHull(rast)) As hull,
    ST_AsText(ST_MinConvexHull(rast)) As minhull
FROM ch07.bag_o_rasters
WHERE rast_name IN('Reo','Reo 1 banded band 2 reclass');
```

The output of this listing follows.

```
rast_name | hull                    |  minhull
----------+-------------------------+--------------------------
Reo       | POLYGON((0 0,600 0,     | POLYGON((0 0,600 0,
          | 600 -878,0 -878,0 0))   | 600 -878,0 -878,0 0))
Reo 1 ban | POLYGON((0 0,600 0,     | POLYGON((75 -104,490 -104,
          | 600 -878,0 -878,0 0))   | 490 -626,75 -626,75 -104))
```

Notice that although both rasters have the same convex hull, the minimum convex hull of the raster occupies a smaller area because pixels with no data on the edges were removed. When `ST_MinConvexHull` is used without a band number, it considers all bands, only considering a pixel as having no data if all of the band values in that pixel have the `nodata` value. When applied to a specific band, `ST_MinConvexHull` only inspects that specific band and considers that pixel as having no data if the pixel value of the band is the `nodata` value. `ST_ConvexHull` always applies to all bands because it never checks pixel values.

7.8 Summary

In this chapter, you got a glimpse into PostGIS's raster functionality. You learned about functions for outputting raster attributes, functions for creating rasters, and functions for reshaping rasters. We also demonstrated how rasters and geometries can work together via clipping, rasterization, and vectorization.

This chapter provides the groundwork for what's to come in later chapters. We didn't touch any real data in this chapter, but just experimented on the PostGIS trademark elephant holding up a globe. In chapter 12 we'll revisit these functions and many more, working with them to solve specific real-world problems. But before we revisit rasters, we'll take a look at geocoding and address standardization utilizing the PostGIS TIGER geocoder extension.

8 PostGIS TIGER geocoder

This chapter covers

- Address normalization
- Geocoding
- Reverse geocoding

What is a geocoder? It's a utility that takes a textual representation of a street address and finds its geographic position using data such as street centerline geometries. Geocoders generally return the longitude and latitude.

In this chapter, we're going to focus on the PostGIS geocoder specifically designed for TIGER. The TIGER acronym stands for Topologically Integrated Geographic Encoding and Referencing, and it's a geospatial database maintained by the U.S. Census Bureau. The database encompasses key features of geographic interest in the entire United States, including political boundaries, lakes, reservations, major and minor roads, rivers, and so on.

POSTGIS TIGER GEOCODER REQUIREMENTS To use the PostGIS TIGER geocoder, you must have PostGIS 2.0 or higher. If this doesn't describe you, stop reading, upgrade, and then rejoin our discussion.

We'll lead you through the following steps in this chapter so that you'll have a fully functioning geocoder at the end:

1. Installing the PostGIS TIGER geocoder
2. Downloading the data from the U.S. Census Bureau for your region of interest
3. Using an address normalizer to prepare your address
4. Geocoding and interpreting the results
5. Reverse geocoding

The U.S. Census Bureau annually updates TIGER data to reflect new constructions. Also, in many years, the data structure itself might be slightly amended. PostGIS tries to keep up with the latest structural changes to TIGER: PostGIS 2.1 handles the 2013 data structure, and the upcoming PostGIS 2.2 handles 2014.

8.1 Installing the PostGIS TIGER geocoder

With the new PostgreSQL extension feature, installing the geocoder involves nothing more than running two SQL commands or making a few clicks in pgAdmin. In psql or the pgAdmin query window, run the following two lines:

```
CREATE EXTENSION fuzzystrmatch;
CREATE EXTENSION postgis_tiger_geocoder;
```

The geocoder relies on string matching to find streets with similar spellings, which is why you need to install the fuzzy-string-match extension.

Because TIGER data is public, you should grant other users unfettered access to read from it, as shown in the following listing.

Listing 8.1 Granting permissions to TIGER

```
GRANT USAGE ON SCHEMA tiger TO PUBLIC;                    <-- ❶ Grant existing permissions
GRANT USAGE ON SCHEMA tiger_data TO PUBLIC;
GRANT SELECT, REFERENCES, TRIGGER
    ON ALL TABLES IN SCHEMA tiger TO PUBLIC;
GRANT SELECT, REFERENCES, TRIGGER
    ON ALL TABLES IN SCHEMA tiger_data TO PUBLIC;
GRANT EXECUTE
    ON ALL FUNCTIONS IN SCHEMA tiger TO PUBLIC;
ALTER DEFAULT PRIVILEGES IN SCHEMA tiger_data
GRANT SELECT, REFERENCES                                  ❷ Grant future permissions
    ON TABLES TO PUBLIC;                             <--
```

First, you grant permissions on existing objects to the PUBLIC role ❶. For future tables created in the tiger_data schema, assign default privileges ❷. Note that by convention we use uppercase for the PUBLIC role to distinguish it from the public schema.

TIGER_DATA CHANGES Versions of postgis_tiger_geocoder prior to PostGIS 2.1.1 didn't create the tiger_data schema during install. For versions prior to 2.1.1, you should either create the tiger_data schema manually or delay setting permissions until you've loaded the TIGER data.

The CREATE EXTENSION postgis_tiger_geocoder; code line, in addition to installing all the necessary skeleton tables and functions, adds the tiger schema to your database search path. But this may not happen if you have your own custom search_path. Before continuing, verify that tiger is in your search_path by disconnecting from your database, reconnecting, and running SHOW search_path; in psql or pgAdmin.

Installing the geocoder doesn't load the TIGER data that you'll need to geocode. That comes next.

8.2 Loading TIGER data

To populate the tables created during geocoder installation, you'll have to visit the U.S. Census FTP site, download the compressed shapefiles, decompress them, and use the shp2pgsql utility to load the files into the appropriate tables. Sounds like many hours of frustration? Fortunately, the geocoder has several functions that will generate scripts to cover all these steps. We'll look at how you can generate and use these scripts for PostGIS 2.1 and above.

The scripts will vary depending on your OS, and they rely on two free additional utilities that must be on your server: Wget and 7-Zip (or unzip). For Linux, Unix, and Mac users, Wget and unzip should already be present. Windows users can install Wget for Windows and 7-Zip. (See chapter 4 for the details on installing these tools.)

8.2.1 Configuration tables

You'll want to edit two tables that control the loader scripts' outputs: tiger.loader_platform and tiger.loader_variables.

The tiger.loader_variables table is a one-record table containing various paths. The only field you should need to edit in this table is the staging_fold field, which specifies the path where you'll download the data and create the temp folder.

The tiger.loader_platform table contains the profiles used to generate the loader scripts. There are two records each uniquely identified by the os field value: windows generates a DOS batch script, and sh generates a Unix sh/bash-compatible script. You can edit the declare_sect field to change database connection strings or paths to the PostgreSQL bin or to shp2pgsql, unzip, and Wget.

8.2.2 Loading nation and state data

Before you can start to load data, you'll need to create a folder to house the downloaded TIGER zip files and a temporary folder to extract and process them. Create a directory called *gisdata* and a subdirectory within it called *temp* in the location you specified in the tiger.loader variables table's staging_fold field. Where you create the directories doesn't matter; just make sure the directories are writeable.

Now connect to your database from the interactive psql console. If you're on Linux, Unix, or Mac, run the code in listing 8.2. If you're on Windows, run listing 8.3. In these listings, change the line \o ...gisdata to start with the folder path you created to house the data.

Listing 8.2 Generate nationscript (for Linux/Unix/Mac)

```
\t
\a
\o /gisdata/nationscript.sh
SELECT loader_generate_nation_script('sh');
\o
```

Listing 8.3 Generate nationscript (for Windows)

```
\t
\a
\o /gisdata/nationscript.bat
SELECT loader_generate_nation_script('windows');
\o
```

Psql will place the script file in the gisdata directory. Open up the file in an editor and make changes to the path and database connection as appropriate. Once you've made the changes and double-checked your typing, go ahead and execute the script file from your OS command line. After you've executed the script, you should see a couple of new tables in your `tiger_data` database schema. The two of most importance are states_all and county_all.

Now that you've had some practice at loading data, let's generate a script to load individual state data. If you're on Linux, Unix, or Mac, run listing 8.4. If you're on Windows, run listing 8.5. If you created a custom profile in the tiger.loader_platform table, use that name instead of `sh` or `windows`. Also, be sure to substitute in your favorite states. Even if you want data for all states, you still have to add them to the array one by one.

Listing 8.4 Generate statescript (for Linux/Unix/Mac)

```
\t
\a
\o /gisdata/statescript.sh
SELECT loader_generate_script(ARRAY['DC','CO'],'sh');
```

Listing 8.5 Generate statescript (for Windows)

```
\t
\a
\o /gisdata/statescript.bat
SELECT loader_generate_script(ARRAY['DC','CO'],'windows');
\o
```

Follow the same editing step as for the nationscript, and then execute the generated script. The script will load data for all the states you chose. You should see new tables in the `tiger_data` schema, all prefixed with the state abbreviation. Should you wish to load additional states later, just regenerate statescript with different states.

After you are done loading data, be sure to run this SQL statement: `SELECT install_missing_indexes();`. That will ensure all the indexes needed by the geocoder functions are in place.

8.3 Normalizing addresses

A preparatory step before geocoding is to parse the address into components such as street numbers, directional prefixes, street names, suffixes, and so on. This step is often referred to as *address standardization* or *address normalization.*

Although address normalization is often done as part of geocoding, you should consider it a separate step. Once you've standardized the addresses, you can pass them to many different geocoders, not just the PostGIS TIGER geocoder. You can even use the standardized addresses to meet postal addressing standards or to remove duplicate addresses. And there's nothing to stop you from performing the quicker standardization step on weekdays and leaving the slower geocoding step to run over the weekend.

8.3.1 Using normalize_address

Standardizing the input addresses to match TIGER conventions greatly improves the accuracy of geocoding. The PostGIS TIGER geocoder includes a function called `normalize_address` for standardizing addresses in accordance with TIGER conventions. You pass in an address as a string, and the output is a composite object called `norm_addy`.

Let's look at an example. The following listing standardizes five addresses.

Listing 8.6 Using `normalize_address`

```
SELECT normalize_address(a) As addy
FROM (
    VALUES
        ('ONE E PIMA ST STE 999, TUCSON, AZ'),
        ('4758 Reno Road, DC 20017'),
        ('1021 New Hampshare Avenue, Washington, DC 20010'),
        ('1731 New Hampshire Ave Northwest, Washington, DC 20010'),
        ('1 Palisades, Denver, CO')
) X(a);
```

The output is the five `norm_addy` objects in the following listing.

Listing 8.7 `normalize_address` output: `norm_addy`

```
                              addy
-------------------------------------------------------
 (,,"ONE E PIMA ST",St,,"STE 999",TUCSON,AZ,,t)
 (4758,,Reno,Rd,,,,DC,20017,t)
 (1021,,"New Hampshare",Ave,,,Washington,DC,20010,t)
 (1731,,"New Hampshire",Ave,NW,,Washington,DC,20010,t)
 (1,,Palisades,,,,Denver,CO,,t)
```

To see some of the constituent parts of norm_addy, you can use the following SQL statement.

Listing 8.8 Viewing parts of norm_addy

```
WITH A AS (
    SELECT normalize_address(a) As addy
    FROM (
        VALUES
            ('ONE E PIMA ST STE 999, TUCSON, AZ'),
            ('4758 Reno Road, DC 20017'),
            ('1021 New Hampshare Avenue, Washington, DC 20010'),
            ('1731 New Hampshire Ave Northwest, Washington, DC 20010'),
            ('1 Palisades, Denver, CO')
    ) X(a)
)
SELECT
    (addy).address As num,
    (addy).predirabbrev As pre,
    (addy).streetname || ' ' || (addy).streettypeabbrev As street,
    (addy).location As city,
    (addy).stateabbrev As st
FROM A;
```

You can clearly see the distinct fields making up norm_addy in the following listing.

Listing 8.9 Parts of norm_addy composite object

```
 num  | pre |       street        |    city    | st
------+-----+--------------------+------------+----
      |     | ONE E PIMA ST St   | TUCSON     | AZ
 4758 |     | Reno Rd            |            | DC
 1021 |     | New Hampshare Ave  | Washington | DC
 1731 |     | New Hampshire Ave  | Washington | DC
    1 |     |                    | Denver     | CO
```

If you want to see all the constituent parts of addy as separate columns, you can replace the selected fields with (addy).*. The downside of using .* is that you have no control over the column names.

8.3.2 Using the PAGC address normalizer

The normalize_address function isn't without its shortcomings. We've seen cases where it fails to parse correctly when addresses have directional prefixes such as North or South or when there are additional elements not relevant to the geocoding, such as floor numbers. PostGIS 2.1 borrows from the Postal Address Geo-coder (PAGC) project to augment the normalize_address function.

Before you can use the PAGC normalizer in PostGIS 2.1, you need to install the extension as follows:

```
CREATE EXTENSION address_standardizer;
```

> **Using address_standardizer in PostGIS 2.2**
>
> In PostGIS 2.1, the address_standardizer extension was a separate project from PostGIS, branched off of the PAGC project. The source code location for the older version and the compile and install directions are documented in the PostGIS 2.1 manual (http://postgis.net/docs/manual-2.1/postgis_installation.html#installing_pagc_address_standardizer). In PostGIS 2.1, only the Windows StackBuilder distribution of PostGIS carries a precompiled version of this extension. Unix, Linux, and Mac users need to compile it for themselves.
>
> In PostGIS 2.2, the address_standardizer extension is incorporated into the PostGIS code base. If you're running PostGIS 2.2, chances are you already have this extension available. As of this writing, PostGIS 2.2 is not out yet.

The `pagc_normalize_address` function is packaged with `postgis_tiger_geocoder` and wraps the more generic `standardize_address` function of the address_standardizer extension to do the standardization work. In order to be swappable with the regular `normalize_address` function, the `pagc_normalize_address` function returns a `norm_addy` custom object just like the `normalize_address` function does, and it also takes the same inputs.

Let's try the same set of addresses with the `pagc_normalize_address` function.

Listing 8.10 Using `pagc_normalize_address`

```
WITH A AS (
    SELECT pagc_normalize_address(a) As addy
    FROM (
        VALUES
            ('ONE E PIMA ST STE 999, TUCSON, AZ'),
            ('4758 Reno Road, DC 20017'),
            ('1021 New Hampshare Avenue, Washington, DC 20010'),
            ('1731 New Hampshire Ave Northwest, Washington, DC 20010'),
            ('1 Palisades, Denver, CO')
    ) X(a)
)
SELECT
    (addy).address As num,
    (addy).predirabbrev As pre,
    (addy).streetname || ' ' || (addy).streettypeabbrev As street,
    (addy).location As city,
    (addy).stateabbrev As st
FROM A;
```

The output follows.

Listing 8.11 The `pagc_normalize_address` output

```
 num  | pre |       street        |    city     | st
------+-----+---------------------+-------------+----
    1 | E   | PIMA ST             | TUCSON      | AZ
 4758 |     | RENO RD             | DC          |
```

```
1021 |      | NEW HAMPSHARE AVE | WASHINGTON | DC
1731 |      | NEW HAMPSHIRE AVE | WASHINGTON | DC
   1 |      |                   | DENVER     | CO
```

If you compare the output of normalize_address and pagc_normalize_address, you'll notice the better handling of the Tucson address in the latter. PAGC can decipher spelled street numbers. Also notice that PAGC always outputs in uppercase. Although the geocoder doesn't care about case, the USPS really hates anything but uppercase.

The PAGC address_standardizer extension was designed with modularity in mind. All standardizers follow a set of rules and use dictionaries for common terms, but these rules differ. For example, USPS normalizers adhere to a list of suffix abbreviations and always capitalize. Instead of having to write a new normalizer for each set of rules, PAGC lets users change standards simply by specifying a different set of tables.

In addition to the input address, the standardize_address function expects as input the names of a rules table, a lexicon table, and a gazetteer table.

The PostGIS TIGER geocoder includes its own set of PAGC-compatible dictionary and rules tables that are used as inputs to the standardize_address function: tiger.pagc_lex, tiger.pagc_gaz, and tiger.pagc_rules. These tables ensure that the output of the normalization process conforms to how TIGER data is structured. We'll describe the structure of these tables in a bit when we discuss the standardize_address function.

Lexicon and gazetteer tables are dictionary tables: A *lexicon* handles generic replacements, such as the word *five* to the number *5*. A *gazetteer* handles geographical name replacements, such as *California* to *CA*. The structure of the lexicon and gazetteer tables are identical, and they must have at least the following columns: id, seq, word, stdword, and token.

The rules table is a table of rules where each row contains an ID and a rule. The ID is just a number. The rule is a sequence of numbers that denote tokens and separators. For more details about what the token numbers correspond to and how rules are set up, refer to the section, "Address Standardizer Rules Table structure," in the PostGIS Manual (http://postgis.net/docs/manual-dev/rulestab.html).

You can create an alternate set of rules, gaz, and lex tables to suit your needs and pass the table names in as inputs to the standardizer. This will allow you to switch between conventional address geocoding and oddballs like the grid-style addresses found in Utah and alphanumeric addresses found in Wisconsin.

The following listing demonstrates a call to standardize_address.

Listing 8.12 Normalizing using standardize_address

```
WITH A(a) AS (
    VALUES
        ('ONE E PIMA ST STE 999, TUCSON, AZ'),
        ('4758 Reno Road, DC 20017'),
        ('1021 New Hampshare Avenue, Washington, DC 20010'),
        ('1731 New Hampshire Ave Northwest, Washington, DC 20010'),
        ('1 Palisades, Denver, CO')
```

```
)
SELECT (s).house_num, (s).name, (s).predir, (s).suftype, (s).sufdir
FROM (
    SELECT standardize_address(
        'pagc_lex','pagc_gaz','pagc_rules', a
    ) As s FROM A
) AS X;
```

The output of listing 8.12 follows.

Listing 8.13 Output of standardize_address

```
 house_num |      name       | predir | suftype | sufdir
-----------+-----------------+--------+---------+--------
 1         | PIMA            | E      | ST      |
 4758      | RENO            |        | RD      |
 1021      | NEW HAMPSHARE   |        | AVE     |
 1731      | NEW HAMPSHIRE   |        | AVE     | NW
 1         | PALISADES       |        |         |
```

The output of the standardize_address function is a composite type object called stdaddr, which is similar in flavor to the norm_addy composite type we already covered. We're only outputting some of the fields that make up stdaddr. If you want to see all the fields, don't itemize but substitute in (s).*.

Speed of standardize_address versus pagc_normalize_address

The output of standardize_address isn't a norm_addy object but rather a stdaddr object, which the PostGIS geocoder can't accept. The pagc_normalize_address function automatically maps stdaddr fields to norm_addy fields so that you can hand off the results to the geocoder, but pagc_normalize_address is an inefficient wrapper around standardize_address. If speed is of importance, we suggest that you call standardize_address directly instead of going through pagc_normalize_address. You'll need to put in the extra work of mapping stdaddr to norm_addy, but the speed you'll gain in the normalization could be up to ten-fold or greater. The PostGIS manual (http://postgis.net/docs/manual-dev/Pagc_Normalize_Address.html) provides an example.

8.4 Geocoding

You have two options when calling the geocode function. You can pass it a norm_addy composite object, or you can pass it an address string. If you opt for the latter, geocode will apply the normalize_address function before geocoding.

This means that if you wish to use pagc_normalize_address, you must standardize first and then pass in a norm_addy object to geocode. Alternatively, you can run the following SQL statement:

```
SELECT set_geocode_setting('use_pagc_address_parser', 'true');
```

This code changes the default behavior of the geocode function permanently to use the pagc_normalize_address function instead of normalize_address when given a plain-text address. Switch this back to false if you need to go back to using normalize_address.

By default, geocode returns up to ten matches with a rating. The lower the rating, the better the match, and a rating of 0 means a perfect match. If you have no additional means of adjudicating among the choices, and you only want the best match, geocode lets you pass in an additional argument indicating the number of records to be returned. If you just want the best match, pass in 1.

8.4.1 Geocoding using address text

This next example uses the geocode function to geocode a plain-text address. Because a plain-text address is passed in, the geocode function standardizes the address before geocoding.

Listing 8.14 Geocode function with a built-in standardization step

```
SELECT
    g.rating As r,                     <-- 1 Rating
     ST_X(geomout) As lon,
    ST_Y(geomout) As lat,
    pprint_addy(addy) As paddress          <-- 2 Pretty-print norm_addy
FROM
    geocode(
        '1731 New Hampshire Avenue Northwest, Washington, DC 20010'
    ) As g;
```

The geocode function takes an address and returns a set of records that are possible matches for the address. One of the columns output by the geocode function ❶ is the rating field. The higher the number, the worse the match. One of the objects is a composite type, norm_addy, and it's output as a field called addy in the returned records. You can pass the returned addy field to a pprint_addy function ❷, which is packaged with the TIGER geocoder, and this will return a pretty-print text version of the address.

The point geometry in longitude and latitude that geocode outputs is called geomout. This point is interpolated along the street segment by its street number. The TIGER data is aware of which side of the street a street number should be on and will add an automatic 10-meter offset from the centerline. The 10-meter offset will be too little for an exclusive estate set off of the road and too much for a roadside lemon stand. The offset combined with the interpolation means that you're not going to achieve surgical bombing accuracy with the geocoder, but perhaps this is a good thing.

The following listing shows the output of listing 8.14.

Listing 8.15 Output of the geocode function

```
r | lon         | lat        | paddress
--+-----------+----------+------------------------------------------
1 | -77.0398..| 38.9133..| 1731 New Ham.. Ave NW, Washin.., DC 20009
8 | -77.0257..| 38.9346..| 3602 New Ham.. Ave NW, Washin.., DC 20010
9 | -77.0098..| 38.9556..| 5407 New Ham.. Ave NW, Washin.., DC 20011
```

If you want individual elements of the addy object, you can write a query as shown in the following listing.

Listing 8.16 Example of geocode function and extracting properties of addy field

```
SELECT
    g.rating As r,
    ST_X(g.geomout)::numeric(10,5) As lon,
    ST_Y(g.geomout)::numeric(10,5) As lat,          <-- Round coordinates
    (g.addy).address As snum,
    (g.addy).streetname || ' '
        || (g.addy).streettypeabbrev As street,      <-- Extract elements of addy
    (g.addy).zip
FROM geocode('1021 New Hampshare Ave, Washington, DC 20009',1) As g;   <-- Intentional misspelling and return single match (1)
```

In listing 8.16 the input address is intentionally misspelled to see if fuzzy string-matching can remedy the mistake (1). As you can see from the results shown in listing 8.17, the geocoder did find a match but assigned it a lower score of 21 compared to the 1 in the listings 8.14 and 8.15.

The code also specified that only one result (the top match) should be returned (1).

Listing 8.17 Output of geocode function extracting norm_addy properties

```
r  | lon        | lat       | snum | street             | zip
---+-----------+----------+------+-------------------+------
21 | -77.03628 | 38.91710 | 2001 | New Hampshire Ave | 20009
```

Finally, the coordinate digits returned were rounded by casting to `numeric(10,5)`: ten digits overall with no more than five to the right of the decimal point. If you find yourself never needing so many significant digits, you can change the `numeric(10,5)` cast setting. A geometric method for rounding the longitude and latitude is to use the PostGIS function expression `ST_X(ST_SnapToGrid( geom ) )`, as shown next:

```
ST_X(ST_SnapToGrid( g.geomout, 0.00001))
ST_Y(ST_SnapToGrid(g.geomout, 0.00001))
```

The `ST_SnapToGrid` function will move the `geomout` point to the closest .00001 degree (both X and Y), and you'll end up with the same rounding as the casting to numeric.

You can also use the plain `round` function and keep your coordinates as double precision.

8.4.2 Geocoding using normalized addresses

You can pass a norm_addy object to the geocoder and save the geocoder from having to first call the normalize_address function. Separating the address normalization from the geocoding also lets you swap in a different normalizer. For example, the following listing uses the pagc_normalize_address normalizer.

Listing 8.18 Geocode with PAGC normalization

```
SELECT g.rating As r, ST_X(geomout) As lon, ST_Y(geomout) As lat
FROM geocode(
    pagc_normalize_address(
        '1731 New Hampshire Avenue Northwest, Washington, DC 20010'
    )
) As g;
```

As mentioned previously, the geocoder will only accept norm_addy objects. You can't pass in the stdaddr object returned by the address_standardize function.

8.4.3 Batch geocoding

Geocoding is rarely done one address at a time. Often you're faced with having to geocode thousands, if not millions, of addresses, and geocoding is not exactly a speedy function. We recommend that when you're faced with overwhelming geocoding tasks, you start your query before going to bed, and wake up to find the job done.

When geocoding in batch, you'll almost always only want the top result. You can easily later delete records where the rating of the top result is too low for you to have confidence in the match.

For an example, let's first create a small table that's populated with addresses to be geocoded and that has output fields readied.

Listing 8.19 Output of geocode function

```
DROP TABLE IF EXISTS addr_to_geocode;
CREATE TABLE addr_to_geocode (
    addid serial NOT NULL PRIMARY KEY,
    rating integer,
    address text,
    norm_address text,
    pt geometry
);
INSERT INTO addr_to_geocode(address)
VALUES
    ('ONE E PIMA ST STE 999, TUCSON, AZ'),
    ('4758 Reno Road, DC 20017'),
    ('1021 New Hampshare Avenue, Washington, DC 20010'),
    ('1731 New Hampshire Avenue Northwest, Washington, DC 20010'),
    ('1 Palisades, Denver, CO');
```

The code in the following listing performs the geocoding and updates the table with the results.

Listing 8.20 Batch geocoding

```
UPDATE addr_to_geocode
SET
    (rating, norm_address, pt) =                         <-- 1 Multicolumn update syntax
     (COALESCE((g).rating,-1 ), pprint_addy( (g).addy), (g).geomout)   <-- Select output fields from geocoder result
FROM
    (SELECT * FROM addr_to_geocode
       WHERE rating IS NULL LIMIT 100) As a               <-- 2 Batches of 100
     LEFT JOIN
    (SELECT addid,  geocode(address, 1) As g
FROM addr_to_geocode As ag
    WHERE rating IS NULL) As g1 ON a.addid = g1.addid
WHERE a.addid = addr_to_geocode.addid;
```

In the preceding listing, you use a multicolumn update, setting one row object to another row object with the code `(...)=(...)` ❶. This syntax is easier to read than many `SET` statements, such as `SET a1=v1, a2=v2, ....`

If you have millions of addresses to contend with, we recommend that you use a scripting language such as pgScript to process them in small batches. The preceding listing limits the geocoding to 100 records at a time ❷. By using small batches, you guard against unhandled errors in the geocoder that could halt your overnight processing. Furthermore, you economize on memory, and should the power go out or the server crash, you won't lose the work already done.

If you're using PostgreSQL 9.3 or later, you can take advantage of the new `LATERAL` construct to write more efficient and succinct queries. The following listing rewrites the geocoding query and throws in a lateral join.

Listing 8.21 Batch geocoding with a lateral construct

```
UPDATE addr_to_geocode
SET
    (rating, norm_address, pt) =
    (COALESCE((g).rating,-1 ), pprint_addy( (g).addy ), (g).geomout)
FROM
    (SELECT * FROM addr_to_geocode WHERE rating IS NULL LIMIT 100) As a
    LEFT JOIN LATERAL
    geocode(a.address, 1) As g          <-- Left lateral join
     ON ((g).rating < 22)
WHERE a.addid = addr_to_geocode.addid;
```

Listing 8.21 is more or less the same as listing 8.20. The main difference is that you spare yourself one subselect by using `lateral`. You also automatically weed out results with a rating worse than 21. To make sure that you don't keep retrying bad matches, you use the SQL `COALESCE` function to replace NULLs with a `-1`.

If you're using PostgreSQL 9.3 psql, you can also use the psql `\watch` command, which allows you to repeat the same update statement several times. If you want to take advantage of the psql `\watch` command as a very lightweight looping engine, remove the semicolon (`;`) at the end of the `WHERE` clause and replace it with `\watch 10`. Then run the command in psql. This will make psql repeat the same update every 10 seconds.

You now know how to geocode when you're starting with a real-world address, but often you'll be starting with longitude and latitude data, such as the locational data smartphone users might pass along. You'll often need to resolve the coordinates to addresses. This process is called *reverse geocoding*, and we'll cover that next.

8.5 Reverse geocoding

Reverse geocoding is the opposite of geocoding. You start with spatial coordinates and resolve them to addresses. The PostGIS geocoder comes with a function called `reverse_geocode`, which takes as input a geometric point in WGS 84 lon/lat coordinates and returns a composite object consisting of an array of `norm_addy` objects in a field called `addy[]` and a text array, `street[]`, consisting of cross-streets for that point.

Computationally, reverse geocoding is much easier than geocoding because there's no fuzzy string match involved. The `reverse_geocode`, to maintain performance, first targets the state, city, and zip area, and then drills down to the streets, filtering your point each step of the way. Once the reverse geocoder is at the street level, the reverse geocoder takes your coordinates and interpolates the street number based on the length of the street and the address range for the respective side of the street.

The trickiest part of reverse geocoding is figuring out which side of the street your point is on, because TIGER streets only have centerlines. Without getting too much into topology, think of TIGER street centerlines as forming a network of connected nodes. In the parlance of topology, the centerlines would be called edges, and the nodes are the intersections of edges. With the U.S. completely partitioned into areas bounded on all sides with streets, a point must lie in one of the areas, or *faces* in topo-speak. If the point falls in the right face relative to the closest edge, it must be on the right side of the street. If the point is on the left face, then it's on the left side. The reverse geocoder will be able to find a unique, closest interpolated numerical street number unless your point lacks sufficient significant digits and ends up on an intersection or is on a multilevel roadway. In cases where the reverse geocoder can't pinpoint a single address, such as if it falls on the corner of two streets, it will return the set of all possible addresses. To help you pick from multiple possible addresses, the reverse geocoder also includes the coordinates of the addresses and the nearest cross-streets.

Listing 8.22 shows reverse geocoding of the addr_to_geocode table created in listing 8.19.

Listing 8.22 Batch reverse geocoding

```
SELECT
    address::varchar(20) as address,
    pprint_addy((rc).addy[1])::varchar(20) As padd_1,      <-- Output primary address
    (rc).street[1]::varchar(12) As cstreet_1               <-- Output first cross-street
FROM (
    SELECT address, reverse_geocode(pt) AS rc
    FROM addr_to_geocode
    WHERE rating between 0 and 20
) AS x;
```

The reverse geocoder returns an array of addresses. The array will only have one member, the primary address, if the reverse geocoding was able to pick without ambiguity. The array could have multiple addresses if your point falls on an intersection or a multilevel roadway. The code in listing 8.22 outputs the primary address along with the cross-streets. The reverse geocoder will provide cross-streets as an array.

The output of listing 8.22 is shown in the next listing. We used `varchar(.)` casting to truncate the text so it could easily fit on the page.

Listing 8.23 Reverse geocoding output

```
       address        |        padd_1        |  cstreet_1
----------------------+----------------------+--------------
 4758 Reno Road, DC 2 | 4760 Reno Rd, Washin | Davenport St
 1731 New Hampshire A | 1733 New Hampshire A | S St NW
```

Note that the reverse geocoded addresses are pretty close to the addresses we geocoded, as you would expect of a reverse process.

8.6 Summary

In this chapter, we covered how to use the packaged PostGIS TIGER geocoder to load U.S. Census TIGER data, how to geocode and reverse geocode U.S. addresses, and how to normalize addresses. If you have data in the U.S., such as a list of customers you need to geocode for targeted marketing, you should find the TIGER geocoder useful. If you have a stream of points, such as GPS points you get from cars beaming location information, the reverse geocoder should be useful for providing meaningful textual address locations for these points. Even if you don't live in the U.S. or have no need for geocoding, the address standardizer package should come in handy for breaking out addresses into house numbers, streets, and postal codes.

We'll move next to learning about spatial relationships. Spatial relationships are the foundation of most spatial operations.

9 Geometry relationships

This chapter covers

- Bounding boxes
- Intersections
- Relationships
- The meaning of equality
- The Dimensionally Extended 9-Intersection Matrix (DE-9IM)

As the old saying goes, "No man is an island," and the same holds true for geometries. In prior chapters, we described geometries in isolation. Going forward, we'll no longer entertain ourselves with one geometry at a time. The richness and power of spatial queries come to light when you start working with more than a singleton.

If we liken geometries to tables, an SQL query that queries a single table can only go so far. It's when you have join operations at your disposal that things become interesting. Mastering join operations is what separates the casual database user from the serious database analyst. Spatial databases have a similar jumping-off point: The casual consumer of a spatial database may use PostGIS to store geometry data or to filter geometries befitting certain conditions. The serious spatial database analyst will be able to write queries that join and morph multiple geometries to solve seemingly intractable problems with brisk elegance.

But as another old saying goes, "No pain, no gain." Working with more than one geometry introduces a new level of conceptual challenges. In non-spatial databases, disparate data interacts through mathematical or string operations. When one number meets another number, you can add, subtract, divide, multiply, or some combination thereof. When one string meets another, you can splice them together or use one to substring the other. In spatial databases, however, when one geometry meets another, things heat up quite a bit. PostGIS offers many ways to consummate their mutual courting, and this chapter explores the most common choices. We'll describe each type of relationship separately, but you should keep in mind that the full analytical power of spatial SQL usually entails disparate relationship functions, operators, and processing functions being applied in unison.

We'll start our discussion with the soul of every geometry—the bounding box.

9.1 Bounding box and geometry comparators

Every geometry has a *bounding box*, the smallest rectangular box with edges parallel to the axes of the coordinate plane that completely encloses the object. What makes PostGIS relationship queries really fast are the box-based comparisons embedded in most of them. Instead of having to compare object to object, comparing bounding boxes often suffices and produces an answer much more quickly.

Raster and geography types have bounding boxes too

Although we're limiting our discussion to geometry bounding boxes, keep in mind that rasters have an outer shell that is a geometry, and that outer shell has a bounding box as well. The fact that both rasters and geometries have the same kind of bounding boxes allows them to be compared to each other using spatial relationship functions.

Geographies also have bounding boxes, but they have a kind of 3D bounding box. You should never relate a `geometry` with a `geography` type using a spatial relationship function without first casting one to `geometry` or the other to `geography`.

9.1.1 The bounding box

Let's demonstrate bounding boxes with a quick example. Suppose you have two multipolygons, one representing the state of Washington and one representing the state of Florida, and you wish to know if Washington is strictly northwest of Florida. If the bounding box of Washington is strictly above and to the left of Florida, then you'll know with certainty that the geometries must share the same relationship as well. The bounding box methodology shortcuts the point-by-point checking by first drawing rectangular boxes around each state and then asking if the box enclosing Washington is above and to the left of the box enclosing Florida. You'll obtain the answer almost instantly.

Furthermore, because a rectangular box is completely specified by the coordinates of the two opposing corners, you can precalculate all of the bounding boxes for geometries in your table and store their coordinates in indexes. Once you have the bounding box of every geometry indexed, comparing any two geometries becomes a simple task of comparing two pairs of numbers.

Bounding boxes are so fundamental to spatial queries that PostGIS always computes them when a geometry changes and has the bounding box stored as part of the geometry. But to make full use of bounding boxes, you'll still need to define spatial indexes.

As useful as bounding boxes are, there will be many instances when they won't do you much good. Suppose you want to know if the centroid of Washington state is to the left of the centroid of Oregon; you can't shortcut yourself to an answer by simply looking at the bounding boxes of the two states. In short, bounding boxes are useful as prechecks for more expensive spatial relationship checks and also as general rule-of-thumb tests.

The next listing contains examples of geometries with their bounding boxes.

Listing 9.1 Box2D and geometries

```
SELECT ex_name, Box2D(geom) As bbox2d , geom
FROM (
VALUES
    ('A line', ST_GeomFromEWKT('LINESTRING (0 0, 1 1)')),
    ('A multipoint', ST_GeomFromText('MULTIPOINT (4.4 4.75, 5 5)')),
    ('A square', ST_GeomFromText('POLYGON ((0 0, 0 1, 1 1, 1 0, 0 0))'))
)
AS x(ex_name, geom);
```

Figure 9.1 illustrates the output of this query, showing the geometries encased in their bounding boxes.

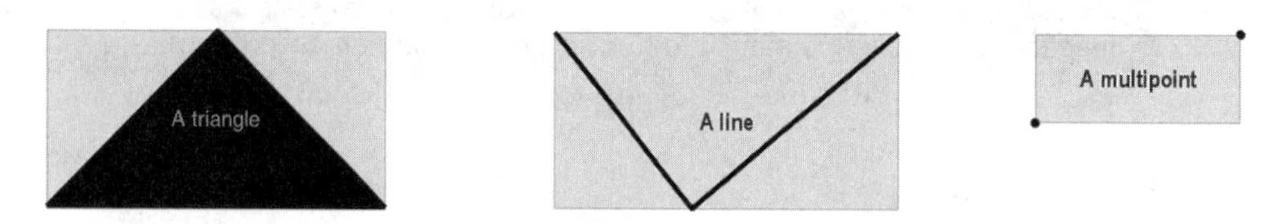

Figure 9.1 Various geometries and their bounding boxes

ST_BOX2D FUNCTION RENAMED TO BOX2D In versions prior to PostGIS 2.0, the `Box2D` function was called `ST_Box2D`.

In the next section, we'll cover operators that work on the bounding boxes of geometries.

9.1.2 Bounding box comparators

PostGIS has always offered geometry bounding box comparators for 2D geometries, and PostGIS 2.0 added comparators for 3D geometries. Some, but not all, of these comparators have counterparts that examine the entire geometry.

PostGIS uses symbols for comparators. For example, `A && B` returns true if the 2D bounding box of `A` intersects the 2D bounding box of `B`, or vice versa. The double ampersand symbol (`&&`) is the intersection comparator. Behind the scenes, PostGIS first checks for a bounding box intersection for many relationship functions such as `ST_Intersects` and `ST_DWithin`. If the bounding boxes fail to intersect, PostGIS can return an answer immediately.

For 3D geometries, the `&&` comparator will compare the 2D footprints. Or, for true 3D bounding box intersection, you can use the `&&&` operator.

Table 9.1 lists the comparators and the kinds of indexes they use, if available. Geometry columns almost always use a gist index. If a geometry doesn't have many points (for example, a single point, short linestring, or small polygon), you could use a B-tree. Keep in mind that you can have both a gist and a B-tree index on the same geometry column.

Table 9.1 PostGIS geometry comparators

Comparator	True condition	Index
&&	If A's 2D bounding box intersects B's 2D bounding box	gist
&&&	If A's 3D bounding box intersects B's 3D bounding box	gist (geometry_ops_nd)
&<	If A's 2D bounding box overlaps or is to the left of B's	gist
&<|	If A's 2D bounding box overlaps or is below B's	gist
&>	If A's 2D bounding box overlaps or is to the right of B's	gist
<<	If A's 2D bounding box is strictly to the left of B's	gist
<<|	If A's 2D bounding box is strictly below B's	gist
=	If A's 2D bounding box is the same as B's	B-tree
>>	If A's 2D bounding box is strictly to the right of B's	gist
@	If A's 2D bounding box is contained by B's	gist
|&>	If A's 2D bounding box overlaps or is above B's	gist
|>>	If A's 2D bounding box is strictly above B's	gist
~-	If A's 2D bounding box contains B's	gist

9.2 Relating two geometries

Two geometries intersect when they have points in common, but sometimes you need to know more than just whether they intersect. Sometimes you need more detail about the points in common, the points not in common, and the points on the boundary. PostGIS has a bevy of functions that describe how two geometries intersect or don't intersect. These functions count on both geometries having the same SRID and assume both are valid. Never trust the output if your inputs contain invalid geometries.

9.2.1 Interior, exterior, and boundary of a geometry

2D intersection functions rely on the geometry concepts of interior, exterior, and boundary:

- *Interior*—The space inside a geometry and not on the boundary
- *Exterior*—The space outside a geometry and not on the boundary
- *Boundary*—The space that's neither interior nor exterior

Any point on a plane with a geometry must be interior, on the boundary, or exterior. It can't be in two places at once. This should be intuitive for polygons. For open linestrings, the boundary is the end points. For closed linestrings and points, the boundary is undefined.

During an intersection operation, PostGIS creates a pairing between interior, boundary, and exterior between the two geometries and examines each pairing separately. For example, it'll check to see if the interior of one intersects the interior of the other, then if the interior intersects the boundary, then if the interior intersects the exterior, and so on, for a total of nine pair-wise checks. The result of an intersection of these nine pairs can be non-dimensional (no intersection), zero-dimensional (punctal), one-dimensional (lineal), two-dimensional (areal), or a combination thereof in the case of collection geometries.

Again, be sure that your input geometries are valid. The concepts of interior, exterior, and boundary completely fall apart otherwise.

9.2.2 Intersections

The idea of *intersection* encompasses a wide range of ways in which geometries can have points in common. We'll delve into the nuances in time, but let's start with the basic definition of intersection: two geometries intersect when they have interior or boundary points in common. The set of all shared points is called the *intersection*.

PostGIS has two functions for 2D intersections. The first is `ST_Intersects`, which returns true or false. The other is `ST_Intersection`, which returns the geometry of the intersected region.

Geometries also have another function called `ST_3DIntersects` to handle 3D geometries. Its inner workings are entirely different from `ST_Intersects`, but it does rely on a 2D bounding-box check to ensure that the footprints of both geometries intersect before performing a more exhaustive 3D check, if necessary.

> **What's an empty geometry?**
>
> An empty geometry is a geometry with no points within it. It's not the same as a database NULL!
>
> You can create an empty geometry with this command:
>
> ```
> ST_GeomFromText('GEOMETRYCOLLECTION EMPTY');
> ```
>
> As of PostGIS 2.0, if you're not completely satisfied with the idea of an empty geometry, and you wish to engage in deep philosophical discussions, you can entertain yourself with `POLYGON EMPTY`, `POINT EMPTY`, and other kinds of emptiness. Here's a Zen-like question for you: if a point and a polygon fail to intersect, is the intersection an empty point, an empty polygon, or Mysterion?

We'll demonstrate the `ST_Intersects` and `ST_Intersection` functions in action with two crafty examples.

SEGMENTING LINESTRINGS WITH POLYGONS

We'll start with a polygon and a linestring and see if they intersect with `ST_Intersects`, and what the resultant intersection geometry looks like with `ST_Intersection`.

This example is quite common in real-world scenarios. The linestring can represent the planned route for a new roadway, and the polygon can represent private property. The `ST_Intersection` function will quickly tell you whether the new road will cut through the private property. If so, you can determine which part of the road falls within the boundaries by using `ST_Intersection` to determine the cost associated with an eminent domain takeover. We'll only look at a simple example, but you can imagine how useful this could be if you have records for all the private properties in a city and you want to determine which properties the road will cut through. The route planner can virtually trace any path through the city and obtain an immediate calculation for the eminent domain purchase.

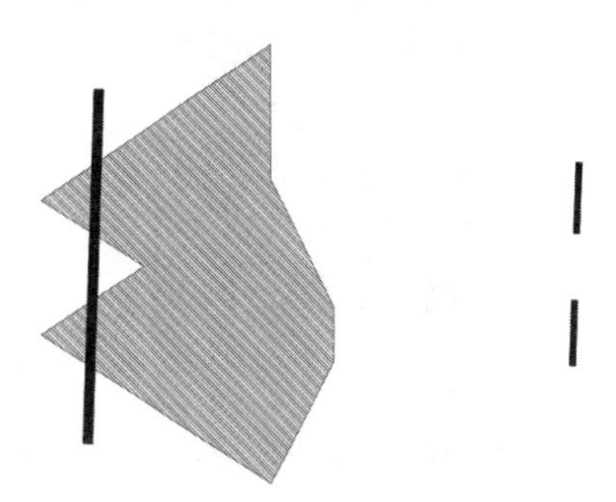

Figure 9.2 The polygon (private property) is overlaid with the linestring (planned road) at left. At right is the intersection of the two. The intersection results in a multilinestring.

Figure 9.2 shows a planned roadway (a linestring), the private land (a polygon), and the resulting intersection geometry.

The code that generates figure 9.2 is shown in the following listing.

Listing 9.2 Segmenting a linestring with a polygon

```
SELECT
    ST_Intersects(g.geom1,g.geom2) As intersect,
    GeometryType(ST_Intersection(g.geom1,g.geom2)) As intersection
FROM (
    SELECT
        ST_GeomFromText('
            POLYGON((
                2 4.5,3 2.6,3 1.8,2 0,
                -1.5 2.2,0.056 3.222,
                -1.5 4.2,2 6.5,2 4.5
            ))'
        ) As geom1,
        ST_GeomFromText('LINESTRING(-0.62 5.84,-0.8 0.59)') As geom2
) AS g;
```

Should you be unimpressed by the previous example, the next one ought to change your mind.

CLIPPING POLYGONS WITH POLYGONS

A common use of the `ST_Intersection` function is to clip polygons. *Clipping* loosely refers to the process of breaking up a geometry into smaller segments or regions. For instance, if you were in charge of sales for a city and had a dozen sales representatives on your staff, you could clip the polygon of the city into 12 sales regions, one for each representative. Another common use of clipping is to make your spatial database queries faster by breaking up your geometries beforehand. If you have data covering more area than you generally need to work with, you can clip the original geometry so you can query against a smaller geometry. For example, if you're working with data covering the entire island of Hispaniola but you only need to report on Haiti, you could clip the island using a linestring to isolate the Haitian half.

We'll start with an example where we break up an arbitrarily shaped polygon (the one used in listing 9.2) into square regions, as shown in figure 9.3.

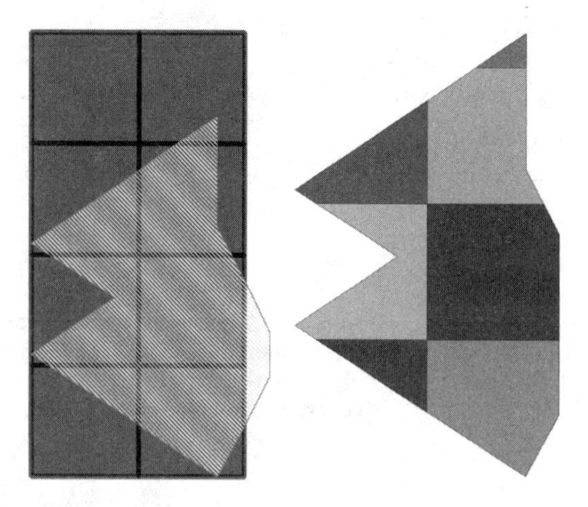

Figure 9.3 The polygon overlaid against square tiles is shown at left. At right is the result of an intersection of square tiles with the region.

To perform this cut-up, you start with a rectangle, break it into eight square cells, and then intersect it with the polygon, as shown in the following listing.

Listing 9.3 Clipping one polygon using another

```
SELECT
    x || ' ' || y As grid_x_y,                  <-- ❶ Squares to use for dicing
    CAST(
        ST_MakeBox2d(
            ST_Point(-1.5 + x, 0 + y),
            ST_Point(-1.5 + x + 2, 0 + y + 2)
        ) As geometry
    ) As geom2
FROM generate_series(0,3,2) As x CROSS JOIN generate_series(0,6,2) As y;

SELECT
    ST_GeomFromText(
        'POLYGON((
            2 4.5,3 2.6,3 1.8,2 0,-1.5 2.2,0.056 3.222,-1.5 4.2,2 6.5,
            2 4.5
        ))'
    ) As geom1;                                 <-- ❷ Region to split
SELECT
    CAST(x AS text) || ' ' || CAST(y As text) As grid_xy,        <-- ❸ Dicing yields multiple records
    ST_AsText(ST_Intersection(g1.geom1, g2.geom2)) As intersect_geom
FROM (
    SELECT
        ST_GeomFromText(
            'POLYGON((
                2 4.5,3 2.6,3 1.8,2 0,
                -1.5 2.2,0.056 3.222,
                -1.5 4.2,2 6.5,2 4.5
            ))'
        ) As geom1
    ) As g1
    INNER JOIN (
    SELECT x, y, ST_MakeEnvelope(-1.5+x,0+y,-1.5+x+2,0+y+2) As geom2
    FROM
        generate_series(0,3,2) As x
        CROSS JOIN
        generate_series(0,6,2) As y
    ) As g2
ON ST_Intersects(g1.geom1,g2.geom2);
```

In this code, you first use `generate_series` to create two series from the minimum X coordinate of the polygon to the maximum X coordinate, skipping two units ❶. You do the same for Y, resulting in eight 2 × 2 squares. The city is the polygon you wish to cut ❷. Then you cross-join the city polygon and the squares and take the intersection ❸, which results in your city polygon being diced.

Table 9.2 lists the WKT for each slice of our Sicilian pizza.

Table 9.2 WKT of sales regions

grid_xy	intersect_geom
0 0	POLYGON((0.5 0.942857142857143...))
2 0	POLYGON((2.5 0.9,2 0,0.5 0.942857142857143,0.5 2,2.5 2,2.5 0.9))
0 2	POLYGON((-1.18181818181818 2,-1.5 2.2...))
2 2	POLYGON((2.26315789473684 4,2.5 3.55...))
0 4	POLYGON((-1.18179959100204 4,-1.5 4.2,0.5 5...))
2 4	POLYGON((2 4.5,2.26315789473684 4,0.5 4,0.5 5.51428571428571...))
2 6	POLYGON((1.23913043478261 6,2 6.5,2 6,1.23913043478261 6))

This example shows how intersections can be useful for partitioning a single geometry into separate records. Notice that the cutting squares didn't need to completely cover the polygon. In this example we left out a few slivers.

Keep in mind that the `geometry` type returned by `ST_Intersection` may look rather different than the input geometries, but it's guaranteed to be of equal or lower dimension (both geometry and coordinate dimensions) than the geometry with the lowest dimension. For example, if you have two polygons that share an edge, then the intersection of the two will be the linestring representing the shared edge. The polygons are two-dimensional, but the resultant linestring is one-dimensional.

Your output may also result in geometry collections even if neither geometry is a geometry collection. For example, you may have two geometries of type `POLYGON` that intersect. If the two polygons share a portion of an edge (as is the case with land parcels), and one portion of the parcel crosses the border of the other parcel (because of a land dispute), then the intersection of the two geometries would be of type `GEOMETRYCOLLECTION`, consisting of a linestring for the agreed-upon border and a polygon for the disputed area.

To summarize, if `A` and `B` are input geometries to `ST_Intersection`, the following points hold true:

- `ST_Intersection` returns the portion shared by `A` and `B`, inclusive of boundaries.
- `ST_Intersection` and `ST_Intersects` are both commutative, meaning that `ST_Intersection(A,B) = ST_Intersection(B,A)` and `ST_Intersects(A,B) = ST_Intersects(B,A)`.
- `A` and `B` need not be of the same geometry subtype.
- The geometry returned by `ST_Intersection` can't have dimensions higher than the lowest dimension between `A` and `B`, `Least(ST_Dim(A),ST_Dim(B))`.
- If `A` and `B` don't intersect, the intersection is an empty geometry.

Now that we've covered the basic concepts of intersections, we'll delve into the finer details of intersecting relationships.

9.2.3 A house plan model

We'll use a house plan example, shown in figure 9.4, to demonstrate more specific and less intuitive intersection relationships. Listing 9.4 generates the house plan.

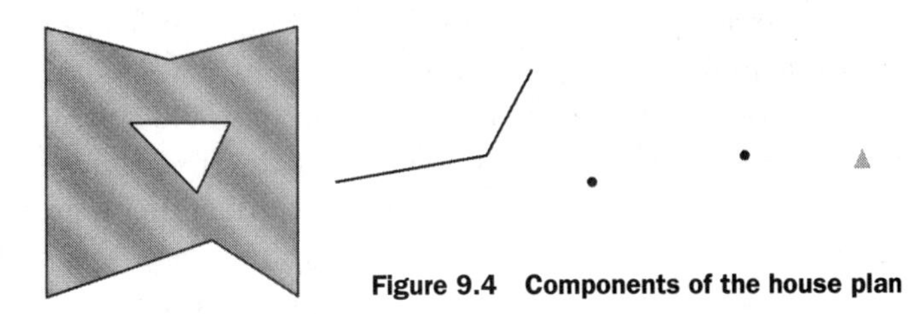

Figure 9.4 Components of the house plan

Listing 9.4 Piecing together the house plan

```
CREATE TABLE example_set(ex_name varchar(150) PRIMARY KEY,
    geom geometry);
INSERT INTO example_set(ex_name, geom)
VALUES
    (
        'A polygon with hole',
        ST_GeomFromText(
            'POLYGON(
                (110 180, 110 335,184 316,260 335,260 180,209 212.51,
                110 180), (160 280,200 240, 220 280,160 280)
            )'
        )
    ),
    ('A point', ST_GeomFromText('POINT(110 245)')),
    (
        'A linestring',
        ST_GeomFromText('LINESTRING(110 245,200 260, 227 309)')
    ),
    ('A multipoint', ST_GeomFromText('MULTIPOINT(110 245,200 260)'));
```

When you view the components in place, the house plan looks like figure 9.5.

In the house, you have four geometries representing different aspects of the house:

- A polygon with a triangular hole represents the building part of the house—the covered structure. The house has a quaint courtyard, which is a part of the house's exterior.
- A linestring represents a red carpet that leads guests through the courtyard to the inner sanctum.
- A point represented by a triangle icon is the front entrance to the house.
- A multipoint represented by two dots marks the two guards stationed at the front entrance and the courtyard, to screen guests.

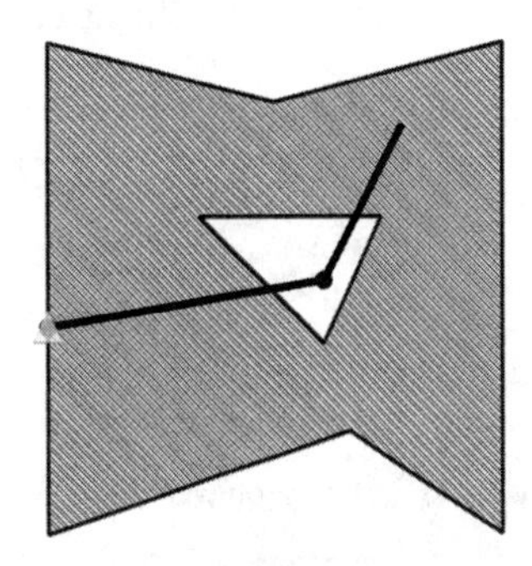

Figure 9.5 House plan with all components in place

In the next section, we'll explore the different spatial relationships that the house, carpet, entrance, and guards have with each other.

9.2.4 Contains and within

When geometry A contains geometry B, no points of B can lie in the exterior of A, and at least one point of B must lie in the interior of A. So if B lies only on the boundary of A, A doesn't contain B. If B lies on the boundary and in the interior of A, A contains B.

One surprising quirk of this definition is that a geometry never contains its own boundary points. For example, a point that is the starting point of an open linestring is not contained by the linestring because it has no points in the interior of the linestring, but if you have a multipoint that contains the starting point and a point somewhere in the middle of the line, then that multipoint is contained by the linestring.

Contains and *within* are inverse relationships. If geometry A is within geometry B, then geometry B contains geometry A. To check contains and within, use the functions ST_Contains and ST_Within. Both of these functions are OGC SQL/MM functions, so you may encounter them in other spatial database products without much difference in meaning.

One of the confusing but necessary conditions for geometry A to contain geometry B is that the intersection of the boundary of A with B can't be B. In other words, B can't sit entirely on the boundary of A. A geometry doesn't contain its boundary, but a geometry always contains itself.

Let's write a query that lists all pair-wise comparisons of the house from the preceding section using ST_Contains and ST_Within. The answers from the comparison will allow you to deduce answers to questions such as "Are both guards inside the house and not in the courtyard? Are they both on the red carpet? Is one still at the front entrance?"

```
SELECT
    A.ex_name As a_name, B.ex_name As b_name,
    ST_Contains(A.geom,B.geom) As a_co_b,
    ST_Intersects(A.geom,B.geom) As a_in_b
FROM example_set As A CROSS JOIN example_set As B;
```

The result of this code is shown in table 9.3.

Table 9.3 Where all intersect but not all contain

a_name	b_name	a_co_b	a_in_b
A polygon with hole	A polygon with hole	t	t
A polygon with hole	A point	f	t
A polygon with hole	A linestring	f	t
A polygon with hole	A multipoint	f	t
A point	A polygon with hole	f	t

Table 9.3 Where all intersect but not all contain *(continued)*

a_name	b_name	a_co_b	a_in_b
A point	A point	t	t
A point	A linestring	f	t
A point	A multipoint	f	t
A linestring	A polygon with hole	f	t
A linestring	A point	f	t
A linestring	A linestring	t	t
A linestring	A multipoint	t	t
A multipoint	A polygon with hole	f	t
A multipoint	A point	t	t
A multipoint	A linestring	f	t
A multipoint	A multipoint	t	t

The example confirms the following:

- All objects intersect. This tells us that at least one guard is at the front entrance, at least one guard is on the red carpet, and at least one guard is wholly within the confines or on the boundary of the building. They can't both be in the courtyard because if they were, they as a whole would not intersect the building. Don't forget that both guards together form the multipoint geometry.
- Because the building doesn't contain the guards, but the guards intersect the building, we know that one guard must be in the courtyard or outside the outer boundary of the building.
- We know that the red carpet isn't completely in the building but intersects it, meaning that the carpet must have some piece in the courtyard or extending beyond the building.
- If geometry `B` sits wholly on the boundary of geometry `A`, geometry `A` doesn't contain geometry `B`. Because the front entrance intersects the building but the building doesn't contain the entrance, we know that the entrance must be on the boundary of the building. The front entrance intersects the red carpet but the carpet doesn't contain the front entrance; therefore the front entrance must be on the boundary of the red carpet (the beginning or end of the carpet).
- The carpet contains both guards, so at most one person can be at the starting or end of the red carpet but not both.
- All geometries contain themselves.

If you were to use `ST_Within`, you'd get the inverse of `ST_Contains`. The column a_co_b would have the opposite values.

9.2.5 Covers and covered by

As you saw in the contains example, containment at the boundaries abides by convention rather than intuition. Most people assert that a geometry should contain its boundary, but instead of changing the OGC SQL/MM meaning of containment, PostGIS introduced the concepts of *covers* and *covered by* to mean *contain with boundary*. The related PostGIS functions are `ST_Covers` and `ST_CoveredBy`; they aren't OGC SQL/MM defined functions.

`ST_Covers` behaves exactly like `ST_Contains` except that it will also return true in the case where one geometry lies completely within the boundary of the other. `ST_CoveredBy` is the inverse function of `ST_Covers` and therefore behaves like `ST_Within`, but excludes the boundary.

Listing 9.5 and table 9.4 demonstrate situations where `ST_Covers` covers a geometry, but doesn't contain it.

Listing 9.5 How `ST_Covers` differs from `ST_Contains`

```
SELECT
    A.ex_name As a_name, B.ex_name As b_name,
    ST_Covers(A.geom,B.geom) As a_co_b,
    ST_Intersects(A.geom,B.geom) As a_in_b
FROM example_set As A CROSS JOIN example_set As B
WHERE NOT (ST_Covers(A.geom,B.geom) = ST_Contains(A.geom,B.geom));
```

The code only outputs those geometries where the `ST_Covers` answer is different from the `ST_Contains` answer. Table 9.4 shows the results.

Table 9.4 Where `ST_Covers` differs from `ST_Contains`

a_name	b_name	a_co_b	a_in_b
A polygon with hole	A point	t	t
A linestring	A point	t	t

Because we limited the results to cases where the answer produced by `ST_Covers` is different from that of `ST_Contains`, we only get the list of cases where `A` covers `B` and `B` sits wholly on the boundary of `A`. Both the red carpet and the building cover the door, but they don't contain the door.

Next we'll look at the `ST_ContainsProperly` function, which provides a more stringent containment check than the `ST_Contains` function.

9.2.6 Contains properly

Contains properly is a concept that's more stringent than the *contains* or *covers* relationships. Geometry `A` contains properly `B` if all points of `B` are within the interior of `A`. Contains properly is faster to compute than other relationship functions because boundaries don't come into play. If you want to be absolutely certain that one geometry is entirely within another, use contains properly. For example, you may want to make sure your new McMansion is properly contained within one municipality to make sure you're not going to be taxed twice.

Contains properly will give you the same result as contains except in the case where any part of geometry `B` sits on the boundary of `A`. Here are a few points to keep in mind about `ST_ContainsProperly`:

- It's not an OGC SQL/MM function; it's a PostGIS-specific function.
- It was introduced in PostGIS 1.4.
- It requires GEOS 3.1 or above. If you're running PostGIS 1.4 with, say, GEOS 3.0.3, no function for you.

Listing 9.6 repeats the previous comparison exercise, except that it lists only the contains properly options where `ST_ContainsProperly` gives a different answer from `ST_Contains`.

Listing 9.6 How `ST_ContainsProperly` differs from `ST_Contains`

```
SELECT
    A.ex_name As a_name, B.ex_name As b_name,
    ST_ContainsProperly(A.geom,B.geom) As a_co_b,
    ST_Intersects(A.geom,B.geom) As a_in_b
FROM example_set As A CROSS JOIN example_set As B
WHERE NOT ( ST_ContainsProperly(A.geom,B.geom) =
    ST_Contains(A.geom,B.geom) );
```

Table 9.5 shows the results of listing 9.6. Observe that `ST_ContainsProperly` gives answers identical to `ST_Contains` except in the case of an areal geometry, a line geometry compared to itself, or a geometry sitting partly on the boundary of another. A geometry never properly contains itself except in the case of points and multipoints. The reason points and multipoints properly contain themselves is that they consist of a finite number of points and therefore have no boundary to speak of. A point can never be sitting partly on its nonexistent boundary.

Table 9.5 Where contains and contains properly are different

a_name	b_name	a_co_b	a_in_b
A polygon with hole	A polygon with hole	f	t
A linestring	A linestring	f	t
A linestring	A multipoint	f	t

You can see from this table that the only cases where the `ST_ContainsProperly` answer is different from that of `ST_Contains` are the cases of a polygon against itself, a linestring against itself, and a point or multipoint that partly sits on the boundary of another. This tells us that in the house, one person must be on the start or end of the red carpet because the red carpet doesn't properly contain both people, but it does contain both people.

9.2.7 Overlapping geometries

Two geometries *overlap* when they have the same geometry dimension, they intersect, and one is not completely contained in the other. The PostGIS overlap function is ST_Overlaps, an OGC SQL/MM function.

If you were to check the house to see if anything overlaps, you'd find that nothing does. Here are the reasons:

- The red carpet is not of the same dimension as the building. One is lineal and the other is areal, so they can't overlap. The same mismatch in dimension holds true between the front entrance and the building and between the front entrance and the red carpet.
- The guards can't overlap with the front entrance because the entrance is contained and covered by one of the guards.
- No self-to-self comparisons overlap because a geometry always contains itself.

9.2.8 Touching geometries

Two geometries *touch* if they have at least one point in common and none of the common points lie in the interior of both geometries. The PostGIS function at play is ST_Touches, an OGC SQL/MM function.

In the house plan, let's see which components touch by running the following query:

```
SELECT
    A.ex_name As a_name,B.ex_name As b_name,
    ST_Touches(A.geom,B.geom) As a_tou_b,
    ST_Contains(A.geom,B.geom) As a_co_b
FROM example_set As A CROSS JOIN example_set As B
WHERE ST_Touches(A.geom,B.geom) ;
```

The result is shown in table 9.6.

Table 9.6 Geometries that touch each other

a_name	b_name	a_tou_b	a_co_b
A polygon with hole	A point	t	f
A polygon with hole	A multipoint	t	f
A point	A polygon with hole	t	f
A point	A linestring	t	f
A linestring	A point	t	f
A multipoint	A polygon with hole	t	f

Let's examine the results in table 9.6:

- The touch relationship is commutative. If A touches B, then B touches A.
- As we can also infer from the results, if two geometries touch, one can't contain the other.
- The building touches the front entrance because the front entrance sits on the boundary of the building. The front entrance itself is the common point. It lies only within one geometry's interior—its own. The same applies to the touching of the front entrance and the red carpet.
- The multipoint and front entrance are missing from the list as expected. The multipoint pair of guards doesn't touch the front entrance because the guards contain the front entrance and the shared point is interior to both geometries. As a general rule, a point can never touch another point or another multipoint because the shared points would always be interior to both.
- The multipoint pair of guards and the polygon building touch because one guard is on the boundary of the building and the other is in the courtyard. The courtyard is part of the exterior of the building and not the interior, so even though one guard is sunning in the courtyard and the other is at the door, as a pair they're touching the building.

9.2.9 *Crossing geometries*

Two geometries *cross* each other if they have some interior points in common but not all. Think of two perpendicular runways here. The function that implements crossing is `ST_Crosses`, an OGC SQL/MM function.

Let's go back to the house plan and see what crosses what:

```
SELECT
    A.ex_name As a_name,B.ex_name As b_name,
    ST_Crosses(A.geom,B.geom) As a_cr_b,
    ST_Contains(A.geom,B.geom) As a_co_b
FROM example_set As A CROSS JOIN example_set As B
WHERE ST_Crosses(A.geom,B.geom) ;
```

Table 9.7 lists the query output.

Table 9.7 Geometries that cross each other

a_name	b_name	a_cr_b	a_co_b
A polygon with hole	A linestring	t	f
A linestring	A polygon with hole	t	f

We can glean a couple of things from this example:

- Only one pair of geometries cross: the red carpet and the building. They don't touch or contain each other, but they do intersect, so they must cross. The shared region contains points interior to both, but one is not completely contained by the other. Note that this cross is made possible by the existence of the courtyard. The red carpet has a strip within the courtyard, so its interior isn't completely contained by the building's interior.

- Geometries that touch can't cross. Compare the crossing output with the touching output.

Now that we've analyzed the various intersects relationships, our last stop will be the only non-intersecting relationship—the disjoint relationship.

9.2.10 Disjoint geometries

The *disjoint* relationship is the antithesis of the *intersects* relationship. Two geometries are disjointed if they have no shared interiors or boundaries. In the case of invalid geometries, it's possible for the `ST_Intersects` and `ST_Disjoint` functions to both return false or both return true. If you encounter such illogical results, your input geometries must be invalid.

PostGIS uses `ST_Disjoint`, an OGC SQL/MM function, to check for disjoint relationships. Although it might appear that `ST_Disjoint` would be used frequently, this isn't the case. The problem with `ST_Disjoint` is that it can't use an index. To check if a set of geometries intersects with another, you're better off performing an unequal join using `ST_Intersects` and filtering for NULLs, as follows:

```
A LEFT JOIN B ON ST_Intersects(A.geom,B.geom) WHERE B.gid IS NULL
```

Because `ST_Intersect` can use indexes, this query will run much faster than using `ST_Disjoint`. Given this superior alternative, we can't say that we find much use for `ST_Disjoint`. Feel free to remove this function from your mind and save room for a more useful function.

Now that we've covered the various ways geometries can intersect, it's time to zoom in on the topic of equality. You'll find that in the spatial realm, equality takes on many forms, and the common equal sign doesn't play the expected role.

9.3 The faces of equality: geometry

In conventional databases, you probably never gave the equal sign (=) a second thought before using it, but this clarity of purpose doesn't carry over to spatial databases. When you compare two spatial objects, equality is a multifaceted notion. You can ask whether geometries occupy the same space. You can ask whether they are represented by the same points. You can even ask if they are enclosed by the same bounding box.

Three basic kinds of equality are specific to 2D geometries in PostGIS:

- *Spatial equality* means that two geometries occupy the same space.
- *Geometric equality* is stronger than spatial equality and means that two geometries occupy the same space and have the same underlying representation.

- *Bounding-box equality* means that the bounding boxes of the two geometries share the same space. This last kind of equality is what is tested when you use the = operator.

We'll explore these facets of equality next.

9.3.1 Spatial equality versus geometric equality

Two geometries are considered *spatially equal* if they occupy the same underlying space. PostGIS uses `ST_Equals` to test for spatial equality; it's an OGC SQL/MM function that you'll find in many spatial database products.

Use `ST_Equals` when the directionality difference of two geometries is unimportant to you. For example, a linestring that starts at point `A` and runs to point `B` and a linestring that starts at point `B` and runs to point `A` are spatially equal. Similarly, `ST_Equals` will disregard the distinction between collection geometries and multigeometries. For instance, the following three geometries are spatially equal:

- Point `A`
- A multipoint with only point `A`
- A geometry collection with only point `A`

Geometric equality is more strict than spatial equality. Not only must the two geometries share the same space, they must also share the same underlying representation. So although an `A`-to-`B` linestring is spatially equal to a `B`-to-`A` linestring, they aren't geometrically equal.

Geometric equality is important for routing. For example, take any interstate highway in the United States. Depending on which side of the road you're traveling on, the interstate is signed as north versus south or east versus west. Although it's the same interstate highway, the direction of travel matters. It matters greatly when you get lost.

For geometric equality comparisons, PostGIS uses `ST_OrderingEquals`, which is not an OGC SQL/MM–compliant function. The next listing demonstrates the difference between `ST_OrderingEquals` and `ST_Equals`.

Listing 9.7 `ST_OrderingEquals` versus `ST_Equals`

```
SELECT
    ex_name,
    ST_OrderingEquals(geom,geom) As g_oeq_g,
    ST_OrderingEquals(geom, ST_Reverse(geom)) As g_oeq_rev,
    ST_OrderingEquals(geom, ST_Multi(geom)) AS g_oeq_m,
    ST_Equals(geom, geom) As g_seq_g,
    ST_Equals(geom, ST_Multi(geom)) As g_seq_m
FROM (
VALUES
    ('A 2D linestring', ST_GeomFromText('LINESTRING(3 5,2 4,2 5)')),
    ('A point', ST_GeomFromText('POINT(2 5)')),
    ('A triangle', ST_GeomFromText('POLYGON((3 5,2.5 4.5,2 5,3 5))')),
    (
```

```
            'An invalid polygon',
            ST_GeomFromText('POLYGON((2 0,0 0,1 1,1 -1,2 0))')
        )
)
AS foo(ex_name, geom);
```

Table 9.8 shows the results of listing 9.7.

Table 9.8 Compare ST_OrderingEquals and ST_Equals

ex_name	g_oeq_g	g_oeq_rev	g_oeq_m	g_seq_g	g_seq_m
A 2D linestring	t	f	f	t	t
A point	t	t	f	t	t
A triangle	t	f	f	t	t
An invalid polygon	t	f	f	f	f

As demonstrated in table 9.8, even an invalid polygon is `ST_OrderingEqual` to itself in PostGIS. Observe also that the multi-geometry variant is not geometrically equal to the singular version, but they are spatially equal.

In the case of invalid geometries, `ST_Equals` may be false when two invalid geometries occupy the same space. Only in this case will you run across the paradox of geometries being geometrically equal (`ST_OrderingEquals` returns true) but not spatially equal (`ST_Equals` returns false). Although PostGIS has no problem comparing the binary bytes that form the geometries to assert that they're geometrically equal, it's unable to form the geometries to see if they overlap. Once again, stay clear of invalid geometries.

Another shortcoming of `ST_OrderingEquals` is that it doesn't work with curved geometries. If you have curved geometries, opt for a binary compare with `ST_AsEWKB(A) = ST_AsEWKB(B)` instead. If you wish to ignore differences in SRIDs, you can use `ST_AsBinary(A) = ST_AsBinary(B)`.

9.3.2 *Bounding-box equality*

In PostGIS, the universally recognized equal sign is reserved for bounding-box equality. If you ask if `geometry A = geometry B`, the answer will be true only if the bounding boxes of `A` and `B` are spatially equal.

Because bounding-box equality uses the equal sign, many people mistake bounding-box equality for spatial or geometric equality. `A = B` doesn't mean that `A` is `B`. Here's an example illustrating the difference:

```
SELECT
    ST_GeomFromText('LINESTRING (0 0, 1 1)')
    =
    ST_GeomFromText('POLYGON ((0 0, 0 1, 1 1, 1 0, 0 0))');
```

The comparison of the polygon and the linestring returns true. How is this possible? Although the geometries are quite different, their bounding boxes are spatially equal.

In contrast, if you use the geometric equality operator, you'll get the expected false answer:

```
SELECT ST_OrderingEquals(
    ST_GeomFromText('LINESTRING (0 0, 1 1)'),
    ST_GeomFromText('POLYGON ((0 0, 0 1, 1 1, 1 0, 0 0))')
);
```

Bounding-box equality is what PostGIS uses as the default equality comparison. You need to be aware of this when using deduping operations such as `UNION`, `DISTINCT`, or `GROUP BY` against geometry columns. The examples in the following listing demonstrate what you should expect.

Listing 9.8 `DISTINCT` is not always distinct

```
SELECT ST_AsText(geom)                    <-- ❶ Returns two records as expected
FROM (
    SELECT ST_GeomFromText('LINESTRING (0 0, 1 1)')
    UNION ALL
    SELECT ST_GeomFromText('POLYGON ((0 0, 0 1, 1 1, 1 0, 0 0))')
) As x(geom);

SELECT ST_AsText(geom)                    <-- ❷ Returns one record
FROM (
    SELECT ST_GeomFromText('LINESTRING (0 0, 1 1)')
    UNION
    SELECT ST_GeomFromText('POLYGON ((0 0, 0 1, 1 1, 1 0, 0 0))')
) As x(geom);

SELECT DISTINCT geom                      <-- ❸ Returns one record
FROM (
    SELECT ST_GeomFromText('LINESTRING (0 0, 1 1)')
    UNION ALL
    SELECT ST_GeomFromText('POLYGON ((0 0, 0 1, 1 1, 1 0, 0 0))')

) As x(geom);

SELECT DISTINCT ST_AsText(geom)           <-- ❹ Returns two records
FROM (
    SELECT ST_GeomFromText('LINESTRING (0 0, 1 1)')
    UNION ALL
    SELECT ST_GeomFromText('POLYGON ((0 0, 0 1, 1 1, 1 0, 0 0))')
) As x(geom);
```

In listing 9.8 you get two records back from `UNION ALL` ❶. `UNION ALL` by definition returns all records—nothing surprising here.

You only get back one record if you use `UNION` ❷. PostgreSQL uses the = operator to dedupe in case of `UNION` for all data types. Therefore all geometry records with bounding-box spatial equality would collapse to a single record. PostgreSQL will choose the first record it encounters as the one to output.

The output of the UNION of the linestring with the polygon would be the linestring because they both have the same bounding box ❷. You also get one record back when using DISTINCT and UNION ALL ❸ for the same reason you get one record when using UNION.

You get two records back when using ST_AsText because the output of ST_AsText isn't a geometry ❹. The textual representation of the geometries differs, and because the PostgreSQL textual representation = requires all characters to match, the records don't collapse into one.

The equal operator also comes into play when you group by geometries. The following listing demonstrates this.

Listing 9.9 A COUNT(DISTINCT) is not always a distinct count

```
SELECT COUNT(DISTINCT geom)                              ❶ Returns 1
 FROM (
    SELECT ST_GeomFromText('LINESTRING (0 0, 1 1)')
    UNION ALL
    SELECT ST_GeomFromText('POLYGON ((0 0, 0 1, 1 1, 1 0, 0 0))')
) As x(geom);

SELECT COUNT(DISTINCT geom)                              ❷ Returns 2
FROM (
    SELECT ST_GeomFromText('LINESTRING (0 0, 1 1.1)')
    UNION ALL
    SELECT ST_GeomFromText('POLYGON ((0 0, 0 1, 1 1, 1 0, 0 0))')

) As x(geom);

SELECT geom                                              ❸ Returns one geometry
FROM (
    SELECT ST_GeomFromText('LINESTRING (0 0, 1 1.1)')
    UNION ALL
    SELECT ST_GeomFromText('POLYGON ((0 0, 0 1, 1 1, 1 0, 0 0))')
) As x(geom)
GROUP BY geom;

SELECT geom                                              ❹ Returns two geometries
FROM (
    SELECT ST_GeomFromText('LINESTRING (0 0, 1 1)')
    UNION ALL
    SELECT ST_GeomFromText('POLYGON ((0 0, 0 1, 1 1, 1 0, 0 0))')
) As x(geom)
GROUP BY geom;
```

In listing 9.9 the DISTINCT count gives an answer of 1 because both geometries share the same bounding box ❶. You get an answer of 2 if the linestring's bounding box differs from the bounding box of the polygon ❷. You get only one geometry back when using GROUP BY if the two geometries have the same bounding box ❸. You get both geometries back when you GROUP BY if they have different bounding boxes ❹.

Why did PostGIS pick bounding-box equality as the flag bearer of the equal sign? We can only guess at the reason: bounding-box comparisons are faster than other equality operations—orders of magnitude faster in some cases. The speed also doesn't deteriorate as geometries grow in complexity. A `GROUP BY`, `UNION`, or `DISTINCT` usually involves an entire column of records, and performing a pair-wise geometry or spatial check with permutations of all the rows could easily test the patience of an unsuspecting user. The likelihood of needing to use one of these SQL operations on a geometry column is also low. A table of geometries usually has other columns storing textual data. Using non-geometry columns for deduping operations makes more sense. For example, if you have a table of countries with possible duplicates, you're better off deduping against the country name column than the geometry column.

What if all you have in your table is a single column, and that column is a geometry column? How would you be able to dedupe with no other column to use? The following listing shows one way to get around the bounding-box comparison by first casting the geometry to a textual representation.

Listing 9.10 Guaranteeing unique geometries

```
CREATE TABLE mygeom_unique(geom geometry);
INSERT INTO mygeom_unique(geom)
SELECT CAST(geom As text)
FROM (
    SELECT ST_GeomFromEWKT('LINESTRING (0 0, 1 1)')
    UNION ALL
    SELECT ST_GeomFromText('POLYGON ((0 0, 0 1, 1 1, 1 0, 0 0))')
    UNION ALL
    SELECT ST_GeomFromText('POLYGON ((0 0, 0 1, 1 1, 1 0, 0 0))')
) As x(geom)
GROUP BY CAST(geom As text);
```

In listing 9.10 you're inserting the text representation of the geometry into a geometry field. The text representation is the HEXEWB displayed when you do a `SELECT` of a geometry. When you insert the HEXEWB into a geometry column, PostGIS silently casts the text to geometry for you.

> **BOUNDING-BOX OPERATORS WITH CURVED AND 3D GEOMETRIES** Bounding-box operators work for curved geometries and for 3D geometries, but the Z coordinate is ignored.

Next we'll look at the underpinnings of relationship functions.

9.4 Underpinnings of relationship functions

The intersects relationship function we covered earlier might have given you the impression that `ST_Intersects` is the most generic relationship between two geometries. In actuality, we can generalize one step further. The underpinning of most 2D geometry relationship functions in PostGIS and most other spatial database products is the Dimensionally Extended 9-Intersection Matrix (DE-9IM), which we'll loosely refer to as the *intersection matrix*. The PostGIS function that can work directly with an intersection matrix is the `ST_Relate` function.

The intersection matrix is the foundation of most geometric relationships supported by the OGC SQL/MM standard, and it's an outgrowth from the work of M.J. Egenhofer and J.R. Herring. To learn more about the intersection matrix, see their article, "Categorizing Binary Topological Relations Between Regions, Lines, and Points in Geographic Databases," at www.spatial.maine.edu/~max/9intReport.pdf.

9.4.1 The intersection matrix

The intersection matrix is a 3 × 3 matrix approach that defines all possible pair-wise combinations of exterior, boundary, and interior when two geometries interact. You can use the matrix in two ways: to state the requirement that must be satisfied by a named relationship, or to describe the relationship that exists between two geometries.

When used to define a named relationship, the matrix cells can take on the following values: T, F, *, 0, 1, or 2. When used to describe two interacting geometries, the matrix cells can take on the following values: F, 0, 1, or 2. Table 9.9 explains what each value represents.

Table 9.9 Possible cell values of an intersection matrix

Value	Description
T	An intersection must exist; the resultant geometry can be 0, 1, or 2 dimensions (point, line, area).
F	An intersection must not exist.
*	It doesn't matter if an intersection exists or not.
0	An intersection must exist, and the intersection must be at finite points (dim = 0).
1	An intersection must exist, and the intersection's dimension must be 1 (finite lines).
2	An intersection must exist, and the intersection's dimension must be 2 (areal).

Figures 9.6–9.8 represent `ST_Disjoint`, `ST_Equals`, and `ST_Within` with intersection matrices.

		B		
		Interior	Boundary	Exterior
A	Interior	F	F	*
	Boundary	F	F	*
	Exterior	*	*	*

Figure 9.6 Intersection matrix of `ST_Disjoint`

		B Interior	B Boundary	B Exterior
A	Interior	T	*	F
A	Boundary	*	*	F
A	Exterior	F	F	*

Figure 9.7 Intersection matrix of `ST_Equals`

		B Interior	B Boundary	B Exterior
A	Interior	T	*	F
A	Boundary	*	*	F
A	Exterior	*	*	*

Figure 9.8 Intersection matrix of `ST_Within`

From the `ST_Within` example, you can see that for a geometry to be within another, the interiors of both must intersect, the interior of `A` can't fall outside `B` (it can't intersect with the exterior of `B`), and the boundary can't fall outside `B` (the boundary can't intersect with the exterior of `B`). The boundaries, however, are free to intersect or not intersect.

To avoid having to draw tic-tac-toe boxes for intersection matrices, you can use the shorthand of nine characters. `ST_Disjoint` would be `FF*FF****`, `ST_Equals` would be `T*F**FFF*`, and `ST_Within` would be `T*F**F***`. Go across and then down the matrix to fill in the slots of the shorthand notation.

For a given named relationship or to describe an existing relationship, the intersection may not be unique. Furthermore, when defining a named relationship, you can chain intersection matrices together with Boolean operators to obtain the exact requirements you need. Incidentally, the intersects relationship requires a minimum of three matrices joined by Boolean `OR`s.

9.4.2 Using ST_Relate

PostGIS has two variants of the `ST_Relate` function. The first variant returns a Boolean true or false that states whether geometries `A` and `B` satisfy the specified relationship matrix. The second variant returns the most constraining relationship matrix satisfied by the two geometries.

In theory, PostGIS could replace all the relationship functions we described with one or more generic `ST_Relate` calls. In practice, PostGIS never internally uses `ST_Relate` for a couple of reasons. For one, `ST_Relate` doesn't automatically use indexes. Second, having separate relationship functions lets PostGIS embed shortcuts that can bypass needing to check all the cells of the intersection matrix.

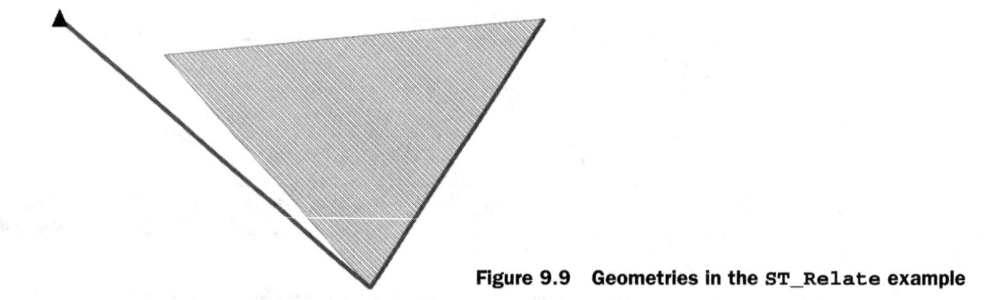

Figure 9.9 Geometries in the ST_Relate example

The following listing exercises both variants of the ST_Relate functions. The geometries used in this example are illustrated in figure 9.9.

Listing 9.11 ST_Relate in action

```
WITH example_set (ex_name,geom) AS (
    SELECT ex_name, geom
    FROM (
        VALUES
            ('A 2D line',
            ST_GeomFromText('LINESTRING(3 5, 2.5 4.25, 1.6 5)')),
            ('A point',
            ST_GeomFromText('POINT(1.6 5)')),
            ('A triangle',
            ST_GeomFromText('POLYGON((3 5, 2.5 4.25, 1.9 4.9, 3 5))'))
    ) AS x(ex_name, geom)
)

SELECT
    A.ex_name As a_name, B.ex_name As b_name,
    ST_Relate(A.geom, B.geom) As relates,
    ST_Intersects(A.geom, B.geom) As intersects,
    ST_Relate(A.geom, B.geom, 'FF*FF****') As relate_disjoint,
    NOT ST_Relate(A.geom, B.geom, 'FF*FF****') As relate_intersects
FROM example_set As A CROSS JOIN example_set As B;
```

Table 9.10 lists the SQL output.

Table 9.10 Results from ST_Relate query

a_name	b_name	Relates	Intersects	Disjoint	Not disjoint
A 2D line	A 2D line	1FFF0FFF2	t	f	t
A 2D line	A point	FF1FF00F2	t	f	t
A 2D line	A triangle	F11F00212	t	f	t
A point	A 2D line	FF0FFF102	t	f	t
A point	A point	0FFFFFFF2	t	f	t
A point	A triangle	FF0FFF212	f	t	f

Table 9.10 Results from `ST_Relate` query *(continued)*

a_name	b_name	Relates	Intersects	Disjoint	Not disjoint
A triangle	A 2D line	FF2101102	t	f	t
A triangle	A point	FF2FF10F2	f	t	f
A triangle	A triangle	2FFF1FFF2	t	f	t

Remember that we mentioned that the intersects relationship requires three intersection matrices. We cheated in our example by taking `NOT ST_Disjoint` instead of computing `ST_Intersects`. This is because intersects implies not disjoint, and not disjoint requires only one intersection matrix to compute.

Let's look at the linestring and the triangle in more detail: figure 9.10 shows the tic-tac-toe notation of this commutative pair of relationships.

Triangle \ 2D line	Interior	Boundary	Exterior
Interior	F	F	2
Boundary	1	0	1
Exterior	1	0	2

2D line \ Triangle	Interior	Boundary	Exterior
Interior	F	1	1
Boundary	F	0	0
Exterior	2	1	2

Figure 9.10 `ST_Relate(triangle,2dline)` and `ST_Relate(2dline,triangle)`

In figure 9.10, notice that if you take FF2101102 and flip the rows and columns, you end up with F11F00212. The intersection matrix is symmetrical. Here are some other observations:

- The interior of the triangle and the interior of the linestring fail to intersect. You can verify this from the image of the geometries in figure 9.10.
- The interior of the triangle doesn't intersect with the boundary of the linestring (recall that the boundary of a line is the start and end points), but the interior of the linestring does intersect with the boundary of the triangle. The dimension of intersection is lineal (dimension of 1).

- You'll find areal intersections at the exteriors of the linestring with both the interior and the exterior of the triangle. This is because the exterior of the linestring encompasses all points not on the linestring, which is an area.

9.5 Summary

In most operations involving spatial databases, geometry relationships play a critical role and are usually a first step before other processing functions, such as `ST_Union` and `ST_Intersection`, are applied. In this chapter, we covered a fair amount of territory related to geometry relationships. We started with bounding boxes and their comparators, and we dug deep into the meaning of equality as it applies to geometries. Intersection and its entourage of functions came next. Finally, we ended with the generic DE-9IM intersection matrix that describes all the aforementioned relationships. After this chapter, you should have a clearer understanding of the various spatial relationships at your disposal and their theoretical underpinnings.

In the next chapter, we'll cover proximity analysis, which covers another set of relationship operators that are used to determine how close things are relative to other things.

Part 2

Putting PostGIS to work

In part 1 of *PostGIS in Action, Second Edition*, you learned about the building blocks you'll need to solve spatial problems. By now you should be able to set up a PostGIS database, populate it with data, and transform data between disparate spatial reference systems. You should also be comfortable using the most common functions in PostGIS and be able to take advantage of their prowess when writing SQL.

In part 2, you'll put the pieces together to solve real problems. The important lessons we want you to take away from part 2 entail how to tackle each problem, starting with building a correct formulation, setting up an appropriate structure to support the analysis, choosing the most appropriate PostGIS functions, and putting it all together using SQL.

Chapter 10 covers the most basic use of PostGIS: finding things and finding them fast.

Chapters 11 and 12 cover various common problems found in vector and raster spatial analyses that you'll come across in building spatial queries for applications. You'll learn how to solve these problems with PostGIS spatial functions and ANSI SQL constructs as well as PostgreSQL-specific enhancements to SQL.

In chapter 13, you'll learn about PostGIS topology and how to use it to manage and fix your spatial data.

Chapter 14 will guide you through various database storage techniques and will take a dive into the topics of triggers and views for maintaining consistency in data.

Chapter 15 focuses on database performance. In this chapter, you'll learn how to speed up queries and how to avoid common SQL pitfalls. You'll learn about the finer points of employing both spatial and non-spatial indexes and fine-tuning PostgreSQL settings. In addition, you'll learn about the often-neglected tactic of simplifying geometries to arrive at "good enough" answers to problems quickly, rather than overly precise answers slowly.

10 Proximity analysis

This chapter covers

- Nearest neighbor searches
- KNN distance operators
- Using KNN with geography
- Geotagging

Once you've located places with a set of coordinates, questions such as the following arise: How far is my house from the nearest expressway? How many burger joints are within a mile drive? What's the average distance that people have to commute to work? Which three hospitals closest to me offer emergency vasectomies? We'll file all these questions under the heading of *proximity analysis*–loosely, the study of how far something is located from something else.

We'll cover both the traditional methods of finding closest neighbors as well as newer methods using KNN indexes. Speed is a concern when performing proximity analyses, and we'll offer techniques and advice on how to speed up slow queries by using bounding boxes.

We'll also cover what you should consider when choosing between a `geography` type, `geometry` type, or hybrid. We'll discuss trade-offs such as performance, features, and ease of use.

We'll end the chapter with geotagging. Geotagging is the labeling of spatial features, usually using data from another spatial feature, such as grouping locations into sales regions, finding all houses located along a street, and so on. Geotagging allows you to aggregate statistics more quickly and to export in formats that are friendly for spreadsheets and charts.

Before we dig in, we want to make clear that all the distances we refer to in this chapter are minimum distances ("as the crow flies"), and are not subject to any path constraints. We'll leave pgRouting, which handles path constraints, to chapter 16.

DATA DOWNLOAD This is a data-intensive chapter, and we gathered the data we'll use from a variety of sources. You can download the data from www.postgis.us/chapter_10_edition_2. The readme.txt file in the data folder details how we groomed the data.

10.1 Nearest neighbor searches

In this section, we'll answer the two most common questions: *which places are within X distance* and *what are the N closest places?* These kinds of problems are often referred to as *nearest neighbor* searches.

10.1.1 Which places are within X distance?

You learned about the versatile `ST_DWithin` function first in chapter 1. Here you'll see some more examples of its use.

You can use `ST_DWithin` to find places that are close to one another or to determine if a place is within *X* units of another. You can pass both `geometry` and `geography` types to the function.

The following listing finds airports within 100 kilometers of a location using the `geography` variant of `ST_DWithin`.

Listing 10.1 Airports within 100 km of a location

```
SELECT name, iso_country, iso_region
FROM ch10.airports
WHERE ST_DWithin(geog, ST_Point(-75.0664, 40.2003)::geography, 100000);
```

Although this query uses the `geography` data type, it runs fairly quickly on a data set of 45,000 airports, returning 631 rows in under 40 milliseconds.

10.1.2 Using ST_DWithin and ST_Distance for N closest results

You can alter listing 10.1 to return the *N* closest airports by adding an order-by-distance clause followed by a limit.

Listing 10.2 Five closest airports to (-75.0664 40.2003)

```
SELECT ident, name
FROM
    ch10.airports
```

```
    CROSS JOIN
    (SELECT ST_Point(-75.0664, 40.2003)::geography AS ref_geog) As r
WHERE ST_DWithin(geog, ref_geog, 100000)
ORDER BY ST_Distance(geog, ref_geog)
LIMIT 5;
```

With this query, you'll need to make sure that your search radius is large enough to return at least five results.

10.1.3 Using ST_DWithin and DISTINCT ON to find closest locations

In many cases, you'll begin with a set of places and need to find the place closest to another set of places; for example, how many emergency medical centers are within 10 miles of all nursing homes in a major city. You can accomplish this by combining ST_DWithin and the PostgreSQL DISTINCT ON construct. DISTINCT ON performs an implicit GROUP BY, but it's not limited to returning just the fields that you grouped on.

The next listing finds the closest navaid (navigational aid) to each airport.

Listing 10.3 Closest navaid to each airport

```
SELECT DISTINCT ON (a.ident)                          <-- ❶ Distinct fields (in parentheses)
    a.ident, a.name As airport, n.name As closest_navaid,
    (ST_Distance(a.geog,n.geog)/1000)::integer As dist_km
FROM ch10.airports As a LEFT JOIN ch10.navaids As n
ON ST_DWithin(a.geog, n.geog,100000)                  <-- ❷ Radius
ORDER BY a.ident, dist_km;                            <-- ❸ Sort by distance
```

In listing 10.3 a comma-separated list of distinct fields in parentheses must follow DISTINCT ON ❶. This same list must appear first in the ORDER BY clause ❸. Then you specify the maximum radius to scan for matches ❷. The wider your radius, the slower the query, but you're more likely to be guaranteed matches. This listing uses a left join instead of an inner join to ensure that even if you find no navaids, the airport will still be in the results ❷. You sort the navaids by dist_km to ensure that the navaid selected for output for each airport is the closest to that airport ❸.

The next listing shows a partial output of listing 10.3.

Listing 10.4 Closest navaid to each airport

```
 ident | airport                    | closest_navaid      | dist_km
-------+----------------------------+---------------------+---------
 00A   | Total RF Heliport          | North Philadelphia  |       7
 00AK  | Lowell Field               | Homer               |      30
 00AL  | Epps Airpark               | Capshaw             |      10
 00AR  | Newport Hospital           | Newport             |       8
```

ST_DWithin can also substitute for the ST_Intersects function. When used this way, you call the approach *intersects with tolerance.*

10.1.4 Intersects with tolerance

Use `ST_DWithin` to check for intersections when you have two geometries that fail to intersect because of differences caused by the number of significant digits. Consider this example:

```
SELECT ST_DWithin(
    ST_GeomFromText(
        'LINESTRING(1 2, 3 4)'
    ),
    ST_Point(3.00001, 4.000001),
    0.0001
);
```

The point and the linestring are close enough that you'll want to ignore the fact that they're only .0001 units apart. You'll find that you end up using intersection with tolerance quite often when working with real data where not everything lines up perfectly.

Using `ST_DWithin` in place of `ST_Intersects` has two more advantages:

- `ST_DWithin` won't choke on invalid geometries as `ST_Intersects` often does, especially if a geometry has self-intersecting regions. `ST_DWithin` doesn't care about validity because it doesn't rely on an intersection matrix. Having said this, you should always carefully inspect the output when you have invalid geometries.
- Since PostGIS 2.1 you can use `ST_DWithin` with curved geometries, whereas `ST_Intersects` doesn't work with curved geometries.

PostGIS 2.0 introduced `ST_3DDWithin` and `ST_3DIntersects`, which you can use against 3D geometries and polyhedral surfaces.

Next we'll look at finding the *N* closest objects using distance bounding-box operators.

10.1.5 Finding N closest places using KNN distance bounding-box operators

A classic nearest neighbor problem is finding the *N* nearest points of interest to a fixed location. PostGIS 2.0 introduced two new KNN (k-nearest neighbor) indexable operators:

- <#>—This is the KNN bounding-box distance operator. `A <#> B` returns the minimum distance between the bounding boxes of `A` and `B`.
- <->—This is the KNN bounding-box centroid distance operator. `A <-> B` returns the distance between the centroids of the bounding boxes of `A` and `B`.

You can use these operators only with `geometry` types. Even though you can pass in 3D geometries, the operators will only consider the 2D XY-plane bounding box. The distance returned should also only be trusted if you're using a measure-preserving planar SRID.

The two KNN operators behave very differently from the commonly used bounding-box intersects spatial operator (`&&`). Unlike `&&`, which utilizes spatial indexes when used in WHERE and JOIN clauses, the KNN operators can only use a spatial index when in the ORDER BY clause and when one side of the operator remains constant through the life of the query. In addition, KNN operators return a numeric value rather than a true/false value like many other operators.

The following listing is the most basic of KNN examples that can utilize a spatial index.

Listing 10.5 Closest ten centroids of geometry bounding boxes

```
SELECT
    pid,
    geom
    <->
    ST_Transform(ST_SetSRID(ST_Point(-71.09368, 42.35857),4326),26986)
FROM ch10.land
WHERE land_type = 'apartment'
ORDER BY
    geom
    <->
    ST_Transform(ST_SetSRID(ST_Point(-71.09368, 42.35857),4326),26986)
LIMIT 10;
```

As with other relationship operators and functions, the spatial reference systems of both geometries need to be the same. In listing 10.5 you pass in a constant point geometry on the right side of the operator. Because both sides must always share the same SRID, you need to transform from 4326 to 26986 (Massachusetts State Plane).

You can also draw values from tables for use in the operator, but one side must return exactly one value. See the following listing.

Listing 10.6 Closest ten; one side is a unique value from a table

```
SELECT pid
FROM ch10.land
WHERE land_type = 'apartment'
ORDER BY geom <-> (SELECT geom FROM ch10.land WHERE pid = '58-162')
LIMIT 10;
```

We mentioned that you must place the operator in the ORDER BY clause in order for the index on the geometry to kick in. This doesn't preclude you from using it elsewhere in the SQL—just know that you won't have the benefit of an index. If you're drawing from a small table, use of the index is immaterial.

Indexes also don't come into play in the SELECT statement and WHERE clause. So if you were to replace the `ORDER BY geom <->ST_Transform(ST_SetSRID(ST_Point (-71.09368, 42.35857),4326),26986) LIMIT 10` in listing 10.5 with `AND geom <->ST_Transform(ST_SetSRID(ST_Point(-71.09368, 42.35857),4326),26986) < 700`, the spatial index couldn't be used.

To work around the requirement that one side of the operator must be a constant geometry, you can use a correlated subquery in the SELECT clause, as shown next.

Listing 10.7 Find closest shopping to each parcel using correlated subquery

```
SELECT
    l.pid, (
        SELECT s.pid
        FROM ch10.land As s
        WHERE s.land_type = 'shopping'
        ORDER BY s.geom <-> l.geom LIMIT 1
    ) As closest_shopping
FROM ch10.land AS l;
```

Listing 10.7 uses the distance centroid operator to find the closest shopping center to each parcel of land.

Unfortunately, because subselects must return a single row when used in `SELECT`, you can't use them to answer the more generic *N* closest where N != 1. In the next listing, the `LATERAL` join allows you to use a correlated subquery in the `FROM`.

Listing 10.8 Find three closest shopping malls using a LATERAL join

```
SELECT l.pid, r.pid As n_closest_shopping
FROM
    ch10.land As l
    CROSS JOIN LATERAL
    (
        SELECT s.pid
        FROM ch10.land AS s
        WHERE s.land_type = 'shopping'
        ORDER BY s.geom <-> l.geom
        LIMIT 3
    ) As r;
```

With lateral joins, you're able to access elements across the join. In listing 10.8 the right side of the join (`r`) draws values from the `geom` column on the left side (`l`) so that for each row of `l` you get a new query `r` where the `l.geom` is treated as a constant geometry.

In all our KNN examples so far, we've been getting the approximate closest results because we've been comparing bounding boxes. For geometries that tend to fill up their bounding boxes or that are very small, these approximations should be fine. To be more exact, you can use KNN to narrow the choices and then apply a distance search.

10.1.6 Combining KNN distance-box operators with ST_Distance

KNN distance-box operators are fast, and `ST_Distance` is much slower. So what should you do if you need the exactitude of `ST_Distance` but also need quick results? You can try a hybrid approach. Start with KNN to narrow your search radius, and then use `ST_Distance` to find the closest locations. For example, if you have a table of all ATM machines in the world and you want to find the five closest, you can use KNN to narrow the choices down to a probable one hundred and then use `ST_Distance` against this much smaller subset.

The following listing demonstrates the approach of using KNN as an approximate filter and then applying `ST_Distance` to the smaller set to get an exact result. It finds the closest five apartment buildings to a particular point.

Listing 10.9 Using KNN to narrow choices and then applying `ST_Distance`

```
WITH x AS (                                          <-- 1 Top 100 by bounding-box distance
    SELECT
        pid,
        geom,
        (SELECT geom FROM ch10.land WHERE pid = '58-162') As ref_geom
    FROM ch10.land
    WHERE land_type = 'apartment'
    ORDER BY geom <#>
        (SELECT geom FROM ch10.land AS l WHERE pid = '58-162')
    LIMIT 100
  )
SELECT
    pid,
    RANK() OVER(ORDER BY ST_Distance(geom, ref_geom)) As act_r,     <-- 2 Order by distance
    ST_Distance(geom, ref_geom)::numeric(10,3) As act_dist,
    RANK() OVER(ORDER BY geom <#> ref_geom) As bb_r,        <-- 3 Order by bounding-box distance
    (geom <#> ref_geom)::numeric(10,3) As bb_dist,
    RANK() OVER(ORDER BY geom <-> ref_geom) As bbc_r,      <-- 4 Order by bounding-box centroid distance
   (geom <-> ref_geom)::numeric(10,3) As bbc_dist
FROM X
ORDER BY act_r        <-- 5 Return top 5 by actual distance
LIMIT 5;
```

In listing 10.9 you use a CTE to limit results to the closest 100 using the KNN bounding-box distance. Then you use the `RANK` window function to order the narrowed set ❶. The closer the apartment building, the lower the rank. This is done three times: using the exact distance computed using `ST_Distance` ❷, using the KNN bounding-box distance ❸, and using the bounding-box centroid distance as a comparison ❹. Finally, you limit the output to the top five by actual distance ❺. The cast to `numeric(10,3)` is used to round the distance outputs for display purposes.

The output of listing 10.9 follows.

Listing 10.10 Comparing exact distance with KNN bounding-box distance

```
  pid    | act_r | act_dist  | bb_r | bb_dist  | bbc_r | bbc_dist
---------+-------+-----------+------+----------+-------+----------
 70-87   |     1 |  515.110  |    1 | 500.886  |     1 |  563.693
 68-74   |     2 |  550.868  |    2 | 543.758  |     2 |  623.308
 48-154  |     3 |  588.216  |    3 | 560.650  |     5 |  675.984
 70-98   |     4 |  610.912  |    4 | 598.233  |     4 |  670.388
 74-3    |     5 |  614.343  |    5 | 600.855  |     3 |  649.738
```

As demonstrated in listing 10.10, the bounding-box distance operator is a better estimate of distance than the bounding-box centroid distance operator for this particular case.

10.1.7 Using window functions to find closest N places

In the previous section, we pulled out the ANSI-SQL RANK window function, which outputs the ordinal ordering of a column. In this section, we'll look at a similar example that demonstrates partitioning first, but uses the ROW_NUMBER function instead of the RANK function.

The problem we're trying to solve here is to find the two closest roads for each school. We need the answer to be absolutely correct, and because long linestrings have bounding boxes that cover very little of the geometry, the KNN provides a very poor approximation of distance. Instead of using a KNN operator to perform the first round of narrowing, we'll use ST_DWithin.

Listing 10.11 Find two closest roads to each school; search 500 meter radius

```
SELECT
    pid, land_type, row_num, road_name,
    round(CAST(dist_km As numeric),2) As dist_km
FROM (
    SELECT
        ROW_NUMBER() OVER (
            PARTITION BY l.pid
            ORDER BY ST_Distance(r.geom,l.geom)
        ) As row_num,                                  ❶ Sequentially number by proximity
        l.pid, l.land_type, r.road_name,
        ST_Distance(r.geom,l.geom)/1000 As dist_km
    FROM
        ch10.land As l
    LEFT JOIN                                          ❷ Left join includes no matches
        ch10.road As r
    ON ST_DWithin(r.geom,l.geom,500)
    WHERE l.land_type = 'education'
) As X
WHERE X.row_num < 3                                    ❸ Limit each window to at most two rows
ORDER BY pid, row_num;
```

Listing 10.11 narrows the set of roads to only those that are within a half kilometer, but the LEFT JOIN ensures that even if there are no roads within half a kilometer of a school, each school will still be represented at least once ❷. This means that you could run into situations where a school has just one road or even no roads. So be it.

The schools are partitioned by unique identifiers, which means the ROW_NUMBER window function will act over each school independently ❶. The ORDER BY ST_Distance forces the sequential numbering to be in order of distance to the school ❶. Finally you limit the results to the closest two ❸. The next listing shows a sampling of the results.

Listing 10.12 Two roads closest to each school

```
pid    | land_type | row_num |     road_name    | dist_km
-------+-----------+---------+------------------+---------
 102-2 | education |       1 | MAGAZINE STREET  |    0.01
 102-2 | education |       2 | CHESTNUT STREET  |    0.03
 104-1 | education |       1 | PLEASANT PLACE   |    0.01
 104-1 | education |       2 | UPTON STREET     |    0.01
 106-1 | education |       1 | FRANKLIN STREET  |    0.00
 106-1 | education |       2 | PEARL STREET     |    0.01
 :
 :
```

RANK versus ROW_NUMBER

The difference between RANK and ROW_NUMBER is in how they handle ties. RANK will mark ties with the same number and skip the subsequent numbers (for example, 1,2,3,3,3,6,7). ROW_NUMBER will arbitrarily break ties so you always have a distinct sequence (1,2,3,4,5,6,7). By PostgreSQL convention, any operation involving ORDER BY will sort NULL values to the end unless the ordering column is followed by NULLS FIRST.

There is another flavor of RANK that we didn't demonstrate called DENSE_RANK. Like RANK, DENSE_RANK will ascribe the same number to the same ORDER BY values, but it won't skip numbers. Instead of a sequence of 1,2,3,3,3,6,7, DENSE_RANK would return a sequence of 1,2,3,3,3,4,5.

Although this example demonstrated the use of ST_DWithin and ST_Distance in conjunction with ROW_NUMBER using geometry types, keep in mind that you can just as easily use this approach with the geography type because geography has the same functions available.

So far you've seen only examples of the geometry and geography types used separately, but it's possible to cast them back and forth to take advantage of the benefits of both. On to the next section.

10.2 Using KNN with geography types

We mentioned at the outset that KNN operators only work against geometry types, but what if you only have geography? Don't fret. You can easily cast between the two types—all you have to do is temporarily convert the geography to geometry. Do what you wish using KNN, and then convert the results back to geography.

What makes it possible to use both geography and geometry functions in the same query is that you can cast between each with the following syntax: geog::geometry for converting geography fields to geometry, or geom::geography for converting geometry fields to geography.

We also said that for KNN to shine, you must have indexes on the underlying column. You can't index a geography column, cast it to geometry, and expect KNN to acknowledge the index. What you need to add is a functional index, where you apply the cast operator to the geography column and index the output. Let's add functional indexes to the airports table:

```
CREATE INDEX idx_airports_geom_gist_cast
    ON ch10.airports USING gist (geometry(geog));
```

CASTING NOTATIONS PostgreSQL offers three different but equivalent syntaxes for casting: `geog::geometry`, `CAST(geog As geometry)`, and `geometry (geog)`. When creating a functional index, if you use `geog::geometry` you need to wrap an additional set of parentheses around it: `gist ( (geog ::geometry) )`.

Now that you have the airport geometry indexes, let's run through an example that casts to geometry to take advantage of the lightning-fast KNN bounding-box centroid operator. In listing 10.13 you're trying to find the five closest airports to a location. This is the same exercise that we did in listing 10.2. You'll see how much faster queries can be with KNN.

Listing 10.13 Five closest airports to a location using bounding-box centroid geometry

```
WITH ref As (
    SELECT ST_Point(-75.0664, 40.2003)::geography AS ref_geog )    <-- Define reference geography

SELECT ident, name
FROM (
    SELECT ident, name, geog
    FROM ch10.airports
    ORDER BY
        (SELECT ref_geog::geometry FROM ref) <-> geog::geometry    <-- Cast to geometry

    LIMIT 20
) AS x
ORDER BY ST_Distance(geog,(SELECT ref_geog FROM ref))    <-- Geog distance check

LIMIT 5;
```

The outputs of listings 10.13 and 10.2 are identical. But by using KNN, the query finishes three times faster (10 ms compared with 30 ms on our machine) with an initial limit of the closest 20. If you're willing to accommodate some false positives and limit the first pass to five, you'll probably see speeds in the single digits.

10.3 Geotagging

Geotagging refers to a class of spatial techniques where you try to situate points located within the context of another geometry. There are two forms this generally takes:

- *Region tagging*—This is a process where you tag a geometry, such as a point of interest, with the name of a region it's in, such as a state.

- *Linear referencing*—This is another kind of tagging, particular to linestrings, whereby you refer to a point of interest by its closest point along a linestring. The tag can be the closest point on the linestring, or a measure such as a mile marker or fractional percent measured from the start of the linestring to the point on the linestring closest to your point of interest.

Geotagging and linear referencing are two common tasks for GIS practitioners because they're preparatory steps for many statistical analyses. For example, suppose you have a list of all McDonalds in California, and you have a table of all counties as geometries. Regional geotagging could involve trying to figure out which counties contain which McDonalds so that you can then easily get a count of McDonalds in each county. If instead you have a list of all major highways in California, linear referencing could involve trying to figure out which highways have access to which McDonalds.

10.3.1 Tagging data to a specific region

One of the more common uses of spatial databases is to tag regions. Often you'll have named regions of space divided into polygons or multipolygons. These could be political districts, sales territories, states, or whatever. You'll also have points with coordinates, and you'll need to figure out which region each point lies within. Ultimately, you'll want to add a column to your points table identifying the matched regions.

Let's look at an example based on the airports table. Suppose that for each airport, you need to find and store its time zone. Your time zone regions will come from a table of multipolygons (ch10.tz_world), and you'll find for each airport what time zone multipolygon it falls in and set its time zone to the time zone value for that region. The following example updates the time zone field of the airport with the time zone value in the corresponding time zone multipolygon:

```
ALTER TABLE ch10.airports ADD COLUMN tz varchar(30);
UPDATE ch10.airports
SET tz = t.tzid
FROM ch10.tz_world As t
WHERE ST_Intersects(ch10.airports.geog, t.geog);
```

After this update is done, most of your airports will have a time zone. This particular update took about three minutes on our machine with PostGIS 2.1, which is a ten-fold improvement over PostGIS 2.0. Yes, each new version brings not only new features but also speed improvements.

To display the time zones in words instead of numerical offsets from GMT, you can use the built-in PostgreSQL time zone functions as follows:

```
SELECT ident, name, CURRENT_TIMESTAMP AT TIME ZONE tz AS ts_at_airport
FROM ch10.airports
WHERE ident IN('KBOS','KSAN','LIRF','OMDB','ZLXY');
```

10.3.2 Linear referencing: snapping points to the closest linestring

One common form of linear referencing returns the closest point on the closest linestring to a reference point. This kind of linear referencing is often referred to as *snapping points to the closest linestring*. You begin with a set of points and a set of linestrings. You then try to associate each point with its closest linestring, and then with the closest point on that linestring. Unlike the region tagging we demonstrated, the point of interest (in the previous case, airports) is almost never on the closest geometry.

For example, say you're driving along erratically, taking GPS readings. Over the course of your journey, you collect points with lots of curves veering both right and left of the street's centerline. You don't want to expose your bad driving habits by simply overlaying your connected GPS points over a map of street centerlines, so you perform linear referencing where each point is snapped to a street centerline.

Paul Ramsey, the founding father of PostGIS, inspired the next example ("Snapping Points in PostGIS," http://blog.cleverelephant.ca/2008/04/snapping-points-in-postgis.html). At the time, Paul only had two functions to work with: `ST_Line_Interpolate_Point` and `ST_Line_Locate_Point` (both renamed to `ST_LineInterpolatePoint` and `ST_LineLocationPoint` in PostGIS 2.1). For this example, we've chosen to use the function `ST_ClosestPoint` instead. Introduced in PostGIS 1.5, `ST_ClosestPoint` is faster than the older linear referencing functions, and the inputs are not limited to points. For this example, you'll be snapping land parcels (polygons) to the closest point on the centerline of the nearest road.

PROXIMITY FUNCTIONS IN 3D PostGIS 2.0 unveiled `ST_3DDWithin`, `ST_3DDistance`, and `ST_3DClosestPoint`, thanks to the efforts of Nicklas Avén. These functions work with 3D points, linestrings, polygons, and polyhedral surfaces. 2D proximity functions will ignore the Z coordinate even if it's included in the input.

The basic approach to the solution is as follows:

1. Use `ST_DWithin` to narrow your choices. If a parcel has no road within 30 meters, eliminate it from consideration.
2. For every pairing of parcel and road, use `ST_ClosestPoint` to pinpoint the closest point on the road to the parcel.
3. Use a combination of `DISTINCT ON` and the `ST_Distance` function to keep only the paired parcel and road that are closest.

When finding closest geometries for anything with a geometry dimension higher than a point, you may not end up with unique answers. For instance, there's an infinite number of points that are closest to each other when you consider two parallel linestrings. `ST_ClosestPoint` will return just one of these. The point selected will always be one of the vertices of the two-point segment returned by `ST_ShortestLine`.

ST_ShortestLine, like ST_ClosestPoint, only returns one answer even if there are multiple answers.

Listing 10.14 Finding the closest point on a road to a parcel of land

```
SELECT DISTINCT ON (p.pid)
    p.addr_num || ' ' || full_str AS parcel,
    r.road_name AS road,
    ST_ClosestPoint(p.geom,r.geom) As snapped_point
FROM ch10.land AS p INNER JOIN ch10.road AS r
ON ST_DWithin(p.geom,r.geom,20.0)
ORDER BY p.gid, ST_Distance(p.geom,r.geom);
```

Figure 10.1 illustrates the original parcels and the snapped points produced by listing 10.14.

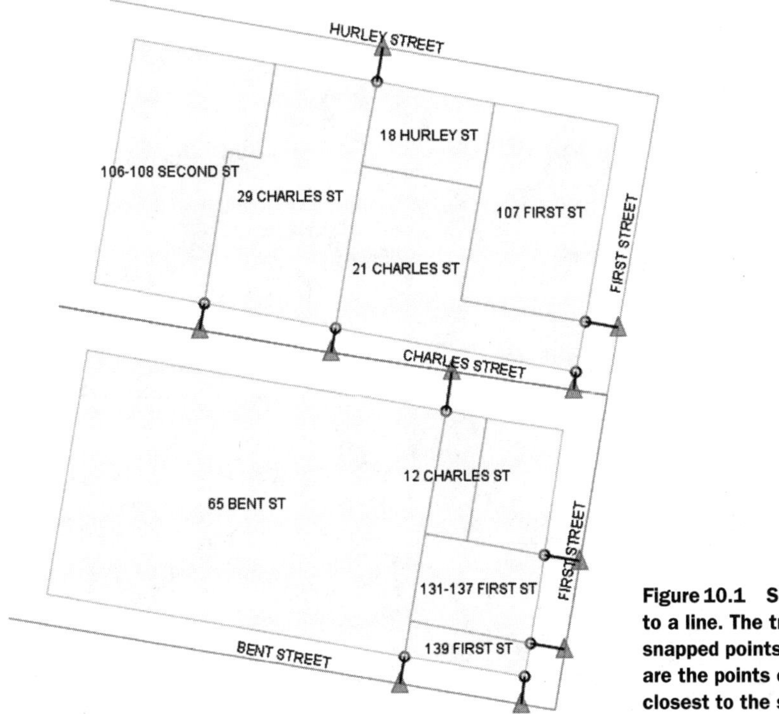

Figure 10.1 Snapping location to a line. The triangles are the snapped points and the circles are the points on the land closest to the snapped points.

For visualizing the original point on the parcel that's closest to the snapped point, we used the companion function ST_ShortestLine.

10.4 Summary

In this chapter, we showcased functions used for proximity analysis. We introduced KNN bounding-box operators, <#> and <->, that can make good use of indexes. We showed how to use KNN operators in the ORDER BY clause. We also proffered a two-step approach where you can first use KNN to narrow your search and then use `ST_DWithin` or `ST_Distance` to be more exacting. If your table has geography columns, we showed you how to cast to geometry to use the KNN operators.

On the SQL front, we introduced the shortcut `DISTINCT ON`, with which you can pick out distinct rows without using a `GROUP BY` and rejoining non-grouped columns. We also showed you how to use the new lateral join, which you can use to access columns across a join.

In the chapters that follow, we'll continue our exploration of common tasks that you'll encounter both in the vector world and the raster world. In the next chapter, we'll explore geometry- and geography-processing functions.

11 Geometry and geography processing

> ***This chapter covers***
> - Spatial aggregation
> - Clipping, splitting, tesselating, and segmentizing
> - Translating, scaling, and rotating geometries (affine operations)
> - Using geometry functions with geography types

This chapter demonstrates techniques for manipulating geometries and geographies, and the end result is generally another geometry or geography. Unless we tell you otherwise, all functions that we demonstrate in this chapter work with both data types.

Through the years, we've amassed a catalog of problems that GIS users encounter, and in this chapter we'll share with you the most common problems and our solutions. Keep in mind that multiple solutions exist for a given problem. We by no means proclaim that our solutions trump all other solutions. In fact, if enough people run into a problem that can be generalized, PostGIS could very well introduce a wrapper function that will resolve the problem with a single call.

The data and code used in this chapter are located here: www.postgis.us/chapter_11_edition_2.

11.1 Using spatial aggregate functions

Aggregation is the process of rolling up several rows of data into one. For any table, aggregation begins by segregating the columns into those that you group by and those that you don't. SQL finds like values across your group-by columns and creates distinct groups. It must then apply an aggregate function to roll up the non-group-by columns, summing them, averaging them, and so on.

In a textual relational database, the most common aggregation functions used are `COUNT`, `SUM`, `MIN`, `MAX`, and `AVG`. With a spatial extender such as PostGIS, many spatial aggregates are added to the mix. The most common `geometry` aggregates are `ST_MakeLine`, `ST_Union`, `ST_Collect`, and `ST_Polygonize`. The `ST_Union` function is by far the most commonly used of the spatial aggregates.

There are currently no spatial aggregates for the `geography` type. In order to use the `geometry` spatial aggregates with geography data, you'll need to cast `geography` to `geometry`.

11.1.1 Creating a multipolygon from many multipolygon records

In many cases, you may have a city where records are broken out by districts, neighborhoods, boroughs, or precincts because you often need to view or report on each neighborhood separately. Sometimes, however, for reporting purposes you need to view the city as a single unit. In this case you can use the `ST_Union` aggregate function to amass one single multipolygon from constituent multipolygons.

For example, the largest city in the United States is New York, made up of the five storied boroughs of Manhattan, Bronx, Queens, Brooklyn, and Staten Island. To aggregate New York, you first need to create a boroughs table with five records—one multipolygon for each of the boroughs with littorals (see figure 11.1).

Then you can use the `ST_Union` spatial aggregate function to group all the boroughs into a single city, as follows:

```
SELECT ST_Union(geom) As city FROM boroughs;
```

Figure 11.2 shows the result of the union operation.

Let's work through an example in the San Francisco area using our table of cities. Listing 11.1 lists cities that straddle multiple records, how many polygons each city straddles, and how many polygons you'll be left with after dissolving boundaries within each city.

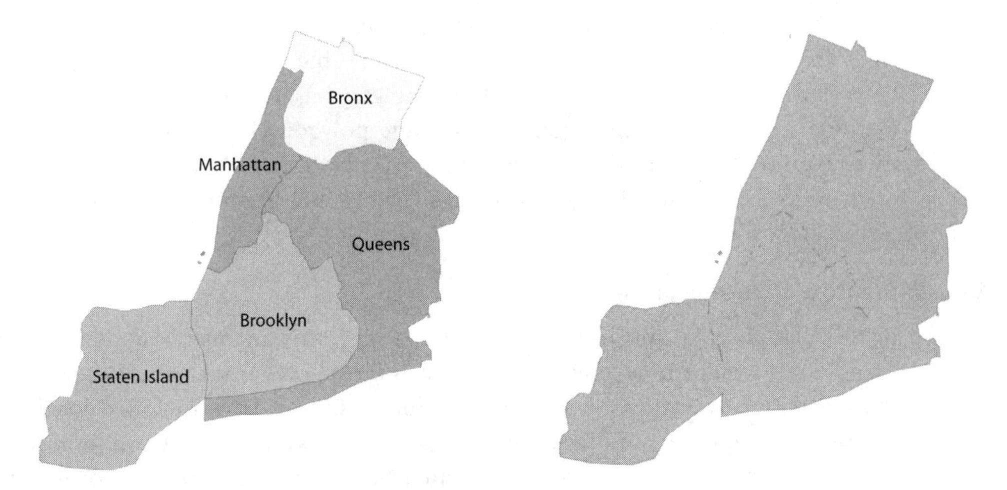

Figure 11.1 Five boroughs of New York City as five records

Figure 11.2 New York City unified

Listing 11.1 Cities with more than one record

```
SELECT
    city,
    COUNT(city) AS num_records,
    SUM(ST_NumGeometries(geom)) AS numpoly_before,
    ST_NumGeometries(ST_Multi(ST_Union(geom))) AS num_poly_after
FROM ch11.cities
GROUP BY city
HAVING COUNT(city) > 1;
```

From the code in listing 11.1, you know that ten cities have multiple records, but you'll only be able to dissolve the boundaries of Brisbane and San Francisco, because only these two have fewer polygons per geometry than what you started out with.

In listing 11.2 you aggregate and insert the aggregated records into a table called ch11.distinct_cities. You then add a primary key to each city to ensure that you have exactly one record per city.

Listing 11.2 Aggregating to one record per city

```
SELECT city, ST_Multi(
    ST_Union(geom))::geometry(multipolygon,2227) AS geom    <-- 1 Make multipolygon
INTO ch11.distinct_cities                                   <-- 2 Type modifier
FROM ch11.cities
GROUP BY city, ST_SRID(geom);

ALTER TABLE ch11.distinct_cities
ADD CONSTRAINT pk_distinct_cities
PRIMARY KEY (city);                                         <-- 3 Primary key
CREATE INDEX idx_distinct_cities_geom
    ON ch11.distinct_cities USING gist(geom);               <-- 4 Spatial index
```

In the preceding listing, you create and populate a new table called ch11.distinct_cities ❶. You use the ST_Multi function to ensure that all the resulting geometries will be multipolygons and not polygons. If a geometry has a single polygon, ST_Multi will upgrade it to be a multipolygon with a single polygon. Then you cast the geometry using typmod to ensure that the geometry type and spatial reference system are correctly registered in the geometry_columns view ❷. For good measure we also put in a primary key ❸ and a spatial index ❹.

11.1.2 Creating linestrings from points

In the past decade, the use of GPS devices has gone mainstream. GPS Samaritans spend their leisure time visiting points of interest (POI), taking GPS readings, and sharing their adventures via the web. Common venues have included local taverns, eateries, fishing holes, and filling stations with the lowest prices. A common follow-up task after gathering the raw positions of the POIs is to connect them to form an unbroken course.

In this exercise, you'll use Australian track points to create linestrings. These track points consist of GPS readings taken during a span of about ten hours from afternoon to early morning on a wintry July day. We have no idea of what the readings represent. Let's say a zoologist fastened a GPS around the neck of a roo and tracked her for an evening. The readings came in every ten seconds or so, but instead of creating one linestring with more than two thousand points, you'll divide the readings into 15-minute intervals and create separate linestrings for each of the intervals.

ST_MakeLine is the spatial aggregate function that takes a set of points and forms a linestring out of them. Since PostgreSQL 9.0, you can add an ORDER BY clause to aggregate functions; this is particularly useful when you need to control the order in which aggregation occurs. In this example, you'll order by the input time of the readings.

Listing 11.3 Creating a linear path from point observations

```
SELECT
    DATE_TRUNC('minute',time) -
        CAST(
            mod(
                CAST(DATE_PART('minute',time) AS integer),15
            ) ||' minutes' AS interval
        ) AS track_period,
    MIN(time) AS t_start,
    MAX(time) AS t_end,
    ST_MakeLine(geom ORDER BY time) AS geom
INTO ch11.aussie_run
FROM ch11.aussie_track_points
GROUP BY track_period
HAVING COUNT(time) > 1;
```

❶ Define track_period as 15 minute intervals

❷ Aggregate points by order of time

❸ Bucket the paths into 15-minute intervals (the track_period)

❹ Only consider tracks with more than one point

```
SELECT
    CAST(track_period AS timestamp),
    CAST(t_start AS timestamp) AS t_start,
    CAST(t_end AS timestamp) AS t_end,
    ST_NPoints(geom) AS np,
    CAST(ST_Length(geom::geography) AS integer) AS dist_m,
    (t_end - t_start) AS dur
FROM ch11.aussie_run;
```

❺ Calculate length, time per period

❻ Cast geometry to geography so you can measure in meters

First you create a column called `track_period` specifying quarter-hour slots starting on the hour, 15 minutes past, 30 minutes past, and 45 minutes past ❶. You allocate each GPS point into the slots and create separate linestrings from each time slot via the `GROUP BY` clause ❸. Not all time slots need to have points, and some slots may have a single point. If a slot is devoid of points, it won't be part of the output. If a slot only has one point, it's removed ❹. For the allocation, you use the `data_part` function and the modulo operator.

Within each slot, you create a linestring using `ST_MakeLine` ❷. You want the line to follow the timing of the measurements, so you add an `ORDER BY` clause to `ST_MakeLine`.

The `SELECT` inserts directly into a new table called aussie_run. (If you're not running this code for the first time, you'll need to drop the aussie_run table first.) Finally, you query aussie_run to find the number of points in each linestring using `ST_NPoints`, subtracting the time of the last point from the time of the first point to get a duration, and using `ST_Length` to compute the distance covered between the first and last points within the 15-minute slot ❺. Note that you cast the `geometry` in longitude and latitude to `geography` ❻ to ensure you have a measurable unit—meters.

Table 11.1 is a sampling from the query.

Table 11.1 Output from querying aussie_run

track_period	t_start	t_end	np	dist_m	dur
2009-07-18 04:30:00	2009-07-18 04:30:00	2009-07-18 04:44:59	33	2705	00:14:59
2009-07-18 04:45:00	2009-07-18 04:45:05	2009-07-18 04:55:20	87	1720	00:10:15
2009-07-18 05:00:00	2009-07-18 05:02:00	2009-07-18 05:14:59	100	1530	00:12:59
2009-07-18 15:00:00	2009-07-18 15:09:16	2009-07-18 15:14:57	45	1651	00:05:41

Now that you know how to make linestrings from points, let's make smaller geometries from larger ones using clipping and splitting.

11.2 Clipping, splitting, tessellating

Clipping uses one geometry to cut another during intersection. We briefly covered the intersection functions in chapter 9 and demonstrated how you can use them for clipping. In this section, we'll explore other functions available to you for clipping and splitting.

11.2.1 Clipping

As the name implies, *clipping* is the act of removing unwanted sections of a geometry, leaving behind only what's of interest. Think of clipping coupons from a newspaper, clipping hair from someone's head, or the moon clipping the sun in a solar eclipse.

Difference and *symmetric difference* are operations closely related to intersection. They both serve to return the remainder of an intersection. `ST_Difference` is a non-commutative function, whereas `ST_SymDifference` is, as the name implies, commutative.

Difference functions return the geometry of what's left out when two geometries intersect. When given geometries `A` and `B`, `ST_Difference(A,B)` returns the portion of `A` that's not shared with `B`, whereas `ST_SymDifference(A,B)` returns the portion of `A` and `B` that's not shared.

Here's a symbolic way to think about it:

```
ST_SymDifference(A,B) =  Union(A,B) - Intersection(A,B)
ST_Difference(A,B) = A - Intersection(A,B)
```

The following listing repeats an exercise similar to the one we did with intersection in chapter 9, except here you're getting the difference between a linestring and polygon instead of the intersection.

Listing 11.4 What's left of the polygon and line after clipping

```
SELECT
    ST_Intersects(g1.geom1,g1.geom2) AS they_intersect,
    GeometryType(
        ST_Difference(g1.geom1,g1.geom2) ) AS intersect_geom_type
FROM (
    SELECT ST_GeomFromText(
        'POLYGON((
            2 4.5,3 2.6,3 1.8,2 0,-1.5 2.2,
            0.056 3.222,-1.5 4.2,2 6.5,2 4.5
        ))'
    ) AS geom1,
    ST_GeomFromText('LINESTRING(-0.62 5.84,-0.8 0.59)') AS geom2
) AS g1;
```

❶ The difference between the polygon and linestring is a polygon

```
SELECT
    ST_Intersects(g1.geom1,g1.geom2) AS they_intersect,
    GeometryType(
        ST_Difference(g1.geom2,g1.geom1) ) AS intersect_geom_type
FROM (
    SELECT ST_GeomFromText(
        'POLYGON((
            2 4.5,3 2.6,3 1.8,2 0,-1.5 2.2,
            0.056 3.222,-1.5 4.2,2 6.5,2 4.5
        ))'
    ) AS geom1,
    ST_GeomFromText('LINESTRING(-0.62 5.84,-0.8 0.59)') AS geom2) AS g1;
```

❷ The difference between the linestring and polygon is a multilinestring

```
SELECT
    ST_Intersects(g1.geom1,g1.geom2) AS they_intersect,

    GeometryType(
        ST_SymDifference(g1.geom1,g1.geom2)
    ) AS intersect_geom_type
FROM (
    SELECT ST_GeomFromText(
        'POLYGON((
            2 4.5,3 2.6,3 1.8,2 0,-1.5 2.2,
            0.056 3.222,-1.5 4.2,2 6.5,2 4.5
        ))'
    ) AS geom1,
    ST_GeomFromText('LINESTRING(-0.62 5.84,-0.8 0.59)') AS geom2) AS g1;
```

The symmetric difference is a geometry collection ❸

In the preceding listing, the first SELECT returns a polygon ❶, which is pretty much the same polygon you started out with. The second SELECT returns a multilinestring composed of three linestrings where the polygon cuts through ❷. Finally, the third SELECT returns a geometry collection as expected, composed of a multilinestring and a polygon ❸.

Figure 11.3 is a diagram of the results of listing 11.4.

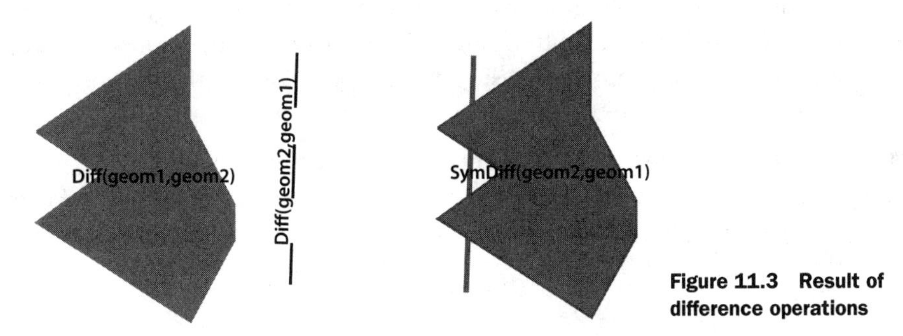

Figure 11.3 Result of difference operations

What remains of the polygon when you remove the linestring is still the original polygon. You can't remove a linestring from a polygon because it has no area.

11.2.2 Splitting

You learned from listing 11.4 that using a linestring to slice a polygon with ST_Difference doesn't work. For that, PostGIS offers another function called ST_Split. The ST_Split function can only be used with single geometries, not collections, and the blade you use to cut has to be one dimension lower than what you're cutting up.

The following listing demonstrates the use of ST_Split.

Listing 11.5 Using ST_Split to split a polygon

```
SELECT (ST_Dump(ST_Split(g1.geom1, g1.geom2))).geom AS geom
FROM (
    SELECT
        ST_GeomFromText(
            'POLYGON((
```

```
                2 4.5,3 2.6,3 1.8,2 0,-1.5 2.2,0.056
                3.222,-1.5 4.2,2 6.5,2 4.5
            ))'
        ) AS geom1,
        ST_GeomFromText('LINESTRING(-0.62 5.84,-0.8 0.59)') AS geom2
) AS g1;
```

The `ST_Split(A,B)` function always returns a geometry collection consisting of all parts of geometry `A` that result from splitting it with geometry `B`, even when the result is a single geometry.

Because of the inconvenience of geometry collections, you'll often see `ST_Split` combined with `ST_Dump`, as in listing 11.5, or with `ST_CollectionExtract` to simplify down to a single geometry where possible.

The output of listing 11.5 is shown in figure 11.4.

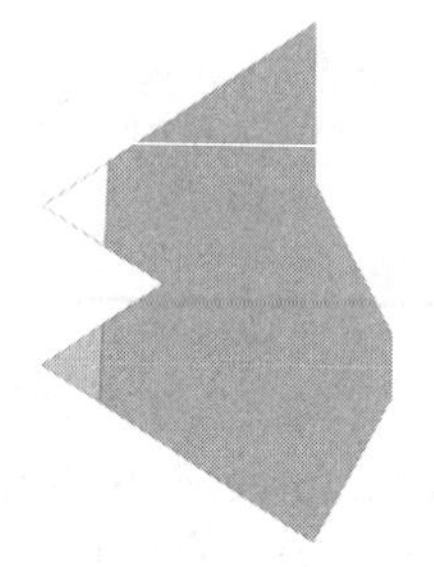

Figure 11.4 Splitting a polygon with a linestring, and then dumping results into separate polygons

11.2.3 Tessellating

Dividing your polygon into regions using shapes such as rectangles, hexagons, and triangles is called *tessellating*. It's often desirable to divide your regions into areas that have equal area or population for easier statistical analysis. In this section, we'll demonstrate techniques for achieving equal-area regions.

CREATING A GRID AND SLICING TABLE GEOMETRIES WITH THE GRID

In this example, you'll slice the United States into small rectangular blocks. Figure 11.5 shows what you're trying to accomplish, and listing 11.6 demonstrates a method that will do the slicing.

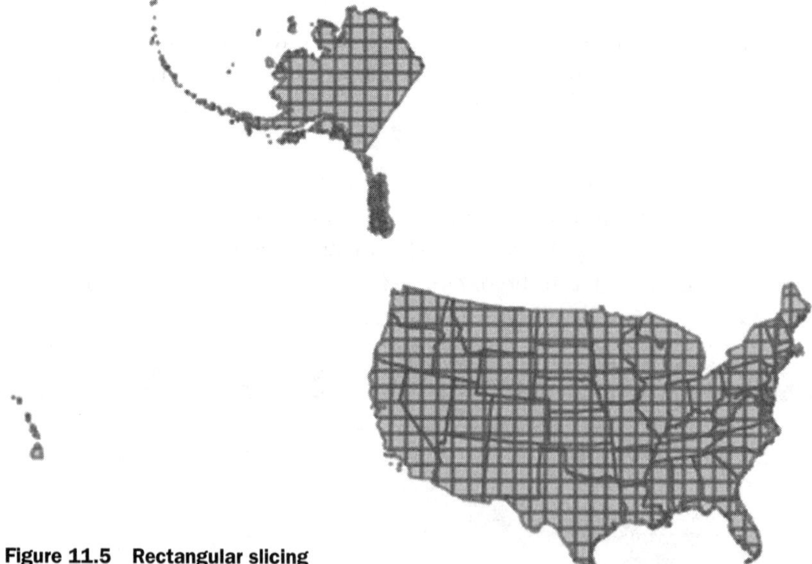

Figure 11.5 Rectangular slicing

Listing 11.6 Dividing the United States into rectangular blocks

```
WITH
    usext AS (
        SELECT
            ST_SetSRID(CAST(ST_Extent(geom) AS geometry),
            2163) AS geom_ext, 60 AS x_gridcnt, 40 AS y_gridcnt
        FROM us.states
    ),
    grid_dim AS (
        SELECT
            (
                ST_XMax(geom_ext)-ST_XMin(geom_ext)
                ) / x_gridcnt AS g_width,
            ST_XMin(geom_ext) AS xmin, ST_XMax(geom_ext) AS xmax,
            (
                ST_YMax(geom_ext)-ST_YMin(geom_ext)
                ) / y_gridcnt AS g_height,
            ST_YMin(geom_ext) AS ymin, ST_YMax(geom_ext) AS ymax
        FROM usext
    ),                                  <-- Create a painting tile
    grid AS (
        SELECT
            x, y,
            ST_MakeEnvelope(
                xmin + (x - 1) * g_width, ymin + (y - 1) * g_height,
                xmin + x * g_width, ymin + y * g_height,
                2163
            ) AS grid_geom              <-- Divide extent into rectangles

        FROM
            (SELECT generate_series(1,x_gridcnt) FROM usext) AS x(x)
            CROSS JOIN
            (SELECT generate_series(1,y_gridcnt) FROM usext) AS y(y)
            CROSS JOIN
            grid_dim
    )
SELECT
    g.x, g.y, state, state_fips,
    ST_Intersection(s.geom, grid_geom) AS geom    <-- Cut grid by state boundary

INTO ch11.grid_throwaway
FROM us.states AS s INNER JOIN grid AS g
ON ST_Intersects(s.geom,g.grid_geom);

CREATE INDEX idx_us_grid_throwaway_geom
ON ch11.grid_throwaway
USING gist(geom);                       <-- Add index
```

Listing 11.6 uses a grid of 60 cells along X and 40 along Y, spanning the full extent. Because the original table is by state, no two states fall into the same final tile (though this is not evident from the figure). The tiles themselves have various shapes and sizes when they are on state boundaries. This may not be ideal if you want all your tiles to be the same size.

CREATING A SINGLE LINE CUT THAT BEST BISECTS INTO EQUAL HALVES

Tessellation is fast and works well when you need many small pieces without paying much attention to the size of each piece. In most scenarios, however, you'll require fewer cuts but ones of equal area.

To create equal-area slices, the first strategy you can employ is one of convergence toward a solution. In listing 11.7 you start by making a trial cut through the area and measuring the area of the cut. If it's larger than what you need, you translate the cut line to get a smaller slice. You keep doing this until you obtain a cut with equal areas.

Listing 11.7 Bisecting Idaho

```
WITH RECURSIVE
x (geom,env) AS (
    SELECT
        geom, ST_Envelope(geom) AS env, ST_Area(geom)/2 AS targ_area,
        1000 AS nit
    FROM us.states
    WHERE state = 'Idaho'
),
T (n,overlap) AS (
    VALUES (CAST(0 AS float), CAST(0 AS float))
    UNION ALL
    SELECT
        n+nit,
        ST_Area(ST_Intersection(geom,ST_Translate(env,n+nit,0)))
    FROM T CROSS JOIN x
    WHERE
        ST_Area(ST_Intersection(geom,ST_Translate(env,n+nit,0)))
        >
        x.targ_area
),
bi(n) AS (SELECT n FROM T ORDER BY n DESC LIMIT 1)
SELECT
    bi.n,
    ST_Difference(geom,ST_Translate(x.env, n,0)) AS geom_part1,
    ST_Intersection(geom,ST_Translate(x.env, n,0)) AS geom_part2
FROM bi CROSS JOIN x;
```

In this query, you use recursive CTEs to perform the iteration. This is more to illustrate the capabilities of PostgreSQL than anything else—for clarity and portability, we advise you to create a function that performs the cut and then calls the function as often as needed to reach the desired cut. The result is shown in figure 11.6.

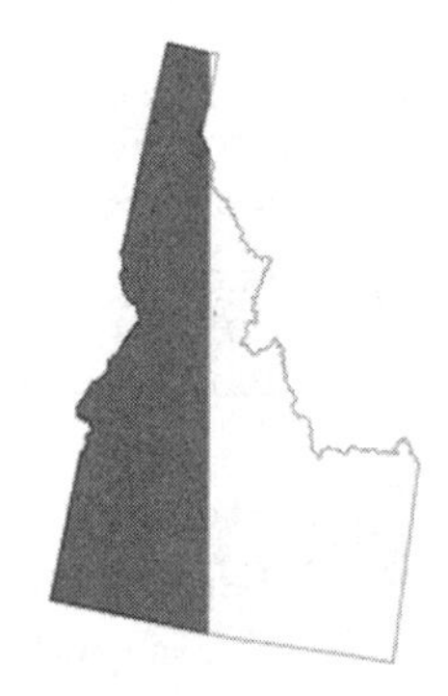

Figure 11.6 State of Idaho bisected

Listing 11.7 presented the basic technique for vertically slicing areas into two equal halves: an eastern half and a western half. You can, of course, create more slices by looping multiple times through the cutter. For slicing into fourths, you'd perform the cut twice. For slices that are multiples of two, you could use another layer of recursion to further bisect your resultant areas until you have the number of slices you want. You could even combine vertical cuts with horizontal cuts by iterating through the Y axis simultaneously to divide an area into quadrants.

CREATING EQUAL AREAS BY SHARDING

In the next approach, we'll use a similar grid cut and accumulate the shards recursively into buckets. When the total area of a set of shards is equal to the desired bucket area or count, it starts a new bucket of shards. It finishes by unioning the shards together by bucket and returning the buckets of geometries as a set of records. When you're finished writing the function, you'll have a function that takes a geometry and the number of buckets as input.

Although this example demonstrates equal-area cuts, you can use the same technique to sum up counts to achieve other equal distributions, such as areas with equal population. Census tracts in the United States are examples of equal-population areas.

You can call the function as follows:

```
SELECT bucket, geom, ST_Area(geom) AS the_area
FROM utility.upgis_slicegeometry(
    (SELECT geom FROM ch11.states WHERE state = 'Oklahoma'),
    4
) AS x;
```

This example will break Oklahoma into four regions of equal area, as you can see in figure 11.7.

You can verify your work by checking the areas, as shown in table 11.2.

Figure 11.7 Oklahoma quartered

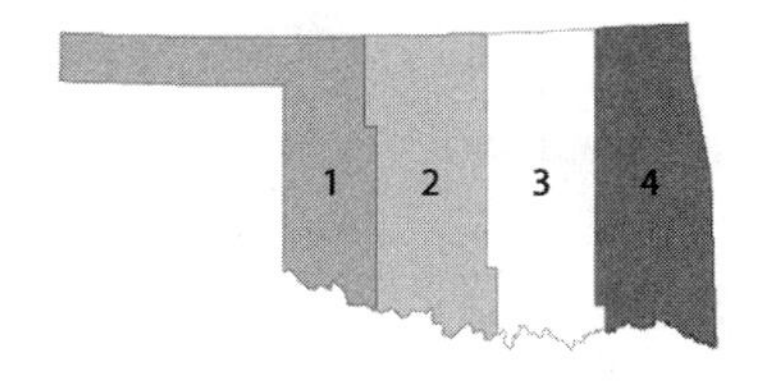

Table 11.2 Area of Oklahoma regions

bucket	the_area
4	45407005343.697
2	45287294131.5032
1	45267841092.5329
3	45214837721.5997

Let's walk through the function and see how it's constructed.

Listing 11.8 upgis_slicegeometry—cuts a geometry into equal areas

```
CREATE OR REPLACE FUNCTION
    utility.upgis_slicegeometry(
        ageom geometry,numsections integer,
        OUT bucket integer, OUT geom geometry)
RETURNS SETOF record AS
$$

WITH RECURSIVE
ref (geom,the_box,targ_area,x_mov,y_mov,        <-- ❶ Define constants
```

```
    x_length,y_length,xmin,ymin) AS (
    SELECT
        geom,
        ST_MakeEnvelope(
            xmin, ymin,
            xmin + CAST(x_length/ngrid_xy AS integer),
            ymin + CAST(y_length/ngrid_xy AS integer),
            ST_SRID(s.geom)
        ) AS the_box,
        ST_Area(geom)/$2 AS targ_area,
        CAST(x_length/ngrid_xy AS integer) AS x_mov,
        CAST(y_length/ngrid_xy AS integer) y_mov,
        s.x_length, s.y_length, xmin, ymin
    FROM (
        SELECT
            $1 AS geom, ST_XMin($1) AS xmin, ST_YMin($1) AS ymin,
            ST_XMax($1) - ST_XMin($1) AS x_length,
            ST_YMax($1) - ST_YMin($1) AS y_length,
            15*$2 AS ngrid_xy) AS s
    ),
X(x) AS (                                    <-- 2 Start position of squares
    VALUES (CAST(0 AS float))
    UNION ALL
    SELECT x + ref.x_mov FROM X CROSS JOIN ref WHERE x <  ref.x_length
),


Y(y) AS (
    VALUES (CAST(0 AS float))
    UNION ALL
    SELECT y + ref.y_mov FROM Y CROSS JOIN ref WHERE y < ref.y_length
),                                           3 Cut into shards
diced AS (
    SELECT ROW_NUMBER() OVER(ORDER BY x,y) AS row_num, g.x, g.y, g.geom
    FROM (
        SELECT
            x, y,
            ST_Intersection(ref.geom,
                ST_Translate(ref.the_box,x,y)) AS geom
        FROM x CROSS JOIN y CROSS JOIN ref
        WHERE ST_Intersects(ref.geom, ST_Translate(ref.the_box,x,y))
    ) AS g
),
T (bucket, row_num, geom, total_area, targ_area,
 remaining_area) AS (                        <-- 4 Bucket the shards

      SELECT
        1 AS bucket, row_num, diced.geom,
        ST_Area(diced.geom) AS total_area,
        ref.targ_area,
        ST_Area(ref.geom) - ST_Area(diced.geom) AS remaining_area
    FROM diced CROSS JOIN ref
    WHERE diced.row_num = 1
```

```
    UNION ALL
    SELECT
        CASE
            WHEN
                T2.total_area + ST_Area(diced.geom) < T2.targ_area
                OR
                T2.remaining_area < T2.targ_area/4
            THEN
                T2.bucket
            ELSE T2.bucket + 1 END AS bucket,
        diced.row_num,
        diced.geom,
        CASE
            WHEN T2.total_area + ST_Area(diced.geom) < T2.targ_area
            THEN T2.total_area + ST_Area(diced.geom)
            ELSE ST_Area(diced.geom)
        END AS total_area,
        T2.targ_area,
        T2.remaining_area - ST_Area(diced.geom) AS remaining_area
    FROM
        diced INNER JOIN
        (SELECT * FROM T ORDER BY row_num DESC LIMIT 1) AS T2
    ON diced.row_num = T2.row_num + 1
)

SELECT bucket, ST_Union(geom) AS geom          <-- 5 Union shards by bucket
    FROM T GROUP BY T.bucket, T.targ_area

$$
LANGUAGE 'sql' IMMUTABLE;
```

This function uses a recursive CTE construct with several subtable expressions, some of which are recursive and some of which are not.

You first define your reusable constants by inspecting the input geometry ❶: `ngrid_xy` defines the number of cuts you'll make along X and Y. If you were to make more cuts, your solution would be slower but more exact. Then you cut `15* numsections` along the X and Y axes.

You then do a recursive query to return X/Y starting positions for each square ❷. You could use `generate_series` instead, but this is slightly shorter.

You use an SQL window `ROW_NUMBER` and `ST_Translate` query to cut up the geometry ❸. The `row_num` column will return sequential unique numbers ordered by `OVER(ORDER ...`. Note that the `ROW_NUMBER OVER(ORDER BY x,y)` controls the cut. If you wanted the cuts going down instead of across, you'd order by `y` and then `x`. You can make intricate cuts by using other functions like `ST_SnapToGrid` or even sinusoidal functions.

You use a recursive query to throw the shards into buckets ❹. The trick here is the SQL `CASE` statement: you keep on adding to the existing bucket until the desired area is exceeded or the remaining area is less than one-fourth of the target area (the one-fourth is arbitrary).

You then union the shards in each bucket ❺. The resulting table will have fields called bucket and geom because that's what the output parameters are called. In PostgreSQL, all arguments to a function are assumed to be input-only parameters unless you explicitly put in OUT or INOUT.

In this section, you've tasted a little bit of what translating geometries can do. In the section that follows, we'll explore a few more tricks with translate and other affine functions.

11.3 Breaking linestrings into smaller segments

In this section, we'll go through a couple of examples for breaking up linestrings. There are several reasons why you might want to break up a linestring into segments:

- To improve the use of spatial indexes—a smaller linestring will have a smaller bounding box.
- To prevent linestrings from stretching beyond one unit measure.
- As a step toward topology and routing to determine shared edges.
- To obtain the directionality of linestrings and for use in conjunction with ST_Azimuth to compute bearings.

11.3.1 Segmentizing linestrings

If you have long linestrings where the vertices are fairly far apart, you can inject intermediary points using the ST_Segmentize function. ST_Segmentize adds points to your linestring to make sure that no individual segments in the linestring exceed a given length. ST_Segmentize has always existed for the geometry type. In PostGIS 2.1 it also became available for the geography type.

For the geometry version of ST_Segmentize, the measurement specified with the max length is in the units of the spatial reference system. For geography, the units are always meters.

In the following listing, you're segmentizing a semicircle into 10,000 meter segments.

Listing 11.9 Segmentizing a geography linestring

```
SELECT
    ST_NPoints(geog::geometry) AS np_before,
    ST_NPoints(ST_Segmentize(geog,10000)::geometry) AS np_after
FROM ST_GeogFromText(
    'LINESTRING(-117.16 32.72,-71.06 42.35,8.67 9.08,120.96 23.70)'
) AS geog;
```

In this listing, you start with a 4-point linestring. After segmentizing, you end up with a 2,447-point linestring where the distance between any two adjacent points is no more than 10,000 meters. You cast the geography object to a geometry to use the ST_NPoints function. The ST_NPoints function does not exist for geography.

11.3.2 Creating two-point linestrings from many-point linestrings

One common task is taking a linestring or multilinestring with various points and breaking it into smaller linestrings, each with two points. The code in the next listing takes GPS-track multilinestrings and converts them to two-point linestrings.

Listing 11.10 Two-point linestrings from a multilinestring

```
SELECT
    ogc_fid, n AS pt_id, (sl.g).path[1] AS nline,
    ST_MakeLine(                                        ❶ Make a two-point line
        ST_PointN((sl.g).geom,n),
        ST_PointN((sl.g).geom,n+1)
    ) AS geom
FROM                                                    ❷ Explode multilinestring
    (SELECT ogc_fid, ST_Dump(geom) AS g                   to linestring
        FROM ch11.aussie_tracks) AS sl
    CROSS JOIN                                          ❸ Iterate points
    generate_series(1,10000) AS n
WHERE n < ST_NPoints((sl.g).geom)                       Limit iteration to
ORDER by ogc_fid, nline, pt_id;                         ❹ number of points
```

The non-aggregate version of the `ST_MakeLine` function is used to construct a two-point linestring ❶. `ST_PointN` then returns the *n*th point on a linestring. (This function only works on a single linestring, not a multilinestring.)

The `ST_Dump` function is used to explode any multilinestrings into linestrings ❷. Because it's a set-returning function, you end up with one row for each linestring in the multilinestring. `ST_Dump` returns a set of `geometry_dump` objects consisting of two fields: `geom` and `path`. `path` is a one-dimensional array indicating the nesting level and order of the component geometry. For example, `path[3,2]` means that the extracted geometry was embedded in the second geometry of the third collection. `ST_Dump` will always drill down to the individual geometry level—a collection will never be one of its outputs. In the case of multilinestrings, there's only one element in the array: the position of the linestring in the multilinestring.

The `generate_series` function generates an iterator between `1` and `10000` ❸, which is used for extracting the points from each linestring output by `ST_Dump`. You need to iterate higher if you have any linestring that has more than 10,000 points. `WHERE n < ST_NPoints...` ensures that for each linestring you never iterate more than the number of points in that linestring ❹.

If you're using PostgreSQL 9.3 or above, you can use the `LATERAL` SQL construct to get rid of the limitation to have the `generate_series` be a fixed `10000`, as shown in this listing.

Listing 11.11 Two-point linestring from multilinestring using `LATERAL`

```
SELECT ogc_fid, n AS pt_id,(sl.g).path[1] AS nline,
    ST_MakeLine(
        ST_PointN((sl.g).geom,n),
```

```
        ST_PointN((sl.g).geom,n + 1)
    ) AS geom
FROM
    (SELECT ogc_fid, ST_Dump(geom) AS g FROM ch11.aussie_tracks) AS sl
    CROSS JOIN LATERAL
    generate_series(1,ST_NPoints((sl.g).geom) -  1) AS n
ORDER by ogc_fid, nline, pt_id;
```

In the lateral version demonstrated in listing 11.11, the `generate_series` can iterate up to the count of points `- 1` in each linestring, bypassing the need to iterate and filter, making this approach faster. We always iterate up to `ST_NPoints(geom) - 1` because the final `n + 1` for each linestring will hold the last point.

11.3.3 Breaking linestrings at point junctions

In this example, we'll demonstrate how, given a table of points and a table of linestrings, you'd go about splitting the linestrings at the intersecting points. This happens, for example, if you're building a routing system for buses, and you want to ensure that the bus stops are represented as nodes in your road network such that each bus stop is the start or end of a road linestring. Although this exercise does make great use of linear referencing functions, people generally don't think of it as a linear referencing activity.

In the simplest case, think of a two-point linestring. In the middle, you have a point slightly off to the side. You must reconfigure your linestring into two so that it becomes a multilinestring consisting of two two-point linestrings.

The basic steps are as follows:

1. Figure out which bus stops are within a specified tolerance distance from the road.
2. If a bus stop is close enough to the street, find the closest point on the road to the bus stop using `ST_LineLocatePoint`.
3. `ST_LineLocatePoint` returns a number between 0 and 1 representing the proportion along the linestring where the closest point lies. For example, .25 would mean that if a line is one kilometer long, one of the closest bus stops would be at the 250 meter mark. We'll call this the *marker.*
4. Once you've determined the marker, you use `ST_LineSubString` to break the linestring into two. For instance, if you have a bus stop at the .25 mark, you'd have a substring that runs from 0 to .25 and another that runs from .25 to 1.
5. Finally, you use `ST_SetPoint` to ensure the starting point of one road linestring is the ending point of the other. This is done because of floating-point precision issues that may result in the fractional linestring endpoint not matching with the start point of the next where it's cut.

So many users have asked for a solution to this problem that we created a generic function in PL/pgSQL. You pass in a linestring and a point, or their multi counterparts, and out comes a new linestring or multilinestring cut at the closest point to the set of points. Our function also lets you specify a tolerance, and any point further than the tolerance from the linestring is ejected. This listing shows our grand oeuvre.

Listing 11.12 Function to cut linestrings and multilinestrings at nearest point junctions

```
CREATE OR REPLACE FUNCTION ch11.upgis_cutlineatpoints(
    param_mlgeom geometry,
    param_mpgeom geometry,
    param_tol double precision
)
RETURNS geometry AS
$$
DECLARE
    var_resultgeom geometry;
    var_sline geometry;
    var_eline geometry;
    var_perc_line double precision;
    var_refgeom geometry;
    var_pset geometry[] :=
        ARRAY(SELECT geom FROM ST_Dump(param_mpgeom));
    var_lset geometry[] :=
        ARRAY(SELECT geom FROM ST_Dump(param_mlgeom));
BEGIN

FOR i in 1 .. array_upper(var_pset,1) LOOP
    FOR j in 1 .. array_upper(var_lset,1) LOOP
        IF
            ST_DWithin(var_lset[j],var_pset[i],param_tol) AND
            NOT ST_Intersects(ST_Boundary(var_lset[j]),var_pset[i])
        THEN
            IF ST_NumGeometries(ST_Multi(var_lset[j])) = 1 THEN
                var_perc_line :=
                ST_Line_Locate_Point(var_lset[j],var_pset[i]);
                IF var_perc_line BETWEEN 0.0001 and 0.9999 THEN
                    var_sline :=
                        ST_Line_Substring(var_lset[j],0,var_perc_line);
                    var_eline :=
                        ST_Line_Substring(var_lset[j],var_perc_line,1);
                    var_eline :=
                        ST_SetPoint(var_eline,0,ST_EndPoint(var_sline));
                    var_lset[j] := ST_Collect(var_sline,var_eline);
                END IF;
            ELSE
                var_lset[j] :=
                    upgis_cutlineatpoints(var_lset[j],var_pset[i]);
            END IF;
        END IF;
    END LOOP;
END LOOP;

RETURN ST_Union(var_lset);

END;
$$
LANGUAGE 'plpgsql' IMMUTABLE STRICT;
```

1 Convert geometries to array

2 Loop through each point

3 Loop through each line

4 If point within tolerance of line, make a cut

5 Recurse if multilinestring

1 Convert geometries to array

We use the design pattern of exploding a multi-geometry into single geometry pieces and then collapsing those into a geometry array for easier processing ❶. This will turn the multilinestring or linestring into an array of linestrings, and multipoints into an array of points.

Next we step through each point ❷ and each line ❸. For each line that intersects the selected point but isn't on the boundary (an endpoint), we perform the steps we outlined previously, using `ST_LineSubstring`, `ST_LineLocatePoint`, and `ST_SetPoint` ❹. Note that if a line is cut multiple times (the multilinestring can expand to more than two pieces), we use the power of recursion to repeat the whole process ❺, so that at any point in time we're always dealing with single linestrings and single points.

> **POSTGIS 2.1 FUNCTION NAME CHANGES** In PostGIS 2.1, the functions `ST_Line_SubString` and `ST_Line_Locate_Point` were deprecated because they didn't conform to the naming standard of PostGIS functions. The new names are `ST_LineSubString` and `ST_LineLocatePoint`.

Now for a simple test to see this function in action. You'll cut roads into two that are within 100 feet of your desired point, and you'll use `ST_Dump` again to explode the multilinestring into individual linestrings.

```
SELECT
    gid, geom AS orig_geom,
    (ST_Dump(
        ch11.upgis_cutlineatpoints(geom, foo.the_pt, 100 )
        )
     ).geom AS changed
FROM
    ch11.stclines_streets AS s
    CROSS JOIN
    (SELECT ST_SetSRID(ST_Point(6011200,2113500),2227) AS the_pt) AS x
WHERE ST_DWithin(s.geom,x.the_pt,100);
```

This query returns the ID of the street that was cut and the individual pieces as separate rows. It also includes the original for comparison. A pictorial view is shown in figure 11.8.

> **Using the ST_Split and ST_Snap functions**
>
> In theory, you could use `ST_Split` and `ST_Snap` in lieu of the custom function shown in listing 11.12. In practice, though, this would only work in a limited number of cases where all the points happen to round nicely. If your geometries take up all the significant digits, `ST_Snap` will end up approximating, and the linestring will not perfectly snap to the point. The other downside of `ST_Split` is that it doesn't work with multilinestrings or multipoints.

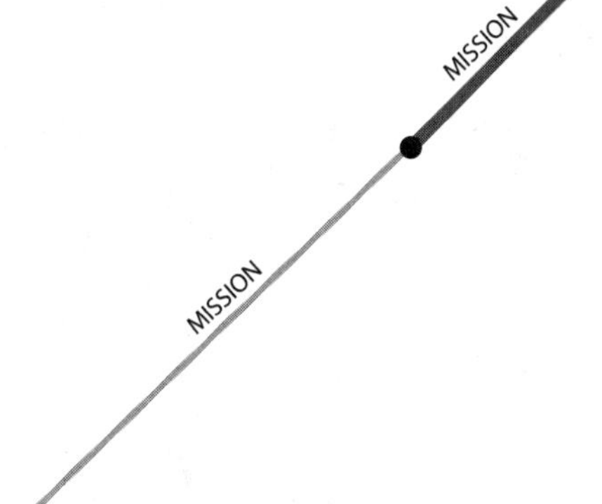

Figure 11.8 Cut Mission Street into two using point within 100 ft of road

11.4 Translating, scaling, and rotating geometries

Do you remember what you learned during your first linear algebra course? Namely, that *shifting*, *scaling*, and *rotating* constitute *affine transformations* on a plane. PostGIS has built-in functions to perform all three: `ST_Translate`, `ST_Scale`, and `ST_Rotate`. All three fall under the umbrella function `ST_Affine`, which lets you explicitly specify the transformation matrix. We won't go into detail about the `ST_Affine` function because it's rarely used directly.

Although you may think of shapes on a map as mostly static objects that don't get repositioned much, these handy functions intrude more often than expected. We've encountered the following common uses and are sure that more creative uses abound:

- Producing heat maps with color variations
- Simulating movement along a road
- Simulating position changes
- Correcting coordinates of a geometry when given shifted data
- Creating parallel road lines or edges to turn a line into a polygon
- Compensating for the lack of Z support in GEOS functions by rotating the axis so you can switch planes of comparison

We'll discuss the three functions in the following sections.

11.4.1 Translating

A common and unintuitive use for `ST_Translate` is to create grids by using one geometry to paint across and down a region. This artificial graticule can then be intersected with a reference geometry to divide it into rectangular regions or other shapes. We call this spatial design pattern the *cookie-cutter grid strategy*.

Take any paper roadmap, and you can see this. The map is often divided into alphabetic and numeric rectangles so that you can find a street in the index and then find it on the map itself. Another common use of an artificial grid is to summarize geometries within each tile to produce what are called *heatmaps*. Now we'll show you how to create artificial cells on a map.

The examples in listing 11.13 create both a honeycomb and a rectangular grid somewhere in the middle of the United States. We won't hold back on using SQL because the awesome power of PostGIS becomes visible only when you make liberal use of SQL's bulk-processing capabilities. This example uses the CTE feature again.

Listing 11.13 Hexagonal and rectangular grids

```
WITH
    center_point(x,y) AS (SELECT -288499, -2718),      ❶ CTE of center_points
    paintbrush(the_hex,the_rect) AS (                  ❷ CTE of hexagonal and rectangular dual paintbrushes
      SELECT
            ST_SetSRID(
                ST_Translate(
```

```
                ST_GeomFromText(
                    'POLYGON((
                        0 0,64 64,64 128,0 192,
                        -64 128,-64 64,0 0
                    ))'
                ), x, y
            ), 2163
        ) AS the_hex,
        ST_SetSRID(ST_Translate(CAST(ST_MakeBox2D(ST_Point(-64,0),
        ST_Point(64,192)) AS geometry), x, y), 2163) AS the_rect
    FROM center_point
)
SELECT xf.x, yf.y,
    ST_Translate(paintbrush.the_hex, xf.x_hex, yf.y_hex) AS hex_tile,
    ST_Translate(paintbrush.the_rect, xf.x_rect,yf.y_rect) AS rect_tile
FROM
    (
        SELECT x,
            x*(ST_XMax(the_hex) - ST_XMin(the_hex)) AS x_hex,
            x*(ST_XMax(the_rect) - ST_XMin(the_rect)) AS x_rect
        FROM generate_series(-50, 50) AS x CROSS JOIN paintbrush
    ) AS xf
    CROSS JOIN
    (
        SELECT y,
            y*(ST_YMax(the_hex) - ST_YMin(the_hex)) AS y_hex,
            y*(ST_YMax(the_rect) - ST_YMin(the_rect)) AS y_rect
        FROM generate_series(-50, 50) AS y CROSS JOIN paintbrush
    ) AS yf
    CROSS JOIN
    paintbrush;
```

Final CTE ❸

This example generates both a hexagonal and a rectangular grid, each with 10,201 records. You use CTEs to break up the steps to prevent repetition of code. First you define a CTE called `center_point` that returns a single-row table with the starting position of the paintbrush ❶. Then you create the paintbrush CTE ❷: `the_hex` to paint hexagons and `the_rect` to paint rectangles.

For the rectangular grid, you use `ST_MakeBox2D` because it's easier and faster to express rectangles as boxes. But because boxes aren't geometries, you must cast to `geometry` when needed. Then you create a grid that will output iterators `x` and `y` as well as two geometries: one representing each rectangular tile and one representing each hexagonal tile ❸. Note that the iterators are multiplied by the width and height of each cell to preclude any overlaps. Alternatively, you could use the stepping variant of `generate_series` to skip ahead by the width and height of the rectangle.

The cross join yields 10,201 records ((50 + 1 + 50) × (50 + 1 + 50)). Both grids are shown in figure 11.9.

Figure 11.9 Samples of the hexagonal and rectangular grids. The highlighted center tiles are the starting locations.

11.4.2 *Scaling*

The scaling family of functions comes in two overloads, one for 2D and one for 3D: `ST_Scale(geometry, xfactor, yfactor)` and `ST_Scale(geometry, xfactor, yfactor, zfactor)`.

Scaling takes every coordinate and multiplies it by the factor parameters. If you pass in a factor between 1 and -1, you shrink the geometry. If you pass in negative factors, the geometry will flip in addition to scaling. The following listing shows an example of scaling a hexagon.

Listing 11.14 Scaling a hexagon to different sizes

```
SELECT
    xfactor, yfactor,
    ST_Scale(hex.geom, xfactor, yfactor) AS scaled_geometry
FROM
    (
        SELECT ST_GeomFromText(
            'POLYGON((0 0,64 64,64 128,0 192, -64 128,-64 64,0 0))'    -- ❶ Original hexagon
        ) AS geom
    ) AS hex
    CROSS JOIN
    (SELECT x*0.5 AS xfactor FROM generate_series(1,4) AS x) AS xf
    CROSS JOIN
    (SELECT y*0.5 AS yfactor FROM generate_series(1,4) AS y) AS yf;    -- ❷ Scaling values
```

In this listing, you start with a hexagonal polygon ❶ and shrink and expand the geometry in the X and Y directions from 50% of its size to twice its size by using a cross join that generates numbers from 0 to 2 in X and 0 to 2 in Y, incrementing .5 for each step ❷. The results are shown in figure 11.10.

As you can see in figure 11.10, the scaling multiplies the coordinates. Because the hexagon starts at the origin, all scaled geometries still have their bases at the origin. Normally when you scale, you want to keep the centroid constant, so you'd use a combination of scaling and translating, as shown in listing 11.15.

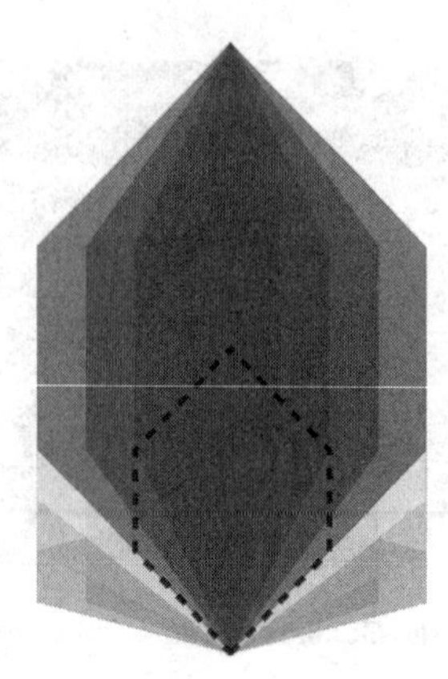

Figure 11.10 The dashed outline is the original hexagon polygon.

Listing 11.15 Combining scaling and translating to prevent shifting of the centroid

```
SELECT xfactor, yfactor,
    ST_Translate(
        ST_Scale(hex.geom, xfactor, yfactor),
        ST_X(ST_Centroid(geom))*(1 - xfactor),
        ST_Y(ST_Centroid(geom))*(1 - yfactor)
    ) AS scaled_geometry
FROM
    (
        SELECT ST_GeomFromText(
            'POLYGON((0 0,64 64,64 128,0 192,-64 128, -64 64,0 0))'
        ) AS geom
    ) AS hex
    CROSS JOIN
    (SELECT x*0.5 AS xfactor FROM generate_series(1,4) AS x) AS xf
    CROSS JOIN
    (SELECT y*0.5 AS yfactor FROM generate_series(1,4) AS y) AS yf;
```

This listing is similar to listing 11.14. Here you scale a hexagon from half to twice its size in the X and Y directions. You then translate the resulting scaled geometry so that the new centroid remains unchanged. See figure 11.11.

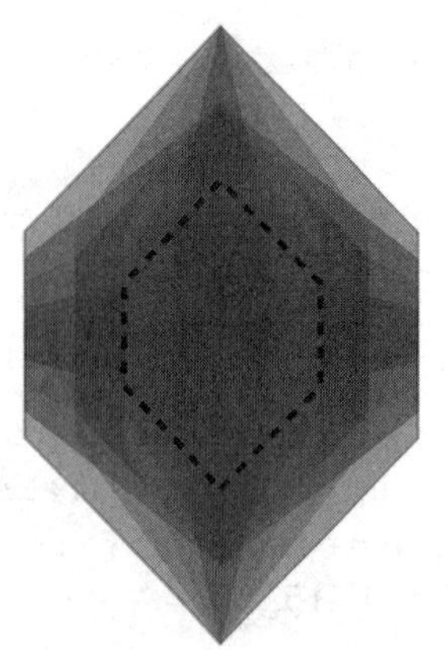

Figure 11.11 Scaling and translating to maintain the original centroid position

11.4.3 Rotating

ST_RotateX, ST_RotateY, ST_RotateZ, and ST_Rotate rotate a geometry about the X, Y, or Z axis in radian units. ST_Rotate and ST_RotateZ are the same because the default axis of rotation is Z.

These functions are rarely used in isolation because their default behavior is to rotate the geometry about the origin rather than about the centroid. In PostGIS 2.0, you can pass in an optional point argument called pointOrigin. When this argument is specified, rotation is about that point; otherwise, rotation is about the origin.

The following listing rotates a hexagon about its centroid in increments of 45 degrees.

Listing 11.16 ST_Rotate rotating a hexagon from 0 to 270 degrees around its centroid

```
SELECT
    rotrad/pi()*180 AS deg,
    ST_Rotate(hex.geom,rotrad,
    ST_Centroid(hex.geom)) AS rotated_geometry
FROM
    (
        SELECT ST_GeomFromText(
            'POLYGON((0 0,64 64,64 128,0 192,-64 128,-64 64,0 0))'
        ) AS geom
    ) AS hex
    CROSS JOIN
    (
        SELECT 2*pi()*x*45.0/360 AS rotrad
            FROM generate_series(0,6) AS x
    ) AS xf;
```

Figure 11.12 shows the 45 degree rotation.

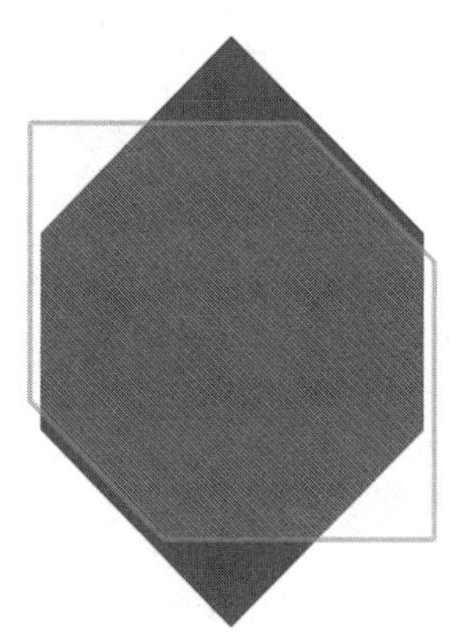

Figure 11.12 Rotating a hexagon from 0 to 270 in 45 degree increments around its centroid. Original and first 45 degree rotation shown.

11.5 Using geometry functions to manipulate and create geographies

There are far more functions for geometry than there are for geography. However, you can apply many geometry functions to geography by first casting your geography to geometry and then casting back.

PostGIS, by design, doesn't implicitly cast from geography to geometry. You need to explicitly use the cast operator :: or longhand CAST(geog As geometry). When casting from geography to geometry, the SRID of the resultant geometry will always be 4326, longitude and latitude. When you cast back to geography from geometry, your geometry must already be in SRID 4326 or unknown SRID 0, and the coordinates must be in bounds of degrees. If you have your geometry data in another spatial reference system, then a transform to 4326 must take place prior to the casting.

In this section, we'll cover some popular geometry functions that aren't available for geography and some alternatives you can take if a geometry function doesn't exist. We'll group our functions into two categories: cast-safe and transformation-recommended.

11.5.1 Cast-safe functions

You can safely use any geometry function against a geography where spatial reference systems don't factor in. Functions such as exploding geometries into subelements or constructor functions fit the bill. For functions that don't perform measurements, you can generally get away with casting without transformation for a small area.

These are some frequently used functions that fall into this category:

- ST_Collect()—This is an aggregate function that groups individual geometries into collections. Unlike ST_Union, ST_Collect doesn't dissolve boundaries. This easily leads to invalid polygons. Use this function with geography as follows:

```
SELECT somefield, ST_Collect(geog::geometry)::geography AS geog
FROM sometable
GROUP BY somefield;
```

- ST_Point(x,y), ST_MakePoint(x,y,z)—These functions return a point. In geography, use longitude and latitude as in ST_Point(lon,lat)::geography.
- ST_MakeEnvelope(minx,miny,maxx,maxy,srid)—This function creates a rectangular polygon geometry from coordinates. To form a geography, use coordinates in SRID 4326 and cast to geography as follows: ST_MakeEnvelope (minlon,minlat,maxlon,maxlat,4326)::geography.
- ST_Transform(geom,srid)—The geography must be in degree coordinates, but once you cast to geometry, you're free to deviate. Use the following syntax: ST_Transform(geog::geometry,srid). Pick an SRID that will minimize the distortion when going from geodetic geography to Cartesian geometry for your particular data set.

11.5.2 Transformation-recommended functions

Many geometry functions rely on a measurement-preserving planar projection. To use these with geography, you first should transform to a suitable SRID. For functions that rely on measurements, such as `ST_Simplify`, you should transform the cast geometry to something other than SRID 4326. Keep in mind that there's always a limit as to how far you can force-fit spherical coordinates onto Cartesian coordinates. If your geographies span the globe, you may have to break them apart before using geometry functions.

Transformation tends to introduce a lot of insignificant digits, and you may wish to use `ST_SnapToGrid` to eliminate the pesky extra digits. Apply `ST_SnapToGrid (processed_geom,0.0001)::geography` once you're ready to cast back to `geography`.

To use a geometry function where you need to transform, such as `ST_Transform (ST_SomeGeomFunc(ST_Transform(geog,some_srid)),4326)::geography`, the syntax of chaining multiple functions together could grow unwieldy. We recommend creating wrapper functions for operations that you'll be using often. Listing 11.17 is a wrapper function that repurposes the `ST_SimplifyPreserveTopology` geometry function introduced in chapter 6 for use with geography.

Listing 11.17 Creating an `ST_SimplifyPreserveTopology` wrapper for geography

```
CREATE OR REPLACE FUNCTION
    ugeog_SimplifyPreserveTopology(geography, double precision)
RETURNS geography AS
$$
SELECT
    geography(
        ST_Transform(
            ST_SimplifyPreserveTopology(
                ST_Transform(geometry($1),_ST_BestSRID($1,$1)),    -- 1 Transform to suitable planar SRID

                $2
            ),
        4326)
    )
$$
LANGUAGE sql IMMUTABLE STRICT
COST 300;
```

Here you use a quasi-private PostGIS function called `_ST_BestSRID` to determine a suitable planar SRID given the geography input ❶. `_ST_BestSRID` returns an internal SRID that you won't find in the spatial_ref_sys table. As such, it should not be used except during intermediary transformations. The function name starts with an underscore to denote this as a private function, but you may on occasion find the need to use PostGIS private functions for building your own custom functions, as is the case with `_ST_BestSRID`.

The `ST_SimplifyPreserveTopology` function you wrapped in listing 11.17, as well as the companion `ST_Simplify`, reduce the number of points used to define a geometry by removing vertices within a specified tolerance. They are important functions for dishing out lightweight geometries to mapping applications. Because these functions are often used for presentation, you shouldn't use them without transformation. We don't know what effect simplification has on geodetic coordinates, but we imagine that your spatial features would look rather unappetizing.

Another function that you may find useful for geography is `ST_Union(geom)`. This is an aggregate function that unions a set of geometries and dissolves boundaries. It relies on the intersection matrix, which exists only for geometries. Over small areas, you may be able to apply `ST_Union` in SRID 4326 directly, but over a large swath you're better off transforming to a planar measure-preserving SRID before unioning.

11.6 Summary

This chapter showed you techniques for solving common problems in geometry and geography. These solutions usually involve applying more than one function, sometimes in iterative loops, until you end up with something that's good enough. Keep in mind that you can arrive at solutions using different techniques. Rarely does one approach trump another.

One aspect we haven't addressed is speed. In real-world scenarios, you'll be working with lots of data, and hopefully lots of people will be interested in what you do with the data. You need to make your application run reasonably fast. Pay attention to indexes, the cost of functions, and the use of simplified geometries.

In the next chapter, we'll focus on techniques for working with raster data.

12 Raster processing

This chapter covers

- Loading raster data
- Spatial aggregate raster functions
- Using geometries to clip rasters
- Accessing pixel values and isolating bands
- Retiling rasters
- Raster statistical functions
- Map algebra functions

In this chapter, we'll focus on the use of raster aggregate functions, functions to manipulate rasters down to the pixel level, and functions for deriving additional rasters and geometries. We'll also demonstrate built-in summary statistics functions that you can use to learn more about the distribution of pixel values. You'll see in the examples that we consistently use geometry to isolate pixel values of interest. Being able to use geometry and raster in tandem is a powerful aspect of PostGIS.

For this chapter, our discussion presumes that you have PostGIS 2.1 or higher. Although we do highlight salient changes between 2.0 and 2.1, we strongly encourage you to upgrade to PostGIS 2.1 (if you haven't already done so) so you can take advantage of the latest functions for rasters. As an added bonus, you'll luxuriate in significant speed gains for some of the most taxing functions.

For many of the examples in this chapter, we used climate data from www.worldclim.org/tiles.php. To learn more about the source, visit www.worldclim.org/formats. We downloaded elevation, precipitation, and mean temperature raster data for UTM Zone 16, centered in Switzerland and extending to most of central Europe. The data came packaged as a generic grid file (.bil), and elevation is in meters, precipitation in millimeters, and temperature in 10X degrees Celsius (each temperature value is multiplied by 10 to avoid decimals). We also made an occasional excursion to Kauai, Hawaii, for which we downloaded elevation data. You can download all the data and code for this chapter at www.postgis.us/chapter_12_edition_2.

12.1 Loading and preparing data

You can start by creating a schema for this chapter, which you'll use to hold the raster data you load:

```
CREATE SCHEMA ch12;
```

You can then use the raster2pgsql command-line tool packaged with PostGIS, which you learned about in chapter 4, to load in the files chunked to 256 × 256 pixel tiles. You can include the filename of the original file by using the `-F` switch, and add `-I` to create a spatial index. Although we don't use the `-R` switch here, which would store the data outside of the database, there are many cases where storing the data out of the database improves performance.

```
raster2pgsql -s 4326 -I -C -M alt/*.bil

-F -t 256x256 ch12.alt | psql
raster2pgsql -s 4326 -I -C -M tmean/*.bil -F -t 256x256 ch12.tmean

| psql
raster2pgsql -s 4326 -I -C -M prec/*.bil -F -t 256x256 ch12.prec | psql
raster2pgsql -s 26904 -I -C -M kauai/*.bil -t 200 ? 200 ch12.kauai

| psql
```

You can use QGIS 2.0 or higher to view the loaded data. Figure 12.1 is a view of the precipitation data from the QGIS DB Manager preview tab.

Our precipitation and temperature data is segregated by calendar month and UTM zone, and each was in a separate file. The filenames are of the form *prec[month]_[zone].bil.*

Because you're storing rasters in the database, you can easily add additional columns to your tables. For example, you can add a column called month to the precipitation and temperature data, and populate it by extracting the month from the filename column, as shown in listing 12.1.

Figure 12.1 QGIS view of UTM Zone 16: Europe precipitation

Listing 12.1 Adding a month column

```
ALTER TABLE ch12.prec ADD COLUMN month smallint;          <-- 1 Add month
UPDATE ch12.prec
SET month = regexp_replace(
    filename,
    E'[a-z]+([0-9]+)\_[0-9]+.bil', E'\\1'
)::integer;                              <-- 2 Update month
```

In listing 12.1, `ADD COLUMN` adds a `month` column to the `prec` table ❶. This listing uses a PostgreSQL back-referencing regular expression in `regex_replace` to populate the month column ❷. The expression `[a-z]+([0-9]+)\_[0-9]+.bil` matches the filename, with `([0-9]+)` being a subexpression for the month. The expression `\\1` is a back-reference to the first subexpression, `([0-9]+)`. The expression replaces the matching string with the subexpression. Then you cast to an integer using `::integer`.

Go ahead and add a month column to the tmean table as well. You'll need the column for later examples.

12.2 Forming larger rasters using spatial aggregate functions

Raster has an `ST_Union` function similar to the `ST_Union` counterpart for geometries. In this section, we'll show you a variety of ways of using `ST_Union` on rasters.

12.2.1 Reconstituting tiled files

In order to improve raster performance, you can chunk large raster files, such as digital elevation model (DEM) files or aerial files, when importing them into the database. For example, you may wish to chunk a file with a 5000 × 5000 pixel raster into one thousand rows of 50 × 50 rasters. When a raster is part of a greater whole, it's often referred to as a *tile*.

When we loaded the climate data with raster2pgsql in section 12.1, we presciently included the `-F` switch. This automatically added a column named filename with the original filename populated. With this information, you can reconstitute the original file by unioning the chunked rasters.

> **Improved raster ST_Union in PostGIS 2.1**
> PostGIS 2.1 introduced two key features for raster `ST_Union`. It improved the speed significantly—often a 100-fold speed improvement. It also applies the unioning operation to all bands if no specific band is specified. This means that if you have a raster with five bands, and you don't specify a band, your end result will be a raster of five bands where same index bands are unioned together, instead of the old 2.0 behavior that gave you a union of band 1 if no band number was specified.

The following listing reconstitutes the precipitation files loaded into PostGIS.

Listing 12.2 Reconstituting the original files

```
SELECT
    filename,
    COUNT(rast) As num_tiles,
    ST_Union(rast) As rast                    <-- ❶ Aggregate rows into a single raster
FROM ch12.prec
WHERE filename IN ('prec1_16.bil','prec2_16.bil')      <-- ❷ Select tiles
GROUP BY filename;
```

Listing 12.2 returns two rows. Each row has a filename, a single raster of all tiles in that file, and a count of the number of tiles in the raster. The `ST_Union` function is used to aggregate all tiles in the result by filename ❶.

`ST_Union` can take an optional argument that dictates the unioning behavior, which can be one of the following in single quotes: `LAST`, `FIRST`, `SUM`, `MEAN`, and `RANGE`. The default behavior of `ST_Union`, when not specified, is to take the `LAST` non-nodata value of overlapping pixels. Writing `ST_Union(rast)` is equivalent to `ST_Union(rast, 'LAST')`. Because this is a reconstitution of a file, there are no overlapping regions, so `LAST` or `FIRST` will return the same raster.

The WHERE condition selects which tiles to aggregate, and this example aggregates by filename all tiles that made up the original file ❷. The count tells you that for each file you're stitching 225 tiles.

12.2.2 Carving out areas of interest using clipping and unioning

Even when you have your rasters chunked into tiles, if you're only interested in a particular area, you can gain significant speed by clipping first and then unioning to carve out just the area of interest. Clipping tends to be faster than unioning, so by clipping first, you limit the number of pixels passed to the union operation.

The following listing shows an example of clipping and unioning to isolate a particular region.

Listing 12.3 Clipping a set of rasters with a geometry and then unioning the clips

```
SELECT ST_Union(ST_Clip(rast,geom)) AS rast          <-- ❶ Clip and union tile
FROM
    ch12.alt
    CROSS JOIN                                           ❷ Define area
    ST_MakeEnvelope(8,47,8.5,47.5,4326) As geom      <--
WHERE ST_Intersects(rast,geom);                      <-- ❸ Select tiles in area
```

Listing 12.3 returns one row with one raster. This raster will only have pixels that intersect the area of interest. The ST_MakeEnvelope function is used to create a bounding rectangle polygon ❷. Next, the ST_Intersects function is used to select tiles that intersect the region of interest ❸. Finally, ST_Clip is used to isolate the portion of each tile that intersects the envelope ❶, followed by a unioning operation, begetting a new tile.

12.2.3 Using specific expression types with ST_Union

To use ST_Union, all rasters must have the same alignment, or more specifically, they must have the same pixel size, the same skew, and the same scale ratio, and their upper-left corners must be set such that their pixels don't cut into each other. We also recommend that they have the same number of bands.

During a union, rasters can completely cover the same area, not intersect at all, or share some area. For example, if you have two identical tic-tac-toe boards, they can be placed side by side for no overlap, one directly on another for complete intersection, or one board could be positioned so that its bottom half overlaps the top half of the other board.

The default behavior of ST_Union is to take the last non-NULL pixel value. This could be rather arbitrary, depending on the order of your input rasters. Imagine three identical tic-tac-toe boards stacked together. ST_Union would produce a single tic-tac-toe board. If the values in the center cell are X, O, and NULL, the unioned board would have a center value of O because it's the last non-NULL value encountered.

In some cases, particularly for overlapping rasters, you'll want some operation to be performed on the non-NULL pixels that intersect: sum, count, average, or some other operation. `ST_Union` has provisions to handle `FIRST`, `LAST`, `SUM`, `COUNT`, `MEAN`, and `RANGE`. For fancier operations, you'll have to resort to map algebra.

For example, our precipitation data covers the same region for 12 months. If you want to find the average annual precipitation, you could use `ST_Union` with a `MEAN` option.

Listing 12.4 Mean precipitation

```
SELECT ST_Union(ST_Clip(rast,geom), 'MEAN') As rast
FROM
    ch12.prec
    CROSS JOIN
    ST_MakeEnvelope(8,47,8.5,47.5,4326) As geom
WHERE ST_Intersects(rast,geom) AND month BETWEEN 1 and 12;
```

❶ Union with mean

Listing 12.4 is similar to listing 12.3, except this listing averages the values in the overlapping cells ❶ instead of reading the last value.

12.3 Working with bands

In this section, we'll demonstrate functions that can create multiple bands from a single band, or conversely, collapse multiple bands down to a single band.

12.3.1 Using ST_AddBand to form multiband rasters from single-band rasters

For related data covering the same area, you may wish to consolidate multiple single-band rasters into one multiband raster. Take an image in the CMYK color space, for instance. You'd be hard pressed to justify storing each band as a separate raster. To output the image, you'd have to union four rows of data.

A few requirements must be met by the individual rasters before you can assemble them into one multiband raster:

- All rasters must have the same alignment, meaning the same cell size and skew.
- All rasters must have the same height and width. With the same alignment, this implies that each raster must have the same number of pixels across and down.
- The ratio between cell dimension and spatial reference system (pixel scale and size) must be the same, and all rasters must cover the same georeferenced area, which implies that the upper-left coordinate must be the same for all rasters.

Let's use the climate data for an example. The data came in as two rasters: one for precipitation and one for temperature. The following listing stacks them together to form a two-band raster.

Listing 12.5 Combining single-band rasters to form one multiband raster

```
CREATE TABLE ch12.tmean_prec (
    rid serial primary key,
    rast raster,
    filename_tmean text,
    filename_prec text,
    month smallint
);                                            <-- 1 Create new table for new raster

INSERT INTO ch12.tmean_prec (rast, filename_tmean, filename_prec, month)
SELECT
    ST_AddBand(t.rast, p.rast) As rast,           <-- 2 Add bands
    t.filename As filename_tmean, p.filename As filename_prec, t.month
FROM ch12.tmean As t INNER JOIN ch12.prec As p
ON t.rast ~= p.rast AND t.month = p.month;       <-- 3 Match same bounding box and month

CREATE INDEX idx_tmean_prec_rast_gist ON ch12.tmean_prec    <-- 4 Add index
USING gist (ST_ConvexHull(rast));
```

Listing 12.5 first creates a new table to hold the multiband rasters ❶. `ST_AddBand` is used to add the temperature band to the one-band precipitation raster ❷, so that you end up with a two-band raster consisting of one band for precipitation and one for temperature. You know that both rasters satisfy the sameness requirement, so the bounding box of a tile in the temperature raster must match the bounding box of a tile in the temperature table.

The ~= raster bounding-box equality operator is used to pair tiles covering the same area ❸. Because you have gist indexes on both rasters, you can use the newer and faster gist bounding-box equality operator (~=) over the older B-tree-based bounding-box equality operator (=). As a last step, you add a spatial index based on the convex hull of each tile ❹.

12.3.2 Using ST_Band to process a subset of bands

To access one band in a raster, you can use `ST_Band`. In the following listing, you pull out the first band (the temperature band) from the two-banded raster created in listing 12.5.

Listing 12.6 Selecting one band from a multiband raster

```
SELECT rid, ST_Band(rast,1) As rast
INTO ch12.tmean2
FROM ch12.tmean_prec;

CREATE INDEX idx_tmean2_rast_gist ON ch12.tmean2
USING gist (ST_ConvexHull(rast));
```

12.4 Tiling rasters

Introduced in PostGIS 2.1, the `ST_Tile` function allows you to divide a larger raster tile into smaller tiles. Suppose you decided 256 × 256 was too big a tile size for the work you're doing. You could retile to 128 × 128 using `ST_Tile`.

`ST_Tile` has many overloads. The following listing shows the most common one.

Listing 12.7 Smaller, evenly blocked tiles

```
CREATE TABLE ch12.tmean_prec_128_128 (
    rid serial primary key,
    rast raster,
    month smallint
);                                      <-- Create new table

INSERT INTO ch12.tmean_prec_128_128 (rast,month)
SELECT ST_Tile(rast, 128, 128, true) AS rast, month    <-- 1 Tile into 128 × 128
FROM ch12.tmean_prec;

CREATE INDEX idx_tmean_prec_128_128_rast_gist
  ON ch12.tmean_prec_128_128 USING gist (ST_ConvexHull(rast));

SELECT AddRasterConstraints(
    'ch12'::name,
    'tmean_prec_128_128'::name,
    'rast'::name
);                                  <-- 2 Add constraints
```

The variant of `ST_Tile` in listing 12.7 takes an optional Boolean parameter (`false`, by default) to denote padding with the `nodata` value. This listing sets the pad-with-`nodata` argument to `true` ❶ because you want all the tiles to be 128 × 128. If you set this to `false` or skip it, then tiles that aren't 128 × 128 wouldn't be padded to guarantee the 128 × 128 size. In this case, the new tile size was chosen to perfectly accommodate the original tile size: 128 divides perfectly into 256. If you were to choose a new tile size such as 200 × 200, pad with `nodata` would come into play. If you set this to `false`, some rows might not have exactly 200 × 200 pixels.

This listing also adds constraints so that pixel types, pixel sizes, and band counts will be correctly registered in the `raster_columns` view ❷. Registration means that PostGIS will enforce the constraints for the raster column. If you were later to append a raster with a different pixel size to the column, for example, the insert would fail.

Tiling out-of-db rasters

Recall that you can't make alterations to out-of-db rasters. In the case of out-of-db rasters, `ST_Tile` only creates new metadata that denotes which portion of the out-of-db raster file corresponds to the tile. As such, `ST_Tile` is one operation that is much faster to do on out-of-db rasters than in-db rasters, because for in-db rasters, the subset of pixels of the original raster is copied to a new raster instead of just the metadata.

12.5 Raster and geometry intersections

PostGIS raster has a rich set of intersection functions that work with both rasters and vectors. We already demonstrated ST_Clip, which returns that portion of a raster intersecting with a geometry. We've also used the ST_Intersects function, which returns true if a raster intersects with a geometry or if two rasters intersect. In this section, we'll explore the ST_Intersection function.

When applied to two rasters, ST_Intersection returns a new raster of the intersection. When applied to a raster and a geometry, ST_Intersection returns a set of geomval objects. Recall that a geomval is a composite PostGIS data type made up of a value and a geometry.

As an example, let's apply ST_Intersection to our Kauai elevation raster and a buffer zone around a point.

Listing 12.8 Intersection of raster with geometry

```
SELECT
    CAST((gval).val As integer) AS val,          ❶ Pixel val
    ST_Union((gval).geom) As geom
FROM (
    SELECT ST_Intersection(                      ❷ Geomval
        ST_Clip(rast,ST_Envelope(buf.geom)),
        1,
        buf.geom
    ) As gval                                    ❸ Intersected output
    FROM ch12.kauai
    INNER JOIN (
    SELECT ST_Buffer(
        ST_GeomFromText('POINT(444205 2438785)',26904),100
    ) As geom) As buf
    ON ST_Intersects(rast,buf.geom)              Pixel val
) As foo
GROUP BY (gval).val
ORDER BY (gval).val;
```

In this listing, you first create a subquery that returns the intersection of all Kauai raster rows that intersect the 100-meter buffer ❸. The intersection returns a set of composite objects called a geomval that contains the properties geom (a geometry) and val (the pixel value of all points in that geometry) ❷. You then format these fields so you can display them in OpenJUMP and use a gradient theming ❶. The reason you CAST to integer is that val returns a double-precision object, which the current version of OpenJUMP treats as text and doesn't permit for gradient theming. You set the theming in OpenJUMP to a Quantile/Equal Number classification so that the color gets darker as the values increase.

The output of listing 12.8 is shown in figure 12.2.

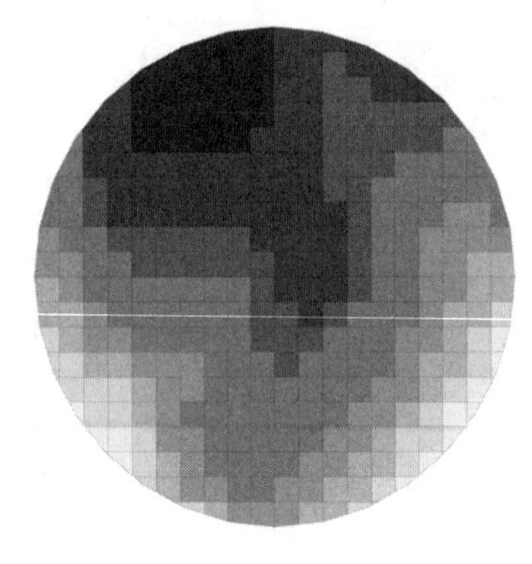

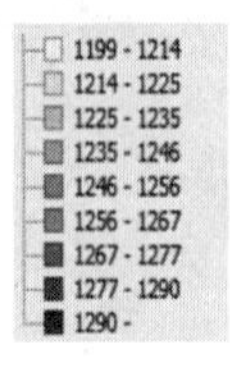

Figure 12.2 Kauai raster intersected with a 100-meter radius buffer. The darker patches represent higher elevations.

12.5.1 *Pixel stats*

One common use of raster analysis is to calculate statistics across raster coverages that intersect a region defined by a geometry. For example, the following listing calculates the average elevation for the previous buffer region.

Listing 12.9 Intersection of raster with geometry: pixel stats

```
SELECT
    SUM((gval).val * ST_Area((gval).geom)) /
    ST_Area(ST_Union((gval).geom)) As avg_elesqm
FROM (
    SELECT ST_Intersection(rast,1,buf.geom) As gval FROM ch12.kauai
     INNER JOIN
    (
        SELECT ST_Buffer(
            ST_GeomFromText('POINT(444205 2438785)',26904),100
        ) As geom
    ) As buf
ON ST_Intersects(rast,buf.geom)) As foo;
```

Running the code should give you an answer of 1258.409. This agrees with a visual check using figure 12.2.

Using ST_Clip versus ST_Intersection

In listings 12.8 and 12.9, if you replace `rast` with `ST_Clip(rast,geom)`, you'll gain about a ten-fold speed improvement. In PostGIS 2.1, `ST_Clip` is implemented in C, whereas `ST_Intersection` still has legacy code in PL/pgSQL. The answers differ slightly due to the fact that `ST_Clip` rasterizes the geometry first, whereas `ST_Intersection` converts the raster to a geometry first.

12.5.2 Adding a Z coordinate to a 2D linestring using ST_Value

A 2D linestring that represents a trail in Kauai can be converted to a 3D linestring with the elevation stored in the Z coordinate. You can do this by dumping all the points that make up the linestring, getting the elevation pixel values at each of these points, and then reconstituting the linestring by adding in the Z coordinate. This gives you a 3D linestring, for which you can calculate length distances relative to other trails.

The next listing will yield a 3D linestring from a 2D linestring.

Listing 12.10 Adding a Z coordinate to a 2D linestring using `ST_Value`

```
SELECT
    ST_AsText(
        ST_MakeLine(                                    ❶ Aggregate points into a line
            ST_Translate(                               ❷ Translate geom Z pixel units
                ST_Force3D((gd).geom),                  ❸ Force points to 3D
                0,0,
                COALESCE(ST_Value(rast,(gd).geom),0)    ❹ Compute elevation at point
            )
        )
    ) As line_3dwkt
FROM
    (
        SELECT ST_DumpPoints(
            ST_GeomFromText(
                'LINESTRING(
                    444210 2438785,434125 2448785,
                    466666 2449780,47000 2459000
                )',
                26904
            )
        ) As gd
    ) As trail                                          ❺ Dump vertices of linestring
    LEFT JOIN
    ch12.kauai
    ON ST_Intersects(rast,(gd).geom);                   ❻ Determine which rasters intersect vertices
```

In this listing, you start with a linestring and dump the constituent vertices to form a virtual table for the trail ❺. For each point on the trail, you determine which raster tiles intersect with the point ❻, and consider only those tiles. The `LEFT JOIN` ensures that you'll still get all points back, even if a point doesn't intersect a tile.

For each point returned, you force the point to 3D using the `ST_Force3D` geometry function ❸, which adds a Z coordinate and initializes it to `0`. You then use the intersecting pixel value (elevation) ❹ corresponding to the `ST_Value` of the vertex location in the Kauai raster to translate along the Z axis ❷. From these new 3D points, you use the `ST_MakeLine` aggregate function to form a 3D linestring ❶, set the spatial reference to be the same as Kauai, and output the result to a well-known text representation.

For this 3D linestring example, you can get an even more accurate 3D linestring by using `ST_Segmentize` on the linestring to yield more points to dump. This would allow you to store more `Z` coordinates along the trail.

ST_FORCE_3D RENAMED TO ST_FORCE3D Prior to PostGIS 2.1, `ST_Force3D` was called `ST_Force_3D`.

12.5.3 Converting 2D polygon to 3D polygon

In this section, we'll demonstrate building 3D polygons. You've already seen one approach to building 3D geometries with rasters: using the `ST_Value` function to add an elevation to each vertex of a 2D linestring. Here we'll look at a second approach using the `ST_Intersection` function to convert a 2D geometry into a set of geomvals. From the geomvals, you can use the pixel value to elevate the geometry into 3D. The `ST_Value` approach is most suited to converting 2D linestrings to 3D linestrings; the `ST_Intersection` approach is better suited for polygons.

Listing 12.11 performs more or less the same operation as listing 12.8, but instead of outputting the pixel value as a separate column, this approach outputs it as the new Z coordinate of each polygon. Listing 12.11 also takes advantage of `ST_Clip` for speedier processing and the `LATERAL` construct for more succinct syntax.

To set up this example, create a table of 2D polygons and add two arbitrary buffer regions to the table:

```
CREATE TABLE ch12.kauai_polys (
    gid serial primary key,
    geom geometry(POLYGON,26904)
);
INSERT INTO ch12.kauai_polys (geom)
SELECT ST_Buffer(ST_GeomFromText('POINT(444205 2438785)',26904),100)
UNION ALL
SELECT ST_Buffer(ST_GeomFromText('POINT(444005 2438485)',26904),10);
```

You can expand those 2D polygons into 3D elevated polygons with the following code.

Listing 12.11 Building 3D polygons from 2D polygons

```
SELECT
    p.gid,
    ST_Translate(                                              -- 1 Move geom up to elevation
        ST_Force3D((r.gval).geom), 0, 0, (r.gval).val          -- 2 Force 2D to 3D geometry
    ) As geom3d
FROM
    ch12.kauai_polys As p,
    LATERAL (
        SELECT ST_Intersection(ST_Clip(rast,1,p.geom),1,p.geom) AS gval
        FROM ch12.kauai
        WHERE ST_Intersects(rast,p.geom)                       -- 3 Get rasters that intersect geometries
    ) As r;                                                    -- 4 Get intersection of polygon and raster
```

Listing 12.11 uses `ST_Intersects` to select all rasters that intersect polygons in the kauai_polys table ❸. For each polygon and raster that intersect, `ST_Intersection` returns a set of geomvals where the `val` is the elevation and `geom` is the 2D geometry with that elevation ❹. The `geom` is converted to ❷ a 3D geometry and the `val` portion is used to elevate the `geom` from 0 to the elevation denoted by `val` ❶. You use `ST_Clip` to accelerate processing ❹.

This example requires PostgreSQL 9.3+ because of the use of the lateral correlated subquery that produces a subtable for each combination of rasters and polygons that intersects ❹.

12.6 Raster statistics

One benefit of storing rasters in a PostgreSQL database, both in-db and out-of-db, is that you can take advantage of the numerous computational functions already present. In this section, we'll focus on the statistical raster functions PostGIS provides, as well as on basic functions for outputting numerical values from a raster.

12.6.1 Extruding pixel values

Pixel accessor functions are those that return pixel values at a particular area. There are two functions commonly used:

- `ST_Value` returns a single value at a given geometric point or raster `column,row`.
- `ST_DumpValues` is new in PostGIS 2.1 and returns a 2D array for each selected band corresponding to the row, column, or pixel value.

ST_VALUE: RETURNING A SINGLE VALUE

The following listing returns the average monthly temperature and monthly precipitation for a location around Switzerland for January and July.

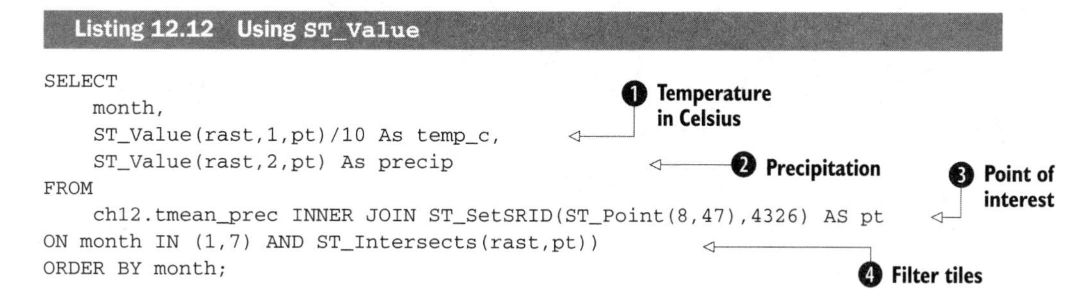

Listing 12.12 Using `ST_Value`

```
SELECT
    month,
    ST_Value(rast,1,pt)/10 As temp_c,
    ST_Value(rast,2,pt) As precip
FROM
    ch12.tmean_prec INNER JOIN ST_SetSRID(ST_Point(8,47),4326) AS pt
ON month IN (1,7) AND ST_Intersects(rast,pt))
ORDER BY month;
```


Listing 12.12 uses the two-band temperature and precipitation raster to retrieve the temperature in Celsius ❶. You divide by 10 because the temperature is stored in 16BSI (16 byte signed integer). The original temperature reading, with one place after the decimal point, was multiplied by 10 to fit into an integer.

The second band is the precipitation band ❷. You join the raster with a geometric point of interest ❸. (The point of interest is in the Swiss Alps, hence the low temperatures and high precipitation.) You use `ST_Intersects` to find the raster tile that contains the point of interest ❹. ST_Value then picks out the particular cell that intersects the point. ST_Value always return a single value, and should the point fall on cell boundaries or corners, ST_Value arbitrarily picks one.

The following listing shows the output of listing 12.12.

Listing 12.13 Temperature and precipitation in January and July

```
 month | temp_c | precip
-------+--------+--------
     1 |   -2.1 |     96
     7 |   14.9 |    131
```

ST_DUMPVALUES: RETURNING AN ARRAY OF VALUES

ST_DumpValues is most suitable if you want to return an area of a raster as a 2D array. You can feed the array output to the ST_SetValues raster function to set more than one pixel in a raster.

In listing 12.14 you use ST_DumpValues to return the precipitation values for your area of interest as an array, where the values are the precipitation values and the cell positions corresponding to the pixels for that area. As with ST_Value, you must specify the band number. Note the tandem use of ST_Union and ST_Clip to isolate the area of interest.

Listing 12.14 Single month precipitation for target area as an array

```
SELECT
    ST_DumpValues(                                    ❶ Dump as array
        ST_Union(ST_Clip(rast,2,geom,false)),
        1
    ) AS ary_precip                                   ❷ Isolate area of raster
FROM
    ch12.tmean_prec
    INNER JOIN
     (
        SELECT
            ST_Buffer(                                ❸ Buffer 1200 meters
                ST_GeogFromText('POINT(8.00 47.00)'),1200
            )::geometry AS geom
    ) AS f
    ON month = 7 AND ST_Intersects(rast,geom);        ❹ July tiles that intersect region
```

In listing 12.14 you use the geography ST_Buffer function to create a 1200-meter buffer zone around a point ❸. You use geography over geometry because ST_Buffer for geometry would require you to specify units in degrees for this projection.

Then you combine ST_Clip and ST_Union and select only the second band ❷. The buffer zone could span multiple tiles, so you use ST_Union to gather all the tiles together.

Then ST_Intersects applies a geometry filter to the data ❹. Finally you dump the pixel values as a 4 × 5 element array ❶.

The output of listing 12.14 is shown in the following listing.

Listing 12.15 Output of single month precipitation for buffered area as an array

```
ary_precip
-----------------------------------
 {{NULL,NULL,NULL,NULL,NULL},
 {132,131,128,127,NULL},
 {131,128,131,130,NULL},
 {NULL,NULL,NULL,NULL,NULL}}
```

The output is a 4 × 5 matrix where the cells contain the precipitation values; the buffer zone hits 20 cells.

You'll see many NULL values in this array. The buffer zone is circular and will only partially cover cells around the border, and for these cells `ST_DumpValues` returns NULL instead of the pixel value. Put another way, `ST_DumpValues` will only output pixel values for cells fully covered by the clipping geometry.

12.6.2 Raster statistics functions

PostGIS 2.1 includes five statistics functions: `ST_Histogram`, `ST_Count`, `ST_ValueCount`, `ST_SummaryStats`, and `ST_Quantile`. All these functions return record sets. They can return statistics on a subset of the data or return exact or approximate stats for one or more bands in a whole raster table.

In this section, we'll cover the `ST_Histogram`, `ST_Count`, and `ST_ValueCount` functions. The `ST_SummaryStats` and `ST_Quantile` functions work much like the `ST_Histogram` function but return different output fields.

HISTOGRAMS

`ST_Histogram` provides a distribution of pixel values. You can set the number breakouts or manually specify bins. You'll often find `ST_Histogram` working in concert with other raster functions, such as `ST_Clip`, `ST_Reclass`, `ST_Union`, and `ST_MapAlgebra`.

The following listing generates a histogram of the maximum mean temperature from January to March for a particular area of interest.

Listing 12.16 Max mean temperature from January through March

```
WITH
    cte AS (
        SELECT
            ST_Histogram(                         <-- 1 Histogram: five bins
                ST_Union(                         <-- 2 Union mean temperature
                    ST_Reclass(                   <-- 3 Reclass temperature to 1/10
                        ST_Clip(p.rast,geom),     <-- 4 Clip area of interest
                        1,
                        '-1000-9000:-100-900',
                        '32BF',-9999
                    ),
                    'MAX'
                ),
                1,
```

```
                5
            ) As hg
        FROM
            ch12.tmean AS p
            INNER JOIN
            ST_MakeEnvelope(8,47,8.5,47.5,4326) As geom
        ON ST_Intersects(p.rast,geom)
        WHERE month between 1 and 3
)
SELECT
    (hg).min::numeric(5,2) As min,
    (hg).max::numeric(5,2) As max,
    (hg).count,
    (hg).percent::numeric(5,2) As percent
FROM cte;
```

❶ Histogram: five bins

In the preceding listing, you use ST_Clip to carve out the area of interest from the intersecting tiles ❹. Next you use ST_Reclass to convert the 10X temperature back to the original values by taking a tenth ❸. ST_Union ❷ computes the MAX across all tiles of interest within the area and month of interest ❶.

The output of listing 12.16 is shown next.

Listing 12.17 Histogram of max mean temperature

```
  min  |  max  | count | percent
-------+-------+-------+---------
 -1.90 | -0.42 |    10 |    0.00
 -0.42 |  1.06 |    11 |    0.00
  1.06 |  2.54 |    70 |    0.02
  2.54 |  4.02 |   918 |    0.26
  4.02 |  5.50 |  2591 |    0.72
```

The output in listing 12.17 shows the pixel values broken out into five bins. For example, the last row tells you that 72% of the pixels have a max temperature falling between 4.02 and 5.5 degrees Celsius during winter.

COUNTS

PostGIS raster has two count functions:

- ST_Count provides a pixel count in an area or raster table. It counts pixels with no data value separately.
- ST_ValueCount outputs both the pixel value and the count of pixels that have that pixel value.

The following listing demonstrates the more informative ST_ValueCount function. This code outputs the number of pixels at each elevation within an area of interest.

Listing 12.18 Count by elevation

```
WITH
    cte AS (
        SELECT
            ST_ValueCount(
```

❶ Compute set of value counts

```
                ST_Clip(p.rast,geom)                    ◁——❷ Clip to area of interest
            ) As pv
        FROM
            ch12.alt AS p                                      ❸ Define area
            INNER JOIN                                           of interest
            ST_MakeEnvelope(8,47,8.5,47.5,4326) As geom     ◁
        ON ST_Intersects(p.rast, geom)
    )
SELECT (pv).value, sum((pv).count) As total_count     ◁     Return value and count
FROM cte                                                   from ST_ValueCount
GROUP BY (pv).value                                      ❹ result
ORDER by total_count DESC                  ◁  Order in reverse
LIMIT 5;                                   ❺ of count limit 5
```

The output of listing 12.18 is shown in the following listing.

Listing 12.19 Output of count by elevation

```
 value | total_count
-------+-------------
   430 |          30
   432 |          27
   433 |          26
   431 |          24
   429 |          23
```

12.7 Map algebra

The term *map* in *map algebra* refers to the rule by which you go from an old pixel value to a new pixel value; it's not *map* in the geographical sense. In chapter 7 you learned about ST_Reclass, which maps pixel values from one set of pixel values to another set of pixel values based on ranges. ST_Reclass, ST_Intersection, and ST_Union are specialized manifestations of a more generalized ST_MapAlgebra function. Think of ST_MapAlgebra as a function of last resort. When no other function can perform the processing you have in mind, ST_MapAlgebra offers hope. But by no means is the function speedy.

ST_MapAlgebra can operate by considering only one pixel at a time or a neighborhood consisting of pixels surrounding a pixel. The operation is repeated for each pixel and one or more raster bands. Regardless of whether processing is based on a single pixel or a neighborhood of pixels, ST_MapAlgebra always returns a new single-band raster that's a function of the pixel values of the original raster. The function can be based on a single band or multiple bands.

When working with ST_MapAlgebra, you have a choice of using expressions or callback functions. Although PostGIS comes with several predefined map algebra callback functions as samples, you're expected to create your own expressions or callback functions. In this section, we'll focus on using ST_MapAlgebra with expressions and build a simple callback function.

12.7.1 Choosing between expression or callback function

The ST_MapAlgebra function is really a suite of functions sharing the same name. It's a super-overloaded function. Regardless of which ST_MapAlgebra permutation you use, at the heart you'll find either a map algebra expression or a map algebra callback function. Think of ST_MapAlgebra as a Zamboni that visits each pixel in your area of interest. At each pixel, it stops and runs the expression or callback function for that pixel only. Once done, it moves on.

In many cases, you have a choice of expression or callback function. For simple operations, you can get by with expressions, but as things get more complex, we advise that you take the time to compose a callback function, both to maintain sanity and also to gain speed improvements. An *expression* can be any PostgreSQL algebraic expression that can accept pixel values or positions. The expression returns the new value for the cell. If what you need to do requires a neighborhood, you have to use callback functions. A *callback function* need not be anything more than a simple expression, but you have the freedom to add complex conditional loops and declare interim variables.

Let's look at some examples of using ST_MapAlgebra.

12.7.2 Using a single-band map algebra expression

Any valid PostgreSQL mathematical expression that can be applied to a pixel value or pixel coordinate can serve as a map algebra expression. You can also include custom functions in your map algebra expression. The simplest case is to map one pixel value to another value.

We'll start with a trivial example. The temperature table we've been using records temperature as 10X Celsius. To remove this shift in decimal point, you can use ST_MapAlgebra with an expression that divides pixel values by 10.

Listing 12.20 ST_MapAlgebra using an expression

```
CREATE TABLE ch12.tmean_cel (                    <-- 1 Create new table
    rid integer primary key,
    rast raster,
    month integer
);

INSERT INTO ch12.tmean_cel(rid, month, rast)
SELECT
    rid, month,
    ST_MapAlgebra(
        rast,
        1,
        '32BF'::text,                     <-- 2 Pixel mapping
        '[rast.val]/10.0'::text,
        -999
    ),
FROM ch12.tmean AS t
WHERE
```

```
    NOT EXISTS (
        SELECT c.rid
        FROM ch12.tmean_cel As c          <-- ❸ Process remaining
        WHERE c.rid = t.rid
    )
LIMIT 10;
```

POSTGIS 2.0 ST_MAPALGEBRAEXPR In PostGIS 2.0, the equivalent map algebra function expression was called `ST_MapAlgebraExpr`. This function is still available in PostGIS 2.1 but it is deprecated; the new name is `ST_MapAlgebra`.

Listing 12.20 creates a new table called `tmean_cel` to house the new rasters ❶. `[rast.val]/10.0` is a map algebra expression that maps the pixel values to 1/10 of their original values ❷. In the process, you also need to change the band type to `float`, because it can no longer be expressed as integers (`32BSI`). You process only the first ten unprocessed tiles ❸. For large tables, you'll want to process and commit piecemeal so that you don't have to wait a long time to see results. You can schedule this to run using crontab or pgAgent. How much you process at a time will depend on how much memory you have allocated to Postgres.

A simple operation like the one in listing 12.20 could be more efficiently achieved using `ST_Reclass`, as we demonstrated in listing 12.16. In addition, the `ST_Reclass` function has two advantages over using expressions: it returns all the bands with only the selected bands changed, and it's about 25–50% faster.

Like other functions we introduced in this chapter, `ST_MapAlgebra` can work on a subset of tiles by combining them with `ST_Clip` and `ST_Union`. One drawback of `ST_MapAlgebra` is that it will always return a single-band raster, although it's capable of reading information in all bands.

12.7.3 Using a single-band map algebra function

The following listing repeats the example from listing 12.20, but this time using a callback function instead of an expression.

Listing 12.21 `ST_MapAlgebra` using a callback function

```
CREATE OR REPLACE FUNCTION ch12.tempdiv_cbf (
    value double precision[][][],
    pos integer[][],
    VARIADIC userargs text[]
)
RETURNS double precision AS                    ❶ Define callback function
$$
BEGIN
    RETURN value[1][1][1]/10.0;
END;
$$
LANGUAGE 'plpgsql' IMMUTABLE COST 1000;

INSERT INTO ch12.tmean_cel (rid, month, rast)
SELECT
```

```
    rid, month,
    ST_MapAlgebra(
        rast,
        1,
        'ch12.tempdiv_cbf(
            double precision[],integer[],text[]
        )'::regprocedure,                          <-- 2 Use callback function
        '32BF'::text)
FROM ch12.tmean AS t
WHERE
    NOT EXISTS (
        SELECT c.rid
        FROM ch12.tmean_cel As c
        WHERE c.rid = t.rid
    )
LIMIT 10;
```

Listing 12.21 is as basic as you can get for a callback function.

A callback function always contains a value matrix ❶. The first dimension of the matrix is the band number, and the second and third are the rows and columns corresponding to pixel coordinates. The value held by the matrix corresponds to the pixel value. In the case of a single-band raster when you're not considering neighborhoods, the band number is `1` and the rest of the matrix will have only one cell.

You apply the callback function by passing it as input to the `ST_MapAlgebra` function ❷.

In our use of `ST_MapAlgebra`, we generally accept most of the defaults. If you intend to make `ST_MapAlgebra` a part of your standard arsenal, study the PostGIS documentation to learn about all the overloads and default settings.

12.7.4 Map algebra with neighborhoods

Sometimes the new value that you need to set a pixel to depends on the values of pixels adjacent to it. Such needs arise when you're performing smoothing; finding slopes, local maxima, and local minima; or playing the Game of Life, as we demonstrate in "PostGIS Day Game of Life celebration" (www.bostongis.com/blog/index.php?/archives/234-GOL.html). To examine adjacent pixels, you pass a neighborhood to the callback function.

A *neighborhood* is a rectangular region of pixels with the pixel of interest at the center, extending *x* pixels to the left and right, and *y* pixels up and down. A neighborhood should always have an odd number of horizontal and vertical pixels unless your neighborhood exceeds the boundary of the raster tile.

The basic syntax of `ST_MapAlgebra` when used with a neighborhood is as follows:

```
ST_MapAlgebra(
raster rast,
integer[] nband,
regprocedure callbackfunc,
text pixeltype=NULL,
text extenttype=FIRST,
raster customextent=NULL,
```

```
integer distancex=0,
integer distancey=0,
text[] VARIADIC
userargs=NULL
);
```

Several neighborhood callback functions are already packaged with PostGIS: ST_Max4ma, ST_Mean4ma, ST_StdDev4ma, and ST_InvDistWeight4ma to name a few. The code in the next listing finds the local maxima within a neighborhood of 5 × 5 pixels.

Listing 12.22 Max value in a neighborhood

```
SELECT
    ST_MapAlgebra(                          <-- 1 Map algebra on envelope raster
        ST_Union(
            ST_Clip(rast,ST_Envelope(buf.geom))      <-- 2 Single raster clipped to envelope
        ),
        1,
        'ST_Max4ma(
            double precision[][][],
            integer[][],
            text[]
        )'::regprocedure,                   <-- 3 Max pixel value callback
        '32BF',
        'FIRST',
        NULL,
        2,
        2                        <-- 4 Neighborhood extending pixels
    )
FROM
    ch12.kauai
    INNER JOIN
    (
        SELECT
            ST_Buffer(
                ST_GeomFromText('POINT(444205 2438785)',26904),100
            ) As geom
    ) As buf
ON ST_Intersects(rast,buf.geom)
GROUP BY buf.geom;
```

For each pixel in the bounding box of the area of interest ❷, the function will return the highest pixel value ❶ from the rectangular pixel range consisting of two to the left and right and two to the top and bottom from the center pixel ❹. What passes to the callback function is a 3D matrix where the first dimension is the band and the second and third dimensions outline the neighborhood ❸.

ST_MAPALGEBRANGB RENAMED ST_MAPALGEBRA AND IMPROVED IN POSTGIS 2.1
In PostGIS 2.0, the ST_MapAlgebra variant for working with neighborhoods was called ST_MapAlgebraNgb, and it only supported single-band rasters.

12.8 Summary

In this chapter, we demonstrated powerful raster functions that are sometimes used exclusively with raster types and sometimes in conjunction with geometry types. Your data could be a raster covering millions of pixels, but if your analysis only requires a few of those pixels, you can use geometry to first isolate the pixels to avoid having to wade through all the pixels you don't need.

Most of the functions we covered in this chapter are more-specialized versions of map algebra. Always use the functions most appropriate for the task at hand, knowing that you can fall back to the generic `ST_MapAlgebra` function if necessary.

Now that you've seen what you can do with rasters, we'll move on to the study of topology.

13 Building and using topologies

This chapter covers

- What a topology is
- Creating a topology
- Building topogeometries
- Loading and editing topogeometries
- Simplification and validation

Topological representation recognizes that, in reality, geometric features rarely exist independently of each other. When you gaze down on large metropolises from a plane, you see a maze of streets outlining blocks, interlocked. With a simple geometry model, you could use linestrings to represent the streets and polygons to represent the blocks. But once you lay out the streets, you know right where your blocks will be. Having to create polygons for the blocks is an exercise in redundancy. Congratulations, you've discovered topology.

In this chapter, you'll learn what a topology is, how to build a topology from scratch, and how to use commonly available geometry data. You'll also learn how to create what are called *topogeometries* (topogeom) in a topology. You'll learn how to detect problems in loaded data, fix problems in spatial data, and create simplified geometries using a topology model that maintains the connectedness of the constituent objects.

We'll be working with two sets of examples in this chapter. The first set will be very simple, created without loading data. This set of examples will give you a feel for how topologies are created and organized. The second set of examples will utilize data from the web. These examples will reflect what you'll commonly do in your work with topology.

For the second set of examples, we'll visit the picturesque city of Victoria, BC, Canada, and convert the geometry representations of the city boundary, neighborhoods, and streets to a PostGIS topology-based representation. Victoria is the birthplace of PostGIS and the capital of British Columbia, Canada. Aside from having historical significance, it's a small city with a complete set of data, well suited for exploratory work. We'll be using municipal data you can find at www.victoria.ca/EN/main/city/open-data-catalogue.html, and we'll load the prepared shapefiles into a staging schema, use the staging data to populate a topology schema, and finally build topogeometry columns and populate those in this chapter's data schema. The staging and data schemas were created with the following commands:

```
CREATE SCHEMA ch13_staging;
CREATE SCHEMA ch13;
```

We've packaged the ch13_staging schema as part of this chapter's download (www.postgis.us/chapter_13_edition_2) and loaded in the tables cityboundary, neighbourhoods, and streetcentrelines. The ch13 schema houses the topogeometry tables for this chapter.

13.1 What topology is

The surface of the earth is finite. We have about 196.9 million square miles (510.1 million square kilometers) to play on, water included. Humans are territorial, so we've divided up all the land into countries, big and small. Excluding Antarctica and a few disputed zones, moving a country's border involves at least two countries. The iron law of geography dictates that when one country gains land, another must cede land. This zero-sum land game is the result of humans having created countries that are collectively exhaustive and mutually exclusive over the earth.

This collectively exhaustive and mutually exclusive division of area is a requirement of topology. With this premise, you don't need to restate the obvious when creating geometries. For example, if you have a plot of land in the country and decide to use the northern half for farming and the other half for non-farming uses, then it follows that some kind of demarcation must be present, dividing the two halves. By creating one polygon for the farmable area, you create another polygon for the non-farmable area, and a linestring to part the two.

Consider another example. In 1790, the U.S. Congress created Washington, D.C., from land ceded by adjoining states. The district is divided into four quadrants with two perpendicular axes radiating from the capitol buildings. The quadrants are appropriately named: Northwest, Northeast, Southwest, and Southeast. Suppose that in the spirit of equality, Congress decided to make all quadrants the same area. This would mean moving the center of the axes to the north and west. If you used a topology in the model, this reorganization would amount to nothing more than moving one point. By shifting this point, your linestrings (the axes) would follow along and the polygons forming the quadrants would either deflate or inflate. You'd achieve all this by simply moving a point!

This is the power of topology: by defining a set of rules for how geometries are interrelated, you save yourself the effort of having to survey the entire landscape anew whenever you make the slightest alteration.

In PostGIS there are two kinds of representations for vector data. There is the more standard *geometry model*, where each geometry stands as a separate unit. In the geometry model, things that are shared, such as borders of land masses, are duplicated in each geometry. Then there is the *topology model*. The benefit of the topology model is that shared borders and areas are modeled as shared. This has a couple of benefits:

- If you simplify an object for distribution, the edges that are simplified are still shared, so that you don't end up with overlaps or gaps where you had none before.
- If you have a set of objects such as buildings, neighborhoods, or land parcels that shouldn't overlap, it's easier to detect and prevent these problems in a topology model.

Now that you have the concept of topologies fresh in your mind, we'll move on to building topologies with PostGIS topology functions.

13.2 Using topologies

Topology is an entirely different take on spatial features than geometries. Think back to your first geometry course: In Euclidean geometry, points, lines, and polygons didn't have coordinate systems as a backdrop. You didn't care about the absolute measurement of things, but rather the relationships between them. The topology model, in a way, reverts back to classical geometry, where you describe how two free geometries interact without any regard to coordinate systems.

Because GIS topology is an outgrowth of graph theory, it subscribes to a different set of terminology. For all intents and purposes, you can think of a *point* in geometry as a *node* in topology, a *linestring* as an *edge*, and a *polygon* as a *face*. Collectively, nodes, edges, and faces are topological primitives, used instead of geometries.

NOTE We use the term *topology* to refer to both topology as a field of study and a topology network.

13.2.1 Installing the topology extension

Before you can create a topology, you must make sure you've installed the topology extension. If you're not sure, look for a schema named topology in your database. This schema contains functions used to create topologies as well as the topology catalog table. If it's missing, you haven't yet installed the extension. Extensions must be installed on a database-by-database basis.

For PostgreSQL 9.1 and above, you can install the topology extension using this command:

```
CREATE EXTENSION postgis_topology;
```

As part of the topology installation, PostGIS adds the topology schema to your database's `search_path`. This means you can reference the topology functions without explicitly prepending `topology`.

In some cases, the role you're logged in as may have its own custom `search_path` setting that will override the database's `search_path`. Before you continue, verify that `topology` is part of your `search_path` by running this SQL statement:

```
SHOW search_path;
```

Once that's done, you can create a topology.

13.2.2 Creating a topology

In this section, you'll create a stylized topology based on the rectangular state of Colorado with an SRID of 4326. The following listing shows how you can create the topology.

Listing 13.1 Create topology in WGS 84 lon/lat

```
SELECT CreateTopology('ch13a_topology',4326);
```

After you execute the SQL in listing 13.1, you'll notice a new schema named ch13a_topology. A new entry will appears in the topology.topology catalog table registering the new topology. When you peek inside the ch13a_topology schema, you'll see four new tables awaiting data: node, edge_data, face, and relation.

PostGIS uses a separate schema to house each topology network—in this case ch13a_topology. The chosen SRID applies to all tables within the schema and all topogeometry columns that will make use of the ch13a_topology schema. Because topology is about relationships between geometries, having differing SRIDs makes no sense.

Within each topology, you'll always find four tables: node, edge_data, face, and relation. The first three are just topo-speak for point, linestring, and polygon. Of these three tables for storing the primitives, edge_data is the one that holds all the information for building the network. When you start to build spatial objects from topology primitives, the relationships of each of these spatial objects with the topology will reside in the relation table.

For Colorado, you can start by adding the linestrings that form the state's four boundaries using the function `TopoGeo_AddLineString`, as shown in the following listing.

Listing 13.2 Building the Colorado topology network

```
SELECT TopoGeo_AddLineString(
    'ch13a_topology',
    ST_GeomFromText(
        'LINESTRING(
            -109.05304 39.195013,
            -109.05304 41.000889,
            -104.897461 40.996484
        )',
        4326
    )
);

SELECT TopoGeo_AddLineString(
    'ch13a_topology',
    ST_GeomFromText(
        'LINESTRING(
            -104.897461 40.996484,
            -102.051744 40.996484,
            -102.051744 40.003029
        )',
        4326
    )
);

SELECT TopoGeo_AddLineString(
    'ch13a_topology',
    ST_GeomFromText(
        'LINESTRING(
            -102.051744 40.003029,
            -102.04874 36.992682,
            -104.48204 36.992682
        )',
        4326
    )
);

SELECT TopoGeo_AddLineString(
    'ch13a_topology',
    ST_GeomFromText(
        'LINESTRING(
            -104.48204 36.992682,
            -109.045226 36.999077,
            -109.05304 39.195013
        )',
        4326
    )
);
```

To make sure you've typed or copied everything correctly, execute the following SQL:

```
SELECT ST_GetFaceGeometry('ch13a_topology',1);
```

The entire state of Colorado is one big face. The preceding SQL should return that face as a perfectly rectangular polygon geometry.

Look inside the tables after running the code in listing 13.2, and you'll see four new edges, four new nodes, and one new face. The `TopoGeo_AddLineString` function automatically generates the topology network using the edge data and fills in the nodes and faces. You now have a topology of the rectangular outline of Colorado.

Two major interstate highways crisscross the state from boundary to boundary: I-25 runs north/south and I-70 runs west/east. You can add I-70 with the following code.

Listing 13.3 Adding highway I-70

```
SELECT TopoGeo_AddLineString(
    'ch13a_topology',
    ST_GeomFromText(
        'LINESTRING(
            -109.05304 39.195013,
            -108.555908 39.108751,
            -105.021057 39.717751,
            -102.051744 40.003029
        )',
        4326
    )
);
```

Upon successfully adding I-70, the `SELECT` will return the ID number of the new edge. You should see the number `5` in the output.

Next, add I-25.

Listing 13.4 Adding highway I-25

```
SELECT TopoGeo_AddLineString(
    'ch13a_topology',
    ST_GeomFromText(
        'LINESTRING(
            -104.897461 40.996484,
            -105.021057 39.717751,
            -104.798584 38.814031,
            -104.48204 36.992682
        )',
        4326
    )
);
```

Because you added I-70 first and then I-25, the latter will bisect I-70, creating two edges for itself and breaking I-70 into two edges. The output will return the ID numbers of the two new edges for I-25: `7` and `8`.

A diagram will be helpful at this point. We used QGIS to produce figure 13.1, which shows the four face IDs, eight edge IDs, and five nodes (each using a different style of numbers).

I-25 (edges 8, 7 with nodes 2, 5, 4) runs north to south. I-70 (edges 5, 6 with nodes 1, 5, 3) runs west to east. The two highways intersect at the state capital, Denver (node 5).

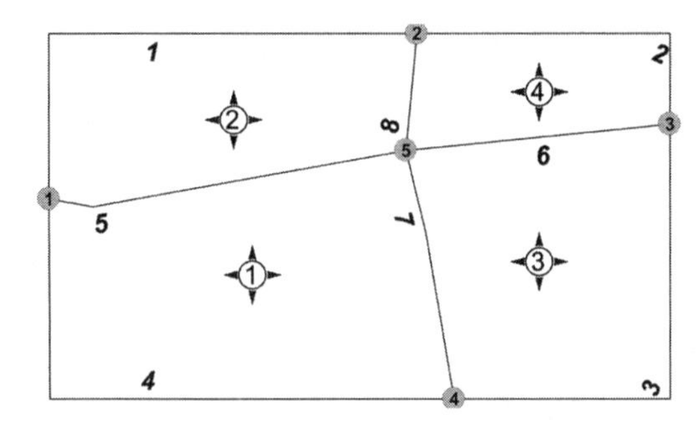

Figure 13.1 Colorado topology network

The addition of the highways splits the original single-face Colorado into four faces. Look carefully at the tables again; PostGIS automatically reorganized your topology. The corner points are no longer nodes, just vertices outlining the edge. PostGIS added a node for Denver where the two highway edges intersect.

> **edge view and edge_data**
>
> The `edge` view is a view that contains a subset of the columns of the edge_data table. The edge _data table contains additional columns not defined in the OGC topology spec, but that are used internally by PostGIS topology. For general uses and to keep in line with the OGC topology standards, the `edge` view should be used instead of directly querying the edge_data table.

We modeled the highways with kinks. For I-25, the kink is at Colorado Springs. For I-70, the kink is at Grand Junction. These kinks are merely vertices used to refine the geometry; they play no part in relationships. As such, they aren't nodes. Edges only intersect at nodes.

You now have a total of eight edges. The two highways slice Colorado into four distinct polygons or faces. The addition of highway I-25 split our original one-edge I-70 (edge 5) into two edges (5 and 6).

If you look in the face table, you'll see each of the faces listed as well as their MBR (minimum bounding rectangle), which is just the bounding box of the face. The face table doesn't store the actual polygons because all the data necessary to derive them can be found in the edge_data table. This storage methodology abides by the database principle of keeping data in only one place.

Remember that topology isn't concerned with describing geometries, but with how they're related. Removing all the superfluous vertices in Colorado creates a skeletal network diagram that you can see in figure 13.2.

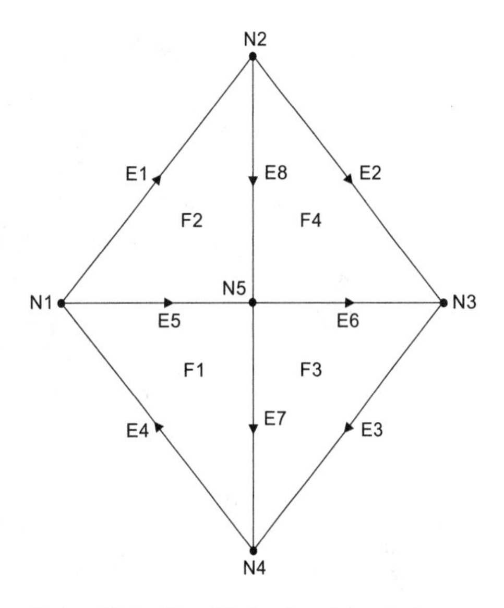

Figure 13.2 Simplified network topology

	edge_id [PK] serial	start_node integer	end_node integer	next_left_edge integer	abs_next_left_edge integer	next_right_edge integer	abs_next_right_edge integer	left_face integer	right_face integer	geom geometry(LineString,4326)
1	1	1	2	2	2	5	5	0	2	0102000020E61000000300C
2	2	2	3	3	3	8	8	0	4	0102000020E61000000300C
3	3	3	4	4	4	-6	6	0	3	0102000020E61000000300C
4	4	4	1	1	1	-7	7	0	1	0102000020E61000000300C
5	5	1	5	-8	8	-4	4	2	1	0102000020E61000000300C
6	6	5	3	-2	2	7	7	4	3	0102000020E61000000200C
7	7	5	4	-3	3	-5	5	3	1	0102000020E61000000300C
8	8	2	5	6	6	-1	1	4	2	0102000020E61000000200C

Figure 13.3 Simplified network topology

Figure 13.3 shows the contents of the edge_data table based on the simplified topology.

13.2.3 The topogeometry type

Once you've constructed your topology, you can group your primitives to constitute *topogeometries* (*layers* in topo-speak).

Let's say you want to collect the four edges making up the highways in the Colorado model. You could start by creating a new table to store topogeometries, as shown in listing 13.5. To this table you could add a topogeometry column using the PostGIS `AddTopoGeometryColumn` function. You should always use the `AddTopoGeometryColumn` function to create new columns because it takes care of registering the new topogeometry column in the topology.layers table.

Listing 13.5 Creating a table to store highways and defining a topogeometry column

```
CREATE TABLE ch13.highways_topo (highway varchar(20) PRIMARY KEY);
SELECT AddTopoGeometryColumn(
    'ch13a_topology',
    'ch13',
    'highways_topo',
    'topo',
    'LINESTRING'
);
```

After running the preceding code, you should see a new entry in the topology.layers table. `AddTopoGeometryColumn` will return the auto-assigned ID of the new layer. Keep in mind that a topogeometry is always tied to a layer.

Once you have your `topogeometry` column, you can add the I-70 highway using the `CreateTopoGeom` function as follows.

Listing 13.6 Defining I-70 topogeometry using `CreateTopoGeom`

```
INSERT INTO ch13.highways_topo (highway, topo)
VALUES (
    'I70',
    CreateTopoGeom(
        'ch13a_topology',
        2,
        1,
```

Define entry for I-70 where the topology elements are formed from ch13a_topology

The type of topogeom: 2 = lineal

The ID of the layer this topogeom belongs to. This is the number returned when you defined the topogeom column.

```
        '{{5,2},{6,2}}'::topoelementarray
    )
);
```

The elements that make up this topogeom. Each element in the array is composed of the element ID and the element type (1 = node, 2 = edge, 3 = face). In this example, all elements are edges.

When defining a new topogeometry column, you need to denote the topogeometry type by one of the following numbers: 1 = point, 2 = lineal, 3 = areal. In the case of topogeometries, polygons and multipolygons are lumped together under the areal type, points and multipoints are the point type, and linestrings and multilinestrings are the lineal type.

If you have geometries to start with, you can use the powerful `toTopoGeom` function to convert geometries to topogeometries and add the newly formed topogeometries to your table in one step, as demonstrated in the following listing.

Listing 13.7 Defining a topogeometry using `toTopoGeom`

```
INSERT INTO ch13.highways_topo (highway, topo)
SELECT
    'I25',
    toTopoGeom(                                  -- 1 Define I-25 using toTopoGeom
        ST_GeomFromText(
            'LINESTRING(
                -104.897461 40.996484,
                -105.021057 39.717751,
                -104.798584 38.814031,
                -104.48204 36.992682
            )',
            4326
        ),                                       -- 2 The geometry; any edges or nodes needed to form the geometry will be created if not present
    'ch13a_topology',                            -- 3 The topology
    1                                            -- 4 The layer
  );
```

In listing 13.7 you add the topogeometry of I-25 using the `toTopoGeom` function ❶. The risk and benefit of using this function is that it will, by default, create new primitive edges, nodes, and faces as needed, if primitives don't exist to form the new topogeometry.

In this example, you already added the primitive edges in listing 13.4, so `toTopoGeometry` shouldn't introduce new edges ❷. You include the name of the topology you're adding to ❸, as well as the layer that this new topogeometry will be associated with ❹. This layer ID must be the same as the one returned when you created the topogeometry column in listing 13.5.

If a node or edge needed to form the new topogeometry doesn't exist, the `toTopoGeom` function will automatically apply a tolerance to find matching nodes or edges before resorting to creating them. In other words, if an existing node is within the snap distance of the linestring geometry, `toTopoGeom` will shift the linestring to incorporate the node as a vertex instead of creating a new node. If you want to override the default tolerance, you can pass in an additional final argument to `toTopoGeom` to apply a tolerance. The default tolerance that `toTopoGeom` uses is a function of the bounding box of the input geometry. This default tolerance is computed internally using the function `topology._ST_MinTolerance`.

To confirm the composition of your new topogeometries, you can use the `GetTopoGeomElements` function, as in the next listing.

Listing 13.8 Querying primitive elements of Colorado highways

```
SELECT highway, (topo).*, GetTopoGeomElements(topo) As el
FROM ch13.highways_topo
ORDER BY highway;
```

This listing outputs the four topogeometry subelement identifiers accessed with `(topo).*` and a set of topoelements using the `GetTopoGeomElements` function.

Listing 13.9 Topogeometry internals

```
 highway | topology_id | layer_id | id | type |  el
---------+-------------+----------+----+------+-------
 I25     |           1 |        1 |  2 |    2 | {7,2}
 I25     |           1 |        1 |  2 |    2 | {8,2}
 I70     |           1 |        1 |  1 |    2 | {5,2}
 I70     |           1 |        1 |  1 |    2 | {6,2}
```

The code in listing 13.8 returns a set of objects called *topoelements* for each topogeometry. Although you only have two rows in the highways_topo table, you get back four rows when you use the `GetTopoGeomElements` function because `GetTopoGeomElements` returns a row for each edge of each highway.

The `TopoElement` object is an integer array domain type with two elements: The first is the ID of the element in the corresponding table. Because edges make up the highways, the IDs are `edge_ids` in ch13a_topology.edge. The second element of a topoelement denotes the layer/class type (`1` = node, `2` = edge, `3` = face, and higher numbers are the IDs of layers).

Establish a naming convention

PostGIS doesn't make a clear distinction between database objects that describe the topological networks versus your own use of topologies in topogeometry columns. We advise you to establish a naming convention. The myriad of schemas and tables supporting topologies can be overwhelming, especially for those charged with maintaining the underlying network.

13.2.4 Recap of using topologies

The PostGIS topology model provides the following features for working with topologies:

- Enabling the topology extension immediately creates the topology schema and functions.
- The topology.topology table records all topologies in your database.
- The topology.layers table records all topogeometry columns (layers) in your database.
- Each topological network has its own network schema.
- Primitives (edges, nodes, faces) have their respective tables in the network schema.
- The relation table in a specific topology network schema (in this case, ch13a_topology.relation) records which topology primitives and layer elements belong in which topogeometry.

Once you've built your topologies, you're free to use them anywhere within the database. You can use them elsewhere in your database by building topogeometries from your topology. The process follows:

- Add topogeometry columns (layers) to your own tables.
- Create topogeometries from primitives or other layers, and add them to your topogeometry column.
- Add topogeometries from geometries and change your underlying network in one step using the `toTopoGeom` function. Keep in mind, though, that once you do this, edges, faces, and nodes are automatically added and existing ones are split. Once your topology is changed this way, simply removing the introduced topogeometry is not sufficient to revert the changes to the topology.

In the next section, you'll learn how to work with data you get from various sources and how to fix faulty topologies caused by introducing less-than-perfect data.

13.3 Topology of Victoria, BC

In this section, we'll present a real-world example of topology use, with Victoria, BC, as our city of choice.

13.3.1 Creating the Victoria topology

The first step in working with topologies is to create a topology. As before, you use the `CreateTopology` function; the first argument is a name for the topology, and the second is the SRID.

The Victoria data came to us in WGS 84 lon/lat (SRID 4326). You can stick with this spatial reference system, but measuring tolerance in degrees is messy, and we prefer making measurements in meters rather than degrees. A decent planar spatial reference system for Victoria is UTM Zone 10N (SRID 32610). UTM allows you to measure in meters, and it's area-preserving.

You can start off by creating the topology to hold the data:

```
SELECT CreateTopology('ch13_topology', 32610, 0.05);
```

This function registers the topology in the topology table, in the topology schema created when you installed the `postgis_topology` extension. It also creates the ch13_topology database schema to house the topology elements.

The preceding code specifies a default tolerance of .05 meters. For functions that take an optional argument of tolerance, if no tolerance is passed in, the function will resort to the default. Roughly, the tolerance is the minimal distance between two points for them to be considered distinct. For instance, if you have a node that's only .01 meters away from another, PostGIS will snap the two together into a single node.

13.3.2 Adding primitives to a topology

In this section, you'll learn how to add primitives to a topology using geometries. PostGIS topology offers three functions that will add topology primitives to your topology, utilizing geometries as the data source: `TopoGeo_AddPoint`, `TopoGeo_AddLineString`, and `TopoGeo_AddPolygon`. Each takes an optional tolerance argument that's in the units of the spatial reference system of the topology and denotes how close primitives that make up the feature need to be to an existing topology primitive or each other to be snapped together with that primitive. If no tolerance argument is passed in, the function looks to the tolerance specified for the topology. If no tolerance is specified for the topology, then the function derives an acceptable tolerance by examining the bounding box of the geometry being added.

These functions may also create other primitives. For example, adding a linestring with `TopoGeo_AddLineString` may create two edges and a face, but only the edges created will be returned in the results.

In the event that you don't want the uncertainty and convenience of automatically adding primitives, you can tap into the following three functions: `AddNode`, `AddEdge`, and `AddFace`. These add one node, one edge, and one face, respectively. These functions are more predictable because they'll never split edges or form faces from edges, and if they're unable to add a primitive to the topology without violating the topology requirements, they'll error out. If you have a blueprint of all primitives and their construction sequence, you should be able to use these lower-level functions.

In this section, you'll learn how to use `TopoGeo_AddLineString` and `TopoGeo_AddPolygon`. The `TopoGeo_AddPoint` function is far less commonly used than the other two and works exactly the same way, except that it takes a point instead of a linestring or polygon.

THE TOPOGEO_ADDLINESTRING FUNCTION

The `TopoGeo_AddLineString` function adds nodes, edges, and faces to the topology from single linestring inputs. We'll start by loading the Victoria city boundary linestrings, as shown in the following listing.

Listing 13.10 Loading linestrings of administrative boundaries

```
SELECT
    gid,
    TopoGeo_AddLineString(
        'ch13_topology', ST_Transform(geom, 32610)
    ) As edge_id                                    <-- ❶ Create edges
FROM (
    SELECT gid, (ST_Dump(geom)).geom FROM ch13_staging.cityboundary
) As f;                                             <-- Expand multilinestrings to linestrings
```

TopoGeo_AddLineString only accepts linestrings, not multilinestrings. This means you need to explode your multilinestring into linestrings using ST_Dump ❶. For the administrative boundaries in the Victoria data, all records are single-line multilinestrings, so you end up with the same number of records in the f subquery as there are rows in the cityboundary table.

The following listing shows the output of listing 13.10.

Listing 13.11 Output of the boundaries query

```
 gid | edge_id
-----+---------
   1 |       1
```

TopoGeo_AddLineString is a set-returning function, which means it has the potential of expanding your row count, because each call may return more than one value.

The topology now consists of two faces, one edge, and one node, as shown in figure 13.4.

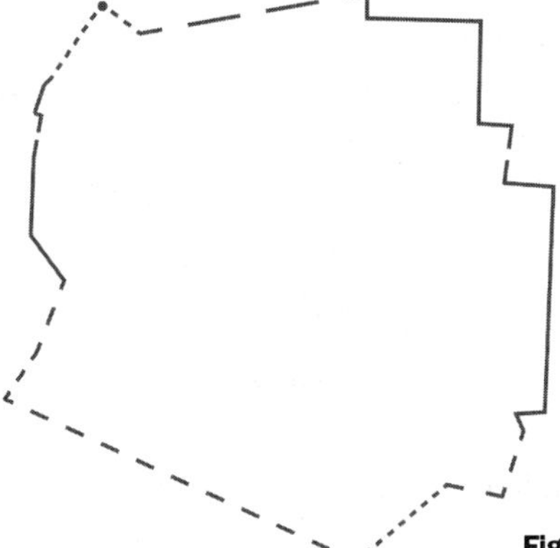

Figure 13.4 Victoria topology with border

The next listing inspects the topology as it currently stands.

Listing 13.12 Count of primitives

```
SELECT 'faces' As type, COUNT(*) As num FROM ch13_topology.face
UNION ALL
SELECT 'edges' As type, COUNT(*) As num FROM ch13_topology.edge
```

```
UNION ALL
SELECT 'nodes' As type, COUNT(*) As num FROM ch13_topology.node
UNION ALL
SELECT 'relations' As type, COUNT(*) As num FROM ch13_topology.relation;
```

The output of listing 13.12 follows:

```
   type     | num
-----------+-----
 faces      |   2
 edges      |   1
 nodes      |   1
 relations  |   0
```

Note that even though you only added linestrings to your topology to create single edges, PostGIS automatically created a face to enclose the edge and a node to demarcate where the edges start and end. A more subtle addition is that of the universal face. Every topology has a *universal face* that encompasses the portion exterior to the topology. Your face count is therefore two: the face of Victoria, and the face that's not Victoria.

THE TOPOGEO_ADDPOLYGON FUNCTION

TopoGeo_AddPolygon creates faces from polygons, though in the process it will most likely create other primitives to fill out the topology. TopoGeo_AddPolygon accepts polygons, not multipolygons, and returns the IDs of the new faces created or the IDs of faces contained within the input polygon.

For this next example, we'll add Victoria neighborhoods.

Listing 13.13 Using AddPolygon with tolerance

```
SELECT
    gid,
    TopoGeo_AddPolygon(
        'ch13_topology', ST_Transform(geom, 32610), 0.05
    ) As face_id
FROM (
    SELECT
        gid,
        (ST_Dump(geom)).geom
    FROM ch13_staging.neighbourhoods
) As f;
```

Listing 13.13 creates 38 faces from 14 single-polygon multipolygons. This example applied a tolerance of 0.05, snapping anything within 0.05 meters.

You may find that when you run TopoGeo_AddPolygon or TopoGeo_AddLineString a second time with the same data set, you'll sometimes end up with more IDs returned than the first time. This is because the first round only returns the IDs of the primitives created. If during the course of running the function, an existing primitive has to be split, you won't see the IDs of the split primitives until the second round. Our advice is not to put much faith in the IDs returned by these functions.

You may also be puzzled by how you ended up with 38 faces from only 14 polygons. This has to do with overlap. Ideally the polygons should be mutually exclusive and collectively exhaustive within the Victoria face. In the real world, data is never so perfect. You'll have to contend with small pockets of polygons where the overlapping happens. In later sections, we'll show you how to realign these polygons to eliminate annoying shards.

13.3.3 Creating topogeometries

The primary reason for building a topology is to have a scaffold for spatial objects we call *topogeometries*. Creating topogeometries is a three-step process:

1. Create a layer by defining a topogeometry column in a table.
2. Create topogeometries by collecting primitive elements, collecting other layer elements, or building them from geometries.
3. Insert the topogeometries into the topogeometry column.

In this section, you'll revisit how to create topogeometry columns and populate them with topogeometries. You'll learn how to do this with existing geometries as well as build from existing elements in a topology. You'll perform these exercises with Victoria data.

Topogeometries are recorded in the topology's relation table.

BUILDING LAYERS WITH ADDTOPOGEOMETRYCOLUMN

The code in the following listing builds a couple of topology layers.

Listing 13.14 Create tables and add topogeometry columns

```
CREATE TABLE ch13.neighbourhoods (feat_name varchar(50) primary key);
SELECT AddTopoGeometryColumn(
    'ch13_topology',
    'ch13',
    'neighbourhoods',
    'topo',
    'MULTIPOLYGON'
);                                  ❶ Topogeometry column for collection of face primitives

CREATE TABLE ch13.cities (feat_name varchar(150) primary key);
SELECT AddTopoGeometryColumn(
    'ch13_topology',
    'ch13',
    'cities',
    'topo',
    'MULTIPOLYGON',
    1
);                                  ❷ Topogeometry column for collection of neighborhoods
```

Listing 13.14 creates two kinds of `topogeometry` columns. You define a column called topo in the neighbourhoods table to store the faces each neighborhood is composed of ❶. You then define a column called topo in the cities table to store the neighbourhoods (layer = 1) that each city is composed of ❷. Each city is defined by a topogeometry. In this Victoria example, you just want one city, so there's only one topogeometry.

You can interrogate the tables with psql using `\d ch13.neighbourhoods` and `\d ch13.cities`.

```
          Table "ch13.neighbourhoods"
  Column    |          Type          | Modifiers
-----------+------------------------+-----------
 feat_name | character varying(50) | not null
 topo      | topogeometry           |
Indexes:
    "neighbourhoods_pkey" PRIMARY KEY, btree (feat_name)
Check constraints:
    "check_topogeom_topo"
    CHECK ((topo).topology_id = 2
    AND (topo).layer_id = 1 AND (topo).type = 3)
```

```
              Table "ch13.cities"
  Column    |          Type          | Modifiers
-----------+------------------------+-----------
 feat_name | character varying(150) | not null
 topo      | topogeometry           |
Indexes:
    "cities_pkey" PRIMARY KEY, btree (feat_name)
Check constraints:
    "check_topogeom_topo"
    CHECK ((topo).topology_id = 2
     AND (topo).layer_id = 2 AND (topo).type = 3)
```

Although it's not evident from the table description that cities are modeled as being composed of neighborhoods, you can inspect the topology.layer table, which lists all the `topogeometry` columns. In it you'll see that the `child_id` field is filled with `1` for the cities layer, showing that each city is made up of child neighborhoods.

CONVERTING GEOMETRIES TO TOPOGEOMETRIES

As you've already seen in the Colorado example, the powerful `toTopoGeom` function will convert a geometry to its topogeometry equivalent. But before you can use it, you must already have a layer—the ID of the layer is a required parameter for `toTopoGeom`, and the layer you pass in must be a layer of primitives. In the Victoria example thus far, this means only the topo column in the neighbourhoods table can be used with `toTopoGeom`. You can't use `toTopoGeom` to add topogeometries to the cities table because the `cities.topo` corresponding topology layer is a hierarchical layer that must be composed of neighborhoods (a non-primitive layer type).

Be forewarned! Each call to `toTopoGeom` could spawn new primitives in the underlying topology if it can't find nodes, edges, and faces within tolerance. Depending on the number of topogeometries you'll be maintaining and the rigor with which you want to control changes to the topology itself, you may not wish to use this function, or at least use it with extreme caution.

For instance, suppose you meticulously created the topology of Beijing's fast-evolving subway network, and you granted your colleagues the right to create topo-geometries. The colleague in charge of stations created a layer of nodes, the colleague in charge of loop lines created a layer of edges, and so on. One day, a bumbling new colleague in charge of the airport subway lines decided to create a layer for his subway line and branches. He downloaded the linestring of Beijing expressways, thinking that what he had were the geometries for the airport express subway line. He used the versatile `toTopoGeom` function and added his linestrings. We'll leave you to figure out how this story ends.

The following example shows how to create the topogeoms from the `neighbourhoods.topo` layer:

```
INSERT INTO ch13.neighbourhoods (feat_name, topo)
SELECT
    neighbourh,
    toTopoGeom(
        ST_Transform(geom, 32610), 'ch13_topology', 1, 0.05
    )
FROM ch13_staging.neighbourhoods;
```

CREATING TOPOGEOMETRIES FROM EXISTING TOPOLOGY ELEMENTS

In situations requiring more rigorous control, such as where the maintainer of the topology is not the same person creating topogeometries, you'll only want to allow the formation of new topogeometries from existing topology elements in your topology. If you know what these elements are or can compute them based on relationships such as geometry containment, then you can use the functions `CreateTopoGeom` and `TopoElementArray_Agg`, as shown in the following listing.

Listing 13.15 Creating topogeometries from non-primitives

```
INSERT INTO ch13.cities (feat_name, topo)
SELECT
    'Victoria',
    CreateTopoGeom(
        'ch13_topology',
        3,                                          -- ❶ Areal
        2,                                          -- ❷ Layer
        (
            SELECT TopoElementArray_Agg(
                ARRAY[(topo).id,(topo).layer_id]
            )                                       -- ❸ Gather all elements
            FROM ch13.neighbourhoods
        )
);
```

Listing 13.15 inserts Victoria into the cities table. `CreateTopoGeom` is the function that puts together the topogeometries. For its parameters in this example, you specify that the new topogeometries will be areal, element type 3 ❶, and that the new topogeometries will belong to the cities topogeometry column, layer 2 ❷.

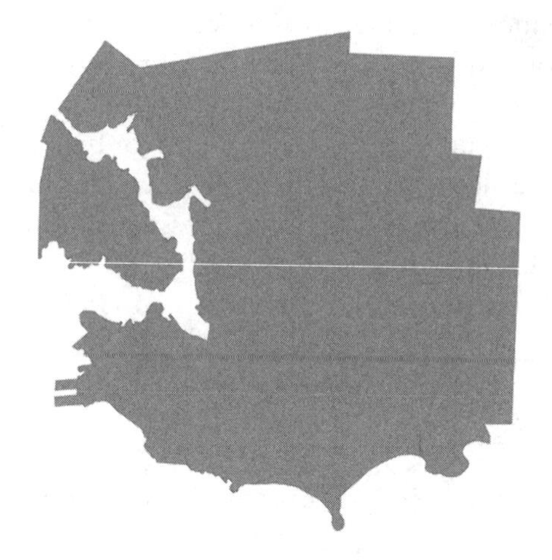

Figure 13.5 Victoria as geometry

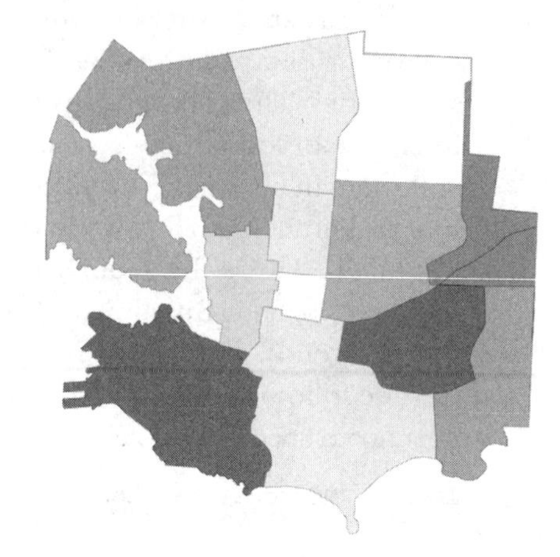

Figure 13.6 Faces of Victoria

In this example, you gather up all the faces in Victoria neighborhoods ❸, but more commonly you'll find that you need to do a containment check using something like `ST_Contains(geom,topo::geometry)`. For example, if your neighbourhoods table also included areas from nearby Sannich, you'd have to use the Victoria polygon to sift out only neighborhoods within Victoria's city boundaries.

Most desktop viewing tools have no concept of topogeometries. To get a picture, you must cast your topogeometries to geometries, as in this example:

```
SELECT topo::geometry FROM ch13.cities WHERE feat_name = 'Victoria';
```

Now you can bring your result into OpenJUMP, as shown in figure 13.5.

To show the neighborhoods, you need to convert each face to a polygon geometry, as in the following example:

```
SELECT face_id, ST_GetFaceGeometry('ch13_topology', face_id)
FROM (
    SELECT (GetTopoGeomElements(topo))[1] As face_id
    FROM ch13.cities
    WHERE feat_name = 'Victoria'
) As x;
```

With theming, the output in OpenJUMP is shown in figure 13.6.

13.4 Fixing topogeometry issues by editing topology primitives

Recall that in listing 13.13 you added 14 polygons and ended up with a total of 38 faces in your topology. The neighborhood polygons either overlapped or the neighborhoods didn't fully fill out the city's polygon. You ended up with shards that are themselves polygons but are too tiny to discern from a map. Besides inherent bad data as the cause, simplification is the usual culprit for misalignments. *Simplification* is a geometry process, so it looks at geometries independent of each other. When you simplify a neighborhood polygon by reducing the number of vertices, PostGIS doesn't care about how adjacent polygons must be altered to avoid introducing small gaps.

NOTE QGIS 2.0 and above have built-in support for viewing and editing topogeometries and topologies. You'll need to have two plug-ins installed: DBManager TopoViewer and PostGIS Topology Editor.

Currently the ch13_topology example has 41 faces, including the universal face. The `neighbourhoods` layer has 14 topogeometries. Using QGIS, you can overlay `neighbourhoods` with `ch13_topology.faces`. In figure 13.7 the neighborhoods are labeled with their names and the faces with their IDs.

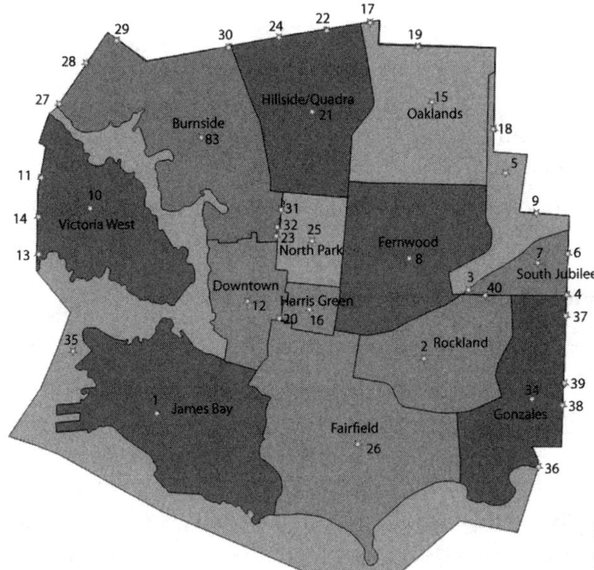

Figure 13.7 Victoria neighborhoods overlaid with faces shown in QGIS

Take a close look at Burnside. It has tiny faces (denoted by numbers 27, 28, 29, 23, 31, 32) that occupy almost no area along its borders. Run the code in the following listing to see all the pesky tiny faces within neighborhoods.

Listing 13.16 Neighborhoods with more than one face

```
SELECT feat_name, COUNT(face_id) As num_faces,
    MIN(
        ST_Area(ST_GetFaceGeometry('ch13_topology',face_id))
    )::numeric(10,2) As min_area,
    MAX(
        ST_Area(ST_GetFaceGeometry('ch13_topology',face_id))
    )::numeric(10,2) As max_area
FROM (
    SELECT feat_name, (GetTopoGeomElements(topo))[1] As face_id
    FROM ch13.neighbourhoods
```

```
) As x
GROUP BY feat_name
HAVING COUNT(face_id) > 1
ORDER BY COUNT(face_id) DESC;
```

The output of listing 13.16 is shown next.

```
    feat_name      | num_faces | min_area |  max_area
-------------------+-----------+----------+------------
 Burnside          |         5 |     1.48 | 2383707.70
 Victoria West     |         4 |     2.22 | 1579455.03
 Gonzales          |         4 |     0.03 | 1366871.65
 North Park        |         3 |    41.29 |  554621.97
 Oaklands          |         3 |     3.53 | 1733012.41
 North Jubilee     |         2 |    39.05 |  629632.96
 Hillside/Quadra   |         2 |    62.23 | 1658097.80
 South Jubilee     |         2 |    78.28 |  378937.43
(8 rows)
```

The code in listing 13.16 listed all neighborhoods with more than one face and counted a total of 25 faces. Not listed are 6 additional neighbors with 1 face each, bringing us to a total of 32 faces that are part of neighborhoods. It's also possible to have faces that don't belong to any neighborhoods, which we evidently have, because we have 41 faces.

13.4.1 Removing faces by removing edges

The ST_RemEdgeNewFace function removes an edge. If the edge splits two faces, the original faces are destroyed and a new face that's the union of the original two is created.

In listing 13.17 you'll use this function recklessly, blindly trying to remove all the edges that form the faces of these small pocket polygons. The main reason you can get away with being reckless here is that the process will fail if the result removes a face used by a topogeometry defined in ch13.neighbourhoods, and that topogeometry doesn't completely cover the new face created. So the result of ignoring failures here is that you'll only have removed edges that don't affect the geometric definition (topo::geometry) of your neighborhoods.

Listing 13.17 Removing extraneous faces with small area

```
DO
LANGUAGE plpgsql
$$
DECLARE r record; var_face integer;
BEGIN
    FOR r IN (
    SELECT DISTINCT abs(
        (ST_GetFaceEdges(
            'ch13_topology',face_id)
        ).edge
    ) As edge
    FROM (
        SELECT feat_name, (GetTopoGeomElements(topo))[1] As face_id
```

```
        FROM ch13.neighbourhoods
    ) As x
    WHERE ST_Area(ST_GetFaceGeometry('ch13_topology',face_id)) < 55000
     )
    LOOP
        BEGIN
            var_face := ST_RemEdgeNewFace('ch13_topology',r.edge);
            EXCEPTION
                WHEN OTHERS THEN
            RAISE WARNING 'Failed remove edge: %, %', r.edge, SQLERRM;
        END;
    END LOOP;
END
$$;
```

In listing 13.17 you raise a warning if a remove step fails, but because it's just a warning, the code continues to run for the remaining edges.

After running listing 13.17, run listing 13.16 again to see how you did.

```
 feat_name   | num_faces | min_area |  max_area
-------------+-----------+----------+------------
 North Park  |         3 |    41.29 |  554621.97
 Burnside    |         3 |    41.29 | 2383714.40
```

From eight neighborhoods with more than one face, you're now down to two. You've mitigated, but not eliminated, your extra faces. Using QGIS as in figure 13.8, you can see that you've got border disputes between North Park and Burnside (around faces 23, 31, and 32). The edges that make up these faces couldn't be destroyed by the previous process because they would have resulted in changing the landscape of North Park and Burnside by either giving land to North Park or taking land away from North Park.

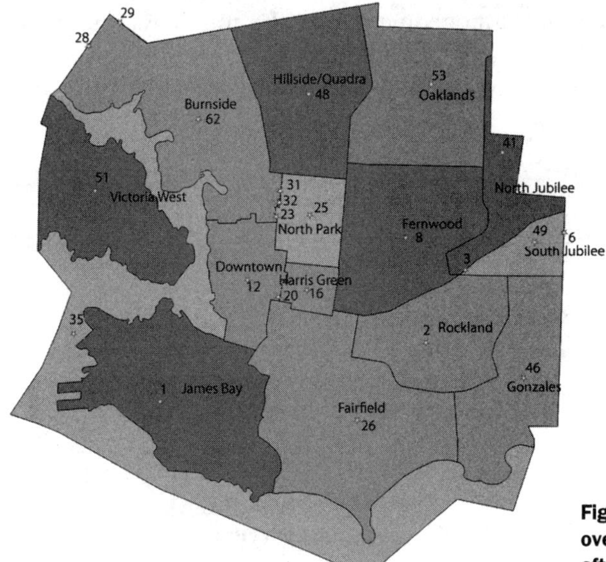

Figure 13.8 Victoria neighborhoods overlaid with faces shown in QGIS after cleanup

13.4.2 Checking for shared faces

It's hard to tell from viewing which of faces 23, 31, or 32, if any, are shared. Using a query is more definitive. The following listing will first dump out the topoelement IDs for the two adjacent neighborhoods, and will only return those faces that are in common.

Listing 13.18 Finding shared faces

```
SELECT (GetTopoGeomElements(topo))[1] As face_id      <-- Face IDs of North Park
FROM ch13.neighbourhoods
WHERE feat_name = 'North Park'
INTERSECT
SELECT (GetTopoGeomElements(topo))[1] As face_id      <-- Face IDs of Burnside
FROM ch13.neighbourhoods
WHERE feat_name = 'Burnside';
```

The output of listing 13.18 is shown next.

```
 face_id
---------
      23
      31
```

You now know, without a doubt, that faces 23 and 31 are shared and that 32 is most likely an unsightly gap between the neighborhoods. This calls for changing the underlying topogeometries so that the neighborhoods don't overlap each other.

13.4.3 Editing topogeometries

The easiest way to fix the overlap is to remove a shared face from each topogeometry. Unfortunately PostGIS 2.1 doesn't offer any functions for doing so; you'll need to work directly with the topology tables. Recall that the ch13_topology.relation table holds all relationships between a topogeometry and the topology. You can edit this table and disassociate faces from your topogeometries.

The following listing deletes shared entries in the relations table corresponding to Burnside and North Park.

Listing 13.19 Removing shared areas from topogeometries

```
DELETE FROM ch13_topology.relation AS r       <-- Remove from relation table
WHERE EXISTS (
    SELECT topo                               <-- Remove face 23 from North Park
    FROM ch13.neighbourhoods As n
    WHERE
        feat_name = 'North Park' AND
        (topo).id = r.topogeo_id AND
        r.element_id = 23 AND
        r.element_type = 3
);

DELETE FROM ch13_topology.relation AS r       <-- Remove face 31 from Burnside
```

```
WHERE EXISTS (
    SELECT topo
    FROM ch13.neighbourhoods As n
    WHERE
        feat_name = 'Burnside' AND
        (topo).id = r.topogeo_id AND
        r.element_id = 31 AND
        r.element_type = 3
);
```

After you're done running listing 13.19, rerun listing 13.17. Now all your neighborhoods should have exactly one face.

13.5 Inserting and editing large data sets

So far you've learned how to insert small sets of polygons and linestrings. When you start loading streets and parcels for large cities, you could easily be looking at tens of thousands of edges and faces. One annoyance when loading large data sets is the possibility of running into topological errors that halt the import process.

PostgreSQL, like most relational databases, is transaction-based. Each insert or update statement runs as a single transaction, meaning all records must succeed or fail; there are no partial updates or inserts. If PostGIS hits one bad record at the end of an hour-long insert, you'll have wasted the entire hour. Our recommendation to get around the all-or-nothing nature of transactions is to perform the inserts or updates in small batches. To implement this, run your process either in a `DO` command or a function:

- The `DO` command will run a single transaction, but it will prompt on each error. If you choose to ignore the error, execution will continue.
- In the function approach, you embed your inserts or updates into a function and then iteratively call the function with small batches of data. Should you hit an error, only the current batch is affected.

The following example demonstrates an enhanced function approach where you also catch errors in the function itself.

First, you need to create a new table with a topology column, as shown in the following listing.

Listing 13.20 Create table to hold streets topogeometry

```
CREATE TABLE ch13.streets (
    gid integer primary key,
    feat_name varchar(50),
    access varchar(20),
    rd_class varchar(20),
    max_speed numeric(10,2)
);                           <-- 1 Streets

SELECT AddTopoGeometryColumn(
    'ch13_topology',
    'ch13',
```

```
    'streets',
    'topo',
    'MULTILINESTRING'
);                          <-- ❷ Add topogeometry

CREATE TABLE ch13.log_street_failures (
    gid integer primary key,
    error text
);                       <-- ❸ Errors table
```

Listing 13.20 creates a table ❶ to hold streets in a topogeometry column ❷. It also creates a table to log topology insert errors during loading ❸.

Next is the logic that does the inserts.

Listing 13.21 Function to load streets in batches

```
CREATE FUNCTION ch13.load_streets() RETURNS void AS
$$
DECLARE r record;
BEGIN
    FOR r IN
        SELECT *
        FROM ch13_staging.streetcentrelines        <-- ❶ Set limit
        ORDER BY gid
        LIMIT 500 OFFSET (SELECT MAX(gid) from ch13.streets)
    LOOP
        BEGIN
            INSERT INTO ch13.streets (
                gid,feat_name,access,rd_class,max_speed,topo)    <-- ❷ Insert
            SELECT
                r.gid,r.streetname,r.access,r.rd_class,
                r.max_speed::numeric,
                toTopoGeom(ST_Transform(ST_Force2D(r.geom),32610),    ❸ Force 2D transform
     'ch13_topology',3,0.05);     ❹ Tolerance
            EXCEPTION WHEN OTHERS THEN
                INSERT INTO ch13.log_street_failures (gid,error)   <-- ❺ Log error and skip
                VALUES (r.gid,SQLERRM);
                RAISE WARNING
                    'Loading of record % failed: %',
                    r.gid,
                    SQLERRM;
        END;
    END LOOP;
END
$$
LANGUAGE plpgsql;
```

Listing 13.21 defines a PL/pgSQL function that on each call will load the next 500 streets. There are about 2,500 streets in the data set, so you limit the function to 500 in each run ❶. The `OFFSET (SELECT MAX(gid))...` code checks the ID of your target table and skips that number in the source table. To take advantage of this snippet, your IDs must be unique and sequential without gaps.

The insert itself is within a FOR loop. The set of records being processed is temporarily stored in the variable r ❷. The source data is in WGS 84, and the input geometry is LINESTRINGZM. You defined ch13_topology as 2D, so it can only accommodate two dimensions. Thus, you force the geometry to 2D by dropping the higher dimensions. You also perform a transform to UTM ❸.

Next you use toTopoGeom to convert the geometry to a topogeometry fashioned after the streets layer (layer ID of 3) ❹. Any streets that fail the insert are skipped and logged in the log_street_failures table ❺.

This function will insert 500 streets at a time, but it doesn't know how many times to run. You need another script to call the function until all streets have been loaded. We've opted to use pgScript, which is a scripting language that's part of pgAdmin. PgScript doesn't run in a single transaction—you can choose any scripting language or agent to call the function, as long as your choice doesn't run as a single transaction. Otherwise, you'd be defeating the purpose of loading in batches.

Listing 13.22 Using pgAdmin pgScript to drive the inserts

```
DECLARE @I;                              ❶ Counter
SET @I = 0;
WHILE @I < 10                            ❷ Run ten times
BEGIN
    SELECT ch13.load_streets();          ❸ Call function
    SET @I = @I + 1;                     ❹ Increment counter
    PRINT @I;
END
```

Listing 13.22 runs ch13.load_streets ten times, which is enough to load all 2,500 or so records.

To run pgScript in pgAdmin, open up a query window and type or copy and paste in the script. Instead of hitting the standard execute button, click the pgScript execute icon identified with the small letters *PGS*.

13.6 Simplifying with topology in mind

Simplification in the realm of topology needs to ensure that you don't end up with things that were connected no longer connecting or with gaping holes.

To simplify in topology, you use ST_Simplify, which is overloaded to accept topogeometries. You'll need at least PostGIS 2.1 to use this function. The ST_Simplify function that takes a topogeometry as input returns a geometry. The difference between the geometry and topogeometry versions of the function is that the topogeometry version applies simplification on the edges that comprise the topogeometry, but prevents simplification that would cause gaps between edges or destroy faces. Because a topogeometry is just a reference to edges, the reconstituted geometries that had shared edges now have simplified shared edges.

Finally, keep in mind that any simplification that takes place for topogeometries won't simplify the underlying topology. The simplification process creates a simplified version of the edges comprised by the topogeometry and reconstitutes a geometry from the simplified edges. Once the function is run, the newly created simplified versions of the edges are thrown away.

We'll look at two examples. In the first, we'll cast the neighborhood topogeometry to geometry and apply `ST_Simplify`. You'll see first-hand how you'll end up with overlaps and gaps. We'll then apply `ST_Simplify` directly to the topogeometry and you'll see how the neighborhoods still fit together harmoniously.

First, we'll simplify against geometry with a tolerance of 150 meters.

Listing 13.23 Geometry-based simplification

```
SELECT feat_name, ST_Simplify(topo::geometry,150) As geom_simp
FROM ch13.neighbourhoods;
```

The visual output is shown in figure 13.9.

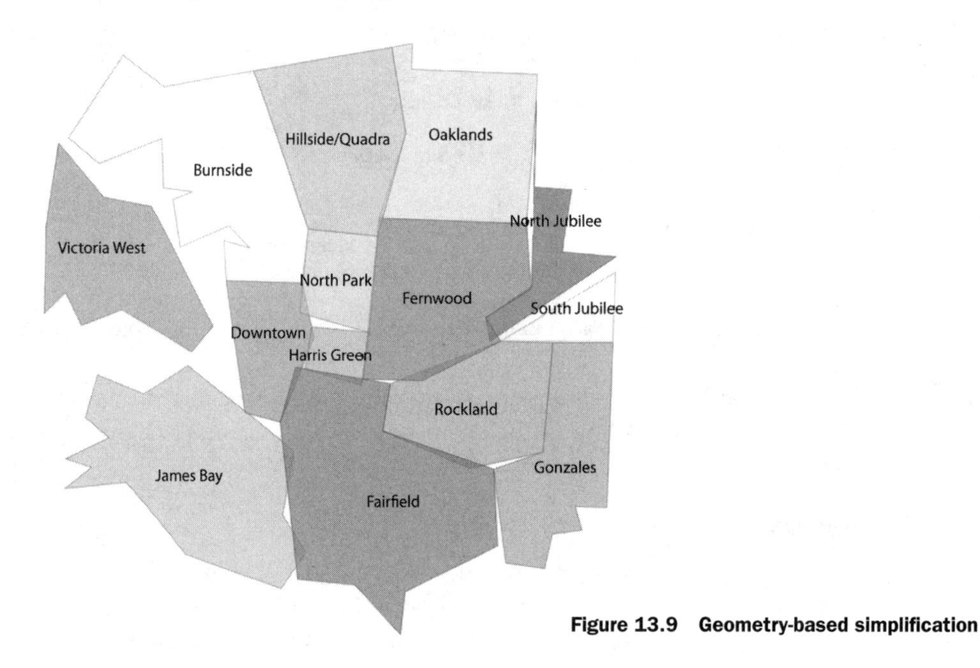

Figure 13.9 Geometry-based simplification

Next, we'll simplify against topogeometry with the same tolerance.

Listing 13.24 Topology-based simplification

```
SELECT feat_name, ST_Simplify(topo,150) As topo_simp
FROM ch13.neighbourhoods;
```

The visual output is in figure 13.10.

As you can see, after the topology simplification process, the neighborhoods maintain their connectedness without overlapping each other, even though their shapes have been altered somewhat.

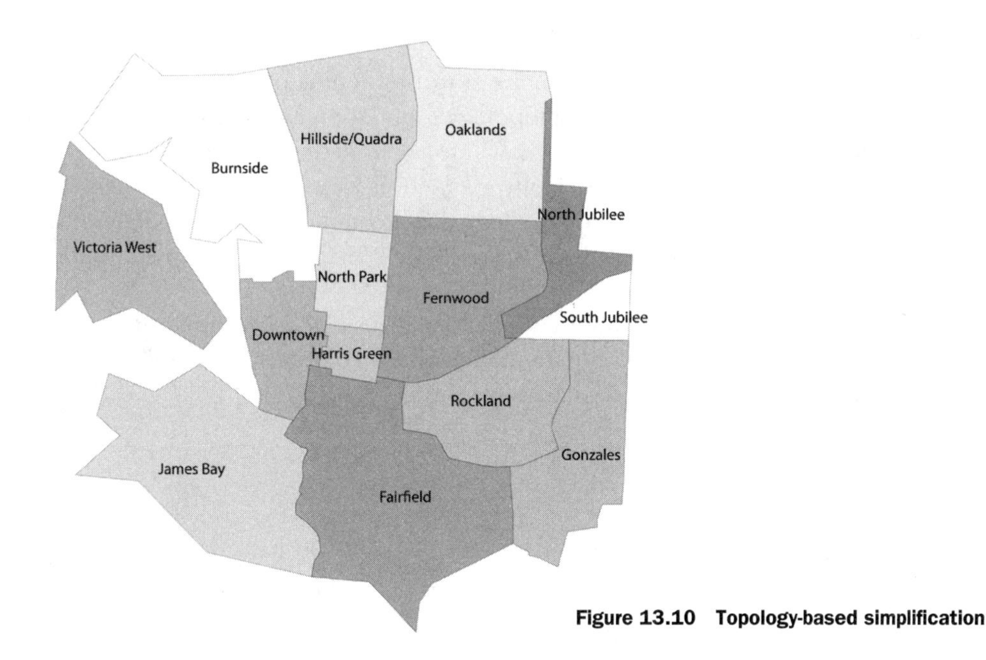

Figure 13.10 Topology-based simplification

13.7 Topology validation and summary functions

In this chapter, we've alluded to many opportunities where your topology could become invalid via an errant edit. We'll now show you two important functions that you should exercise regularly to keep tabs on your topology.

`ValidateTopology` notifies you if there are "issues" with your base topology. It doesn't inspect topogeometries! Here's an example:

```
SELECT ValidateTopology('ch13_topology');
```

Keep in mind that the standard definition of *validity* is rather loose. Solitary elements that aren't interconnected will pass a validity test. You may consider developing additional validity checks that include `ValidateTopology` as a step.

`TopologySummary` is another useful management function that provides you with a basic summary of your topology and layers without having to look into the tables. Run it with code such as this:

```
SELECT TopologySummary('ch13_topology');
```

The output of `TopologySummary` follows:

```
Topology ch13_topology (2), SRID 32610, precision 0.05
2070 nodes, 3137 edges, 1074 faces, 2395 topogeoms in 3 layers
Layer 1, type Polygonal (3), 14 topogeoms
 Deploy: ch13.neighbourhoods.topo
Layer 2, type Polygonal (3), 1 topogeoms
 Hierarchy level 1, child layer 1
 Deploy: ch13.cities.topo
Layer 3, type Lineal (2), 2380 topogeoms
 Deploy: ch13.streets.topo
```

13.8 Summary

In this chapter, we took a deeper dive into the depths of topology. Always keep in mind the distinction between the topology foundation and topogeometry layers that you add. A topology network underlies all topogeometries.

We demonstrated how to fix faulty geometries by using a topology network. Most exciting, we demonstrated using topology that a common spatial problem of simplifying data and maintaining connectedness was largely resolved by using a topologically aware data model.

Now that we've covered all the spatial types PostGIS has to offer and how to work with them, we'll next focus on data model design considerations and the use of triggers and views to better encapsulate logic.

14 Organizing spatial data

This chapter covers

- Options for structuring spatial data
- Modeling a real city
- Data abstraction with views
- Triggers on tables and views

In chapter 2 we walked through all the possible geometry, geography, and raster types PostGIS offers, and how you can create and store them. In this chapter, we'll continue our study by demonstrating the different table layouts you can design to store spatial data. Then we'll apply these various design approaches to a real-world example (Paris, France). We'll finish the chapter with a discussion and examples of using views for database abstraction and using triggers to manage inserts and updates in tables and views. Our main focus will be the geometry type, which is still the most commonly used type in PostGIS.

You can download all the data and code for this chapter at www.postgis.us/chapter_14_edition_2. Before we start, you'll need to create a schema to hold data for this chapter:

```
CREATE SCHEMA ch14;
```

14.1 Spatial storage approaches

In database design, there's always a healthy dose of compromise. Many considerations factor into the final structure you settle on, such as the analysis it must support, the speed of the queries, and so forth. With a spatial database, a few additional considerations enter the design process: availability of data, the precision at which you need to store the data, and the mapping tools your database needs to be compatible with. Unlike databases with numerical and text data, where a poor design leads to slow queries, poor design in a spatial database could lead to queries that will never finish in your lifetime. It also goes without saying that many factors can't be determined at the outset. You may not know exactly how much or what type of spatial data will eventually reside in the database. You may not even know how the users will query the data. As with all decision making, you do the best you can with the information you have at the time. You can always rework your design as needs change, but as any database practitioner knows, getting the design more or less right the first time saves hassles down the road.

In this section, we'll cover three common ways to organize data in a spatial database: heterogeneous spatial columns, homogeneous spatial columns, and inheritance. We'll explain how you'd go about setting up your database structure using each of these approaches and point out the advantages and disadvantages of each. These approaches are by no means exhaustive, and you should feel free to find your own hybrid that fits your specific needs. We'll also mainly focus on geometry data types over any of the other spatial types. Geometry data types are by far the predominant data types in PostGIS, and they're the foundation for topology and raster data types. Finally, geometry types are inherently faster for most spatial computations than the other types in the spatial family. All this may change as the other spatial types mature, but you'll find the general concepts we cover in this section to be applicable to other spatial types too.

14.1.1 Heterogeneous columns

You can't mix geometry, geography, raster, and topogeometry in the same table column unless you go completely hog wild by defining a byte array (`bytea`) column and cast to the various data types as needed. And even that approach will only allow you to mix geometry, geography, and raster. We won't explore that approach because it has utility only in rare (and mostly temporary) storage use cases.

Within each base spatial type you can constrain yourself as little or as much as you want. For example, to store geographic features in a city, you could create a bare-bones geometry table column and be done. In this single column, you could store geometry points, linestrings, polygons, collections of 2D/3D, or any other geometry type for that matter, but you couldn't throw a geography type in a column defined as geometry.

You may wish to mix subtypes if you're more interested in geographically partitioning the city. For example, Washington, D.C., as well as many other planned cities, is divided into quadrants: NW, SW, SE, NE. A city planner can employ a single table with quadrant names in a text column and use another generic geometry column to store the geometries within each quadrant. With the data type as the generic geometry type, the column can store polygons for the many polygonal shaped government edifices in D.C., linestrings to represent major thoroughfares, and points for metro stations.

There are varying degrees in the heterogeneous approach. Using a base spatial column without any subtype doesn't necessarily mean having no additional constraints. You should still judiciously apply constraints (or type modifiers) to ensure data integrity. We advise that you at least enforce the spatial reference system, the coordinate dimension, and the number and type of band constraints, because the vast majority of all non-unary functions in PostGIS and all aggregate functions will assume a certain degree of sameness.

PROS OF HETEROGENEOUS COLUMNS

The heterogeneous column approach has a couple of main benefits:

- It allows you to run a single query of several features of interest without giving up the luxury of modeling them with the most appropriate spatial subtype.
- It's simple. You could conceivably cram all your geometries into one column in a table if their non-spatial attributes were more or less the same.

CONS OF HETEROGENEOUS COLUMNS

There are also drawbacks to the heterogeneous column approach:

- You run the risk of having someone insert an inappropriate geometry for an object. For example, if you've obtained data for subway stations that should be modeled as points, an errant linestring in the data could enter your heterogeneous table. Furthermore, if you don't constrain the spatial reference system or coordinate geometry and unwittingly end up with more than one of each, your queries could be completely incorrect or break.
- Many third-party tools can't deal with heterogeneous spatial type columns. As a workaround, you may need to create views against this table to make it appear as separate tables and add a geometry type, band number, or spatial reference index, or ensure that your queries select only a single grouping from the heterogeneous column.
- For cases where you need to extract only a certain kind of geometry, you'll need to filter by geometry type. For large tables, this could be slow and annoying to have to keep doing over and over again.
- Throwing all your geometry data into a single table could lead to an unwieldy number of self-joins. For example, suppose you placed points of interest (POIs) in the same table as polygons outlining city neighborhoods; every time you needed to identify which POIs fall into which neighborhoods, you'd need to perform a self-join on this table. Not only are self-joins taxing for the processor, they're also taxing for the mind. Imagine a scenario where you have 100 POIs

and two neighborhoods, for a total of 102 records. Determining which POIs fall into which neighborhood requires that a table of 102 rows be joined with a table of 102 rows (itself). If you had separated out the neighborhoods into their own table, you'd only be joining a table of 100 rows with a table of 2 rows.

With the disadvantages of the heterogeneous storage approach fresh in your mind, let's move on to the homogenous spatial columns approach.

14.1.2 Homogeneous columns

A strict homogeneous approach for geometry and geography avoids mixing the different subtypes in a single column. Polygons must be stored in columns of only polygons, multipolygons must be stored in columns of only multipolygons, and so on. This means that each spatial subtype must reside in its own column at the least, but it's also common to break up different spatial subtypes into entirely separate tables.

If in the D.C. example you care more about the type of feature than the quadrant each feature is located in, you could employ the homogeneous columns design. One possible table structure would be to define a features table with a name column and three geometry columns. You'd constrain one column to store only points, one to store only linestrings, and one to store only polygons. If a feature is point data, you'd populate the point column, leaving the other two columns NULL; if it's linestring data, you'd populate the linestring column only, and so on. But you don't necessarily need to cram all of your columns into a single table. A more common design would be to use three distinct tables, storing each type of geometry in a separate table.

PROS OF HOMOGENEOUS COLUMNS

The homogeneous geometry columns approach offers the following benefits:

- It enforces consistency and prevents the unintended mixing of spatial subtypes and spatial reference systems.
- Third-party tools rely on consistency in spatial types, and some may go so far as to only allow one spatial column per table. The popular Esri shapefile supports only one geometry per record, so you'd need to explicitly state the geometry column should you ever need to dump data into shapefile format. Many tools that render or output raster data rely on it being homogeneous, meaning it's evenly blocked, of the same spatial reference system, of the same band pixel types, of the same number of bands, and of the same pixel dimensions, especially when displaying coverages.
- In general, you get better performance when joining tables having large geometries and few records with tables having smaller geometries and many records than vice versa.
- Should you be working with monstrous data sets, separate tables also allow you to reap benefits from placing your data on separate physical disks for each table by means of tablespaces.

> **What is a PostgreSQL tablespace?**
>
> In PostgreSQL, a *tablespace* is a physical folder location, as opposed to a schema, which is a logical location. In the default setup, all tables you create go into the same tablespace, but as your tables grow, you may want to create additional tablespaces, perhaps on separate physical disks, and distribute your tables across the different tablespaces to achieve maximum disk I/O versus cost of disk. One common practice is to group rarely used large tables into their own tablespace and place them on slower, cheaper, bigger disks.
>
> In PostgreSQL 9.0, tablespaces were enhanced to allow you to set `random_page_cost` and `seq_page_cost` settings by tablespace. In older versions, you could set these only at the server or database level. The query planner uses these two parameters to discern whether data will source from a slow disk or a fast disk.

CONS OF HOMOGENEOUS COLUMNS

On the con side, by choosing the homogeneous geometry columns approach, you may face the following obstacles:

- When you need to run a query that draws multiple geometry types, you'll have to resort to a union query. This can add to the complexity and reduce the speed of the query. For example, if 99% of the queries you write for the D.C. example involve querying by quadrant only, you should stick with the heterogeneous approach.
- If you choose the homogeneous approach but decide on hosting multiple spatial columns per table, you might run into performance issues. Multiple spatial columns in a single table mean wider, fatter rows. Fatter rows make for slower queries, on both selects and updates. In the case of updates, because PostgreSQL creates a new row for the updated record and spatial columns tend to be especially fat, even making an update on a simple attribute column like a name or date for large numbers of records takes a lot more time than for thinner tables.

14.1.3 Typmod versus constraints

Typmod is short for *type modifier.* It's a facility for building constraints straight into the data type. Typmods and constraints are different ways of enforcing homogeneity. We covered typmods in chapter 2.

In the case of PostGIS geometries, a column defined as `geometry(POINT,4326)` is of the `geometry` data type with a type modifier restriction that it be a `POINT` and have an SRID of `4326`. You can also have a geometry defined as `geometry(Geometry,4326)`, meaning it's a `geometry` with only the SRID constrained by a type modifier.

PostGIS 2.0 brought typmods to the geometry scene, but you still have the option of using the more laborious constraint-based method. Geography started out with typmods, and there are no management functions to aid in adding constraints. To use the old constraint-based method, you'd have to add constraints manually and create a table to register all your constraints.

Although the constraint method is falling out of style, there are several cases where the typmod model just doesn't work or isn't as efficient as the constraint model.

ISSUES WITH TYPMODS

Although using typmods is the most recommended way of defining your columns, there are some cases where it doesn't work:

- Dropping and adding constraints is generally faster than changing a data type via a typmod. Also, with constraints you have the option of creating a constraint as `NOT VALID`, which means the constraint will only be checked for future inserts and updates, speeding up validation. This is particularly useful for large tables because validating existing data to ensure it doesn't violate the newly created check constraint could be a lengthy process requiring an access lock. If, for whatever reason, you don't require old data to abide by new rules, then using a check constraint is your only option. Later on, to ensure the validity of older records, you could run `ALTER TABLE sometable.somecolumn VALIDATE CONSTRAINT` *`constraint_name`*`;`.
- Certain kinds of triggers don't work with typmods. For example, let's say you had defined a trigger that does the following: When a user tries to insert or update a geometry in a table, the trigger determines the geometry's centroid to guarantee the resulting geometry is a point. The trigger then stores the generated centroid instead of the user-provided geometry in the geometry column. If you defined the geometry column as `geometry(POINT,4326)`, guess what? Your trigger would fail if the user tried to update with anything other than a point of SRID 4326. If the column's geometry subtype is constrained with a typmod, any geometry you try to insert that isn't a point would fail before it even gets to your trigger because the type modifier check kicks in before the geometry even hits your table—the geometry of the `NEW` trigger row itself is defined as a constrained typmod geometry. If you use constraints, your point-fixing trigger (using the centroid to force a geometry to a point) would work because the constraint check doesn't kick in until the record is about to be added to the table.
- If you plan to use table inheritance where each child table is constrained to have a different geometry subtype, you can't have geometries with different subtypes when you use a typmod. You can define check constraints at the child level that the parent doesn't have, and the child can also inherit check constraints defined at the parent level. If you use a typmod to constrain the geometry column subtype of the parent, then all its children must abide by the same typmod subtype requirement, and you can't have a typmod column definition for the child column that's different from the parent.

WHY USE TYPMODS

Despite all the issues we've outlined with typmods, why should you use them for most cases? For the following reasons:

- Typmods can be created with `CREATE TABLE` and short column definitions, which means you don't need an extra step to add the geometry column or memorize a lengthy constraint list to include in your `CREATE TABLE`.
- If you build a view that selects a typmod column, the column properties of that view column are correctly displayed in the geometry_columns table. For constraint-only enforced base table columns, the geometry_columns table will be missing all the other key attributes, such as subtype, dimensionality, and SRID. This restriction may change in future versions of PostGIS.
- Similarly, with typmods you can use the more standard `ALTER TABLE .. USING` syntax to change a geometry type in single step.

14.1.4 Table inheritance

The final design approach we'll consider is using table inheritance. This is by far the most versatile of the various storage approaches, but it's slightly more involved than the previous two. One unique strength of PostgreSQL is its support for table inheritance. You can tap into this gem of a feature to distill the positive aspects of both the homogeneous and heterogeneous column approaches.

Table inheritance means that a table can inherit its structure from a parent table. The parent table doesn't need to store any data, relegating all the data storage to the child tables. When used this way, the parent table is often referred to as an *abstract table* (from the object-oriented concept of abstract classes). Each child table inherits all the columns of its parent, but in addition it can have columns of its own that are revealed only when you query the child table directly. Check constraints are also inherited, but primary keys and foreign key constraints aren't. PostgreSQL supports multiple inheritance, where a child table can have more than one parent table, with columns derived from both parents. PostgreSQL doesn't place a limit on the number of generations you can have. A parent table can have parents of its own, and so forth.

To implement a table inheritance storage approach, you can create an abstract table that organizes data along its non-geometric attributes, and then create inherited child tables with constrained geometry types. With this pattern, end users can query from the parent table and see all the child data, or query from each child table when they need only data from the child tables or child-specific columns.

In our D.C. example, the table of the single generic heterogeneous geometry column could serve as a parent table. You could then create three inherited child tables, each constrained to hold points, linestrings, and polygons. If you need to pull data of a specific geometry, you would query one of the child tables.

Only with PostgreSQL can you orchestrate such an elegant solution. No other major database offerings support direct table inheritance, at least not yet.

> **Constraint exclusion**
>
> PostgreSQL has a configuration option called `constraint_exclusion`, which is often used in conjunction with table inheritance. When this option is set to `On` or `Partition` (which is the default in PostgreSQL 8.4 and above), the query planner will check the table constraints of a table to determine if it can skip a table in a query. The `Partition` setting saves query-planning cycles by only performing constraint exclusion checks when doing queries against tables in an inheritance hierarchy or when running a `UNION` query.

PROS OF TABLE INHERITANCE

There are several benefits to using table inheritance:

- You can query a hierarchy of tables as if they were a single table or query them separately as needed.
- If you partition by geometry type, you can query for a specific geometry type or query for all geometry types as needed.
- With the use of PostgreSQL constraint exclusions, you can cleverly skip over child tables if none of the rows qualify under your filtering conditions. For example, suppose you need to store data organized by countries of the world. By partitioning the data into a child table for each country, any query you write that filters by country name would completely skip unneeded country tables as if they didn't exist. This can yield a significant speed boost when you have large numbers of records.
- Inheritance can be set and unset on the fly, making it convenient when performing data loads. For instance, you can disinherit a child table, load the data, clean the data, add any necessary constraints, and then re-inherit the child table. This prevents queries slowing down on other data while data loading is happening.
- Most third-party tools will treat the parent table as a bona fide table even though it may not have any data, as long as relevant geometry columns are registered and primary keys are set on the parent table. Inheritance works seamlessly with OpenJUMP, QGIS, GeoServer, and MapServer. Any tool that polls the standard PostgreSQL metadata should end up treating parent tables like any others.

CONS OF TABLE INHERITANCE

Table inheritance also has a number of disadvantages:

- Table inheritance isn't supported by other major databases. Should you ever need to switch away from PostgreSQL to another database, your application code may not be portable. This isn't as big a problem as it may initially appear, because most database drivers will see a parent table as a single table with all the data of its children. Your opting to desert PostgreSQL is the bigger problem!

- Primary key and foreign key constraints don't pass to child tables, though check constraints do. In the D.C. example, if you place a primary key constraint on the parent feature table, dictating that each place name must be unique, you can't expect the child tables to abide by the constraint. Even if you were to assign primary key constraints to the children, you still couldn't guarantee unique results when querying multiple child tables or querying the parent table together with its child tables.
- If you use table inheritance, and each of your child tables holds a different geometry subtype in the geometry column, you need to use check constraints to enforce the geometry subtype requirement. You can't use the typmod feature that allows you to define a column as geometry and the geometry type in one `CREATE TABLE`. But you can use a hybrid of the form `geometry(geometry, SRID)` to constrain the SRID with a typmod and then use constraints to constrain the geometry subtype. PostGIS is not special in this regard. You'd have similar issues with `varchar` and `numeric`. You can't have a parent table with a column defined as `varchar(60)` and then have each child redefine the column as `varchar(50)`, `varchar(40)`, and so on. You'd have to use constraint checks to enforce the lower requirements in child tables.
- To maintain the table inheritance hierarchy when adding data, you must take extra steps to make sure that rows are appropriately added to the parent table or one of its child tables. For table updates, you may want to put in logic that automatically moves a record from one child table to another child table, should an update cause a check violation. This generally means having to create rules or triggers to insert into a child table when inserting into a parent table, or vice versa. We'll cover this in detail in section 14.4.3. Thankfully, PostgreSQL inheritance is smart enough to automatically handle updates and deletes for most situations. When you update or delete against a parent table, it will automatically drill down to its child tables, but updates to move data from one child to another need to be managed with rules or triggers on the child table. You can, if you choose, go through the trouble of creating update and delete triggers to figure out which records in child tables need to be updated when an update or delete call is made on the parent table. This often yields a speed improvement over relying on the automated drill-down of PostgreSQL inheritance.
- If you use constraint exclusions to skip tables entirely, you'll face an initial performance hit when the query is executed for the first time.
- You need to be watchful of the total number of tables in your inheritance hierarchy. Performance begins to degrade noticeably after a couple hundred tables. Since PostgreSQL 9.0, the planner will generate statistics for the inheritance hierarchy. This should boost performance when querying against inherited tables.

A TABLE INHERITANCE EXAMPLE

Listing 14.1 demonstrates how you'd go about implementing a table inheritance model. In this example, you first create a parent table for all roads in the United States. In this parent table, the SRID and the geometry type are set. You then beget two child tables. The first will store roads in the six New England states; the second will store roads in the Southwest states. You then populate only the child tables with data, leaving the parent table devoid of any rows.

Listing 14.1 Partition roads into various states

```
CREATE TABLE ch14.roads(
    gid serial PRIMARY KEY,
    road_name character varying(100),
    geom geometry(LINESTRING,4269), state varchar(2)
);

CREATE TABLE ch14.roads_NE (CONSTRAINT pk PRIMARY KEY (gid))    <-- 1 Child table
INHERITS (ch14.roads);

ALTER TABLE ch14.roads_NE
ADD CONSTRAINT chk CHECK (state IN ('MA','ME','NH','VT','CT','RI'));    <-- 2 Constraints

CREATE TABLE ch14.roads_SW (CONSTRAINT pk_roads PRIMARY KEY (gid))
INHERITS (ch14.roads);

ALTER TABLE ch14.roads_SW
ADD CONSTRAINT chk CHECK (state IN ('AZ','NM','NV'));

SELECT gid, road_name, geom FROM ch14.roads WHERE state = 'MA';    <-- 3 Constraint exclusion
```

In listing 14.1 you create a child table to the roads table ❶. You then add constraints to the table ❷, which will be useful for speeding up queries when you have `constraint_exclusion` set to `Partition` or `On`. It will ensure that the roads_NE table is skipped if the requested state isn't in MA, ME, NH, VT, CT, or RI.

Finally, you write a simple `SELECT` to pull all roads in Massachusetts ❸. With constraint exclusion, only the child table with roads in New England will be searched. You can see this by running an explain plan or by looking at the graphical explain plan in pgAdmin III.

We've now examined three ways of organizing spatial data. In the next section of this chapter, we'll put these ideas to work by modeling a real-world city using these approaches.

14.2 Modeling a real city

In this section, you'll apply what you learned in the previous section by exploring various ways to model a real city. We'll abandon the quadrants of D.C. and states of the United States and cross the Atlantic to Paris, the city of lights (or love, depending on your preference) for our extended example. We chose Paris because of the importance placed on arrondissements.

For those of you unfamiliar with Paris, the city is divided into 20 administrative districts, known as *arrondissements*. Unlike people in other major cities, Parisians are keenly aware of their administrative districts. It's not unusual for someone to say that they live in the *n*th arrondissement, fully expecting their fellow Parisians to know what general area of Paris is being spoken of. Unlike what are often referred to as *neighborhoods* in other major cities, arrondissements are well defined geographically and so are well suited for GIS purposes. On top of it all, Parisians often refer to the arrondissements by their ordinal numbers rather than their ascribed French names, making numerically minded folk like us extra happy.

The geography of the basic Paris arrondissements is illustrated in figure 14.1. The arrondissement arrangement is interesting in that it spirals clockwise from the center of Paris, reflecting the pattern of growth since the 1800s as the city annexed adjacent areas.

We downloaded our Paris data from GeoCommons (http://geocommons.com) as well as OpenStreetMap (OSM; http://www.openstreetmap.org). We transformed all the data to SRID 32631 (WGS 84 UTM Zone 31). All of Paris fits into this UTM zone, and because UTM is meter-based, we have measurements at our disposal without any additional effort.

As a starting point, we modeled each arrondissement as a multipolygon and inserted all of them into a table called arrondissements. The table contains exactly 20 rows. Not only will this table serve as our base layer, but we'll also use it to geotag additional data into specific arrondissements. You can load up the table in your database by running in psql this chapter's ch14_data.sql download file.

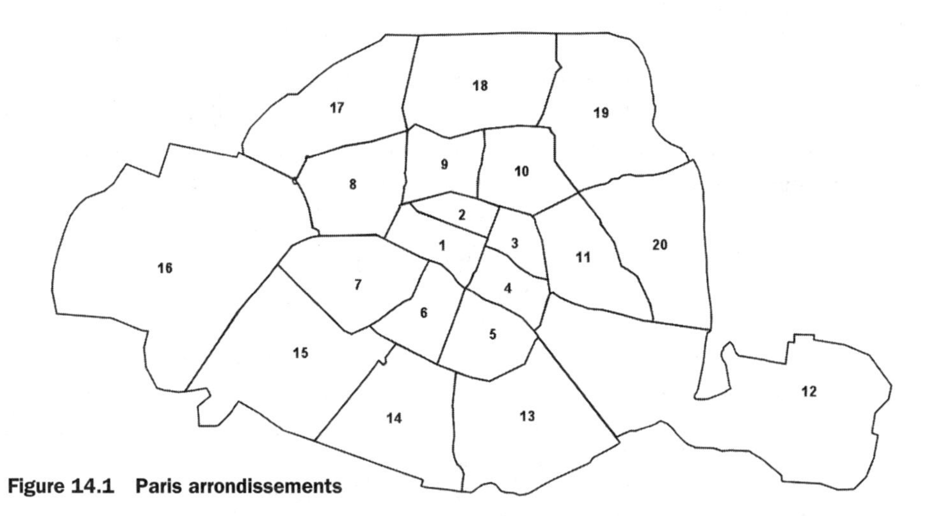

Figure 14.1 Paris arrondissements

Paris data transformation

The original file in raw_files/paris_-_arrondissement.zip that we started out with was in WGS 84 lon/lat (EPSG:4326), and we performed the following exercises after loading it with shp2pgsql to get it to the form you see in ch14_data.sql:

```
ALTER TABLE ch14.arrondissements
ALTER COLUMN geom TYPE geometry(MultiPolygon,32631)
USING ST_Transform(geom,32631);

ALTER TABLE ch14.arrondissements
ADD COLUMN ar_num integer;

UPDATE ch14.arrondissements
SET ar_num = (regexp_matches(name, E'[0-9]+'))[1]::integer;
```

14.2.1 Modeling using heterogeneous geometry columns

If you mainly need to query your data by arrondissements without regard to the type of feature, you can employ a single geometry column to store all of your data. Create this table:

```
CREATE TABLE ch14.paris_hetero (
    gid serial NOT NULL,
    osm_id bigint,
    geom geometry(Geometry,32631),
    ar_num integer,
    tags hstore,
    CONSTRAINT paris_hetero_pk
    PRIMARY KEY (gid)
);
```

Notice how a constraint or typmod restricting the type of geometry is decidedly missing. This geometry column will be able to contain points, linestrings, polygons, multigeometries, geometry collections—in short, any geometry type you want to put in it. Note that the preceding code does take the extra step to limit the column to only SRID 32631 using a typmod.

You'll also notice a data type called `hstore`. Hstore is a data type for storing key/value pairs, similar in concept to associative arrays. Much like geometry columns, `hstore` can be indexed using the gist index.

OSM makes wide use of tags for storing properties of features that don't fit elsewhere. To bring in the OSM data without complicating the table, we used the osm2pgsql utility with the `--hstore` switch to map the OSM tags to an hstore column.

The hstore data type and PostgreSQL

The `hstore` data type is a contrib module found in PostgreSQL 8.2 and above. To enable this module for PostgreSQL 9.1 or higher, use this SQL statement:

```
CREATE EXTENSION hstore;
```

> Since PostgreSQL 9.3, `hstore` has been enhanced to include new functions (`hstore_to_json` and `hstore_to_json_loose`) for easy conversion to the `json` data type. The PostgreSQL 9.4 `hstore` extension added more functions to convert `hstore` to the new binary JSON format, `jsonb`, with functions like `hstore_to_jsonb`.

The ch14.paris_hetero table includes a column called ar_num for holding the arrondissement number of the feature. Unfortunately, this attribute isn't maintained by OSM. But no worries—you can intersect the OSM data with your arrondissement table to figure out which arrondissement each OSM record falls into. Although you can determine the arrondissements on the fly, having the arrondissements figured out beforehand means you can query against an integer instead of having to constantly perform spatial intersections later on.

The next listing demonstrates how to intersect arrondissements with the OSM data to yield an `ar_num` value.

Listing 14.2 Region tagging and clipping data to a specific arrondissement

```
INSERT INTO ch14.paris_hetero (osm_id, geom, ar_num, tags)
SELECT o.osm_id, ST_Intersection(o.geom,a.geom) As geom,
    a.ar_num, o.tags
FROM
    (
        SELECT osm_id, ST_Transform(way,32631) As geom, tags
        FROM ch14_staging.planet_osm_line
    ) AS o
    INNER JOIN
    ch14.arrondissements AS A
    ON (ST_Intersects(o.geom, a.geom));
CREATE INDEX idx_paris_hetero_geom
ON ch14.paris_hetero USING gist(geom);
CREATE INDEX idx_paris_hetero_tags
ON ch14.paris_hetero USING gist(tags);
VACUUM ANALYZE ch14.paris_hetero;
```

❶ Insert data and clip to specific arrondissement

❷ Add indexes and update statistics

In listing 14.2 you load in all the OSM data you downloaded into the paris_hetero table ❶. The listing only shows the insert from the planet_osm_line table, but you'll need to repeat this for OSM points and OSM polygons. The full code is available in this chapter's download file.

Features such as long linestrings and large polygons will straddle multiple arrondissements, but the intersection operation will clip them, so you'll end up with one record per arrondissement. For example, the famous Boulevard Saint-Germain passes through the fifth, sixth, and seventh arrondissements. After the clipping exercise, the record with a single linestring will have been broken up into three records, each with shorter linestrings, for each of the arrondissements that the original linestring passed through.

Finally, you perform the usual indexing and update statistics after the bulk load ❷.

As we've demonstrated, by not putting a geometry type constraint on the geometry column, you can stuff linestrings, polygons, points, and even geometry collections into the same table if you want. This model is nice and simple in the sense that if you wanted to pick or count all features that fit in a particular user-defined area, for mapping or statistical purposes, you could do it with one simple query. Here's an example that counts the number of features within each arrondissement:

```
SELECT ar_num, COUNT(DISTINCT osm_id) As compte
FROM ch14.paris_hetero
GROUP BY ar_num;
```

This yields the following answer.

```
 r_num | compte
-------+--------
     1 |      4
     2 |      4
     7 |      7
     8 |   1121
     9 |      9
    16 |   1060
    17 |   2067
    18 |      5
```

We should mention that for this example, we extracted from OSM only the area of Paris surrounding the Arc de Triomphe, which is at the center of arrondissements 8, 16, and 17. As a result, most of our features tend to be in those three regions. Figure 14.2 shows a map we quickly generated in OpenJUMP by overlaying the planet_hetero table atop the arrondissement polygons.

The main advantage of using hstore to hold miscellaneous attribute data is that you don't have to set up bona fide columns for attributes that could be of little use later on, just so you can import data. You can first import the data and then cherry-pick which attributes you'd like to promote to columns as your needs grow. Using hstore also means that you can add and remove attributes without fussing with the data structure.

The drawback becomes apparent when you do need attributes to be full-fledged columns. You can't query inside an hstore column as easily as you can a character or numeric column or enforce numeric and other data type constraints on the hstore values. Also remember that hstore is a PostgreSQL data type, not to be found elsewhere. Few mapping tools will accept columns in hstore natively.

A simple way to overcome the drawbacks of hstore columns is to create a view that will map attributes within an hstore column into virtual data columns, as shown here:

```
CREATE OR REPLACE VIEW ch14.vw_paris_points AS
SELECT
    gid, osm_id, ar_num, geom,
    tags->'name' As place_name,
    tags->'tourism' As tourist_attraction
FROM ch14.paris_hetero
WHERE ST_GeometryType(geom) = 'ST_Point';
```

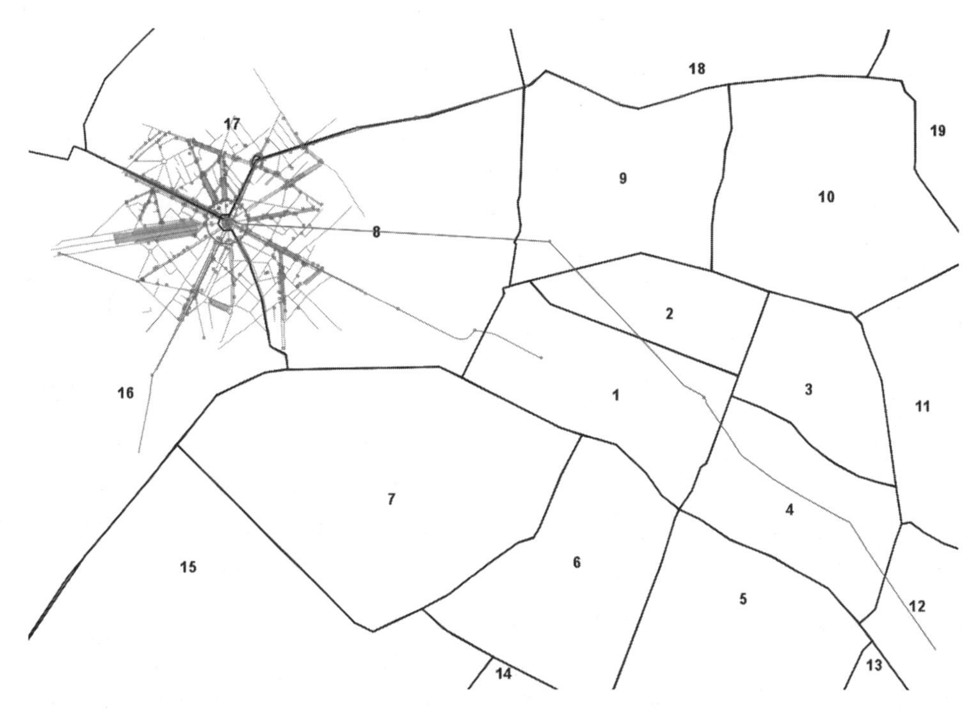

Figure 14.2 The paris_hetero dataset overlaid on the arrondissements

In this snippet, you create a view that promotes the two tags, `name` and `tourism`, into two text data columns. In PostGIS 2 or higher, geometry_columns is no longer a table that you can manually update; it now reads from system catalogs. Because the only thing that is typmoded is `geometry,32612`, your view will show `vw_paris_points` as a geometry of SRID 32631.

To work with tools that don't understand mixed geometry subtype tables, you'll need to make your view register as a point table. If you wanted to have the view correctly register the type as a `POINT` in geometry_columns, you could define the view instead as shown in the following listing.

Listing 14.3 Using typmod in casting to correctly register a view in geometry_columns

```
CREATE OR REPLACE VIEW ch14.vw_paris_points_tmod
    WITH (security_barrier=true) AS
    SELECT
        gid, osm_id, ar_num,
        CAST(geom As geometry(POINT,32631)) As geom,
        tags->'name' As place_name,
        tags->'tourism' As tourist_attraction
    FROM ch14.paris_hetero
    WHERE ST_GeometryType(geom) = 'ST_Point';

CREATE INDEX idx_paris_hetero_geom_pt ON ch14.paris_hetero
USING gist ( (geom::geometry(POINT,32631)) )
WHERE ST_GeometryType(geom) = 'ST_Point';
```

1. Security barrier enforces that the view filter is checked before any other operations in the view happen
2. Cast on points ST_GeometryType (geom) = 'ST_Point' to POINT geometry type
3. Add index so a spatial index can be used

In order for the view's geom column to be registered as a point geometry subtype, you need to cast it to a point geometry ❷. Casting it makes the original geometry index ineffective, so you need to create a partial spatial index that only applies to point geometries ❸. It has to be partial because a linestring and polygon can't be cast to a point without applying some processing function.

In the view you also apply a security barrier ❶. The security barrier feature was introduced in PostgreSQL 9.0, and although it was designed foremost to prevent people from applying functions on data that isn't part of the view output, it accidentally serves another purpose. It forces the `ST_GeometryType` filter to be applied before any other conditions.

Without the security barrier in place, if you ran a query of the following form,

```
SELECT *
FROM ch14.vw_paris_points_tmod
WHERE ST_DWithin(geom,ST_SetSRID(ST_Point(453121,5413887),32631),4000);
```

it might apply the cast operation on a polygon or a linestring if it applied the spatial filter first. This would cause the cast, and your query, to fail.

14.2.2 Modeling using homogeneous geometry columns

The homogeneous columns approach stores each geometry type in its own column or table. This style of storage is more common than the heterogeneous approach, and it's the one most supported by third-party tools. Having distinct columns or tables for different geometry types allows you to enforce geometry type constraints or to use typmods fully, preventing different geometry data types from inadvertently mixing. The downside is that your queries will have to enumerate across multiple columns or tables, should you ever wish to pull data of different geometry types.

The following listing uses the homogeneous columns approach for the Paris data.

Listing 14.4 Breaking data into separate tables with homogeneous geometry columns

```
CREATE TABLE ch14.paris_points(
    gid SERIAL PRIMARY KEY,
    osm_id bigint,
    ar_num integer,
    feature_name varchar(200),
    feature_type varchar(50),
    geom geometry(Point, 32631)
);                                      <-- ❶ Typmod point geometry column

INSERT INTO ch14.paris_points (
    osm_id,     ar_num,     geom,
    feature_name, feature_type
)                                       <-- ❷ Add points
SELECT
    osm_id, ar_num, geom,
    tags->'name' As feature_name,
    COALESCE(
        tags->'tourism',
```

```
        tags->'railway',
        tags->'station',
        'other'
    )::varchar(50) As feature_type
FROM ch14.paris_hetero
WHERE ST_GeometryType(geom) = 'ST_Point';
```

You start by creating a table to store point geometry type data having the spatial reference system UTM for Paris (SRID 32631) ❶. Finally, you perform the insert ❷, but instead of starting from the OSM data, you take advantage of the fact that you already have the data you need in the paris_hetero table, and you selectively pick out the tags you care about and morph them into the columns you want. If you wanted to have a completely homogeneous solution, you'd create similar tables for paris_polygons and paris_linestrings.

If you wanted to get a count of all features by arrondissement, your query would need to union all the different tables together, as shown here:

```
SELECT ar_num, COUNT(DISTINCT osm_id) As compte
FROM (
    SELECT ar_num, osm_id FROM paris_points
    UNION ALL
    SELECT ar_num, osm_id FROM paris_polygons
    UNION ALL
    SELECT ar_num, osm_id FROM paris_linestrings
) As X
GROUP BY ar_num;
```

UNION versus UNION ALL

When performing union operations, you'll generally want to use `UNION ALL` rather than `UNION`. `UNION` has an implicit `DISTINCT` clause built in, which automatically eliminates duplicate rows. If you know that the sets you're unioning can't or need not be deduped in the process, `UNION ALL` will be faster.

We'll now move on to an inheritance-based storage design where you'll see that by expending some extra effort, you'll reap the benefits of both the heterogeneous and homogeneous approaches.

14.2.3 Modeling using inheritance

Table inheritance is a feature that's fairly unique to PostgreSQL. We gave you a quick overview earlier. Now we'll apply it to the Paris example.

You can begin by creating an abstract parent table to store attributes that all of its children will share, as shown in the following code:

```
CREATE TABLE ch14.paris (
    gid SERIAL PRIMARY KEY,
    osm_id bigint,
    ar_num integer,
```

```
    feature_name varchar(200),
    feature_type varchar(50),
    geom geometry(geometry, 32631)
);
```

This code goes to the extra effort of adding a primary key on the parent table, even though you may never plan to add data to it. Child tables can't inherit primary keys, so why take the extra step? Besides the good practice of having a primary key on every table, abstract or not, many client tools rely on all tables having a primary key.

With the parent table in place, you can create child tables. Keep in mind that you'll need to do this for paris_points and paris_linestrings or any other geometry type you have data for, but for the sake of brevity we'll only look at creating the child table for storing polygons.

Listing 14.5 Creating a child table

```
CREATE TABLE ch14.paris_polygons (
    tags hstore,                                  -- 1 Create an inherited table
    CONSTRAINT paris_polygons_pk
    PRIMARY KEY (gid)
)
INHERITS (ch14.paris);

ALTER TABLE ch14.paris_polygons NO INHERIT ch14.paris;   -- 2 Disinherit from parent

INSERT INTO ch14.paris_polygons (
    osm_id,ar_num,geom,tags,
    feature_name,feature_type
)                                                 -- 3 Load
SELECT
    osm_id, ar_num, ST_Multi(geom) As geom, tags,
    tags->'name',
    COALESCE(
        tags->'tourism',
        tags->'railway',
        'other'
    )::varchar(50) As feature_type
FROM ch14.paris_hetero
WHERE ST_GeometryType(geom) LIKE '%Polygon';

SELECT populate_geometry_columns(
    'ch14.paris_polygons'::regclass,
    false
);                                                -- 4 Add constraints
ALTER TABLE ch14.paris_polygons INHERIT ch14.paris;   -- 5 Re-inherit
```

In listing 14.5 you create a polygon table and declare it as inheriting from the paris table ❶; you need only add the additional columns (in this case, tags) beyond what are already defined in the parent. You also add a primary key to the child table because primary keys don't automatically inherit.

Then you disinherit the child from the parent ❷. Disinheriting doesn't remove inherited columns. Once a child table inherits from a parent table, the structure of the parent is passed down permanently. The disinheritance simply disengages the child from the parent so that queries against the parent don't drill down to the child. We find it a good idea to disinherit a child table prior to performing large bulk loads on the child table. This prevents someone from querying a child table while it's in the process of being loaded.

Next you load the table, taking rows from paris_hetero, where the geometry type is polygon or multipolygon ❸. You finish up by calling the `populate_geometry_columns` function (using `false` for the `use_typmod` argument) to automatically add the geometry constraints that make the table appear properly in the `geometry_columns` view ❹. Then you re-inherit from the parent ❺.

Note that if you didn't pass in `false` to the `populate_geometry_columns` function ❹, the function would have converted your geometry column to a completely typmoded column, which would prevent you from re-inheriting. Because you didn't use typmod (you used constraints instead), it looked at the data in the table and added constraints that made it display correctly in the `geometry_columns` view.

Listing 14.6 repeats the same code for linestrings, but it omits the loading of data and the adding of the tag column. (We omitted these extra steps because they're the same as what is done for points. We'll leave that as an exercise for you to do.) Because you aren't populating the table immediately, you can constrain the geometry column to store only linestrings, so that your `populate_geometry_columns` function can use this check constraint to properly register the geometry column.

Listing 14.6 Creating a child table

```
CREATE TABLE ch14.paris_linestrings (          <-- ❶ Create an inherited table
    CONSTRAINT paris_linestrings_pk
    PRIMARY KEY (gid)
) INHERITS (ch14.paris);

ALTER TABLE ch14.paris_linestrings             <-- ❷ Add constraints
ADD CONSTRAINT enforce_geotype_geom
    CHECK (geometrytype(geom) = 'LINESTRING'::text);
```

As you did with polygons, you create a table that inherits from paris to store your linestrings ❶. You aren't ready to load data yet, but you want to constrain the table to just linestrings, so you add a geometry type constraint ❷. You don't need to add a dimension or SRID constraint because these are inherited from the parent via typmods. Because you have a geometry constraint, the table will be displayed correctly in the `geometry_columns` view as `LINESTRING`.

At last, you reap the fruits of your labor. With inheritance, your count query is identical to the simple one you used in the previous heterogeneous model:

```
SELECT ar_num, COUNT(DISTINCT osm_id) As compte
FROM ch14.paris
GROUP BY ar_num;
```

With inheritance in place, you have the added flexibility to query just the polygon table, should you care about only the counts there:

```
SELECT ar_num, COUNT(DISTINCT osm_id) As compte
FROM ch14.paris_polygons
GROUP BY ar_num;
```

As you can see, inheritance requires an extra step or two to set it up properly, but the advantage is that you're able to keep your queries simple by judiciously querying against the parent table or one of the child tables. As one famous Parisian might have said, "Let them have their cake and eat it too."

ADOPTION

More often than not, inheritance comes as an afterthought rather than as part of the initial table design. As an example, suppose you had already set up a paris_points table to store point geometries and had gone to great lengths to populate the table with data. You wouldn't want to drop your points table and re-create it for it to be a legitimate child of the paris table. The following listing demonstrates how you can make an existing table a child of paris.

Listing 14.7 Creating a child table

```
ALTER TABLE ch14.paris_points DROP COLUMN gid;          ❶ Drop old gid
ALTER TABLE ch14.paris_points
    ADD COLUMN gid integer                              ❷ Add new gid based on parent's sequence
        PRIMARY KEY NOT NULL DEFAULT nextval('ch14.paris_gid_seq');
ALTER TABLE ch14.paris_points
ALTER COLUMN geom TYPE geometry(geometry,32621);

SELECT populate_geometry_columns('ch14.paris_points', false);

ALTER TABLE ch14.paris_points INHERIT ch14.paris;       ❸ Adoption
CREATE INDEX idx_paris_points_geom
ON ch14.paris_points USING gist (geom);                 ❹ Add a spatial index
```

There are a couple of considerations when a parent "adopts" a new child table. Before being adopted, the child table must first ensure that its set of columns is a superset of the columns found in the parent's table. The new parent must not have any columns not found in the child. Although it's not an absolute necessity, it's useful for all of the child's primary keys to be unique across the hierarchy. One way to ensure that is to make them use the same sequence as the parent—a family genetic sequence, so to speak.

To reassign the gid of the points table to use the family sequence, you drop the gid columns entirely ❶. Next, you add the column back, but this time you specify that the sequence must come from the sequence of the parent ❷. Then you make paris_points a child of paris ❸. Finally, you add a spatial index for good measure ❹. If you're doing bulk loads, you may wish to add the index afterward, not before, so the loading can run as quickly as possible.

ADDING COLUMNS TO THE PARENT

When you add a new column to the parent table, PostgreSQL will automatically add the column to all inherited children. If the child table already has that column, PostgreSQL issues a gentle warning.

In listing 14.6, you created a paris_polygons table with a tags column, but the parent table and none of the other child tables had this column. Let's try adding tags to the paris table:

```
ALTER TABLE ch14.paris ADD COLUMN tags hstore;
```

When you do this, you'll get a notice:

```
merging definition of column "tags" for child
                  "paris_polygons"
```

This informs you that the child paris_polygons table already has this column. Remember how you purposely omitted the tags column when creating the paris_linestrings child table? After adding tags to the parent, paris_linestrings now also has a tags column. Check for yourself.

14.3 Making auto-updateable views

PostgreSQL 9.3 and above allow you to create views that are updatable without any additional work. A view is generally updatable if it involves only one table.

For example, you can create a view called `ch14.subways`:

```
CREATE OR REPLACE VIEW ch14.subways AS
SELECT gid, osm_id, ar_num, feature_name, geom
FROM ch14.paris_points
WHERE feature_type = 'subway';
```

In order to update records in the view, you'd run an update statement such as this:

```
UPDATE ch14.subways
SET feature_name = 'subway 1'
WHERE osm_id = 243496729;
```

Similarly, you can delete from the view without writing any triggers or rules:

```
DELETE FROM ch14.subways WHERE feature_name = 'subway 1';
```

Although you can also insert into the view, for this particular example we're not exposing the `feature_type`, so the insert would never result in a record that satisfies the filter condition. In order to guarantee that all new records are tagged with `feature_type = 'subway'`, you'll need to use a rule or trigger.

Auto-updateable views can have default values for columns that are different from the parent table. For example, if you wanted all newly added subways to be called subway if no `feature_name` is specified, then you'd change the view as follows.

Listing 14.8 Auto-updateable view

```
ALTER VIEW ch14.subways ALTER COLUMN feature_name SET DEFAULT 'subway';
```

For cases where your view involves multiple tables or calculated fields, or you need to do additional processing beyond what's provided by the default view-update behavior, you'll need to employ the use of rules or triggers. Although rules and triggers can be used wherever the situation calls for them, we find that they're invaluable in working with inheritance hierarchies.

PostgreSQL 9.4 WITH CHECK OPTION

Although views can be auto-updateable as of PostgreSQL 9.3, it's possible to update a value such that it will no longer appear in the view. For example, if you exposed the feature_type column as part of the `SELECT` clause, you could then update the feature_type to something else, like bus, which would make the updated record disappear from the view. This is often an undesirable side effect.

PostgreSQL 9.4 introduced a new feature called `WITH CHECK OPTION` that will ensure that any updates or inserts into the view that won't be visible when querying the view (based on the view's `WHERE` clause) will throw an error. The format of the view-creation statement is

```
CREATE OR REPLACE VIEW name_of_view
 AS ... WITH CHECK OPTION
```

14.4 Using rules and triggers

Sophisticated RDBMSs usually offer ways to catch the execution of certain SQL commands on a table or view and allow some form of conditional processing to take place in response to these events. PostgreSQL is certainly not devoid of such features and can perform additional processing when it encounters the four core SQL commands: `SELECT`, `UPDATE`, `INSERT`, and `DELETE`. The two mechanisms for handling this conditional processing are *rules* and *triggers*.

At this point, we assume you've worked through the examples and have in your test database the four tables paris, paris_points, paris_linestrings, and paris_polygons. We'll now enhance the Paris example by adding rules and triggers.

14.4.1 Rules versus triggers

Both rules and triggers respond to events, so they overlap in functionality. You could often use a trigger instead of a rule and vice versa, but they were created with different intents. Although there are no steadfast guidelines on when to use one over the other when you have a choice, the underlying purposes of the two separate event-response mechanisms will help you decide.

RULES

A *rule* in PostgreSQL is an instruction on how to rewrite an SQL statement. For this reason, people sometimes refer to *rules* as *rewrite rules*. A rule is completely passive and only transforms one SQL statement into another SQL statement, nothing more.

Unbeknownst to many people, views are nothing more than one or more rewrite rules nicely packaged together. When you execute a SELECT command from a view, the view portion of your SQL statement is rewritten to include the view definition before the command is run. For example, suppose you create a view as follows:

```
CREATE OR REPLACE VIEW some_view AS
SELECT * FROM some_table;
```

When you then select from the view using a simple statement like this,

```
SELECT * FROM some_view;
```

the rule rewriter substitutes the some_view part of the SELECT with the definition you used to create the view, so that your SELECT is rewritten to be something like this:

```
SELECT * FROM (SELECT * FROM some_table) AS some_view
```

Because a view is nothing more than a packaging of rewrite rules, you're free to use views far beyond a simple SELECT statement. You can have your views manipulate data. You're free to use UPDATE, INSERT, and DELETE commands at will within your view rules. Furthermore, a view need not have just one SQL statement but can process an entire chain of statements, combining SELECT, UPDATE, INSERT, and DELETE statements. Calling it a *view* in PostgreSQL belies its underlying capability to do much more than view data.

TRIGGERS

A trigger is a piece of procedural code that does one of the following:

- Prevents something from happening, such as canceling an INSERT, UPDATE, or DELETE if certain conditions aren't met
- Does something instead of the requested INSERT, UPDATE, or DELETE
- Does something else in addition to the INSERT, UPDATE, or DELETE command

Triggers can never be applied to SELECT events.

> **TRIGGERS ON VIEWS, AUTO-UPDATEABLE VIEWS** Since PostgreSQL 9.1, views can have triggers. From 9.1 onwards, the use of triggers is favored over the use of rules even when applied to views.

Triggers are based on rows, statements, or data definition language (DDL) events. Row-based triggers are executed for each row participating in an INSERT, UPDATE, or DELETE operation. Statement-based triggers are rarely used except for statement-logging purposes, so we won't cover them here. Statement-based triggers get called once for each UPDATE, DELETE, or INSERT statement. DDL event triggers are a new feature in PostgreSQL 9.3 and are used in response to DDL events, such as the creation of a table, constraint, table column, view, and so on.

In PostgreSQL, you have many language choices for writing triggers, except for SQL. Only rules support SQL; triggers must be standalone functions. Popular languages for authoring functions in PostgreSQL are PL/pgSQL, PL/Python, PL/R, PL/V8, and C. You could even develop your own language should you choose to do so. You can also have multiple triggers on a table with each trigger written in a different language that's better suited for each particular task.

WHEN TO USE RULES AND WHEN TO USE TRIGGERS

Broadly speaking, triggers are more powerful than rules, but they must be executed for each row. For bulk loads, rules can often be faster because they're called once per `UPDATE` or `INSERT` statement, whereas triggers are called for each row needing an `UPDATE` or `INSERT`. In situations where only a few rows are involved, the speed difference between rules and triggers is negligible.

In certain situations, only rules can be used. Should you need to bind to a view, only rules will work for versions of PostgreSQL prior to 9.1.

Triggers are more predictable in behavior than rules and are also found in other databases. The general trend of the PostgreSQL community is to use triggers for most things where rules were formerly used, and in the future to deprecate rules or possibly remove them entirely.

Here are some general rules of thumb we follow. Use rules in the following situations:

- When creating a select-only view. This is automatically done for you.
- When making a view updatable prior to PostgreSQL 9.1. Since PostgreSQL 9.1, you should generally use triggers to make views updatable.
- When doing bulk loads, if that's all you're doing.

Use triggers in these situations:

- When redirecting inserts from parent tables to child tables.
- When preprocessing data such as converting lon/lat to geometry/geography or geotagging data.
- When doing complex validation, or in situations where your logic is better written in a procedural language other than SQL.
- When you need to run `CREATE TABLE` or other DDL statements in response to changes in data.

The most important thing to keep in mind is that despite their overlap in achieving the same goal, rules and triggers are fundamentally different. Rules rewrite SQL statements. Triggers (the common row-based triggers) run a function for each affected row.

14.4.2 Using rules

In the auto-updateable view created in listing 14.8, the default insert behavior isn't what you'd want, because the feature_type columns won't be set. To fix that issue, you can override the default insert behavior with a `DO INSTEAD` rule, as follows:

```
CREATE OR REPLACE RULE rule_subway_insert AS
ON INSERT TO ch14.subways
DO INSTEAD
```

```
    INSERT INTO ch14.paris_points (
        gid, osm_id, ar_num, feature_name, feature_type, geom
    )
    VALUES (
        DEFAULT,
        NEW.osm_id,
        NEW.ar_num,
        NEW.feature_name,
        'subway',
        NEW.geom
    );
```

To test this insert rule, you can re-add the station you deleted:

```
INSERT INTO ch14.subways(osm_id, geom)
SELECT osm_id, geom
FROM ch14.paris_hetero WHERE osm_id = 243496729;
```

If you query the view for that subway, you'll find it, and for PostgreSQL 9.3, the default column value for feature_name is used, even though you didn't explicitly insert into the feature_name column.

14.4.3 Using triggers

When it comes to triggers, we must expand the three core events of `INSERT`, `UPDATE`, and `DELETE` to six: `BEFORE INSERT`, `AFTER INSERT`, `BEFORE UPDATE`, `AFTER UPDATE`, `BEFORE DELETE`, and `AFTER DELETE`. `BEFORE` events fire prior to the execution of the triggering command, and `AFTER` events fire upon completion.

Should you wish to perform an alternative action, as you can with a `DO INSTEAD` rule, you'd create a trigger and bind it to the `BEFORE` event but throw out the resulting record. If you need to modify data that will be inserted or updated, you also need to do this in a `BEFORE` event. An `AFTER` trigger would be too late.

Should you wish to perform some operation that depends on the success of your main action, you'll need to bind to an `AFTER` event. Examples of this are if you need to insert or update a related table on the success of an `INSERT` or `UPDATE` statement, as when logging changed records or sending emails on the completion of a task.

In the case of DDL triggers, there are far more events. The creation, deletion, and alteration of PostgreSQL object types such as tables, views, constraints, and so on each have their own events. For the full list of DDL events supported in PostgreSQL 9.3+, refer to the PostgreSQL event-triggering matrix (www.postgresql.org/docs/current/interactive/event-trigger-matrix.html). We describe one use case for DDL event triggers in the article, "Materialized geometry_columns using Event Triggers," in the Postgres OnLine Journal (www.postgresonline.com/journal/archives/314-Materialized-geometry_columns-using-Event-Triggers.html).

PostgreSQL triggers are implemented as a special type of function called a *trigger function* and then are bound to a table or DDL event. This extra level of indirection means you can reuse the same trigger function for different events, tables, and views.

The slight inconvenience is that you face a two-step process of first defining the trigger function and then binding it to a table, view, or DDL event.

PostgreSQL allows you to define multiple triggers per event per table, but each trigger must be uniquely named across the table. Triggers fire in alphabetical sequence. If your database is trigger-happy, we recommend developing a convention for naming your triggers to keep them organized.

We'll now move on to a series of examples showcasing how you can use triggers in a variety of situations to fortify your data model. Triggers are powerful tools, and your mastery of them will allow you to develop database applications that can control business logic without the need to touch the front-end application.

REDIRECTING INSERTS WITH BEFORE TRIGGERS

For our first trigger example, we'll demonstrate how to redirect inserts on a parent table to the child tables. This is a common need when working with inherited tables.

Recall that in an inheritance hierarchy with abstract parents, you want people to think they're inserting into the parent table, but you don't want any data going into it. To accomplish this, you can use a `BEFORE INSERT` trigger to redirect inserts into child tables. The function checks the geometry type of the record being inserted into the table, and depending on the geometry type, you redirect the insert to one of the child tables. For geometry types that don't fit, you toss them into a rejects table created with the following code:

```
CREATE TABLE ch14.paris_rejects (
    gid integer NOT NULL PRIMARY KEY,
    osm_id integer,
    ar_num integer,
    feature_name varchar(200),
    feature_type varchar(50),
    geom geometry, tags hstore
);
```

The accompanying `BEFORE INSERT` trigger is shown in the following listing.

Listing 14.9 PL/pgSQL `BEFORE INSERT` trigger function to redirect inserts

```
CREATE OR REPLACE FUNCTION ch14.trigger_paris_insert()
RETURNS trigger AS
$$
DECLARE
    var_geomtype text;
BEGIN
    var_geomtype := geometrytype(NEW.geom);            <-- 1 Use temporary variables
    IF var_geomtype IN ('MULTIPOLYGON', 'POLYGON') THEN
        NEW.geom := ST_Multi(NEW.geom);
        INSERT INTO ch14.paris_polygons(
            gid,osm_id,ar_num,feature_name,feature_type,geom,tags
        )
        SELECT gid,osm_id,ar_num,feature_name,feature_type,geom,tags
        FROM (SELECT NEW.*) As foo;                    <-- 2 NEW is alias for table that contains new record
    ELSIF var_geomtype = 'POINT' THEN
```

```
        INSERT INTO ch14.paris_points (
            gid,osm_id,ar_num,feature_name,feature_type,geom,tags
        )
        SELECT gid,osm_id,ar_num,feature_name,feature_type,geom,tags
        FROM (SELECT NEW.*) As foo;
    ELSIF var_geomtype = 'LINESTRING' THEN
        INSERT INTO ch14.paris_linestrings (
            gid,osm_id,ar_num,feature_name,feature_type,geom,tags
        )
        SELECT gid,osm_id,ar_num,feature_name,feature_type,geom,tags
        FROM (SELECT NEW.*) As foo;
    ELSE
        INSERT INTO ch14.paris_rejects (
            gid,osm_id,ar_num,feature_name,feature_type,geom,tags
        )
        SELECT gid,osm_id,ar_num,feature_name,feature_type,geom,tags
        FROM (SELECT NEW.*) As foo;        <-- 3 Nonstandard geometry types go into rejects table

    END IF;
    RETURN NULL;        <-- 4 Cancel original insert
END;
$$
LANGUAGE 'plpgsql' VOLATILE;
```

In listing 14.9 you declare a temporary variable to hold intermediary information ❶. This can reduce processing time for long-running functions, plus you end up with clearer code.

During an insert operation, PostgreSQL automatically dumps the new record into a single-row table, aliased `NEW`, with the same structure as the table being inserted into. You then take advantage of this alias to read the values of the geometry type of the new record coming in to decide which child table to redirect the insert to ❷. If the geometry type is something like a geometry collection or some type you don't have a specific table set up for, you dump it into a paris_rejects table ❸.

Normally when you finish with a `BEFORE` trigger, you return the new record, which you may have changed in the trigger. This signals to PostgreSQL that it can continue with the `INSERT`. In this case, however, you want to halt the `INSERT` into the parent table altogether, so you return `NULL` instead of `NEW` ❹. Returning the `NEW` record is usually only done in a `BEFORE` trigger, because in an `AFTER` trigger the event has already happened, so there's no hope of being able to change the record being inserted or updated. This is a common mistake people make—defining an `AFTER` trigger and then trying to change the `NEW` record. PostgreSQL will let you do that, but the changes will never make it into the underlying table.

Remember that trigger functions do you no good unless they're bound to a table event. To bind the previous trigger function to the `BEFORE INSERT` of the paris table, you can run this statement:

```
CREATE TRIGGER trigger1_paris_insert BEFORE INSERT
ON ch14.paris FOR EACH ROW
EXECUTE PROCEDURE ch14.trigger_paris_insert();
```

Using NEW.* without specifying column names in rules and triggers

In trigger functions, you'll often see the use of `NEW.*` as shorthand to pick up all the columns of the record being inserted. The single-row NEW table not only has the same structure, but it also has the same column order as the triggering table. This often allows you to use the following insert syntax without worrying about listing each column:

```
INSERT INTO ch03.paris_rejects VALUES(NEW.*);
```

For the Paris example, we chose not to use this syntax. This syntax is extremely powerful because you can use it in any trigger function without knowing beforehand what the columns are or will be, but it's not without danger.

The danger of this approach arises when you're redirecting inserts to child tables. A child table may have more columns than its parent, or the same columns in a different order; this syntax will fail in such cases.

Let's take this new trigger for a test drive. But before you do, you need to delete any data you have thus far, to get a clean start. As long as you have no foreign-key constraints, you can use the fast SQL `TRUNCATE` clause to delete data from the parent table and all of its child tables:

```
TRUNCATE TABLE ch14.paris;
```

Now when you perform your insert with the trigger in place, the records will sort themselves into child tables befitting their respective geometry types.

```
SELECT osm_id, geom, tags FROM ch03.paris_hetero;
```

Because you never created a child table for multilinestrings, these records will end up in the paris_rejects table.

CREATING TABLES ON THE FLY WITH TRIGGERS

Triggers allow you to do something you can't do with rules. You can generate SQL statements on the fly and execute them as part of your trigger function. You can even run SQL that will create new database objects, which is what we'll demonstrate in the next example.

Dynamic table creation in triggers

Dynamic table creation in a trigger is overkill for the few arrondissements in our example, and the same applies if you know the tables you'll need beforehand. It's more efficient to create the tables at the outset than to have each insert check and then create tables as needed, but you could imagine cases where this may not be possible. For example, you might have a large amount of financial data that you'd like to break out into weekly tables. If you anticipate your database being in use for 10 years, you'd have to prepare 520 tables at the start. Not only that, but on the first day of the eleventh year, your database would fail.

Suppose you want to partition your Paris data by arrondissements in addition to geometry type, but you're too lazy to create all 60 geometry-arrondissement tables beforehand. You can delegate the work to a trigger function. As you insert new records into the parent table, it will redirect inserts to each geometry-type child table, which in turn will redirect inserts to each geometry-arrondissement grandchild table as appropriate. Furthermore, if the particular grandchild geometry-arrondissement table doesn't exist, the trigger function will create it.

The following listing shows a trigger that creates tables as needed.

Listing 14.10 Trigger that dynamically creates tables as needed

```
CREATE OR REPLACE FUNCTION ch14.trigger_paris_child_insert()
RETURNS TRIGGER AS
$$
DECLARE
    var_sql text;
    var_tbl text;
BEGIN
    var_tbl :=
        TG_TABLE_NAME || '_ar' || lpad(NEW.ar_num::text,2,'0');      -- 1 Assign destination table name to variable
    IF NOT EXISTS (
        SELECT *
        FROM information_schema.tables                               -- 2 Check if destination table exists
        WHERE table_schema = TG_TABLE_SCHEMA AND table_name = var_tbl)
    THEN
        var_sql :=
            'CREATE TABLE ' || TG_TABLE_SCHEMA || '.' || var_tbl ||
            '(CONSTRAINT pk_' || var_tbl ||
            ' PRIMARY KEY(gid)) INHERITS (' || TG_TABLE_SCHEMA ||
            '.' || TG_TABLE_NAME  || '); CREATE INDEX idx_' ||
            var_tbl || '_geom ON ' || TG_TABLE_SCHEMA || '.' ||
            var_tbl || ' USING gist(geom); ALTER TABLE ' ||
            TG_TABLE_SCHEMA || '.' || var_tbl ||
            ' ADD CONSTRAINT chk_ar_num CHECK (ar_num = ' ||
            NEW.ar_num::text || ');';
        EXECUTE var_sql;                                              -- 3 Create destination table if absent
    END IF;
    var_sql :=
        'INSERT INTO ' || TG_TABLE_SCHEMA || '.' || var_tbl ||
        '(gid,osm_id,ar_num,feature_name,feature_type,geom,tags) ' ||
        'VALUES($1,$2,$3,$4,$5,$6,$7)';                               -- 4 Prepare and execute insert SQL
    EXECUTE var_sql
    USING
        NEW.gid,NEW.osm_id,NEW.ar_num,NEW.feature_name,
        NEW.feature_type,NEW.geom,NEW.tags;
    RETURN NULL;                                                      -- 5 Cancel original insert
END;
$$ language plpgsql;
```

Before you do anything, you must settle on a naming convention for all of your geometry-arrondissement grandchild tables. In this example, we chose paris_points_ar01 through paris_points_ar20, paris_linestrings_ar01 through paris_linestrings_ar20, and paris_polygons_ar01 through paris_polygons_ar20. You then formulate the destination table name of the new record ❶. Notice how PostgreSQL provides a `TG_TABLE_NAME` variable that tells you the table to which the current trigger is bound. Without this, you'd have to further test the geometry type of the new record to figure out the destination table.

Next, you check to see if the destination table is present ❷. If not, you create it ❸. Now you're assured that the destination table must be present, and you can proceed with the insert ❹. Normally you'd return `TRIGGER` if you wanted the insert into the child table to complete, but because you replaced it with an alternative insert, you return `NULL` to cancel the original insert ❺.

Once you have the trigger function, you can bind it to the three child tables: paris_points, paris_linestrings, and paris_polygons, as shown in the following listing.

Listing 14.11 Binding the same trigger function to multiple tables

```
CREATE TRIGGER trig01_paris_child_insert BEFORE INSERT
ON ch14.paris_polygons FOR EACH ROW
EXECUTE PROCEDURE ch14.trigger_paris_child_insert();

CREATE TRIGGER trig01_paris_child_insert BEFORE INSERT
ON ch14.paris_points FOR EACH ROW
EXECUTE PROCEDURE ch14.trigger_paris_child_insert();

CREATE TRIGGER trig01_paris_child_insert BEFORE INSERT
ON ch14.paris_linestrings FOR EACH ROW
EXECUTE PROCEDURE ch14.trigger_paris_child_insert();
```

Once in place, these three triggers will prevent data from being inserted into the child tables and instead will have the data flow to arrondissement-specific grandchild tables. If the grandchild is missing, it's created on the fly.

To test the new trigger, you can delete all the data you've inserted and start anew:

```
TRUNCATE TABLE ch14.paris;
TRUNCATE TABLE ch14.paris_rejects;
```

Then perform the insert:

```
INSERT INTO ch14.paris(osm_id, geom, tags, ar_num)
SELECT osm_id, geom, tags, ar_num
FROM ch14.paris_hetero;
```

After you've finished, and provided you have data to fully span all 3 geometry types and 20 arrondissements, you should end up with 60 tables. Our particular data set will only require the creation of 9 tables.

Before bringing this discussion of rules and triggers to an end, let's revisit constraint exclusions. Remember how before we began the preceding extended example, we described the usefulness of having the constraint exclusion enabled? To test that the constraint exclusion is working correctly, run the following query and look at the pgAdmin graphical explain plan:

```
SELECT * FROM ch14.paris WHERE ar_num = 17;
```

The graphical explain plan output for this query is shown in figure 14.3.

Observe that although there are tables such as paris_points_ar01, paris_polygons_ar08, and so on, the planner strategically skips over those tables because we asked only for data found in ar_17 tables. Constraint exclusion works!

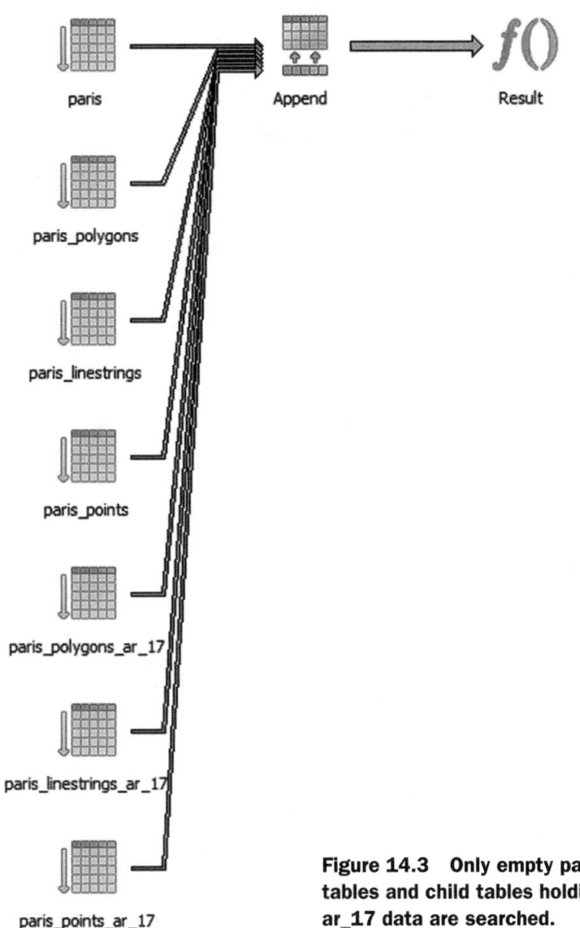

Figure 14.3 Only empty parent tables and child tables holding ar_17 data are searched.

14.5 Summary

In this chapter, we discussed some approaches you can use for storing PostGIS geometry data in PostgreSQL relational tables, as well as for managing this data. We also demonstrated the use of the PostgreSQL custom key/value `hstore` data type for implementing schemaless models. We followed up by applying these approaches to storing Parisian data.

We demonstrated in this chapter that PostGIS geometry columns are like other columns you'll find in relational tables. They have indexes and are stored along with other related data, such as text columns. Like other data types, they take advantage of all the facilities that the database has to offer, such as inheritance, triggers, rules, indexes, and so forth. In addition, you can inspect geometries using various geometry functions designed for them and can even use them in SQL join conditions as you would other relational data types.

This chapter also reinforced the use of some of the PostGIS functions we explored in prior chapters. In the next chapter, we'll focus on performance tuning.

15 Query performance tuning

This chapter covers

- Planner basics
- Reading plans
- Common query patterns
- Spatial processing for better performance
- Influencing plans

When dealing with several tables at once—especially large ones—tuning queries becomes a major consideration. The way you write your queries is also important. Two queries can return exactly the same data, but one can take a hundred times longer to finish. The complexity of spatial objects, memory allocation, and even storage affects performance.

In this chapter, you'll learn

- How to use the planner and read query plans
- How to write efficient queries
- How to monitor query performance
- How to organize spatial data to improve query performance

Much of this information has more to do with PostgreSQL proper and SQL in general, but PostGIS piggybacks on PostgreSQL. Learning more about PostgreSQL and how it executes queries will not only make your non-spatial queries faster, but will also improve your spatial queries significantly.

The data and code used in this chapter can be found at www.postgis.us/chapter_15_edition_2. Some examples also use data from prior chapters.

15.1 The query planner

All relational databases employ a query planner to digest the raw SQL statement prior to executing the query. But the planner isn't perfect, and it can optimize some SQL statements better than others.

The query planner parses SQL into execution steps and decides which indexes, if any, and which search strategies it should use. It bases its plans on various heuristics and on its knowledge of the data distribution. It knows something that you often don't know: how your data is distributed at any point in time. It won't, however, relieve you of having to write efficient queries.

The query planner has many options to choose from, especially when joining tables. The planner can choose certain indexes over others, the order in which it navigates these indexes, and which navigation strategies (nested loops, bitmap scans, sequential scans, index scans, hash joins, and the like) it will use. All these play a role in the speed and efficiency of the queries.

It's only partly true that SQL is a declarative language that allows you to state a request without worrying about the way it's eventually implemented. The database planner may use one approach one day and a different approach the next day for the same query because the distribution of data has changed. In practice, the way you state your question can greatly influence the way the planner answers it. The plan that the planner chooses has a direct impact on speed. This is why all high-end databases provide *explain plans* or *show plans* to give you a glimpse of the planner's strategy. SQL only allows you to ask questions and not to define explicit steps, but you should still take care in how you ask your questions.

15.1.1 Different kinds of spatial queries

The spatial world of PostGIS offers some classic examples of how asking the same question in different ways results in vastly different performance. Here are some examples.

N-CLOSEST THINGS WITHIN A DISTANCE RANGE

One such example is asking for the top five closest objects, which we covered in chapter 10. If you ask this literally, you force the PostgreSQL planner to do a table scan of all records, rank them all by distance, and pick the top five. Alternatively, you can ask for the top five closest within 10 miles and achieve the same result but much faster. In the second case, the planner can use a spatial index to throw out all objects that aren't within ten miles (10 × 1609 meters) and then scan the remaining objects. You don't necessarily care about the ten miles and don't want to make that a requirement, but it makes the planner's task simpler.

An example of what the two different SQL statements look like is shown in the following code. First, the fast way:

```
SELECT restaurant_name
FROM restaurants
WHERE ST_DWithin(ST_GeogFromText(...),restaurants.geog,10*1609)
ORDER BY ST_Distance(ST_GeogFromText(...),restaurants.geog)
LIMIT 5;
```

Next is the slower but more obvious way:

```
SELECT restaurant_name
FROM restaurants
ORDER BY ST_Distance(ST_GeogFromText('),restaurants.geog)
LIMIT 5;
```

Granted, the faster way does require you to have some knowledge of the data: that there are at least five restaurants within ten miles.

THINGS NOT NEAR ANYTHING

Another example is what we call the left-handed trick (or anti-join). In this case, you want to know everything that doesn't fit a particular criterion, but the straightforward way often leads to inefficient planner strategies. Instead, you ask to collect all objects that meet a criterion that's capable of using an index, as well as the ones that don't, and throw out the ones meeting the criterion. Surprisingly, this works pretty well for most relational databases, whereas the straightforward question isn't as often converted to an efficient strategy.

Here's an example of the left-handed trick that gives you all restaurants further than 100 meters from any road:

```
SELECT restaurant_name
FROM restaurants LEFT JOIN roads
ON ST_DWithin(restaurants.geog,roads.geog,100)
WHERE roads.gid IS NULL;
```

The way it works is that a left join always returns all records from the left table (restaurant, in this case) and creates one NULL row with NULL placeholders where there's no match for the right table (roads). So in this case the roads primary key will be NULL if the "within 100 meters" condition is not met.

N-CLOSEST THINGS REGARDLESS OF RANGE

Since PostgreSQL 9.1 and PostGIS 2.0, we've gained the KNN GiST bounding box (<#>) and bounding-box centroid (<->) distance operators, which have reduced the need for doing `ST_DWithin` for geometry types. You saw an example of this in chapter 10. A KNN GiST query allows you to not specify a range of proximity and instead order by proximity. All the index action happens in the `ORDER BY` clause.

These distance operators have a couple of limitations:

- They only compare bounding-box or centroid bounding-box proximity, so they're only exact for point geometry to point geometry comparisons.
- They only work for the geometry type, and one of the geometries has to be kept constant in the query.

You can partly compensate for the constant geometry issue by using subqueries, or in PostgreSQL 9.3 by using a LATERAL clause, which you saw examples of in chapter 10.

A KNN GiST query takes the following form:

```
WITH x AS (
    SELECT restaurant_name, geom FROM restaurants
    ORDER BY ST_GeomFromText(...) <#> restaurants.geom
    LIMIT 100
)
SELECT restaurant_name FROM x
ORDER BY ST_Distance(ST_GeomFromText(''), restaurants.geom) LIMIT 5;
```

15.1.2 Common table expressions and how they affect plans

Another important feature you've learned about is common table expressions (CTEs), which are demonstrated in the prior example and discussed in appendix C. We've also used them in various places in the book. CTEs allow you to break a complex query into more manageable subqueries and reuse any subqueries in subsequent CTE subexpressions and the final result.

CTEs are not only syntactical sugar; they also affect how the planner plans things for both good and bad. All table expressions in the CTE are materialized, meaning that a temporary work table is created behind the scenes, and generally each subexpression is planned as if it were a separate query. Materialization is good if you have costly expressions like distance, because the computation will be done only once. But if your subexpression returns a huge table, that table probably utilizes much more memory than a similar subquery embedded in a larger query.

Because a CTE subexpression is treated as a single unit of work and is materialized, subsequent references to it can't take advantage of whatever indexes it used in the base tables, as would happen if a subquery within the main query were used. As such, if you use CTEs heavily and run into performance issues with a CTE, you should try rewriting them using regular subqueries or minimize the number of rows each of your subtable expressions returns.

We'll delve into some of these different ways of writing queries later in this chapter along with other planner topics, such as PostgreSQL settings, as we examine real case scenarios.

15.2 Planner statistics

The planner uses data statistics as well as various server configurations (allocated memory, shared buffers, random page costs, and the like) to make its decisions. Most relational databases use planner statistics as input to their planner cost strategies. Planner statistics are updated in PostgreSQL when you do a

```
vacuum analyze sometable;
```

or during one of PostgreSQL's automated vacuum runs if you have autovacuum enabled. Note that from PostgreSQL 8.3 on, autovacuum is enabled unless you explicitly disable it in your postgresql.conf file. In addition, from PostgreSQL 8.3 on, you can selectively set the frequency of vacuum runs or turn off automated vacuuming for certain tables if you want. Selectively controlling vacuum settings for problem tables is a better option than disabling autovacuum altogether.

A `vacuum analyze` will both get rid of dead rows as well as update planner statistics for a table. For bulk inserts and updates, it's best to do a `vacuum analyze` of the table after a large load rather than waiting for PostgreSQL's vacuum run.

You can also do a plain

```
analyze sometable verbose;
```

if you want to update the statistics without getting rid of dead tuples and want to see the progress of the analyze.

If you call `analyze` or `vacuum analyze` without a table name, it will analyze all tables in the database.

Planner statistics are a summary of the distinct values in a table and a simple histogram of the distribution of common values in a table. You can get a sense of what they look like by first updating the statistics with this command:

```
vacuum analyze ch01.restaurants;
```

Then run the following query.

Listing 15.1 Planner statistics query

```
SELECT
    attname As colname,
    n_distinct,
    array_to_string(most_common_vals, E'\n') AS common_vals,
    array_to_string(most_common_freqs, E'\n') As dist_freq
FROM pg_stats
WHERE schemaname = 'ch01' AND tablename = 'restaurants';
```

The result of listing 15.1 is shown next.

Listing 15.2 Output for the planner statistics query

```
 colname   | n_distinct | common_vals | dist_freq
-----------+------------+-------------+------------
 id        |         -1 |             |
 franchise |         10 | MCD        +| 0.274433  +
           |            | BKG        +| 0.1479    +
           |            | TCB        +| 0.1248    +
           |            | WDY        +| 0.122767  +
```

```
            |         | PZH      +| 0.122467   +
            |         | KFC      +| 0.107233   +
            |         | JIB      +| 0.0408333 +
            |         | HDE      +| 0.0354333 +
            |         | CJR      +| 0.02       +
            |         | INO       | 0.00413333
geom        |      -1 |           |
```

Having -1 in the n_distinct column means that the values are more or less unique across the table in that column. A number less than 1 but greater than 0 in the n_distinct column tells you the percentage of records that are unique. If you see a number greater than 1 in n_distinct, that's usually the exact number of distinct records found. The common_vals array column lists the most commonly observed values, and the corresponding dist_freq denotes the percentages of those common values.

For example, the value of 10 for franchise in the n_distinct column tells us that there are 10 franchises represented, with the value MCD being about 27% of the records, as denoted by 0.274433 in the dist_freq column. This is useful to the planner, because it can use this information to decide the order in which it will navigate tables and apply indexes as well as to plan the strategy. It can determine whether using an index or doing a sequential scan is faster. If most values in the column are the same, and a common value is filtered for in the WHERE, the planner would generally opt to do a sequential scan. It can also guess whether a nested loop is more efficient than a hash by looking at the WHERE and JOIN conditions of a query and estimating the number of results from each table.

Planner statistics sampling

The planner analyzes a sample of the records when analyze is run. The number of records sampled is usually about 10% but varies depending on the size of the table and the default_statistics_target.

You can set planner statistics separately for each column in a table if you want more or fewer records to be sampled. You do this using

```
ALTER TABLE ALTER COLUMN somecolumn SET STATISTICS somevalue
```

We'll cover this in more detail in appendix D.

In the next section we'll look into the mind of the planner and investigate how it reasons about the queries it has to assess.

15.3 Using explain to diagnose problems

There are a few items you should look for when troubleshooting query performance:

- What indexes, if any, are being used?
- What is the order of function evaluation?

- In what order are the indexes being applied?
- What strategies are used; for example, nested loop, hash join, merge join, bitmap, sequential scan?
- What are the calculated versus the actual costs?
- How many rows are scanned?

The explain plan (particularly `explain analyze`, which gives the actual plan) of a query answers all these questions. In this section, you'll see various explain plans of queries. You'll look at both plain-text explain outputs and graphical outputs. As you look at these plans, we want you to consider the explain output and observe what answers it gives to the previous questions.

PostgreSQL, like most relational databases, allows you to view both actual and planned execution plans.

There are three levels of explain plans in PostgreSQL:

- `EXPLAIN` doesn't try to run the query but provides the general approach that will be taken, without extensive analysis.
- `EXPLAIN ANALYZE` runs the query but doesn't return an answer. It generates the true plan and timings without returning results. As a result, it tends to be much slower than a simple `EXPLAIN` and takes at least the amount of time needed to run the query (minus any network effects of returning the data). In addition to the rows estimated, it provides actual row counts and timings for each step. It also indicates the amount of memory used. Comparing the actual row counts against the estimated ones is a good way of telling if your planner statistics are out of date.
- `EXPLAIN ANALYZE VERBOSE` does an in-depth plan analysis that also includes more information, such as the columns being output.

15.3.1 Text explain versus pgAdmin graphical explain

There are two kinds of plan displays you can use in PostgreSQL: textual explain plans and graphical explain plans. Each caters to a different audience or a different state of mind. We enjoy using both, but generally we find the graphical explain plans easier to scan, more visually appealing, and, as a rule of thumb, a good place to focus our efforts.

In this section, we'll experiment with both. There are many PostgreSQL tools that provide graphical explain plans and textual explain plans, and all are different in look, ability to print, and so on. For this study we'll focus on the pgAdmin III graphical explain plan, which is often packaged with PostgreSQL and available as a free download, and on the native raw text explain plan output by PostgreSQL.

WHAT IS A TEXT EXPLAIN?

A text explain is the raw format of an explain output by the database. This is a common feature that can be found in most relational databases. The text explain in

PostgreSQL is presented as indented text to demonstrate the ordering of operations and the nesting of suboperations. You can output it using psql or pgAdmin III. For outputting nicely formatted text explains, the psql interface tends to be a bit better than pgAdmin III. There's also an online plan analyzer that outputs text plans nicely and highlights rows that you should be concerned about; it's available at http://explain.depesz.com/help.

PostgreSQL since version 9.0 has had the ability to output the text explain in XML, JSON, and YAML formats. This provides more options for analyzing and viewing explain plans. We have an example of prettifying and making the JSON plan interactive using JQuery on the Postgres OnLine Journal at www.postgresonline.com/journal/archives/174-pgexplain90formats_part2.html.

A textual explain plan generally provides more information than a graphical explain plan, which we'll discuss next, but tends to be harder to read and even sometimes provides too much information.

WHAT IS A GRAPHICAL EXPLAIN?

A graphical explain is a diagrammatic view of a text explain. You can glean information such as how the planner navigated the data, which functions it processed, and what strategies it chose. The pgAdmin III graphical explain plan is replete with eye candy, with distinct icons to represent aggregations, hash joins, bitmap scans, and CTEs. Tooltips pop up to guide you when you mouse over elements. PgAdmin III thoughtfully varies the thickness of the arrows linking one step to another, with thicker arrows representing more costly steps. With versions of pgAdmin III above 1.10, you can even save the plan as an image file.

In the next set of exercises, we'll scrutinize plans and elaborate on what they're telling you. We'll examine both textual plans and graphical explain plans.

15.3.2 The plan with no index

We purposely didn't index our tables, so that we could demonstrate what a plan without an index looks like. A text explain is a tree composed of plan nodes that define basic strategy. At the bottom of the tree are scan nodes that collect the data. The very top of the tree shows costs, which are the sums of all nodes below.

Listing 15.3 EXPLAIN query sans index

```
EXPLAIN
SELECT t.town, r.rt_number
FROM
    ch15.ma_towns AS t
    INNER JOIN
    ch15.ma_roads As r
    ON ST_Intersects(t.geom,r.geom)
WHERE r.rt_number = '9';
```

The result of listing 15.3 is shown in the next listing.

Listing 15.4 Planner sans index output of EXPLAIN

```
QUERY PLAN
-----------------------------------------------------------
Nested Loop (cost=0.00..613.09 rows=1 width=28)
    Join Filter: ((t.geom && r.geom) AND _st_intersects(t.geom, r.geom))
    -> Seq Scan on ma_roads r
        (cost=0.00..3.38 rows=1 width=52)
        Filter: ((rt_number)::text = '9'::text)
    -> Seq Scan on ma_towns t
        (cost=0.00..283.43 rows=1243 width=8287)
(5 rows)
```

The text explain plan in listing 15.4 tells you the planner's strategy and estimates the cost for each step. EXPLAIN doesn't execute the query, so it's faster than EXPLAIN ANALYZE.

The planner internally decomposed the ST_Intersects function into two functions: an && operator to perform an initial bounding-box intersection check and _ST_Intersects to perform the intersection check proper. The planner can only peek inside functions written in the SQL language (not other PLs). This procedure is called *inlining a function.* The planner removes the function definition and treats the code within the function as SQL statements. Inlining allows the planner to decompose and reorder the SQL to achieve better performance. For the most part, inlining is beneficial, though we've seen a few cases where it distracts the planner from more through analysis or engages a superfluous index.

In the next listing, we repeat the query in listing 15.3 but use EXPLAIN ANALYZE.

Listing 15.5 Planner sans index EXPLAIN ANALYZE query

```
EXPLAIN ANALYZE
SELECT t.town, r.rt_number
FROM
    ch15.ma_towns AS t
    INNER JOIN
    ch15.ma_roads As r
    ON ST_Intersects(t.geom,r.geom)
WHERE r.rt_number = '9';
```

The result of the preceding EXPLAIN ANALYZE is shown in the following listing.

Listing 15.6 Planner sans index output of EXPLAIN ANALYZE

```
QUERY PLAN
---------------------------------------------------------------
Nested Loop
    (cost=0.00..613.09 rows=1 width=28)
    (actual time=162.391..1976.342 rows=28 loops=1)
    Join Filter: ((t.geom && r.geom) AND _st_intersects(t.geom, r.geom))
    Rows Removed by Join Filter: 1215
    -> Seq Scan on ma_roads r
        (cost=0.00..3.38 rows=1 width=52)
```

```
        (actual time=0.024..0.082 rows=1 loops=1)
        Filter: ((rt_number)::text = '9'::text)
        Rows Removed by Filter: 29
    -> Seq Scan on ma_towns t
        (cost=0.00..283.43 rows=1243 width=8287)
        (actual time=0.010..4.208 rows=1243 loops=1)
Total runtime: 1976.920 ms
(8 rows)
```

You can see that EXPLAIN ANALYZE provides more information than EXPLAIN alone. In addition to the plan, it reports the actual time each step took, the total time, the number of rows that the planner had to scan, and the number of rows removed by filters.

In the preceding example, the slowest step of the query is the nested loop. Nested loops tend to be the most time-consuming steps in a query because the planner has to wade through the records row by row. Furthermore, for each row, it must scan another set of records. Loops are unavoidable, but you'll want to filter out as many rows as possible before your query reaches the loop.

Now let's add VERBOSE to the explain. In the next listing, we'll repeat the query from listing 15.3 but use EXPLAIN ANALYZE VERBOSE.

Listing 15.7 Planner sans index EXPLAIN ANALYZE VERBOSE query

```
EXPLAIN ANALYZE VERBOSE
SELECT t.town, r.rt_number
FROM
    ch15.ma_towns AS t
    INNER JOIN
    ch15.ma_roads As r
    ON ST_Intersects(t.geom,r.geom)
WHERE r.rt_number = '9';
```

The result of the preceding EXPLAIN ANALYZE VERBOSE is shown in the next listing.

Listing 15.8 Planner sans index output of EXPLAIN ANALYZE VERBOSE

```
QUERY PLAN
-----------------------------------------------------------
Nested Loop
    (cost=0.00..613.09 rows=1 width=28)
    (actual time=145.660..1883.420 rows=28 loops=1)
    Output: t.town, r.rt_number
    Join Filter: ((t.geom && r.geom) AND _st_intersects(t.geom, r.geom))
    Rows Removed by Join Filter: 1215
    -> Seq Scan on ch15.ma_roads r
        (cost=0.00..3.38 rows=1 width=52)
        (actual time=0.018..0.033 rows=1 loops=1)
        Output: r.gid, r.admin_type, r.rt_number, r.shape_len, r.geom
        Filter: ((r.rt_number)::text = '9'::text)
        Rows Removed by Filter: 29
    -> Seq Scan on ch15.ma_towns t
        (cost=0.00..283.43 rows=1243 width=8287)
```

```
        (actual time=0.003..1.784 rows=1243 loops=1)
        Output: t.gid, t.town, t.town_id, t.pop1980, t.pop1990,
            t.pop2000, t.popch80_90, t.popch90_00, t.type, t.island,
            t.coastal_po, t.fourcolor, t.fips_stco, t.ccd_mcd,
            t.fips_place, t.fips_mcd, t.fips_count, t.acres,
            t.square_mil, t.pop2010, t.popch00_10, t.shape_area,
            t.shape_len, t.geom
Total runtime: 1883.818 ms
(11 rows)
```

The VERBOSE version tells you which columns are in the output of each step. Notice that the query is much faster than for the EXPLAIN ANALYZE run, which may be puzzling. The speed gain is due to caching. The planner is smart enough to know that if you give it the same query twice, it doesn't need to replan the second time around. Moreover, the data retrieved from the first run may still be in shared buffer memory.

The planner pays attention to whether a function is marked as *immutable* or not. A function marked as immutable should yield the same output for the same input. It can't rely on any dynamic variables that are constantly changing, such as CURRENT_TIMESTAMP. When the planner encounters an immutable function, it leans toward caching the data, because it knows that the output shouldn't vary with subsequent runs. With this in mind, you need to exercise discretion in marking functions as immutable. If your function is nothing but a series of mathematical operations, by all means, mark the function as immutable. One plus one will always equal two. But if your function draws data and you mark it as immutable, you may not always end up with the most current records.

Depending on the size of your shared_buffers setting, the planner may cache a fair amount of data in RAM. The planner will then retrieve the results from RAM rather than from disk, and this can be an order of magnitude quicker. The planner is smart enough to identify the data it needs, regardless of the query. For example, let's say you query a table of all the country names in the world. The planner retrieves the two hundred or so rows from disk and stores them in a shared buffer. If your subsequent query only asks for countries starting with the letter A, the planner will know to search in the shared buffer.

Using shared buffers to store common lookup tables leads to the concept of *prewarming*. Because accessing the memory is very fast, prewarming allows you to load small, frequently used lookup tables into shared buffers during database startup. PostgreSQL offers an extension to do exactly this: pg_prewarm. To find out more, see the article, "Caching in PostgreSQL" on the Relational Database Technologies blog: http://raghavt.blogspot.com/2012/04/caching-in-postgresql.html. pg_prewarm is included as a packaged extension in PostgreSQL 9.4+.

Now let's turn our attention to graphical explains. To summon a graphical explain in pgAdmin III, highlight the SQL statement in the query window and click the Explain Query menu option. You can optionally check the Analyze and Verbose options, as shown in figure 15.1. Note that graphical explain can't handle VERBOSE output, so if you check it, you'll end up with a text explain.

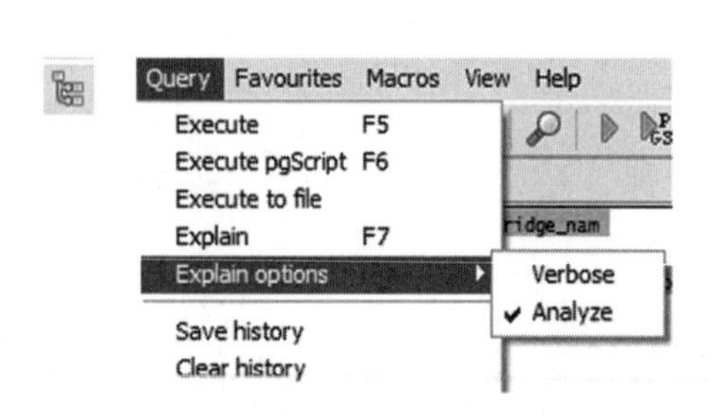

Figure 15.1 Graphical explain controls

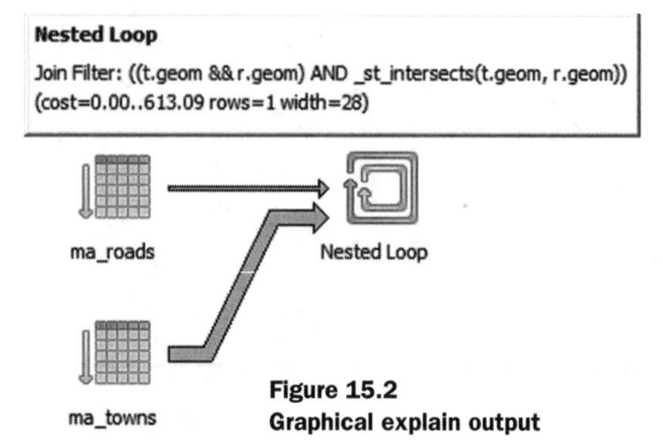

Figure 15.2 Graphical explain output

Figure 15.2 shows the diagram generated by the graphical explain.

You can follow the graphical explain from left to right. The nested loop is the last operation and is therefore in the right-most position. One nicety about the graphical explain is the way it uses the thickness of the arrows to convey the cost of a step: the thicker the arrow line, the more costly the step. Hovering over an icon in the diagram brings up a tooltip, which provides some of the details found in the text explain. The tooltips declutter the output. You can review each step one at a time, instead of having all the details of all the steps displayed in one long piece of continuous text.

In the next section, you'll see what a plan with indexes looks like by rerunning the same query after adding spatial indexes and vacuum analyzing tables.

15.4 Planner and indexes

The main families of indexes in PostgreSQL are B-tree, generalized search tree (GiST), and generalized inverted tree (GIN). Data type, organization of the data within the table, and query practices dictate which kind of index will be most useful. PostGIS, pgSphere, and full test search (FTS) objects all can use GiST. FTS and hstore can also use GIN.

GIN indexes tend to take up more space than GiST, but they aren't lossy. Spatially speaking, this means the GIN indexes the geometry itself rather than just the bounding box.

New to market is the spatial GiST index (SPGiST). Currently only built-in PostgreSQL geometry types (not PostGIS types), text, and pg_trgm can use SPGiST. SPGiST support is on the roadmap for PostGIS 2.2.

B-tree is the most popular index for basic PostgreSQL data types, such as character varying and numbers. Hash indexes have fallen out of favor because they're slower than B-tree and GiST with no compensating advantages.

In this chapter, we'll focus on GiST. This should be the index of choice for PostGIS spatial types (geometry, geography, raster). Unlike the previous section, here you'll need to make sure you have spatial indexes in place.

15.4.1 The plan with a spatial index

You already saw examples of how the planner performs without the help of indexes. In the next examples, we'll help the planner out by adding spatial indexes to the table. Observe how the planner reacts to this positive change of events.

Listing 15.9 Planner with index

```
CREATE INDEX idx_ch15_ma_towns_geom
ON ch15.ma_towns USING gist (geom) WITH (FILLFACTOR=90);      <-- ❶ Add spatial indexes

CREATE INDEX idx_ch15_ma_roads_geom
ON ch15.ma_roads USING gist (geom) WITH (FILLFACTOR=90);

EXPLAIN ANALYZE VERBOSE
SELECT t.town, r.rt_number                <-- ❷ Show explain
FROM
    ch15.ma_towns AS t
    INNER JOIN
    ch15.ma_roads As r
    ON ST_Intersects(t.geom, r.geom)
WHERE r.rt_number = '9';
```

Here you index the tables ❶. Then you run `EXPLAIN ANALYZE VERBOSE` on the query to see how the plan changed as a result of adding indexes ❷.

The following listing shows the explain plan with an index in place. Compare this to the plan of the same query without an index shown in listing 15.4.

Listing 15.10 Planner with index output of `EXPLAIN ANALYZE VERBOSE`

```
QUERY PLAN
----------------------------------------------------
Nested Loop
    (cost=0.14..11.80 rows=180 width=11)
    (actual time=69.609..646.638 rows=28 loops=1)
    Output: t.town, r.rt_number
    -> Seq Scan on ch15.ma_roads r
        (cost=0.00..3.38 rows=1 width=68346)
        (actual time=0.013..0.031 rows=1 loops=1)
        Output: r.gid, r.admin_type, r.rt_number, r.shape_len, r.geom
        Filter: ((r.rt_number)::text = '9'::text)
        Rows Removed by Filter: 29
    -> Index Scan using idx_ch15_ma_towns on ch15.ma_towns t
        (cost=0.14..8.41 rows=1 width=8287)
        (actual time=68.357..645.262 rows=28 loops=1)
        Output: t.gid, t.town, t.town_id, t.pop1980, t.pop1990,
            t.pop2000, t.popch80_90, t.popch90_00, t.type, t.island,
            t.coastal_po, t.fourcolor, t.fips_stco, t.ccd_mcd,
            t.fips_place, t.fips_mcd, t.fips_count, t.acres,
            t.square_mil, t.pop2010, t.popch00_1, t.shape_area,
            t.shape_len, t.geom
        Index Cond: (t.geom && r.geom)
```

```
        Filter: _st_intersects(t.geom, r.geom)
        Rows Removed by Filter: 151
Total runtime: 648.023 ms
```

The plan now specifically uses indexes. These are the salient differences:

- A spatial index scan replaced a sequential scan.
- The planner decomposed `ST_Intersects` into two parts: the `&&` part, which uses the spatial index scan, goes first; the more costly `_ST_Intersects` goes second.
- The planner listed the count of rows removed by the spatial join filter, `_ST_Intersects`. You'll notice that the count is much lower than without the index. This implies that the spatial index scan performed during the `&&` operation was more effective with an index than without. Putting it another way, because more rows were caught by `&&`, `_ST_Intersects` needs to check fewer rows.

In a spatial query, you should always look at the plan to make sure an index scan is taking place, and as early on as possible. Not taking advantage of a spatial index is the number one reason for slow queries. In the preceding example, the planner decomposed `ST_Intersects` and executed the part with the index scan first. This is optimal.

The planner sometimes employs a common programming tactic called *short-circuiting*. Short-circuiting occurs when a program processes only one part of a compound condition if processing the second part doesn't change the answer. For example, if the first part of the logical condition `A and B` returns false, the planner knows it doesn't have to evaluate the second part because the compound answer will always be false. This is a common behavior of relational databases and many programming languages. But unlike many programming systems that implement short-circuiting, relational databases (PostgreSQL included) generally don't check A and B in sequence. They first check the one they consider the cheapest.

In the previous example with the index, you can see that the planner now considers `&&` cheaper than `_ST_Intersects`, so it processes that one first. Only after that will it process `_ST_Intersects` for those records where geomA `&&` geomB is true. With `AND` conditions, it often looks at the cost of a function and uses that to forecast how costly the operation is relative to others, but for `OR` compound conditions, function costs are ignored. Sometimes the cost of figuring out the cost is too expensive, and in those cases it simply processes the conditions in order. So even though the query planner may not process conditions in the order in which they're stated, it's still best for you to put the one you think is quickest to evaluate first.

15.4.2 Options for defining indexes

In PostgreSQL, you have several options for defining indexes. Some of these you can mix and match together:

- You can index on a single column of a table, which you saw earlier in this chapter.

- You can index only a subset of data via a *partial index* that dictates the records to be indexed based on a WHERE filter condition that is specified as part of the index definition.
- You can define an index that uses multiple columns via a *compound index.*
- You can define an index based on an expression that can draw from one or more columns of the table, but can't involve multiple rows. This is also often referred to as a *functional index* because it's a derivative of the input columns and most often accomplished with a function.
- You can define an index as a Unique index, which would prevent duplicate data in the columns used in the index. Related to the concept of the unique index are what are called *primary keys* and *unique keys*. These all have a unique index behind the scenes.

In the subsections that follow, we'll elaborate on these options and on what you need to watch for when using them.

PARTIAL INDEX

A partial index allows you to define criteria, and only data meeting that condition will be indexed. The main advantages of this approach are as follows:

- A partial index is smaller, taking up less storage space.
- Because it's smaller, it has a better chance of caching the entire index in a shared buffer.
- It steers the planner toward a more optimal strategy. For example, if your data is the same in 90% of the rows and different in 10%, and you expect this to be the case for future data, you can place a partial index on the 10%. It's more efficient for the planner to scan the index for the 10% and scan the table for the 90%.

Partial indexes also have limitations:

- The WHERE condition of your query has to be *compatible* with the partial index. For instance, if you index on a column of last names, but you always query by the full name, the index is useless. This holds true for all indexes, not just partial indexes.
- In versions earlier than PostgreSQL 9.2, prepared statements and parameterized queries often can't use partial indexes if the parameterized argument involves a column used in the partial index filter condition. For instance, if you have parameterized queries of the form SELECT ... FROM some-table WHERE status = $1, even if you place a partial index on status, the planner won't recognize it. In PostgreSQL 9.2, the planner has less rigidity and can handle more variations in the WHERE. To read more about the handling of dynamic SQL in PostgreSQL 9.2 and earlier, refer to Hubert Lubaczewski's blog entry, "Prepared Statements Gotcha," at www.depesz.com/2008/05/10/prepared-statements-gotcha/.
- You can't cluster on a partial index.

Here's an example of a partial index:

```
CREATE INDEX idx_sometable_active_type
ON sometable
USING btree (type) WHERE active = true;
```

This situation presents itself when you only care about the type column when the record is active.

COMPOUND INDEX

PostgreSQL, like most other relational databases, gives you the option of creating an index sourcing from more than one table column. This type of index is called a *compound index*. You can combine compound indexes with partial and functional indexes.

PostgreSQL 8.1 introduced a bitmap index plan strategy that gave planners the freedom to use more than one index in a plan. This minimized the need for compound indexes, because the planner could use a bitmap index scan strategy to take advantage of two columnar indexes simultaneously using `AND` and `OR` bitmap operations. Still, in some cases, you might get better performance with a compound index, because an index scan is generally quicker than the bitmap index scan strategy.

You can't include common textual and numeric data types in a gist index because they lack compatible operators. If you have the `btree_gist` PostgreSQL extension installed, you can create a gist compound index by combining a spatial column with a textual or numeric column, which is often done. Here's a sample index definition:

```
CREATE INDEX idx_ch15_ma_roads_geom_rt_number
ON ch15.ma_roads
USING gist(geom, rt_number);
```

FUNCTIONAL INDEX

Functional indexes, sometimes called *expression indexes*, index a calculated value. They have three notable restrictions:

- The arguments to the function need to come from columns in the same table.
- You can't index on aggregate functions.
- The function must be marked immutable, which means that the same input always returns the same output.

> **WHEN IMMUTABLE FUNCTIONS CHANGE** If you change the definition of an immutable function, and this function is used in an index, you should re-index your table. Otherwise you could end up with unreliable output.

Functional indexes come in handy for spatial queries. In prior chapters, we used `ST_Transform` in a functional index of the following form:

```
CREATE INDEX idx_sometable_geom_2163
ON sometable
USING gist(ST_Transform(geom,2163));
```

Strictly speaking, `ST_Transform` is not an immutable function because it looks up data in the spatial_ref_sys table.

Other common uses for functional indexes in the spatial world are calculations with `ST_Area`, `ST_Length`, or `ST_GeoHash`. You may not want to store derived columns such as area or length but still want to enjoy the speed gain from an index—use a functional index.

PRIMARY KEYS, UNIQUE KEYS, UNIQUE INDEXES, AND FOREIGN KEYS

You rely on primary keys, unique key constraints (*unique keys* for short), and unique indexes to enforce referential integrity. The planner relies on them to know when to stop scanning for matches.

Both primary keys and unique keys have an implicit unique index built in. There isn't much difference between a primary key and a unique key except that you can have multiple unique keys and only one primary key per table. Primary keys, unique keys, and unique indexes can all draw from more than one column. All three serve the purpose of ensuring uniqueness in your column.

There are some subtle differences between primary and unique keys versus unique indexes:

- Only primary keys and unique keys can take part in foreign key relationships as the *one* side of a one-to-many relationship.
- A materialized view can have a unique index, but it can't have either a primary or a unique key.
- A unique index can be computed, making it qualify also as a functional index. Primary and unique keys can't.
- A unique index can be qualified with a `WHERE`, making it a partial index as well. Primary and unique keys must apply to all rows.
- Unique indexes can contain NULLs, but primary and unique keys can't. Unique indexes will ignore NULL values.

What about foreign keys that enforce referential integrity? Many people claim they impact performance, and they do, but only for update, insert, and delete operations. Think of them as insurance. The performance hit is the premium you pay to ensure against bad data. Specifically, foreign keys offer the following benefits:

- They prevent orphan records, which generally means fewer records for the planner to scan through.
- With cascade updates and deletes, you can offload some maintenance to the database itself.
- They're self-documenting. A user who knows nothing about your database can look at a foreign key relationship and understand how tables are related.
- Third-party GUI query builders take advantage of foreign keys. When a user drags and drops two tables in a third-party query builder, the tables become automatically linked.

INDEX NOT BEING USED

The planner should take advantage of the indexes you've created, but sometimes it doesn't. There are two common causes.

First, your index might be set up incorrectly. This is especially prevalent with B-tree indexes because they vary from one version of PostgreSQL to another.

Second, the planner may opt for a table scan on a small table even if you have an index. For example, it would take less time for the planner to loop through a table of ten records than to loop through an index on a table of ten records and then fetch the records.

15.5 Common SQL patterns and how they affect plans

In this section, we'll take a look at three common SQL constructs and how they affect the planner. PostgreSQL fully implements the SQL standard and more. This means you usually have a few ways to accomplish the same task. When working with large tables, writing your SQL in the most efficient way becomes pivotal.

The four constructs we'll explore are as follows:

- PostgreSQL lets you use subqueries in the `SELECT` portion of your SQL. This is convenient, but overuse of subqueries can slow your query to a crawl. If you find yourself using too many subqueries, consider using a `CASE` statement.
- CTEs organize complicated queries into separate components. But there's a downside—the planner materializes all CTEs. This means that all records in the CTE will be pulled, even if the CTE isn't used at all in the main query.
- PostgreSQL offers window functions that are useful for outputting row numbers and running totals. Although these can often be accomplished with self-joins, the window approach is generally faster.
- `LATERAL` joins are new in PostgreSQL 9.3. In most cases, you can accomplish the same outputs using an alternative syntax, but in many cases the `LATERAL` syntax is shorter and much more efficient. You'll see some examples of where `LATERAL`s can be used and how they can both shorten code and improve performance.

15.5.1 SELECT subqueries

A subquery can appear in the `SELECT`, `WHERE`, or `FROM` part of a query. You should avoid using subqueries that return a large number of rows in the `SELECT` or `WHERE` clauses. When you have a subquery, especially if it's correlated, the planner must process the subquery for each row of the main query. For subqueries returning a small number of records, the nested loop is generally not an issue, but we still suggest that you limit your subqueries to the `FROM` clause if for no other reason than that it's easier to read subqueries in the `FROM` than when they're placed elsewhere. Always remember that you can probably accomplish the same results with a join.

The first exercise we'll look at is the classic example of how many objects intersect with a reference object.

EXERCISE 1: HOW MANY STREETS INTERSECT EACH NEIGHBORHOOD?

For this exercise, we'll use two vastly different queries to determine how many streets intersect each neighborhood. The first is the naive way in which people new to relational databases approach this problem, putting the subquery in the `SELECT`. In some cases, despite the expectations of most database folk, this performs better or as well as the conventional `JOIN` approach. The second approach doesn't use a subquery and uses the power of joins instead. Although these strategies are vastly different, the timings are pretty much the same for this data set.

Here is the subquery approach:

```
EXPLAIN ANALYZE
SELECT
    n.neighborho,
    (
        SELECT COUNT(*) AS cnt
        FROM ch15.stclines_streets As s
        WHERE ST_Intersects(n.geom,s.geom)
    ) As cnt
FROM ch15.planning_neighborhoods As n
ORDER BY n.neighborho;
```

The output of the preceding analyze is as follows:

```
QUERY PLAN
--------------------------------------------------------------------
Sort
    (cost=472.02..472.12 rows=37 width=100)
    (actual time=844.146..844.157 rows=37 loops=1)
    Sort Key: n.neighborho
    Sort Method: quicksort  Memory: 27kB
    -> Seq Scan on planning_neighborhoods n
        (cost=0.00..471.06 rows=37 width=100)
        (actual time=19.661..843.894 rows=37 loops=1)
        SubPlan 1
            -> Aggregate
                (cost=12.47..12.48 rows=1 width=0)
                (actual time=22.797..22.798 rows=1 loops=37)
                -> Bitmap Heap Scan on stclines_streets s
                    (cost=4.29..12.47 rows=1 width=0)
                    (actual time=2.523..22.467 rows=456 loops=37)
                    Recheck Cond: (n.geom && geom)
                    Filter: _st_intersects(n.geom, geom)
                    Rows Removed by Filter: 242
                    -> Bitmap Index Scan on stclines_streets_geom_gist
                        (cost=0.00..4.29 rows=2 width=0)
                        (actual time=0.458..0.458 rows=697 loops=37)
                        Index Cond: (n.geom && geom)
Total runtime: 846.336 ms
```

Now we'll ask the same query, but not using a subquery at all:

```
EXPLAIN ANALYZE
SELECT n.neighborho, COUNT(n.gid) AS cnt
```

```
FROM
    ch15.planning_neighborhoods As n
    LEFT JOIN
    ch15.stclines_streets As s
ON ST_Intersects(n.geom,s.geom)
GROUP BY n.neighborho
ORDER BY n.neighborho;
```

Here's the result:

```
Sort
    (cost=450.00..450.09 rows=37 width=17)
    (actual time=877.121..877.132 rows=37 loops=1)
    Sort Key: n.neighborho
    Sort Method: quicksort  Memory: 27kB
    -> HashAggregate
        (cost=448.67..449.04 rows=37 width=17)
        (actual time=876.969..876.990 rows=37 loops=1)
        -> Nested Loop Left Join
            (cost=0.28..447.71 rows=191 width=17)
            (actual time=6.076..850.368 rows=16855 loops=1)
            -> Seq Scan on planning_neighborhoods n
                (cost=0.00..9.37 rows=37 width=5831)
                (actual time=0.005..0.073 rows=37 loops=1)
                -> Index Scan using stclines_streets_geom_gist on
                    stclines_streets s
                    (cost=0.28..11.84 rows=1 width=32)
                    (actual time=2.314..22.544 rows=456 loops=37)
                    Index Cond: (n.geom && geom)
                    Filter: _st_intersects(n.geom, geom)
                    Rows Removed by Filter: 242
Total runtime: 878.307 ms
```

Using a JOIN generally becomes faster than a SELECT subquery as your query outputs more records. When used in views, however, the planner is usually smart enough not to compute the column if it's not asked for. In these cases, it's better to put the subquery in the SELECT if you don't need other fields from the subquery table and you know your subquery calculated column is rarely asked for.

This is another reason to avoid the greedy SELECT *, especially with views: you have no idea what complicated formula could be stuffed into a column.

EXERCISE 2: HOW MANY NEIGHBORHOODS HAVE STREETS, HOW MANY STREETS, AND HOW MANY ARE LONGER THAN 1000 FEET?

In this exercise, we'll demonstrate the danger of subqueries. When you find yourself having multiple subqueries in your SELECT clause, ask yourself if they're really necessary.

Once again we'll demonstrate this query using two different approaches, shown in the following listings. Listing 15.11 shows the naive subselect way, and listing 15.13 shows the JOIN approach, with CASE WHEN statements.

Listing 15.11 Subqueries gone too far

```
EXPLAIN ANALYZE
SELECT
    n.neighborho,
    (
        SELECT COUNT(*) AS cnt FROM ch15.stclines_streets As s
            WHERE ST_Intersects(n.geom,s.geom)
    ) As cnt,
    (
        SELECT COUNT(*) AS cnt
        FROM ch15.stclines_streets As s
        WHERE ST_Intersects(n.geom,s.geom) AND ST_Length(s.geom) > 1000
    ) As cnt_gt_1000
FROM ch15.planning_neighborhoods As n
WHERE EXISTS (
    SELECT s.gid
    FROM ch15.stclines_streets As s
    WHERE ST_Intersects(n.geom,s.geom)
)
ORDER BY n.neighborho;
```

The result of the preceding listing is shown next.

Listing 15.12 Explain plan of subqueries gone too far

```
Sort
    (cost=484.25..484.25 rows=1 width=5827)
    (actual time=1094.885..1094.896 rows=37 loops=1)
    Sort Key: n.neighborho
    Sort Method: quicksort Memory: 27kB
    -> Nested Loop Semi Join
    (cost=0.28..484.24 rows=1 width=5827)
    (actual time=42.124..1094.708 rows=37 loops=1)
        -> Seq Scan on planning_neighborhoods n
            (cost=0.00..9.37 rows=37 width=5827)
            (actual time=0.007..0.070 rows=37 loops=1)
        -> Index Scan using stclines_streets_geom_gist on
            stclines_streets s
            (cost=0.28..11.84 rows=1 width=32)
            (actual time=2.158..2.158 rows=1 loops=37)
            Index Cond: (n.geom && geom)
            Filter: _st_intersects(n.geom, geom)
            Rows Removed by Filter: 5
        SubPlan 1
            -> Aggregate
                (cost=12.47..12.48 rows=1 width=0)
                (actual time=21.764..21.765 rows=1 loops=37)
                -> Bitmap Heap Scan on stclines_streets s_1
                    (cost=4.29..12.47 rows=1 width=0)
                    (actual time=2.346..21.442 rows=456 loops=37)
                    Recheck Cond: (n.geom && geom)
                    Filter: _st_intersects(n.geom,geom)
                    Rows Removed by Filter: 242
```

```
                        -> Bitmap Index Scan on
                            stclines_streets_geom_gist
                            (cost=0.00..4.29 rows=2 width=0)
                            (actual time=0.441..0.441 rows=697 loops=37)
                            Index Cond: (n.geom && geom)
        SubPlan 2
            -> Aggregate
                (cost=12.48..12.49 rows=1 width=0)
                (actual time=5.627..5.628 rows=1 loops=37)
                -> Bitmap Heap Scan on stclines_streets s_2
                    (cost=4.29..12.48 rows=1 width=0)
                    (actual time=2.954..5.598 rows=16 loops=37)
                    Recheck Cond: (n.geom && geom)
                    Filter:
                        ((st_length(geom) > 1000::double precision) AND
                        _st_intersects(n.geom, geom))
                        Rows Removed by Filter: 681
                        -> Bitmap Index Scan on
                            stclines_streets_geom_gist
                            (cost=0.00..4.29 rows=2 width=0)
                            (actual time=0.435..0.435 rows=697 loops=37)
                            Index Cond: (n.geom && geom)
Total runtime: 1097.019 ms
```

To the untrained eye, this looks impressive because it uses complex constructs such as subqueries, exists, and aggregates all in one query. In addition, the planner is making full use of index scans—and more than one, at that. To the trained eye, however, this is a recipe for a slow and long-winded query.

The graphical explain plan, shown in figure 15.3, looks particularly beautiful, we think.

Even though this does look convoluted, it has its place. It's a slow strategy, but for building things like summary reports where your count columns are totally unrelated to each other except for the date ranges they represent, it's not a bad way to go. It's an expandable model for building query builders for end users where flexibility is more

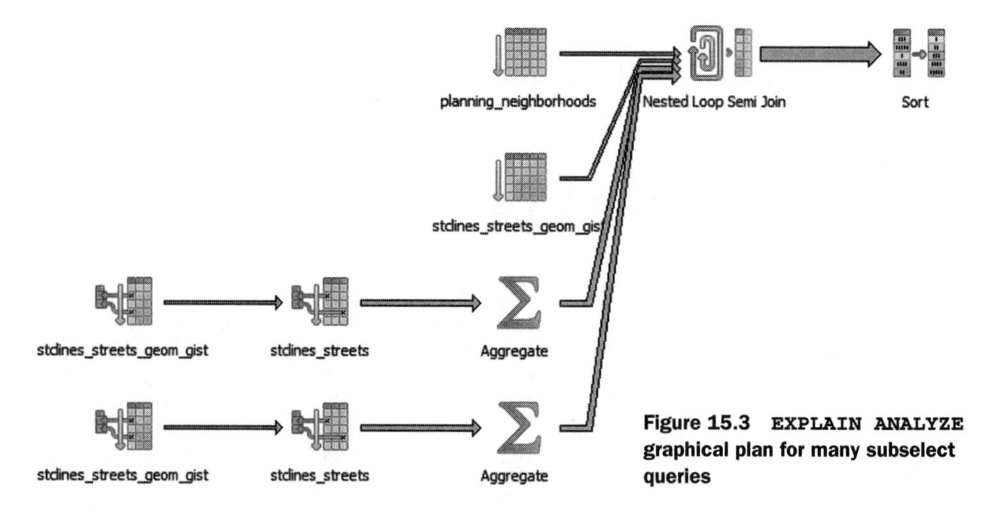

Figure 15.3 `EXPLAIN ANALYZE` **graphical plan for many subselect queries**

important than speed and where no penalty is paid if the column isn't asked for. PostgreSQL 9.0+ introduced the join removal optimization, which made the query planner smart enough to skip joins if no fields are selected from the joined table and the joined result would not affect the resulting answer.

Listing 15.13 solves the same problem as listing 15.11, but with a CASE statement instead of a subselect. A CASE statement is particularly useful for writing cross-tab reports, where you use the same table over and over again and aggregate the values slightly differently.

Listing 15.13 Using CASE instead of subquery

```
EXPLAIN ANALYZE
SELECT
    n.neighborho,
    COUNT(s.gid) AS cnt,
    COUNT(
        CASE WHEN ST_Length(s.geom) > 1000 THEN 1 ELSE NULL END
    ) As cnt_gt_1000
FROM
    ch15.planning_neighborhoods As n
    INNER JOIN
    ch15.stclines_streets As s
ON ST_Intersects(n.geom,s.geom)
GROUP BY n.neighborho
ORDER BY n.neighborho;
```

The result is shown in the following listing.

Listing 15.14 Query plan using CASE instead of subquery

```
Sort
    (cost=451.43..451.52 rows=37 width=49)
    (actual time=892.323..892.334 rows=37 loops=1)
    Sort Key: n.neighborho
    Sort Method: quicksort  Memory: 27kB
    -> HashAggregate
        (cost=450.10..450.47 rows=37 width=49)
        (actual time=892.158..892.183 rows=37 loops=1)
        -> Nested Loop
            (cost=0.28..447.71 rows=191 width=49)
            (actual time=6.135..839.497 rows=16855 loops=1)
            -> Seq Scan on planning_neighborhoods n
                (cost=0.00..9.37 rows=37 width=5827)
                (actual time=0.006..0.071 rows=37 loops=1)
                -> Index Scan using stclines_streets_geom_gist
                    on stclines_streets s
                    (cost=0.28..11.84 rows=1 width=36)
                    (actual time=2.295..22.240 rows=456 loops=37)
                    Index Cond: (n.geom && geom)
                    Filter: _st_intersects(n.geom, geom)
                    Rows Removed by Filter: 242
Total runtime: 893.614 ms
```

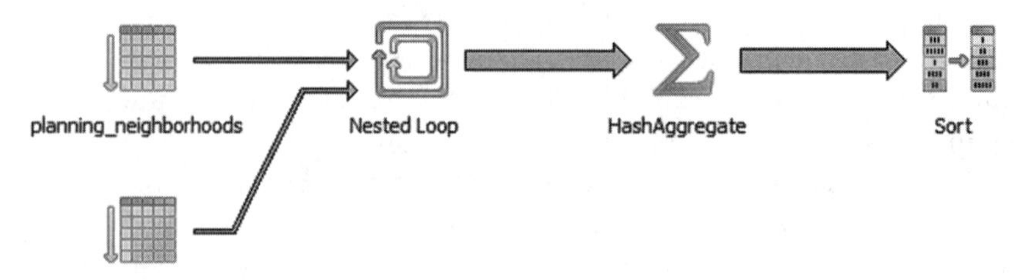

Figure 15.4 Graphical query plan using CASE instead of subquery

As you can see, this query is not only shorter than listing 15.11, but also faster. Also observe that you're doing an `INNER JOIN` instead of a `LEFT JOIN`. This is because you care only about cities with streets.

The results are shown in figure 15.4.

> **The PostgreSQL 9.4 FILTER construct**
>
> PostgreSQL 9.4 introduced the aggregate `FILTER` construct, which can be used to replace `CASE WHEN` clauses in aggregate use. The syntax of `FILTER` is a bit cleaner and generally performs faster than the equivalent `CASE WHEN`. It's also very useful when aggregating arrays, because NULL values will be automatically stripped out, so you don't end up with NULLS in your final array. This is something you can't do with the `CASE WHEN` when an aggregate considers NULLs as values.
>
> The following two statements are equivalent, with the second using the aggregate `FILTER` construct:
>
> ```
> COUNT( CASE WHEN ST_Length(s.geom) > 1000 THEN
>                         1 ELSE NULL END)
>
> COUNT(1) FILTER(WHERE ST_Length(s.geom) > 1000)
> ```

15.5.2 FROM subqueries and basic CTEs

A `FROM` subselect is a favorite of SQLers old and new. It allows you to compartmentalize all these complex calculations as computed columns, assigning alias names to both the subquery and the computed columns. For example, the following subselect can be used elsewhere in your overall query:

```
(SELECT neighborhood, AVG(house_value) AS total GROUP BY
                  neighborhood) As neigh_house
```

Another kind of subselect is called the *common table expression* (CTE), which allows you to reuse the same subselect in as many places as you want in your SQL statement without repeating its definition.

A couple of things about subqueries used in `FROM` and CTEs aren't entirely obvious, even to those with extensive SQL backgrounds:

- Although you write a subselect in a `FROM` as if it's a distinct entity, it's often not. It often gets collapsed (rewritten, if you will). It's not always materialized, and the order of its processing isn't guaranteed.
- For the PostgreSQL CTE incarnation, although the ANSI specs don't require it, a CTE always seems to result in a materialization of the work table, but you can't tell this from the plan, because it shows a CTE strategy.

CTE GOTCHA Be careful with CTEs because, as stated, they always result in a materialization of the table expressions. Try to avoid table expressions within your CTEs that return a lot of records, unless you'll be returning all those records in your final output. If your subquery returns many records and can be compartmentalized in the `FROM` clause, then you'll generally be better off with a subselect in the `FROM` rather than a CTE. This behavior may change in future.

For small subselect tables with complex function calculations, such as spatial function calculations, you'll generally want the subselect to be materialized, although for large data sets you generally won't. You can't directly tell PostgreSQL this, but you can write your queries in a way that will sway it in one direction or another. You can write expressions as CTE subexpressions to force a materialization of the subselect.

We've used CTEs and basic subqueries throughout the book. For some basic examples, refer to appendix C.

Now that we've covered the use of subqueries and CTEs, we'll explore window functions and joins.

15.5.3 Window functions and self-joins

The window function support introduced in PostgreSQL 8.4 is closely related to the practice of using self-joins; the two approaches are often interchangeable but yield very different performance. For cases where you can use a window, using a window frame approach is generally much more efficient and results in shorter code than using a self-join.

To compare the speeds, we'll write the same query in two ways: listing 15.15 uses a CTE and self-join to rank results, and listing 15.16 demonstrates using a window frame and function to rank results. The window approach is about three times faster (20 ms) than the self-join approach (90 ms) for this case and is much shorter.

Listing 15.15 Rank results using the self-join approach

```
WITH main AS (                                   <-- 1 CTE main
    SELECT
        p1.neighborho As nei_1,
        p2.neighborho As nei_2,
        p1.geom As p1_geom,
        p2.geom As p2_geom,
        p2.gid As p2_gid,
        ST_Distance(p1.geom,p2.geom) As dist,
        p1.gid As p1_gid
```

```
    FROM
    (
        SELECT neighborho, gid, geom
        FROM ch15.planning_neighborhoods
        WHERE neighborho = 'Chinatown'
    ) As p1
    INNER JOIN
    ch15.planning_neighborhoods AS p2
    ON p1.gid <> p2.gid AND ST_DWithin(p1.geom,p2.geom,2500)
)

SELECT COUNT(p3.gid) As rank, main.nei_2, main.dist
FROM
    main                                          <-- ❷ Use main
    INNER JOIN
    ch15.planning_neighborhoods As p3
    ON ST_DWithin(main.p1_geom,p3.geom,2500)          <-- ❸ Self-join
WHERE
    (main.p2_gid = p3.gid
        OR ST_Distance(main.p1_geom,p3.geom) < main.dist)
    AND
    main.p1_gid <> p3.gid
GROUP BY main.p2_gid, main.nei_2, main.dist
ORDER BY rank, main.nei_2;
```

In the preceding listing, you employ lots of techniques in unison. You use a CTE called `main` to define a virtual worktable ❶ that will be used to determine what neighborhoods are within 2,500 feet of Chinatown. You then use `main` in the final output of your query ❷.

Instead of using a CTE, you could have defined `main` as a subselect within the main body of the query. For this particular case, defining it as part of the main query would prevent materialization and would also result in slower performance (192 ms vs. 90 ms). This is because the costly distance check isn't recalculated if you use a CTE, but it is if you don't use a CTE.

Next, you do a self-join to collect and count all the neighbors that are closer to Chinatown than your reference `p2` in `main` ❸. Note that the `main.p2_gid = p3.gid OR` ensures the `RANK` will count at least the reference geom even if there's no closer object.

This is more efficiently done with a window statement, which is a feature supported in many enterprise relational databases and PostgreSQL 8.4+. The next example is the same query written using the `RANK` window function.

Listing 15.16 Using window frame to number results

```
SELECT
    RANK() OVER w_dist As rank,                    <-- ❶ Use window frame
    p2.neighborho As nei_2, ST_Distance(p1.geom, p2.geom) As dist
FROM
    ch15.planning_neighborhoods As p1
    INNER JOIN
    ch15.planning_neighborhoods As p2
    ON p1.gid <> p2.gid AND ST_DWithin(p1.geom,p2.geom,2500)
```

```
WHERE p1.neighborho = 'Chinatown'
WINDOW w_dist AS (
    PARTITION BY p1.gid ORDER BY ST_Distance(p1.geom, p2.geom)
)
ORDER BY RANK() OVER w_dist, nei_2;
```

❷ Define window frame

This window frame implementation using the RANK function is a bit cleaner-looking and also runs much faster. This runs in about 20 ms, and the larger the geometries, the more significant the speed differences between the previous self-join hack and the window frame rank.

In this example, you see the PostgreSQL declaration of WINDOW ❷—WINDOW naming doesn't exist in all relational database products supporting windowing constructs. It allows you to define your partition, order by frame, and reuse it across the query instead of repeating it where you need it ❶.

The output of listings 15.15 and 15.16 is the same and is shown in the following listing.

Listing 15.17 Output of ranking results using self-join or window

```
 ank |         nei_2         |       dist
-----+-----------------------+-----------------
   1 | Downtown/Civic Center |                0
   1 | Financial District    |                0
   1 | Nob Hill              |                0
   1 | North Beach           |                0
   1 | Russian Hill          |                0
   6 | South of Market       | 1726.01750301085
```

Another kind of correlated subquery is the LATERAL clause. We'll examine laterals next.

15.5.4 Laterals

PostgreSQL 9.3+ introduced the LATERAL construct, which is used in the FROM join clause. LATERAL allows you to create correlated subqueries in the FROM clause of an SQL statement or to use a set-returning function in the FROM clause that takes input from another table in the FROM clause.

We demonstrated the use of lateral constructs in chapter 10. They allowed you to use the KNN gist index by forcing the constant geometry in the lateral correlated subquery. Aside from allowing the planner to use a spatial index that it couldn't normally use, a lateral construct is useful for preventing a set-returning function from running multiple times per call if the set-returning function returns multiple columns. For PostgreSQL 9.2 or lower, in order to prevent a set-returning multicolumn function from running multiple times, if you need more than one column from the result, you'd have to create a subselect or CTE and then select the elements from the function result.

In the next set of exercises, we'll demonstrate three ways of exploding San Francisco neighborhoods into points.

Listing 15.18 uses the naive and slowest way of exploding that people mistakenly use. This is the slowest because by using `(ST_DumpPoints(geom)).*`, the `ST_DumpPoints` function is called for each column output by `ST_DumpPoints`. So because `ST_DumpPoints` outputs two columns, each `(ST_DumpPoints(geom)).*` will make two calls to `ST_DumpPoints` functions.

`ST_DumpPoints` is pretty fast in PostGIS 2.1+, and the `ST_DumpPoints` time is a relatively small percentage of the time required for the overall query, so you'll only notice slight differences in speed between this approach and `LATERAL` for this particular task.

> **NOTE** Note that for these exercises we're showing the `EXPLAIN ANALYZE VERBOSE` time, which excludes network effects of returning the data to the client. In practice, most of the time spent in dumping is spent returning data to the client, so the time can jump about ten-fold or more depending on how close the server and client are and the speed of memory.

Listing 15.18 Exploding the naive way: don't do this

```
EXPLAIN ANALYZE VERBOSE
SELECT
    p1.neighborho As nei_1,
    (ST_DumpPoints(p1.geom)).geom As geom,
    (ST_DumpPoints(p1.geom)).path[1] As poly_index,
    (ST_DumpPoints(p1.geom)).path[2] As poly_ring_index,
    (ST_DumpPoints(p1.geom)).path[3] As pt_index
FROM ch15.planning_neighborhoods As p1;
```

The problem with listing 15.18 is that it will call `ST_DumpPoints` for each column output. Even if you were to revise to `(ST_DumpPoint(geom)).*`, it would still do a call for geom and path output. This example took a little over 79 ms (330 ms if you consider network transfer) to run on our development box. The output is shown in the next listing.

Listing 15.19 Explain plan output for exploding the naive way

```
Seq Scan on ch15.planning_neighborhoods p1
    (cost=0.00..194.56 rows=37000 width=5827)
    (actual time=0.264..75.849 rows=13254 loops=1)
    Output: neighborho, (st_dumppoints(geom)).geom,
        (st_dumppoints(geom)).path[1], (st_dumppoints(geom)).path[2],
        (st_dumppoints(geom)).path[3]
Total runtime: 79.735 ms
```

Unfortunately, you can't tell from the explain output that `ST_DumpPoints` is being called multiple times unless you put logging inside the `ST_DumpPoints` function. You'll get a hint that you aren't getting the best performance if you compare to the next approach, which yields the same answer.

One way to avoid multiple calls to your function is to wrap the call in a subselect, as shown in the following listing.

Listing 15.20 Exploding using subselect

```
EXPLAIN ANALYZE VERBOSE
SELECT
    nei_1,
    (gp).geom,
    (gp).path[1] As poly_index,
    (gp).path[2] As poly_ring_index,
    (gp).path[3] As pt_index
FROM (
    SELECT p1.neighborho As nei_1, ST_DumpPoints(p1.geom) As gp
    FROM ch15.planning_neighborhoods As p1
) As x;
```

The output of this listing follows.

Listing 15.21 Explain plan output for exploding using subselect

```
Subquery Scan on f
    (cost=0.00..564.28 rows=37000 width=45)
    (actual time=0.120..37.836 rows=13254 loops=1)
    Output: f.nei_1, (f.gp).geom, (f.gp).path[1], (f.gp).path[2],
        (f.gp).path[3]
    -> Seq Scan on ch15.planning_neighborhoods p1
        (cost=0.00..194.28 rows=37000 width=5827)
        (actual time=0.111..21.455 rows=13254 loops=1)
        Output: p1.neighborho, st_dumppoints(p1.geom)
Total runtime: 41.635 ms;
```

Observe that the timing of this subselect approach is almost twice as fast as the naive approach demonstrated in listing 15.19.

Next we'll try the same exercise using the lateral construct. The lateral construct is a little shorter to write and generally a bit faster than the subselect approach. LATERAL is an optional keyword, but we like to use it as a more explicit declaration of what we're doing. Without the keyword, the planner is smart enough to figure out that if you have a correlated subquery or function (one that depends on another table in the FROM condition), then you are asking for a LATERAL.

Listing 15.22 shows the neighborhood explosion exercise using the lateral construct.

Listing 15.22 Exploding using lateral (requires PostgreSQL 9.3+)

```
EXPLAIN ANALYZE VERBOSE
SELECT
    p1.neighborho As nei_1,
    (gp).geom,
    (gp).path[1] As poly_index,
    (gp).path[2] As poly_ring_index,
    (gp).path[3] As pt_index
FROM
    ch15.planning_neighborhoods As p1,
    LATERAL
    ST_DumpPoints(p1.geom) As gp;
```

The output of the preceding listing is shown next.

Listing 15.23 Explain plan output for exploding using lateral

```
Nested Loop
    (cost=0.00..749.37 rows=37000 width=77)
    (actual time=0.689..30.664 rows=13254 loops=1)
    Output: p1.neighborho, gp.geom, gp.path[1], gp.path[2], gp.path[3]
    -> Seq Scan on ch15.planning_neighborhoods p1
        (cost=0.00..9.37 rows=37 width=5827)
        (actual time=0.010..0.046 rows=37 loops=1)
        Output: p1.gid, p1.neighborho, p1.geom
    -> Function Scan on public.st_dumppoints gp
        (cost=0.00..10.00 rows=1000 width=64)
        (actual time=0.337..0.450 rows=358 loops=37)
        Output: gp.path, gp.geom
        Function Call: st_dumppoints(p1.geom)
Total runtime: 34.305 ms
```

Observe that the lateral approach is more than twice as fast as the naive approach and a little faster and shorter than the subselect approach.

In addition to improving performance by rewriting your queries, you can control the behavior of the planner by setting properties on functions and also disabling various plan strategies to encourage it to use others. We'll discuss these settings in the next section.

15.6 System and function settings

Most system variables that affect plan strategies can be set at the server, session, database, or function levels.

To set these variables at the server level prior to PostgreSQL 9.4, edit the postgresql .conf file and restart or reload the PostgreSQL daemon service (using the SQL construct `SELECT pg_reload_conf();`).

If you're running PostgreSQL 9.4 or above, you can set the variables at the system level by using the `ALTER SYSTEM` SQL construct instead of directly setting postgresql .conf:

```
ALTER SYSTEM SET somevariable=somevalue;
```

With the `ALTER SYSTEM` construct, your custom settings are stored in a file called postgresql.auto.conf, and thus are easier to distinguish from default settings and to migrate when you upgrade.

To set system variables at the session level, use the following command:

```
SET somevariable TO somevalue;
```

To set them at the database level, use this command:

```
ALTER DATABASE somedatabase SET somevariable=somevalue;
```

To set them at the function level, use this command:

```
ALTER FUNCTION somefunction(type1, type2) SET somevariable=somevalue;
```

To see the current value of a parameter, use this command:

```
show somevariable;
```

Now let's look at some system variables that impact query performance.

15.6.1 *Key system variables that affect plan strategy*

In this section, we'll cover the key system variables that most affect query speed and efficiency. For many of these, particularly the memory ones, there's no specific right or wrong setting.

A lot of the optimal settings depend on whether or not your server is dedicated to PostgreSQL work, what CPU you have, how much motherboard RAM you have, and even whether your loads are connection-intensive versus query-intensive. Do you have more people hitting your database asking for simple queries, or is your database a workhorse dedicated to generating data feeds?

You may want to adjust many of these settings for specific queries and not across the board. We encourage you to do your own tests to determine which settings work best under what loads.

CONSTRAINT_EXCLUSION

In order to take advantage of inheritance partitioning effects, the `constraint_exclusion` variable should be set to `partition`, which is the default. This can be set at the server or database level, as well as at the function or statement level. It's generally best to set it at the server level so you don't need to remember to do it for each database you create.

The difference between the older `on` value and the new `partition` value is that with `partition` the planner doesn't check for constraint exclusion conditions unless it's looking at a table that has children. This saves a few planner cycles over the previous `on` setting. The `on` setting is still useful, however, with union queries.

MAINTENANCE_WORK_MEM

This variable specifies the amount of memory to allocate for indexing and vacuum analyze processes. When you're doing lots of loads, you may want to temporarily set this to a higher value for a session and keep it lower at the server or database level. You can set it as follows:

```
SET maintenance_work_mem TO 512000;
```

The `shared_buffers` and `work_mem` variables covered next are also set in units of bytes.

SHARED_BUFFERS

`shared_buffers` sets the amount of memory the database server uses for shared memory. `shared_buffers` is what makes things such as shared reads possible. It allows the server to cache data in motherboard memory to be used by other PostgreSQL processes. The more of it you have, the more of your database can be loaded in onboard memory for faster retrieval.

You'll generally want this variable to be set much higher than the default and to be set to as much as 20% of available onboard RAM for a dedicated PostgreSQL box. This setting can only be set in the postgresql.conf file or via `ALTER SYSTEM` and requires a restart of the service after setting. You'll get diminishing returns after about 8 GB.

WORK_MEM

`work_mem` is the maximum memory used for each sort operation, and it's set as the amount of memory (in KB) for each internal sort operation. If you have a lot of onboard RAM, do a lot of intensive geometry processing, and have few users doing intensive things at the same time, this number should be fairly high. This is also a setting you can set conditionally at the function level or connection level, so keep it low for general inexperienced users and high for specific functions.

```
ALTER DATABASE postgis_in_action SET work_mem=120000;
ALTER FUNCTION somefunction(text, text) SET work_mem=10000;
```

ENABLE (VARIOUS PLAN STRATEGIES)

The `enable` strategy options all default to true/on. You should rarely change these settings at the server or database level, but you may find it useful to set them at the session or function level if you want to discourage a certain plan strategy that's causing query problems. It's rare that you'd ever need to turn these off.

Some PostGIS users have experienced great performance improvements by fiddling with these settings on a case-by-case basis:

- `enable_bitmapscan`
- `enable_hashagg`
- `enable_hashjoin`
- `enable_indexscan`
- `enable_mergejoin`
- `enable_nestloop`
- `enable_seqscan`
- `enable_sort`
- `enable_tidscan`

The `enable_seqscan` option is one that's useful to turn off for troubleshooting because it forces the planner to use an index that it seemingly could use but refuses to. It's a good way of knowing if the planner's costs are wrong in some way, if a table scan is truly better for your particular case, or if your index is set up incorrectly so the planner can't use it.

In some cases, even when you turn off a setting, the planner will use it anyway. This is because the planner has no other valid options. Turning the following settings off will discourage the planner from using them but won't guarantee it:

- `enable_sort`
- `enable_seqscan`
- `enable_nestloop`

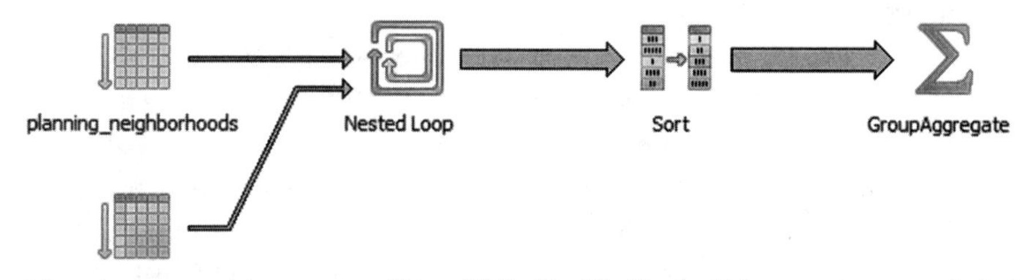

Figure 15.5 Disabling hashagg forces a group app strategy

To play around with these and other planner settings, set them before you run a query. For example, turn off hashagg like this,

```
set enable_hashagg = off;
```

and then rerun the `CASE` query from listing 15.13 that used a hashagg. This change in settings will cause it to use a `GroupAggregate`, as shown in figure 15.5.

Disabling specific planner strategies is useful for certain critical queries where you know a particular planner strategy yields slower results. By compartmentalizing these queries in functions, you can control the strategies with function settings.

Functions also have specific settings relevant only for functions. We'll go over these in the next section.

15.6.2 Function-specific settings

The `COST` and `ROWS` settings have the estimated values for the cost of the function and the number of returned rows for the function. These settings are available only to functions. They're part of the definition of the function and not set separately like the other parameters. The form is

```
CREATE OR REPLACE FUNCTION somefunction(arg1,arg2 ..)
RETURNS type1 AS
....
LANGUAGE 'c' IMMUTABLE STRICT
COST 100 ROWS 2;
```

COST

The `COST` setting is a measure of how costly you think a function is relative to other functions.

Versions of PostGIS prior to 1.5 didn't have these cost settings explicitly set, so under certain situations, such as big geometries, functions such as `ST_DWithin` and `ST_Intersects` behaved badly, and sometimes the more costly process ran before the less costly `&&` operations. To fix this, you can set these costs in your install. You'll want to set the costs high on the non-public side of `_ST_DWithin`, `_ST_Intersects`, `_ST_Within`, and other relationship functions. A cost of 200 for the aforementioned seems to work well in general, although no extensive benchmarking has been done on these functions to determine optimal settings.

ROWS

The ROWS setting is relevant only for set-returning functions. It's an estimate of the number of rows you expect the function to return.

IMMUTABLE, STABLE, VOLATILE

As shown previously, you can use IMMUTABLE when writing a function to state what kind of behavior is expected of the output. If you don't, the function is assumed to be VOLATILE. These settings have both a speed as well as a behavior effect.

An immutable function is one whose output is constant over time, given the same set of arguments. If a function is immutable, then the planner knows it can cache the result, and if it sees the same arguments passed in, it can reuse the cached output. Because caching generally improves speed, especially for pricy calculations, marking such functions as immutable is useful.

A STABLE function is one whose output is expected to be constant across the life of a query, given the same inputs. These functions can generally be assumed to produce the same result, but they can't be treated as immutable because they have external dependencies that could change, such as dependencies on other tables. As a result, they perform worse than IMMUTABLE functions, all else being equal, but faster than VOLATILE functions.

A VOLATILE function is one that can give you a different output with each call, even with the same inputs. Functions that depend on time or some other randomly changing factor, or that change data, fit into this category because they change state. If you mark a volatile function, such as random(), as non-volatile, it will run faster but not behave correctly because it will be returning the same value with each subsequent call.

Now that we've covered the various system settings you can employ to impact speed, we'll take a closer look at the geometries themselves. Can you change a geometry so that applying spatial predicates and operations to it is speedier, but the geometry is still accurate enough for your needs?

15.7 Optimizing spatial data

Generally speaking, spatial processes and checks on spatial relationships take longer with bigger or invalid spatial data. Spatial relationship checks are often slower, give wrong answers, or just don't work if your geometry data is invalid.

For any kind of spatial data object, whether it be geometry, geography, raster, or topology, spatial checks take longer as the size of your spatial data increases. Part of the reason is that there's just more data to deal with. If your spatial data objects get large enough, they are often internally chunked and stored in TOAST (which stands for *The Oversized-Attribute Storage Technique* and is used when an object grows beyond 8 KB). Each 8 KB fragment is essentially stored as a separate row in a TOAST table. When data is toasted, in order to do more involved operations such as intense ST_Intersects checks or processes like ST_Union, the data needs to be de-toasted, which takes more time.

The other concern with storing large spatial objects, particularly with smaller attribute data, is that even when you're not updating the spatial object, it will significantly impact the speed of updating other data columns. This is because of the way PostgreSQL implements MVCC: it creates a new record for each `UPDATE` and marks the old deleted record as inactive. One benefit of storing rasters using the out-of-db approach, if much of what you are updating is the related attribute data, is that you can significantly improve update and insert performance because the raster representation during the copy of the record will be just raster metadata and not the actual raster.

In this section, we'll go over some of the more common techniques for validating, optimizing, and simplifying your spatial data.

15.7.1 Fixing invalid geometries

The main reason to fix invalid geometries is that you can't use GEOS relationship checks and many processing functions that rely on the intersection matrix with invalid geometries. Functions like `ST_Intersects`, `ST_Equals`, and so on return false or throw a topology error for certain kinds of invalidity, regardless of the true nature of the intersection. The same holds true for union, intersection, and the powerful GEOS geometry process functions. Many won't work with invalid geometries.

Most of the cases of invalid geometries involve polygons. In PostGIS 2.0, there's a function called `ST_MakeValid` that can be used to fix invalid polygons, multipolygons, multilinestrings, and linestrings.

In addition to making sure that geometries are valid, you can improve performance by reducing the number of points in each geometry.

15.7.2 Reducing the number of vertices by simplification

In PostGIS there are two functions, `ST_Simplify` and `ST_SimplifyPreserveTopology`, that can be used to reduce the number of vertices in a polygon or linestring. We covered these in chapter 6.

15.7.3 Clustering

Clustering can refer to two totally different optimization tricks that sound similar and even use the same terminology but mean different things. We'll refer to the first as *index clustering* and the second as *spatial clustering* (or bunching; the term *bunching* is more colloquial).

- *Index clustering*—This refers to the PostgreSQL concept of clustering on an index. You maintain the same number of rows, but you physically order your table by an index (in PostGIS, usually the spatial one). This guarantees that your matches will be in close proximity to each other on the disk and will be easy to pick. Your index seeks will be faster because each data page will have more matches.

- *Spatial clustering (bunching)*—This is usually done with point geometries, and it reduces the number of rows. It's done by taking a set of points, usually close to one another or related by similar attributes, and aggregating by collecting them into multipoints. For example, you could be talking about 100,000 rows of multipoints versus 1,000,000 rows of points, which can be both a great space saver as well as a speed enhancer, because you need fewer index checks.

The index-clustering concept is fairly common and is similarly named in other databases.

Pointcloud

A project called *Pointcloud* (https://github.com/pramsey/pointcloud) takes the bunching concept to extremes and defines a new spatial data type called a `PCPatch` that collects many *n*-dimensional points into a single unit. A `PCPatch` has its own set of analysis and accessor functions and also can cast to PostGIS geometry types. It's often used to store and analyze LIDAR data.

INDEX CLUSTERING ON GEOHASH FUNCTIONAL INDEX OR GIST SPATIAL INDEX

We've talked about GeoHash before in other chapters, but it's worthwhile revisiting it. Why would you want to physically sort your data on disk by a spatially based index like a functional index of GeoHash or the gist geometry index you built?

When PostgreSQL (and, in fact, many relational databases) query data, they do it in batches called *pages*. A page may house many records depending on the size of each record. If you can keep data commonly asked for together on the same data page or nearby pages, your retrieval performance will be better because your disk seeks become more efficient. For spatial queries, you commonly ask for things that are spatially close to each other. As such, you want them to be physically close to each other on disk as well for faster retrieval.

There are two kinds of spatial indexes commonly used for database clustering in PostGIS: the `GeoHash` cluster, which is most beneficial for small objects and requires data to be in WGS 84 lon/lat (EPSG 4326), and the more common, all-purpose R-tree cluster, which is just a cluster on the gist index you create on a table.

> **MORE ABOUT GEOHASH AND R-TREE** For more details on GeoHash versus the standard R-tree cluster, see the "Clustering on Indices" workshop module of Boundless's Introduction to PostGIS: http://workshops.boundlessgeo.com/postgis-intro/clusterindex.html: Clustering on Indices.

The GeoHash cluster works best for small objects, such as points or small polygons and linestrings, and becomes unusable for larger objects unless you base it on something like `ST_GeoHash(ST_Centroid(geom))`. The reason it's not usable or is of minimal use for larger objects is that as an object gets bigger, its GeoHash representation gets smaller until it shrinks to nothing. The GeoHash implemented by PostGIS is the GeoHash of the bounding box.

Listing 15.24 demonstrates a slight twist to the standard GeoHash index. This index combines both a GeoHash and street name in the index so that when you cluster the data, the data will first be spatially clustered, and for streets that have the same GeoHash, you'll have similarly named streets closer together.

Listing 15.24 Cluster by compound index consisting of GeoHash and street name

```
CREATE INDEX idx_stclines_streets_ghash_street                  ❶ Create index
ON ch15.stclines_streets (ST_GeoHash(ST_Transform(geom,4326)),street);

CLUSTER ch15.stclines_streets
    USING idx_stclines_streets_ghash_street;                    ❷ Cluster on index
```

In listing 15.24 you create a compound index composed of the GeoHash of the street centerline and the name ❶. The advantage of a compound index is that long streets are often broken into smaller segments and stored as separate rows. You want streets that are continuations to be closer together if they have the same GeoHash. Data doesn't physically get resorted until you cluster on the index ❷.

> **Cluster not maintained after updates or inserts**
>
> PostgreSQL doesn't maintain the physical order of the table to match the cluster index during inserts and updates. If you have a table that you update fairly frequently, you'll want to run `CLUSTER` *`table_name`* to force a reordering of the table on the index you clustered on.
>
> If you need to recluster all the tables that have clusters defined, just run `CLUSTER verbose`. The `verbose` is optional but will show you the table names and the clustering index as each table is reclustered. It will also show you stats on the number of pages and rows.

If you decided to change your cluster later to the R-tree index, you'd run this command:

```
CLUSTER ch15.stclines_streets USING stclines_streets_geom_gist
```

This would force a reclustering of the table using your gist index called `stclines_streets_geom_gist`, and for future cluster operations where no cluster index is specified, it would use this index.

If you have a small table such as ch15.stclines_streets, with ~15,000 rows, it's hard to see a performance difference between clustered and nonclustered. If your data set is fairly small, it fits into onboard RAM, so disk seeks are less common.

15.8 Summary

In this chapter, we covered a variety of ways of improving the performance of spatial queries. We discussed various approaches for writing spatial queries, how to troubleshoot query performance, how to optimize geometries, and several common settings in PostgreSQL that can be changed to improve performance. Although many of these techniques focused on spatial queries, many can be applied to non-spatial queries as well.

PostGIS and PostgreSQL aren't islands. They intermingle with various applications and software. The power of PostGIS can only be fully appreciated when you combine it with other tools to build applications or to view outputs. In the chapters that follow, we'll take a closer look at how PostGIS interacts with other tools for building applications. In chapter 16, we'll demonstrate additional PostgreSQL extensions that can be used in conjunction with PostGIS.

Part 3

Using PostGIS with other tools

In part 2 you learned the basics of solving problems with spatial queries, and performance tips for getting the most speed out of your spatial queries. But PostGIS is a seductive mistress widely courted by both commercial and open source tools. In part 3, you'll learn about some of the more common open source server-side tools that are used to complement and enhance PostGIS.

Chapter 16 covers other PostgreSQL extensions commonly used with PostGIS. You'll learn about the procedural languages PL/R, PL/Python, and PL/V8. These are common favorites in GIS for leveraging the wealth of statistical functions and plotting capabilities of R, the numerous packages for Python, and the brisk elegance of JavaScript in the database. You'll learn how to write stored functions in these languages and use them in SQL queries. In addition, we'll cover pgRouting, which is another package of SQL functions used to build routing applications and solve various kinds of traveling-salesperson problems.

In chapter 17, you'll learn about server-side mapping servers and client-side mapping frameworks, which are commonly used to display PostGIS data on the web. You'll learn how to display PostGIS data with third-party mapping layers, such as OpenStreetMap, Google Maps, and Microsoft Bing, using the open source JavaScript mapping APIs Leaflet and OpenLayers. You'll also learn the basics of setting up GeoServer and MapServer and configuring them as WMS/WFS services.

16 Extending PostGIS with pgRouting and procedural languages

This chapter covers

- pgRouting
- PL/R
- PL/Python
- PL/V8

In this chapter, we'll cover PostgreSQL extensions commonly installed with PostGIS. Extensions expand what you can do with PostGIS beyond the base installation. Each extension can come packaged with additional functions and data types (PostGIS is itself an extension). Each extension has a specific mission. It may allow you to script in an additional language, add specific functionality, or replace existing functions with faster implementations.

In this chapter, we'll discuss the following extensions:

- *pgRouting*—A library of functions used in conjunction with PostGIS to solve problems such as shortest path, driving directions, and geographic constrained resource allocation problems, such as the legendary traveling salesman problem (TSP).
- *PL/R*—A procedural language handler for PostgreSQL that allows you to write stored database functions using the R statistical language and graphical environment. With this extension you can generate elegant graphs and make use of a breadth of statistical functions to build aggregate and other functions within your PostgreSQL database. This allows you to inject the power of R into your queries.
- *PL/Python*—A procedural language handler for PostgreSQL that allows you to write PostgreSQL stored functions in Python. This allows you to leverage the breadth of Python functions for network connectivity, data import, geocoding, and other tasks.
- *PL/V8 (a.k.a. PL/JavaScript)*—A procedural language handler for PostgreSQL that allows you to write PostgreSQL stored functions in JavaScript. This means you can use the same language on the server that you'd commonly use with client-side web applications, and even reuse some of these functions. PL/V8 utilizes the Google V8 engine, which is also the plumbing used for NodeJS.

After you've finished this chapter, you'll better appreciate the benefits of implementing solutions directly in your database instead of exporting your data for external processing.

The data and code used in this chapter can be found at www.postgis.us/chapter_16_edition_2. To follow along with the upcoming examples, you'll need to run the data/ch16_data.sql script from this chapter's download file. It's best to use psql to load the file. The script will both create the schema for this chapter and load in the tables used in this chapter.

16.1 Solving network routing problems with pgRouting

Once you have all your data in PostGIS, what better way to show it off than to find solutions to routing problems such as the shortest path from one address to another or the famous traveling salesman problem. PgRouting lets you do just that. All you have to do is add a few extra columns to your existing tables to store parameters and solutions. Then execute one of the many functions packaged with pgRouting. PgRouting makes it possible to get instant answers to seemingly intractable problems. Without pgRouting, you'd have to resort to expensive desktop tools such as ArcGIS Network Analyst or pay-per-use web services.

PgRouting is a FOSS project in its own right, but it relies on PostGIS for spatial analysis functions. PgRouting underwent significant improvements in its version 2.0, with new functions and easier installation. Function names in version 2.0 also differ from those in 1.0. As a general rule, functions in pgRouting 2.0 begin with the prefix *pgr_*.

16.1.1 Installing pgRouting

Installing pgRouting 2.0 is simpler than installing version 1.0. Many distributions of PostGIS offer pgRouting now. If you're using Windows, the PostGIS 2.1+ stack builder installs pgRouting binaries along with PostGIS. Refer to the pgRouting site (http://pgrouting.org/download.html) for binaries for other distributions.

Once you've procured the binaries and installed them, add pgRouting to your database as an extension with SQL:

```
CREATE EXTENSION pgrouting;
```

For more details on working with pgRouting, visit the pgRouting site: http://pgrouting.org.

16.1.2 Basic navigation

The most common use of routing is to find the shortest route among a network of interconnected roads. Anyone who has ever sought driving directions from a GPS unit should be intimately familiar with this application.

For a first example, we picked the North American cities of Minneapolis and Saint Paul. Picture yourself as a truck driver who needs to find the shortest route through the Twin Cities. As with most industrialized cities in the world, highways usually bifurcate at the boundary of a metropolis, offering a perimeter route that encircles the city and multiple radial routes into the city. Altogether, highways form a spoke-and-wheel pattern.

The Twin Cities have one of the most convoluted patterns of all the major cities in the United States. A truck driver trying to pass through the cities via the shortest route has quite a few choices to make; furthermore, the shortest choice isn't apparent from just looking at a map. See figure 16.1. A driver entering the metropolitan area from the south and wishing to leave via the northwest has quite a few options. We'll use pgRouting to point the driver to the shortest route.

BUILDING THE NETWORK TOPOLOGY

The first step in routing problems is to create a network topology from your table of linestrings, or *edges* in topo-speak. You'll build a network topology using the `pgr_CreateTopology` pgRouting function. This comprehensive function loops through all the records and assigns each linestring two integer identifiers: one for the starting point and one for the ending point. `pgr_CreateTopology` makes sure that identical points receive the same identifier even if it's shared by multiple linestrings.

In order for the `pgr_CreateTopology` function to have somewhere to store the identifiers, you need to have two placeholder columns readied: a source column for the starting point and a target column for the ending point. Listing 16.1 demonstrates adding the source and target columns and populating those columns using `pgr_CreateTopology`.

> **WARNING** Keep in mind that pgRouting topology is completely unrelated to the `topology` data type in PostGIS.

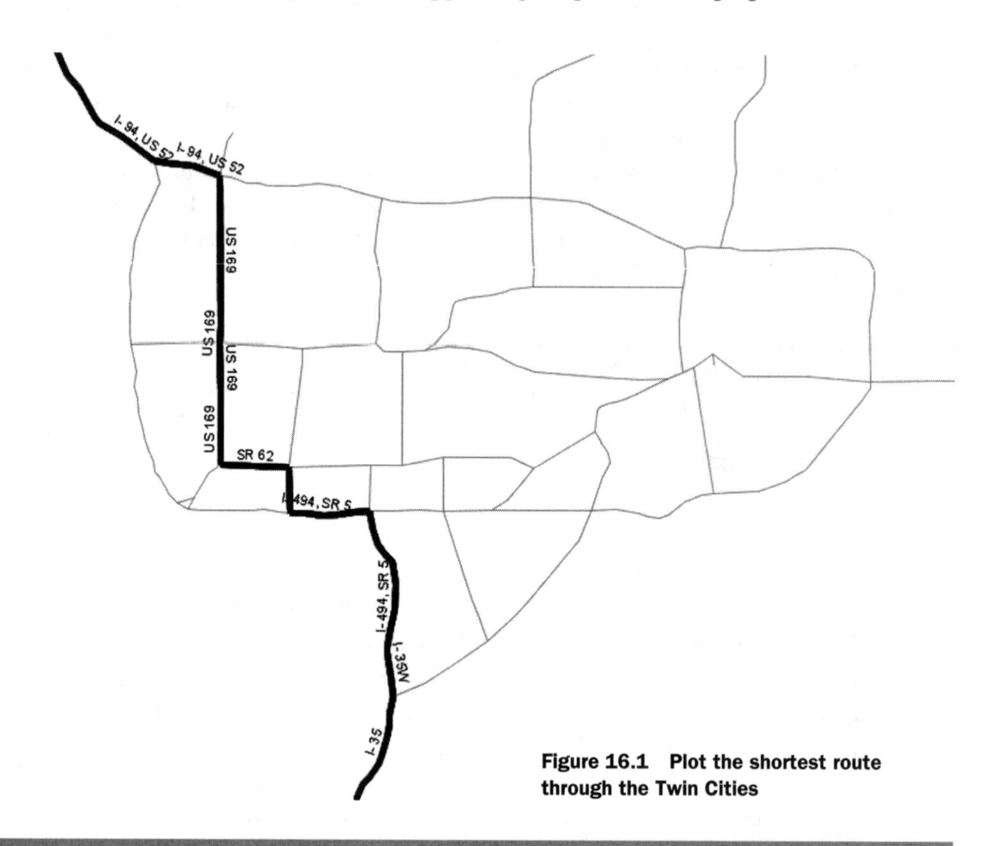

Figure 16.1 Plot the shortest route through the Twin Cities

Listing 16.1 Building a network topology

```
ALTER TABLE ch16.twin_cities ADD COLUMN source integer;
ALTER TABLE ch16.twin_cities ADD COLUMN target integer;
SELECT pgr_CreateTopology(
    'ch16.twin_cities',
    0.000001,
    'geom',
    'gid',
    'source',
    'target'
);
```

❶ Add source
❷ Add target
❸ Populate fields

In this listing, you create source ❶ and target columns ❷, which will hold the node identifiers for the nodes' connecting edges. Then you populate the source and target columns by specifying a tolerance value that defines how close the start and end points need to be for them to be considered the same node. You use the edge identifier column, gid, to uniquely identify each edge and a geometry column, geom, that has the edge linestring ❸. In addition to populating the source and target columns of the twin_cities table, pgRouting creates a table of nodes called ch16.twin_cities_vertices_pgr to store the nodes as point geometries.

DIJKSTRA SHORTEST PATH ALGORITHM

PgRouting weighs routes using costs, and there are many kinds of costs. You can assign costs to segments based on length, speed limit, directionality (one-way or two-way), gradient, and so forth. From these costs, you can optimize your travel to produce a route with a minimum cost. The most prevalent cost measure, and the one we'll use here, is distance.

You begin by assigning costs to each linestring. Because you're looking at distance, you'll create a column to hold length, take the spheroidal length of each linestring, and fill in the length column, as shown in the following listing.

Listing 16.2 Assigning costs to edges

```
ALTER TABLE ch16.twin_cities ADD COLUMN length float8;          <-- Add length
UPDATE ch16.twin_cities
SET length = ST_Length(ST_Transform(geom,4326)::geography);       <-- Update value
```

To get an accurate length, you cast your linestrings in longitude and latitude to `geography` and use the geography `length` function, which returns length in meters.

Although it's not shown in this first example, you can easily use different cost factors to weigh the linestrings. For example, you could weigh highways by a speed limit so that slower highways have a higher cost. You could even get live feeds of traffic conditions so that routes with major traffic congestion would receive a higher cost.

The Dijkstra algorithm is one approach for arriving at an exact solution for travel from one node to another in your network based on given costs. For small networks like this one, exact solutions are possible in real time. For large networks, approximate solutions are often good enough and cut down computation time.

With the network prepared and the costs assigned, all it takes is the execution of a pgRouting function to return the answer with the minimum cost.

```
SELECT pd.seq, e.geom, pd.cost, pd.id1 As node
INTO ch16.dijkstra_result
FROM
    pgr_Dijkstra(
        'SELECT gid AS id, source, target, length As cost
        FROM ch16.twin_cities',                          <-- 1 Network SQL
        134,                              <-- 2 Source node
Target node 3 -->   33,
        false,                               <-- 4 Not directed
No reverse cost 5 -->  false
    ) As pd                               <-- 1 Network SQL
    LEFT JOIN
    ch16.twin_cities As e
    ON pd.id2 = e.gid
ORDER BY pd.seq;
```

`pgr_Dijkstra` takes as input a query with the following columns: edge ID, source (origin) node, target (destination) node, and cost ❶. If directed ❹ is set to true and reverse cost is set to true ❺, then it must have an additional reverse-cost column. The source node `134` is on Interstate 35, south of the city ❷, and the target node `33` is on Interstate 94, northwest of the city ❸.

Dijkstra is merely one of many algorithms available in pgRouting for routing. To see the ever-growing list of algorithms available (or to contribute your own), visit the main pgRouting site at http://pgrouting.org. For large networks, don't forget to add spatial indexes to your table prior to executing any algorithms.

The shortest-route problem is a general class of cost-minimizing or profit-maximizing problems. What you define as cost or profit is entirely up to you. Don't limit yourself to traditional measures. Be creative. For example, you can easily download a table of calories from your local McDonald's, group the food items into sandwiches, drinks, and sides, and query for the least fattening meal you can consume, provided that you must order something from each group—the McRouting problem.

16.1.3 Traveling salesman

Many times in our programming ventures, we've come across the need to find solutions to TSP-related problems. Often we've given up because nothing was easy to integrate. Although algorithms are available in many languages, setting up a network and pairing the algorithm with whichever database we were using at the time was much too tedious. We often resorted to suboptimal SQL-based solutions. How often we have hoped that something like pgRouting would come along!

The classic description of a TSP problem involves a salesman having to visit a wide array of cities to sell widgets. Given that the salesman has to visit each city only once, how should he plan his itinerary to minimize the total distance traveled?

To demonstrate TSP using pgRouting, we'll pretend that we're a team of inspectors from the International Atomic Energy Agency (IAEA), the United Nations' nuclear energy watchdog, and our task is to inspect all the nuclear plants in Spain. A quick search on Wikipedia (circa 2011) shows that seven plants are operational on the entire Iberian Peninsula.

You can create a new table as follows:

```
CREATE TABLE spain_nuclear_plants(
    id serial,
    plant varchar(150),
    lat double precision,
    lon double precision
);
```

The data to populate the table is included with the chapter's downloads.

For TSP, you need your table to have X and Y coordinates (longitude and latitude will do). Each row will represent a node that the nuclear inspectors must visit. Another requirement of the TSP function is that each node must be identified using an integer identifier. For this reason, the table includes an ID column and assigns each plant a number from 1 to 7.

With all these pieces in place, you can execute the TSP function.

Listing 16.3 Traveling to nuclear power plants in Spain using TSP

```
SELECT seq, t.id1, p.id, p.plant
FROM
    pgr_tsp(
        'SELECT id, lon AS x, lat AS y
        FROM ch16.spain_nuclear_plants',          <-- 1 Locations
Start 2 -->  1,
        7           <-- 3 End
    ) As t
    INNER JOIN
    ch16.spain_nuclear_plants As p
    ON t.id2 = p.id           <-- 4 Rejoin with ch16.spain_nuclear_plants
ORDER BY seq;
```

The TSP function call in listing 16.3 is a little unusual in that the first parameter is an SQL string ❶. This string must return a set of records with the columns id, x, and y: id is the site identifier, and x and y are the geographic coordinates. The column names output by the SQL statement must always have these column names, but can have additional columns. Additional columns will be ignored.

The second parameter of 1 (Alamaraz) is the identifier of the site to start at ❷. There is an optional ending node you can provide if you don't want your trip to start and end in the same spot. In this example, the ending node is set to 7, Vendellios ❸.

The TSP function returns a set of pgr_CostResult objects made up of three fields: seq, id, and id1. The seq is the order of travel; id, which is not really relevant for this case, is the depth into the distance matrix; and id2 is the site identifier. You rejoin by site id to get back the plant names ❹.

The results follow. The visual representation of these results is shown in figure 16.2.

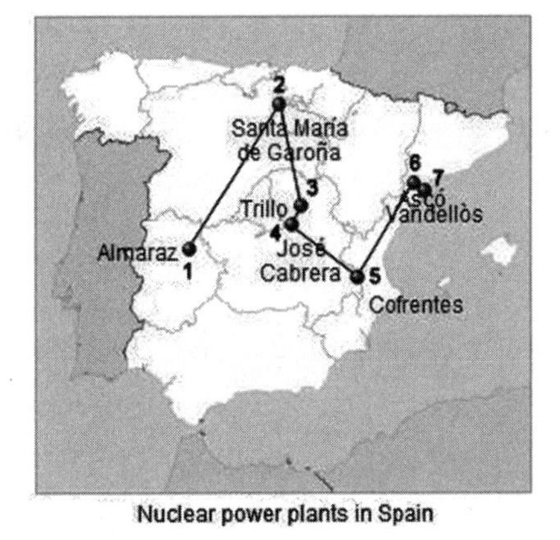

Figure 16.2 Traveling to nuclear power plants in Spain

```
 seq | id1 | id | plant
-----+-----+----+----------------------
   0 |   0 |  1 | Almaraz
   1 |   4 |  5 | Santa Maria de Garona
   2 |   5 |  6 | Trillo
   3 |   3 |  4 | Jose Cabrera
   4 |   2 |  3 | Cofrentes
   5 |   1 |  2 | Asco
   6 |   6 |  7 | Vandellios
```

There are other variants of the TSP function provided by pgRouting. Because we provided a table of geographic locations, pgRouting used standard Euclidean math to compute a distance matrix for each combination. If you don't want Euclidean distance, you could provide a distance matrix populated with a cost for each site-to-site pairing.

This section has illustrated the convenience resulting from pairing a problem-solving algorithm with a database. Imagine that you had to solve the shortest route or TSP problem on some set of data using just a conventional programming language. Without PostGIS or pgRouting, you'd have to define your own data structure, code the algorithm, and find a nice way to present the solution. Should the nature of your data change, you'd have to repeat the process.

In the next sections, we'll explore PL languages. The marriage of PL languages and SQL combines the expressiveness of an all-purpose or domain-specific language suited for certain classes of problems with the power of SQL.

16.2 Extending PostgreSQL with PLs

One thing that makes PostgreSQL unique among the various relational databases is its pluggable procedural language (PL) architecture. Many Samaritans have created PL handlers for PostgreSQL, allowing you to write database stored functions in languages like Perl, Python, Java, TCL, R, JavaScript, and Sh (shell script), in addition to the built-in C, PL/pgSQL, and SQL.

Stored functions are directly callable from SQL statements. This means

- You can write stored functions in a language more suited for a particular task, or a language that you're well versed in.
- You can perform certain tasks much more easily than you would if you had to extract the data, import it into these language environments, and push it back into the database.
- You can write aggregate functions and triggers, and use functions developed for these languages right in your database.
- You can use various functions together in a single SQL query even if the functions are written in different languages.
- The code you'd write to define the PL function is pretty much the same as what you'd normally write in the language, except for the additional hooks into the PostgreSQL database.

These PL languages are prefixed with *PL*: PL/Perl, PL/Python, PL/Proxy, PL/R, PL/Sh, PL/Java, PL/V8. The list of PLs is growing.

16.2.1 Basic installation of PLs

In order to use each non-built-in PL language in your database, there are three prerequisites:

- The language environment must be installed on your PostgreSQL server.
- The PL handler library (which generally starts with the filename prefix *pl* and suffix *.so* or *.dll*) must be installed in your PostgreSQL instance.

- The language handler must be installed in the databases you'll use them in. In older versions, this was done with a script that included at a minimum the `CREATE LANGUAGE` statement. In PostgreSQL 9.1 or later, you install these languages using `CREATE EXTENSION` *`name-of-language;`*.

The functionality of a PL extension is usually packaged as a .so/.dll file whose filename starts with `pl*`. It negotiates the interaction between PostgreSQL and the language environment by converting PostgreSQL data sets and data types into the most appropriate data structure for that language environment. It also handles the conversion back to a PostgreSQL data type when the function returns with a record set or scalar value.

16.2.2 What you can do with PLs

Each PL achieves varying degrees of integration with the PostgreSQL environment. PL/Perl is the oldest and probably the most common and most tested PL you'll find.

PLs are registered in two flavors: *trusted* and *untrusted.* PL/Perl can be registered as both trusted and untrusted. PL/V8 offers just the trusted variant. Most of the other PLs you'll come across offer just the untrusted variant.

What's the difference between trusted and untrusted?

A trusted PL is a sandboxed PL, meaning provisions have been made to prevent it from accessing other parts of the OS outside the database cluster. A trusted language function can run under the context of a non-superuser, but certain features of the language are disabled.

An untrusted language is one that can potentially wreak havoc on the server, so great care must be taken. It can delete files, execute processes, and do all the things that the PostgreSQL daemon/service account has the power to do. Untrusted language functions must run in the context of a superuser, which also means that you must be a superuser to create them. To permit non-superusers to execute the functions, you must mark the functions as `SECURITY DEFINER`.

In the sections that follow, we'll demonstrate PL/Python, PL/R, and the newer PL/V8. We've chosen these particular languages because they have the largest offerings of spatial packages. We also think they're pretty cool languages in their own right. They're favorites among geostatisticians and GIS programmers. PL/Python and PL/R only come in the untrusted form; PL/V8 only comes trusted.

Python is a dynamically typed, all-purpose procedural language. It has elegant approaches for creating and navigating objects, and it supports functional programming, object-oriented programming, the building of classes, metaprogramming, reflection, map reduce, and all those chic programming paradigms you've probably heard of.

R, on the other hand, is more of a domain language. R is specifically designed for statistics, graphing, and data mining, so it draws a large following from research institutions. It has many built-in statistical functions or functions you can download and install via the built-in package manager. You'll be hard-pressed to find R functionality in other FOSS languages; we've seen them in pricy tools such as SAS, MATLAB, and Mathematica. You'll find tasks such as applying functions to all items in a list and matrix algebra operations will become second nature once you get into the R mindset. In addition to manipulating data, R packs a graphical engine that allows you to generate polished graphs with only a few lines of code. You can even plot in 3D.

Using in-database PLs that can call out to external environments, such as PL/R and PL/Python, has many advantages over writing similar logic outside of the database. Here are a few that come to mind:

- You can write functions in PLs that pull data from the PostgreSQL environment without any messy database connection setup and have them return sets of records, or update sets of records. You can also return scalars.
- You can write database triggers in PLs that use the power of these environments to run tasks in response to changes of data in the database. For example, you can geocode data when an address changes or have a database trigger to regenerate a map tile on a change of data in the database without ever touching the application edit code. This is impossible to accomplish with just the languages and a database connection driver.
- You can write aggregate functions with these languages that will allow you to pass in a set of rows to an aggregate function that in turn uses functions available only in these languages to summarize the data. Imagine an aggregation function that returns a graph for each grouping of data, all done with a single `SELECT` query.

Our ensuing examples will only have a slight GIS bent. Our intent here is to show you how to get started integrating these in your PostgreSQL database and give you a general feel of what's possible with these languages. We'll also show you how you can find and install libraries that can expand PLs.

16.3 PL/R

PL/R is a PL using the R statistical language and graphical environment. You can tap into the vast statistical packages that R provides, as well as the numerous geospatial add-ons. R is a darling among statisticians and researchers because operations can be applied to an entire matrix of data just as easily as to a single value. Its built-in graphing environments mean you need not resort to yet another software package. R also supports data imports from a variety of formats.

We'll just touch the surface of what PL/R and R can do here. To explore further, we suggest reading *R in Action, Second Edition* by Robert I. Kabacoff (Manning, 2015) or *Applied Spatial Data Analysis with R* by Roger Bivand, Edzer Pebesma, and V. Gómez-Rubio (Springer, 2013). Appendix A also provides more links to useful R sites.

For what follows, we used R 3.0.2. Most of our examples should work on earlier versions as well.

16.3.1 Getting started with PL/R

To set up PostgreSQL for R, do the following:

1. Install the R environment on the same computer as PostgreSQL. R is available for Unix, Linux, Mac OS X, as well as Windows. Unix/Linux users may need to compile PL/R, but for Windows and Mac OS X users there are precompiled binaries. You can download source and precompiled binaries of R from www.r-project.org. Any R version from R 2.5 through R 3.02 should work fine (for these exercises we used R 3.0.2).

   PL/R also assumes that the R libraries and the R binaries are in the environment `path` setting of the server.

   If you're running a 64-bit version of PostgreSQL, then you'll need a 64-bit version of R. For PostgreSQL 32-bit, you'll need to run a 32-bit version of R, even if you're running on a 64-bit OS.
2. Compile the source or download binaries via Package and then install the plr library by copying it into the lib directory of your PostgreSQL install. If you're using an installer, this will probably already be done for you. If you're running under Linux, R should be configured with the option `-enable-R-shlib`. As with other PostgreSQL extensions, you must use the plr library version compiled for your version of PostgreSQL. However, the same plr library will generally work for the same R version as long as they are the same 32/64-bit compiled. You can download the binaries and source from www.joeconway.com/plr. You may need to restart the PostgreSQL service before you can use PL/R in a database.
3. In the database in which you'll be writing R stored functions, run the SQL command `CREATE EXTENSION plr;`. You need to repeat this step for each database you want to use R in. Keep in mind that language extensions need to be installed by a superuser.

PL/R relies on an environment variable called `R_HOME` to point to the location of the R install. The `R_HOME` variable must also be accessible by the `postgres` service account. After the install, check that `R_HOME` is specified correctly by running the following command: `SELECT * FROM plr_environ();`. This should already be set for you if you're using an installer. If you're a Linux/Unix user, you can set this with `export R_HOME = ...` and include it as part of your PostgreSQL initialization script. You may need to restart your Postgres services for the new settings to take effect.

If any of this is confusing or you get stuck, check out the PL/R wiki installation tips guides at www.joeconway.com/web/guest/pl/r/-/wiki/Main/Installation+Tips.

16.3.2 Saving data sets and plotting

Now let's take PL/R for a test drive.

SAVING POSTGRESQL DATA TO R DATA FORMAT

For this first example, we'll pull data out of PostgreSQL and save it to R's custom binary format (RData). There are two common reasons to do this:

- It makes it easy to interactively test different plotting styles and other R functions in R's interactive environment against real data before you package them in a PL/R function.
- If you're providing sample data sets, you may want to provide your data sets in a format that can be easily loaded in R by users.

Listing 16.4 uses the PostgreSQL `pg.spi.exec` function and R's `save` function.

The `pg.spi.exec` function is a PL function that allows you to convert any PostgreSQL data set into a form that can be consumed by the language environment. In the case of PL/R, this is usually an R `data.frame` type structure.

The `save` command in R allows you to save many objects to a single binary file, as shown in listing 16.4. These objects can be data frames (including spatial data frames), lists, matrices, vectors, scalars, and all of the various object types supported by R. When you want to load these in an R session, you run the command `load("filepath")`.

Listing 16.4 Saving PostgreSQL data in an R data format with PL/R

```
CREATE OR REPLACE FUNCTION ch16.save_places_rdata() RETURNS text AS
$$
places_mega <<- pg.spi.exec("
    SELECT name, latitude, longitude FROM ch16.places WHERE megacity = 1
")

nb <<- pg.spi.exec("
    SELECT name, latitude, longitude
    FROM ch16.places
    WHERE ST_DWithin(geog,ST_GeogFromText('POINT(7.5 9.0)'),1000000)
")
save(places_mega, nb, file="C:/Temp/places.RData")
return("done")
$$
LANGUAGE 'plr';
```

❶ Store results in R variables

❷ Save variables to R data file

In listing 16.4 you create two data sets that contain world places, one based on attributes and one based on a spatial `data.frame` ❶. You then save this to a file called places.RData ❷. *RData* is the standard suffix for the binary R data format, and in most desktop installs, when you launch it, it will open R with the data loaded.

To run this example, run `SELECT ch16.save_places_rdata();`.

You can load this saved data in R by clicking the file or by opening R and running a load call in R. Table 16.1 lists some quick commands you can try in the R environment.

Table 16.1 Some R commands

Description	Command
Load a file in R and clear all variables in memory	`rm(list=ls()) and then load("C:/Temp/places.RData")`
List contents loaded in memory in R	`ls()`
View a data structure in R	`summary(places_mega)`
View data in R	`nb (type the name of the data variable)`
View a set of rows in a variable in R	`places_mega[1:3,]`
View columns of data in an R variable	`places_mega[1:4,]$name`

If you append <- to the command, the output goes to an R variable instead of being printed to the screen. Figure 16.3 shows a snapshot of these commands.

```
> rm(list=ls())
> load("C:/Temp/places.RData")
> ls()
[1] "nb"          "places_mega"
> summary(places_mega)
     name              latitude          longitude
 Length:45          Min.   :-37.820   Min.   :-123.12
 Class :character   1st Qu.:  6.132   1st Qu.: -17.47
 Mode  :character   Median : 23.723   Median :  18.43
                    Mean   : 19.987   Mean   :  14.92
                    3rd Qu.: 39.927   3rd Qu.:  47.98
                    Max.   : 60.176   Max.   : 174.76
> nb
          name   latitude  longitude
1  Porto-Novo  6.4833110  2.6166255
2        Lome  6.1319371  1.2227571
3      Niamey 13.5167060  2.1166560
4       Abuja  9.0033331  7.5333280
5    Ndjamena 12.1130965 15.0491483
6      Malabo  3.7500153  8.7832775
7  Libreville  0.3853886  9.4579650
8     Yaounde  3.8667007 11.5166508
9     Cotonou  6.4000086  2.5199906
10   Sao Tome  0.3334021  6.7333252
11      Accra  5.5500346 -0.2167157
12      Lagos  6.4432617  3.3915311
> places_mega[1:3,]
        name latitude longitude
1     Kigali  -1.95359  30.06053
2      Kyoto  35.02999 135.75000
3 Montevideo -34.85804 -56.17105
> places_mega[1:4,]$name
[1] "Kigali"     "Kyoto"      "Montevideo" "Lome"
> |
```

Figure 16.3 Output of running the previous statements in R

DRAWING PLOTS WITH PL/R

R excels in plotting. Many people, even those who could care less about statistics, are attracted to R by its sophisticated scriptable plotting and graphing environment. The following listing demonstrates a bit of this by generating a random data set in PostgreSQL and plotting it.

Listing 16.5 Plotting PostgreSQL data with R using PL/R

```
CREATE OR REPLACE FUNCTION ch16.graph_income_house() RETURNS text AS
$$
randdata <<- pg.spi.exec("
    SELECT x As income,AVG(x*(1+random()*y)) As avgprice
    FROM
        generate_series(2000,100000,10000) As x
        CROSS JOIN
        generate_series(1,5) As y
    GROUP BY x
    ORDER BY x
")                                                          ❶ Create random data
 png('C:/temp/housepercap.png',width=500,height=400)        ❷ Create PNG file
 opar <- par(bg="white")                                    ❸ Set background
 plot(x=randdata$income,y=randdata$avgprice, ann=FALSE,type="n")   ❹ Draw plot

yrange = range(randdata$avgprice)
abline(
    h=seq(yrange[1],yrange[2],(yrange[2]-yrange[1])/10),
    lty=1,col="grey"
)                                                           ❺ Prep plot space
lines(x=randdata$income,y=randdata$avgprice,
 col="green4",lty="dotted")                                 ❻ Draw grid lines

points(x=randdata$income,y=randdata$avgprice,bg="limegreen",pch=23)   ❼ Draw lines
title(
    main="Random plot of house price vs. per capita income",
    xlab="Per cap income",ylab="Average House Price",
    col.main="blue",col.lab="red1",font.main=4,font.lab=3
)
dev.off()                                                   ❽ Draw points

return("done")
$$
LANGUAGE 'plr';
```

This code creates a stored function written in PL/R that will create a file called housepercap.png on the C:/temp folder of the PostgreSQL server. It first creates random data by running an SQL statement using the PostgreSQL `generate_series` function and dumps this into an R variable called `randdata` ❶.

Then it creates a PNG file using the R `png` function (note that other functions such as `pdf`, `jpeg`, and the like can be used to create other formats), which all the plotting will be redirected to ❷. Then it sets the background color to white using the `par` parameter setting function ❸. Next it draws the plot ❹. The `n` type means there is no plot; it just prepares the plot space so that you can then draw grid lines ❺, lines ❻, and points ❼ on the same grid.

Finally you close writing to the file with `dev.off()` ❽ and then return some text saying `done`.

> **Unable to start device devWindows**
> It's common to get a *can't start device* error, even though the same command runs perfectly fine in the R GUI environment. This is because PL/R runs in the context of the `postgres` service account. Any folder you wish to write to from PL/R must have read/write access from the `postgres` service/daemon account.

Run the function in listing 16.5 with the following SQL statement:

```
SELECT ch16.graph_income_house();
```

Running this command generates a PNG file, as shown in figure 16.4.

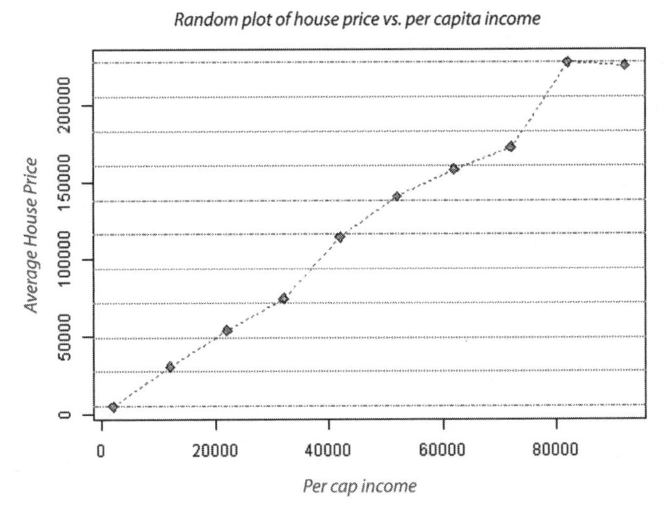

Figure 16.4 Result of `SELECT ch16.graph_income_house();`

16.3.3 Using R packages in PL/R

The R environment has a whole gamut of functions, data, and data types you can download and install. They're distributed in packages and are often referred to as *libraries*.

You can see all installed packages in the library folder of your R installation. R also makes finding, downloading, and installing additional libraries easy using the Comprehensive R Archive Network (CRAN). Once a package is installed, you can use its components in PL/R functions.

What's particularly instructive with R is that many packages come with demos showcasing features. They also often come with something called *vignettes*, which are quick tutorials on using a package. Demos and vignettes make R a fun, interactive learning environment. In order to use a vignette or demo, you first have to use the library command to load the library. The commands to load and view these packages are listed in table 16.2.

Table 16.2 Commands for installing and navigating packages

Command	Description
`library()`	Displays a list of packages already installed
`library(package-name)`	Loads a package into memory
`update.packages()`	Upgrades all packages to the latest versions
`install.packages("package-name")`	Installs a new package
`available.packages()`	Lists packages available in default CRAN
`chooseCRANmirror()`	Allows you to switch to a different CRAN
`demo()`	Shows a list of demos in loaded packages
`demo(package = .packages(all .available = TRUE))`	Lists all demos in installed packages
`demo(name-of-demo)`	Launches a demo (you must load the package first)
`help(package=some-package-name)`	Gives summary help for a package
`help(package=package-name,function-name)`	Gives detailed help for an item in a package
`vignette()`	Lists tutorials in packages
`vignette("name-of-vignette")`	Launches a PDF of exercises

In order to test the CRAN install process, we'll install two packages: *sp* (http://cran.r-project.org/web/packages/sp/index.html), which provides spatial classes for R data, such as spatial data frames and charting functionality; and another called *rgeos* bindings (http://cran.r-project.org/web/packages/rgeos/index.html), which provides GEOS functions such as conversion and spatial predicate functions in R. Recall that the GEOS library is one that PostGIS leverages for many of its spatial functions.

To install packages in R, you can use the R command line or the graphical R interface, Rgui. For this example, we'll use the command line.

To enter the R console, type `R` at a command line. Then, enter the following command to load the sp library:

```
library(sp)
```

If that command fails, use the following commands to install sp and then load it:

```
install.packages("sp")
library(sp)
```

After installing R, you'll likely have to exit R and come back in to run any commands.

To get help about the sp library, run this command:

```
help(package=sp)
```

To quit the R console, enter this command:

```
q()
```

Repeat the same steps for rgeos. Once it's loaded, you can verify the version of GEOS you're running with:

```
version_GEOS()
```

That command should output something like this:

```
[1] "3.4.2-CAPI-1.8.2 r3921"
```

Restart needed after installing packages
For this particular installation and some more complex packages, you may need to restart R before you can use the libraries. To use these libraries from PL/R, you also need to restart the PostgreSQL service. These steps aren't necessary for all R packages.

Next we'll test drive the sp and rgeos installations by writing a PL/R function calling their functions.

16.3.4 Converting geometries into R spatial objects and plotting spatial objects

The sp package contains classes to represent geometries as R objects. It has lines, polygons, and points. It also has spatial polygon, line, and point data frames. Data frames are similar to PostgreSQL tables with geometry columns.

The rgeos package is an R wrapper for the GEOS library, which is the same library that PostGIS relies on. One of the functions exposed by rgeos is called `readWKT`, and it converts a well-known text (WKT) representation to an sp geometry. In the next example, we'll combine sp and rgeos to convert PostGIS geometries into a form that can be charted in R.

In the next listing, you'll convert the previous pgRouting results for the Twin Cities into R spatial objects and then plot them directly in R.

Listing 16.6 Plotting linestrings with R

```
CREATE OR REPLACE FUNCTION ch16.plot_routing_results()
RETURNS text AS
$$
library(sp)
library(rgeos)
geodata <<- pg.spi.exec("
```

```
    SELECT gid, route, ST_AsText(geom) As geomwkt
    FROM ch16.twin_cities
    ORDER BY gid
")
```
Create an R data frame with a column for WKT of highway

```
ngeom <- length(geodata$gid)
row.names(geodata) = geodata$gid
for (i in 1:ngeom) {

    if (i == 1) {
        geo.sp = readWKT(geodata$geomwkt[i],geodata$gid[i])
    }
    else {
        geo.sp = rbind(
            geo.sp,readWKT(geodata$geomwkt[i],geodata$gid[i])
        )
    }
}
```
Convert WKT linestring to sp line

Convert WKT linestring to sp line

```
sdf <- SpatialLinesDataFrame(geo.sp, geodata[-3])
georesult <<- pg.spi.exec("
    SELECT ST_AsText(ST_LineMerge(ST_Collect(geom))) As geomwkt
    FROM ch16.dijkstra_result
")
```
Create spatial data frame

Collect result as single geometry WKT row

```
sdf_result <- SpatialLinesDataFrame(
    readWKT(georesult$geomwkt[1],"result"),
    data = data.frame(c("result")),
    match.ID=FALSE
)
```
Convert to SpatialLinesDataFrame with id=result

```
png('C:/temp/twin_bestpath.png',width=500,height=400)
plot(sdf,xlim=c(-94,-93),ylim=c(44.5,45.5),axes=TRUE);
lines(sdf_result,col="green4",lty="dashed",type="o")
title(
    main="Travel options to Twin Cities",font.main=4,col.main="red",
    xlab="Longitude",ylab="Latitude"
)

dev.off()
return("done")
$$
LANGUAGE 'plr' VOLATILE;
```
Create PNG file for plotting

Plot highways with lon/lat axis

Plot Dijkstra solution from pgRouting example

Add captions

Figure 16.5 shows the result of running this query:

```
SELECT ch16.plot_routing_results();.
```

The sp package has its own plot function as well, called `spplot`, which was designed with spatial data in mind and has niceties beyond the basic R plot. We encourage you to check out the demo by running the following commands from the R console:

```
library(sp)
demo(gallery)
```

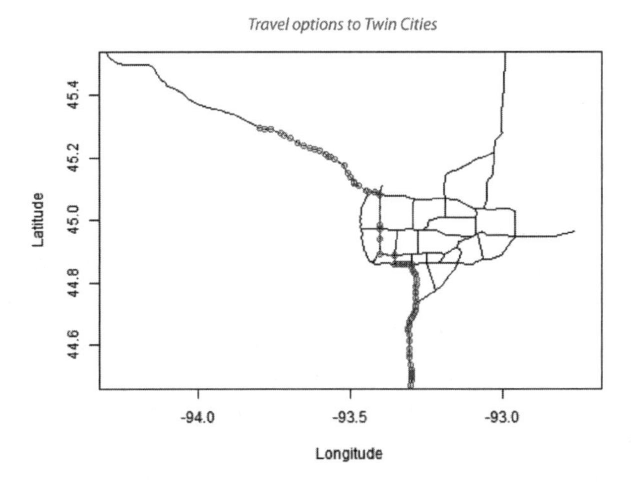

Figure 16.5 pgRouting Twin Cities results plotted with PL/R

16.3.5 Outputting plots as binaries

In the previous plotting examples, you generated the plot and manually saved it in a graphics format. If, however, you need to send the plot to a web browser, you'll need to output the file directly from the query. We're aware of three ways you can do this.

The first approach uses RGtk2 and a Cairo device, and you output a graph as a byte array. This approach is documented on the PL/R wiki and requires installing both the RGtk2 and Cairo libraries. Both libraries are large and require the installation of yet another graphical toolkit called *GTK*. For us, experimenting on Windows, loading the library often fails inexplicably. Of course, YMMV. This approach does generate nicer-looking graphics and avoids the need to temporarily save to disk. It's a self-contained, single-step process.

The next approach is to save the file to disk and let PostgreSQL read the file from disk. There's a superuser function in PostgreSQL called `pg_read_binary_file` and its older text-outputting sibling `pg_read_file`, but they're limited to reading files from the PostgreSQL data cluster. To implement this approach, we created a tablespace to hold all R-generated files and then used `pg_read_binary_file`.

Finally, you can use a PL language with more generalized access to the filesystem, such as PL/Python or PL/Perl. Doing so does require the extra step of wrapping your PL/R function in a PL function of another language.

16.4 PL/Python

Python is another favored language of GIS analysts and programmers. These days, most popular GIS toolkits have Python bindings. You'll see its use in open source GIS desktop and web suites such as QGIS, OpenJUMP, and GeoDjango, and even in commercial GIS systems such as Safe FME and ArcGIS.

PL/Python is the procedural language handler in PostgreSQL that allows you to call Python libraries and embed Python classes and functions right into a PostgreSQL database. A PL/Python stored function can be called in any SQL statement. You can even create aggregate functions and database triggers with Python. In this section, we'll show you some of the highlights of PL/Python.

16.4.1 Installing PL/Python

For the most part, you can use any feature of Python from within PL/Python. This is because the PostgreSQL PL/Python handler is a thin wrapper that only marshals messaging between PostgreSQL and the native Python environment. This means that any Python package you install can be accessed from your PL/Python stored functions. Unfortunately, not all mappings from database data types to PL/Python objects are supported. This means you can't return a complex Python object back to PostgreSQL unless it can be easily coerced into a custom PostgreSQL data type.

In order to use PL/Python, you must have Python installed on your PostgreSQL machine. Because PL/Python runs within the server, any client connecting to it, such as a web application or a client PC, need not have Python installed to be able to use PostgreSQL functions written in PL/Python.

The precompiled PostgreSQL PL/Python libraries packaged with most PostgreSQL distributions are compiled against Python 2.5 through 2.7, and the extension would be named `plpython2u` or simply `plpythonu`. If you're using PL/Python 3 (`plpython3u`), you'll need a Python 3 major version. Python language extensions work only with the Python minor version they were compiled against, so if your PL/Python is compiled with Python 2.7, then you need Python 2.7. If it's compiled with Python 3.2, then you need 3.2, and so on.

If you're running a 64-bit version of PostgreSQL, then you'll need a 64-bit version of Python. For a 32-bit version of PostgreSQL, you'll need to run a 32-bit version of Python, even if you're running on a 64-bit OS.

> **Windows one-click installer PL/Python support**
>
> If you're a Windows user, you'll find that the one-click installers for PostgreSQL 9.3 and 9.4 no longer offer the `plpython2u (plpythonu)` extension. You'll have to move up to PL/Python 3 (`plpython3u`). PostgreSQL 9.3 is compiled against Python 3.2, and PostgreSQL 9.4 is compiled against Python 3.3.

If you're using the PostgreSQL Yum repository (http://yum.postgresql.org) for the PostgreSQL installation, install PL/Python with the following command from the OS:

```
yum install postgresql92-plpython
```

Similarly, the PostgreSQL Apt repository (http://wiki.postgresql.org/wiki/Apt) has packages for Ubuntu and Debian users.

Once you have Python and the plpython.so or plpython.dll file installed on your server, execute one of the following statements to enable the language in your database:

```
CREATE EXTENSION plpythonu;
```

```
CREATE EXTENSION plpython3u;
```

If you run into problems enabling PL/Python, refer to our PL/Python help links in appendix A. The most common issue people face is that the required version of Python isn't installed on the server, or the plpython.so or plpython.dll file is missing.

> **PLPYTHON2U VERSUS PLPYTHON3U** Although Python 3 is not generally backward compatible with older versions, it doesn't hurt to try. The examples we have in this chapter all use `plpython3u`, but if you only have `plpython2u` (`plpythonu`), replace `plpython3u` and see if PostgreSQL accepts your function.

Although it's possible to have both `plpython2u` and `plpython3u` installed in the same database, you can't run functions written in both during the same database session because of global name conflicts.

16.4.2 *Writing a PL/Python function*

Because PL/Python is an untrusted language, it can interact with the filesystem of the OS. And PL/Python has plenty of file and network management functions for you to use.

PostGIS raster can output rasters in numerous formats, but the stock PL/pgSQL won't allow you to save them to the filesystem. The following listing uses PL/Python to save a binary BLOB generated from a raster.

Listing 16.7 Saving binary files to disk

```
CREATE OR REPLACE FUNCTION ch16.write_bin_file(
    param_bytes bytea,
    param_filename text
)
RETURNS text AS
$$
f = open('C:/temp/' + param_filename, 'wb+')      -- Open file for binary write
f.write(param_bytes)                              -- Write bytes
f.close()
return param_filename                             -- Return filename
$$ LANGUAGE plpython3u IMMUTABLE;
```

To use this function, call it with any raster output format function, such as `ST_AsPNG` or `ST_AsJPEG`:

```
SELECT
    ch16.write_bin_file(
        ST_AsPNG(ST_AsRaster(ST_Collect(geom),300,300,'8BUI')),
        'dijkstra_result.png'
    )
FROM ch16.dijkstra_result;
```

The preceding code outputs the content of the byte array to the folder specified.

Although we're demonstrating with raster outputs, you can use PL/Python to output any document stored in the database. You can even write a query that selects records from a table holding documents, generating a separate file for each record. See the following example:

```
SELECT write_bin_file(doc_obj,doc_file_name) FROM documents;
```

16.4.3 Using Python packages

The standard Python installation comes with no frills. What makes Python so versatile is the wide array of packages that can handle anything from matrix manipulation to web service integration. A good starting point for uncovering the available packages is the Python CheeseShop package repository.

You'll first need to install a tool called *Easy Install* before you can sample the CheeseShop. Download Easy Install from the Python site (http://pypi.python.org/pypi/setuptools#downloads) or use your Linux repository update.

> **EASY INSTALL ON WINDOWS** Once installed, the easy_install.exe file is located in the C:\Python32\scripts folder for Windows users.

Let's now try installing some packages and creating Python functions that use them.

IMPORTING AN EXCEL FILE WITH PL/PYTHON

For this example, we'll use the xlrd package, which will allow you to read Excel files in any OS. Grab this from the CheeseShop at http://pypi.python.org/pypi/xlrd.

Prior to installing xlrd, make sure you've already installed Easy Install; then, from the OS command line, execute `easy_install xlrd`. (If you're on Windows, xlrd comes with a setup.exe file that lets you bypass using Easy Install.)

Listing 16.8 tests your installation by importing a test.xls file that has a header row and three columns of data. Versions of PostgreSQL prior to PostgreSQL 9.0 didn't support SQL `OUT` parameters for PL/Python, but PostgreSQL 9.0+ offers the same `OUT` parameter functionality that PL/pgSQL has had for much longer. This allows you to return `SETOF` records from PL/Python and define the columns of the result set with `OUT` parameters, rather than having to first `CREATE TYPE` and return `SET OF` whatever type.

Listing 16.8 Reading an Excel file of points

```
CREATE OR REPLACE FUNCTION ch16.fngetxlspts(
    param_filename text,
    OUT place text, OUT lon float, OUT lat float
)
RETURNS SETOF RECORD AS
$$
import xlrd                                    <-- 1 Import package
book = xlrd.open_workbook(param_filename)
sh = book.sheet_by_index(0)
for rx in range(1,sh.nrows):                   <-- 2 Skip headers
yield(
```

```
    sh.cell_value(rowx=rx,colx=0),
    sh.cell_value(rowx=rx,colx=1),
    sh.cell_value(rowx=rx,colx=2)
)
$$
LANGUAGE 'plpython3u' VOLATILE;
```

❸ Append to result

You first import the xlrd package so you can use it ❶. For this example, we'll assume there's data in only the first spreadsheet. Next you loop through the rows of the spreadsheet, skipping the first row ❷ and using the Python yield function to append to the result set ❸. In the final yield, the function will return with all the data.

You can use this data and query the Excel file as if it were a table:

```
SELECT place, ST_SetSRID(ST_Point(lon,lat),4326) As geom
FROM ch16.fngetxlspts('C:/Temp/Test.xls') AS foo;
```

The Excel file path has to be accessible by the postgres daemon account because the PL/Python function runs under the context of that account.

IMPORTING SEVERAL EXCEL FILES WITH PL/PYTHON

Now let's imagine you have several Excel files to import. They all have the same structure and all sit in one folder, and you want to import them all in one step.

First you need to create a Python function to list all the files in a directory. Then you'll write another query that treats this list like a table and applies a filter to the list. Finally you'll write one SQL function to insert all the data using this list.

The next listing shows a function that lists the files in a directory path.

Listing 16.9 List files in directory

```
CREATE FUNCTION ch16.list_files(param_filepath text) RETURNS SETOF text
AS
$$
import os
return os.listdir(param_filepath)
$$
LANGUAGE 'plpython3u' VOLATILE;
```

The import os line in listing 16.9 allows you to run OS commands. PL/Python takes care of converting the Python list object to a PostgreSQL set of text data types.

You can then use the function within a SELECT statement, much like you can do with any table, applying LIKE to the output to further reduce the records returned:

```
SELECT file
FROM ch16.list_files('C:/temp') As file
WHERE file LIKE '%.xls';
```

The following listing passes this list to the Excel import function to get a distinct set of records.

Listing 16.10 Reading multiple Excel files

```
SELECT DISTINCT pt.place, pt.lon, pt.lat
FROM
    ch16.list_files('C:/temp') AS file,          <-- 1 List of files

    LATERAL                                      2 For each file,
    ch16.fngetxlspts('C:/temp/' || file) As pt   <-- get records
WHERE file LIKE '%.xls'       <-- 3 Limit file listing to XLS files
```

This example is similar to listing 16.9, except that you're doing three interesting things. For each file in your Temp directory ❶ that ends with .xls, it's selecting the records, but it's only selecting distinct values across all the files, using the `DISTINCT` SQL predicate.

Note that listing 16.10 only works in PostgreSQL 9.3+ because of the use of `LATERAL` ❷. The `LATERAL` clause allows you to use each filename output in the `fngetxlspts` function so that you get a different set of records for each file. The `LIKE` condition ensures that only files ending in *.xls* are considered ❸.

16.4.4 Geocoding example

PL/Python is a great tool for enabling geocoding within your database using a third-party service such as OpenStreetMap, Google Maps, MapQuest, Yahoo Maps, or Bing. You can find numerous Python packages at the CheeseShop to do just that.

One fine example is the Python geopy package, which you can download from https://pypi.python.org/pypi/geopy/0.97. This particular package needs to be installed using *pip*, a package management system for Python. If you don't have pip installed, you can install it using `easy_install pip`. Geopy has support for OpenStreetMap, Nominatim, Google Geocoding API (V3), Yahoo OSS, geocoder.us, Bing Maps API, and Esri ArcGIS. The package supports both Python 2 and Python 3, so if you have Python 2 installed, just change `plpython3u` to `plpythonu` in the code.

Once you have pip installed, you can install geopy from the command line using `pip install geopy`. All the geocoders in geopy return the same output format, but take slightly different initializations. The next listing is a wrapper function for the Google V3 geocoder.

Listing 16.11 Geocoder wrapper function

```
CREATE FUNCTION ch16.google_geocode(
    param_addr text,
    OUT address text, OUT lon numeric, OUT lat numeric    <-- Output columns
)

RETURNS record
AS
$$
from geopy.geocoders import GoogleV3          <-- Load GoogleV3 class
```

```
geoc = GoogleV3()
address,
(latitude,longitude) = geoc.geocode(param_addr)
return (address, longitude, latitude)
$$
LANGUAGE 'plpython3u';
```

Geocode and store in variables

Return variables in OUT parameters

Now you can use that function in an SQL statement similar to how you used the TIGER geocoder function:

```
SELECT *
FROM ch16.google_geocode(
    '1731 New Hampshire Avenue Northwest, Washington, DC 20010'
);
```

It produces this output:

```
 address                           |lon        |lat
-----------------------------+----------|---------
 1731 New Hampshire Avenue...|-77.027...|38.932...
```

If you wanted to use this `googlemaps` class in Python outside of PostgreSQL, you'd have to take these steps:

- Establish a connection to your PostgreSQL database with a few lines of Python code and a connection string.
- Pull the data out of your database.
- Loop through the database, retrieve the raw address, geocode, and update the database with the coordinates.

By packaging your Python code as a function, you'll never need to leave the environs of PostgreSQL. You can reuse this same function easily in any query. You can even use it in reporting tools that lack access to Python.

16.5 PL/V8, CoffeeScript, and LiveScript

PL/V8 (a.k.a. PL/JavaScript) is a trusted language that's been available since PostgreSQL 8.4. Several distributions now bundle it in PostgreSQL 9.3 and later offerings. Should your distribution not have it, you can compile it from source as described in the PL/V8 project page (https://github.com/plv8/plv8). PL/V8 relies on the Google V8 engine, so in order to compile and use it, you need to have V8 installed.

Here are some features only found in PL/V8:

- You can get away with fewer lines of code to accomplish the same task.
- For folks fluent in JavaScript, you'll feel right at home. You can reuse many existing JavaScript libraries with little or no modification.
- PL/V8 is generally faster for mathematical processing than PL/pgSQL or SQL.
- PL/V8 comes with built-in support for JSON, making it a natural choice for ingesting data from (and sending data to) web applications.

- Because PL/V8 is a trusted language, non-superusers can use it to create functions. This is not the case with PL/Python or PL/R.
- PL/V8 is the only language other than C and PL/R that supports creating window functions. Most languages, including PL/Python and SQL, can create aggregate functions that can be used as window aggregates, but not window functions such as `row_number`, `lead`, `lag`, `rank`, and the like.

16.5.1 Installing PL/V8

Once you've installed the V8 engine and PL/V8 binaries, you need to enable PL/V8 in a database. Connect to your database and run the following SQL statement:

```
CREATE EXTENSION plv8;
```

If you prefer the syntax of CoffeeScript (http://coffeescript.org) or LiveScript (http://livescript.net), PL/V8 automatically installs these two as extensions: plcoffee and plls. These dialects offer additional syntactic sugar over PL/V8 and still compile to V8 bytecode.

To enable CoffeeScript, run the following statement:

```
CREATE EXTENSION plcoffee;
```

To enable LiveScript, run this statement:

```
CREATE EXTENSION plls;
```

If you're on Windows, we've compiled PL/V8 and provided binary packages for PostgreSQL 9.2, 9.3, and 9.4 in both 32-bit and 64-bit versions, which include both the V8 engine and the plv8 extension. You can download these from the Postgres OnLine Journal Windows Extensions page at www.postgresonline.com/winextensions.php. Also check out our various articles on writing PL/V8 functions on the Postgres OnLine Journal at www.postgresonline.com/journal/categories/72-plv8js.

16.5.2 Using other JavaScript libraries and functions in PL/V8

Perhaps the most compelling reason to use PL/V8 is that you can leverage the vast body of existing JavaScript code simply by cutting and pasting the source code of these functions and libraries. With the preeminence of web technology, there's probably now more JavaScript code in the world than any other language. Many of these functions and libraries can be used without modification.

For a first example, we'll show you how to paste in a function called `parse_gps` from Stack Overflow: "Converting latitude and longitude to decimal values" (http://stackoverflow.com/questions/1140189/converting-latitude-and-longitude-to-decimal-values). All you need to do to make it work in PostgreSQL is to wrap a PostgreSQL function body around it. The revised code is shown in the following listing.

Listing 16.12 Parse GPS

```
CREATE OR REPLACE FUNCTION ch16.parse_gps(input text)
RETURNS float8[] AS
$$
    if (
        input.indexOf('N') == -1 && input.indexOf('S') == -1 &&
        input.indexOf('W') == -1 && input.indexOf('E') == -1
    ) {
    return input.split(',');
    }
    var parts = input.split(/[°'"]+/).join(' ').split(/[^\w\S]+/);
    var directions = [];
    var coords = [];
    var dd = 0;
    var pow = 0;

    for (i in parts) {
        if (isNaN(parts[i])) {
            var _float = parseFloat( parts[i] );
            var direction = parts[i];
            if (!isNaN(_float)) {
                dd += ( _float / Math.pow( 60, pow++ ) );
                direction = parts[i].replace( _float, '' );
            }
            direction = direction[0];
            if (direction == 'S' || direction == 'W')
                dd *= -1;
                directions[ directions.length ] = direction;
                coords[coords.length] = dd;
                dd = pow = 0;
        }
        else {
            dd += (parseFloat(parts[i]) / Math.pow( 60, pow++));
        }
    }

    if (directions[0] == 'W' || directions[0] == 'E') {
        var tmp = coords[0];
        coords[0] = coords[1];
        coords[1] = tmp;
    }

    return coords;
$$
LANGUAGE plv8;
```

To use the preceding function in an SQL statement, you'd execute it like this:

```
SELECT ch16.parse_gps('36°57''9" N 110°4''21" W') ;
```

That statement outputs `{36.9525,-110.0725}`.

PL/V8 is a trusted language, so it can't access additional JavaScript libraries on the system. If you're just copying and pasting individual snippets of JavaScript code, this isn't an issue. But entire JavaScript libraries with tens of thousands of lines of code and interdependent functions don't lend themselves to being easily copied and pasted.

To load JavaScript libraries, we use a technique espoused by Andrew Dunstan in his article "Loading Useful Modules in PL/V8" (http://adpgtech.blogspot.com/2013/03/loading-useful-modules-in-plv8.html). Andrew's approach is to use a table to store these modules as plain text JavaScript. Each row defines a separate module, and the code field contains all the functions in the module. During session startup, you loop through the table and use the PL/V8 `eval` function to create these functions on the fly for each module.

WARNING We use the terms *libraries*, *modules*, and *add-ons* loosely and synonymously when talking about PL/V8.

For the next example, you'll embed a library called *Chance* (http://chancejs.com). Chance is a suite of random generator functions useful for generating dummy data for testing.

The first step is to create a table to house the plv8 modules:

```
CREATE TABLE ch16.plv8_modules(
    modname text PRIMARY KEY,
    load_on_start boolean,
    code text
);
```

The second step is to load the Chance module into this table as a single-row entry with an SQL `INSERT`. The following code shows a snippet of the entire SQL:

```
INSERT INTO ch16.plv8_modules(modname, load_on_start,code)
VALUES('chance', true, '//  Chance.js 0.5.4
//  http://chancejs.com
//  (c) 2013 Victor Quinn
//  Chance may be freely distributed or modified under the MIT license.

(function () {
:
:')
```

MORE ABOUT THE SQL INSERT If you're wondering how we came up with the SQL `INSERT`, see the *README* file included with the code downloads for the chapter. There are a few different ways you can generate the insert depending on your OS and your tools.

The third step is to create a startup function that compiles the module and makes it available as a global PL/V8 object.

Listing 16.13 PL/V8 module compiler and loader

```
CREATE OR REPLACE FUNCTION ch16.plv8_startup()
RETURNS void AS
$$
```

❶ Load all the modules marked for loading on start

```
    var rows = plv8.execute(
        "SELECT modname, code " +
        " FROM ch16.plv8_modules WHERE load_on_start"
    );
    for (var r = 0; r < rows.length; r++) {
        var code = rows[r].code;
        eval("(function() { " + code + "})")();        <-- 2 Compile
    };
$$
LANGUAGE plv8;

SELECT ch16.plv8_startup();        <-- 3 Load the modules
```

Listing 16.13 creates a PL/V8 function that loops through the plv8_modules table and extracts the text of the function from the code field of each row marked as `load_on_startup = true` ❶. For each row, you apply the built-in JavaScript `eval` function to compile and instantiate each function ❷. Then you run the function, making it live in the PL/V8 memory context as the variable `chance` ❸.

For libraries that you use often, you'd want to execute the `ch16.plv8_startup()` function ❸ during startup of the PL/V8 procedure handler. To do so, place this call in your postgresql.conf file:

```
plv8.start_proc = 'ch16.plv8_startup'
```

Now you're ready to use Chance. You can use the PostgreSQL `DO` command to execute a snippet of PL code without having to wrap it in a function. In the next listing you create a table to store people and then use `chance` to generate random beings all over the globe.

Listing 16.14 Creating dummy people with Chance

```
CREATE TABLE ch16.people(
    id serial primary key,        <-- Create table to hold fictitious people
    first_name varchar(50), last_name varchar(50),
    gender varchar(15), geog geography(POINT,4326)
);

DO LANGUAGE plv8
$$        <-- 1 Parameterized SQL insert
    var sql =
        "INSERT INTO ch16.people(first_name,last_name,gender,geog)
        VALUES($1,$2,$3,ST_Point($4,$5)::geography)"        <-- 2 Prepared statement for insert
    var iplan = plv8.prepare(
        sql,
        ['text','text','text','numeric','numeric']
    );        <-- Beget 10,000 people around the globe

    for (var i=0; i < 10000; i++) {
        iplan.execute([
            chance.first(),
            chance.last(),
```

```
                chance.gender(),
                chance.longitude(),
                chance.latitude()
            ]);
    }
$$;
```

Listing 16.14 demonstrates a couple of standard features in PL/V8, in addition to the use of third-party modules. Like other PLs, PL/V8 lets you write dynamic SQL statements ❶, which you can vary with different arguments using a loop ❷. After you're done running the code in listing 16.14, you should find 10,000 people in your people table.

Note that, like many PL languages, PL/V8 can be run as an anonymous one-type function using the PostgreSQL `DO` command, as you saw in listing 16.14.

16.5.3 Using PL/V8 to write map algebra functions

PL/V8 can also be used to build map algebra functions. To demonstrate, we'll simplify the built-in `ST_Range4MA` map algebra function using PL/V8. This simplified version, which is shown in listing 16.15, will ignore the `userargs` and `position` input variables. But although it won't use these variables, it still needs to have them as inputs, because all map algebra functions must follow the function input signature: `value float8[][][], pos integer[][][],userargs text[])`.

> **somevariable[][][] versus somevariable[]**
>
> Although raster map algebra machinery assumes a 3D array for some args, in PostgreSQL the dimensionality of the input arg signature is not maintained. So you'll see your `float8[][][]` converted to `float8[]` when you look again at your definition. As such, you can write it as `float8[]` to save keystrokes, but we write it here as `float8[][][]` for clarity.

Listing 16.15 PL/V8 range map algebra function

```
CREATE FUNCTION ch16.plv8_st_range4ma(
    value float8[][][],
    pos integer[][][],
    VARIADIC userargs text[] DEFAULT NULL::text[]
)
RETURNS double precision AS
$$
    return(Math.max.apply(null,value) - Math.min.apply(null,value));
$$
LANGUAGE plv8 IMMUTABLE;
```

The following listing shows the same function written in SQL.

Listing 16.16 SQL range map algebra function

```
CREATE FUNCTION ch16.sql_st_range4ma(
    value float8[][][],
    pos integer[][][],
    VARIADIC userargs text[] DEFAULT NULL::text[]
)
RETURNS double precision AS
$$
    SELECT MAX(v) - MIN(v) FROM unnest($1) As v;
$$
LANGUAGE sql IMMUTABLE;
```

To compare the performance of PL/V8, SQL, and PL/pgSQL, we ran these queries on an image (included as part of this chapter's download).

Listing 16.17 Compare speed of range functions

```
SELECT
    ch16.write_bin_file(
        ST_AsPNG(
            ST_MapAlgebra(
                ST_Clip(
                    rast,
                    ST_Expand(ST_Centroid(rast::geometry),300)
                ),
                1,
                'ch16.plv8_st_range4ma(
                    double precision[][][],
                    integer[][],
                    text[]
                )'::regprocedure,
                '8BUI','FIRST',NULL,2,2
            )
        ),
        RID::TEXT || '_plv8_range2.png'
    )
FROM ch16.pics;                           <-- ❶ PL/V8 range 2,776 ms

SELECT
    ch16.write_bin_file(
        ST_AsPNG(
            ST_MapAlgebra(
                ST_Clip(
                    rast,
                    ST_Expand(ST_Centroid(rast::geometry),300)
                ),
                1,
                'ch16.sql_st_range4ma(
                    double precision[][][],
                    integer[][],
                    text[]
                )'::regprocedure,
                '8BUI','FIRST',NULL,2,2
```

```
                )
            ),
            RID::TEXT || '_sql_range2.png'
        )
FROM ch16.pics;                        ❷ SQL range 5,959 ms

SELECT
    ch16.write_bin_file(
        ST_AsPNG(
            ST_MapAlgebra(
                ST_Clip(
                    rast,
                    ST_Expand(ST_Centroid(rast::geometry),300)
                ),
                1,
                'st_range4ma(
                    double precision[][][],
                    integer[][],
                    text[]
                )'::regprocedure,
                '8BUI','FIRST',NULL,2,2
            )
        ),
        RID::TEXT || '_builtin_range2.png')    ❸ PostGIS packaged
FROM ch16.pics;                                 PL/pgSQL range 13,463 ms
```

The performance of the PL/V8 variant ❶ is about five times faster than the PL/pgSQL version ❸ and twice as fast as the SQL version ❷. The examples also utilized the PL/Python function in listing 16.7 to write out the range images to disk.

All the range results were equivalent. The output is shown in figure 16.6.

Be careful when using PL/V8 to build map algebra callback functions, because the *n*-dimensional arrays passed in collapse to one-dimensional arrays. In many cases, such as when you're trying to extract the maximum value from a neighborhood of pixels, this collapsing isn't important. For cases where you need to keep the positional information, you'll probably need to write a wrapper SQL function to track the information lost during the collapse.

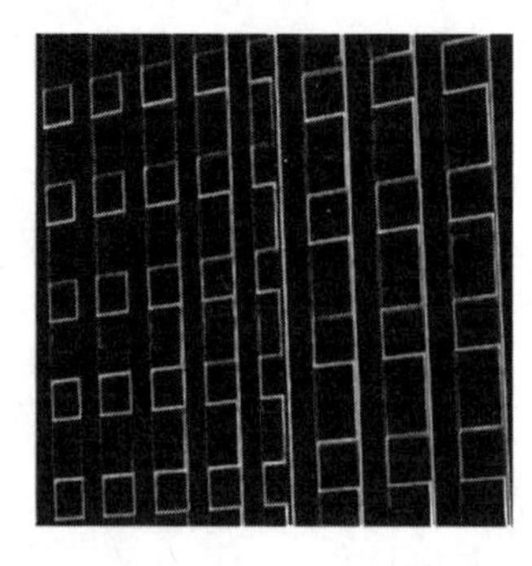

Figure 16.6 Before and after range operation

Map algebra function speed

The handling of `userargs` and `position` in the PostGIS packaged PL/pgSQL map algebra functions `ST_Range4ma`, `ST_Mean4ma`, and so on adds overhead. Stripping the handling of `userargs` and `position` alone improves the PL/pgSQL speed about two-fold and allows you to rewrite `ST_Range4ma` and `ST_Mean4ma` as SQL functions, yielding yet another 20% improvement in speed. Rewriting in PL/V8 improves the speed even more.

16.6 Summary

In this chapter, we demonstrated how you can solve routing problems using pgRouting. We demonstrated various PL languages (PL/R, PL/Python, and PL/V8) that allow you to do things not possible in PL/pgSQL or SQL, or that allow you to do some things more succinctly. We also demonstrated how you can tap into the extensive network of prepackaged functions that R, Python, and JavaScript offer and use them directly from PostgreSQL. We hope we piqued your curiosity enough that you'll further explore these tools and discover other treats they hold in store.

Next we'll talk about another set of server-side tools for displaying GIS data to the world and allowing the world to edit your data via a web interface or desktop tool. We'll leave the safe confines of the database and expose more of our data to the world to savor.

17 Using PostGIS in web applications

This chapter covers

- Shortcomings of conventional web solutions
- MapServer, GeoServer, QGIS Server
- OpenLayers 2 and 3, Leaflet

In the short span of 15 years, the World Wide Web has emerged as the leading method of information delivery, threatening to replace printed media altogether. For GIS, this has been a godsend. Not only did the web introduce GIS to the popular imagination, but it also provides a delivery mechanism for GIS data that wouldn't have been possible via traditional printed media. Only a few years ago, a GIS practitioner wishing to share data would have had to print out large maps on oversized printers. And then came the web.

Conventional web technologies suffice to deliver textual and image data, but for the ultimate GIS web-surfing experience, you need additional tools, both on the delivery end (the server) and on the receiving end (the client).

In this chapter, we'll cover web tools that work with PostGIS. We'll start with three server tools—MapServer, GeoServer, and QGIS Server—that can read data from PostGIS and serve images or data according to OGC standards. We'll then move on to the client side of the equation, where we'll look at OpenLayers, a JavaScript-based tool that greatly enriches the viewing experience for the user. Along with OpenLayers, we'll check out Leaflet, another JavaScript-mapping framework that competes with OpenLayers in many arenas. Both are open source with generous licensing terms. OpenLayers is an older, more mature platform, whereas Leaflet is a newer framework recently adopted by projects such as OpenStreetMap (www.openstreetmap.org) and CartoDB (http://cartodb.com), to name just two. Leaflet is a bit lighter weight than OpenLayers, but it has a large crowd developing plug-ins for it.

The code and data used in this chapter can be downloaded from www.postgis.us/chapter_17_edition_2.

17.1 Limitations of conventional web technologies

Conventional web technologies work well for static data and images, but what if you need a website where users can extract your map at various zoom levels? Using conventional web server technology, you'd have to limit the user to a fixed set of zoom levels, generate the images beforehand, and serve them as requested. Now consider what would happen if the user would like to see only subsections of the map: you'd have to slice up your maps beforehand and restrict users to picking from one of your prepared slices.

There are two big problems here: First, you can't possibly predict what portions of the map the user would like to see. Second, even if you were to generate thousands of subsections for the user to pick from, your server would most likely run out of storage space after just a few maps. Add in zoom levels, and the problem becomes intractable. The client side of the picture isn't much rosier. For zoom-level selectors, you could use standard HTML combo boxes, but the drop-down list would have to be changed from map to map. If a map has three zoom levels, you'd have to prepopulate your combo box with three values. If the next map has 30 zoom levels, you'd have to have 30 rows in the combo box for the user to pick from. Using various programming technologies now available, such as Python, PHP, and ASP.NET, you can dynamically generate the HTML combo box, but this requires that the mapping person also be a web programmer—and not in just one language. The demands become even more challenging if users have to be able to draw rectangles around subsections to be blown up, add their own markers, or have pop-up description balloons when hovering over certain points of interest. These interface features would all require extensive programming on the client side.

If server-side programming hasn't already discouraged the GIS specialist, the client-side programming surely will. What you need is a suite of client tools with useful controls for map viewing and editing already built in. Sure, the suite will dictate the overall appearance and functionality, but this is preferable to building your own solution from the ground up. After all, your goal is to disseminate maps, not to program web servers.

17.2 Mapping servers

Mapping servers have one central purpose: to render images for delivery to a client on the fly. As mentioned previously, conventional web servers can't serve up images unless they already exist, but generating and storing all possible subsections and zoom levels associated with a map is in many cases impractical. Mapping servers solve this problem by quickly generating the static images only when requested by the client and caching previously generated images for future requests.

There are many open source mapping-server products to choose from that support PostGIS in addition to other spatial databases. Some popular ones are MapServer, GeoServer, the fairly new QGIS Server, Degree, and MapGuide OpenSource.

Because mapping servers are rarely the starting point of a GIS project, people generally start from a need to spatially extend existing web applications or to disseminate existing data via the web. To decide which server products to use, we recommend that you judge how easily each fits into your current infrastructure and data landscape. You should consider the following:

- Will the selected product require a major change in the existing platform?
- Which OGC web services, if any, do you need to provide?
- How well will the server connect to the data sources you already have, be they PostGIS, Oracle Spatial/Locator, Microsoft SQL Server, SpatiaLite, MySQL, shapefiles, raster files, or something else?

What are web services?

Loosely speaking, a *web service* is a standard for function calls across the internet. The service accepts requests from clients usually using HTTP and standard messaging streams (`GET`, `PUT`, `POST` in standard formats: XML, JSON, and the like) and returns the processed output.

To adhere to standards set by the W3C, a web service must make known which requests it can fulfill. In the case of OGC web services, the services available are published via what is called a GetCapabilities response, which is returned as an XML document.

To consume web services, the requester application generally creates stub classes to make the web service call indistinguishable from a local function call. Many tools are available to autogenerate stub classes, sparing you the pain of having to write them yourself. A stub class contains methods to pass data from the client to the service for each kind of capability the service offers, and handles the serialization/deserialization of objects into XML or some other format (usually JSON), so that they can traverse the internet.

17.2.1 Platform considerations

Some of the most important deciding factors for choosing a tool are the platform requirements. If you're on a shared web host, you may not be able to use anything that requires installation. Even if you have complete control over your server, you may shy away from technologies that require additional installation.

Table 17.1 outlines the prerequisites for each mapping server. *No** means the server doesn't require the service for general use, but you get more features if you have it.

Table 17.1 Mapping-server prerequisites

Service	MapServer	GeoServer	QGIS Server
Java runtime (JRE)	No	Yes	No
Python	No*	No	No*
PHP	No*	No	No
.NET	No*	No	No
CGI/Fast-CGI	Yes	No	Yes

MapServer is our favorite of the aforementioned mapping servers because it contains a lot of functionality and can run under practically any web server without requiring installation. Just drop the compiled .so/.dlls/.exe file into the CGI or some other web-server-executable folder, and you have a completely functional web-mapping service. MapServer also offers an API called *MapScript* in many flavors, with PHP MapScript, Python MapScript, and C# MapScript being the most common. This provides more granular control by allowing you to create layers and other map objects from PHP, C#, VB.NET, and Python server-side code. The downside of the MapScript interface is that it also requires writing more code in general than using the mapserv executable.

GeoServer is built on Java servlets. Some binary distributions of GeoServer come packaged with their own mini web server called *Jetty*. GeoServer requires an existing installation of the Java 5+ JRE, although the newest version of GeoServer (version 2.6) requires Java 7. If you need to run GeoServer under the context of an existing web server service, you'll need to get a servlet plug-in for your web server, such as Tomcat, and install the Java web archive (WAR) version. Unlike many other mapping servers, GeoServer comes packaged with a user-friendly, web-based administrative interface. This makes GeoServer a popular option for those who prefer GUIs and wizards over configuration scripts.

QGIS Server is a mapping server often packaged with the popular QGIS Desktop. A key benefit of the QGIS server is that it allows you to export your QGIS workspaces as web-mapping services. The QGIS site has more info about setting up and configuring QGIS Server: http://hub.qgis.org/projects/quantum-gis/wiki/QGIS_Server_Tutorial.

We'll only be demonstrating GeoServer and MapServer in this chapter because those are the most commonly used open source mapping servers, and from experience, they're the easiest to set up on most platforms.

If you'd like an easy environment in which you can try all three servers and additional ones, you may want to try out the OSGeo-Live DVD distribution (http://live.osgeo.org/en/overview/overview.html). The Live DVD comes installed with the GeoServer, MapServer, QGIS Server, and Degree mapping servers. In addition to web-mapping servers, you'll also find PostGIS, SpatiaLite, and the various desktop offerings: QGIS Desktop, OpenJUMP, GRASS, and several others.

17.2.2 OGC web service support

You may recall from earlier chapters that OGC is short for the Open Geospatial Consortium, the accepted standards organization in the world of GIS. OGC has outlined a series of web services that mapping servers should provide. By adhering to these standard OGC web services, mapping servers won't limit end users to their particular web or desktop client.

All the open source web-mapping clients and the desktop tools we covered in chapter 5 consume OGC web services. Even proprietary desktop applications such as Manifold, Cadcorp, and MapInfo nowadays offer decent support for OGC web-mapping services. These are the most common of the web services defined by OGC:

- *Web Mapping Service (WMS)*—Renders vector and raster data as map images in JPEG, PNG, TIFF, or some other raster format. This is suitable if you want to show a map of an area, but downloading and rendering the data would be too processor-intensive. For example, if you want to display maps on a mobile device with limited processing power, retrieving ready-made images from a WMS server makes more sense than pulling the raw vector data and performing visual rendering on the fly. WMS also defines a mechanism called GetFeatureInfo for getting basic information in HTML or some other text format. This is useful for info pop-ups.
- *Web Map Tile Service (WMTS)*—Renders vector and raster data as map images in JPEG, PNG, TIFF, or some other raster format, at fixed scales that can be easily cached and reused by other clients. It serves much the same purpose as the standard WMS, but it's a newer standard that is less taxing on the server because it defines a mechanism for caching and reusing tiles. It's closely related to the WMS-C standard (Web Map Service Cache), which is still alive but considered legacy at this point. WMTS trades the flexibility of custom map rendering for scalability, so it's best suited for things like the base map layers or commonly asked for maps that are time-consuming to generate. Tiles are often only provided in one spatial projection and at fixed scales and tile sizes.
- *Web Feature Service (WFS)*—Outputs vector data, generally using some XML standard such as GML or KML. Geography JavaScript Object Notation (GeoJSON) is another output format commonly supported by WFS that's more

processor-friendly for consumption by JavaScript because it's a native JavaScript format. The GeoJSON format includes both the geometry represented as JSON encoded, as well as the standard database column attributes like dates, numbers, and strings encoded as JSON. WFS is most suitable if users need to highlight regions of a map and display attribute info or styling options, without making round trips to the server. WFS is often used in conjunction with WMS, where WMS would be used to show aerial images or large zoomed-out regions of a map, and WFS is used to overlay key commonly changing features on a map, or features whose styling you may want to control.

- *Web Feature Service Transactional (WFS-T)*—Allows you to edit vector data in transactional mode. This is necessary if you expect end users, such as web users or desktop applications, to edit geometry data in the database without giving them direct access to the database.

There are other web services as well, such as Web Tiling Services (WTS) and Web Coverage Services (WCS). Table 17.2 offers a brief summary of the key OGC web services, and indicates which tools support them.

Table 17.2 Web services support

Service	MapServer	GeoServer	QGIS Server
WMS	Yes	Yes	Yes
WMTS	Yes[a]	Yes	No
WFS	Yes	Yes	Yes
WFS-T	Yes[b] (for PostGIS)	Yes	Yes
Custom[b]	Yes	Yes	Yes

a. Support is available via an extra downloadable plug-in or library.
b. The product has its own custom protocols that provide functionality beyond what is defined in the OGC standards.

The REST architecture is a lighter-weight interface than WFS and relies on the concepts of `GET`s, `PUT`s, and `DELETE`s to update data and output XML streams. A WFS that supports `GET` requests can be considered for all intents and purposes to be a REST service.

17.2.3 Supported data sources

All maps are derived from data. The WMS/WFS/WFS-T protocols allow various data sources to be accessed via one web interface. They provide an abstract interface for GIS data, similar to ODBC and JDBC drivers for databases.

All web-mapping server tools support various data formats. Table 17.3 describes which tools support which formats, so you can make an informed choice. They all support PostGIS geometries and Esri shapefiles out of the box, so we left those out of the table.

Table 17.3 Data source formats supported

Service	MapServer	GeoServer	QGIS Server
Oracle Spatial/Locator	Yes*	Yes*	Yes*
SQL Server 2008/2012	Yes*	Yes*	Yes
PostGIS geography	Yes	Yes	Yes
PostGIS raster	Yes	Yes*	Yes
Basic raster	Yes	Yes	Yes
MrSID	Yes*	Yes*	Yes*
SpatiaLite	Yes*	Yes	Yes
MySQL	Yes*	Yes*	Yes

* Support is available via an extra downloadable plug-in or library.

17.3 Mapping clients

Once the web-mapping services have been set up, you need client applications to consume them. Client applications come in two flavors: desktop and web. Web applications are often implemented using Ajax and a mix of web-scripting languages.

Many desktop mapping toolkits are also capable of consuming standard OGC web-mapping services. A desktop client can either be an open source desktop tool, such as QGIS, uDig, gvSIG, OpenJUMP, and countless others, or a proprietary desktop tool such as Manifold, MapInfo, Cadcorp SIS, and ArcGIS desktop, to name a few .

As far as web-mapping clients go, OpenLayers and Leaflet tend to be the most popular, particularly in the open source GIS arena. The main reason for this is that both give you the ability to overlay proprietary non-OGC-compliant mapping layers with OGC WMS, WFS, and WFS-T layers.

OpenLayers is often extended to create more advanced or specific toolkits. One common one that builds on top of OpenLayers is GeoExt, which is used by OpenGeo's GeoExplorer. GeoExt is a web-mapping JavaScript framework that combines OpenLayers with ExtJS to provide a web client interface with more of a desktop feel.

17.3.1 Proprietary services

We'd be remiss if we failed to mention that the most popular web-mapping services around are still proprietary, such as Google Maps, Bing, and MapQuest. These services package server, client, and data together in a slick, easy-to-use interface, and they make mapping accessible to the general public. Though these packages are easy to use, each has its own proprietary JavaScript API providing limited control over overlaying data.

The proprietary and inflexible nature of these services, even on the data level, is a serious drawback. You can't remove one core feature. For example, if you wanted to display foliage density over a region instead of the usual streets and places, you couldn't do so with these popular packages.

You also can't suppress the commercial licensing clause of these packages. For recreational use, these packages are in most cases free, but once you start to use them for profit or for non-public websites, you'll find yourself needing to cough up a rather exorbitant licensing fee. Because each has its own custom API that's incompatible with any other one, you'll have to rewrite much of your custom data-overlay logic when deciding to swap services.

Despite their commercial bent, we must pay homage to these popular services for planting the seeds of GIS in the popular imagination. They were the first to show the world the power of dynamic mapping on the internet, and they continue to lead the way in the development of display technologies. This book is devoted to open source solutions, so we won't cover these proprietary JavaScript APIs, but we advise you to not lose sight of the important role they play on the web today.

Each of these web GIS tools provides a lot of functionality out of the box. They do so by limiting you to certain protocols when you interact with your database and other spatial data. For many solutions that need only light support for maps but heavier support for data, you may want to forgo web-mapping services altogether and build the logic to display PostGIS data right in your application. In the sections that follow, we'll go into detail on the basics of setting up and using MapServer and GeoServer as well as creating solutions that don't require you to host your own web-mapping service.

If you wanted to do some heavy lifting by showing thousands of hefty features, outputting vector features would be slow and cumbersome. In such a case, it's better to output image tiles using a web-mapping service or tile service. As a user zooms in, you might want to complement this with either a vector output using a direct PostGIS query with PHP, Python, .NET or some other web server language, or with a WFS. We'll demonstrate how to do that next with MapServer.

The rise of vector tiles

There is a new trend gaining steam in the mapping arena called *vector tiles*, and it's spearheaded by MapBox. Vector tiles are distributed as tiles much as current tile services distribute raster tiles, but they have binary vectors inside of the tiles. The benefit of vector tiles is that they allow for local styling on the client, they can include attribute data in each tile, and they can gracefully support multiple resolutions with a single zoom.

For example, if you have a particular focus of interest, you might provide data for that area in zoom levels as high as 20 (which would require a great deal of storage for a large area), and for surrounding areas only up to 14 (significantly less storage required). If someone zooms to 20 on a low-res area (only having a zoom of 14), the vector data can gracefully resize on the client to support a zoom of 20.

More details about the spec can be found at https://github.com/mapbox/vector-tile-spec.

(continued)

On a related note, there's a new output format coming in PostGIS 2.2 (already available in the PostGIS development version), called *TWKB* (tiny well-known-binary), which builds on some of the same ideas as vector tiles. In particular, both the current implementations of vector tiles and PostGIS TWKB utilize the Google `varint` encoding scheme (https://developers.google.com/protocol-buffers/docs/encoding#varints) to minimize the size of vectors. The PostGIS output functions for TWKB are `ST_AsTWKB` and `ST_ASTWKBAgg`. OfflineMap (https://github.com/nicklasaven/offlineMap) demonstrates using PHP to create TWKB-formatted data and consuming this data in a Leaflet web client.

17.4 Using MapServer

MapServer was the first mapping server to support PostGIS as a data source. It is fairly lightweight and can run under almost any web server. In the following example, we'll demonstrate using MapServer's WMS features. The version we'll be using for these exercises is MapServer 6.4.

17.4.1 Installing MapServer

MapServer is a mature product, and as such there's little need to compile from scratch unless you want to. There are already precompiled binaries for most any operating system, and you can find them here: http://mapserver.org/download.html#binaries.

WINDOWS INSTALL

For MS Windows installations, several options are available. OSGeo4W is a very popular but bulky installation because it includes an Apache server and various other GIS open source packages. The 64-bit version of OSGeo4W is fairly new as of this writing, and it doesn't have as many features as the 32-bit version. This will change in the future.

We like using the GISInternals package because it's much lighter weight and has the latest developer version available. It has both 32-bit and 64-bit versions, both compiled with most data drivers supported by MapServer. It also includes the C# Interop extensions to allow the use of MapScript from an ASP.NET (VB.NET or C#) environment. In addition to MapServer, the GISInternals package includes the full GDAL toolkit.

To deploy GISInternals on a Windows IIS server as CGI, we usually do the following:

1. Download one of the zip files from GISInternals (www.gisinternals.com/), extract the contents into a folder such as C:\Mapserv, and give execute permissions to IIS accounts (usually called IIS_IUSRS, IUSR, or IIS_WPG) for this folder. (There is also an msi file if you prefer standard installation.) To avoid having to set environment variables for MapServer, copy the contents of bin/ms/apps to the root bin folder of C:\MapServ, so that the .dlls and mapserve.exe are all in same folder.

2. Verify that all the dependencies are in place: open up a command line, `cd` into the bin folder, and run `mapserv -v`. That should output all the supported features.
3. You'll need to reference the path to bin/proj/share in your MapServer map file later, but it doesn't need to be web accessible.
4. Open up IIS Manager, and in the ISAPI and CGI Restrictions, add the path to mapserv.exe with a Description something like `MapServ 6.4`.
5. Create a virtual application path in IIS Manager to C:\MapServ\bin and call it `mapserv`.
6. In Handler Mappings, add a new Module Mapping with a request path of `*.exe`, a module of `FastCGI`, and an executable path of `C:\MapServ\bin\mapserv.exe`. Call it something like `MapServ` or `Mapserv 6.4`.
7. Click the Request Restrictions button on Module Mapping, and on the Mapping tab check the Invoke Handler Only if Request Is Mapped To check box and check File. On the Verbs tab choose Only One of the Following, and in the text box, type `GET,HEAD,POST`. On the Access tab choose Script.

SECURITY CONSIDERATIONS

If you're going to have PostGIS layers, you may need to put the PostgreSQL login username and password in the map file or in a file included in the map file. You don't want this information to be readable, and you may not want your map files readable at all for copyright reasons.

There are a couple of safeguards to prevent passwords and other sensitive content from being readable by website users. Please do at least one of these. You may want to do all of them for full protection:

- Don't put your map file in a folder that's web accessible. Admittedly, we tend to break this rule because of the convenience of keeping everything related together.
- Use the msencrypt executable packaged with MapServer to encrypt the password, and use only the encrypted password.
- Use an `INCLUDE` clause in your map file, and make sure the `INCLUDE` file is of an extension type that isn't served by a web server. For example, we use the .config extension in IIS because ASP.NET will never serve a file with this extension. Using an `INCLUDE` for the PostGIS connection string is also convenient, at least if all your PostGIS layers use the same database. This saves you from having to repeat the same information over and over again.
- If you have control over your own web server, you can block dishing out .map files by editing your httpd.conf, or in IIS by mapping the files to a 404.dll or some other IIS ISAPI processor.

17.4.2 Creating WMS and WFS services

MapServer supports its own non-OGC API as well as WMS, WFS, WCS, and other web service interfaces. We're going to focus on its OGC WMS and WFS functionality and its offerings in version 6.4. For the OGC WMS/WFS features, you don't need template files. A correctly configured map file with WFS/WMS metadata sections, a set of fonts (http://mapserver.org/mapfile/fontset.html#fontset), a symbol set, and proj_lib will do.

For our map files, we like to use `INCLUDE`s for sections that we reuse repeatedly within the map or reuse across several maps, such as for the PostGIS connection string, or for general configurations like the location of the projection library.

The following listing shows what such a map file looks like.

Listing 17.1 Map with `INCLUDE`s

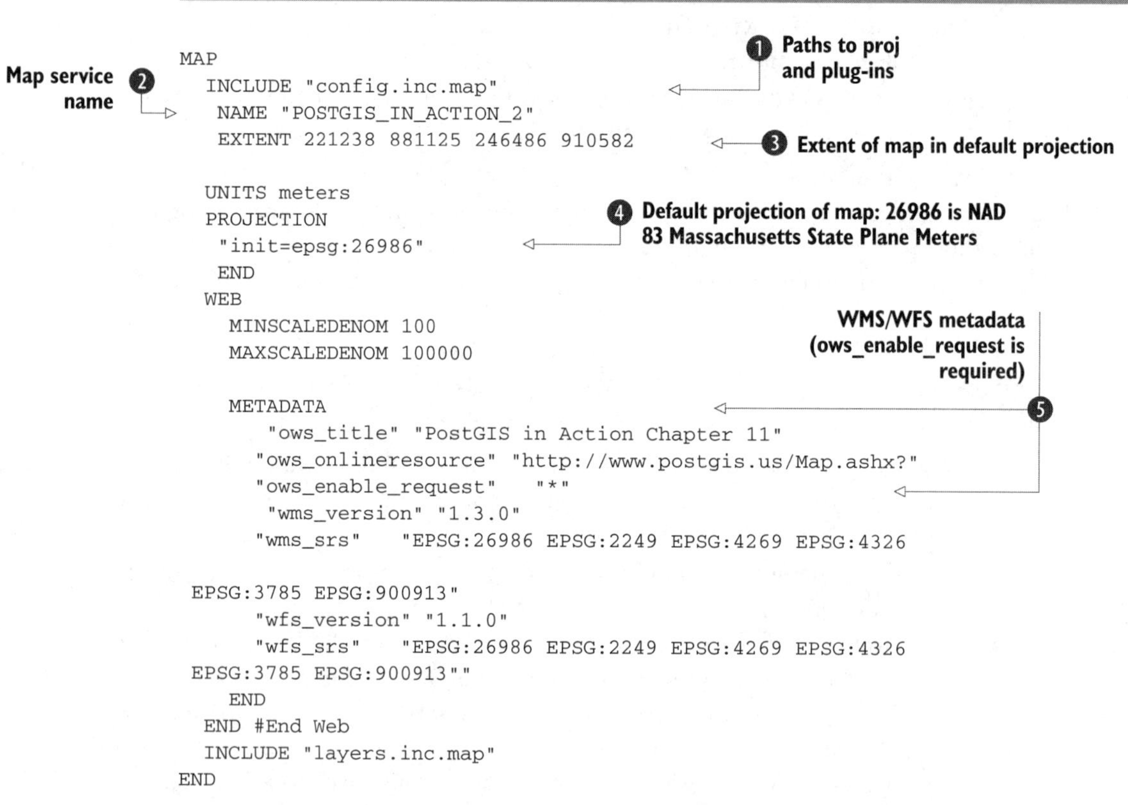

```
MAP
  INCLUDE "config.inc.map"
   NAME "POSTGIS_IN_ACTION_2"
   EXTENT 221238 881125 246486 910582

  UNITS meters
  PROJECTION
   "init=epsg:26986"
   END
  WEB
    MINSCALEDENOM 100
    MAXSCALEDENOM 100000

    METADATA
        "ows_title" "PostGIS in Action Chapter 11"
      "ows_onlineresource" "http://www.postgis.us/Map.ashx?"
      "ows_enable_request"    "*"
       "wms_version" "1.3.0"
      "wms_srs"    "EPSG:26986 EPSG:2249 EPSG:4269 EPSG:4326

 EPSG:3785 EPSG:900913"
      "wfs_version" "1.1.0"
      "wfs_srs"    "EPSG:26986 EPSG:2249 EPSG:4269 EPSG:4326
 EPSG:3785 EPSG:900913""
    END
  END #End Web
  INCLUDE "layers.inc.map"
END
```


Listing 17.1 is a basic map file with includes ❶. The config.inc.map file contains the paths to the projection library, symbol set, font set, and additional plug-ins not built into the core. All `INCLUDE`s are relative to the location of the file they're included in.

The `NAME` property is the map service name that appears in the logs ❷. The `EXTENT` property defines the extent of the map in units of the default projection of the map ❸. This defines the default output projection of the map if none is given. Each layer can be in a different projection, but they'll be reprojected to the map projection when the map is called ❹. This projection is often overridden in WMS calls with the SRS parameter.

The metadata section is particularly important, because this makes the map file behave like a true WMS/WFS. The `ows_*` elements are shorthand for WFS and WMS, so properties that are the same for both don't have to be specified twice. WFS version 1.0.0 can have only one SRS, but WFS version 1.1.0 allows you to specify a preferred SRS. The WMS standard allows many SRSs, and the ones listed are the ones the WMS service will allow to be passed in for the `SRS` URL parameter. The online resource gets displayed in the WMS capabilities as the URL to call to access the service. The `ows_enable_request` property is required for MapServer 6.2+ ❺. It defines what services are allowed; if it's set to `*`, that means all services are allowed.

The config.inc.map file defines the location of the symbol set, proj library, and fonts. It's shown in the following snippet:

```
CONFIG PROJ_LIB "C:/mapserv/bin/proj/SHARE/"
SYMBOLSET "symbols/postgis_in_action.sym"
FONTSET "fonts/fonts.list"
```

`PROJ_LIB` is always an absolute physical path, but `SYMBOLSET` and `FONTSET` can be absolute or relative to the location of the map file. If you're on Windows, you can copy the fonts you'll use from your Windows/fonts folder into your mapserv fonts folder, and then list them in the fonts.list file (as shown on the MapServer fontset page: http://mapserver.org/mapfile/fontset.html).

For the symbol set, you can use map symbol-set codes or images. A sample of both is packaged in the MapServer source download file. For this example, we used some freely available, public domain, true type fonts found at 1001 Free Fonts (http://www.1001freefonts.com). These are packaged as part of the chapter's download.

The following listing shows one of the layers in the layers.inc.map file. Note that you can include layers directly in the main map file.

Listing 17.2 Sample vector layer from layers.inc.map

```
LAYER
 NAME major_roads                  <-- ❶ Name and type
  TYPE LINE
 STATUS ON
 DUMP TRUE                              ❷ Database config
 INCLUDE "postgis.config"     <--
  DATA "geom from ch17.ma_eotmajroads using unique gid using srid=26986"
 PROJECTION
   "init=epsg:26986"
 END
 LABELITEM "rt_number"
 METADATA
   ows_title "Massachusetts Major Roads"
   gml_include_items "all"
   ows_featureid "gid"
 END
```

```
CLASS
 COLOR 255 0 0
 LABEL
  TYPE truetype
  FONT boston
  MINDISTANCE 50
  POSITION AUTO
  ANGLE AUTO                     <-- 3 Angle text around lines
   SIZE 6
  COLOR 0 0 0
 END
END
```

Every map layer starts with LAYER and has a NAME and TYPE ❶. The TYPE for PostGIS layers is usually LINE, POINT, POLYGON, or ANNOTATION. Then you include a file called postgis.config ❷, which you'll include for each of the PostGIS layers to define the connection string to the PostGIS database.

MapServer supports angled text, which is useful for labeling streets. Using ANGLE AUTO, the labels will wrap along the line segments ❸. For this example we used a font called *boston* that we downloaded.

The postgis.config file looks something like this:

```
CONNECTIONTYPE POSTGIS
CONNECTION "host=localhost dbname=somedb user=someuser

 port=5432 password=something"
PROCESSING "CLOSE_CONNECTION=DEFER"
```

CLOSE_CONNECTION=DEFER ensures that if multiple PostGIS layers are asked for, the connection will be reused instead of creating a new connection. This results in faster performance.

You now have a map file, but how do you turn this map file into a WMS/WFS service? You call the MapServer CGI with the map file as an argument.

17.4.3 Calling a mapping service using a reverse proxy

When you call the MapServer CGI, the call will look something like this:

```
http://localhost/mapserv/mapserv.exe?map=c:/mapserv/maps/

postgis_in_action.map&REQUEST=GetCapabilities&

SERVICE=WMS&VERSION=1.1.1
```

Specifying a map file for each call is often undesirable. Many people prefer to set up either a CGI script, a URL rewrite command in an .htaccess file, or a reverse proxy so that the map file doesn't have to be explicitly named. You can do more with a reverse proxy than with a CGI script.

What is a reverse proxy?

A *reverse proxy* is a server that behaves as a client and has access to other services, such as web-mapping servers, that a requesting client can't directly access. Reverse proxies are often used for load balancing by accepting requests from a web browser on the outside and funneling them to the least-busy mapping server. In addition, a reverse proxy can call services on other ports on the same machine.

If you use a reverse proxy, or a URL rewrite, the long map URL example can be reduced to something like this:

```
http://localhost/Map.ashx?REQUEST=GetCapabilities&SERVICE=WMS
&VERSION=1.1.1
```

Listing 17.3 demonstrates what a simple reverse proxy written in C# looks like. This is just a snippet. This reverse proxy just deals with `GET` requests, which are generally what most WMS servers use. For `POST`s you can do a check on the request method by looping through the `REQUEST` and `POST` variables.

Listing 17.3 Snippet of a reverse proxy in C#

```
string mapURLStub = "http://yourserver/cgi-bin/mapserv.exe?map=";
string mapfile = "c:/mapserver/maps/postgis_in_action.map";
System.IO.StreamReader sr;
System.Net.HttpWebResponse WebResponseObject;
System.Text.StringBuilder sb = new System.Text.StringBuilder();
sb.Append(mapURLStub + mapfile);
foreach (var key in context.Request.QueryString.AllKeys) {
   sb.Append("&" + key + "=" + context.Request.QueryString[key])
 }
 WebRequestObject = (System.Net.HttpWebRequest)
  System.Net.WebRequest.Create(sb.ToString());
WebRequestObject.Method = "GET";
WebResponseObject = (System.Net.HttpWebResponse)

 WebRequestObject.GetResponse();
if (context.Request["REQUEST"].ToLower() == "getcapabilities"

|| context.Request["REQUEST"].ToLower()
   == "getfeatureinfo") {
  sr = new System.IO.StreamReader(

WebResponseObject.GetResponseStream());
   context.Response.ContentType = "application/xml";
  context.Response.Write(sr.ReadToEnd());
}
else {
  context.Response.ContentType =
     context.Request["format"].ToString();
   System.IO.Stream outs =
     WebRequestObject.GetResponse().GetResponseStream();
```

❶ Loop request variables

❷ XML request to MapServer

❸ Image request to MapServer

```
    byte[] buffer = new byte[0x1000];
    int read;
    while ((read = outs.Read(buffer, 0, buffer.Length)) > 0){
         context.Response.OutputStream.Write(buffer, 0, read);
     }
}
```

Listing 17.3 loops through all the arguments received via the client query string ❶. The code then checks to see if the OGC request is `GetCapabilities` or `GetFeatureInfo` ❷, and if the request is, the code assumes that the result returned by your internal server is XML. If the request is something other than `GetCapabilities` or `GetFeatureInfo`, then the code assumes it's an image and processes it as such ❸.

Reverse proxy in other languages

We have code equivalent to listing 17.3 in the source download packaged for VB.NET and the full C# code. If you're using PHP, you can implement similar logic using curl. This reverse proxy code can also be used to set up GeoServer web-mapping services, such as to run GeoServer on its own Apache or Jetty web server on a local port, or even on a separate server in your internal network, while keeping the regular port 80 for a regular Apache or IIS server.

A WMS call to generate an image that has both open space and major roads would look like the following.

Listing 17.4 PostGIS MapServer WMS layer call using proxy

```
http://yourserver/Map.ashx?LAYERS=openspace&STYLES=&TRANSPARENT=true
&FORMAT=image%2Fpng&SERVICE=WMS&VERSION=1.1.1&REQUEST=GetMap&
EXCEPTIONS=application%2Fvnd.ogc.se_inimage&SRS=EPSG%3A3857&
BBOX=-7912678.2752033,5204927.2982632,-7912475.239347,5205061.6602269
&WIDTH=340&HEIGHT=225
```

MapServer doesn't support WFS-T out of the box or for all data sources, but it does support WFS-T for PostGIS via a plug-in called *TinyOWS* (http://mapserver.org/tinyows/index.html#tinyows)

We'll next take a look at GeoServer and see how it compares to MapServer.

17.5 Using GeoServer

GeoServer is similar in flavor to MapServer, except that it's a bit heftier and comes with an administrative user interface, so there's not as much need for manually configuring files with a text editor. It also supports WFS-T.

17.5.1 Installing GeoServer

GeoServer has several installation packages that can be downloaded from http://geoserver.org:

- Installers for Windows and Mac guide you through the setup. They come with the mini web server Jetty.
- Java binaries are available for all operating systems. You need only extract them to a folder and manually set the environment variables. Jetty is included too.

  A web application archive (WAR) is available for those who already have a servlet engine installed on their server and just want to run GeoServer as another servlet application. This one doesn't come with Jetty.

We chose the Java binary GeoServer 2.5-RC1 version for our installation. To set it up, you need to do the following:

1. Make sure you have Java JDK 1.5+ installed.
2. Extract the folder into the root; for example, C:\geoserver or /usr/local/geoserver.
3. On Windows, set the appropriate system environment variables. `JAVA_HOME` would be something like C:\Program Files\Java\jdk1.6.0_16 (or whatever JDK you have).
4. `cd` into the geoserver\bin folder, and from the command line run startup.bat (for Windows) or startup.sh (for Linux/Unix).
5. You should now be able to get to the administrative panel by navigating to the following link in your web browser: http://localhost:8080/geoserver.

17.5.2 Setting up PostGIS workspaces

Once you've got GeoServer installed, you need to set up a GeoServer workspace to house your tables and then register PostGIS tables with GeoServer. Follow these steps:

1. From the menus, select Admin > Data > Workspaces, and click Add a New Workspace. The New Workspace screen should look something like figure 17.1.

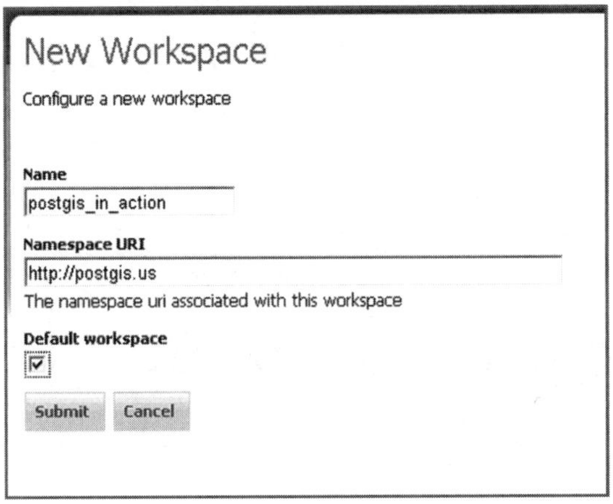

Figure 17.1 Setting up a GeoServer workspace

2. From the left navigation menu choose Data > Stores.

3 Click the Add New Store menu option and then choose PostGIS from the list of options shown in figure 17.2.

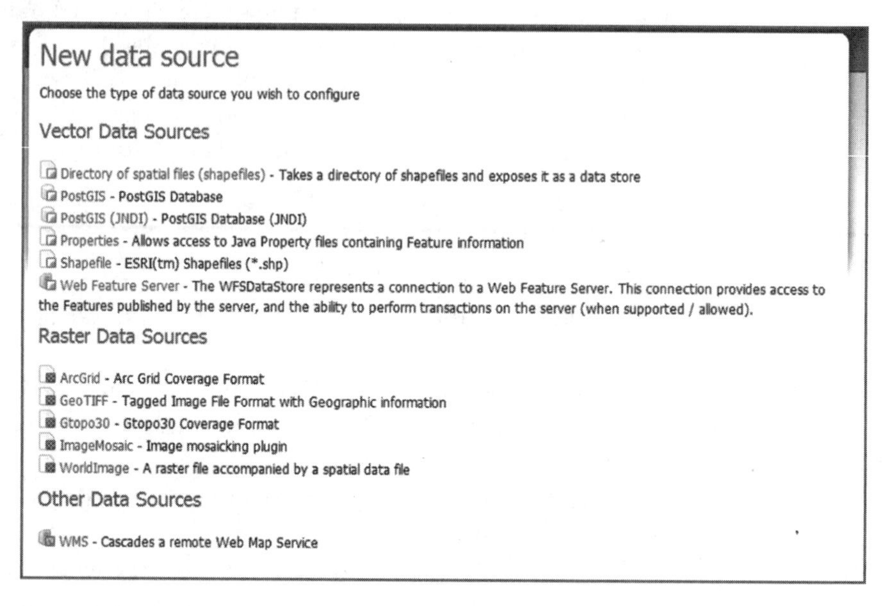

Figure 17.2 Adding a GeoServer PostGIS data store

4 Give the data source a name—we used ch17—and fill in all the credentials asked for. By default, GeoServer uses the public schema, which means it will list only layers from that schema. If you want it to list a different schema, like ch17 in our case, replace `public` with `ch17`.

5 Select Admin > Layers > Add a New Resource, and choose the postgis_in_action store you created previously. Your screen should look something like figure 17.3.

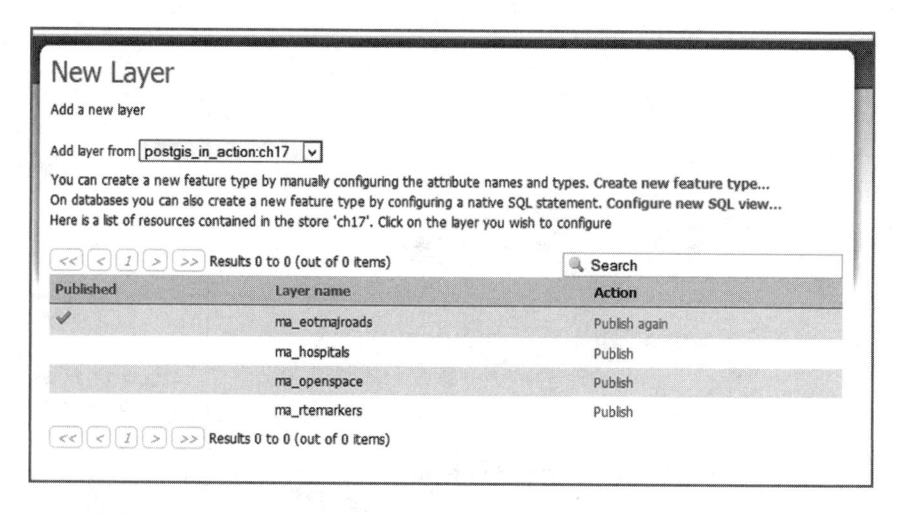

Figure 17.3 Selecting PostGIS layers

6. Publish the layer you want by clicking the Publish action for the appropriate layer (see figure 17.3). Make sure you choose Compute From Data and Compute From Native Bounds on the layer edit screen.
7. Click the Add New Resource link.
8. Repeat steps 6 and 7 for each layer you want to publish.

> **GeoServer data stores from other schemas**
>
> It's possible to leave the schema setting blank in GeoServer for PostGIS, and the layer chooser will list them all. However, we've found that publishing layers in a schema other than public will throw an error. Be sure you create a different data store for each schema you want to publish.

17.5.3 Accessing PostGIS layers via GeoServer WMS/WFS

Once you've published your PostGIS layers, you can quickly see them via the Layer Preview menu link. Figure 17.4 shows what that screen looks like. Note that it also shows the OpenLayers code to be used to call the layer, and it shows GeoJSON as a direct WFS output format.

As you can see in figure 17.4, GeoServer autogenerates OpenLayers sample JavaScript code to display each of your layers. OpenLayers and Leaflet are both popular web-mapping client companions for GeoServer and MapServer. Both provide basic mapping functionality for loading layers, editing widgets, and so forth. These two frameworks are useful for commercial web services, for tile services, for WMS services offered by GeoServer, MapServer, and other mapping servers, and for scripted applications with languages such as ASP.NET, PHP, or NodeJS. In the next section, we'll introduce you to OpenLayers and Leaflet JavaScript-mapping client toolkits.

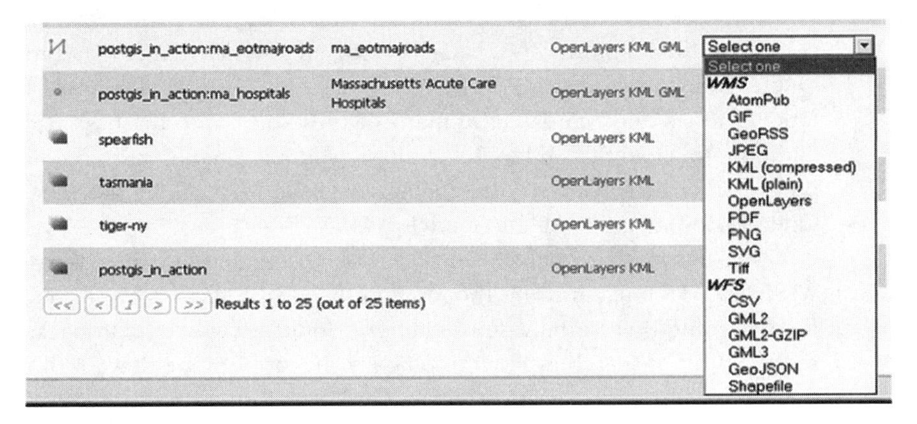

Figure 17.4 Layer preview screen of GeoServer

17.6 Basics of OpenLayers and Leaflet

In the beginning, mapping services like Google Maps, Virtual Earth, MapQuest, and Yahoo had their own proprietary JavaScript APIs to access their data. This was a Bad Thing, because if you decided you liked the maps of service A better than the maps of service B, or if usage and pricing became too cumbersome, then you had to rewrite everything to switch services. Worse yet, if you wanted to feed your own data via an OGC WMS or ArcGIS/IMS server for your area of interest, it was hard to integrate the base layers provided by these services with your custom study-area layers.

OpenLayers (http://openlayers.org) and Leaflet (http://leafletjs.com) changed the landscape quite a bit by allowing layers provided by different vendors with vastly different APIs to be accessed using the same API, or, better yet, to be used together in the same map.

OpenLayers started life as an incubation project of MetaCarta (which then became part of Nokia, which then got partly bought out by Microsoft), because it needed to create an easy-to-use toolkit for customers to digest its map product offerings. OpenLayers is now an incubation project of OSGeo.

Leaflet is another JavaScript API that came on the scene some years after OpenLayers. As a result of not having old JavaScript baggage, the Leaflet JavaScript API is considered by many to be a fresher, more modern API with HTML5 very much in it's design from the outset. Leaflet's focus is mostly on simplicity.

Both APIs have a lot of overlapping features, with Leaflet generally having less built-in functionality than OpenLayers and relegating additional functionality to Leaflet plug-ins. The latest version of OpenLayers (the OpenLayers 3 series) is a complete rewrite of OpenLayers with a more modern JavaScript API very similar in pattern to Leaflet. In talking about the two, we need to compare Leaflet (version 0.7), OpenLayers 2.13 (the second generation), and OpenLayers 3 (version 3.1), the new contender.

What do OpenLayers and Leaflet give you that you can't easily get elsewhere?

- Layer classes that allow you to access many of the proprietary non-OGC-compliant tile map offerings, such as Google Maps, Virtual Earth (Bing), MapQuest, Yahoo, and ArcGIS Rest, using the same interface for all. Both the OpenLayers 2 and 3 series have many of these built into the base package (in addition to OpenStreetMap tile layers) whereas Leaflet requires additional plug-ins. The only tile layer drivers built into the base Leaflet download are for OpenStreetMap and WMS tile services.

  Layer classes that enable you to access OGC-compliant map servers WMS, WFS, and WFS-T, again using the same fairly consistent map layer creation call. Keep in mind that in the case of Leaflet, a lot of these aren't prepackaged and require a bit of searching for the plug-ins. In case of OpenLayers (both 2 and 3), most of the layer classes you'll need are packaged in the base download.
- The ability to overlay all these competing proprietary services in one map.

- Various controls to build custom menus, toolbars, and widgets to enable map editing. OpenLayers 2 has most of these features built-in, and OpenLayers 3 has many missing at this point, requiring you to build your own or find an OL plug-in. Leaflet has just the most rudimentary controls, requiring you to look at the additional plug-in offerings.

All these things are wonderful, and that's why OpenLayers and Leaflet have become so popular. But most great things aren't without their tradeoffs:

- It's hard to get to the deep features of a proprietary service when using Leaflet or OpenLayers to access the proprietary service, such as the 3D street views provided by Google Maps and Bing. This may change as new OpenLayers and Leaflet layer classes are added to support these features.
- There's yet another API to learn, with the hope that you won't have to learn any other APIs.

When comparing Leaflet and OpenLayers, which should you choose? As with all things, it depends.

For a lightweight and flashy-looking modern interface, many people seem to prefer Leaflet. Products such as CartoDB and CloudMade, needing their own customized API, tend to build on Leaflet. Even Esri has a customized Leaflet set of classes called *Esri Leaflet* that are used in conjunction with the base Leaflet script to work with their ArcGIS Online services (http://esri.github.io/esri-leaflet).

OpenLayers, on the other hand (particularly the 2 series), has a lot of the things you'll need, even for a big app, already built in. There's no searching for and comparing of competing plug-ins. There are also a lot more examples to look at with OpenLayers, although this is changing rapidly, and the Leaflet API is better documented, with examples displayed alongside the documentation of the classes and methods.

In this section, we'll demonstrate a basic map using OpenLayers 2.13, OpenLayers 3, and Leaflet. This first set of maps will just give you a feel for what each looks like. In subsequent sections, we'll add PostGIS layers and PostGIS queries that output JSON.

OpenStreetMap tiles: publicly available tiles versus building your own

For the base layers, we'll use OpenStreetMap public tile servers for the exercises that follow. Because OpenStreetMap public tile servers run on donations, you may be cut off if you make a lot of calls to them. The tile usage policy is detailed at http://wiki.openstreetmap.org/wiki/Tile_usage_policy.

If you have heavy traffic, you should build your own tiles, or use tiles from a commercial service, such as MapQuest OSM tiles (http://wiki.openstreetmap.org/wiki/Mapquest#MapQuest-hosted_map_tiles), CloudMade (http://cloudmade.com), or Mapbox (http://mapbox.com), which also provide storage and tools for building custom tiles. If you want to build and host your own tiles, you can do so using the OSM Mapnik kit or TileMill. Both are described on the SWITCH2OSM page (http://switch2osm.org), which also details other tile providers.

17.6.1 OpenLayers primer

The OpenLayers 2 series is currently at version 2.13 (http://openlayers.org/two/). OpenLayers 3 (http://openlayers.org) is the new code base for OpenLayers moving forward, and it's a complete rewrite of OpenLayers. As such, there's no backward compatibility between the two versions. OpenLayers 3 is currently at version 3.1.1.

Class documentation is available on each site, although you'll probably find the numerous code samples to be much more useful for getting started. Because OpenLayers is nothing more than a glorified JavaScript file, you can download the file and use it directly from your web server. Alternatively, you can link your code directly with the version on OpenLayers.

One thing that OpenLayers is particularly good at is allowing you to integrate various map sources from disparate services. Both versions have classes for accessing the Google, Bing (Virtual Earth), OpenStreetMap (OSM), MapQuest, and MapServer APIs, as well as standard OGC-compliant WMS and WFS services produced with tools like MapServer, GeoServer, Degree, and TinyOWS.

OPENLAYERS 2.13

For a first example, we'll demonstrate adding an OpenStreetMap base layer and a WMS layer we created. Note that you can easily swap out MapServer for GeoServer in these examples.

Listing 17.5 OpenLayers 2.13 general setup: postgis_in_action_ol2_1.htm

```
<!doctype html> <html lang="en">   <head>     <style>        #map {
        height: 600px;
        width: 100%;
      }
    </style>     <link rel="stylesheet" href="http://openlayers.org/api/
     2.13.1
/theme/default/style.css" type="text/css">   </
     head>   <body>     <div id="map" class="map"></div>
 <script src="http://openlayers.org/api/2.13.1/OpenLayers.js"
 type="text/javascript"></script>     <script type="text/
     javascript">          map = new OpenLayers.Map("map", {
            projection: new OpenLayers.Projection("EPSG:3857")
        });
        var l1 = new OpenLayers.Layer.OSM("OSM Map");

        var l2 = new OpenLayers.Layer.WMS("Open Space / Major Roads"
           , 'Map.ashx',
          { 'LAYERS': 'major_roads,openspace',
              'styles': "", 'FORMAT': "image/png", 'transparent': true
          },
        { 'isBaseLayer': false, 'visibility': true, 'buffer': 1,
          'singleTile': false, 'attribution': 'MassGIS data' });
        map.addLayers([l1,l2]);
        map.addControl(new OpenLayers.Control.LayerSwitcher());
```

1. Position map on page
2. Link to API
3. Instantiate map and set projection
4. Add OSM base layer
5. Add WMS layers from PostGIS
6. Add Layer switcher panel to map

```
    var lonLat =
      new OpenLayers.LonLat(-71.0636, 42.3581).transform(
        new OpenLayers.Projection("EPSG:4326"),
        map.getProjectionObject());
     map.setCenter(lonLat, 15);

</script>   </body> </html>
```

❼ **Project lon/lat point to projection of map, and zoom to location**

Listing 17.5 positions the div on the HTML page that will be used to display the maps ❶. The code also includes the link to the source OpenLayers.js file ❷, which contains all the functions needed for the map. If you want to customize or fully control this script, you should download and reference it locally. The JavaScript code defines a `map` variable, instantiates the map in the div called `map`, and sets the map projection to EPSG 3587 (web mercator) ❸. The `OpenLayers.Layer.OSM` layer class is used to instantiate an OpenStreetMap layer and set the base map to OpenStreetMap ❹. The `OpenLayers .Layer.WMS` layer class is used to overlay layers from a PostGIS-driven WMS service ❺. The `map.addControl>` call adds a layer switcher control that allows the user to toggle map layers on and off ❻. `var lonLat` holds a user-input lon/lat which is used by `map.getProjectionOjbect` to project that location to the projection of the map ❼.

The output of listing 17.5 is shown in figure 17.5.

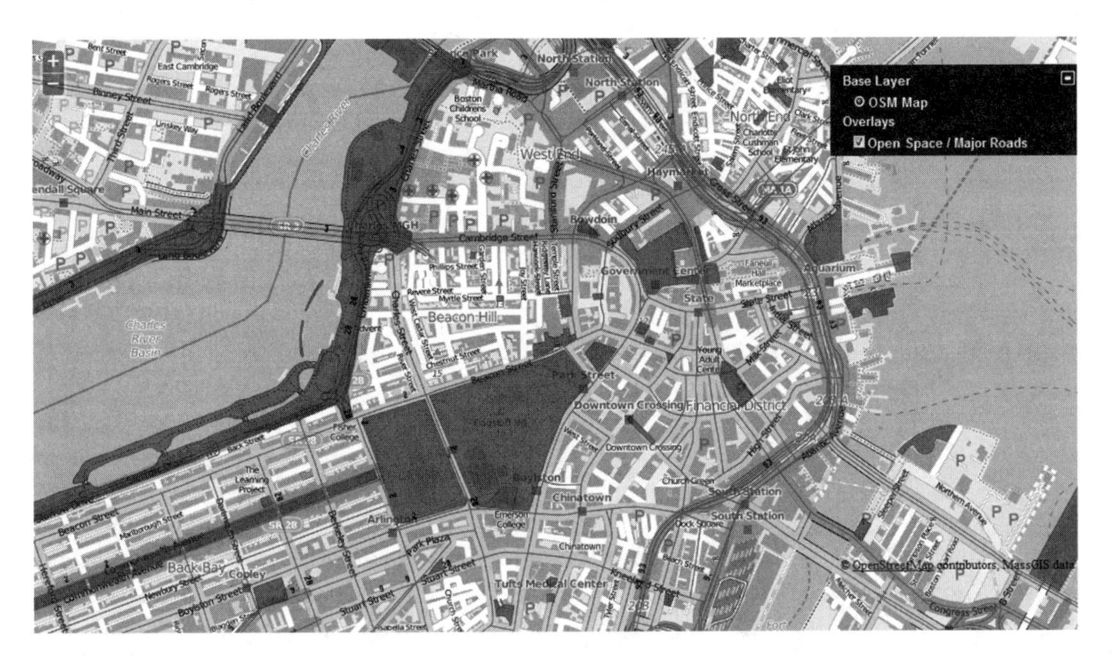

Figure 17.5 Output of OpenLayers 2.13 example

OpenLayers 3

For this next exercise, we'll display the same information as we did in listing 17.5, but using OpenLayers 3 instead. One thing we'll leave out for this exercise is the layer switcher. The layer-switcher control is not yet built into OpenLayers 3, even as of the

3.1 version, although there is a LayerSwitcher control extension you can download from https://github.com/walkermatt/ol3-layerswitcher.

Listing 17.6 OpenLayers 3 general setup: postgis_in_action_ol3_1.htm

```
<!doctype html> <html lang="en">   <head>     <link rel="stylesheet"
      href="http://ol3js.org/en/master/css/ol.css" type="text/css">
     <style>       #map {
        height: 600px;
        width: 100%;
      }
    </style>     <script src="http://ol3js.org/en/master/build/ol.js"
      type="text/javascript"></script>
 </head>   <body>     <div id="map" class="map"></
     div>     <script type="text/
     javascript">          var l1 = new ol.layer.Tile({
          source: new ol.source.OSM(
            {url:'//{a-c}.tile.osm.org/{z}/{x}/{y}.png'}
           )
        });

        var l2 = new ol.layer.Tile({
            source: new ol.source.TileWMS(({
                 url: 'Map.ashx',
                params: { 'LAYERS': 'openspace,major_roads'},
                serverType: 'mapserver',
                attributions: [new ol.Attribution({
                    html: 'MassGIS data'
                }
            }))
        });

        var map = new ol.Map({
            target: 'map',
             layers: [l1, l2],
             view: new ol.View2D({
                center: ol.proj.transform([-71.0636, 42.3581]
                 , 'EPSG:4326', 'EPSG:3857'),
                 zoom: 15
            })
        });
        map.addControl(new ol.control.Zoom());
     </script>   </body> </html>
```

1. Link to OL3 API JS and CSS
2. Create OpenStreetMap layer
3. Create PostGIS WMS layers
4. Load map
5. Add layers
6. Center reprojecting WGS lon/lat to OSM projection

Add zoom in/zoom out control

First, you add the link to the OL3 CSS and JS files ❶. Again you have the choice of using a hosted version or downloading and using one on your server. You then add an OpenStreetMap tile layer ❷. The `url` property is optional and defaults to the OpenStreetMap tile server when not specified. You next add two layers from your WMS mapping server ❸. As part of the load map ❹, add the two layers ❺ to the map, and ❻ reproject to map units.This particular WMS layer call adds the layers as tiles of the same size as the OpenStreetMap tile. If you wanted single tiles to minimize on query calls to your server, you'd use `ol.Layer.Image` in conjunction with `ol.source.ImageWMS`.

The output of listing 17.6 is shown in figure 17.6.

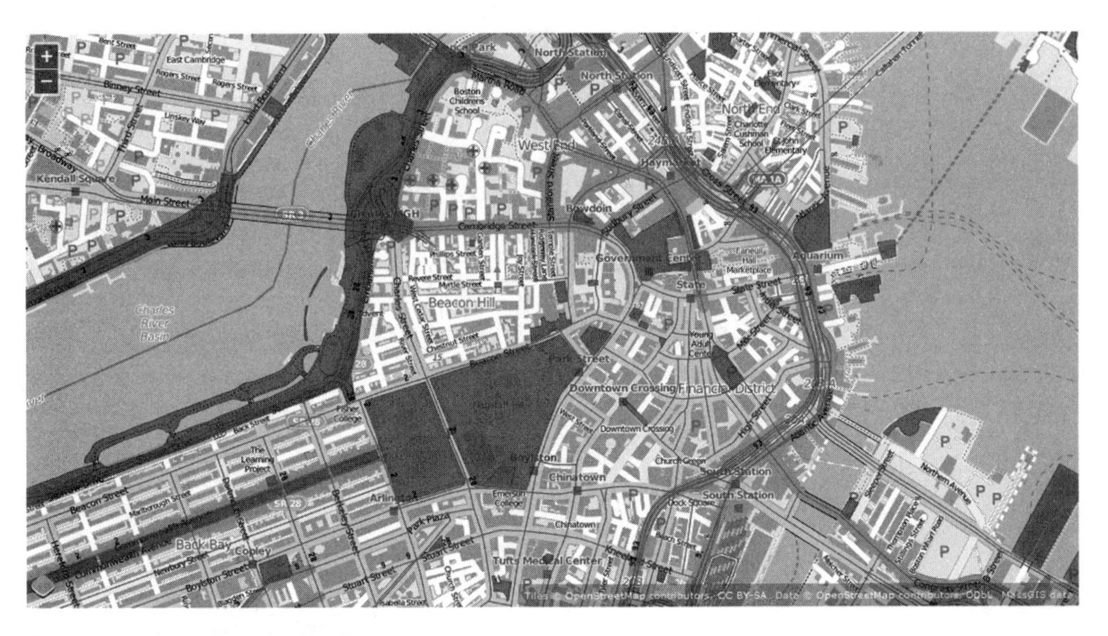

Figure 17.6 Output of OpenLayers 3.0 example

As you can see, the output from OpenLayers 2.13 and OpenLayers 3.0 look much the same, except the OpenLayers 3 example (figure 17.6) is missing the layer switcher that allows the user to turn on and off layers. The OpenLayers 3 version also has a slightly more prominent OpenStreetMap attribution and has a small link back to the OpenLayers 3 website.

The code for OpenLayers 2.13 (listing 17.5) and OpenLayers 3 (listing 17.6) show much the same elements, except for the following distinctions:

- OpenLayers 3 calls the base API component `ol`, whereas OpenLayers 2.13 uses the much longer `OpenLayers`. In general, the syntax of OpenLayers 3 is more succinct than that of OpenLayers 2, except for how you specify the data source attribution information.
- The +/- zoom control is by default added in OpenLayers 2.13 unless you start with a blank controls container, so you don't need to explicitly add it. In OpenLayers 3.0 you have to explicitly add it.
- The layer-adding syntax is very different between the two versions, and for the WMS layer you're outputting in the more popular tile approach.
- OpenLayers 2.13 still has a lot more controls built in than OpenLayers 3. One we demonstrated was the layer-switcher control.

Though it's not demonstrated in these figures, both OpenLayers 2.13 and OpenLayers 3 add mouse-wheel scroll behaviors for zooming in and out by default, so you don't need to explicitly add those.

In the next section, we'll take a look at Leaflet and see how it compares to OpenLayers 2.13 and 3.

17.6.2 Leaflet primer

Leaflet is a lighter-weight mapping API than OpenLayers. It's also a newer API. The current version, as of this writing, is 0.7.

For many apps where you want a tile-based layer and want to draw your own layers on top using something like GeoJSON objects, Leaflet often suffices and provides a slicker, less busy interface, and is generally much faster to get up to speed with than OpenLayers (2 or 3). You can also expand Leaflet's functionality by adding other Leaflet plug-ins.

Let's perform the same exercise as we did with OpenLayers, but using Leaflet instead.

Listing 17.7 Leaflet general setup: postgis_in_action_leaflet_1.htm

```
<!doctype html> <html lang="en"><head>  <link rel="stylesheet" href="http://
     cdn.leafletjs.com

//leaflet-0.7/leaflet.css" />
   <script src="//cdn.leafletjs.com/leaflet-0.7/leaflet.js">
   </script> <style> #map {height: 600px;width: 100%;}</style>     </
     head>     <body> <div id="map"></div> <script type="text/
     javascript">  var l1 = L.tileLayer(
    'http://{s}.tile.osm.org/{z}/{x}/{y}.png', {
     attribution: 'Map data &copy; OpenStreetMap contributors',
     maxZoom: 18
 });
 var map = L.map('map', { layers: [l1] })
             .setView([42.3581, -71.0636], 15);

 var l2 = L.tileLayer.wms("Map.ashx", {
      layers: 'major_roads,openspace',
     format: 'image/png',
     transparent: true,
     version: '1.3.0',
     attribution: "MassGIS data"
 });
 var baseMaps = { "OpenStreetMap": l1 }
  var overlayMaps = { "Open Space / Major Roads": l2 }
  L.control.layers(baseMaps, overlayMaps,
  { collapsed: false }).addTo(map);
 </script>     </body> </html>
```

❶ Link to Leaflet API JS and CSS
❷ Create OpenStreetMap layer
❸ Load map and center on location
❹ Create PostGIS WMS layers
❺ Add layers control with base layer and overlays

The Leaflet code is slightly more succinct than that for OpenLayers 2 and 3, but in many cases it's much the same. Listing 17.7 follows steps similar to the OpenLayers 2 example. First, you reference the location of the Leaflet CSS and JavaScript API files ❶. Then you create the OpenStreetMap layer ❷. You load the map, initialized with the OpenStreetMap layer, mark it as an active layer, and center it on a location using `setvView` ❸.

One difference between OpenLayers and Leaflet is that Leaflet `setView` coordinates are specified in lat/lon instead of database/OpenLayers lon/lat. The `setView`

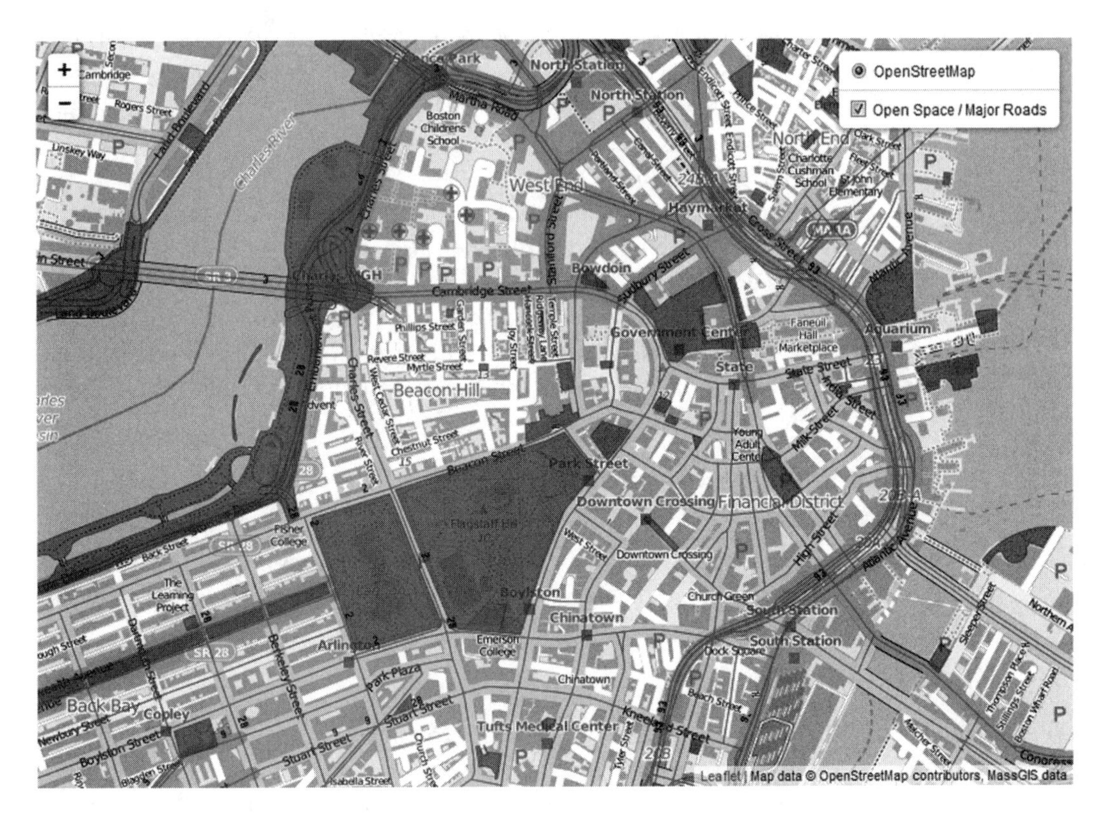

Figure 17.7 Output of Leaflet

syntax is a bit shorter than the transform, center, zoom approach of OpenLayers, but this is not without sacrifice. Leaflet, out of the box, assumes you want to show your data in Web Mercator, whereas OpenLayers gives you the choice of what projection to use and what your input projections are.

Next you create the WMS layer ❹, which can be MapServer, GeoServer, or any other OGC-compliant WMS. Then you specify which will be base layers and which will be overlays, create a layer control to manage these, and add the control to the map ❺. The Leaflet layers control is equivalent to the OpenLayers 2 layer-switcher control.

The output of listing 17.7 is shown in figure 17.7.

Similar to OpenLayers 2.13, Leaflet does have a built-in layer control. Figure 17.7 looks much the same as the outputs from OpenLayers, but with slightly different styling for the controls and attribution. Both of these can be controlled by changing the CSS in any of these toolkits.

17.6.3 Synopsis of the three different APIs

This section demonstrated three different APIs at work. The OpenLayers 2 series is a long-time favorite of many open source web mappers. Leaflet is the up-and-coming favorite with a generally lighter and more modern API than OpenLayers 2. You also saw OpenLayers 3, which is a complete rewrite of OpenLayers 2. It's still relatively new, but it promises to be a good mix of feature-richness, faster speed, and streamlined API. We demonstrated that with these three APIs, not only can you query common web-mapping services such as OpenStreetMap tile services, but you can also overlay a WMS server powered by your PostGIS data.

Although WMS and WFS servers are great for dishing out often-changing mapping data, they limit the queries you can do, and they also tend to add hefty overheads to your infrastructure. A common practice nowadays is to leave the static, commonly used layers to tile services and prerendered tiles. You can then use raw database calls for things like saving data and displaying constantly changing features. In the next section, we'll use PHP to do direct PostGIS queries and demonstrate how these can be overlaid on a map.

17.7 Displaying data with PostGIS queries and web scripting

We're now going to demonstrate how you can use the functions built into PostgreSQL and PostGIS to overlay spatial data on a map. The assumption for this section is that you're using PostgreSQL 9.2+ and PostGIS 2.1+.

17.7.1 Displaying PostGIS rasters using raster queries

Unfortunately, support for the PostGIS `raster` type in WMS servers is still pretty lackluster or nonexistent. Fortunately, you can simulate a WMS server by doing direct query calls to your database and utilizing the built-in functions that PostGIS raster provides.

Listing 17.8 shows a PostgreSQL function that simulates a WMS server to serve up PostGIS raster data. In order to work with multiple bands, you'll need PostGIS 2.1+, because the `ST_Union` function of PostGIS in 2.0 only supports single bands.

Listing 17.8 In-DB WMS raster tile generator

```
CREATE OR REPLACE FUNCTION ch17.get_rast_tile(
    param_format text,
    param_width integer,
    param_height integer,
    param_srid integer,
    param_bbox text,
    param_schema text,
    param_table text
)
RETURNS bytea AS
$$
DECLARE
    var_sql text; var_result raster; var_srid integer;
    var_env geometry; var_erast raster;
BEGIN
    EXECUTE
        'SELECT ST_MakeEnvelope(' || array_to_string(('{' ||
```

```
        param_bbox || '}')::float8[],',') || ',' || param_srid ||
        ')'
    INTO var_env;                                   <-- ❶ Bounding-box window
    var_sql :=
        'SELECT srid, ST_AsRaster($4,$5,$6,pixel_types,nodata_values,nodata_v
     alues) As erast
        FROM raster_columns
        WHERE r_table_schema = $1 AND r_table_name = $2 AND r_raster_column=$
     3';
    EXECUTE var_sql INTO var_srid, var_erast
    USING param_schema, param_table, 'rast', var_env, param_width, param_heig
     ht;                                            <-- ❷ SRID of raster,
                                                        create blank
    var_sql :=                                          bounding-box raster
        'WITH r AS (SELECT ST_Clip(rast,' ||
        CASE
            WHEN var_srid = param_srid THEN '$3'
            ELSE 'ST_Transform($3,$2)'
        END || ') As rast FROM  ' ||
        quote_ident(param_schema) || '.' ||
        quote_ident(param_table) || '
        WHERE ST_Intersects(rast,' ||
        CASE
            WHEN var_srid = param_srid THEN '$3'
            ELSE 'ST_Transform($3,$2)'
        END || ') limit 15)
        SELECT ST_Clip(ST_Union(rast), $3) As rast      ❸ Parameterized
        FROM (SELECT ST_Resample(' ||                      query
        CASE                                               transform,
            WHEN var_srid = param_srid THEN 'rast'         resample,
            ELSE 'ST_Transform(rast,$1)'                   union, clip
        END ||
        ',$6,true,''CubicSpline'') As rast FROM r) As final';  <--

    EXECUTE var_sql INTO var_result

    USING
        param_srid,
        var_srid,
        var_env,
        param_width,
        param_height,
        var_erast;                          <-- ❹ Execute parameterized query

    IF var_result IS NULL THEN
        var_result := var_erast;
    End If;

    RETURN
        CASE
            WHEN param_format ILIKE 'jp' THEN ST_AsJPEG(var_result)
            ELSE ST_AsPNG(var_result)
        END;
END;
$$
LANGUAGE plpgsql IMMUTABLE;
```

Listing 17.8 is a PL/pgSQL function that, given a bounding-box area of interest and a raster table ❶, will look up the SRID from `raster_columns` to formulate a blank bounding-box raster ❷. It will formulate a parameterized query that will return a single raster by unioning tile areas from the table that intersect the bounding box and clipping to the bounds of the box ❸. If the requested output projection is different from the raster table projection, it will do a transformation and resampling. The resampling is to get the raster in the same resolution as what is represented by the input raster/geometry bounds. It will then execute the parameterized query, inputting the area of interest and SRID ❹. If there is a result, it will return that; otherwise it will return an empty raster.

Next you need to create a web script that gets called like a WMS and passes the standard WMS variables to the `ch17.get_rast_tile` function. Note that this function takes an additional variable called `schema`, which isn't normally passed by a WMS. Luckily both Leaflet and OpenLayers allow you to pass additional variables that can be captured by the WMS.

The script shown in listing 17.9 is written in PHP, but you could use ASP.NET, Python, Java, or any other language that supports querying PostgreSQL.

Listing 17.9 PGMap.php: web script to call DB stored tile function

```
<?php
    include_once("config.inc.php");                    ❶ Include DB connection info

    $param_format = $_REQUEST['FORMAT'];               ❷ Read variables from request

    $param_width = (int) $_REQUEST['WIDTH'];
    $param_height = (int) $_REQUEST['HEIGHT'];
    $param_bbox = $_REQUEST['BBOX'];
    $param_schema = $_REQUEST['SCHEMA'];
    $param_table = $_REQUEST['LAYERS'];
     if ( !empty($_REQUEST['VERSION'])
          && $_REQUEST['VERSION'] == '1.1.1' ) {

        $param_srid = (int) str_replace('EPSG:', ''
             , $_REQUEST['SRS']);                      ❸ CRS/SRS based on WMS version
    }
    else {

        $param_srid = (int) str_replace('EPSG:', ''
             , $_REQUEST['CRS']);
    }

    $dbconn = pg_connect(DSN);                         ❹ Connect to database

    pg_query('SET bytea_output = "escape";');          ❺ Force database to output in escape mode

    $res = pg_query_params($dbconn,
       'SELECT ch17.get_rast_tile($1, $2, $3, $4,
        $5, $6, $7) As result',
        array($param_format, $param_width, $param_height,
```

```
                    $param_srid, $param_bbox,
                    $param_schema, $param_table ));
    $val = pg_fetch_result($res,0,0);

    header('Content-type: ' . $param_format);
     echo pg_unescape_bytea($val);
?>
```

❻ **Call parameterized query with inputs**
❼ **Fetch results**
❽ **Denote type of outputting image**
❾ **Decode bytea back to binary**

The first part of listing 17.9 includes the file config.inc.php ❶, which contains the connection string to the database and looks like this:

```
<?php
define("DSN", "host=localhost dbname=postgis_in_action

  user=postgis_in_action port=5432 password=whatever");
?>
```

The REQUEST object is used to read variables passed in via the page request ❷. There is also some conditional logic to handle projection field naming ❸. For the case where the call is a WMS 1.3.0-like call, the projection variable is called CRS; WMS 1.1.1 and lower use SRS. You also assume the projection will be an EPSG-coded one so you can easily look up the SRID by stripping off EPSG. For example, if the request is of the form SRS=EPSG:4326, you'd convert that to 4326 and look up 4326 in the spatial_ref_sys table.

Next you create a connection to the database ❹. Because the PHP pg_unescape_bytea function can't properly handle the newer default PostgreSQL 9.0+ bytea hex output, you force the connection to output binary data in the old escape format ❺.

Then you run the parameterized function created in listing 17.8, with parameters passed in by web call ❻, and you fetch the results into a PHP variable ❼. The output will be a bytea-escaped PNG or JPEG based on the image format the user requested in the FORMAT request variable ❽. The final step is to decode the image binary from the escaped format to binary format ❾.

CALLING A RASTER WMS FROM OPENLAYERS 2.13

Calling a custom raster WMS from OpenLayers 2.13 is similar to calling a GeoServer WMS or MapServer WMS, except that there's an additional SCHEMA parameter; the layers parameter only supports one layer at a time; and the layer must be a table name.

Listing 17.10 OpenLayers 2.13 raster layer

```
var l3 = new OpenLayers.Layer.WMS("NOAA", 'PGMap.php',
  { 'LAYERS': 'noaa', 'SCHEMA': 'ch17',
      'styles': "", 'FORMAT': "image/png"
  },
 { 'isBaseLayer': true, 'visibility': false, 'buffer': 1
            , 'singleTile': false });
```

The result of adding the new layer is shown in figure 17.8.

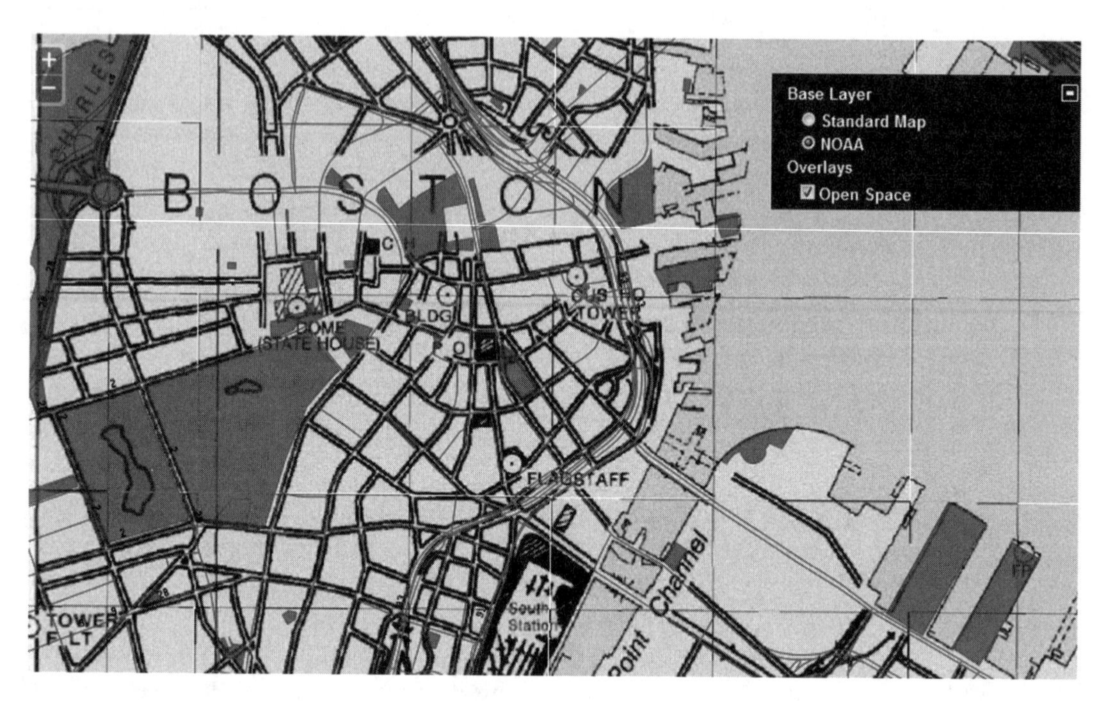

Figure 17.8 Output of OpenLayers 2.13

CALLING A RASTER WMS FROM OPENLAYERS 3

Calling a custom raster WMS from OpenLayers 3 is shown in the next listing.

Listing 17.11 OpenLayers 3.0 raster layer tiles

```
var l3 = new ol.layer.Tile({
    source: new ol.source.TileWMS(({
        url: 'PGMap.php',
        params: {'SCHEMA': 'ch17', 'LAYERS': 'noaa' }
    }))
});
```

As noted earlier, if you want just a single image back instead of tile calls, you use the `ImageWMS` source, as shown in the following listing.

Listing 17.12 OpenLayers 3.0 raster layer as single image

```
var l3 = new ol.layer.Image({
      source: new ol.source.ImageWMS(({
          url: 'PGMap.php',
          params: { 'SCHEMA': 'ch17', 'LAYERS': 'noaa' }
      }))
  });
```

CALLING A RASTER WMS FROM LEAFLET

In order to call a raster function from Leaflet, you add a layer much like you'd add any WMS layer.

Listing 17.13 Leaflet raster layer

```
var l3 = L.tileLayer.wms("PGMap.php", {
   layers: 'noaa', 'SCHEMA': 'ch17',
   format: 'image/png',
   transparent: true,
   version: '1.3.0'});
```

17.7.2 Using PostGIS and PostgreSQL geometry output functions

A common feature of web mapping is to highlight the features clicked on or selected on a map and show descriptive information about the feature clicked. For this kind of functionality, you need a web feature service or something like a GeoJSON query that returns both vector and attribute data.

For this next exercise, we'll demonstrate how you can generate GeoJSON right in the database for output on a map. These are the basic steps:

1. Create a PL/pgSQL stored function called `get_features` to output GeoJSON. This function relies on the JSON support introduced in PostgreSQL 9.2 as well as numerous PostGIS functions, such as the `ST_AsGeoJSON` and `ST_GeomFromGeoJSON` functions.
2. Create a PHP script that grabs parameters from the request, passes them to a function, and returns the PL/pgSQL function output.
3. Utilize Leaflet in conjunction with jQuery to query the PHP script and draw the selected feature and properties on the map.

The PL/pgSQL function is shown in the following listing.

Listing 17.14 PL/pgSQL `get_features` function

```
CREATE OR REPLACE FUNCTION ch17.get_features(
    param_geom json,
    param_table text,
    param_props text,
    param_limit integer DEFAULT 10
)
RETURNS json AS
$$
DECLARE
    var_sql text; var_result json; var_srid integer; var_geo geometry;
    var_table text; var_cols text; var_input_srid integer;
    var_geom_col text;
BEGIN
    SELECT
        f_geometry_column,
        quote_ident(f_table_schema) || '.' || quote_ident(f_table_name)
```

```
FROM geometry_columns                                              -- Verify table is a geometry table (1)
INTO var_geom_col, var_table
WHERE f_table_schema || '.' || f_table_name = param_table
LIMIT 1;

IF var_geom_col IS NULL THEN
    RAISE EXCEPTION 'No such geometry table as %', param_table;
END IF;
var_geo := ST_GeomFromGeoJSON($1::text);                           -- Convert location to geometry (2)
var_input_srid := ST_SRID(var_geo);
If var_input_srid < 1 THEN                                         -- Get SRID of requested location (3)
    var_input_srid = 4326;
    var_geo := ST_SetSRID(
    ST_GeomFromGeoJSON($1::text),var_input_srid);
END IF;

var_sql := 'SELECT ST_SRID(geom) FROM ' || var_table || ' LIMIT 1';  -- Get SRID of table (4)

EXECUTE var_sql INTO var_srid;

SELECT string_agg(quote_ident(trim(a)), ',')
INTO var_cols                                                      -- Sanitize column names (5)
FROM unnest(string_to_array(param_props, ',')) As a;

var_sql :=
    'SELECT row_to_json(fc)
    FROM (
        SELECT
            ''FeatureCollection'' As type,
            array_to_json(array_agg(f)) As features
        FROM (
            SELECT
                ''Feature'' As type,
                ST_AsGeoJSON(ST_Transform(
                    lg.' || quote_ident(var_geom_col) || ', $4)
                )::json As geometry,
                row_to_json(
                    (SELECT l FROM (SELECT ' || var_cols || ') As l)
                ) As properties
            FROM ' || var_table || ' AA lg
            WHERE ST_Intersects(lg.geom,ST_Transform($1,$2)) LIMIT $3
        ) As f
    ) As fc;';                                                     -- Build parameterized SQL (6)

    EXECUTE var_sql INTO var_result                                -- Execute parameterized SQL using variables, output to var_result, and return (7)
    USING var_geo, var_srid, param_limit, var_input_srid;

    RETURN var_result;
END;
$$
LANGUAGE plpgsql;
```

Listing 17.14 takes as input a location in GeoJSON format and a geometry table. The code first checks in the geometry_columns table to verify that the requested table has a geometry column and is visible by the user account the stored function runs under ❶. If not, an exception is raised, ending execution of the function.

The code converts the input location ❷ to a geometry and assumes the geometry is in lon/lat if no SRID is provided ❸. It then gets the SRID by assuming all geometries in the table column have the same SRID ❹. Note that you could revise the code to read the SRID from geometry_columns, but for views based on tables with constraints, this information might not be available in geometry_columns.

The `string_to_array` PostgreSQL function is then used to convert columns to an array of elements, and then the `quote_ident` function is used on each element of the array, and they are reconcatenated back into a comma-separated list with `string_agg` ❺. This is done to prevent an SQL injection attack.

Next you build a parameterized SQL statement that uses the table and column names ❻. The executed SQL returns a GeoJSON feature collection when parameters `var_geo`, `var_srid`, `param_limit`, and `var_input_srid` are provided and replaced in the corresponding slots (`$1,$2,$3,$4`) of the parameterized SQL statement ❼. It will return a single GeoJSON object composed of at most `param_limit` features.

This listing uses several PostgreSQL 9.2+ JSON functions and PostGIS `ST_AsGeoJSON` calls to build a single JSON object ❻. It does so by aggregating all the feature rows (`f`) into an array using `array_to_json`, converting the array to a JSON object, and then converting the final single row (`fc`) into a JSON object.

A sample call to the PL/pgSQL function would look something like this:

```
SELECT ch17.get_features('{"type":"Point",
 "coordinates":[-71.06575012207031,42.35299407336028]}',
  'ch17.ma_openspace','site_name, gis_acres') As result;
```

It will produce a GeoJSON feature collection output that looks something like this:

```
{"type":"FeatureCollection",
 "features":[{"type":"Feature","geometry":
   {"type":"MultiPolygon",
    "coordinates":[[[[-71.0655781086837,42.3524959163772],
 [-71.0669188706842,42.352579208964],
 [-71.0665996076648,42.3527625658689],...,
 [-71.0655781086837,42.3524959163772]]]]},
 "properties":{"site_name":"Central Burying Ground",
 "gis_acres":1.57214290}}]}
```

Outputting geography in GeoJSON

The example in this section assumes that you're working with geometry data. If more than one geometry column exists in the table, the function will arbitrarily pick one geometry column.

This function can just as easily work with geography by changing the `ST_GeomFromGeoJSON(...)` to `ST_Transform(ST_GeomFromGeoJSON(...),4326)::geography`.

For this exercise, we're just working with point location clicks, but the PL/pgSQL function is designed to work with any arbitrary geometry, such as a circle buffer or a polygon drawn by a user, and it will return all features that intersect the region of interest.

A PHP script that will collect the inputs, call the PL/pgSQL function, and output the result is shown in the following listing.

Listing 17.15 Contents of get_features.php

```
<?php
    include_once("config.inc.php");
    $param_geom = $_REQUEST['geom'];
    $param_table = $_REQUEST['table'];
    $param_props = $_REQUEST['props'];
    $dbconn = pg_connect(DSN);

    $res = pg_query_params($dbconn,
       'SELECT ch17.get_features($1,$2,$3) As result ',
         array($param_geom, $param_table,$param_props));
    $val = pg_fetch_result($res,0,0);
    echo $val;
?>
```

You can revise the original Leaflet page from listing 17.7 and add a link to jQuery right after the Leaflet API `include`:

```
<script src="//code.jquery.com/jquery-1.10.2.min.js"></script>
```

Right after *l2.addTo(map);*, you can add the lines in the following listing.

Listing 17.16 Additional contents to make postgis_in_action_leaflet_3.htm

```
var popup = L.popup();                               ❶ New pop-up and placeholder
       var lgeojson;                                   for geoSON layer
  function onMapClick(e) {                           ❷ Onclick event function
     var lgeoJsonLoc = '{"type":"Point","coordinates":['
     + e.latlng.lng                                  ❸ Convert clicked location
                                                       to GeoJSON
     + ',' + e.latlng.lat + ']}'
    $.getJSON("get_features.php", { 'geom': geoJsonLoc,   ❹ Get the features

    'table': 'ch17.ma_openspace',
       'props': 'site_name, gis_acres'
    })
      .done(function (data) {
          var popupContent = ''
          if (lgeojson != null){
                map.removeLayer(lgeojson);
          }
          lgeojson = L.geoJson(data, {               ❺ JQuery returned output

          onEachFeature: function (feature, layer) {     ❻ Add to pop-up content

    popupContent += '<b>Site:</b> '
                 + feature.properties.site_name
                 + '<br /><b>Acres:</b> '
```

```
                + feature.properties.gis_acres
          }, style: { "color": "blue", "weight":10 }
      });             popup.setLatLng(e.latlng)
        .setContent(popupContent)
        .openOn(map);
       geojson.addTo(map);
   });
}
map.on('click', onMapClick);
```

Add features to map

Bind event handler to click event of map

❼ Position pop-up location and content and open

Listing 17.16 is additional code that defines a new pop-up to be moved around the screen ❶. The core is an onclick event handler function ❷ that, when the user clicks on the map, will create a GeoJSON point ❸ that you will use to locate open-space features that intersect. Note that although a point is used here, any GeoJSON geometry will work with the PL/pgSQL and PHP combo.

You use the jQuery `getJSON` Ajax function to call the get_features.php script with the geometry, table, and fields you want ❹. When jQuery is done, it will return the output of the PL/pgSQL function ❺, which is a GeoJSON feature collection. For each feature returned, the name and number of acres is added to the pop-up ❻. The most important piece is the click event handler ❼, which binds the `onMapClick` event function you created with the `click` event of the map.

The output of clicking on an open-space feature is shown in figure 17.9.

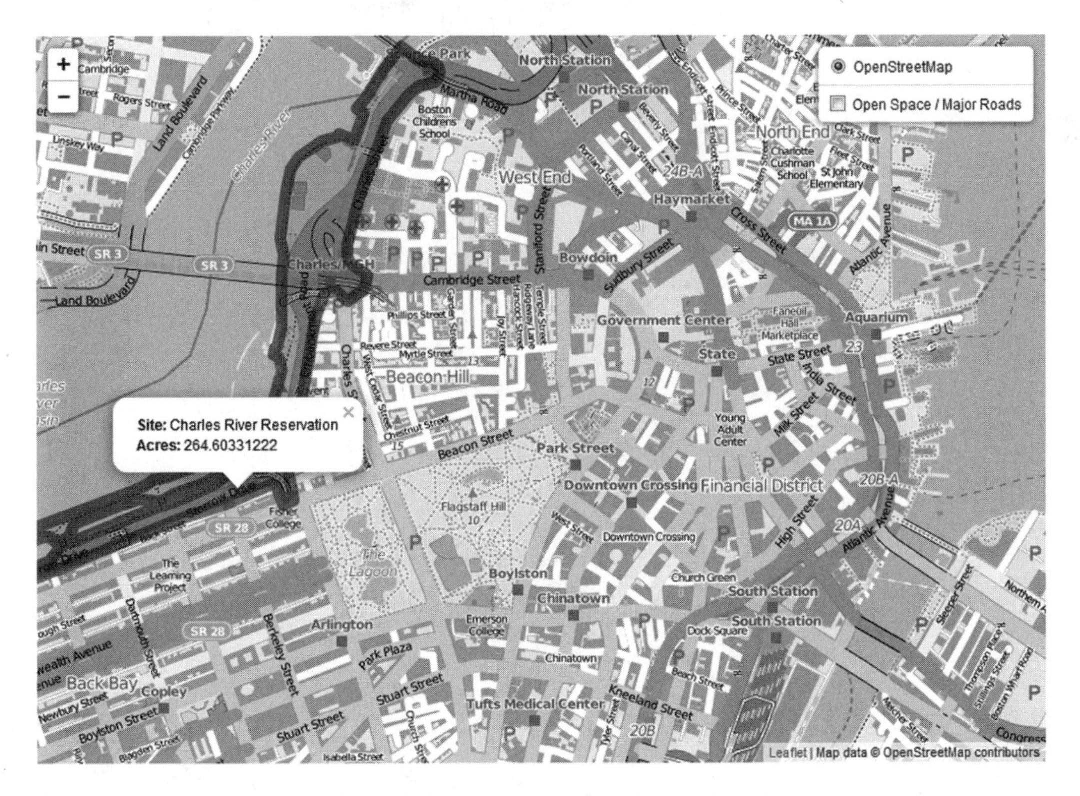

Figure 17.9 Output of Leaflet with onclick event: postgis_in_action_leaflet_3.htm

17.8 Summary

In this chapter, we explored the various ways you can consume PostGIS data in web applications. We demonstrated the commonly available WMS/WFS mapping servers and how you could utilize these in OpenLayers and Leaflet. We also demonstrated how to query PostGIS raster data with SQL and display the rendered output on OpenLayers and Leaflet. In addition, we looked at how you can leverage the power of PostgreSQL and PostGIS to output fully formed GeoJSON feature collections or raster images, and how to consume this in concert with PHP, jQuery, and Leaflet.

This concludes our study of PostGIS. You should now have all the knowledge you need to put PostGIS to work in common spatial analysis as well as use it as a tool for integrating spatial awareness in your web applications. If you have any questions about what you've read in these chapters, please don't hesitate to post a comment in this book's forum at https://forums.manning.com/forums/postgis-in-action-second-edition.

appendix A
Additional resources

This appendix includes links to resources useful for PostGIS users of all walks of life. We've mentioned some of these links in previous chapters, but they're also listed here for easy reference.

A.1 Planet sites

The best sources of timely information and tutorials are the various planet sites. The following ones are most relevant to PostGIS:

- *Planet PostGIS* (http://planet.postgis.net)—Many PostGIS bloggers hang out and are aggregated here. You'll learn about upcoming features, learn how to use and install them, find commentary, hear first-hand from core PostGIS developers, and more.
- *Planet OSGeo* (http://planet.osgeo.org)—You'll find many bloggers working on various OSGeo projects here. Many of the core PostGIS developers are aggregated here, as well as on Planet PostGIS. You'll also find content about related projects such as MapServer, QGIS, MapGuide, and GeoServer.
- *Planet PostgreSQL* (http://planet.postgresql.org)—Many bloggers working with PostgreSQL come here. You'll find many of the core PostgreSQL developers blogging and sharing details of new features and security updates. You'll also find PostgreSQL power users discussing tricks for getting the most out of PostgreSQL.

A.2 Open source tools and offerings

PostGIS has garnered more support in the free, open source GIS arena than any other spatial database, far exceeding the spatial offerings of MySQL. There are too many PostGIS open source tools to list. We covered the more well-known offerings in chapters 5 and 17. As you can see, PostGIS already has a strong and growing commercial support belt, as well.

You can find some of the tools covered in this book and others, as well as popular web-mapping servers that support PostGIS, listed on the PostGIS website's Features page: http://postgis.net/features.

A.2.1 Self-contained GIS suites that include PostGIS

The following GIS suites contain PostGIS as part of an integrated GIS desktop or web-mapping tool stack. They include one-click installers, fully contained application stacks, and single-download virtual machines.

- *KyngChaos for Mac users* (www.kyngchaos.com/software/unixport)—This site has binaries for Mac OS X graciously supplied by KyngChaos. The offerings include PostgreSQL, PostGIS, and some other useful open source GIS toolkits such as MapServer, GRASS, QGIS, Python GIS modules, and so on.
- *Boundless OpenGeo Suite* (http://boundlessgeo.com/solutions/opengeo-suite/)—This stack contains GeoServer, GeoExt, GeoEditor, GeoWebCache, PostGIS, PostGIS GUI shapefile loader, and optional extensions for ArcSDE and Oracle Spatial. It has one-click installers available for Windows, Mac OS X, and Linux. The GeoEditor is a web-based GIS editor that allows you to edit PostGIS data via the web interface. It comes in both Enterprise and Community editions. The main difference is that Enterprise includes support, training, and Service Level Assurances (SLA), as well as hand-holding help with upgrades for those new to GIS or who need more predictable professional support. The stack also comes prepackaged with sample data to get you started. The Community edition is a free, open source and binary download for the more experienced users, student users, or consultants looking for an easy-to-configure stack for a client or to extend with their own web product. The Boundless site offers a comparison between the Community and Enterprise editions.
- *OSGeo Live* (http://live.osgeo.org)—OSGeo Live is a self-contained suite that comes in the following flavors: bootable DVD, USB thumb drive (often distributed in FOSS4G conferences), or VM. The distribution is based on the Xubuntu variant of Ubuntu. It contains fairly new versions of many OSGeo and related open source GIS products, including PostGIS + pgRouting, MapServer, GRASS, OpenJUMP, GeoServer, SpatiaLite, and Rasdaman, to name a few. It's great for training or for experimenting with all that OSGeo has to offer. It's also kind of hefty (~4 GB) because it includes the whole OS.
- *Portable GIS (for Windows)* (www.archaeogeek.com/portable-gis.html)—This is GIS on a USB flash drive just for Microsoft Windows users. The package is a bit hefty (~750 MB), but it contains a lot and is runnable from a USB flashdrive on a Windows machine. It comes packaged with QGIS, FWTools (GDAL/OGR), Apache2, PHP5, PostgreSQL with PostGIS, MapServer, Python with GDAL bindings, and loader for Ordnance Survey's MasterMap data. It also has portable Firefox, a PDF reader, and a text editor.

A.2.2 Open source desktop tools

There are many open source desktop tools that work with PostGIS. The following list is just a brief sampling of the more commonly used open source desktop viewing and editing tools:

- *OpenJUMP* (www.openjump.org)—This is one of our favorite desktop GIS tools and what we used to render many of the ad hoc spatial queries in this book. It's a Java-based GIS desktop toolkit based on a plug-in architecture, and it has many user-contributed plug-ins. It runs on Linux, Windows, and Mac OS X.
- *QGIS* (www.qgis.org)—This is perhaps the most popular of the free, open source desktop tools, and it also has a plug-in architecture. QGIS is written in C++ but offers a rich Python scripting environment and various GRASS integration options. It also includes drivers for connecting to PostGIS data as well as various other GIS data sources. QGIS is GNU GPL licensed.
- *gvSIG* (www.gvsig.com)—This Java-based desktop platform offers lots of integration features for ArcIMS and other Esri services.
- *uDig* (http://udig.refractions.net)—This is an Eclipse-based Java desktop application and SDK. It has lots of integration features for OGC-compliant web services and more advanced cartography.
- *GRASS GIS* (http://grass.osgeo.org/)—GRASS (Geographic Resources Analysis Support System) is probably the oldest and one of the most advanced free and open source tools for analyzing vectors, rasters, and other GIS data. It's designed more for the advanced GIS analyst than a new GIS or pure spatial database user. Although it's not set up specifically for PostGIS, there are many avenues of integration, such as the PostGRASS driver, JGRASS, and QGIS GRASS integration tools.

A.2.3 Open source extract-transform-load (ETL)

This section lists open source tools for loading data into PostGIS:

- *GDAL/OGR* (http://gdal.org)—This is the most popular all-purpose, free, open source ETL tool. It's licensed under the MIT license, which is similar to BSD. GDAL/OGR binaries can be downloaded from the GDAL page: http://trac.osgeo.org/gdal/wiki/DownloadingGdalBinaries. If you're running PostgreSQL 9.3 or above, you can also enjoy OGR as a PostgreSQL foreign data wrapper using the ogr_fdw PostgreSQL extension, and query external spatial vector sources right from the comfort of your PostgreSQL database using SQL. Code for the PostgreSQL ogr_fdw extension can be found at pgsql-ogr-fdw (https://github.com/pramsey/pgsql-ogr-fdw). Ogr_fdw allows you to join local PostgreSQL tables (both PostGIS and non-PostGIS) with spatial vector files or other spatial vector databases and web services supported by GDAL/OGR using SQL. Ogr_fdw is currently not distributed with any PostGIS packages, but it should be in at least the Windows StackBuilder and Boundless installers in upcoming PostGIS 2.2.

- *GeoKettle* (http://sourceforge.net/projects/geokettle)—This LGPL-released open source ETL loader is based on Pentaho Data Integration (formerly known as Kettle ETL) (http://community.pentaho.com/projects/data-integration/). It currently has built-in support for PostGIS, Oracle Spatial, MySQL, and Esri shapefiles.

A.3 Proprietary vendors that support PostGIS

Proprietary vendor support for PostGIS is now just as strong as what you'll find available for Oracle, SQL Server, or IBM DB2. The following proprietary vendors currently support PostGIS in their desktop and web products:

- *CadCorp*—CadCorp partially funded the raster support in PostGIS. The CadCorp tools are a favorite among modelers for both desktop and web-based apps. CadCorp supports more than 160 formats, including direct support for all other high-end spatial database offerings.
- *Safe*—Safe contributes both monetary and developer support for GEOS and makes extract-transform-load (ETL) tools for GIS data, which makes moving GIS data to different formats and databases a simple drag, drop, and schedule exercise. Its FME desktop and cloud-based ETL tools are a favorite for high-end ETL transactions. The latest versions of their FME tools support PostGIS rasters.
- *Manifold*—Manifold released support for PostGIS in its Manifold 8.0 Desktop tool, and Manifold is a favorite of many spatial database analysts and people who like SQL in all its glory. Manifold supports Oracle Locator/Spatial, PostGIS, SQL Server 2008, IBM DB2, MySQL, and its own extender for SQL Server 2005.
- *Esri*—Esri, in ArcGIS 9.3, introduced support for PostGIS in both the desktop and server tool, although this requires an ArcSDE Server license for PostGIS and works only with PostGIS 1.4 and below. In ArcGIS 10, SDE is no longer required for ArcMap desktop or ArcServer. The direct read via the query layer menu works for the PostGIS 1 and 2 series. ArcGIS has support only for the PostGIS `geometry` spatial type and not the `geography` or `raster` spatial types.

  There is also an open source BSD licensed plug-in called *AmigoCloud* GDAL/OGR Plugin for ArcGIS (https://github.com/RBURHUM/arcgis-ogr). The site has binaries for Windows, and you can compile for other OSs if you have the ArcGIS SDK. This plug-in allows you to load any GDAL-supported format as a layer into ArcMap. This includes PostGIS and SpatiaLite among other GDAL-supported formats.
- *Pitney Bowes*—Pitney Bowes introduced support for PostGIS in its MapInfo 10 offering. MapInfo is a popular tool for GIS VB programmers using its MapBasic interface. It enjoys a rich history of integration with MS Office products. It's a favorite of lightweight GIS users and database analysts because of its rich query options and easy data-import menus.

A.4 Places to get free data

There are many places to get free data, and since the first edition of this book even more have shown up. In chapter 4 we grab data from some of these places to demonstrate how to load up on spatial data:

- *OpenStreetMap* (www.openstreetmap.org)—This community-driven spatial database and map repository has contributions from people all over the world. You can think of OSM as a free and open source Google map that has both web services and data you can download. It has base map information you can access via tile services as well as other crowd-sourced information such as biking trails and other GPS traces and waypoints in GPX format. You can use it as an overlay directly on your maps using something like OpenLayers.
- *GeoNames* (www.geonames.org/)—The GeoNames geographical database covers all countries and contains over eight million place names (cities, postal codes, countries) that are available for download free of charge. Most data is in tabular format. It also has REST APIs for doing place name and other searches. The data is licensed under Creative Commons 3.
- *Mapzen* (https://mapzen.com/metro-extracts/)—This is another site offering OpenStreetMap packages. It provides data in OSM/PBF and Esri shapefile formats for popular cities. Its updates are done usually every week or so. You'll find touristy hotspots like Paris, Boston, and Florence, each available in a self-contained package.
- *Geofabrik* (http://download.geofabrik.de)—This is another source of prepared OpenStreetMap data. This distribution is generally built nightly and comes in OSM XML, pbf, and shapefile (for very popular areas) formats. The breakdown is usually by state or country.
- *Natural Earth* (www.naturalearthdata.com/)—This site offers public domain map data sets that contain both raster and vector data. Most data can be used in any manner for private or commercial consumption. The data currently offered includes world administrative boundaries, city and town points with populations, and various natural land and water geometries.
- *U.S. Census TIGER data* (www.census.gov/geo/maps-data/data/tiger.html)—If you're in the U.S. or doing research on a U.S. population, then the Census TIGER data site should be one of your first stops. It contains data in Esri shapefile format updated annually or semiannually. This data has U.S. road networks, which are great for geocoding (and it is, in fact, the source used by the PostGIS packaged TIGER geocoder).

  For researching, the more important data is the Census tract population grouping, which is often combined with data from American FactFinder (http://factfinder2.census.gov) to formulate population stats about housing, ethnicity, income, population, job makeup, and so on.

- *National Elevation Dataset* (http://ned.usgs.gov)—If you're looking for raster elevation data covering the United States, look no further than NED.
- *PRISM Climate Group* (www.prism.oregonstate.edu/mtd/)—This site provides fairly current and historical climate data in .bil and .asc raster formats for the continental United States.

appendix B
Installing, compiling, and upgrading

There are several ways to install PostgreSQL/PostGIS. When we started out, the only way was to compile the code yourself, but life has since become much simpler, and now the average user doesn't need to experience the joys and frustrations of compiling their own source code. Most people who just want to use PostGIS take the easy road of acquiring and installing prebuilt binaries via packaged installers. A brief synopsis of the more common PostGIS installer offerings is detailed on the PostGIS site: http://postgis.net/install.

Compiling from source is still an important and adventurous journey if you want to be a contributor to the PostGIS project. If you wish to compile from source code, refer to the directions on "PostGIS source download page," http://postgis.net/source.

B.1 Installing PostgreSQL and PostGIS

It goes without saying that you'll need a functioning PostgreSQL server to use PostGIS. The installation options we'll discuss here describe the base PostgreSQL installation as well as the additional PostGIS installation.

As a general rule, you'll want to get your PostGIS binaries from the same source you get your PostgreSQL binaries so that they're guaranteed to work together. If you're not happy with the version of PostGIS available from your distribution of choice, you can still use the PostgreSQL binaries and compile PostGIS yourself, as long as you also install the postgresql-dev package that commonly gets distributed with PostgreSQL binary distributions. You'll also need a working gcc/g++ compiler to compile.

You should also try to get PostgreSQL 9.3 or 9.4. To take advantage of the `LATERAL` feature, which is very important for PostGIS KNN gist queries, you'll need 9.3+. PostgreSQL 9.4 has a couple of neat new features that are useful for spatial queries. It also has numerous new JSON and JSONB types that make feeding and consuming web data much easier. Also new in 9.4 is the `REFRESH CONCURRENTLY` feature for materialized views, which allows rebuilding a view without blocking queries currently reading from the view.

B.1.1 Desktop Linux, Windows, Mac OS X using one-click installers

There are two popular offerings of PostGIS that support Linux, Windows, and Mac OS X desktops.

ENTERPRISEDB ONE-CLICK INSTALLERS

If you're on a Windows system, the easiest way to get started is to use one of the one-click installers provided by EnterpriseDB at www.enterprisedb.com/products/pgdownload.do and use the packaged Application StackBuilder to install the PostGIS extension. The EnterpriseDB PostGIS extension application installer for Windows is one we maintain, and we keep it fairly up to date. You can also download the same binaries and installers from the PostGIS site (http://postgis.net/windows_downloads) or use one of the experimental Windows binaries built whenever there's a change in the PostGIS development code base. For other operating systems, the EnterpriseDB PostGIS offering isn't always the latest stable release.

EnterpriseDB one-click installers will work for any desktop Linux system (32-bit and 64-bit), Windows 32-bit and 64-bit systems (2000, XP, 2003, 2008), and Mac OS X. The installer comes with the following prepackaged goods:

- PostgreSQL Server
- pgAdmin III (GUI database administration tool)
- Application StackBuilder—Allows you to install PostgreSQL add-ons such as PostGIS, JDBC, and ODBC, plus application development environments such as Apache and Ruby on Rails, the PostgreSQL Tuning Wizard (to help you quickly configure memory and other settings for your desired profile), and the MySQL Migration Wizard (requires Java to be installed)

Turn off User Account Control

If you run into issues installing on Windows, try turning off User Account Control (UAC) located in Control Panel > User Accounts. In most cases, the newer PostgreSQL installers seem capable of creating a Postgres account on their own. You can also run the setup as Administrator by right-clicking and selecting Run as Administrator.

If you're trying to install using the Linux one-click installer, make sure you make the .bin file executable by running `chmod 777` on the .bin file.

BOUNDLESS OPENGEO SUITE

If you want a more encompassing GIS package that includes the GeoServer mapping server, editor, PostgreSQL, and PostGIS, then the OpenGeo Suite (http://boundlessgeo.com/solutions/opengeo-suite/) might be the best one for you. There are packages for Windows, Mac OS X, and Linux.

These come in two flavors with the only difference being support. The Community edition is free and comes with the binaries. The Enterprise edition includes binaries, various tiers of support for installation, deployment, training, tuning, expedited services for bug fixing, and support for other spatial databases.

B.1.2 Installing on a Linux server (Red Hat EL, CentOS) using YUM

If you're running a variant of Red Hat Enterprise Linux, Fedora, CentOS, or Scientific Linux, the PostgreSQL Yum repository is a great option. It has the latest and greatest of the main and beta versions of PostgreSQL. In addition to core PostgreSQL, the Yum repository has packages, such as PostGIS and other add-ons such as pgRouting, all available via http://yum.postgresql.org.

The Yum repository is most suitable for command-line server installs, but it can also be used for desktop installs via the Yum installer. The Yum repository generally has the latest PostGIS stable offering, but it usually only offers one version of PostGIS for each version of PostgreSQL. This means that if you want PostGIS 2.0+, you'll need to install PostgreSQL 9.1 or 9.2. If you have PostgreSQL 9.3 or 9.4, you'll get PostGIS 2.1.

You can check out our various guides to Yum on the Postgres OnLine Journal site: www.postgresonline.com/journal/categories/53-yum.

B.1.3 Mac OS X–specific installers

If you're a Mac user, you might want to check out KyngChaos: www.kyngchaos.com/software:postgres. KyngChaos has packages for the latest stable releases of PostGIS, PostgreSQL, and pgRouting. Packages are usually for the latest versions of Mac OS X (currently Lion+) as well as the PostgreSQL pgRouting extension. KyngChaos generally stays up to date with the latest and greatest PostGIS stable offerings and has them available right after the PostGIS source is officially released.

Another offering that a lot of Mac users seem to like is Postgres.app (http://postgresapp.com), supported by Heroku. Postgres.app is a Mac distribution of PostgreSQL and popular PostgreSQL extensions like PostGIS and PL/V8. Installing and experimenting with it is described in the 'sproke blog: http://sproke.blogspot.com/2012/07/setting-up-postgresapp-with-postgis.html. The PostgreSQL server service of Postgres.app can be launched and shut down with a click, making it great for development.

If you use any of these, make sure to get your PostgreSQL version from the same source as PostGIS, or your PostGIS may not be compatible with your PostgreSQL.

B.1.4 PostgreSQL APT repository

The PostgreSQL development group (PGDG) has a repository for the Ubuntu and Debian APT packaging system. More details of how to add the PGDG APT repository can be found at https://wiki.postgresql.org/wiki/Apt. Once you add this APT repository to your list of repositories, you can install/upgrade PostgreSQL and PostgreSQL extensions via the standard APT package manager.

The PGDG APT repository comes packaged with the latest versions of PostgreSQL and many add-ons, such as pgAdmin and common PostgreSQL extensions. It also includes packages for PostGIS. There's generally only one PostGIS per major version of PostgreSQL. PostgreSQL 9.3 and 9.4 are the latest, and both carry PostGIS 2.1.

B.1.5 Other available binaries and distros

Most of the other distros such as Ubuntu and Debian make PostgreSQL and PostGIS available via their package managers, though the ones from the official repositories are sometimes antiquated.

B.1.6 Compiling and installing from PostGIS source

If you want the most bleeding-edge version of PostGIS, compiling it yourself is still generally the way to go. This is covered in the PostGIS manual and wiki:

- The Installation chapter of the official PostGIS manual covers standard compilation on Linux systems; see http://postgis.net/docs/manual-dev/postgis_installation.html.

  Although you can compile your own PostgreSQL, you don't need to if you're on Linux, even if you want to compile PostGIS yourself. But you will need the PostgreSQL development headers (usually packaged in something called postgresql-devel) and you'll need to install postgresql and postgresql-server, which you can do using a Linux packager, such as Yum, YatZ, apt-get, or whatever your distribution uses for software install. The Yum, YatZ, and apt-gets of the world are similar in concept to Windows Update and provide precompiled binaries of PostgreSQL and PostGIS for your particular Linux distribution from well-defined repositories.
- There is a whole user-contributed section on the PostGIS wiki with details on compiling PostGIS on various operating systems; see http://trac.osgeo.org/postgis/wiki/UsersWikiInstall.
- For Windows, as of this writing headers aren't available because Windows PostgreSQL versions are compiled with Visual C++. You must compile your own PostgreSQL under MinGW if you want to compile PostGIS. The PostGIS user wiki covers this: http://trac.osgeo.org/postgis/wiki/UsersWikiWinCompile.

PostGIS Windows 64-bit support

PostGIS 2.0 was the first PostGIS release to support PostgreSQL 64-bit for Windows. It's available on StackBuilder and the PostGIS website, and is compiled with the MinGW-w64 toolchain (http://mingw-w64.sourceforge.net). The PostGIS 2.1 bundle for Windows (32-bit and 64-bit) contains both PostGIS and pgRouting as a single install.

If you don't want to experience the joys and pains of compiling code and don't mind waiting for a package maintainer to compile and prepare a package for general consumption, then stick with the prepackaged versions.

B.2 Creating a PostGIS database

You can create a spatial database by first creating a template database with the postgis extension installed, and use that for future databases. But it's easier to just use the new extension feature introduced in PostgreSQL 9.1:

```
CREATE EXTENSION postgis;
```

For versions of PostgreSQL 9.1+, the default `CREATE EXTENSION` approach picks the latest version of the postgis extension installed in your PostgreSQL server.

If you prefer a different version, such as if you want to experiment with PostGIS 2.2.0 and you have it already compiled and installed, you can use a variation like the following:

```
CREATE EXTENSION postgis VERSION "2.2.0dev";
CREATE EXTENSION postgis_topology VERSION "2.2.0dev";
```

`CREATE EXTENSION` can be used to spatially enable an existing database as well.

B.2.1 Spatializing a PostgreSQL 9.0 or lower database or PostGIS without raster

PostgreSQL 9.0 and below don't have the simpler `CREATE EXTENSION` that comes packaged with PostgreSQL 9.1+. Also, if you installed PostGIS without raster support, you won't be able to install PostGIS using `CREATE EXTENSION`. In either case, you can still install PostGIS by running the installation scripts that come packaged with PostGIS. The general steps are outlined in the Installation chapter of the official PostGIS manual: http://postgis.net/docs/postgis_installation.html#create_new_db.

Listing B.1 demonstrates how to create a template PostGIS database for pre-9.1 databases. This approach would also be necessary if you didn't compile with raster support, because postgis extension files aren't created in that case.

Listing B.1 Creating a template_postgis database

```
CREATE DATABASE template_postgis_21
WITH TEMPLATE = template1 ENCODING = 'UTF8';
\c template_postgis_21;                              -- Create and connect to database
\cd /usr/share/pgsql/contrib/postgis-2.1             <-- cd scripts
\i postgis.sql;
\i spatial_ref_sys.sql;                              -- Basic PostGIS support
\i postgis_comments.sql;                             <-- Function descriptions
\i rtpostgis.sql;                                    <-- Raster support
\i raster_comments.sql;
\i topology.sql                                      <-- Topology support
\i topology_comments.sql
UPDATE pg_database SET datistemplate = TRUE          <-- Mark as template
```

```
WHERE datname = 'template_postgis_21';
GRANT ALL ON geometry_columns TO PUBLIC;
GRANT ALL ON spatial_ref_sys TO PUBLIC;
```

You use listing B.1 at the psql command line to create a new template PostGIS database and give permissions to geometry_columns and spatial_ref_sys so that when a database is created using the template database as a template, new geometry columns can be registered by the user and new spatial_ref_sys records can be added as needed.

In order to use this template database to create a new spatial database, you'd run a command such as this:

```
CREATE DATABASE mygisdb
    WITH TEMPLATE = template_postgis_21;
```

When you're done, you can exit out of the psql console with the `\q` command.

> **Different versions of PostGIS can coexist on the same data cluster**
> Multiple versions of PostGIS can be installed on the same PostgreSQL server instance, but each database can have only one version of PostGIS. You can work with various versions (for example, PostGIS 1.5 for legacy projects, 2.1 for newer projects, and 2.2 for development projects). Just keep in mind that if you plan to run various versions on the same database server cluster, you'll need to be using the same version of GEOS and Proj for all of them.

B.3 Upgrading PostGIS

Upgrading PostGIS from one minor version to another is straightforward. Install the new binaries and execute an `ALTER EXTENSION` command. Upgrading from one PostGIS major version to another, such as 1.5 to 2.0, requires a dump and restore of the PostgreSQL database.

B.3.1 PostGIS soft upgrade using extensions

If you're upgrading PostGIS from a minor version 2.0 to another minor version 2.1.*, or a microversion such as from 2.1.4 to 2.1.5, you can accomplish this without doing a backup and restore of your database. Doing an in-place upgrade is referred to as a *soft upgrade.*

If you're running PostgreSQL above 9.1 with extensions support, start by updating your PostGIS binaries via the same system you used in your original install of PostGIS. Next, execute the following command, making sure to adjust the version number for your version of PostGIS:

```
ALTER EXTENSION postgis UPDATE TO "2.1.5";
```

If you want to move up to the most recently installed version of PostGIS and are not sure of the version number, you can leave out the specification of the version number, as shown in the next example. You'll want to be cautious with this approach if you have multiple versions of PostGIS installed on your server. For example, you may want a PostGIS 2.0.4 database to be only upgraded to PostGIS 2.0.6 and not to PostGIS 2.1.5.

```
ALTER EXTENSION postgis UPDATE;
```

If you also have topology installed, run this command in addition:

```
ALTER EXTENSION postgis_topology UPDATE TO "2.1.5";
```

For the in-development versions of PostGIS, which aren't versioned like released versions, you can take advantage of the extension feature using `next`, which is a dummy packaging that forces running of the upgrade script:

```
ALTER EXTENSION postgis UPDATE TO "2.2.0devnext";
ALTER EXTENSION postgis_topology UPDATE TO "2.2.0devnext";
```

The next time you need to update your 2.2.0dev install, you would go back to the regular name without the `next`:

```
ALTER EXTENSION postgis UPDATE TO "2.2.0dev";
ALTER EXTENSION postgis_topology UPDATE TO "2.2.0dev";
```

B.3.2 Upgrading PostGIS from 1.X to 2.X

If you're upgrading from PostGIS 1.X to PostGIS 2.X, then a dump and restore of your database is unfortunately required. There are two approaches to this.

The recommended clean way involves using a Perl script

PostGIS comes packaged with a script called postgis_restore.pl, which will allow you to restore using PostgreSQL's custom compressed backup format. This will take care of several issues, such as fixing up SRIDs and converting deprecated constraint calls to new constraint calls. This approach is well documented in the official PostGIS manual: http://postgis.net/docs/postgis_installation.html#hard_upgrade.

The no-Perl-script upgrade approach

For many users with lower attention spans, smaller databases, a distaste for anything involving a command line, or who don't have Perl installed on their server, this approach will be noisier but will work. This approach will generate errors you can safely ignore because it will try to restore old functions not available in the latest binaries.

1. Make a custom backup of your database using `pg_dump -Fc` or pgAdmin choosing Format: *Custom.*
2. Create a new PostGIS 2+ database using `CREATE EXTENSION postgis;` or the various PostGIS install scripts.
3. Run the legacy.sql script packaged with PostGIS. You can opt for legacy_minimal.sql instead of legacy.sql if you know you weren't using too many legacy functions in your code. Most legacy functions lacked the prepended `ST_`, so if you used a lot of those, you might need the full legacy.sql. If in doubt, just run the legacy.sql version.
4. Restore your backup over this new database.

5. *Do not forget to do this last part.* Run just the drop command statements at the end of the postgis_upgrade_*_minor.sql script. This drops old functions that would otherwise conflict with new functions. Functions that fall in this category are functions that got additional arguments in the new versions.

appendix C SQL primer

PostgreSQL supports almost the whole ANSI SQL 92, 1999 standard logic, as well as many of the SQL:2003, SQL:2006, SQL:2008 constructs, and some of the SQL:2011 constructs. In this appendix, we'll cover some of these as well as some PostgreSQL-specific SQL language extensions. Because we'll remain fairly focused on standard functionality, the content in this appendix is also applicable to other standards-compliant relational databases.

C.1 information_schema

The `information_schema` is a catalog introduced in SQL 92 and enhanced in each subsequent version of the spec. Although it's a standard, sadly most commercial and open source databases don't completely support it. We know that the following common databases do: PostgreSQL (7.3+), MySQL 5+, and Microsoft SQL Server 2000+. Oracle and IBM do via user-supported contributions.

The most useful views in this schema are `tables`, `columns`, and `views`; they provide a catalog of all the tables, columns, and views in your database. To get a list of all non-system tables in PostgreSQL, you can run the following query (the `information_schema.tables` view in PostgreSQL will list only tables that you have access to):

```
SELECT table_schema, table_name, table_type
    FROM information_schema.tables
    WHERE table_schema NOT IN('pg_catalog', 'information_schema')
    ORDER BY table_schema, table_name;
```

The preceding query will work equally well in MySQL (except that in MySQL *schema* means *database* and there's only one `information_schema` shared across all MySQL databases in a MySQL cluster). MS SQL Server behaves more like PostgreSQL in that each `information_schema` is unique to each database, except that in SQL Server the system views and tables aren't queryable from `information_schema`, whereas they are in PostgreSQL.

The `columns` view will give you a listing of all the columns in a particular table or set of tables. The following example lists all the columns found in a table called ch01.restaurants.

Listing C.1 List all columns in ch01.restaurants

```
SELECT c.column_name, c.data_type, c.udt_name,
       c.ordinal_position AS ord_pos,
       c.column_default AS cdefault
    FROM information_schema.columns AS c
    WHERE table_schema = 'ch01' and table_name = 'restaurants'
    ORDER BY c.column_name;
```

The results of this query look something like the following.

Listing C.2 Results of query in listing C.1

```
column_name |  data_type   | udt_name | ord_pos |  cdefault
------------+--------------+----------+---------+--------------------------
 franchise  | character    | bpchar   |       2 |
 geom       | USER-DEFINED | geometry |       3 |
 id         | integer      | int4     |       1 | nextval('ch01...)
```

One important way that PostgreSQL is different from databases such as SQL Server and MySQL Server that support `information_schema` is that it has an additional field called `udt_name` that denotes the PostgreSQL-specific data type. Because PostGIS `geometry` is an add-on module and not part of PostgreSQL, you'll see the standard ANSI data type listed as `USER-DEFINED` and the `udt_name` field storing the fact that it's a geometry.

The `information_schema.columns` view provides numerous other fields, so we encourage you to explore it. We consider these to be the most useful fields:

- `table_name` *and* `column_name`—These should be obvious.
- `data_type`—The ANSI standard data type name for this column.
- `udt_name`—The PostgreSQL-specific name. Except for user-defined types, you can use `data_type` or `udt_name` when creating these fields except in the case of series. Recall that we created `id` as a serial data type in chapter 1, and behind the scenes PostgreSQL created an integer column and a sequence object and set the default of this new column to the next value of the sequence object: `nextval('ch01.restaurants_gid_seq'::regclass)`.
- `ordinal_position`—This is the order in which the column appears in the table.
- `character_maximum_length`—With character fields, this tells you the maximum number of characters allowed in the field.
- `column_default`—The default value assigned to new records. This can be a constant or the result of a function.

The `tables` view lists both tables and views (virtual tables). The `views` view gives you the name and the view definition for each view you have access to. The view definition gives you the SQL that defines the view, and it's very useful for scripting the definitions. In PostgreSQL, you can see how the `information_schema` views are defined, though you may not be able to in other databases such as SQL Server, because the information_schema is excluded from this system view.

```
SELECT table_schema, table_name, view_definition,
    is_updatable, is_insertable_into
    FROM information_schema.views
    WHERE table_schema = 'information_schema';
```

In the preceding examples, we've demonstrated the common meta-tables you'd find in the ANSI information_schema. We also demonstrated the most fundamental of SQL statements. In the next section, we'll look at the anatomy of an SQL statement and describe what each part means.

C.2 Querying data with SQL

The cornerstone of every relational database is the declarative language called *Structured Query Language* (SQL). Although each relational database has a slightly different syntax, the fundamentals are pretty much the same across all relational DBMSs.

One of the most common things done with SQL is to query relational data. SQL of this nature is often referred to as a Data Manipulation Language (DML) and consists of clauses specifically designed for this purpose. The other side of DML is updating data with SQL, which we'll cover in section C.3.

C.2.1 SELECT, FROM, WHERE, and ORDER BY clauses

For accessing data, you use a SELECT statement, usually accompanied with a FROM and a WHERE clause. The SELECT part of the statement restricts the columns that will be returned, the FROM clause determines where the data comes from, and WHERE restricts the number of records to be returned.

When returning constants or simple calculations that come from nowhere, the FROM clause isn't needed in PostgreSQL, SQL Server, or MySQL, whereas in databases such as Oracle and IBM DB2, you need to select FROMdual or sys.dual or some other dummy table.

Basic SELECT

A basic select looks something like this:

```
SELECT gid, item_name, the_geom
    FROM feature_items
    WHERE item_name LIKE 'Queens%';
```

Keep in mind that PostgreSQL is by default case sensitive, and if you want to do a non-case-sensitive search, you'd do the following (or use the non-portable ILIKE PostgreSQL predicate):

```
SELECT gid, item_name, the_geom
    FROM feature_items
    WHERE upper(item_name) LIKE 'QUEENS%';
```

There's no guaranteed order for results to be returned in, but sometimes you'll care about order. The SQL ORDER BY clause satisfies this need for order.

Following is an example that lists all items starting with *Lion* and orders them by item_name:

```
SELECT DISTINCT item_name
    FROM feature_items
    WHERE upper(item_name) LIKE 'LION%'
    ORDER BY upper(item_name);
```

For versions of PostgreSQL prior to 8.4, you should uppercase your ORDER BY field, but PostgreSQL 8.4 provides a new per-database collation feature that makes this not as necessary, depending on the collation order you've designated for your database.

SELECT * IS NOT YOUR FRIEND

Within a SELECT statement you can use the term *, which means "select all the fields in the FROM tables." There is also the variant sometable.* if you want to select all fields from only one table and not all fields from the other tables in your FROM.

We highly recommend you stay away from this with production code. It's useful for seeing all the columns of a table when you don't have the table structure in front of you, but it can be a real performance drain, especially with tables that hold geometries. If you have a table with a column that's unconstrained by size, such as a large text field or geometry field, you'll be pulling all that data across the wire and pulling from disk even when you don't care about the contents of all the fields. It's also dangerous to use * when you have multiple tables in a join that have the same column names, because the column names would be output, and whatever code you're running might arbitrarily pick the wrong column, depending on the language you're using.

INDEXES

The WHERE clause often relies on an index to improve row selection. If you have a large number of distinct groupings of records that have the same value in a field, it's useful to put an index on that field. For a few distinct groupings of records by a column, the index is more harmful than helpful, because the planner will ignore it and do a faster table scan, and updating will incur a heavy performance penalty.

ALIASING

In listing C.1 using information_schema, we demonstrated the concept of aliasing. Aliasing is giving a table or a column a different name in your query than how it's defined in the database.

Aliasing is done with an AS clause. For table aliases, AS is optional for most ANSI SQL standard databases including PostgreSQL. For column aliases, AS is optional for most ANSI SQL databases and PostgreSQL 8.4+ but required for PostgreSQL 8.3 and below.

Aliasing is indispensable when doing self-joins (where you join the same table twice) and you need to distinguish between the two, or where the two tables you have may have field names in common. The other use of aliases is to make your code easier to read and to reduce typing by shortening long table and field names.

WHY USE AS WHEN YOU DON'T NEED TO

Although AS is an optional clause, we like to always put it in for clarity, but it's really a matter of preference. To demonstrate, which of the following is more understandable?

```
SELECT b.somefield a FROM sometable b;
```

or

```
SELECT b.somefield AS a FROM sometable AS b;
```

C.2.2 Using subselects

The SQL language has built-in support for subselects. Much of the expressiveness and complexity of SQL consists of keeping subselects straight and knowing when and when not to use them. For PostgreSQL, most valid `SELECT ...` clauses can be used as subselects, and when used in a `FROM` clause, the subselect must be aliased. For some databases, such as SQL Server, there are some minor limitations; for example, SQL Server doesn't allow an `ORDER BY` in a subselect without a `TOP` clause.

A subselect statement is a full `SELECT ... FROM ...` statement that appears within another SQL statement. It can appear in the following locations of an overall SQL statement:

- *In a* `UNION`, `INTERSECT`, *or* `EXCEPT`—You'll learn about these shortly.
- *In a* `FROM` *clause*—When used in a `FROM`, the subselect acts as a virtual table, and it needs to have an alias name to define how it will be called in other parts of the query. Also, in versions prior to PostgreSQL 9.3, the subselect can't reference other `FROM` table fields as part of its definition. Some databases allow you to do this under certain conditions, such as SQL Server's 2005+ `CROSS/OUTER APPLY` and the `LATERAL` clause in PostgreSQL 9.3+. Note that for PostgreSQL 9.3+, the `LATERAL` clause term is optional, and you can simply use a subselect that references other tables in the `FROM`. We'll demonstrate `LATERAL`s later in this appendix.
- *In the definition of a calculated column*—When used in this context, the subselect can return only one column and one row. This pretty much applies to all databases, but PostgreSQL has a somewhat unique feature because of the way it implements rows. Each table has a data type that contains all the columns of its row. As such, a table can be used as a data type of a column. In addition, a row, even one coming from a subselect, is a composite type. This allows you to get away with returning a multicolumn row as a field expression. This isn't a feature you'll commonly find in other databases, so we won't cover it in this appendix. You can, however, return multiple rows as an array if they contain only one column by using `ARRAY` in PostgreSQL. This will return the column as an array of that type. We demonstrate this in various parts of the book. Again, this is a feature that's fairly unique to PostgreSQL and is very handy for spatial queries.
- *In the* `WHERE` *part of another SQL query*—Subselects can be used in `IN`, `NOT IN`, and `EXISTS` clauses.

- *In a* WITH *clause*—A SELECT query in a WITH clause is loosely defined as a subselect but is not strictly thought of that way. Note that the WITH clause is available only in PostgreSQL 8.4+. You'll also find it in Oracle, SQL Server 2005+, IBM DB2, and Firebird. You won't find it in MySQL.

  One caution with subselects in WITH clauses when used in PostgreSQL is that they're always materialized. WITH materialization is still the case in PostgreSQL 9.4, but it isn't necessarily the case with other databases that support the construct. Materialization is both good and bad. It's good because you can use it as a kind of HINT to the planner to materialize, but bad because if you just consider it to be syntactic sugar, you could slow down your queries significantly.

WHAT IS A CORRELATED SUBQUERY?

A correlated subquery is a subquery that uses fields from the outer query (the next level above the subquery) to define the subquery. Correlated subqueries are often used in column expressions and WHERE clauses. They're generally slower than non-correlated subqueries because they have to be calculated for each unique combination of fields and have a dependency on the outer query.

The following listing shows some examples of subselects in action. Don't worry if you don't completely comprehend them, because some require an understanding of topics that we'll cover shortly.

Listing C.3 Subselects used in a table alias

```
SELECT s.state, r.cnt_residents, c.land_area
    FROM states As s LEFT JOIN
        (SELECT state, COUNT(res_id) As cnt_residents
            FROM residents
            GROUP BY state) AS r ON s.state = r.state
    LEFT JOIN (SELECT state, SUM(ST_Area(the_geom)) As land_area
            FROM counties
            GROUP BY state) As c
        ON s.state = c.state;
```

This statement uses a subselect to define the derived table we alias as r. This is the common use case.

The same statement is demonstrated in the following listing using the PostgreSQL 8.4 WITH clause. The WITH clause, sometimes referred to as a *common table expression* (CTE), is an advanced ANSI SQL feature that you'll find in SQL Server, IBM DB2, Oracle, and Firebird, to name a few.

Listing C.4 The same statement written using the WITH clause

```
WITH
        r AS (
            SELECT state, COUNT(res_id) As cnt_residents
                FROM residents
            GROUP BY state),
```

```
    c AS (
        SELECT state, SUM(ST_Area(the_geom)) As land_area
            FROM counties
        GROUP BY state)
SELECT s.state, r.cnt_residents, c.land_area
FROM states As s LEFT JOIN
    r ON s.state = r.state
LEFT JOIN c
    ON s.state = c.state;
```

Now let's look at the same query written using a correlated subquery.

Listing C.5 The same statement written using a correlated subquery

```
SELECT s.state,
        (SELECT COUNT(res_id)
            FROM residents
            WHERE residents.state = s.state) AS cnt_residents
    , (SELECT SUM(ST_Area(the_geom))
        FROM counties
         WHERE counties.state = s.state) AS land_area
    FROM states As s ;
```

Although you can use any of these variations to get the same results, the strategies used by the planner are very different. Depending on what you're doing, one can be much faster than another. If you expect large numbers of returned rows, you should avoid the correlated subquery approach, although in certain cases it can be necessary to use a correlated subquery, such as when you need to prevent duplication of counts. You also don't want to use a CTE for expressions that would result in many rows that you won't always return. This is because the CTE will materialize the subexpression and will also not be able to employ indexes on the underlying table for subsequent uses in later expressions.

C.2.3 *JOINs*

PostgreSQL supports all the standard `JOIN`s and sets defined in the ANSI SQL standards.

A `JOIN` is a clause that relates two tables, usually by a primary and a foreign key, although the join condition can be arbitrary. In spatial queries, you'll find that the `JOIN` is often based on a proximity condition rather than on keys. The clauses `LEFT JOIN`, `INNER JOIN`, `CROSS JOIN`, `RIGHT JOIN`, `FULL JOIN`, and `NATURAL JOIN` exist in the ANSI SQL specifications, and PostgreSQL supports all of these. SQL Server supports them as well, but MySQL lacks `FULL JOIN` support. Oracle supports them as well.

LEFT JOIN

A `LEFT JOIN` returns all records from the first table (M) and only records in the second table (N) that match records in the first table (M). The maximum number of records returned by a `LEFT JOIN` is $m \times n$ rows, where m is the number of rows in M

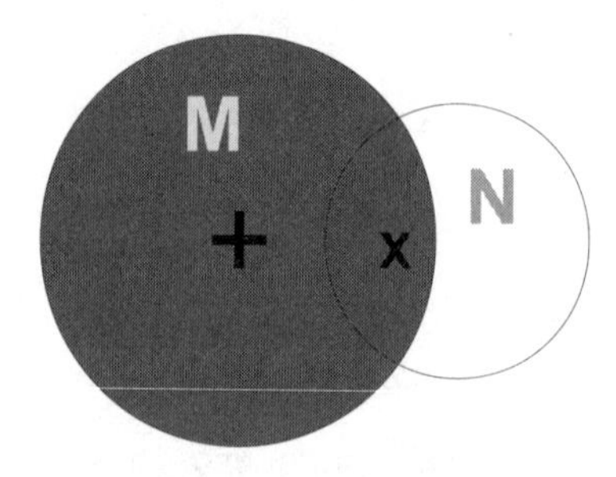

Figure C.1 Diagram of a `LEFT JOIN`. The darkened region represents the portion of records returned by a `LEFT JOIN`. The × stands for multiplication and the + is additive. The first circle is M and the second circle is N.

and *n* is the number of rows in N. The number of columns is the number of columns selected from M plus the number of columns selected from N.

Generally speaking, if your M table has a primary key that's the joining field, you can expect the minimum number of rows returned to be *m* and the maximum to be $m + m \times n$.

NULL placeholders are put in table N's columns where there's no match in the M table. You can see a diagram of a `LEFT JOIN` in figure C.1.

Let's look at some examples of `LEFT JOIN`s:

```
SELECT c.city_name, a.airport_code,a.airport_name, a.runlength
    FROM city As c
        LEFT JOIN airports As a ON a.city_code = c.city_code;
```

This query will list both cities that have airports and cities that don't have airports, based on `city_code`. We assume `city_code` to be the city table's primary key and a foreign key in the airports table. If the `LEFT JOIN` were changed to an `INNER JOIN`, only cities with airports would be listed. With a `LEFT JOIN`, cities that have no airports will get a NULL placeholder for the airport fields.

One trick commonly used with `LEFT JOIN`s is to return only unmatched rows by taking advantage of the fact that a `LEFT JOIN` will return NULL placeholders where there's no match. When doing this, make sure the field you're joining with is guaranteed to be filled in when there are matches; otherwise, you'll get spurious results. For example, a good candidate would be the primary key of a table. Here's an example of such a trick:

```
SELECT c.city_name
    FROM city AS c
    LEFT JOIN airports AS a ON a.city_code=c.city_code
    WHERE a.airport_code IS NULL;
```

In this example, you're returning all cities with no matching airports. You're making the assumption that the `airport_code` is never NULL in the airports table. If it were ever NULL, this wouldn't work.

INNER JOIN

An `INNER JOIN` returns only records that are in both the M and N tables, as shown in figure C.2. The maximum number of records you can expect from an inner join is $(m \times n)$. Generally speaking, if your M table has a primary key, and that field is used to

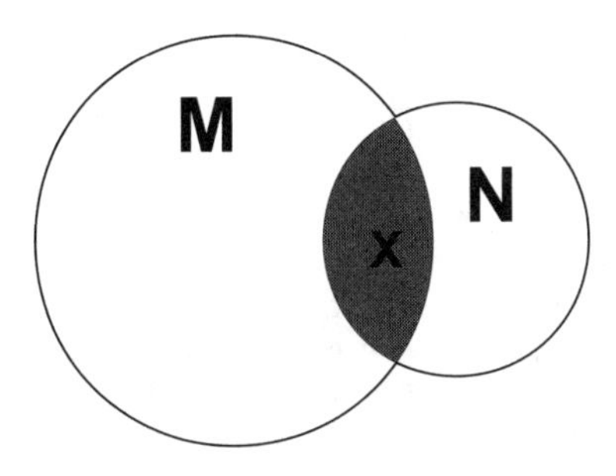

Figure C.2 Diagram of an INNER JOIN. The darkened region represents the portion of records returned by the INNER JOIN. The × denotes that it's multiplicative.

join with a field in table N, you can expect the maximum number of rows to be *n*. A classic example is customers joined with orders. If a customer has only five orders, the number of rows you'll get back with that customer ID and name is five.

Following is an example of an `INNER JOIN`:

```
SELECT c.city_name, a.airport_code, a.airport_name, a.runlength
    FROM city AS c
        INNER JOIN airports a ON a.city_code = c.city_code;
```

In this example, you list only cities that have airports and only the airports in them. If you had a spatial database, you could do a `JOIN` using a spatial function such as `ST_Intersects` or `ST_DWithin` and you could find airports in proximity to a city or in a city region.

RIGHT JOIN

A `RIGHT JOIN` returns all records in the N table and only records in the M table that match records in N, as shown in figure C.3. In practice, `RIGHT JOIN`s are rarely used because a `RIGHT` can always be replaced with a `LEFT`, and most people find reading join clauses from left to right easier to comprehend. The `RIGHT JOIN`'s behavior is a mirror image of the `LEFT JOIN`, flipping the table order in the clause.

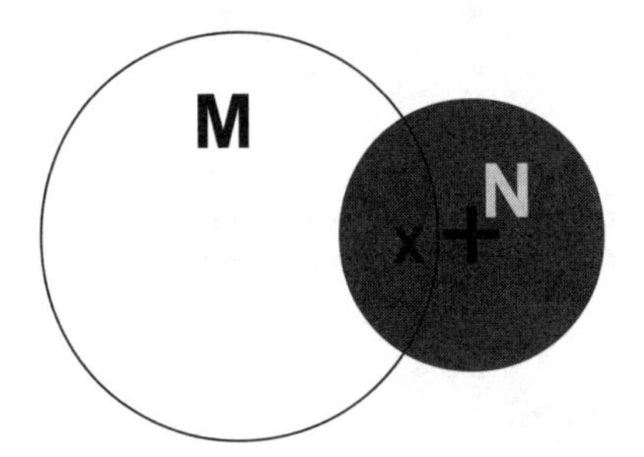

Figure C.3 Diagram of a RIGHT JOIN. The darkened region represents the portion of records returned by a RIGHT JOIN. The × stands for multiplication and the + is additive.

FULL JOIN

The `FULL JOIN`, shown in figure C.4, returns all records in M and N and uses NULLs as placeholders in fields where there's no matching data. There's a lot of debate about the usefulness of `FULL JOIN`s. In practice they're rarely used, and some people are of the opinion that they should never be used because they can always be simulated with

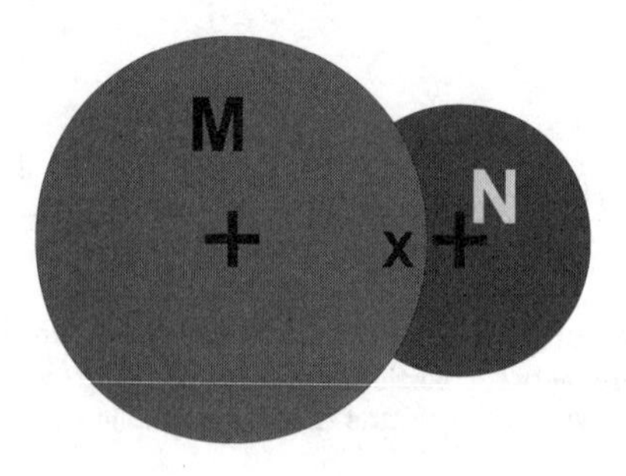

Figure C.4 Diagram of a FULL JOIN. The darkened region represents the portion of records returned by a FULL JOIN. The × stands for multiplication and the + is additive.

a UNION [ALL]. Although we rarely use FULL JOINs, in some cases we find them clearer to use than a UNION [ALL].

The number of columns returned by a FULL JOIN is the same as for a LEFT, RIGHT, or INNER join; the minimum number of rows returned is $\max(m,n)$ and the maximum is $(\max(m,n) + m \times n - \min(m,n))$.

FULL JOINs on spatial relationships—forget about it

While in theory it's possible to do a FULL JOIN using spatial functions like ST_DWithin or ST_Intersects, in practice this isn't currently supported, even as of PostgreSQL 9.4 and PostGIS 2.1.

CROSS JOIN

The CROSS JOIN is the cross product of two tables, where every record in the M table is joined with every record in the N table, as illustrated in figure C.5. The result of a CROSS JOIN without a WHERE clause is $m \times n$ rows. It's sometimes referred to as a *Cartesian product.*

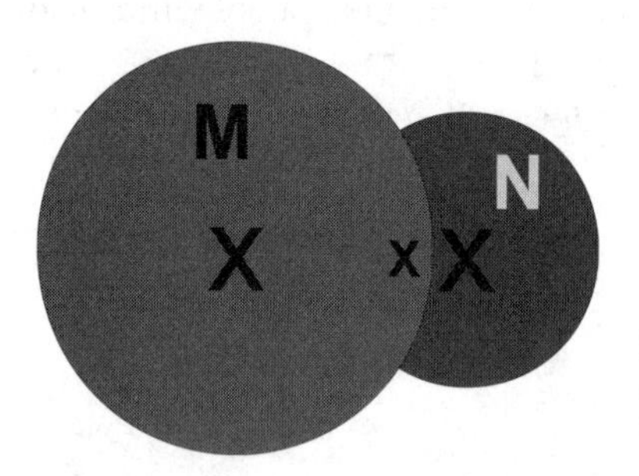

Figure C.5 Diagram of a CROSS JOIN. The darkened region represents the portion of records returned by the CROSS JOIN. The × stands for multiplication.

Here's an example of a good use for a CROSS JOIN. This statement calculates the total price of a product, including state tax, for each state:

```
SELECT p.product_name, s.state,
       p.base_price * (1 + s.tax) As total_price
    FROM products AS p
    CROSS JOIN state AS s;
```

It can also be written as follows:

```
SELECT p.product_name, s.state,
       p.base_price * (1 + s.tax) As total_price
    FROM products AS p, state AS s
```

Note that table1 INNER JOIN table2 ON (table1.field1 = table2.field2) can be written with the table1 CROSS JOIN table2 or table1,table2 syntax and then followed with a WHERE table1.field1 = table2.field2 part, but we prefer the more explicit INNER JOIN because it's less prone to mistakes.

When doing an INNER JOIN with CROSS JOIN syntax, you put the join fields in the WHERE clause. Primary keys and foreign keys are often put in the INNER JOIN ON clause, but in practice you can put any joining field in there. There's no absolute rule about it. The distinction becomes important when doing LEFT JOINs, as you saw with the LEFT JOIN orphan trick.

NATURAL JOIN

A NATURAL JOIN is like an INNER JOIN without an ON clause. It's supported by many ANSI-compliant databases. The NATURAL JOIN automagically joins same-named columns between tables, so there's no need for an ON clause.

JUST SAY NO TO THE NATURAL JOIN

We highly suggest you stay away from using NATURAL JOINs. It's a lazy and dangerous way of doing joins that will come back to bite you when you add fields with the same names as fields in other tables that are totally unrelated. We feel so strongly about not using NATURAL JOINs that we won't even demonstrate their use. So when you see one in use, instead of thinking *cool*, just say *no*.

CHAINING JOINS

The other thing with JOINs is that you can chain them almost ad infinitum. You can also combine multiple JOIN types, but when joining different types, either make sure you have all your INNER JOINs before the LEFTs or put parentheses around them to control their order.

Here's an example of JOIN chaining:

```
SELECT c.last_name, c.first_name, r.rental_id, p.amount, p.payment_date
    FROM customer As C
      INNER JOIN rental As r ON C.customer_id = r.customer_id
      LEFT JOIN payment As p
       ON (p.customer_id = r.customer_id
        AND p.rental_id = r.rental_id);
```

This example is from the PostgreSQL pagila database. The pagila database is a favorite for demonstrating new features of PostgreSQL. You can download it from "PostgreSQL sample databases" (www.postgresql.org/ftp/projects/pgFoundry/dbsamples).

In the preceding example, you find all the customers who have had rentals, and you list the rental fields as well (note that the INNER JOIN excludes all customers who haven't made rentals). You then pull the payments they've made for each rental. You'll get NULLs if no payment was made but the rental exists.

C.2.4 Sets

The set predicates UNION [ALL], EXCEPT, INTERSECT, like a JOIN, can contain multiple tables or subqueries. What distinguishes the set class of predicates from a JOIN is that they chain together SQL statements that can normally stand by themselves to return a single data set. The set class defines the kind of chaining behavior. Keep in mind that when we talk about sets here, we're not talking about the `SET` clause you'll find in `UPDATE` statements.

PostgreSQL supports all three set predicates, though many databases support only `UNION [ALL]`.

One other distinguishing thing about sets is that the number of columns in each `SELECT` has to be the same, and the data types in each column should be the same too, or autocast to the same data type in a non-ambiguous way.

SPATIAL PARALLELS

One thing that confuses new spatial database users is the parallels between the two terminologies. In general SQL lingua franca, you have `UNION`, `INTERSECT`, and `EXCEPT`, which talk about table rows. When you add space to the mix, you have parallel terminology for geometries: `ST_Union` (which is like a `UNION`), `ST_Collect` (which is like a `UNION ALL`), `ST_Intersection` (which is like `INTERSECT`), and `ST_Difference` (which is like `EXCEPT`) serve the same purposes for geometries.

UNION AND UNION ALL

The most common type of set includes the `UNION` and `UNION ALL` sets, illustrated in figure C.6. Most relational databases have at least one of these, and most have both. A `UNION` takes two `SELECT` statements and returns a `DISTINCT` set of these, which means no two records will be exactly the same. A `UNION ALL`, on the other hand, always returns $n + m$ rows, where n is the number of rows in table N and m is the number of rows in table M.

Figure C.6 `UNION ALL` versus `UNION`. The thick-bordered light-gray box is M, and the thin-bordered dark-gray box is N. On the left, the `UNION ALL` shared regions are duplicated; in the `UNION` on the right, only one of the shared regions is kept, resulting in a distinct set.

A union can have multiple chains, each separated by a `UNION ALL` or a `UNION`. `ORDER BY` can appear only once and must be at the end of the chain. `ORDER BY` is often denoted by numbers, where the number denotes the column number to order by.

A union is generally used to put together results from different tables. The example in the following listing will list all water and land features greater than 500 units in area and all architecture monuments greater than 1000 dollars, and will order the results by item name.

Listing C.6 Combining water and land features

```
SELECT water_name As label_name, the_geom,
       ST_Area(the_geom) As feat_area
    FROM water_features
    WHERE ST_Area(the_geom) > 10000
    UNION ALL
    SELECT feat_name As label_name, the_geom,
```

```
    ST_Area(the_geom) As feat_area
FROM land_features
WHERE ST_Area(feat_geometry) > 500
UNION ALL
SELECT arch_name As label_name, the_geom,
    ST_Area(the_geom) As feat_area

FROM architecture
WHERE price > 1000
ORDER BY 1,3;
```

This example will pull data from three tables (water_features, land_features, and architecture) and return a single data set ordered by the name of the feature and then the area of the feature.

UNION IS OFTEN MISTAKENLY USED

The plain `UNION` statement is often mistakenly used because it's the default option when `ALL` isn't specified. As stated, `UNION` does an implicit `DISTINCT` on the data set, which makes it slower than a `UNION ALL`. It also has another side effect of losing geometry records that have the same bounding boxes. In general, you'll want to use a `UNION ALL` except when deduping data.

INTERSECT

`INTERSECT` is used to join multiple queries, similar to `UNION`. It's defined in the ANSI SQL standard, but not all databases support it; for example, MySQL doesn't support it, and neither does SQL Server 2000, although SQL Server 2005 and above do.

`INTERSECT` returns only the set of records that is common between the two result sets, as shown in figure C.7. It's different from `INNER JOIN` in that it isn't multiplicative and in that both queries must have the same number of columns. In figure C.7, the shaded area represents what's returned by an SQL `INTERSECT`. Later we'll look at a spatial intersection involving an intersection of geometries rather than an intersection of row spaces.

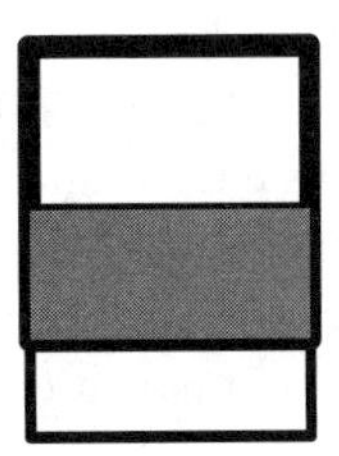

Figure C.7 `INTERSECT`—the darkened region is the intersection of two data sets returned by an `INTERSECT` clause.

`INTERSECT` is rarely used, and there are a few reasons for that:

- Many relational databases don't support it.
- It tends to be slower than doing the same trick with an `INNER JOIN`. In PostgreSQL 8.4, the speed of `INTERSECT`s has been improved, but in prior versions it wasn't that great.
- In some cases, it looks convoluted when you're talking about the same table.

In some cases, though, INTERSECT does make your code clearer, such as when you have two disparate tables or when you chain more than two queries. The following listing demonstrates INTERSECT and the equivalent query using INNER JOIN.

Listing C.7 INTERSECT compared to INNER JOIN

```
SELECT feature_id                         <-- ❶ INTERSECT example
        FROM water_features
       WHERE ST_Area(geom) > 500
    INTERSECT
    SELECT feature_id
        FROM protected_areas
        WHERE induction_year > 2000;

    SELECT wf.feature_id                  <-- ❷ INNER JOIN version
     FROM water_features As wf
        INNER JOIN
        protected_areas As pa ON wf.feature_id = pa.feature_id
    WHERE ST_Area(wf.geom) > 500
    AND pa.induction_year > 2000;
```

The first query uses the INTERSECT approach to list all water features greater than 500 square units that are also designated as protected areas inducted after the year 2000 ❶.

The second approach demonstrates the same query, but using an INNER JOIN instead of an INTERSECT ❷. Note that if the feature_id field isn't unique in both tables, the INNER JOIN runs the chance of multiplying records. To overcome that, you can change the SELECT to SELECT DISTINCT.

The next example demonstrates chaining INTERSECT clauses:

```
SELECT r
        FROM generate_series(1,3) AS r
    INTERSECT
    SELECT n
        FROM generate_series(3,8) AS n
    INTERSECT
    SELECT s
        FROM generate_series(2,3) AS s;
```

Keep in mind that you can mix and match with UNION and EXCEPT as well. The order of precedence is from top query down, unless you have subselect parenthetical expressions.

EXCEPT

An EXCEPT chains queries together such that the final result contains only records in A that aren't in B. The number and type of columns in each chained query must be the same, similar to UNION and INTERSECT. The shaded section in figure C.8 represents the result of the final query.

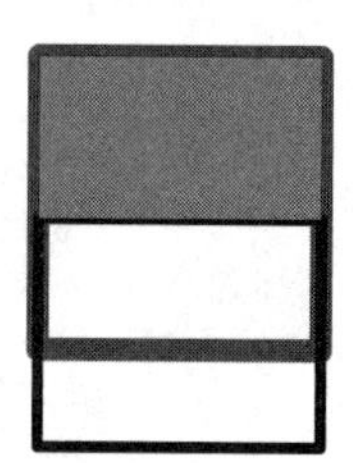

Figure C.8 A demonstration of EXCEPT

`EXCEPT` is rarely used, but it does come in handy when chaining multiple clauses:

```
SELECT r
        FROM generate_series(1,3) AS r
    EXCEPT
    SELECT n
        FROM generate_series(3,8) AS n
    INTERSECT
    SELECT s
        FROM generate_series(2,3) AS s;
```

C.2.5 Using SQL aggregates

Aggregate functions roll a group of records into one record. In PostgreSQL, the standard `SUM`, `MAX`, `MIN`, `AVG`, `COUNT`, and various statistical aggregates are available out of the box. PostGIS adds many more for `geometry`, `raster`, and `topology` types, of which `ST_Collect`, `ST_Union`, `ST_MakeLine`, and `ST_Extent` are the most commonly used. In this section, we'll focus on using aggregates. How you use aggregates is pretty much the same regardless of whether they're spatial or not.

Aggregates in SQL generally have the following parts:

- `SELECT` *and* `FROM`—This is where you select the fields and where you pull data from. You also include the aggregated functions in the select field list.
- `SOMEAGGREGATE(DISTINCT somefield)`—On rare occasions, you'll use the `DISTINCT` clause within an aggregate function to denote that you use only a distinct set of values to aggregate. This is commonly done with the `COUNT` aggregate to count a unique name only once.
- `WHERE`—Non-aggregate filter; this gets applied before the `HAVING` part.
- `HAVING`—Similar to `WHERE`, but used when applying filtering on the already aggregated data.
- `GROUP BY`—All fields in the `SELECT` that are non-aggregated and function calls must appear here (pre-PostgreSQL 9.1).
- `SOMEAGGREGATE(somefield ORDER BY someotherfield1, ... someotherfieldn)`—This is a feature new in PostgreSQL 9.0. It's most useful for aggregates that return output composed of subelements, and it controls the order in which these are returned. In common PostgreSQL usage, you'll often see this used with `string_agg` or `array_agg`. In the PostGIS world, you'll see this used commonly with the `ST_MakeLine` aggregate function where you need to control the order of the line's points by time or some other column. The `ORDER BY` construct can be combined with `DISTINCT` in the form `SOMEAGGREGATE(DISTINCT somefield ORDER BY somefield)`. Note that in the `DISTINCT` form, similar to a regular `SELECT DISTINCT`, the `ORDER BY` columns need to be inputs to the function.

WARNING With geometries, what is `DISTINCT`ed is the bounding box, so different geometries with the same bounding box will get thrown out.

GROUP BY FUNCTIONAL DEPENDENCY ENHANCEMENT

PostgreSQL 9.1 introduced the functional dependency feature, which means that if you're already grouping by a primary key of a table, you can skip grouping by other fields in that table. This feature is defined in the ANSI SQL 99 standard. It saves some typing as well as makes it easier to port some MySQL apps.

FAST FACTS ABOUT AGGREGATE FUNCTIONS

There are some important things you should keep in mind when working with aggregate functions. Some of these facts are standard across all relational databases, some are specific to PostgreSQL, and some are a consequence of the way PostGIS implements = for geometries:

- For most aggregate functions, NULLs are ignored. This is important to know, because it allows you to do things such as `COUNT(geom) AS num_has_geoms` and `COUNT(neighborhood) AS num_has_neighborhoods` in the same `SELECT` statement.
- If you want to count all records, use a field that's never NULL to count; for example, `COUNT(gid)` or a constant such as `COUNT(1)`. You can also use `COUNT(*)`. Prior to PostgreSQL 8.1, the `COUNT(*)` function was really slow, so long-time PostgreSQL users tend to avoid that syntax out of habit.
- When grouping by geometries, which is very rare, it's the bounding box of the geometry that's actually grouped on (although the first geometry with that bounding box is used for output), so be very careful and avoid grouping by geometry if possible, unless you have another field in the `GROUP BY` that's distinct for each geometry, like the primary key of the table the geometry is coming from.

The following listing is an example that mixes aggregate SQL functions with spatial aggregates.

Listing C.8 Combining standard SQL and spatial aggregates

```
SELECT n.nei_name,
        SUM(ST_Length(roads.geom)) as total_road_length,
        ST_Extent(roads.geom) As total_extent,
        COUNT(DISTINCT roads.road_name) As count_of_roads
    FROM neighborhoods As n
        INNER JOIN roads ON
            ST_Intersects(neighborhoods.geom, roads.geom)
    WHERE n.city = 'Boston'
        GROUP BY n.nei_name
        HAVING ST_Area(ST_Extent(roads.geom)) > 1000;
```

The query for each neighborhood specifies the total length of roads and the extent of all roads. It also includes a count of unique road names and counts only neighborhoods where the total area of the extent covered is greater than 1,000 square units.

C.2.6 Window functions and window aggregates

PostgreSQL 8.4 introduced the ANSI-standard window functions and aggregates, and PostgreSQL 9.0 improved on this by expanding the functionality of `BETWEEN ROWS` and `RANGE`. PostgreSQL 9.4 improves even more on this feature by adding `percentile_cont` and `percentile_dist` as well as the complementary `WITHIN GROUP (ORDER BY somefield)` to go along with these new functions.

Window functionality allows you to do useful things such as sequentially number results by some sort of ranking; calculate running subtotals based on a subset of the full set using the concept of a window frame; and, for PostGIS 1.4+, perform running geometry `ST_Union` and `ST_MakeLine` calls, which are perhaps solutions in search of a problem but nevertheless intriguing.

A window frame defines a subset of data within a subquery using the term `PARTITION BY`, and then within that window you can define orderings and sum results to achieve rolling totals and counts. Microsoft SQL Server, Oracle, and IBM also support this feature, with Oracle's feature set being the strongest and SQL Server's being weaker than that of IBM DB2 or PostgreSQL. Check out our brief summary comparing these databases on the Postgres OnLine Journal to get a sense of the differences: www.postgresonline.com/journal/archives/122-Window-Functions-Comparison.html

PostgreSQL also supports named window frames that can be reused by name.

The example in the following listing uses the `ROW_NUMBER` window function to number streets sequentially within one kilometer of a police station, ordered by their proximity to the police station.

Listing C.9 Find roads within 1 km of each police station and number sequentially

```
SELECT  ROW_NUMBER() OVER (                    <-- ❶ Number rows
          PARTITION BY loc.pid                 <-- ❷ Restart numbering for each pid
              ORDER BY ST_Distance(r.geom, loc.geom)      <-- ❸ Order numbers by distance
                , r.road_name) As row_num,
    loc.pid, r.road_name,
          ST_Distance(r.geom, loc.geom)/1000 As dist_km
       FROM land As loc
          LEFT JOIN  road As r
                ON ST_DWithin(r.geom, loc.geom, 1000)
   WHERE loc.land_type = 'police station'
   ORDER BY pid, row_num;
```

In this listing, you use the window function called `ROW_NUMBER` to number the results ❶. The `PARTITION BY` clause forces numbering to restart for each unique parcel ID (identified by `pid`) that uniquely identifies a police station ❷. The `ORDER BY` defines the ordering ❸. In this case, you increment based on proximity to the police station. If two streets happen to be at the same distance, then one will arbitrarily be *n* and the other *n*+1. The `ORDER BY` includes `road_name` as a tie breaker.

Table C.1 shows a subset of the resulting table for two police stations.

Table C.1 Results of the window query in listing C.9

row_num	pid	road_name	dist_km
1	000010131	Main Rd	0.228687666823197
2	000010131	Curvy St	0.336867955509993
3	000010131	Elephantine Rd	0.959190964077745
1	000040128	Elephantine Rd	0.587036350160092
2	000040128	Main Rd	0.771250583026646

C.2.7 LATERALs

New in PostgreSQL 9.3 is the LATERAL clause. The LATERAL clause is an ANSI SQL feature that allows you to specify tables, functions (particularly set-returning functions), or subqueries in the FROM clause that reference columns from preceding FROM items. A common use of the LATERAL clause in PostGIS work is to expand spatial objects into component parts. LATERAL is also used in conjunction with KNN gist operators <-> and <#> to overcome the constant reference geometry issue, and doing limit queries where, for example, for each record location you want to return the five closest items from another set of data. We demonstrated some examples of its use in distance searching in chapter 10, and in chapter 8 for batch geocoding.

The basic use of LATERAL in conjunction with KNN operators such as <-> is shown in the following example, which returns the closest three hospitals for each location:

```
SELECT loc.address, hosp.name
FROM loc CROSS JOIN
  LATERAL (SELECT name FROM hospitals
  ORDER BY hospitals.geom <-> loc.geom LIMIT 3) As hosp
```

As with all LATERAL constructs, the hosp subquery relies on column geom from the loc table, and each value of loc.geom begets a new subtable. loc.geom is used as a constant in the subquery, so it can utilize spatial indexes.

In cases where you aren't sure if a subquery will return a result for each record in your preceding FROM table, you can combine LATERAL with a LEFT JOIN, as this next example demonstrates:

```
SELECT loc.address, hosp.name
FROM loc LEFT JOIN
  LATERAL (SELECT name FROM hospitals
  ORDER BY hospitals.geom <-> loc.geom LIMIT 3) As hosp ON true
```

In the next section, you'll learn about another key component of SQL. SQL is good for querying data, but it's also useful for updating and adding data.

C.3 UPDATE, INSERT, and DELETE

The other feature of a DML is the ability to update, delete, and insert data. SQL's UPDATE, DELETE, and INSERT statements can combine the predicates you learned about for selecting data. They can perform cross updates between tables or formulate a virtual table (subquery) to insert data into a physical table. In the exercises that follow, we'll demonstrate simple constructs as well as more complex ones.

C.3.1 UPDATE

You can use the SQL UPDATE statement to update existing data. You can update individual records or a batch of records based on some WHERE condition.

SIMPLE UPDATE

A simple UPDATE will update data to a static value based on a WHERE condition. Here's a simple example of this:

```
UPDATE things
    SET status = 'active'
    WHERE last_update_date > (CURRENT_TIMESTAMP - '30 day'::interval);
```

UPDATE FROM OTHER TABLES

A simple UPDATE is one of the more common update statements used. In certain cases, however, you'll need to read data from a separate table based on some sort of related criteria. In this case, you'll need to use joins within your UPDATE statement.

Here's a simple example that updates the region code of a point data set if the point falls within the region:

```
UPDATE things
        SET region_code = r.region_code
        FROM regions As r
    WHERE ST_Intersects(things.geom, r.geom);
```

UPDATE WITH SUBSELECTS

A subselect, as you learned earlier, is like a virtual table. It can be used in UPDATE statements the same way you use regular tables. In a regular UPDATE statement, even involving statements with table joins, you can't update a table value with an aggregate such as the SUM of another table field. A way to get around this limitation of SQL is to use a subselect.

Following is an example that tallies the number of objects in a region:

```
UPDATE regions
   SET total_objects = ts.cnt
 FROM (SELECT t.region_code, COUNT(t.gid) As cnt
        FROM things AS t
         GROUP BY t.region_code) As ts
    WHERE regions.region_code = ts.region_code;
```

If you're updating all rows in a table, it's often more efficient to build the table from scratch and use an INSERT statement rather than an UPDATE statement. The reason for this is that an UPDATE is really an INSERT and a DELETE. Because of the multi-version concurrency control (MVCC) implementation of PostgreSQL, PostgreSQL will remove the old row and replace it with the new row in the active heap.

Next you'll learn how to perform INSERTs.

C.3.2 INSERT

Just like the UPDATE statement, you can have simple INSERTs that insert constants as well as more complex ones that read from other tables or aggregate data. We'll demonstrate some of these constructs.

SIMPLE INSERT

The simple INSERT just inserts constants, and it comes in three basic forms.

The single-value constructor approach has existed in PostgreSQL since the 6.0 days and is pretty well supported across all relational databases. Here you insert a single point:

```
INSERT INTO points_of_interest(fe_name, geom)
        VALUES ('Highland Golf Club',
                ST_SetSRID(ST_Point(-70.063656, 42.037715), 4269));
```

The next most popular approach is the multi-row VALUES constructor syntax introduced in SQL 92, which we demonstrate often in this book. This syntax was introduced in PostgreSQL 8.2 and IBM DB2, has been supported for a long time in MySQL (we think since 3+), and was introduced in SQL Server 2008. As of this writing, Oracle has yet to support this useful construct.

The multi-row VALUES constructor is useful for adding more than a single row or as a faster way of creating a derived table with just constants. Listing C.10 shows an example of a multi-row VALUES insert. It's similar to the single insert. It starts with the word VALUES, and then each row is enclosed in parentheses and separated with a comma.

Listing C.10 Multivalue row INSERT: two insert facilities

```
INSERT INTO poi(poi_name, poi_geom)
    VALUES ('Park',
            ST_GeomFromText('POLYGON ((86980 67760,
                     43975 71292, 43420 56700, 91400 35280,
          91680 72460, 89460 75500, 86980 67760))') ),
    ('Zoo',  ST_GeomFromText('POLYGON ((41715 67525, 61393 64101,
       91505 49252, 91400 35280, 41715 67525))') );
```

The last kind of simple INSERT is one that uses the SELECT clause, as shown in listing C.11. In the simplest example, it doesn't have a FROM. Some people prefer this syntax because it allows you to alias what the value is right next to the constant. It's also a necessary syntax for the more complex kind of INSERT we'll demonstrate in the next section.

Listing C.11 Simple value INSERT using SELECT instead of VALUES

```
INSERT INTO poi(poi_name, geom)
SELECT 'Park' AS poi_name,
    ST_GeomFromText('POLYGON ((86980 67760,
                    43975 71292, 43420 56700, 91400 35280,
        91680 72460, 89460 75500, 86980 67760))') As geom
UNION ALL
SELECT 'Zoo' As poi_name,
    ST_GeomFromText('POLYGON ((41715 67525, 61393 64101, 91505 49252,
       91400 35280, 41715 67525))')  As geom;
```

This is the standard way of inserting multiple rows into a table. It was the only way to do a multi-row `INSERT` before PostgreSQL 8.2. This syntax is supported by PostgreSQL (all versions), MySQL, and SQL Server. To use it in something like Oracle or IBM DB2, you need to include a `FROM` clause, like `FROMdual` or `sys.dual`.

ADVANCED INSERT

The advanced `INSERT` is not that advanced. You use this syntax to copy data from one table or query to another table. In the simplest case, you're copying a filtered set of data from another table. It uses the `SELECT` syntax, usually with a `FROM` and sometimes accompanying joins.

This example inserts a subset of rows from one table into another:

```
INSERT INTO polygons_of_interest(fe_name, geom, interest_type)
    SELECT pid, geom, 'less than 300 sqft' As interest_type
    FROM parcels WHERE ST_Area(geom) < 300;
```

A slightly more advanced `INSERT` is one that joins several tables together. In this scenario, the `SELECT FROM` is just a standard SQL `SELECT` statement with joins, or one that consists of subselects. Listing C.12 is a somewhat complex case: given a table of polygon chain link edges, it constructs polygons and stuffs them into a new table of polygons.

Listing C.12 Construct polygons from line work and insert into polygon table

```
INSERT INTO polygons(polyid, geom)
    SELECT polyid, ST_Multi(final.geom) As geom
    FROM (SELECT pc.polyid,
       ST_BuildArea(ST_Collect(pc.geom)) As geom
        FROM
    (SELECT p.right_poly as polyid, lw.geom
            FROM polychain p INNER JOIN linework lw ON
                lw.tlid = p.tlid
            WHERE (p.right_poly <> p.left_poly OR p.left_poly IS NULL)
        UNION ALL
        SELECT p.left_poly as polyid, lw.geom
            FROM polychain p INNER JOIN linework lw ON
                lw.tlid = p.tlid
            WHERE (p.right_poly <> p.left_poly OR p.right_poly IS NULL)
    ) As pc
    GROUP BY poly.polyid) As final;
```

SELECT INTO AND CREATE TABLE AS

Another form of the INSERT statement is what we commonly refer to as a *bulk* INSERT. In this kind of INSERT, not only are you inserting data, but you're also creating the table to hold the data in a single statement. PostgreSQL supports two basic forms of this:

- The standard SELECT ... INTO is supported by a lot of relational databases. We prefer this approach because it's more cross-platform (it will work on SQL Server as well as MySQL, for example).
- The CREATE TABLE ... AS SELECT ..., approach isn't as well supported by other relational databases.

In both cases, any valid SELECT or WITH statement can be used. The following listing shows examples of the same statement written using SELECT INTO and CREATE TABLE AS.

Listing C.13 Examples of SELECT INTO and CREATE TABLE

```
SELECT t.region_code
 , COUNT(t.gid) As cnt              <-- Cross-platform bulk insert
      INTO thingy_summary
     FROM things AS t
   GROUP BY t.region_code;

CREATE TABLE thingy_summary AS                <-- Less cross-platform way
      SELECT t.region_code, COUNT(t.gid) As cnt
         FROM things AS t
      GROUP BY t.region_code;
```

C.3.3 DELETE

When doing a DELETE, there are four basic forms: a simple delete that just involves one table, a medium delete that involves deleting data USING matching data in another table or subselect, and the NOT IN or IN approach, which utilizes a correlated or uncorrelated subquery. Finally, there's the TRUNCATE TABLE approach, which is the fastest and deletes all data in a table, but only works if your table has no related foreign-key constraints in other tables.

SIMPLE DELETE

A simple DELETE has no subselects but usually has a WHERE clause. All the data in a table is deleted and logged if you're missing a WHERE clause.

Following is an example of a standard DELETE:

```
DELETE FROM streets WHERE fe_name LIKE 'Mass%';
```

DELETE BASED ON DATA IN ANOTHER TABLE WITH USING

PostgreSQL has a USING clause that can be used in a DELETE. The USING clause denotes tables that should be used for filtering only, and not deleted from. Tables or subqueries that appear in the USING clause can be used in the WHERE clause of the DELETE.

In this next example, you first delete all streets in the current streets table that appear in the new_streets data set in preparation for reload:

```
DELETE FROM streets USING new_streets WHERE streets.tlid = new_streets.tlid;
```

DELETE WITH SUBSELECT IN WHERE

In PostgreSQL, as in many other relational databases, you can't use a JOIN in the FROM clause to determine what to delete based on another table. You can, however, overcome this restriction by either using a subselect in the WHERE clause or using the PostgreSQL-specific USING clause. The WHERE approach is more cross-platform and the one we'll demonstrate next. The subselect approach is useful for cases where you need to delete all data in your current table that's also in the table you're adding from, or you need to delete duplicate records.

The following example deletes duplicate records:

```
DELETE
    FROM sometable
    WHERE someuniquekey NOT IN
        (SELECT  MAX(dup.someuniquekey)
            FROM  sometable As dup
              WHERE dup.dupcolumn1 = sometable.dupcolumn1
                AND dup.column2 = sometable.dupcolumn2 A
                ND dup.column3 = sometable.dupcolumn3
            GROUP BY dup.dupcolumn1, dup.dupcolumn2, dup.dupcolum3);
```

TRUNCATE TABLE

In cases where you want to delete all the data in a table, you can use the much faster TRUNCATE TABLE statement. TRUNCATE TABLE is considerably faster because it does much less transaction logging than a standard DELETE FROM, but it can be used only in tables that aren't involved in foreign-key relationships. Here's an example of it at work:

```
TRUNCATE TABLE streets;
```

appendix D PostgreSQL features

In this appendix, we'll give you a taste of the uniqueness and versatility of PostgreSQL that makes it stand apart from the other databases you may be familiar with. This is by no means the extent of what is offered by PostgreSQL, and we encourage you to reference its very detailed and extensive manuals when you need to learn more about a specific feature.

D.1 What makes PostgreSQL special?

PostgreSQL has many features that are rarely found in other databases, and some of its features don't exist in *any* other databases. It also has perhaps the most extensible type and index architecture of any relational database. This extensible architecture is the main reason it was chosen as a vehicle to house PostGIS functionality.

D.1.1 PostgreSQL's unique features

PostgreSQL has features you'll rarely find in other databases. Here are the key ones that set it apart it from most other databases you may have worked with:

- *Support for using various languages to write database functions and triggers*—No open source or commercial database, to our knowledge, can compete with PostgreSQL in this regard. Commonly used languages are the built-in SQL, PL/pgSQL, and C. In addition, PL/Perl, PL/Python, PL/TCL, PL/SH, PL/R, and PL/Java are also often used. In PostgreSQL 9.2 and above, you may also find PL/V8 (a.k.a. PL/JavaScript). These require additional environment installs such as Perl, Python, TCL, Java, R, or the Google V8 engine. IBM DB2 and Microsoft SQL Server allow .NET functions, but this isn't quite as elegant as being able to write the code right in the database. Oracle supports PL/SQL, Java, and for an additional cost to enterprise customers, R (Oracle R Enterprise) via the Oracle Advanced Analytics Option module. In addition, the PostgreSQL PL platform is the most extensible of any database platform, making it easy to register new language handlers.
- *Support for arrays*—PostgreSQL, Oracle, and IBM DB2 are fairly unique among databases in that arrays are first-class citizens. In PostgreSQL, you can define any table column as comprising an array of strings, numbers, dates, geometries, rasters, or even your own data types. This comes in handy for

matrix-like analysis or aggregation. In addition, you can convert any single-column row list to an array, which is particularly useful when manipulating geometries and rasters.

- *Support for loosely defined (a.k.a. schemaless) structures*—PostgreSQL for a long time has had the `hstore` data type, which you can install with `CREATE EXTENSION hstore`. `hstore` is a key/value store type commonly used with GIS applications like OpenStreetMap. Examples of its use are shown in chapter 14. Not only can you create key/value structures from scratch, but you can convert any data row to an `hstore` key/value object and expand your `hstore` to a set of key/value rows. This makes it trivial to flip your data, converting columns to rows for easier consumption by applications.

  If a key/value store is too simple for your unstructured needs, PostgreSQL 9.2 introduced built-in support for the `json` data type, and PostgreSQL 9.3 added many more functions to support the `json` type. PostgreSQL 9.4 sweetened the JSON pot by introducing a binary JSON type called `jsonb`, with `gin` index bindings for more compact storage and much faster traversal of in-database `jsonb` columns. As with `hstore`, it's fairly trivial to morph database rows into JSON data structures right in the database for compact delivery to client applications. You can see this at work in chapter 17 with a PostgreSQL function that outputs queries as GeoJSON feature collections. In PostgreSQL 9.3+ and 9.4, you have the `hstore_to_json` and `hstore_to_jsonb` functions packaged with the hstore extension that allow you to convert `hstore` structures to `json/jsonb` structures.
- *Table inheritance*—PostgreSQL has a feature called *table inheritance*, which is something like object multi-inheritance. Table inheritance allows you to treat a whole set of tables as a single table, as well as define nested inheritance hierarchies. It's often used for table-partitioning strategies. Table inheritance is demonstrated in chapter 14.
- *Ability to define aggregate functions that take more than one column*—When you think of aggregates, you think of them as taking only one column as input. The multi-column feature isn't commonly exploited and thus is hard to visualize, but multicolumn aggregates have existed for some time in PostgreSQL. We have a couple of examples on our Postgres OnLine Journal site that demonstrate it: "How to create multi-column aggregates" (www.postgresonline.com/journal/archives/105-How-to-create-multi-column-aggregates.html) and "Making SVG plots with PLPython and multi-column aggregates" (www.postgresonline.com/journal/archives/107-PLPython.html).
- *Range types*—These were introduced in PostgreSQL 9.2, and they allow for defining expiration periods, scheduling periods as a table column, and being able to do fast overlaps and intersection checks with a very simple syntax. This allows for very sophisticated constraint keys, like ensuring two scheduled flights utilizing the same plane don't book the plane at intersecting times.

D.1.2 Basic enterprise features

In addition to its unique features, PostgreSQL also sports basic enterprise features that make managing mission-critical information easier:

- *Exceptional ANSI-SQL compliance, even compared to the commercial offerings*—If you're familiar with other relational database systems, you should feel at home using PostgreSQL.
- *A fairly sophisticated query planner and indexing support for complex objects*—The indexing support is good for optimizing intricate joins and aggregations without the need for hints. The speed is comparable to enterprise-class DBMSs for even the hairiest of SQL statements.
- *Ability to define new data types fairly easily*—You can define a new data type using the `CREATE TYPE` SQL construct.
- *Ability to update data via views*—You can write rules for relational views that handle inserts, updates, and deletes of data from these views. These rules can also handle non-single table and rollup views. PostgreSQL 9.1+ also supports triggers on views, where the triggers can be written in almost any supported language. PostgreSQL 9.3 introduced auto-updateable views that can be updated without triggers or rules. This feature is covered in chapter 14.
- *Advanced transactional support*—PostgreSQL uses a multiversion concurrency control system, which is the same model that Oracle and Microsoft SQL Server 2005+ use. It also has features such as transaction save points.
- *Thousands of built-in functions and extension libraries*—These are used for anything from string manipulation, regular expressions, and regression analysis to analyses of astronomical data.
- *Similarity to PL/SQL*—If you're coming from an Oracle background, you'll be surprised at how similar Oracle's PL/SQL language is to PostgreSQL's native PL/pgSQL. In addition to PL/pgSQL and numerous other languages, PostgreSQL has a built-in SQL function language, which other databases lack and which is much easier to write for simple set-returning or calculation functions. Unlike other language functions, an SQL function isn't a black box to the PostgreSQL planner, which means it can be incorporated in the plan strategy. The logic is frequently inlined in the query, similar to a macro in C. This often makes it more efficient than a PL/pgSQL or other language function, while still hiding the complexity from the person utilizing the function.
- *Ability to run on multiple platforms*—PostgreSQL is supported on Unix, Linux, Windows, Mac OS X, and various other OSs.
- *Ability to write functions with optional arguments*—This allows you to write a single function that has a default argument value if no value is passed in for that argument. So `getMyElephant('blue')` and `getMyElephant()` would use the same function, but `getMyElephant()` would use the default color defined in the function. PostgreSQL 9.0 extends the ways you can call functions by allowing a

named argument call notation similar to what you'll find in languages like VB and Python: `getMyElephant(color := 'blue')`.

PostGIS contains many functions with optional arguments to minimize the set of functions in the PostGIS code base. If it weren't for the default argument support, the PostGIS function list could easily be twice what it is now without providing any additional functionality.

- *Ability to write variadic functions*—PostgreSQL allows you to define variadic functions, which are functions that take an unspecified number of arguments of the same data type (http://en.wikipedia.org/wiki/Variadic_function). Functions of this type look very similar in definition to a function that takes an array of values, except the argument would be defined as `VARIADIC userargs text[]` instead of `userargs text[]`. Instead of passing an array to a variadic function, you'd pass the elements as separate arguments to the function. For example, a function that takes an array as an argument would be called like `myfunc('{hello,world}'::text[])` and `myfunc('{hello,world,how,are,you}'::text[])`, whereas comparable variadically defined function calls would be `myfunc('hello', 'world')` and `myfunc('hello','world','how', 'are', 'you')`. You'll see variadic functions employed by some PostGIS raster functions.

D.1.3 Advanced enterprise features

In addition to the basic enterprise features that PostgreSQL sports, it offers advanced enterprise features you'll rarely find in other open source databases. Some of these features are also more advanced than the equivalents in commercial database offerings:

- *Ability to easily write your own aggregate functions in almost any supported language, including SQL*—This feature is particularly useful for something like spatial analysis. The simplicity and ease of writing aggregates will come as a shock for those who have come from other databases that allow this but require immense amounts of code.
- *ANSI standard windowing functionality*—This was introduced in PostgreSQL 8.4 and further enhanced in 9.0–9.4. Many of the high-end commercial databases such as IBM DB2 and Oracle have had this functionality, and Microsoft SQL Server introduced it in SQL Server 2005. This functionality is useful for OLAP and data warehouse applications, and it's even more important for nearest-neighbor searches. In PostgreSQL 9.0 this feature was enhanced to include numbered `ROWRANGES`, thus coming closer to the capabilities of Oracle's windowing functionality and far surpassing the SQL Server 2012 windowing functionality. In PostgreSQL 9.4, new window functions were added, along with the `ORDERED SET (WITHIN GROUP)` construct (see www.depesz.com/2014/01/11/waiting-for-9-4-support-ordered-set-within-group-aggregates/).
- *Ability to create new window analytic functions*—Window analytic functions are functions like `ROW_NUMBER` and `RANK` that can apply operations across a window frame. PL/V8 and PL/R allow you to define new window analytic functions using

JavaScript or R. You can also build window analytic functions with C. Building window functions is a feature that is rare or nonexistent in most other databases.

- *Ability to write CTEs and recursive queries*—Recursive common table expressions (CTEs) for writing recursive queries (useful for navigating trees) and CTE functionality were introduced in PostgreSQL 8.4, enhanced in 9.1 to support updating, and further enhanced in 9.3 to allow their use in views. These are found in the popular high-end commercial databases. One important thing about CTEs is that PostgreSQL's implementation follows the ANSI SQL 2003 standard, so it's almost exactly what you'd write in Microsoft SQL Server and IBM DB2. Oracle has had its own nonstandard variant for hierarchical queries almost since its inception, called `CONNECT BY`. Oracle in its 11GR2 offering introduced ANSI-compliant recursive CTEs that follow the same CTE syntax as PostgreSQL, SQL Server, and IBM DB2. PostgreSQL 9.1 introduced writable CTEs that allow for including `UPDATE/INSERT` statements in a CTE and recursive CTE. MS SQL Server 2005+ has similar functionality.
- *Foreign data wrappers (FDWs)*—These were introduced in PostgreSQL 9.1 and further refined in PostgreSQL 9.2, 9.3, and the upcoming 9.5. FDWs are an ANSI standard feature not found in most other databases. They allow you to query external data sources like web services, other relational databases, and files as if they were local database tables.
- *Built-in warm standby and streaming replication*—This was introduced in PostgreSQL 9.0 and enhanced in later versions.
- *In-place upgrade*—This was introduced in PostgreSQL 8.4 and enhanced in later versions.

D.1.4 More features in PostgreSQL 9.3, 9.4, and coming in 9.5

PostgreSQL 9.3 and 9.4 introduced many more sort-after features, both for enterprise applications and for ease of use.

- `LATERAL` *ANSI standard construct*—Introduced in PostgreSQL 9.3, this feature is similar in concept to SQL Server's `CROSS APPLY` and `OUTER APPLY`. It allows you to use in a `JOIN` clause a function or subquery that changes based on a field value in the preceding table in the `FROM`. In prior versions, these clauses would have to be put in the `SELECT` and often required nested subqueries to maintain efficiency.
- *Recursive views*—An embellishment to the recursive CTEs is the ability to use them in a view definition.
- *Automatically updatable views*—PostgreSQL 9.3 introduced this feature, so simple views now are automatically updatable. PostgreSQL 9.4 improved on this feature with the `WITH CHECK OPTION` to prevent updates that would cause a record to no longer be visible in a view. This is covered in chapter 14.

- *Replication improvements*—PostgreSQL 9.3 introduced streaming-only remastering, which allows you to promote a slave to be a master even if that slave does not have physical access to the write-ahead logs of the original master. PostgreSQL 9.4 introduced replication slots notification, which allow standbys to provide information to the primary or upstream cascading standby. This allows you to keep fewer WAL logs because the primary doesn't need to guess how many WAL logs to keep around to ensure that all slaves are up to date.
- *Ability to query PostgreSQL databases*—PostgreSQL 9.3 introduced the PostgreSQL foreign data wrapper (FDW), which allows for querying and updating remote PostgreSQL servers.
- *Materialized views via the new* `CREATE MATERIALIZED VIEW` *construct*—This is very useful for those expensive rollup views. PostgreSQL 9.3 introduced the feature, and PostgreSQL 9.4 improved on it with the `REFRESH VIEW CONCURRENTLY` option, which allows the view to be readable while data is being reloaded.
- *Improved ability to work with and create JSON objects*—PostgreSQL 9.3 introduced more JSON functions, such as `json_populate_record`, `json_populate_recordset`, and `json_each`.
- *Ability to update other remote data sources*—Writeable FDW API support allows FDW developers to build in logic to update foreign tables. This feature is employed by the commonly packaged `postgres_fdw` and other FDWs such as `hadoop_fdw`, an FDW for querying and updating Hadoop data sources, and `cstore`, which is a column data store implemented as an FDW.

  PostgreSQL 9.5 enhances the FDW API further with the ANSI-SQL–compliant `IMPORT FOREIGN SCHEMA` API addition for pulling in a set of tables from a foreign data source.

D.2 Useful PostgreSQL resources

In this section, you'll find a list of key PostgreSQL resources that cover general PostgreSQL usage as well as add-on tools and performance.

D.2.1 General resources

The following resources provide tips for using PostgreSQL features:

- *PostgreSQL wiki* (http://wiki.postgresql.org/wiki/Main_Page)—User-contributed articles about various PostgreSQL topics ranging from administration, performance tuning, and writing queries to using PostgreSQL in various application and programming environments. Check out the code snippets repository for lots of useful PostgreSQL functions that you can copy and paste into your database (http://wiki.postgresql.org/wiki/Category:Snippets).
- *Planet PostgreSQL* (www.planetpostgresql.org/)—A blogroll of PostgreSQL-specific blogs. Learn from hard-core long-time PostgreSQL users about how to get the most out of PostgreSQL. Also learn what's new and hot in PostgreSQL.

- *Our Postgres OnLine Journal blog/journal* (www.postgresonline.com)—We try to cater to new PostgreSQL users, programmers, and database users coming from other database systems such as MySQL, SQL Server, or Oracle.
- *PostgreSQL main site* (www.postgresql.org)—You can download the source from here as well as get flash news. You can also download the manual in PDF form or leaf through the HTML version online. The manual is huge and consists of five volumes.
- *PostgreSQL books* (www.postgresql.org/docs/books)—A fairly recent couple of books on PostgreSQL are written by 2ndQuadrant consultants who are major contributors to PostgreSQL. We've also written one on PostgreSQL 9.2 that you'll find listed. Other PostgreSQL books are also listed here.

D.2.2 PostgreSQL-specific tools

The following are PostgreSQL-specific tools for administering, loading, and exporting data:

- *Psql, pg_dump, pg_dump_all, and pg_restore (packaged with PostgreSQL)*—These are command-line utilities for querying, backing up, and restoring PostgreSQL databases. You can get them from your Linux or Mac OS X distribution or from EnterpriseDB one-click installers, or you can download the source from the PostgreSQL core site and compile them yourself.
- *PgAdmin III* (www.pgadmin.org)—Comes packaged with PostgreSQL, but binaries and source can be downloaded separately if you need to install it on a workstation without a PostgreSQL server. It's also available via the common OS distributions.
- *PhpPgAdmin* (http://phppgadmin.sourceforge.net/)—A PHP web-based database administration tool for PostgreSQL, patterned after phpMyAdmin.

D.3 Connecting to a PostgreSQL server

Before you can create a spatial database (or any database, for that matter), you need to be able to log in to your PostgreSQL server via pgAdmin III or psql. In this section, we'll cover the basics along with the most common problems and how to work around them.

D.3.1 Core configuration files

If you're starting out and have just installed your PostgreSQL server, you'll want to pay attention to the postgresql.conf and pg_hba.conf files, which are both located in the data cluster of your installation.

LOCATION OF DATA CLUSTER

PostgreSQL has a data cluster that determines the default location for new data, and it's also where you'll find many of the configuration files. The location of this folder is not consistent across OSs and is also user-configurable. Following are some suggestions about how to determine your data cluster location:

- For Windows users, this is the data directory you're prompted for during install. If you don't change it, the location is C:\Program Files\PostgreSQL\9.2\data.
- For other users, you likely had to do an `initdb`, and the path you gave to the `-D` option is the location of the data cluster. Alternatively, the location may have been set by your distribution via a sysconfig file, which is generally located at /etc/sysconfig/pgsql/postgresql-9.2, where 9.2 is the PostgreSQL minor version number.

THE POSTGRESQL.CONF FILE

The postgresql.conf file is the most important configuration file. It contains all the memory configurations and defaults, as well as the listening addresses and ports. If you're running multiple versions of PostgreSQL or just multiple instances, you need to have them listening on different ports or different addresses, or the first one to start will prevent others from starting. You can have multiple instances sharing the same binaries as long as they have a different data cluster, but in practice that's rarely done.

The two settings of most importance for getting started are `listen_addresses` and `port`.

If you want to allow your server to be accessed by remote computers without the need for SSH tunneling, then set `listen_addresses` as follows:

```
listen_addresses = '*'      # what IP address(es) to listen on;
                            # comma-separated list of addresses;
                            # defaults to 'localhost', '*' = all
                            # (change requires restart)
```

The port setting defaults to 5432, but if you want to run multiple PostgreSQL services, you'll need to set each one differently. For example, we run PostgreSQL 8.2, 8.3, and 8.4 on our servers for testing. We have our port for 8.4 set to something like this:

```
port = 5434
```

We discuss some of the other important settings in the postgresql.conf file in chapter 15.

> **PostgreSQL 9.4 postgresql.auto.conf**
>
> PostgreSQL 9.4 introduced an `ALTER SYSTEM` SQL construct, which largely eliminates the need to manually change the postgresql.conf file. All `ALTER SYSTEM` changes are recorded in a new file called postgresql.auto.conf, and whatever settings are found in this file supersede whatever is set in postgresql.conf.

THE PG_HBA.CONF FILE

The pg_hba.conf file controls which users on which IP address ranges can connect to the PostgreSQL service/daemon, as well as which authentication scheme is allowed for them. Examples of lines you'll find and can add are detailed in the PostgreSQL Manual's pg-hba-conf section (www.postgresql.org/docs/current/static/auth-pg-hba-conf.html).

D.3.2 Launching psql

If you're using a Linux server with just a command-line console (which is standard for most production web and app servers), you'll need to use psql at least once on the server to get everything rolling.

From the server, do the following to verify that you can connect:

```
psql -h localhost -U postgres
```

If you can't connect, refer to section D.3.4, which discusses connection difficulties.

D.3.3 Launching pgAdmin III

For new users, we highly recommend the pgAdmin III GUI. If you installed PostgreSQL using one of the one-click desktop installers, pgAdmin III is usually included. On Windows you can find it under Start > Programs > PostgreSQL 89.4 > pgAdmin III. For Linux distributions, the path varies.

You can also install pgAdmin III on a regular desktop PC that doesn't have a PostgreSQL server installed. Download one of the available binaries from the pgAdmin download site: www.pgadmin.org/download/.

For versions of pgAdmin III 1.10 and above, you can also launch psql for that specific database within pgAdmin III. This is useful for taking advantage of special psql features, like redirecting output to files or importing data from files.

To access psql from pgAdmin III, follow these steps:

1. Select the database.
2. Under the Plug-ins icon, choose psql. If the wrong version of psql launches, you can change it in the plugins.ini file in the pgAdmin III install folder, or by changing the bin location in the Options tab. This is discussed briefly in the article, "PgAdmin III Plug-in Registration: PostGIS Shapefile and DBF Loader," on the Postgres OnLine Journal (www.postgresonline.com/journal/archives/145-PgAdmin-III-Plug-in-Registration-PostGIS.html).

In pgAdmin III 1.13 and above, the plug-in architecture has changed a bit to allow easier adding of more plug-ins without affecting prior or distributed ones. Instead of a single plugins.ini file, there's a plugins.d folder where you can put all the INIs for your plug-ins. These INIs can be given descriptive names. We discuss this change in our article, "PgAdmin III 1.13 - Change in Plugin Architecture and PostGIS Plugins," at www.postgresonline.com/journal/archives/180-PgAdmin-III-1.13-change-in-plugin.html, which also covers registering more custom plug-ins.

D.3.4 Connection difficulties

If you're connecting to the server from a separate desktop PC, then the server needs to listen on one or more IP addresses and should allow remote connections. After making the required changes to configuration files, you must restart the PostgreSQL service. On Windows, you go into Services Manager and restart.

On Linux, if you installed PostgreSQL as a service, which is usually the case if you installed from Yum, apt-get, or a one-click installer, you can usually enter the following from a shell prompt: `psql -d somedb`.

CONNECTION REFUSED

The most common error you'll get when trying to connect to a PostgreSQL server is a connection-refused message, when you try to do the following:

```
service postgresql restart
```

If you get an error in pgAdmin III like this,

```
could not connect to server: Connection refused (0x0000274D/10061)
Is the server running on host "blah blah blah"
and accepting TCP/IP connections on port 5432?
```

then most likely you have one of the following problems:

- Your PostgreSQL server is not started.
- Your PostgreSQL server service is only listening on localhost or a non-accessible IP address.
- Your PostgreSQL server is not listening on the port you think it's listening on.
- Your firewall is getting in the way. Generally for firewall issues you can set up an SSH tunnel, which we describe briefly in our article, "Putty for SSH Tunneling to PostgreSQL Server" (www.postgresonline.com/journal/archives/38-PuTTY-for-SSH-Tunneling-to-PostgreSQL.html). Some third-party PostgreSQL tools also have SSH tunneling built in. Newer versions of pgAdmin III have SSH tunneling.

NO ENTRY IN PG_HBA.CONF

If you get a no-entry error, this means your pg_hba.conf file isn't configured correctly for remote connections or contains errors. We generally set our configuration to something like the example pg_hba.conf in listing D.1 and allow all local connections to be trusted. This means that if you connect from the local machine, you don't need to provide a password, only a valid PostgreSQL username. If you're very security conscious, you could leave out the `trust` line and require `md5` or some other security scheme. To make connecting a bit easier, you can set up a .pgpass file, which we'll discuss shortly.

Listing D.1 Example pg_hba.conf—trust all local connections

```
# TYPE  DATABASE     USER         CIDR-ADDRESS           METHOD

# IPv4 local connections:
host    all          all          127.0.0.1/32           trust
# IPv6 local connections:
#host   all          all          ::1/128                md5
host    all          all          0.0.0.0/0              md5
```

Keep in mind that the order of these statements is important because PostgreSQL will check each one in order and apply the first matching rule that meets the credentials of the person trying to connect. This means that if you accidentally put the 0.0.0.0/0 MD5 rule above all the others, you'll have to provide a password even when connecting locally.

D.3.5 Enabling advanced administration for pgAdmin III

In order to be able to do administration tasks via pgAdmin III from a remote computer, you need to run adminpack.sql first, which is located in the contrib folder of your PostgreSQL install or can be installed in PostgreSQL 9.1+ using `CREATE EXTENSION`.

Run the following command from the command line or via pgAdmin III after connecting to the postgres database. This extension should be installed in the postgres database:

```
CREATE EXTENSION adminpack;
```

From then on, to access the administrative postgresql.conf and pg_hba.conf files from within pgAdmin from any desktop, do the following:

1. Register the server in pgAdmin III.
2. Choose Tools > Server Configuration. You should see both config files there.

D.4 Controlling access to data

There are two parts to access control in PostgreSQL. First, you can control who can log in and how they can log in, which you saw a glimpse of earlier. Then, once a person is logged in, you can control what kind of data can be accessed, created, deleted, and edited.

D.4.1 Connection rules

The connection rules are controlled by three files:

- *Postgresql.conf*—This file controls on which ports and IP addresses the server listens and whether a Secure Socket Layer (SSL) connection is required. For LDAP-like connectivity, it also holds information such as the Kerberos settings to use to connect to a Kerberos authenticating server.
- *Pgpass.conf or .pgpass*—This is a local configuration file that stores the usernames, server, and passwords for the database that you connect with. If you're using pgAdmin, then pgAdmin creates this for you automatically, and you can export its contents using the File > Open pgpass.conf menu option. Under Windows, this file generally exists in %APPDATA%\postgresql\pgpass.conf, and on Linux and Unix systems the file is called .pgpass and should be in ~/.pgpass. This file will be used by psql, pg_dump, and pg_restore to automatically log you into a PostgreSQL server without prompting for a username or password. A pgpass file is useful to have if you don't have trust enabled and you need to schedule backup jobs and the like. Keep in mind that the file must exist under the account doing the work, so if you're doing backups under a service account

such as `postgres` or `Administrator`, then you'll need to copy the file into the respective home directories of these accounts.

- *Pg_hba.conf*—This file controls whether people can connect based on their IP range and specifies what kind of authentication is required for each connection. Common authentication schemes include the following:
  - `md5`—MD5 encryption; what most people use, particularly for web apps.
  - `trust`—Ignores the password. Never use this except in a tightly secured local network, or on a local PC that has good firewall protection against IP spoofers or that listens only on a local port.
  - `ident`—Trusts a user based on their local identity determined by the OS. Again, this is generally used only for local authentication.
  - `reject`—This kind of authentication doesn't allow you to authenticate. You use this if you want to ban certain IP ranges or everyone who isn't on your network but who would otherwise be allowed by a broader IP range rule. In such cases, you'd put this rule above the broader rule so that it's resolved first.

  The following are less common schemes, but they're particularly useful if you're in an enterprise network using LDAP or Active Directory (there are even more, such as PAM and some others):
  - `krb4/5`—Kerberos connection. This is deprecated; don't use it.
  - `sspi`—Supported only on Windows and requires the PostgreSQL server to be running on Windows. It's designed for connecting via Windows or NT authentication. It sits on top of Kerberos.
  - `gss`—Industry-defined protocol similar to SSPI but doesn't require a Windows server; it sits on top of Kerberos.
  - `ldap`—Authentication via an LDAP directory service such as Active Directory or Novel directory service. The user must exist in the PostgreSQL server, but the password verification uses LDAP.
  - `pg_ident.conf`—Allows you to map an authenticated user to a database-defined user/login. For example, you might want `root` to log in as `postgres`.

D.4.2 Users and groups (roles)

The PostgreSQL security model from PostgreSQL 8.1+ is composed of roles, and roles sit on the server level, not the database level. Prior versions of PostgreSQL had groups and users instead of roles.

Roles can inherit from each other, can have login rights, and can contain other member roles. A user is a role with login rights. Unlike most databases, PostgreSQL doesn't make a distinction between a user and a group. You can easily morph a user into a group by adding members to the roles. Roles are all there is.

In a relational database system, you create users (roles) and grant rights using a kind of SQL called Data Control Language (DCL). DCL varies significantly from one database product to another because of the idiosyncrasies in how each database manages security. There are ANSI SQL standards dictating the syntax, but these are less frequently followed than those for Data Manipulation Language (DML) and Data Definition Language (DDL). PostgreSQL does try to follow the standard as much as possible, but it also deviates, like most relational databases. In this section, we'll go over PostgreSQL security concepts and also demonstrate PostgreSQL's specific dialect of DCL. In terms of roles, Oracle is probably closest in syntax to PostgreSQL.

The general user database concepts and their equivalents in PostgreSQL are listed in table D.1.

Table D.1 PostgreSQL role concepts and parallels to other databases

General concept	PostgreSQL equivalent
User (login)	A role with login rights that generally contains no member roles.
Group	A role with member roles. This kind of role generally has no login rights.
Database user	A role with the ability to grant rights to a database object.
Sys DBA	A role that has `SUPERUSER` rights.
Public	The built-in role that all authenticated users belong to. SQL Server has such a role too, and it's also called `Public`.

There also exist ANSI standard information_schema tables for interrogating roles, privileges, and so forth, but each DBMS we've worked on arbitrarily implements the ones they prefer in this regard, to the point that relying on any of the role-/privilege-based tables in information_schema is not very portable between DBMSs.

D.4.3 *Rights management*

PostgreSQL roles can contain and be contained by many other roles. In other words, each role/user/group can have many parents or belong to many groups. Roles in PostgreSQL don't necessarily inherit rights from their parent roles, which is a cause of confusion for many people. We'll go over this shortly.

CORE SERVER RIGHTS

A role can have core rights that are granted at the server level. These rights are not inheritable, so if you add a user to a group role with these rights, that user won't by default be able to do these things even if you mark them as inheriting from their roles. To relinquish these rights, prefix them with `NO`, such as `NOSUPERUSER` or `NOINHERIT`.

A list of core server rights follows:

- `SUPERUSER`—Has superpowers (to relinquish superuser rights, use `NOSUPERUSER`).
- `INHERIT`—When marked as `INHERIT`, the role inherits the rights of its parent roles. This is the default behavior in PostgreSQL.

- CREATEDB—This gives a role the ability to create a database.
- CREATEROLE—This gives a role the ability to create other roles that are not superuser roles and that it's not a member of. Only a superuser can create other superusers.
- LOGIN—This gives the role rights to log in. Generally speaking, people create group roles by not giving the group role rights to log in, though in theory you can have a group role that has rights to log in. In practice, having group roles that can log in is confusing, so pgAdmin prevents you from doing this via the GUI interface.

ROLES AND SUPERPOWERS

People often mistakenly assume that a member of a role with superpowers always has superpowers. This is never the case, because SUPERUSER rights and the other aforementioned core server rights are never inheritable. This prevents you from causing damage by adding a user to a group. When your boss demands, "I need the power to do everything," as bosses often demand, you can nod and say, "I've added you to a group that has the power to do everything," and blissfully walk away.

The following exercise demonstrates this superuser without superuser powers:

```
CREATE ROLE office_of_president SUPERUSER;

CREATE ROLE regina INHERIT LOGIN PASSWORD 'queen';
GRANT office_of_president TO regina;

CREATE ROLE leo LOGIN PASSWORD 'lion king' SUPERUSER;
```

This simple script creates a group called office_of_president with two users, leo and regina. Leo has superuser rights, and Regina is a member of a group that has superuser rights. Leo is always omnipotent. Regina is only omnipotent when she summons her powers of omnipotence. We'll demonstrate this with two scenarios.

First, Leo logs in and creates a database called kingdom by running this command:

```
CREATE DATABASE kingdom;
```

He is successful.

Then Regina logs in and tries to create a database called fortress:

```
CREATE DATABASE fortress;
```

She gets this message:

```
ERROR: permission denied to create database
```

She's frustrated. She's a member of the mighty role of office_of_president and she's marked as inheriting rights. She must be able to create a database, but how?

First, recall that SUPERUSER rights are never inheritable, but they can be summoned. Regina summons her powers of office_of_president and then creates the database:

```
SET ROLE office_of_president;
CREATE DATABASE fortress;
```

Now she succeeds.

Being dissatisfied with this state of affairs, she summons her powers to put things into order:

```
SET ROLE office_of_president;
ALTER ROLE leo NOSUPERUSER;
ALTER ROLE regina SUPERUSER;
```

Now Leo is powerless, and Regina is always omnipotent without the need to summon superpowers.

TO INHERIT OR NOT TO INHERIT

One thing that makes PostgreSQL stand out from other databases is this idea of `INHERIT` and `NOINHERIT`, as well as the fact that, as we mentioned earlier, some rights are never inheritable. You can define a user that belongs to many groups but does not inherit the permissions of those groups. This little idiosyncrasy dumbfounds people because they often accidentally mark login roles as not inheriting rights from the parent roles and then scratch their heads when the user complains that they can't do anything.

Why would anyone ever create a user that doesn't inherit rights from its membership groups?

One reason is for testing. Let's imagine that you created a user that's a member of every single group role under the sun, but that user (login role) doesn't inherit rights from any role it's a member of. What can this user do? It can, for a specific session, promote itself to have the rights of any role it's a member of, much like Regina promoted herself to the rights of her powerful group. This can be useful for testing different membership rights or for giving a user only certain rights within an application. As we also demonstrated earlier, this prevents you from doing superuser damage without trying to deliberately do superuser damage.

SESSION AUTHORIZATION

`SET SESSION AUTHORIZATION` is similar to `SET ROLE`, but the distinction is that in `SET ROLE` you summon your powers as a member of a role, whereas with `SET SESSION AUTHORIZATION` you become that role. Basically you're impersonating another user.

Only a superuser can impersonate another user, but any member of a role can do a `SET ROLE` to the roles of which they're a member. Impersonation is useful when you're creating a bunch of objects that you want to be owned by a specific user without having to change ownership to that person for each creation. Another example would be when you want to run commands but limit yourself to the rights that user has, just to verify what a user can do.

GRANTING RIGHTS TO OBJECTS

As with other databases, PostgreSQL allows you to grant rights to specific objects in a database. The database owner or the owner of an object can grant rights to others, and in addition to granting rights to objects, they can give others the right to grant rights to objects using `WITH GRANT OPTION`.

GRANT, as you saw in the previous examples, is also used to add a user to a group role. If a user is granted rights to a role WITH ADMIN OPTION, then the user can add or remove users to or from that role.

Listing D.2 lists the common GRANT usages.

Listing D.2 Common GRANT options

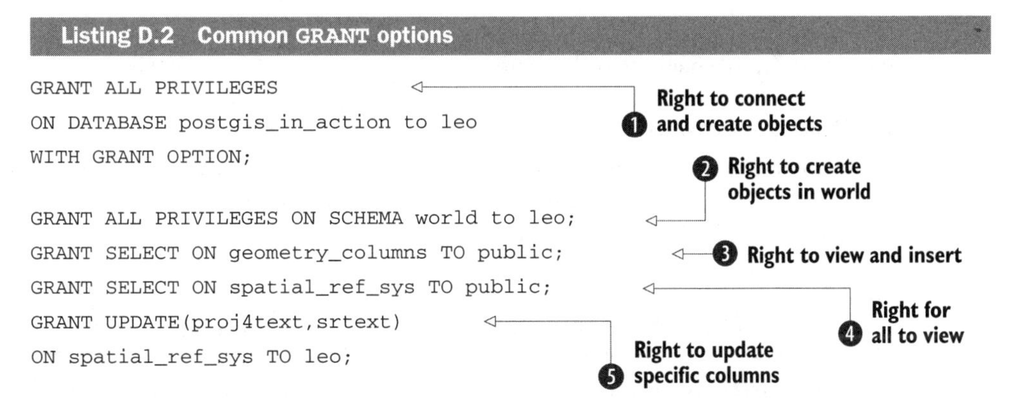

GRANT ALL PRIVILEGES
ON DATABASE postgis_in_action to leo
WITH GRANT OPTION;
GRANT ALL PRIVILEGES ON SCHEMA world to leo;
GRANT SELECT ON geometry_columns TO public;
GRANT SELECT ON spatial_ref_sys TO public;
GRANT UPDATE(proj4text,srtext)
ON spatial_ref_sys TO leo;
1 Right to connect and create objects
2 Right to create objects in world
3 Right to view and insert
4 Right for all to view
5 Right to update specific columns

This listing first grants all rights to Leo for the database and also allows him to give grant rights to whomever he chooses ❶, but this only means that Leo can connect to the database and create new schemas. It doesn't give him the right to view existing tables, for example, or to create objects in schemas for which he doesn't have rights.

Next, Leo is given all rights to the world schema ❷. This doesn't allow him to view or edit existing data, but it does allow him to create new objects in world.

The next few lines give Leo the right to view and add data in geometry_columns but not to update or delete ❸, give everyone the right to view data in spatial_ref_sys ❹, and give Leo the right to update the proj4text and srtext columns in spatial_ref_sys ❺.

This is all good and fine if you only have a couple of tables to contend with, but as you add more tables and objects to your database, this quickly becomes unmanageable. Luckily PostgreSQL 9.0+ introduced new management constructs: ALTER DEFAULT PRIVILEGES IN SCHEMA *some_schema* allows you to grant privileges for future objects, and GRANT .. ON ALL .. IN SCHEMA *someschema* allows you to grant privileges on all existing objects of a type in a specific schema.

To use these, you would do something of this form:

```
GRANT USAGE ON SCHEMA fortress TO leo;
GRANT ALL ON ALL TABLES IN SCHEMA fortress TO leo;
ALTER DEFAULT PRIVILEGES IN SCHEMA fortress
    GRANT ALL ON TABLES TO leo;
```

REVOKING RIGHTS

You can revoke rights just as easily as you can grant rights. You revoke rights with the REVOKE command. The REVOKE command is used to revoke any kind of permission that's granted with the GRANT command.

Our favorite REVOKE command involves revoking connection rights from the Public group. As we mentioned, the Public group is the group that everyone belongs to and that, in general, most databases allow connect access to when created. What this means is that any authenticated user can connect to the database and browse the structure of the tables. This isn't always desirable. To prevent this, you can run the following command:

```
REVOKE CONNECT ON DATABASE postgis_in_action FROM public;
```

Now that we've covered the basics of security, we'll cover something perhaps even more important: backup and restore.

D.5 Backup and restore

PostgreSQL has perhaps the richest backup and restore tools of any open source database, and they rival and often surpass those offered by commercial relational database systems.

Backing up is accomplished with the following tools:

- *Pg_dump*—This can do custom compressed backups, SQL backups, as well as selective backups of schemas and other objects all in a single command line. SQL backups are restored with psql, and compressed and tar backups are restored with pg_restore. PostgreSQL 9.3 introduced parallel backups, which write to a directory rather than a single tar or custom backup file and can parallelize the backup process for much speedier backups.
- *Pg_dumpall*—This does only SQL backups and system server configuration backups, such as backups of users, tablespaces, and the like. It can also do a whole backup of the server—all databases included. The backup is a regular SQL backup, so it doesn't allow the selective restore that's possible with pg_dump. Backups done with pg_dumpall are restored with psql.
- *Pg_basebackup*—This does a filesystem data cluster backup. This is generally the preferred way of creating a consistent snapshot of your whole server instance (in lieu of the very verbose pg_dumpall). The backup created by pg_basebackup is usually a compressed tar file. This kind of backup is also used for building slave servers.

For restoring data, PostgreSQL comes packaged with psql and pg_restore:

- *Pg_restore*—This is used for restoring compressed and tar backups created with pg_dump. Pg_restore will allow you to restore select objects and also to generate a

> **Improvements to pg_restore in 8.4**
>
> In PostgreSQL 8.4, pg_restore was enhanced to include a `jobs=` option. This option is particularly useful for large backups and defines the number of parallel threads used to do a restore. If you back up a database with PostgreSQL 8.4+ pg_dump, then you can specify `jobs=2` or more. This does a parallel restore. Depending on your disk I/O and CPU, setting this can reduce the time of a restore by half or more. For example, a restore of a PostGIS 800 GB database would take about 12 hours in prior versions and only 6 hours or less in version 8.4.

list of objects backed up in a backup. You can then edit this list to fine-tune what you'd like to restore from the backup.

- *Psql*—This is used for restoring or running an SQL file, such as those generated by pg_dumpall or pg_dump when SQL mode is chosen or by the PostGIS shp2pgsql shapefile import tool.

Next we'll look at the various backup and restore commands you can use with the PostgreSQL pg_restore, pg_dump, and psql tools.

D.5.1 Backup

The pg_dump command-line tool packaged with PostgreSQL is our preferred tool for database backups. It creates a nice compressed backup and allows for selective restore of objects. Most of the time, a restore is needed because a user accidentally destroyed data, and in those cases you don't want to have to restore the whole database.

The following listing shows some common pg_dump and pg_dumpall statements used for backing up data.

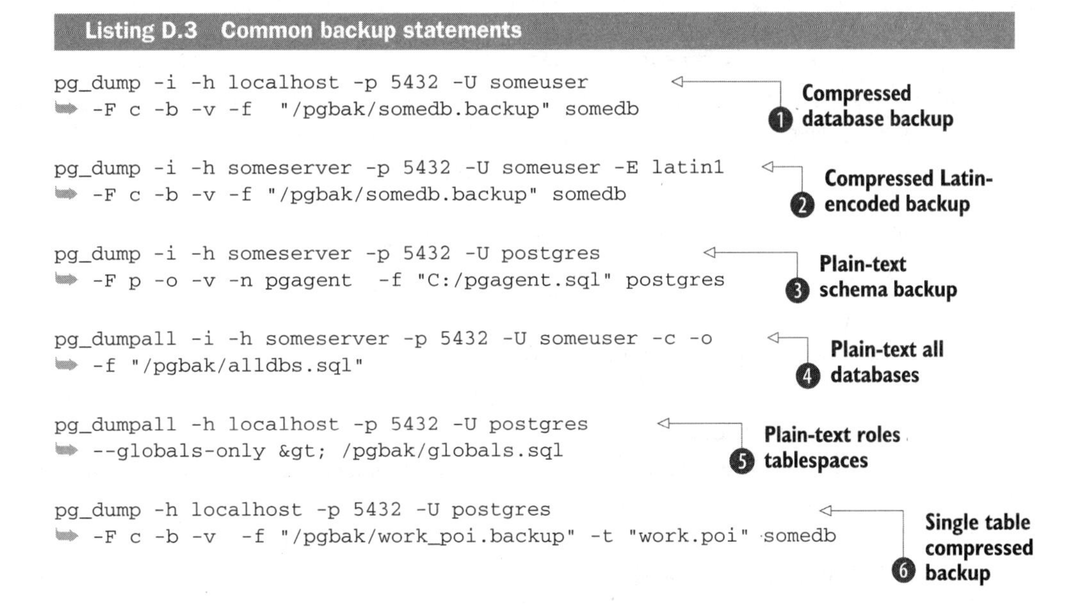

Listing D.3 Common backup statements

```
pg_dump -i -h localhost -p 5432 -U someuser
➥ -F c -b -v -f  "/pgbak/somedb.backup" somedb

pg_dump -i -h someserver -p 5432 -U someuser -E latin1
➥ -F c -b -v -f "/pgbak/somedb.backup" somedb

pg_dump -i -h someserver -p 5432 -U postgres
➥ -F p -o -v -n pgagent  -f "C:/pgagent.sql" postgres

pg_dumpall -i -h someserver -p 5432 -U someuser -c -o
➥ -f "/pgbak/alldbs.sql"

pg_dumpall -h localhost -p 5432 -U postgres
➥ --globals-only &gt; /pgbak/globals.sql

pg_dump -h localhost -p 5432 -U postgres
➥ -F c -b -v  -f "/pgbak/work_poi.backup" -t "work.poi" somedb
```


The preceding listing shows several backup variations:

- Dump the database in compressed format; include BLOB and show verbose progress (-v) ❶
- Dump the database in Latin1 encoding, which is useful if you want to restore a database but want to use a different encoding in the new database ❷
- Back up the pgagent schema or any schema of the Postgres DB in plain-text copy format, and maintain object identifiers (oids) ❸
- Dump all databases—note that pg_dumpall can only output to plain text ❹

- Back up users/roles and tablespaces ❺
- Back up a single table in compressed format ❻

D.5.2 Restore

In order to restore a backup of PostgreSQL, you use pg_restore to restore compressed and tar backups, and you use psql to restore SQL backups. If you have a compressed or tar backup, you can use pg_restore to restore select portions of a backup file.

The following listing demonstrates some common restore examples.

Listing D.4 Common restore statements

```
psql -h localhost -p 5432 -U postgres
➥ -c "CREATE DATABASE somedb"
pg_restore -h localhost -p 5432 -U postgres
➥ --dbname=somedb --jobs=2 /pgbak/somedb.backup
pg_restore --schema=us --dbname=somedb
➥ -U postgres /pgbak/somedb.backup
pg_restore --list /pgbak/somedb.backup
➥ --file=/pgbak/somedb_list.txt
psql -h localhost -p 5432 -U postgres -d postgres
➥ -f /pgbak/globals.sql
pg_restore -h localhost -p 5432 -U postgres
➥ -t "work.poi" /pgbak/somedb.backup
```

❶ Create database and restore backup
❷ Restore specific schema
❸ Generate table of contents
❹ Restore plain-text backup
❺ Restore single table

The preceding listing shows several restore variations:

- Create a new database and restore the backup file to this new database using two threads for restore ❶.
- Restore only a specific schema, in this case the us schema ❷.
- Generate a table of contents for a backup file and store it in the file somedb_list.txt ❸.
- Restore user accounts and custom table spaces. You can specify any SQL file here, such as the one created to back up all databases ❹.
- Restore a single table from backup. In this case, you're restoring the poi table in the work schema ❺.

In the next section, we'll provide some tips for automating the backup process.

D.5.3 Setting up automated jobs for backup

There are two common ways of automating backups for PostgreSQL, and they vary slightly depending on your OS:

- Use an OS-specific scheduling agent, such as cronjob in Unix/Linux or Windows Scheduler in Windows.
- Use pgAgent, a free scheduling agent for PostgreSQL, manageable from pgAdmin III.

We prefer the pgAgent method because it's cross-platform, it allows us to manage backups the same way we manage and view other parts of PostgreSQL (via the pgAdmin III tool), and it's also designed for running SQL jobs. On the downside, it's sometimes more finicky to set up. We describe the details of the setup and also how to define a backup script for Windows and Linux in our article, "Setting Up PgAgent and Doing Scheduled Backups," on the Postgres OnLine Journal at www.postgresonline.com/journal/index.php?/archives/19-Setting-up-PgAgent-and-Doing-Scheduled-Backup. html.

Note that because the backup scripts use only shell commands for their respective Unix/Linux/Windows environments, you can also run them with your scheduling agent of choice.

D.6 Data structures and objects

PostgreSQL, like many sophisticated relational databases, has a rich collection of objects you can use to accomplish different tasks. In addition to database objects, it has built-in data types, many of which you'll find in other relational databases, as well as some data types that are unique to it. As if that isn't enough, PostgreSQL allows you to extend the system and define new data types to suit your needs. The PostGIS family of data types is an extension of the core set. In this section, we'll go over all this.

D.6.1 PostgreSQL objects

When we speak of *objects*, we're not talking about data types but rather about a set of objects of which a data type is one type. Data types are used to define columns in a table, but objects are part of the core makeup of PostgreSQL. Objects are tables, views, schemas, data types, columns, foreign data wrappers, extensions, and so on. Some of these you've already been exposed to.

The following list gives a brief synopsis of the core PostgreSQL objects and their functions:

- *Server service/daemon*—This is PostgreSQL itself, which houses everything.
- *Tablespaces*—These are physical locations of data that map to a named location in the server. When you run out of disk space, objects can be moved to different locations on disks by moving them to a different tablespace. You can define the default for these by setting the Global User Control (GUC) variables `default_tablespace` and `temp_tablespace`. These can even be set at the user level so that you can control the disk space used by groups of users or use fast non-redundant disks for temporary tables and so forth. It's also fast and easy to move even a single table to a different tablespace using pgAdmin or with the SQL command `ALTER TABLE sometable SET TABLESPACE newtablespace`. We describe this in our article, "Managing Disk Space Using Tablespaces": www.postgresonline.com/journal/index.php?/archives/123-Managing-disk-space-using-table-spaces.html.

- *Database*—Both a physical and a logical entity, a database has a root folder in the filesystem, and database data in any tablespace is always stored in a folder, such as <tablespace path>/<databaseoid>/objectoid.
- *Schemas*—These are the logical locations of tables, views, and functions. They have no relation to physical location, but SQL statements reference the logical name, and you can control the default schemas at the server, database, or user levels in PostgreSQL 8.2+. In PostgreSQL 8.3+ you can also control the default at the function level via the `search_path` configuration. This allows you to maintain a logical separation without having to schema-qualify commonly used schemas. Think of a schema as a database within the database. The first schema in the `search_path` is the one where new objects are created by a user. If you have two objects with the same name in different schemas, and you reference them without qualifying the schema, the first one in the search path will be chosen.
- *Roles*—These include users and groups. They sit at the database level and are granted rights to objects in a database.
- *Rules*—Rules rewrite `SELECT`, `INSERT`, and `UPDATE` statements. They're unique to PostgreSQL and serve a purpose similar to triggers. In some cases, such as the way PostgreSQL implements views, rules are the only option.
- *Views*—Views are virtual tables. They are windows to the real data and allow you to see summaries or a subset of data by selecting from an abstracted virtual table. A view generally consists of only an `INSTEAD OF SELECT` rule, which is a rule that defines the `SELECT` statement of the view. An updatable view will also have rules on the `UPDATE`, `INSERT`, and `DELETE` actions of a view.
- *Triggers*—Triggers are actions that are performed when data changes. They're often used to update additional data. A common example in PostGIS would be if you have an application that updates a lon/lat field and uses a trigger to update the geometry field when these values change. You may have another trigger to store a line in a separate table when points are added to one table.
- *Data types*—Data types are the micro-storage structure of data, and their definitions can comprise other data types. Table columns are composed of things with the same data type. The rows of a table itself are implemented in PostgreSQL as a composite data type. You'll notice when you look at the list of types in a database with a tool like pgAdmin III that every PostgreSQL table has a corresponding type with the same name as the table.
- *Casts*—Casts are the objects that allow you to implicitly or explicitly convert from one data type to another. PostgreSQL is fairly distinctive among relational databases in that it allows you to define the casting behavior for your custom-created data types. If an implicit cast is in place (a cast with no qualification), and if there's an unambiguous autocast type, then when data of a specific data type is fed to a function that expects a different data type, the data will be automatically cast for you. Take care when doing this. Because of the overloading features of PostgreSQL, it's possible to have two functions with the same name

but different data types. In this case, if an object that has an autocast for both is used without an explicit casting, you'll get an "ambiguous" error. You do an explicit `CAST` by using the ANSI SQL–compliant `CAST(mybox As geometry)` or the PostgreSQL non-ANSI SQL–specific shorthand `mybox::geometry`.

- *Operators*—These are things like =, >, and <, and again PostgreSQL allows you to define custom operator behavior for your custom types. Some operators have special meanings, such as =, >, and <, which are used by internal SQL querying to define `ORDER BY` and `GROUP BY DISTINCT` ordering. These are useful to override if you're building custom data types and want them to sort in a certain way. As you can see in earlier chapters, PostGIS overrides = to order by the bounding box of geometries and geographies.
- *Functions*—Functions can be used within an SQL statement. PostgreSQL comes with a lot of built-in and contributed functions, such as the `soundex` function, which is packaged in the fuzzystrmatch extension, and those provided by PostGIS. You can also build your own. Functions can return simple data types, sets, or arrays. There are three core classes of functions: regular functions, aggregate functions, and trigger functions.
- *Sequences*—If you've worked with Oracle, then a sequence object will be very familiar to you. It's a counter that can be incremented and used to get the next ID for a column. MySQL folks will recognize this as `AUTO_INCREMENT`, except in PostgreSQL a sequence object need not be tied to a single table. You can use it for multiple tables and increment it separately from a table. SQL Server people will recognize this as an `IDENTITY` field, which is tied to a specific table. SQL Server 2011 introduced support for sequences as well, which follow the same ANSI SQL standard as Oracle and PostgreSQL. If you wanted a sequence to be tied to a specific table in PostgreSQL, you'd create the column as `serial` or `serial8`, which behind the scenes will create a sequence object and set the default of the column to the next value of the sequence.

D.6.2 Built-in data types

PostgreSQL comes packaged with a lot of built-in data types. Some of these are pretty standard across all relational databases:

- `int4`, `int8`—These go by more familiar names such as int, integer, and bigint.
- `float`, `double precision`—This is another class of number types that don't necessarily exist in other databases but are common.
- `serial`, `serial8`—You can use this in the `CREATE TABLE` statement, but it's not a true type. It's shorthand for "give me an integer with a sequence object to increment it." It's still an integer. The parallel in MySQL would be marking the column as `AUTO_INCREMENT` or in SQL Server setting the `Identity` property to `Yes`.
- `numeric`—This has a scale and precision and is named the same in other relational databases. It's also often referred to as *decimal* in other databases.

- `varchar, text`—This means character-varying. Unlike most other relational databases, PostgreSQL doesn't put a limit on the maximum length of a varchar or a text variable. Varchar and text behave much the same, except that text has no maximum limit and varchar may or may not have a specified maximum limit. Some other databases decide on storage-handling based on the specified size of a field. For example, in SQL Server if text is noted, then a pointer to the text field is stored and the data is stored elsewhere, outside the table. The closest parallel in SQL Server is the `varchar(MAX)` option. PostgreSQL doesn't care about this and bases storage considerations on the size of data actually stored in the field. Only if a field goes beyond its allotted storage size is storage relegated to toast tables. This means, as many PostgreSQL people will argue, that there's no penalty for using text over varchar with a limit. But if you care about interoperability, we argue that there's a big penalty. For exporting purposes, such as tab-delimited and so forth, it's important to have a limit on the size of a field, and if you export to another system often, you'll want your size limits to mirror those of the other side. If you use autogenerated screens with screen painters, such applications refer to system tables to determine the width for fields on the screen, and if everything is text, you'll end up with big text boxes everywhere. If you use an ODBC driver, such as in MS Access, a varchar is treated very differently from text—it will allow you to sort by varchar but not by text.
- `char`—These are padded characters. If you say it's a `char(8)`, then the field will always be of length 8. This is the same in almost all relational databases. This is more a presentation feature than a storage consideration in PostgreSQL because PostgreSQL presents padded eight characters but doesn't actually store eight characters if the text is shorter. Most other relational databases store eight characters.
- `date`—This is a date without time. MySQL has this, Oracle has this, and SQL Server 2008+ has this. (In prior versions of SQL Server you couldn't have a date without time.)
- `timestamp, timestamp with timezone`—Again, these are very similar in other relational databases, although they may be called *datetime* or some other name. SQL Server introduced timezone in SQL Server 2008, so prior to that no timezone information was stored.
- `arrays`—Arrays are not quite so common in other relational databases. As far as we know, only Oracle and IBM DB2 have them. Arrays in PostgreSQL are typed. For example, `date[]` would be an array of dates. For any custom type you build, you can define a table column as an array of that type and use it in functions as well. Arrays play an important role in building aggregate functions, because many of the tricks for building aggregate functions involve wrapping data in an array to be processed by a terminal function. Some quick ways of building arrays are `ARRAY(SELECT somefield FROM sometable WHERE something_is_true)`, `ARRAY[1,2,3,4]`, or in PostgreSQL 8.4+ the `array_agg` ANSI SQL–compliant

aggregate function that will create an array for each row in a `GROUP BY ...`. Note that IBM DB2 also has an `array_agg` function as defined by the ANSI SQL 2003 specs.

- `row`—This is more of an abstract data type, similar to an array. A typed row is a row in a table or a specific type. You can cast compatible rows to compatible types, as we'll demonstrate shortly.

D.6.3 Anatomy of a database function

Stored functions and procedures are useful for compartmentalizing reusable nuggets of functionality and embedding them in SQL statements. Unlike most relational databases, PostgreSQL doesn't make a distinction between a stored procedure and a stored function. In other databases, stored procedures are things that can update data and generally return a cursor or nothing for their output. In PostgreSQL, there only exist functions, and functions may return nothing (void) or something, and they can update data as well as return something at the same time.

PostgreSQL allows you to write stored functions in various languages. Its language offering is probably richer than that of any relational database system you'll find, both commercial and open source. Common favorites are SQL, PL/pgSQL, PL/Perl, PL/V8, and for GIS users PL/Python and PL/R are the most popular. There are more esoteric languages that are designed more for specific domains, such as PL/SH (which allows you to write stored functions that run bash/shell commands) and PL/Proxy (designed by Skype Corporation and freely provided, designed to replicate commands between PostgreSQL servers).

The only languages preinstalled in all PostgreSQL databases are SQL and C. PostgreSQL allows you to bind a C function in a C library to a stored function wrapper so that it can be used in an SQL statement. Most PostGIS functions are C functions.

A PostgreSQL database function has a couple of core parts regardless of what language the function is written in:

- *The function argument declaration*—This defines the list of input and output arguments.
- *The* `RETURNS` *declaration*—This dictates the return of the function; for functions that don't return anything, it's void.
- *The body*—This is the meat of the function. As of PostgreSQL 8.1+, the general convention is to use what is referred to as dollar-quoting syntax to encapsulate the body. Dollar quoting has the form *$somename$*. Oftentimes people leave out the *somename*, so it reduces down to `$$ body goes here $$`. This works for all languages. Prior versions of PostgreSQL required quoting with a single quote mark (`'`), which required a lot of escaping if you had single quotes in the function. $$ quoting is a much more readable and painless way of writing functions.
- *The language*—This is always `LANGUAGE 'somelanguage'`.

- ROWS *expected and* COST—This denotes the number of rows expected to be returned by the function. The COST is a measure of how costly a function is expected to be in some metric of processor time.
- *Cachability*—Designated as IMMUTABLE, STABLE, or VOLATILE, this allows PostgreSQL to know under what conditions the results can be cached. IMMUTABLE means that with the same inputs you can always expect the same output. STABLE within the same query means that you can expect the same inputs to result in the same outputs. VOLATILE means it should never be cached because it either updates data or the results vary even given the same function inputs.
- *The security context*—If not specified, the function is assumed to be run using the security rights of the user. If you denote a function as SECURITY DEFINER, that means the function is allowed to do anything that the owner of the function can do. This allows you, for example, to create logic that can be executed by a non-superuser that has logic that requires superuser rights, such as reading files from the filesystem.

The PostgreSQL 9.0 DO command

In PostgreSQL 9.0+, the DO command was introduced. It allows you to write one-off anonymous functions that contain only a body and no name, and that can be run straight from the command line. It currently supports only PL/pgSQL, PL/Python, and PL/Perl.

Next we'll demonstrate how to define custom data types.

D.6.4 Defining custom data types

Defining custom data types is fairly simple in PostgreSQL. As we mentioned earlier, when you create a new table, you create a new data type as well.

Listing D.5 is a simple example that creates a data type called vertex that contains x and y attributes. It creates instances of vertex and then pulls out just one of its attributes.

Listing D.5 Create a simple type and use it

```
CREATE TYPE vertex AS                              -- ❶ Create type
(x double precision,
y double precision);
SELECT CAST(ROW(x,y*0.02) As vertex) As myvert     -- ❷ Convert row to type
FROM generate_series(1,10) As x
CROSS JOIN generate_series(10,20,2) As y;

SELECT (myvert).y                                  -- ❸ Get element of typed object
FROM (
SELECT CAST(ROW(x,y*0.02) As vertex) As myvert
FROM generate_series(1,10) As x
CROSS JOIN generate_series(10,20,2) As y
) As foo;
```

In listing D.5 you define a new type called `vertex` that has an `x` attribute and a `y` attribute ❶. Then you create a query that returns two columns, and then cast that to a vertex by first packaging each as an anonymous row ❷. Finally, you pull out the `y` attribute of the table ❸.

This is similar to what we do often with `ST_Dump`. We often do a `(ST_Dump(the_geom)).geom` to grab just the geom attribute, or a `(ST_Dump(the_geom)).*` to explode all the attributes into separate columns.

D.6.5 Creating tables and views

Creating tables and views is done just like in any other relational database. Listing D.6 shows some simple examples that create a table and view in the assets schema.

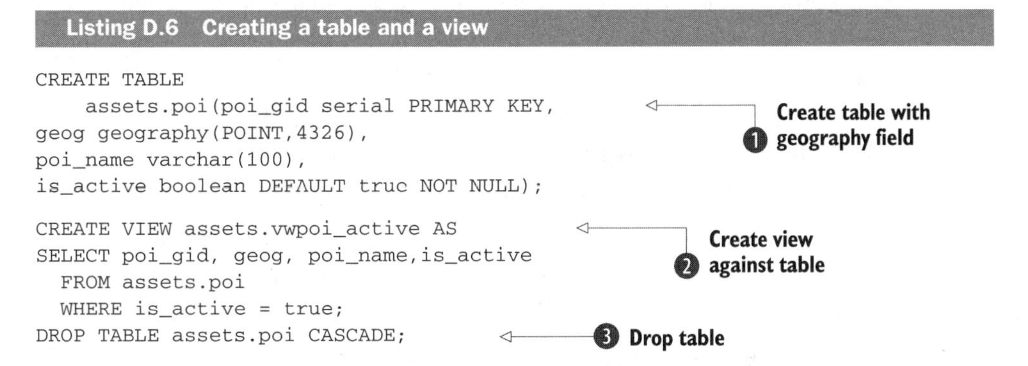

Listing D.6 Creating a table and a view

```
CREATE TABLE
    assets.poi(poi_gid serial PRIMARY KEY,
geog geography(POINT,4326),
poi_name varchar(100),
is_active boolean DEFAULT true NOT NULL);

CREATE VIEW assets.vwpoi_active AS
SELECT poi_gid, geog, poi_name,is_active
  FROM assets.poi
  WHERE is_active = true;
DROP TABLE assets.poi CASCADE;
```


In this listing, you first create a table with a geography field that is of type `POINT` and WGS 84 lon/lat, with an autoincrement primary key called `poi_gid` and an active flag that defaults to true for new entries ❶. Then you create a view against this new table that will list only active records ❷. Next you drop the table and include the `CASCADE` command ❸, which will drop all dependent objects such as the view you created earlier ❷. When using `CASCADE`, proceed with caution because you could be dropping a lot of dependent objects. Without the `CASCADE`, you'd be informed that `assets.vwpoi_active` depends on `assets.poi` and thus can't be dropped. You'd have to drop the view first and then the table.

Now that we've covered the basic features of PostgreSQL, let's go into greater detail about functions and rules.

D.7 Writing functions in SQL

PostgreSQL is probably the only relational database system that allows you to write stored procedures in pure SQL. This is very different from the PL/SQL supported by IBM DB2 and MySQL in that the PostgreSQL SQL function language has no support for procedural control structures. What other databases call *PL/SQL* is closer in family to PostgreSQL's PL/pgSQL.

It would seem on first glance that not allowing procedural control in a stored function language would be an undesirable thing, but the main benefit of this is that an SQL function can be treated like any other SQL statement and can be optimized by the SQL planner. In many cases, very useful pieces of reusable code can be compartmentalized in such a simple structure.

D.7.1 When to use SQL functions

The most important attribute of SQL functions that makes them stand out from functions written in other procedural languages is that they are often inlined in the overall query. This means the query planner can see inside an SQL function and embed its definition in the query. Essentially, it treats SQL functions like macros, much like the way C macros are expanded where they're used. This means that if your function uses an indexable expression, the planner can use an index, and if your SQL function contains a subexpression within a query, the planner can collapse the expression. A common example is the `&&` operator, which is used in many PostGIS functions. If you use two functions with `&&`, the planner will see `&&` and `&&` and will collapse the two into a single `&&`.

As a general rule of thumb, here's when to use an SQL function:

- When you use constructs that could benefit from an index
- When logic is fairly simple and short

There's one situation where you absolutely can't use SQL to write a function even if you wanted to, and that's for a trigger function. This may change in later versions of PostgreSQL, but as of PostgreSQL 9.0, you can't write triggers in the SQL language.

D.7.2 Creating an SQL function

An SQL function, like all other functions, contains an argument list, a return argument type, and a function body.

Unlike other languages, SQL functions can't have variables. This makes them fairly limited but easy to fold into a larger SQL statement. The other disadvantage is that you can't use the argument inputs by their names in versions of PostgreSQL prior to 9.2; you have to reference them by `$1`, `$2`, and so on. In other PL languages such as PL/pgSQL, PL/Perl, PL/Python, and PL/R, you can reference by position or name.

The following listing is a trivial function that returns the squares of numbers starting with the first and ending with the last.

Listing D.7 Example SQL function that returns squares

```
CREATE OR REPLACE FUNCTION
 fnsquare(param_start integer,
       param_end integer)
  RETURNS SETOF integer
AS
$$
SELECT CAST(POWER(i,2) As integer)
  FROM generate_series($1,$2) As i;
$$
language sql
IMMUTABLE;
```

❶ Define set-returning function

```
SELECT i, fnsquare(i,i + 3) As squared_range
FROM generate_series(1,3) As i;
```

❷ **Use function in SELECT**

```
SELECT *
FROM fnquare(1,10) As foo;
```

❸ **Use function in FROM**

In this listing, you define a function that takes a range and returns the square of each number in the range ❶. You use the function in the `SELECT` part of a query ❷. This is only legal with set-returning functions in PostgreSQL prior to 8.4 if written in SQL or C. For PostgreSQL 8.4+, you can do this with PL/pgSQL and other functions as well. Finally, you call the set-returning function in the standard way ❸.

> **SQL and variables**
>
> While it's true that you can't declare variables in an SQL function, for PostgreSQL 8.4+ you can significantly compensate for this by using CTEs to define sub steps, as we've demonstrated throughout this book.

D.7.3 *Rules*

Rules are objects that are bound to tables or views. They're often used in place of triggers, and for views in PostgreSQL 9.0 and below, you can only use rules. Rules don't perform any actions but they help in rewriting SQL statements to do something in addition to or instead of what the SQL statement would normally do.

The classic use of rules is in defining views. For example, you can create a view in PostgreSQL using standard ANSI syntax of this form:

```
CREATE OR REPLACE VIEW assets.vwpoi_active AS
SELECT poi.poi_gid, poi.geog
 , poi.poi_name, poi.is_active
FROM poi
WHERE poi.is_active = true;
```

PostgreSQL, behind the scenes, changes it to something that has a `SELECT` rule. If you were ever nosy enough to inspect your view, you'd see this curious thing attached to it:

```
CREATE OR REPLACE RULE "_RETURN" AS
ON SELECT TO vwpoi_active
DO INSTEAD
SELECT poi.poi_gid, poi.geog
 , poi.poi_name, poi.is_active
 FROM poi  WHERE poi.is_active = true;
```

In PostgreSQL 9.1, triggers can be bound to views to update, insert, or delete data, and they are preferred instead of rules for these events. In PostgreSQL 9.3+, views became auto-updateable if they only involve one table and no computed columns, so in many cases you don't even require triggers.

D.7.4 Creating aggregate functions

Aggregate functions are a special type of function that is used to roll up data. Some built-in aggregate functions are MAX, MIN, and AVG. PostgreSQL allows you to create your own custom aggregate functions, even with a language as simple as SQL. This is one of the coolest features of PostgreSQL. Part of the power of doing this results from the malleability of the PostgreSQL array model.

To demonstrate the ease with which you can create an aggregate function in PostgreSQL, listing D.8 shows an example that simulates the MS Access First and Last aggregate functions (and improves on them, we think). It's excerpted from one of our articles titled "More Aggregate Fun: Who's on First and Who's on Last," available at www.postgresonline.com/journal/archives/68-More-Aggregate-Fun-Whos-on-First-and-Whos-on-Last.html.

Listing D.8 Creating first and last aggregate functions

```
CREATE OR REPLACE FUNCTION
 first_element_state(                    <-- 1 State function
 anyarray, anyelement)
RETURNS anyarray AS
$$
SELECT CASE WHEN array_upper($1,1) IS NULL
 THEN array_append($1,$2) ELSE $1 END;
$$
LANGUAGE 'sql' IMMUTABLE;

CREATE OR REPLACE FUNCTION first_element(anyarray)    <-- 2 FINALFUNC function
RETURNS anyelement AS
$$  SELECT ($1)[1] ;$$  LANGUAGE 'sql' IMMUTABLE;

CREATE OR REPLACE FUNCTION last_element(              <-- 3 State function
 anyelement, anyelement)
RETURNS anyelement AS
$$  SELECT $2;  $$ LANGUAGE 'sql' IMMUTABLE;

CREATE AGGREGATE first(anyelement) (                  <-- 4 Aggregate for first
SFUNC=first_element_state,STYPE=anyarray,
FINALFUNC=first_element);

CREATE AGGREGATE last(anyelement) (                   <-- 5 Aggregate for last
SFUNC=last_element,STYPE=anyelement);
```

As you can see in listing D.8, an aggregate function is composed of at least one state function ❶ ❸ whose name is specified in the SFUNC argument of the CREATE AGGREGATE statements (❹, ❺). In addition, the CREATE AGGREGATE statement must specify a state type (STYPE), which is used to denote the type of the value that is output by a state function. An additional final state function ❷ specified in the ❹ FINALFUNC argument is needed if the result of each subsequent state is not enough, or the data type of the final output of the state function is different from the data type of the state outputs. In the CREATE AGGREGATE statements, ❹ and ❺, you define the first and last aggregate functions with these elements, and in the next listing you take them for a test drive.

Listing D.9 Putting `first` and `last` to work

```
SELECT max(age) As oldest_age, min(age) As youngest_age,
count(*) As numinfamily, family,
first(name) As firstperson, last(name) as lastperson
FROM (SELECT 2 As age , 'jimmy' As name, 'jones' As family
UNION ALL SELECT 50 As age, 'c' As name , 'jones' As family
UNION ALL SELECT 3 As age, 'aby' As name, 'jones' As family
UNION ALL SELECT 35 As age, 'Bartholemu' As name,
  'Smith' As family
) As foo
GROUP BY family;
```

You put the functions to work with a simple query. This example and the creation of aggregates work in most versions of PostgreSQL, even back to 8.1.

D.8 Writing functions in PL/pgSQL

The PostgreSQL PL/pgSQL procedural language is probably closest in form to Oracle's PL/SQL. PL/pgSQL, like Oracle's PL/SQL and the other relational database procedural languages, is a language that allows you to declare variables, employ other control flow such as `FOR` and `WHILE` loops, use cursors, `RAISE` errors, and so on, and also write SQL.

Unlike the pure SQL language, PL/pgSQL is not transparent to the planner and is treated like a black box. Inputs go in and outputs come out. Like the SQL language and other PL languages, PL/pgSQL allows you to dictate attributes such as volatility, cost, and security so that the planner can decide whether a choice of order is allowed, how costly the function is to evaluate relative to other functions, and what kind of rights are allowed within the function.

D.8.1 When to use PL/pgSQL functions

PL/pgSQL is desirable for functions where using an outer index gives no benefit, such as when the values that go into the function are already filtered by a `WHERE` condition, or when very fine-grained step-by-step control is needed.

As a general rule of thumb, here's when to use a PL/pgSQL function:

- When no use of the function output could benefit from an outer index check.
- When the logic is complex and needs several breaks, or you need variables or the ability to raise errors.
- In a trigger, because you can't use SQL in a trigger. Although you can use other languages, such as PL/Python, PL/R, or PL/Perl for writing triggers, PL/pgSQL tends to be more stable and also has more integration with PostgreSQL. Therefore, PL/pgSQL is generally a better language for writing triggers unless you need to leverage specific functionality only offered in the other languages.

As mentioned earlier, you can't write rules with PL/pgSQL, and in earlier versions of PostgreSQL (before 8.4), you can't use a set-returning PL/pgSQL function in the `SELECT` clause of a statement, whereas you can use an SQL function.

D.8.2 Creating a PL/pgSQL function

Listing D.10 is a simple PL/pgSQL function. This is the `utmzone` function we use often in the book, and it offers a good example of when to use a PL/pgSQL function. Let's study its parts.

Listing D.10 The `utmzone` function

```
CREATE OR REPLACE
    FUNCTION utmzone(geometry)                 ❶ Function envelope
    RETURNS integer AS
$$
DECLARE                                        ❷ Variables
 geomgeog geometry;
 zone int;
 pref int;
BEGIN                                          ❸ Function body
 geomgeog:= ST_Transform($1,4326);
 IF (ST_Y(geomgeog))>0 THEN
    pref:=32600;
 ELSE
    pref:=32700;
 END IF;
 zone:=floor((ST_X(geomgeog)+180)/6)+1;
 RETURN zone+pref;
END;
$$ LANGUAGE 'plpgsql' IMMUTABLE
COST 100;
```

The first part of a PL/pgSQL function, like any function, is the envelope, which defines the parameters that go into the function and the return type ❶. Then there's the `DECLARE`, which is part of the body, the place where you declare the variables you'll use through the rest of the function ❷. SQL functions don't have this; other languages may, but they specify it differently. Then comes the meat of the function, which is encapsulated between `BEGIN` and `END` and generally ends with a `RETURN` that returns the output ❸.

We haven't gone through any of the control flow logic, but the `BEGIN` and `END` section uses `FOR` loops, and the `RETURN` statement may contain a `RETURN NEXT` loop when returning a set.

For PostgreSQL 8.3+ there's also `RETURN QUERY`, which allows you to return the results of precompiled SQL, and version 8.4 introduced `RETURN QUERY EXECUTE`, which allows you to return the results of dynamic SQL. An example of the 8.4 construct is demonstrated in Pavel Stehule's blog entry "EXECUTE USING feature in PostgreSQL 8.4" (http://okbob.blogspot.com/2008/06/execute-using-feature-in-postgresql-84.html). These newer constructs are more efficient and shorter to write than the older `RETURN NEXT`, but if you need finer-grained control of which records you return, `RETURN NEXT` will still be needed.

D.8.3 Creating triggers

Triggers, like rules, have an available record called NEW or OLD or both, and they also have a variable called TG_OP, which holds the kind of operation that triggered the trigger. There are also other TG_ variables. If you're reusing the same trigger across multiple tables, TG_TABLE_NAME and TG_TABLE_SCHEMA are useful as well. The NEW and OLD objects have the same column structure as the table the trigger is being applied to. Trigger functions can be shared across tables.

Triggers in PostgreSQL 8.4 and below can't be written using SQL; they must be written in PL/pgSQL or some other language. Not all languages support triggers, but PL/Python, PL/Perl, and PL/R do, to name a few. How the NEW and OLD data is referenced varies from language to language.

The following list describes the kinds of triggers and what data is available to each. A trigger is either a row-level or statement-level trigger and is triggered on the UPDATE, INSERT, or DELETE event or a combination of them:

- *Statement trigger*—Run for each kind of SQL statement on a table. No data is available to it, so the best you can do is log that a statement has been run and what kind of statement it is. It's not often used.
- INSERT *row-level trigger*—Run on the insert of data and once for each row. The NEW object is available to it and contains the new data. An INSERT trigger can be marked as BEFORE INSERT or AFTER INSERT. In a BEFORE INSERT, you can change the values in the NEW object, and these will get propagated to the actual insert. In an AFTER INSERT, PostgreSQL lets you set values in NEW, but this data gets thrown away and isn't propagated to actually affect the insert. A common mistake is trying to set values of fields in the NEW row in the AFTER INSERT trigger.
- UPDATE *row-level trigger*—You can think of an update as a delete followed by an insert. Therefore, the UPDATE trigger has both OLD and NEW variables available to it. OLD contains data that is deleted or to be deleted, and NEW has data to be added or that is added. Again, an UPDATE trigger can be marked as BEFORE or AFTER, and for BEFORE UPDATE, changes to the NEW record will get propagated to the table; for AFTER UPDATE, your NEW changes go into a black hole when the trigger is completed.
- DELETE—Just the OLD object is available.

Listing D.11 shows an example trigger that will update a geography column whenever longitude and latitude are updated or a new record is added. It will also log changes to a log table. Keep in mind that you can do other useful things, such as geocode records when address information is updated. In PostgreSQL, triggers are a kind of function, and the function is separate from the actual trigger that the trigger function is bound to. The benefit of this approach is that a trigger function can be shared across many tables. The downside is that you can't just write the trigger function as part of the table definition as you can in some other databases.

Listing D.11 Trigger function applied to geography table in PL/pgSQL

```
CREATE TABLE
    poi(gid serial PRIMARY KEY,                    <-- ❶ Table
 geog geography(POINT,4326),
 poi_name varchar(100),
 longitude float, latitude float);

CREATE TABLE poi_log(logid SERIAL PRIMARY KEY,
 logdt timestamp with time zone DEFAULT CURRENT_TIMESTAMP,
 logtype varchar(20), geogtable varchar(100), geog_gid integer,
 old_geog geography, new_geog geography);

CREATE OR REPLACE FUNCTION trig_set_thegeog_pt()          <-- ❷ Trigger function

RETURNS trigger AS $$
DECLARE
changed boolean := false;
oldgeog geography := NULL;
BEGIN
IF tg_op = 'INSERT' AND NEW.longitude IS NOT NULL         <-- ❸ Insert conditional code
  AND NEW.latitude IS NOT NULL THEN
 changed = true;
ELSIF COALESCE(NEW.longitude, -1000)                      <-- ❹ Update conditional code
     != COALESCE(old.longitude, -1000)
OR COALESCE(NEW.latitude, -1000)
  != COALESCE(old.latitude, -1000) THEN
    changed = true;
END IF;
IF changed THEN
  IF NEW.longitude IS NOT NULL AND NEW.latitude IS NOT NULL THEN
    NEW.geog :=
        ST_GeographyFromText('SRID=4326;POINT('
      || NEW.longitude || ' ' || NEW.latitude || ')');
ELSE
NEW.geog = NULL;
END IF;
INSERT INTO poi_log(logtype, geogtable, geog_gid,         <-- ❺ Log change
    old_geog, new_geog)
VALUES(TG_OP, TG_TABLE_NAME, NEW.gid, oldgeog, NEW.geog);
END IF;
RETURN NEW;
END;
$$
LANGUAGE 'plpgsql' VOLATILE;

CREATE TRIGGER step01_trigupdpt                           <-- ❻ Bind trigger to table events
BEFORE INSERT OR UPDATE
ON poi
FOR EACH ROW
EXECUTE PROCEDURE trig_set_thegeog_pt();

INSERT INTO poi(poi_name, longitude, latitude)            <-- ❼ Test trigger
VALUES('My back yard', -72.1234, 41.3456);

SELECT gid, ST_AsText(geog) As wktgeog
FROM poi;
```

```
UPDATE poi SET longitude = -72.555 WHERE gid = 1;

SELECT gid, ST_AsText(geog) As wktgeog
FROM poi;
SELECT * FROM poi_log;
```

First you create a test table that you'll later apply your trigger to ❶. Then you create a trigger function. The first part declares a state variable you initialize to `false` because you don't want to make any unnecessary updates ❷.

Next, you check to see what kind of event caused the trigger to fire; if it's an insert, you need to update if the longitude and latitude values are not NULL ❸. If it's an update, you need to either update the geography column or wipe out the contents ❹. You use `COALESCE` here to set NULLs to `-1000` so as to never compare NULLs. NULLs are tricky to compare because even when two NULLs are compared, the comparison returns false. To shorten the code, you use the `COALESCE` hack.

You then log the change to the log table ❺. In general, logging should be done as an `AFTER TRIGGER` event so that the logging sees the final record data. In this case, because you have only one trigger, it's simpler to add the logging into the `BEFORE` event with the assumption that your `NEW` record represents the final data.

Next you bind the trigger function to the `INSERT` and `UPDATE` events of the table ❻. Note that a table can have multiple triggers, and they run in alphabetical order based on the triggering event. Sometimes, especially if you have complex triggers shared by many tables, it's advantageous to categorize your triggers by functionality rather than writing a big body of logic. In those cases, you just have to keep track of the order in which the triggers are fired by naming them accordingly, such as step01_..., step02_..., and so on. Each subsequent `BEFORE` trigger will see the change of the previous trigger if the previous one makes sure to return `NEW`; otherwise trigger execution stops.

Then you test the trigger to make sure it's working ❼. The `SELECT` should show something like `POINT(-72.555 41.3456)`, and you should see two records in the log table, which includes the name of the table from the `TG_TABLE_NAME` variable.

This example just scratches the surface of what you can do with triggers in PostgreSQL in general and PL/pgSQL in particular. Triggers are also capable of triggering other triggers, so that you can have recursive triggers. Recursive triggers are particularly useful for maintaining the positioning of a parent object, so that when you move a parent object, its child component parts move accordingly. We hope that we've demonstrated enough here for you to envision the potential they hold.

PostgreSQL 9.0 introduced ANSI SQL column-level triggers, which allow specifying a `WHEN` condition that can contain column names and will be executed only when the `WHEN` condition evaluates to `true`. This feature saves a bit of processing time because the body of the trigger doesn't always need to be checked.

Next we'll cover some key elements for achieving optimal performance for your PostgreSQL database by creating useful indexes.

D.9 Index performance

In chapter 15 we talked a bit about performance. Now we'll cover some of the loose ends we left out of that chapter.

Just like in other databases, PostgreSQL uses indexes to improve performance. There are various flavors of indexes to choose from, as well as additional index options you can specify that you may or may not find in other relational databases. The key ones are listed here:

- *Partial indexes*—These are indexes with a `WHERE` clause where the `WHERE` constrains the data that's actually indexed.
- *Functional indexes*—You can choose to index a function calculation such as `UPPER`, `LOWER`, `soundex`, or `ST_Transform`, where the arguments to the function can be any of the columns in a row. You can't go across rows, but your function can take multiple columns. The function must also be marked immutable, which means given a set of inputs, the function is guaranteed to return the same output.
- *Kinds of indexes*—These include B-tree, gist, GIN, and hash. The most common is the B-tree index. The kind of index controls how the index leaves are structured.

D.9.1 B-tree index gotchas

A B-tree index is the most commonly used of all index types in PostgreSQL.

This next example creates an index on the `item_name` field so that when you use `item_name='something' or item_name > 'something'`, this index will be used:

```
CREATE INDEX idx_item_name ON items USING btree(item_name);
```

Under certain conditions where you'd expect the basic B-tree index to be used, it's not. These conditions are probably very unintuitive to people coming from databases that are not necessarily case sensitive. In case-insensitive DBMSs, a `WHERE` condition such as `item_name='LION'` would match database values `lion`, `LION`, and any permutation of uppercase characters you have. If you had a regular B-tree index as shown, the index would kick in, but you may not get all the matches you expect. Because PostgreSQL is case sensitive, you would have to specify a condition such as `upper(item_name)='LION'` to account for all permutations. Because the aforementioned index is on `item_name` and not on `upper(item_name)`, the index will not be used.

You need to change the index to the following:

```
CREATE INDEX idx_item_name ON items USING btree(upper(item_name));
```

If you use operations like `LIKE`, then you can't use an unqualified B-tree. You need one with `varchar_pattern_ops`. Prior to PostgreSQL 8.4, a `varchar_pattern_ops` was not able to service `item_name = 'something'`. To handle both equality and pattern matching using `LIKE`, you needed two indexes. In newer versions, `varchar_pattern_ops` can support both, though standard B-tree is generally more efficient for equality operations. Read Tom's note on this thread in our article, "Why Is My Index Not

Being Used," to get the gory details: www.postgresonline.com/journal/index.php?/archives/78-Why-is-my-index-not-being-used.html#c503.

D.9.2 Functional index gotchas

Functional indexes (sometimes called *expression indexes*) are indexes that are built from a function rather than raw data. Common functional indexes are things like this:

```
CREATE INDEX idx_item_name ON items USING btree(upper(item_name));
```

The main gotcha with functional indexes is that you can only index functions marked as `IMMUTABLE`. This means the function outputs don't change, given the same arguments. The main reason for this limitation is that once an index is calculated, the index value is changed only if the input fields to the functions change.

You can, of course, lie about a function being immutable by marking it as immutable to get around this restriction, and PostgreSQL, even as of version 9.4, will not try to validate whether the function demands dynamic things such as tables. We demonstrated that by doing an index on `ST_Transform`. If you do such a thing, you'll need to be careful to ensure that in most cases the function is immutable.

The other gotcha with functional indexes is that if you redefine a function to do something other than what it was doing before, such as changing the output value, PostgreSQL will not go back and reindex the affected tables. So if you change a function used in an index, and you know that change will affect the output, you need to go back and re-index the affected tables.

It's fairly easy to determine which tables are affected, particularly in pgAdmin, by using the dependents tab of a function.

index

Symbols

Numerics

A

B

C

D

E

H

I

S

T

W

X

Y

Z